Baedeker's

NETHERLANDS, BELGIUM & LUXEMBOURG

A SPECTRUM BOOK

PRENTICE-HALL, Inc., Englewood Cliffs, New Jersey 07632

Cover Picture: Dutch windmill, Kinderdijk near Rotterdam

167 colour photographs
72 maps and plans
1 large road map

Text:
Werner Fauser (Music, part; Folklore)
Dr Udo Duhr (General, Animal and Plant life, Introduction to the Netherlands, Belgium and Luxembourg, Population, History, Literature, Music, Economy, the Netherlands, Belgium and Luxembourg from A to Z)
Gerald Sawade (Climate)
Christine Wessely (Art)

Editorial work:
Baedeker–Stuttgart
English language: Alec Court

Cartography:
Huber & Oberländer, Munich

Design and Layout:
Creativ + Druck GmbH, Stuttgart

Conception and general direction:
Dr Peter Baumgarten,
Baedeker Stuttgart

English translation:
Edgar Knobloch

© Baedeker Stuttgart
Original German edition

© The Automobile Association
United Kingdom and Ireland

© Jarrold and Sons Ltd
English Language edition Worldwide

Licensed user:
Mairs Geographischer Verlag GmbH & Co.,
Ostfildern-Kemnat bei Stuttgart

Reproductions:
Gölz Repro-Service GmbH
Ludwigsburg

The name *Baedeker* is a registered trademark

Source of illustrations:

Most of the colour photographs were provided by the Belgian Tourist Office in Düsseldorf, or by the General Commissariat for Tourism in Brussels, the Dutch Tourist Office in The Hague, and the Luxembourg Tourist Office in Düsseldorf, or by the National Tourist Office of the Grand Duchy of Luxembourg.

Allianz-Archiv (pp. 278, 280).
Anthony-Verlag, Starnberg (cover picture: Krautwurst; p. 311: W. Schmidt)
Bavaria-Verlag, Gauting (K. Thiele: p. 141, D. Pittius: p. 315)
Commission des Communautés Européennes, Direction Générale de l'Information, Division Télévision-Radio-Film, Fototeca, Brussels (pp. 126; 207, bottom)
De Efteling, Kaatsheuvel (p. 253)
Henri Gehlen, Luxembourg (pp. 93; 250, bottom)
Lestrade, Luxembourg (pp. 130; 135; 140, bottom; 206; 207, top; 220, top and bottom; 251)
Locus, Brussels (p. 117, top)
Philips-Evoluon, Eindhoven (p. 142)
Steigenberger Kurhaus Hotel, Scheveningen (p. 244)
Zentrale Farbbild Agentur (ZEFA), Düsseldorf (p. 279, top and bottom).

In a time of rapid change it is difficult to ensure that all the information given is entirely accurate and up to date and the possibility of error can never be entirely eliminated. Although the publishers can accept no responsibility for inaccuracies and omissions they are always grateful for corrections and suggestions for improvement.

Printed in Great Britain by Jarrold & Sons Ltd, Norwich ★

0–13–056028–6 paperback
0–13–056036–7 hard cover

How to Use this Guide

The principal towns and areas of tourist interest are described in alphabetical order. The names of other places referred to under these general headings can be found in the very full index.

Following the tradition established by Karl Baedeker in 1844, sights of particular interest and hotels and restaurants of particular quality are distinguished by either one or two asterisks.

The abbreviations used should give no difficulty. In the list of hotels, b.=beds; r.=rooms; rest.=restaurant

The symbol ⓘ indicates addresses from which further information can be obtained.

This guidebook forms part of a completely new series of the world-famous Baedeker Guides to Europe.

Each volume is the result of long and careful preparation and, true to the traditions of Baedeker, is designed in every respect to meet the needs and expectations of the modern traveller.

The name of Baedeker has long been identified in the field of guidebooks with reliable, comprehensive and up-to-date information, prepared by expert writers who work from detailed, first-hand knowledge of the country concerned. Following a tradition that goes back over 150 years to the date when Karl Baedeker published the first of his handbooks for travellers, these guides have been planned to give the tourist all the essential information about the country and its inhabitants: where to go, how to get there and what to see. Baedeker's account of a country was always based on his personal observation and experience during his travels in that country. This tradition of writing a guidebook in the field rather than at an office desk has been maintained by Baedeker ever since.

Lavishly illustrated with superb colour photographs and numerous specially drawn maps and street plans of the major towns, the new Baedeker Guides concentrate on making available to the modern traveller all the information he needs in a format that is both attractive and easy to follow. For every place that appears in the gazetteer, the principal features of architectural, artistic and historic interest are described, as are its main areas of scenic beauty. Selected hotels and restaurants are also included. Features of exceptional merit are indicated by either one or two asterisks.

A special section at the end of each book contains practical information, details of leisure activities and useful addresses. The separate road map will prove an invaluable aid to planning your route and your travel within the country.

Introduction to Holland, Belgium & Luxembourg

An old windmill in Kempen, Belgium

Benelux Countries

**Belgium
The Netherlands
Luxembourg**

The **Benelux countries**, Belgium, the Netherlands and Luxembourg, are in West-Central Europe. They border on the German Federal Republic in the east and on France in the south. In the west, Belgium and the Netherlands border on the North Sea.

The Kingdom of **Belgium**, the Kingdom of the **Netherlands** and the Grand Duchy of **Luxembourg** are parliamentary democracies and constitutional monarchies.

The Benelux countries are linked together by an economic and customs union. Each is a member of the United Nations (UN), a founder member of NATO, and of the European Communities (EEC). They are also members of the Council of Europe.

The Benelux countries, Belgium, the Netherlands and Luxembourg, form the heartland of the European Communities. They are rich in places of interest. In this part of Western Europe two substantial cultural realms meet and intersect. There are unusual geological formations, as well as a variety of cultural attractions inviting visitors at any time of the year. The Dutch flower fields are a popular destination for short trips when the tulips are in bloom. The seaside resorts along the Dutch and Belgian North Sea coast offer extensive, pleasant beaches and picturesque dunes. Entertainment is provided by a great number of artistic and folk festivals and sporting events. The art lover will delight in the superb museums and galleries in Belgium and the Netherlands, in their old towns, often criss-crossed or surrounded by canals, and in their impressive architectural monuments, churches, monasteries or secular buildings. Those who are interested in technical achievements, will find fascinating port installations, bridges, locks, dikes and canals. The flat country along the coast has a special charm underlined by the characteristic landmark, the windmill. But the undulating and hilly regions further inland in Belgium and Luxembourg have unexpected impressions in store for the tourist. The attraction of the many culinary specialities and other gastronomic delights should not be underestimated. Visitors with children will find many pleasure grounds and amusement parks. The colourful local markets and well-stocked shops in the big cities are a real paradise for souvenir hunters and compulsive shoppers.

Because of their natural character and their economic, social and cultural mixture, the regions around the estuaries of the Rhine, the Maas and the Schelde rank among the most remarkable places in Europe. They have an excellent position in the most favoured section of the North Sea coast, the best communications, and a hinterland extending far into Central Europe. The river estuaries are accessible to sea-going vessels deep into the interior, and a network of natural and artificial waterways connects distant cities with the sea.

The sea and the navigable rivers provide the basis for economic development, but they are at the same time a constant danger to man. Along the coast behind a band of dunes, not always continuous, lies a wide strip of flat country below sea level, stretching from Friesland in the north to Zealand and Flanders in the south. This is the so-called Fens or polders. Rivers flowing from the interior, and stormy seas with unpredictable tides, have threatened human life since people first settled here around 1000 B.C. The inhabitants had to fight the floods without respite. Long periods of laborious land reclamation were again and again interrupted by destructive, catastrophic floods. Even the era of modern technology did not bring much change, as the burst dikes in 1953 and their devastating effects have shown. On the whole, the inhabitants of the polders have remained victorious, although the costs were enormous. They have provided one of the most impressive examples of man's resistance against the elementary forces of the sea.

The polders are bordered by higher, dry, sandy plains, river terraces and glacial moraines called Geest, in Dutch also "Zand". Further south in Belgium, Luxembourg and the Limburg tip of the Netherlands, follow the widely diversified and scenic foothills of Central European mountain ranges which then continue into France and Germany.

But the special position of the Benelux countries is not due only to their natural characteristics. Their history and evolution made the three countries an extraordinary part of Europe. Situated between Germany and France and looking across the sea towards the estuary of the Thames, they have built, developed, maintained and advanced a character of their own.

Belgium, the Netherlands and Luxembourg form a transitional zone between France on one side and Germany and Britain on the other. The linguistic frontier between the Romance and Germanic languages runs across Belgium south—north from Lorraine to Limburg at Verviers, and then west to French Flanders and to the coast at Dunkerque. This was

The Principal Waterways and Highlands in the Benelux Countries

the dividing line which stabilised in the Merovingian era after the great mixing of the migration of nations, and separated the two language groups. On one side of it, Frankish dissolved into Romance; on the other the Gallo-Roman remains were absorbed into Germanic. Quite independent from the geographical divisions, this line in Belgium hardly changed after it was established. Walloon to the south of it is a French dialect with Germanic mixtures, rich in ancient forms, but nowadays almost completely suppressed by French. Dutch north of it became a Germanic language in its own right, still containing quite a few Romanisms in its vocabulary.

The lands along the Meuse/Maas, around Liège, Maastricht and Aix/Aachen, where today three languages are spoken, formed in the Middle Ages the heart!and of Charlemagne's Western empire which comprised both Romania and Germania. After its collapse the French and German nations became established in the west and east. In between, a tendency towards independence from either emerged, which does not necessarily go back to the Partition Agreement of Verdun (843) by which Lotharingia was created. The political antagonism of the French, German and English helped in many important respects to strengthen this striving for freedom.

Just as the Belgae in antiquity separated from the Gauls in the Basin of the Seine and the Germans on the Lower Rhine, the seafaring Frisians on the coast have preserved their individuality against the Franks and the Saxons since the Middle Ages. In the 13th c. Flanders and its cities became opposed to the French crown, of which it was then the fief. On the other hand, the Germanic centralising power of the Holy Roman Empire was, well before the beginning of the modern era, hardly noticeable in the territories of what was to become the Burgundian sphere extending from Friesland via Holland to Brabant. And yet only after the Reformation did the North achieve its independence as a nation, when the Dutch General States (Joint Assembly of the Estates; since 1588 Dutch provinces which broke away from Spain), succeeded in defeating the Spanish Habsburgs. Enjoying supremacy of the sea, the young state soon became a world power. Unlike Holland, the Southern Netherlands (Brabant, Flanders and in particular Liège and Luxembourg), remained for centuries in a position of vacillating dependence. The Congress of Vienna at last brought all these countries together in the Kingdom of the United Netherlands. However, the contrasts between the Flemish–Dutch north, and the Walloon south became too strong in the course of time, and the country soon broke up into its component parts. The uprising of 1830 led to the creation of the Kingdom of Belgium, and gained the Grand Duchy of Luxembourg, a remnant of the once powerful imperial territory of the Middle Ages, its independence within the present-day frontiers.

When the creation of the Congress of Vienna, the Kingdom of the United Netherlands, disintegrated, the present Benelux countries seemed at first to draw further and further apart. And yet the great suffering which had afflicted Belgium and Luxembourg in the First World War and which struck all three countries in the Second, together with the loss of their colonies, brought them closer again and revived the desire for a cultural and economic rapprochement. Belgium and Luxembourg formed an Economic Union in 1921; in 1944 they signed a treaty with the Netherlands which, together with some later agreements, became the foundation of the "Union Douanière Bénélux". An economic union between the three countries has existed since 1958. This, with all its problems and achievements, can be regarded as a test case for European unification attempts. The three countries are members of the European Coal and Steel Community, and the European Economic Community. In 1967 the executive organs of the ECSC merged with those of the EEC and of EURATOM.

By area and population, the Benelux countries are not very large. The Netherlands has a population of approximately 14 million, and an area of 33,899 sq. km (13,088 sq. miles); Belgium has a population of just 10 million, and an area of 30,521 sq. km (11,784 sq. miles). The population of Luxembourg is approximately 360,000 and its area is 2586 sq. km (998 sq. miles). However, the population density in Belgium and the Netherlands reaches 322 and 412 per sq. km (834 and 1067 per sq. mile) respectively, the highest in the world after Monaco. To this corresponds also the intensive economic exploitation of their arable land which is second to none. But it is not only because of their taming of the sea and cultivation of reclaimed land that the Benelux countries are one of the most highly developed regions in the world. Industry, too, which in the last century spread from Belgium all over the rest of Europe, has reached in all three countries a standard ranking among the highest in the world.

The points for modern development were already set in the Middle Ages. It was then that the Flemish and the Dutch began to make use of their excellent position on the North Sea coast and around the estuaries of the rivers, opening up the interior of the continent and exploiting in various ways its communications potential. The development of their cities followed – from Bruges, Ghent, Antwerp and Dordrecht to Amsterdam and Rotterdam. Unlike the cities along the Meuse and the Rhine, the medieval European cities of Flanders had characters of their own, not based on any models from Mediterranean antiquity. Although the soil in Flanders around the cities of merchants and craftsmen, such as Ypres and Ghent, was of inferior quality, it was intensively cultivated as early as the 15th c. and could support an astonishingly large population.

Incomparable old towns, most of them preserved, still reflect the wealth and the high degree of spiritual and cultural achievement accomplished in the previous centuries. The best examples of medieval urban development can be found in the Flemish part of Belgium. In the Netherlands, long hampered by the exhausting struggle against nature, Amsterdam and many other ports and merchant cities reached their full prosperity only centuries later, in the age of the great adventurers and discoverers.

A feature of Dutch, Flemish and Northern French towns is the **belfry** (in Dutch, *belfort*; French, *beffroi*), a high rectangular tower which was the symbol of the town's freedom and power. Its bells called the citizens to work, to meetings or to arms. The belfry is usually connected with the Town Hall or other buildings. Sometimes it stands on its own.

The **carillon** (in Dutch, *beiaard*; French, *carillon*) which calls, even at night, every quarter or half hour, from the belfries or towers of the churches and public buildings in Belgium and in the Netherlands, owes its origins to the installation of public clocks, the first of which appeared about 1370. The need appeared to attract attention to the forthcoming hourly stroke, by preceding it with a few strokes of small bells. When a greater number of such bells was used, their striking was co-ordinated and mechanically controlled, and about 1500 it was found that simple ringing could be made into a melodious overture. The carillon as we know it, was created only when a keyboard was installed. The first of these is documented in Oudenaarde around 1510. In several Belgian towns carillon concerts take place regularly. There is even a carillon school in Mechelen.

Climate

The Netherlands and Belgium which extend along the North Sea have an oceanic climate with relatively cool summers and mild winters. The prevalent westerly and south-westerly winds accentuate the maritime influence. Transitional oceanic/continental climate exists only in Luxembourg which is far from the sea; it is much less pronounced in south-east Belgium, which rises to 700 m (2297 feet), and in the Dutch province of Limburg.

The lowest **temperatures** averaging annually 6·5–7°C (43–44°F) are found in the high Ardennes. An annual average of 8–9°C (46–48°F) can be found in the valleys of the Ardennes (Rochefort 8·5°C (47°F)), in the Hautes Fagnes (Spa 8·1°C (46°F)) and in the Luxembourg Ösling (Clervaux 7·8°C (46°F)); also in certain places in the Northern Netherlands (Leeuwarden 8·8°C (47·8°F), Hoorn 8·9°C (48°F), Zutphen 8·8°C (47·8°F)). The annual averages along the coast are between 9–9·9°C (48–49·8°F); Den Helder 9·2°C (48·5°F), Katwijk aan den Rijn 9·1°C (48·3°F), Flushing 9·8°C (49·6°F) and Ostend 9·7°C (49·5°F)). The highest annual averages will be found further inland (Amsterdam and Rotterdam 10°C (50°F) each, Antwerp 10·1°C (50·1°F), Ghent 10·2°C (50·4°F)), and at Maastricht (10·1°C (50·1°F)). Most other places have annual averages of between 9–10°C (48–50°F) (Groningen 9·2°C (48·5°F), Breda 9·3°C (48·7°F), Brussels, 9·7°C (49°F), Luxembourg 9·4°C (49°F)). The lowest monthly average (mostly January, and in about one-third, also February), are in the high Ardennes (−2°C (28°F)) and in Ösling (Clervaux −1·5°C (29°F)). The highest January/February averages, i.e. the mildest winters, are in the coastal areas of the Southern Netherlands (Flushing 3·4°C (38°F)) and of Belgium (Ostend 3·5°C (38·3°F)); also in Antwerp (3·5°C (38·3°F)). In the rest of the country the temperature decreases in January/February from

south to north: Maastricht 3·2°C (37·7°F), Rotterdam 2·8°C (37°F), Amsterdam 2°C (35·6°F), and Groningen 1·6°C (34·8°F). The highest monthly averages (mostly July, rarely August) are at Echternach on the Moselle, shielded by the Ardennes (18·4°C (65°F)). This is followed by Rotterdam 18·2°C (64·7°F), Groningen 18·1°C (64·6°F), Amsterdam, Maastricht and Luxembourg, 18°C (64°F) each, Ghent 17·6°C (63·6°F), Brussels and Flushing with 17·2°C (63°F); Ostend, Breda and Den Helder with 16·3°C (61·3°F); Spa with 15·7°C (60°F), and last, the high Ardennes with 14–15°C (57·6–59°F). The annual average, the main criterion for oceanic and continental climate, varies in the Benelux countries from 12·8°C (55°F) in Ostend, 14–15°C (57–59°F) in most places in the plains and uplands, and Groningen (16·5°C (61·7°F)) up to 17·7°C (63·8°F) (Clervaux) in the Grand Duchy of Luxembourg (Echternach 17·2°C (63°F), Luxembourg 17°C (62°F)).

Precipitation reaches an annual average in the Netherlands of between 650 mm (25·6 in.) and 750 mm (29·5 in.), with a maximum on the coast of North Holland and in Groningen (744 mm (29·2 in.)), and a minimum, leeward of the coastal dunes in Amsterdam (648 mm (25·5 in.)) and in Den Helder (665 mm (26·3 in.)). In Belgium the annual average is a little higher (Ostend 820 mm (32·3 in.), Antwerp 713 mm (28·0 in.), Brussels 835 mm (32·9 in.)). In the hilly south-east it can rise suddenly with increasing rain, to 1114 mm (44 in.) at Spa, and over 1400 mm (55 in.) in the high Ardennes (Carlsbourg, north of Bouillon 1251 mm (49 in.)). Leeward of the Ardennes it drops again to some 950–800 mm (37–31 in.) in Ösling (Clervaux 865 mm (34 in.)), to 739 mm (29 in.) in Luxembourg, and to 719 mm (28 in.) in Echternach. The rainiest month is October with 70–90 mm (2·7–3·5 in.) near the Dutch coast (Amsterdam 70 mm (2·7 in.); Katwijk aan den Rijn 88 mm (3·4 in.)); less frequently November (Rotterdam 82 mm (3·2 in.); further east and in Zealand, August (Groningen

83 mm (3·3 in.), Zutphen 85 mm (3·4 in.), Flushing 76 mm (3 in.)); in the Belgian plains and hills, July (Antwerp 75 mm (2·9 in.), Brussels 87 mm (3·4 in.)); in Ostend, July and December (80 mm (3·2 in.) each); in Ghent, July and October (82 mm (3·2 in.) each). In the Hautes Fagnes and the Ardennes, most rain falls in high summer and in November or December (Spa, July and November, 115 mm (4·6 in.) each, Rochefort, July 84 mm (3·3 in.)). The maximum is reached in Carlsbourg (December, 130 mm (5·1 in.)). In the Grand Duchy of Luxembourg it rains most in July (Luxembourg city 70 mm (2·9 in.)); in Clervaux in August (96 mm (3·7 in.)); and in Echternach in December (79 mm (3 in.)). The driest season is spring in the North-East Netherlands, in the Ardennes and in Luxembourg (Den Helder, April 36 mm (1·4 in.), Groningen, March 39 mm (1·5 in.), Amsterdam and Rotterdam also March 48 mm (1·9 in.)). In all other areas it rains least in February (Zutphen 44 mm (1·7 in.), Flushing 38 mm (1·5 in.), Breda 44 mm (1·7 in.), Ostend and Ghent, 45 mm (1·8 in.), Brussels 51 mm (2 in.), Maastricht 40 mm (1·6 in.)).

Plant Life

The Benelux countries belong to the Euro-Siberian floral region. Inside this region several sections can be distinguished, for example the Atlantic European and the Central European floral areas. Their common border forms a transitional belt some 20–40 km (12–25 miles) wide running parallel with the coast across Belgium and the Netherlands. This borderline reflects the oceanity of the climate, decreasing proportionally with the distance from the coast.

Next to climate, regional and local differences in soil quality and geological character influence the range of floral elements. Most remarkable here are the Ardennes which lie in the Central European floral region, but because of their altitude their vegetation is mainly Atlantic.

The transitional zone between the Atlantic European and the Central European floral areas does not form in any way a clear-cut borderline. Some plants such as holly, ivy, gorse, foxgloves and bell heather, which are characteristic of the Atlantic zone, exist also in Luxembourg far from the sea. The only better known exception is the bog myrtle. The border zone, therefore, separates only areas in which the characteristic floral elements are either more or less common.

The plant world of the Benelux countries is additionally enriched by influences from neighbouring floral areas. From the south, offshoots of Mediterranean flora, and from the south-east those of Pontic plant life penetrate via Lorraine, Luxembourg and the middle Meuse region as far as the Meuse/Rhine Valley. A characteristic Mediterranean element is the wall germander, which appears in Luxembourg and in the foothills of the Ardennes.

Typical examples of the Pontic vegetation are the anemone and the sea holly which extend as far as the polders. From the boreal region of Scandinavia several marsh plants penetrate as far as Kempen; for example, the cranberry, which comes from the north, represents a typical boreal element in the Ardennes.

Natural vegetation survives only sporadically in the Benelux countries because vast areas of it have been converted into farmland. On the sand soils of the Geest in the Atlantic region, the original vegetation was birch, oak or mixed forests which in the course of time were degraded by cultivation to extensive Atlantic heath, and in recent decades have been re-planted with pines. The natural deciduous forest on the loess and loess-chalk soil of Belgium (oak, hornbeam), and in the Ardennes (beech) were largely replaced with evergreens (pine and firs) which grow faster and, therefore, make forestry more profitable. The leeward lying Luxembourg part of the Ardennes (Ösling) possesses as its natural vegetation oak and copper beech. Oak and hornbeam forest is characteristic of Gutland. On the less fertile soil of the Luxembourg sandstone, and also on the sand soils of the Dutch/Belgian Geest plains, the original woods were birch and oak.

Especially interesting vegetation is in the marshes, dunes and polders along the North Sea coast, and in the few still existing fens in Holland. The typical beach plants are the so-called halophytes which need salt for life and prosper therefore only where the soil is saline. The best known examples of this family are the salt aster and some other beach plants which are not only the first to occupy the newly reclaimed polders, but also grow all over the flooded coastal region. In the dunes, planted with dune grass, sea couch grass and dwarf pines to protect against erosion, the characteristic plant next to halophytes is *Viola rupestris* (Teesdale violet). As the salinity of the marsh soil decreases, the halophytes are replaced with pasture. In the final stage the area of the former marshes changes into farmland and lush meadow grass. A special characteristic feature is the high moor which nowadays is mostly drained and cultivated, except in parts of the Peel. A high moor forms independently from the ground water-level. It is created by continuous growth of peat mosses which absorb the rainwater and act like a sponge to raise it above ground level. The bottom parts of the mosses die, and in due course turn into peat. Typical accompanying plants of this biotope are cotton grass and sedge, crowberry and wild rosemary. In an advanced stage appear also heathers and finally trees, especially alder, pine and birch.

Unlike the high moors, the low moors (in the south-east of Friesland and in the north-west of Overijssel), are fed by means of the ground water-level. They are, therefore, much more fertile, and the vegetation differs accordingly. Typical here are reed, reed-mace, rush, sedge, shrubs and mosses. In the stage of reclamation, low moors change into marsh meadows, marsh woods and meadow woods.

Animal Life

The original animal world of the Benelux countries, which was never distinguished by a great variety of species, has been much reduced by man's cultivation of this area down to its remotest parts. Natural plant formations have been mostly preserved in areas too small to support large animal species. However, as beasts of prey disappeared, the roe, stag and boar lost their natural enemies, and without the interference of man their population would have risen to unbearable numbers.

The roe deer, which is the most common large mammal, prefers sparse woodland with dense undergrowth, from the cover of which it can venture into open country and even near human settlements. It can, therefore, be found only in the Dutch Geest regions and in the woods south of the Sambre/Meuse Valley. It does not appear in the open fenlands of Flanders, Zealand, Holland and Friesland. The stag prefers large areas of forest even more than the roe. It is common, therefore, in the Belgian Ardennes and in the Luxembourg Ösling. Wild boar can be found only in the Ardennes. In the Netherlands it is practically extinct.

The wildcat has become rare and it can only be found sporadically in the Southern Ardennes where it hides during the day in abandoned foxholes. A little more common is the tree-marten, which exists also in the larger woods in the Netherlands. A beast of prey, which is rarely seen by the inhabitants of the interior, is the seal. During the day seal packs can be seen on the sandy stretches along the coast; by night they go hunting.

Among the rodents, two species should be emphasised because they have become relatively rare. First, the hamster, which prefers the Belgian loess regions. It makes its burrows in the soft and yet remarkably solid soil usually where there is a very low ground water-level. Second, the dormouse, whose habitat is limited to the southern part of Belgium and Luxembourg. Its behaviour has been relatively little explored.

The Waddenzee between the Dutch mainland and the West Frisian Islands is a paradise for water birds, and is in many ways unique in Europe.

Particularly interesting mainland birds here are the hoopoe and the tree-creeper. They are faithful to their habitat and can be found almost exclusively either in the farm and meadowland north of the Sambre/Meuse Valley, or in the compact wooded areas south of it.

A very rare reptile is the wall lizard which came here from the Mediterranean. It can live only in dry, warm places, and can, therefore, be found mainly in Southern Luxembourg (Gutland and the Valleys of the Moselle and the Sûre). Occasionally it can also be found in sheltered spots in the Condroz and in Southern Limburg.

The fish population in inland waters has been much reduced because of increasing pollution. The salmon, which was once a delicacy from the Rhine and the Meuse, has almost disappeared. Much more common is the crayfish. In the Waddenzee there are eels and mussels; also a whole range of crustaceans which can only be found in sea water.

The Birds of the Waddenzee

The most characteristic birds of Central European shallow seas are the many species of gulls. The most common is the **herring gull** with a yellow beak, white breast and grey upper parts. Very common, too, is the *great black-backed gull*, a daring predator whose favourite prey is the eiderduck chicks, but it also hunts other sea birds. The great black-backed gull can be recognised by its white breast and black upper parts.

The West Frisian Islands are the largest breeding grounds in Europe of the **gannet**. When hunting it flies with lowered head above water, and then suddenly dives when it spots its prey. The Island of Texel is the breeding ground of the **spoonbill**, a large long-legged bird which elsewhere in Europe can only be seen in Austria and Hungary.

A flying spoonbill can be distinguished from a *heron*, which is equally common because it flies with its neck extended.

Among the most conspicuous coastal birds is the **oyster catcher**, up to 43 cm (17 inches) high. This wader can crack mussels with its orange-coloured knife-sharp beak. Frequent visitors to the West Frisian Islands are many species of **geese** and **ducks**, the *yellow-legged ringed plover* and the somewhat less conspicuous *Kentish plover*.

Finally, the *curlew sandpiper* must also be mentioned. It is a small wader which appears in large flocks in the Waddenzee. In winter its upper parts are striped grey/brown, and its breast is white and grey. In summer its plumage is chestnut-brown and black striped on the upper parts.

The **Kingdom of Belgium** – in Dutch, *Koninkrijk Belgie*; in French *Royaume de Belgique* – consists of nine provinces, comprising altogether 43 districts. A proposed constitutional reform will divide the country into three regions (Flanders, Wallonia and Brussels). Regional parliaments and cultural councils will be created to satisfy the demands of various parts of the population (the Dutch-speaking Flemish, the French-speaking Walloons, and the German-speaking people in East Belgium: all predominantly Catholic).

According to the Constitution of 1931, Belgium is a constitutional monarchy. The executive power is, vested in the King (since 1951 Baudouin/ Boudewijn I, born 1930). The legislative power is vested in the King and parliament. In practice, however, the King's part in the business of government is limited to representative and official functions.

The parliament consists of two Houses, the Senate (in Dutch, Senaat; in French, Senat; 187 members), and the Lower House (in Dutch, Kamer von Volksvertegenwoordigers; in French, Chambre des Représentants; 212 members). Senators and Members of the Lower House are elected for four years. The Council of Ministers is headed by the Prime Minister, who is the head of government. The Council is composed of an equal number of Dutch- (Flemish) and of French-speaking members.

The capital Brussels (bilingual; a special French/Dutch region), is the seat of numerous international organisations, including the Council of Ministers of the EEC, the European Commission, the EEC Economic and Social Committee, and the General Secretariat of the North Atlantic Treaty Organisation (NATO).

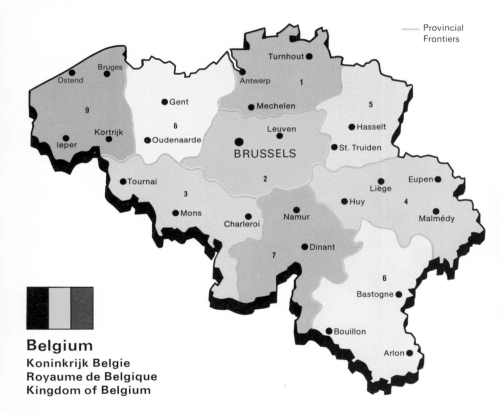

— Provincial Frontiers

Belgium
Koninkrijk Belgie
Royaume de Belgique
Kingdom of Belgium

BELGIUM extends from its short coast, only 60 km (37 miles) long, deep inland to the south-east beyond the Meuse to the western forehills of the Middle-German mountain ranges. Its varied landscape is divided into parallel east–west bands. In the north, the band of dunes along the North Sea coast, the Fens and the Geest, are the natural continuation of the Netherlands. These three geographical formations constitute together what is usually described as Lower Belgium. Middle Belgium is a hilly country with sandy, clay and lime layers from the tertiary and cretaceous geological periods. Its southern plains are overlaid with a compact, thick layer of loess, which makes them, like the neighbouring Rhineland and Northern France, a rich and fertile agricultural country. High Belgium, the region of the Ardennes, begins beyond the Valley of the Meuse and the Sambre, and is divided into the Low and High Ardennes. This ancient mountain range composed of slate, greywacke and chalk, forms the western outpost of the Rhine slate range. In the south, High Belgium merges into the Uplands of Lorraine, the north-east rim of the Paris basin. These uplands consists of horizontal rock layers of different hardness overlaying each other in steps.

In **Lower Belgium**, the coast with its fine sandy beaches consists of a continuous band of dunes with very few openings to the sea. One of these is the estuary of the Yser at Nieuwpoort. The width of the dunes varies and their maximum height, reached in the large dune field of De Panne, is 30 m (98 feet). This strip is one of the best known and most popular seaside areas in Europe. It extends on both sides of the ferry port of Ostend.

Lace-maker in Bruges

Behind the dunes, and along the Westerschelde, the south bank of which is part of the Netherlands called Zealand Flanders, is a stretch of reclaimed marshes narrower than in Holland. At Blankenberge it is only some 12 km (7 miles) wide. Mostly it is well cultivated and in no danger of flooding. Old sea inlets which previously penetrated deep into the country have been drained. This was, for example, the fate of the Zwin, which once reached from the mouth of the Schelde to **Bruges**, the great medieval sea port of Flanders. Its silting was the main cause of Bruges' decline. The unique townscape of the city has survived almost untouched from that time. The port of Zeebrugge, built in 1900 in the dunes, and linked with Bruges by a canal, could not revive the city's former greatness. Bruges, although criss-crossed with canals, is a town of the flat, sandy Geest just like Ghent and Antwerp.

Geest (in its proper meaning of sandy, alluvial land), is mainly the region of Kempen (in French, Campine), east of the Schelde and the Dijle and north of the Demer, the north part of which belongs to the Netherlands. It is the least densely populated part of Belgium, with heath and sandbanks sparsely planted with pines and suitable for army training grounds. Its villages are scattered on poor soil, and there are only a few small towns. In the Middle Ages that remote area was eminently suitable for monasteries. In modern times it became the seat of various industries such as lead and tin foundries,

radium plants and the nuclear research complex at Mol, which were either environmentally detrimental or preferred to keep their distance from inhabited places. In the subsoil between Maastricht and Antwerp are important coal deposits. This mining area of Limburg and Kempen is the northern branch of the large European coal seam which divides at Aix/Aachen. Its location beneath a massive blanket of rock requires large-scale mining. Seven productive pits have been sunk here since 1920, but only a small part of the existing resources has been tapped. The heart of the area is around Genk. Miners have been recruited from elsewhere and settled in new villages that can be seen from the high pyramid-shaped slag heaps.

In the west in Flanders, the Geest is partly a newly formed, flat area, and partly a land of low, sandy-clay hills between the Schelde, the Leie and the fen belt. Whereas Kempen has along the Demer a sharp geographical divide which separates it from the fertile lands of Middle Belgium, in the west (in Brabant and Flanders) there is a gradual transition to the higher and more fertile regions of Middle Belgium, more or less along the line Louvain–Brussels–Kortrijk. Geest-Flanders was originally woodland, and it is still partly covered with heath on bleached sandy soil, but it has been since the Middle Ages densely populated and carefully cultivated. Small individual farms, in groups or rows, are the typical

Province District	Area in sq. km (sq. miles)	Population	Main Town
1 Antwerp	2867 (1107)	1,571,000	Antwerp
Antwerp	1001 (386)	926,000	Antwerp
Mechelen	510 (197)	292,000	Mechelen
Turnhout	1365 (527)	353,000	Turnhout
2 Brabant	3358 (1297)	2,217,000	Brussels
Brussels	162 (63)	1,016,000	Brussels
Halle-Vilvoorde	943 (364)	511,000	Halle/Vilvoorde
Leuven	1163 (449)	410,000	Leuven
Nivelles	1090 (421)	280,000	Nivelles
3 Hainaut	3788 (1463)	1,313,000	Mons
Ath	487 (188)	78,000	Ath
Charleroi	555 (214)	446,000	Charleroi
Mons	585 (226)	262,000	Mons
Mouscron	101 (39)	73,000	Mouscron
Soignies	518 (200)	168,000	Soignies
Thuin	934 (361)	141,000	Thuin
Tournai	603 (233)	145,000	Tournai
4 Liège	3863 (1492)	1,008,000	Liège
Huy	659 (254)	88,000	Huy
Liège	798 (308)	615,000	Liège
Verviers	2016 (778)	245,000	Verviers
Waremme	390 (151)	60,000	Waremme
5 Limburg	2422 (935)	705,000	Hasselt
Hasselt	907 (350)	348,000	Hasselt
Maaseik	884 (341)	183,000	Maaseik
Tongeren	631 (244)	174,000	Tongeren
6 Luxembourg	4441 (1715)	222,000	Arlon
Arlon	317 (122)	49,000	Arlon
Bastogne	1043 (403)	36,000	Bastogne
Marche-en-Famenne	955 (369)	41,000	Marche-en-Famenne
Neufchâteau	1353 (522)	52,000	Neufchâteau
Virton	77 (30)	44,000	Virton
7 Namur	3666 (1415)	402,000	Namur
Dinant	1592 (615)	88,000	Dinant
Namur	1165 (450)	257,000	Namur
Philippeville	909 (351)	57,000	Philippeville
8 East Flanders	2982 (1151)	1,328,000	Ghent
Aalst	469 (181)	263,000	Aalst
Dendermonde	343 (132)	179,000	Dendermonde
Eeklo	334 (129)	80,000	Eeklo
Gent	943 (364)	486,000	Ghent
Oudenaarde	418 (161)	112,000	Oudenaarde
Sint-Niklaas	475 (183)	208,000	Sint-Niklaas
9 West Flanders	3134 (1210)	1,076,000	Bruges
Bruges	651 (251)	253,000	Bruges
Diksmuide	362 (140)	47,000	Diksmuide
Ieper	550 (212)	104,000	Ieper
Kortrijk	403 (156)	271,000	Kortrijk
Ostend	292 (113)	133,000	Ostend
Roeselare	272 (105)	136,000	Roeselare
Tielt	329 (127)	85,000	Tielt
Veurne	275 (106)	47,000	Veurne
Kingdom of Belgium	30,514 (11,781)	9,840,000	Brussels

Landscape in West Flanders

despite the poor soil, is extremely in-tensive. In some places it is spade and hoe farming, for example in the vegetable-growing Waasland around Sint-Niklaas. Since long ago domestic crafts – such as cloth-making, inherited from ancient times, or the making of lace which was then retailed by traders in the open towns such as Lokeren or Tielt – have been practised here alongside farming. Fields of flax line the banks of the Leie, which provides water for the retteries (places where flax is softened by soaking). Today large towns, especially Ghent, are the locations for modern textile mills.

form of rural settlements. Hedges and lines of poplars surround the adjacent fields and restrict the view on all sides. Farming,

The famous medieval ports and merchant cities of Flanders made use of the advantageous transport position of their country. Trade from the coast and the rivers moved by sea. To the south there were roads through flat, open country across the Picardian threshold into Champagne, and via Burgundy to the Alpine passes and the Mediterranean. Flanders linked the North Sea countries with the distant Baltic and Southern Europe until historical incidents closed all the sea and land routes, and the country's economy retrenched and declined. **Ghent**, lying on the confluence of the Schelde and the Leie a little above the tidal zone, overlooked by St Peter's Hill, has preserved from its period of prosperity its sumptuous churches and patrician houses, and also the grim Castle of the Counts. Modern Ghent is a sober 19th c. industrial textile city and a sea port, thanks to the canal of Terneuzen on the Schelde.

View across the Schelde towards Sint-Amands

Antwerp inherited the role of Bruges towards the end of the Middle Ages and became the most prosperous city in Northern Europe until the closing of the Schelde by the newly independent Dutch (1648) severed its lifeline for two centuries. It lies on the higher outer bank in a bend of the Schelde, its old business front turned towards the open stream. The river is here up to 500 m (1641 feet) wide, and has a strong tidal movement (up to 4 m (13 feet) between ebb and flow). In the first half of the 20th c. Antwerp rose again to be a world port. Large harbour docks, provided with locks, were built upstream in the river marshes.

Among the inland towns of Flanders, the smaller ones often have highly diversified business activity while others like Ypres, have never overcome the decline of the medieval textile crafts. Others in their role

as border fortresses against France, were repeatedly destroyed in wars.

Central Belgium has a very varied landscape and, together with the Valley of the Meuse and the Sambre between Liège and Charleroi, may be considered to be the heart of the country. It is a tertiary and cretaceous plateau rising gradually from less than 100 m (328 feet) in the north to 200 m (656 feet) in the south. The northern part, although lower, is rather hilly and deeply incised by the valleys of the Dijle, Senne, Dender and Schelde. The youngest topmost layer in the hills is made of late tertiary hard conglomerate rock which protects the individual hills from being eroded. This is the case, for example, of the Pellenberg near Louvain on the edge of the Hageland, of the Kemmelberg south-west of Ypres, and of the Mont St Aubert which dominates the country around Tournai. The set of tertiary layers is not very thick, and in the valleys which are less than 100 m (328 feet) deep, the underlying very ancient massif of Brabant already shows. It consists partly of crystalline rocks which are worked in large quarries (near Lessines). Over and above the tertiary rocks, clay and sandy soil formed, which is somewhat more productive than the Geest-type sandy soil in Northern Flanders. In addition, fertile loess appears on the slopes and hills, but only in unconnected patches. Such is the character of Central Brabant. Large individual farms are scattered in undulating, intensely cultivated fields and meadowland, with an abundance of trees. In between, some large forests have been preserved, such as the Forêt de Soignes south of Brussels.

To the south, the landscape rises slowly to the vast open plains covered with a continuous blanket of loess, the Hesbaye in the east and the Hainaut in the south. Here, large compact villages lie in the valleys. Vast treeless fields of wheat and sugar-beet span the plateaux: a perfect picture of rich, fertile country like that of the Rhineland or of Picardy.

But there are also local difference. If there are tertiary clays under the loess, the land is richer in water and the ratio of pastureland increases, for example, in the wet Hesbaye north of St Trond, and also in parts of Hainaut. If, on the other hand, the subsoil is chalk and lime, the country is drier and better for farming. This applies especially to the dry Hesbaye around Tongres and Waremme. The Meuse/Sambre Valley belongs geologically to the Ardennes. It has ploughed a wide furrow in the soft carboniferous layers on their edges, and connects individual coal-mining areas. In between the chalk protruding from below, the carboniferous layers produce narrow rocky valleys like those below Namur. West of Charleroi, the coal country changes into the farmland of Hainaut.

The cultural and geographical significance of the Central Belgian regions has changed in many ways. Population was concentrated in the fertile areas from the earliest Prehistoric times up to the Roman period, and there were close connections with the civilisations of inland Europe. There were almost no contacts with the lands of the Northern Geest. The great Roman road from Cologne to Reims passed through agricultural country east–west from Maastricht via Tongres and Gembloux to Bavai in France. *Tongres*, the Roman Civitas Tungrorum, is the oldest town in the country. At the end of antiquity, the Valley of the Meuse became more important. The successor of Tongres was first *Maastricht*, and after it Liège, unknown until then, which became the seat of a Bishop and of a feudal authority. The agricultural country was by no means abandoned, but the traffic moved from the disused road to the waterway of the Meuse and the Sambre. In the west, *Tournai* (the Civitas Nerviorum of Julius Caesar and the first capital of the Franks) managed to hold its ground, thanks to its position on the Schelde. On the Meuse, Huy and Dinant became important places. Only later, after the early Middle Ages, the wastes of Flanders were colonised along the waterways, and the coastal country developed into a dominant economic area.

This was the time when **Brussels** became the political focus of the country due to its position half-way between the farmlands and Lower Belgium, accessible from the sea by the Senne, and at the same time connected with the naturally more endowed south. When the Flemish cities declined, cut off from the sea by the silting of their waterways, Brussels became the court town of Brabant and the first city of the country. Although it lay in the Flemish part of Brabant, the court introduced into it a strong French influence. This contrast is clearly reflected in the difference between the Flemish Lower Town with a city hall and the Upper Town. In the 19th c. when the great boulevards and parks were laid out, Brussels began to look like another Paris, and yet it did not quite lose its Flemish character.

Today, linked to the River Schelde and the sea by a canal whose banks are crowded with industrial plants, Brussels is a city with a million inhabitants. The linguistic frontier separating the Walloons and the Flemish bisects the Central Belgian region less than 30 km (19 miles) south of Brussels and cuts right across the agricultural countryside. Characteristically, it runs through open country which has long been colonised, but has been in no way central in the cultural and political scenes. The absence of any geographically natural dividing line has always kept the two linguistic groups in close contact. The fact that the great medieval territories, the Episcopal principality of Liège, Hainaut, Brabant, Flanders and Luxembourg, contained parts of both linguistic areas, is part of the same phenomenon. The administration of the young Belgian state of 1830 was, of course, wholly French in its orientation. This and the current opinions of the 19th–20th c. have influenced to some extent the fight of the Flemings for their language, though political and economic motives also played a part. Flemish now enjoys equality, especially since the language frontier was fixed in 1963, though there are linguistic struggles from time to time mainly in the area of Brussels.

On the divide between Middle and High Belgium lies the Valley of the Meuse and the Sambre. Before industrialisation it was a pleasant country with palaces and gardens, vineyards, hop plantations and orchards on the slopes, and castles on rocky spurs. Coal, now on its way out, was mined here very early, as in the Ruhr, but there was little use for it as the ironworks had avoided the main valley. They preferred to settle by the little streams coming from the Ardennes. Coal belongs to the main seam extending from the Ruhr across Aix/Aachen, Belgium and Northern France to England. In Belgium it runs south of the Brabant massif which separates it from the coalfields of Kempen. In the tectonic border zone between the massifs of Brabant and the Ardennes, the coal is much folded and partly covered

The Begijnhof Sint-Amandsberg

In many old Flemish towns of Belgium there still exists the so-called **Beguinage** (in Dutch, Begijnhof; French, Béguinage). Its origins go back to the Middle Ages. It is in principle an enclosed group of houses like a nunnery, where devout women live in a community either collectively in larger houses, or individually in small cottages. The beguines do not take any lifelong vows. Nevertheless, withdrawals are rare. They must abide by the rules of the community. They may go out on their own by day, but must return to the Beguinage in the evening.

The Beguinages first appeared late in the 12th c, and their peak period was the 13th–14th c. Originally they were free associations of working women, created for economic and religious reasons. They were given their rules by the Church and accommodated in enclosed precincts with a chapel or a church. Eventually such a community became a parish and finally a Beguinage. Because of their links with the Church, they escaped in 1311 the condemnation by Pope Clement V, whereas similar communities in Germany were affected by it.

The Beguinage is headed by a Superior appointed by the Bishop, called "Grootjuffrouw" or "Grande Dame". The sisters live at first in convents and work together as lace-makers, seamstresses, etc. After six years they are allowed to move into a separate house with two–four apartments. Collective services are held two or three times a day. Blue garments and white kerchiefs of the beguines give them a quaint solemnity and charm. When the beguines leave the house, they wear a black Flemish coif (hat – in Dutch falie; French, faille).

with earlier rocks. This causes higher production costs offset to some extent by lesser depth. From east to west there are the mining districts of Liège, Charleroi, the Bassin du Centre and the Borinage near Mons.

Industrialisation began in the first half of the 19th c. when for the first time on the European continent the coal mines were combined with foundries and iron mills (Cockerill Works in Seraing). Technically and economically, this had an important effect on the entire European industry.

As the coal seams will shortly be exhausted, the industrial range has been extended to include glassworks, non-ferrous metals, large chemical plants and highly specialised manufacturing industries. Their locations are influenced by waterways accessible to large ships, such as the Albert Canal between Liège and Antwerp, and by the canalisation of the Meuse and the Sambre. The important Canal du Centre from Brussels to Charleroi still awaits widening. Iron ores come mostly from Lorraine (Minette). **Liège**, with its old churches going back to the Carolingian and early Romanesque eras, and the much more recent fortress town of Charleroi, named after Charles II of Spain, have both grown to half a million inhabitants, but no statistics will show it because in Belgium all the small communities surrounding large towns have remained administratively independent.

High Belgium is, in fact, the Ardennes. They belong to the western outposts of the Rhine slate range and are a continuation of the Eifel massif. The Ardennes are a fraction of an ancient mountain range, the surface of which cuts across the folded strata. Their mountain character can only be recognised by their steep and deep valleys. Earlier they were remote and had only a few roads, but now they are fully accessible and have become a favourite resort area ("villégiature") for the inhabitants of the northern towns.

The **NETHERLANDS** show a clear, natural division from the sea to the interior. The coastal dunes ("duinen") – which in the Frisian island region are separated from the inner coast by the shallows of the "wadden" – then the sea and river marshes (polders), the Geest with its sandy plains and heath ("hoog veen"), Limburg in the south, the loess-covered lowlands, and finally the edge of the mountain range, can all be clearly discerned.

By its origin, the older and higher country, the Geest, is an enormous glacial alluvial area formed by the Rhine and the Maas with its tip approximately at the point where the rivers leave the highlands. It covers in a triangular shape the lowlands between the estuary of the Eems in the north-east, and the Schelde in the south-west. It originally reached as far as the Dogger Bank, far into the North Sea, but today it nowhere touches on the open seas. It now borders with a low profile a former coastline, that of the later fens which were pushed seawards in front of it. The Geest is composed of gravels and sands. In the Ice Age the north and the east were covered with a Scandinavian inland glacier which brought about two kinds of Geest country, the Glacial Geest and the Fluvial Geest. The glaciers modified the fluvial deposits and where they stood still, garland-shaped hilly chains formed. The most western of them can be traced from Krefeld to Xanten, and from Elten via Cleve to Nijmegen, and from Rhenen as far as the old Zuiderzee coast at Huizen. In the north the former islands Urk and Wieringen, and also Texel, have a glacial core. Inland-facing steps arranged north to south, extend across Veluwe from Arnhem to Zwolle, over 100 m (328 feet) high, and east of Deventer across Overijssel. The gravel and sand ground was partly overlaid with a clay-sand moraine in the Ice Age. In Hondsrug near Groningen the moraine table descends steeply to the old fens of the Eems lowland and the marshes. Water from the melting ice brought in sand, and the wind formed irregular fields of dunes now covered with heath and wood, as was originally the whole country. Extensive high moors formed in wide channels where ground water was dammed up. That is why the regions of Veluwe, Overijssel and Drente have the same features as the North German Emsland and the Luneburg Heath. The fluvial Geest of the Rhine-Maas country in the south-west was untouched by ice, and is therefore even more monotonous, but it has basically the same appearance. Sandy patches and inland dunes alternate with strips of fen lowlands.

The Geest is an ancient human habitat. It offers only sparse bleached soil for farming, and dry pastures, but is elevated and safe for living. On the Geest are the megalithic tombs of prehistoric civilisations. Here were the ancient villages on inferior but permanently farmed soil, with sheep grazing on extensive heath and moors. Old roads crossed the Geest inland, and small towns like those in Overijssel and North Brabant grew up along them. Traditional crafts were the spinning and weaving of wool, which later on became the basis for the textile industry. The modern development of the Geest, agricultural and industrial alike, can only be interpreted by the stimuli coming from the fens, the heartland of the country.

The fens and dunes in the region of the North Sea coast are geologically the youngest parts of the country. They emerged less than 10,000 years ago after the end of the last Ice Age, and their formation is still not complete. The rise in the sea level and the sinking of the land which went with it caused, after the Ice Age, a slow but irresistible penetration of the sea from the Dogger Bank, then still part of the mainland, to the south. The formation of the English Channel strengthened the tides. On the gentle slope of the sea bottom sandbanks formed near the coast, and, from the steep promontory of the Cap Blanc Nez near Calais, a spit of land extended, along which sand and debris were pushed by currents and coastal rubble in a north-easterly direction. The dry sand on the coast was then blown into dunes. This can still be observed on a hot summer day at low tide. Behind the dunes in coves and bays and in the river estuaries, the fine mud came down and formed the soil of the fens.

The dunes are rapidly changing formations. So, for example, in Holland between 's-Gravenzande and Haarlem there are older dunes of brownish weathered sand running at an angle to the present coast (the Dutch call them Geest). On them lie the tulip fields of

The Netherlands
Kingdom of The Netherlands
Koninkrijk der Nederlanden

— Provincial Frontiers

Province	Area in sq. km (sq. miles)			Population	Main Town
	Total[1]	Land	Inland Waters		
1 Groningen	2593 (1001)	2335 (902)	55 (21)	551,350	Groningen
2 Friesland	3808 (1470)	3353 (1295)	207 (80)	578,250	Leeuwarden
3 Drenthe	2681 (1035)	2654 (1025)	26 (10)	416,000	Assen
4 Overijssel	3925 (1515)	3812 (1472)	113 (44)	1,009,500	Zwolle
5 Gelderland	5129 (1980)	5010 (1934)	118 (46)	1,680,650	Arnhem
6 Utrecht	1396 (539)	1332 (514)	64 (25)	885,800	Utrecht
7 Noord-Holland	2936 (1134)	2668 (1030)	214 (83)	2,299,200	Haarlem
8 Zuid-Holland	3344 (1291)	2907 (1122)	362 (140)	3,063,700	Den Haag
9 Zeeland	2745 (1060)	1794 (693)	88 (34)	344,400	Middelburg
10 Noord-Brabant	5107 (1972)	4912 (1897)	150 (58)	2,030,950	's-Hertogenbosch
11 Limburg	2209 (853)	2166 (836)	42 (16)	1,065,500	Maastricht
12 Zuidelijke IJsselmeer Polder	1135 (438)	955 (369)	180 (69)	58,750	Dronten
Kingdom of the Netherlands (including persons with no fixed domicile; excluding Dutch Antilles)	41,160 (15,892)	33,899 (13,088)	1620 (625)	13,985,600	The Hague/Amsterdam

[1] Including inland waters which belong to communes; apart from that there are in the Netherlands, 4152 sq. km (1603 sq. miles) of inland waters not belonging to any particular commune.

The **Kingdom of the Netherlands** (in Dutch, *Koninkrijk der Nederlanden*) comprises five regions with eleven provinces and the South IJsselmeer Polder (Flevoland). To these, several West Indian islands, the Dutch overseas territories must be added. There are altogether 850 communes grouped in 129 so-called economic geographical areas. The communes enjoy a relatively large local autonomy. Apart from this, the country has been divided into eighty key areas for reasons of social restructuring, and further into forty regions introduced by the Co-ordinating Commission for Regional Research (COROP).

According to the Constitution of 1815, the Netherlands are a constitutional monarchy. Executive power is vested in the Crown and the legislative power in the Crown and parliament. The role of the Royal Family is today restricted to representative and official functions.

The Parliament (Staten-General), consists of two Houses: "Eerste Kamer" and "Tweede Kamer". The First Chamber consists of fifty members elected by provincial parliaments for six years; the Second Chamber of 100 members elected directly by the population. In questions of legislation, the State Council (Raad van State), headed by the monarch (since 1980 Queen Beatrix, born 1938), has a consultative function.

Next to the indigenous Dutch (40% Catholics, 38% Protestants), many coloured people who have come from the former overseas territories (Indonesians, Moluccans and Surinamese) live in the country. There is also the Frisian minority in the north-east and many Europeans from various countries.

The capital of the country is Amsterdam, but the seat of the government is The Hague, which is also the seat of the International Court of Justice.

Haarlem. The more recent white dunes can be up to 5·5 km (3 miles) wide and more than 50 m (164 feet) high. They are and were the natural protection of the fens and are therefore protected in Belgium as in the Netherlands. Some of the fishing villages on them have become famous seaside resorts (Zandvoort, Scheveningen, etc.). On the inner side lies **The Hague**, the old hunting preserve of the Counts of Holland ('s-Gravenhage), and later the royal residence. Another important function of the dunes is to preserve the fresh-water level created by seeped-in rainwater. As the fens are poor in drinking water this was formerly of great importance to the population.

The fens consist of silt and mud soil which has accumulated in tidal ponds (sea fens, or "zeeklei"), or stretched far inland along the river estuaries (fluvial fens or "rivierklei"). The thick clayish mass is aired and made fertile by gravel and lime shells of innumerable small crustaceans which die in brackish water. The fens of the more recent polders form particularly good farmland. The older fens in Holland are frequently covered with low moor and serve as pastures.

The sea and the rivers from the interior are equally dangerous to the low-lying fenland. The *Rhine* carries, at an average level, some 2400 cu. m (84,744 cu. feet) of water per second, at high water 10,000–12,000 cu. m (353,100–423,720 cu. feet) per second. The *Maas* which is much smaller, carries only 150 cu. m (5297 cu. feet) per second, but at high water almost twenty times as much. The protecting dune belt has not remained intact because the waters of the Rhine, Maas and Schelde, together with the tides, ripped large gaps in it, and so exposed the fens to the twin dangers of flooding by the rivers and by the sea. This was the region of the funnel-shaped river estuaries which split the provinces of Zealand and South Holland between the Schelde and the Rhine into numerous islands. The rim of dunes from the Hook of Holland to the tip of Den Helder was continuous, but later openings had to be enclosed by dikes. The river estuaries show a remarkable tendency to change; the openings to the south-west have become naturally deeper and therefore more important, whereas the north-eastern ones have become gradually silted up. The reason for this is that the tides move from the Channel in a north-easterly direction, and the ebb currents which are important for the deepening of the river bed always affect the southern river branches first. Above all, the estuaries of the Rhine and the Maas in Holland shifted in stages southwards. The Roman estuary near Leyden ("Oude Rijn") has long become silted. The Rhine branches at Rotterdam, which as the Waal and the Lek carry most of the Rhine's water into the sea, still bear their earlier name of the Maas because they had originally been the main estuary of the Maas. Now the Maas water reaches the sea further south opposite the Schelde by the estuaries of Haringvliet and Krammer.

When the land was threatened by flooding, people could not settle there. Only when they learned to throw up artificial mounds did the first permanent settlements appear in the marshes about 2000 B.C. The natural fertility of the soil here was much superior to that of the Geest whether it was used for pasture or for ploughing. On these man-made mounds, called "warft" or "terpen", the inhabitants built farms, then villages, and finally whole towns such as *Leeuwarden*, the capital of Friesland. But their living space became safe only when, in the Middle Ages, they at last learned to build dikes. This was particularly difficult in the Netherlands because there it was not only necessary to fight off the sea and drain the marshes; the main dangers were the innumerable branches of the Rhine and the Maas which criss-crossed the country, continually changing course. The endangered territory begins below Emmerich where the streams divide. The

Drawbridge in Nieuwersluis

Geldersche IJssel, carrying about one-ninth of the Rhine water, flows from here through a wide glacial valley to the north and opens into the IJsselmeer. The Rhine

Land Reclamation

In earlier times vast expanses of water often lying 5 m (16 feet) or more below sea level could not be controlled. The use of windmills in the 17th–18th c. made it possible to drain four large lakes in North Holland, the *Schermer, Beemster, Wormer* and *Purmer*. But it was only when steam power came into use that the Haarlemmer Meer (183 sq. km – 71 sq. miles) and also the large areas of the *IJ* at Amsterdam could be pumped out. The procedure for this drainage ("droogmakerijen") is simple: a dike is built around the area, then a ring canal, made partly with mobile dikes, takes in the pumped-out water. The bottom of these "seas" is very fertile and the dried-up area provides excellent farmland equalled only by the most recent polders on the edge of the Frisian "wadden". The boggy parts of the fens can only be used as pastures.

The biggest venture of land reclamation, made possible only with 20th c. technology, was the draining of the former Zuiderzee, formed in the Middle Ages by the penetrating sea. In 1924 the narrow channel between North Holland and the Island of Wieringen was closed. In 1932 the enormous dam over 30 km (19 miles) long between Wieringen and Friesland was completed. Technically, this was a gigantic enterprise. The sea moved several cubic kilometres of water with ebb and flow twice daily in and out of the Zuiderzee. As the dike advanced both from the north-east and the south-west and the gap narrowed, the impact of the tides on it became progressively stronger.

Since the **Enclosing dike** (*Afsluitdijk*) was completed, the Zuiderzee ceased to exist and the IJsselmeer has been gradually turning into a

fresh-water lake. It has become relatively simple to turn the cut-off sea into polders but it required, and still requires, massive investment of money and labour. First the corner between North Holland and the Island of Wieringen was drained (20,000 hectares – 49,420 acres). In 1942 the first actual Zuiderzee Polder was completed, the North-east Polder (47,600 hectares – 117,620 acres), next to the provinces of Friesland and Overijssel. The western part of the fishermen's island of *Urk* became part of the dike. From the enclosures at the south bank two polders have so far emerged; first the East Flevoland (54,000 hectares – 133,434 acres) and the second, South Flevoland (43,000 hectares – 106,253 acres). Between the polders and the coast, a strip of water remains free in order not to cut off some ancient coastal towns, such as Harderwijk and Elburg from the sea, and also to prevent the lowering of the ground water-level in the more elevated mainland. The last polder here will be Markerwaard (40,000 hectares – 98,840 acres) off the coast of North Holland. It was to have been completed in 1980. However, various environmental protection groups objected to the draining of the Markerwaard Polder and the government promised to re-examine the project. The remaining IJsselmeer will nonetheless have an area of 110,000 hectares (271,810 acres).

The draining of the Zuiderzee is the largest ever coastal reclamation enterprise. Another project is the **Delta plan** approved in 1957. It will enclose the open estuaries of the Rhine, the Maas and the Schelde and thus consolidate the islands of South Holland and Zealand. The construction of the dikes is well advanced, and completion is foreseen for 1981. The catastrophic flood of 1 February 1953, reminiscent of the tidal waves of the earlier centuries, made this task particularly urgent.

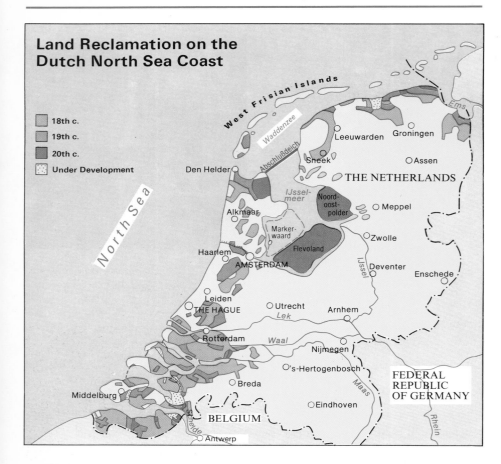

Land Reclamation on the Dutch North Sea Coast

- 18th c.
- 19th c.
- 20th c.
- Under Development

West Frisian Islands

Waddenzee

Abschlußdeich

North Sea

Den Helder

Leeuwarden
Groningen

Sneek
Assen

THE NETHERLANDS

IJssel-meer

Alkmaar

Noord-oost-polder

Meppel

Marker-waard

Zwolle

Haarlem

Flevoland

AMSTERDAM

Deventer

Enschede

IJssel

Leiden

Utrecht

Arnhem

THE HAGUE

Lek

Rotterdam
Waal

Nijmegen

's-Hertogenbosch

FEDERAL
REPUBLIC
OF GERMANY

Breda

Maas

Middelburg

Eindhoven

Schelde

BELGIUM

Rhein

Antwerp

Ems

itself here splits into the Nederrijn and the Waal; the latter, with about two-thirds of the water, is the main stream. Lower down the streams split into many branches. Most of these still exist and have their own names. Among them are the present-day estuaries which are often called by different names (Lek, Merwede, Noord, Dutch IJssel, etc.) and many others such as the "Kromme" and the "Oude" Rhine; originally also the Eem in its glacial Gelder Valley, and several streams with names of their own, such as the Linge, Vecht and Amstel. All these branches are called dike rivers because they deposit sediments brought from the interior, gradually raising their bed and banks until they seem to flow on dikes. At high tide they flood the low-lying country on both sides. This danger can be eliminated only by the construction of dikes, which dike and polder communities have built over many centuries.

But the building of dikes along the coast and the river banks was only part of the job. Because the country lies so extraordinarily low, the usual principle of drainage (to let the excess ground and rainwater escape through sluices at low tide) could be applied only to a limited extent. Holland could only increase its population when windmills became available, to continually lift water from the deep polders, a technique which became known only in the later Middle Ages. Over the entire country, the water-level was now tightly controlled. Only in the main branches of the Rhine, the Lek and the Waal, and in the estuaries of Zealand and

Haringvliet – Locks and Dam

Flour Mill near Nieuwenhorn

islands with the mainland. After thousands of years of natural destruction and centuries of struggle when victory and defeat were in the balance, the inhabitants of the fens will now shortly be nature's masters. But that does not mean that they can relax for a moment. A latent threat still exists along the coastal dunes which are exposed, especially in winter, to the destructive effects of the surf attacking them from the south and south-west, and gradually pushing them back. The church in Scheveningen, a former fishing village and now a fashionable seaside resort, provides one of the most chilling portents. It once stood well inland, but in the course of about 150 years, as the coastline receded, it has been engulfed by the sea. Recently built concrete seafronts in the resorts already stand out from the unstrengthened parts of the coast.

South Holland were the streams allowed to flow freely at first. All other streams are canals ("boezem"), and the basic technical device is the lock. The meandering of the streams betrays that these were once free-flowing rivers, as for example the Amstel in Amsterdam. These streams, flowing at different levels, form a very complicated system but represent at the same time a highly useful network of waterways. For instance, milk obtained on the pastures deep in the polders where the cows graze, travels by water to the farm, then to the dairy and from there to any place in the country where it is required. The same applies to fruit and vegetables and other crops moved from the fields to auction and then to the town markets. The high-lying canals criss-crossing the country, in earlier times navigated by brightly coloured sailing vessels, belong to the most typical and impressive sights of the Dutch landscape. The windmills which appear so often in Dutch landscape paintings have now almost disappeared, being replaced by modern motor pumps. They have been preserved only here and there as romantic mementoes.

The islands off the Dutch coast with their quaint little old towns, once remote and isolated, can now be reached without any difficulty by the new dams and bridges. As a result tourism has increased by leaps and bounds. Great numbers of hotels, summer houses, holiday villages, camping sites and marinas have been built in the last few years. A motorway (highway), recently completed, connects the

Clog-maker in Aalsmeer

The Dutch fen belt has become the economic and political heart of the country because of its geographical position and the communications advantages that go with it, and because its soil is much more fertile than elsewhere. This has led to the rise of the cities as commercial capitals. The amphibious area was at first totally unsuitable for any higher civilisation. On the other hand, it was also impregnable at least to mainland enemies. The fight for independence of the Geuze benefited, therefore, from some natural advantages. The Spaniards were able to attack *Haarlem* which lies on the edge of the dunes, but could never reach Amsterdam. Louis XIV was also unable to cross the estuaries of the Rhine and the Maas.

As far as communications are concerned, *Leyden* (Lugdunum) was the Roman town in the Rhine estuary. *Utrecht*, situated somewhat higher, was the river crossing (trajectum), and, as a heritage from antiquity, also a bishopric. Later on two kinds of Dutch fen towns evolved: those orientated towards the Rhine and Maas estuaries, and those on the Zuiderzee. The early medieval trading towns situated on the rivers just above the tidal zone were *Wijk-bij-Buurstede* on the Lek, *Tiel* on the Waal and later *Dordrecht*, much further out in the Delta, which acted as a trans-shipment place between the Rhine and the Thames. The Zuiderzee, a bay reaching deep into the interior, was once more important than the Rhine estuaries. Around it grew *Deventer* and *Kampen* on the IJssel, *Hoorn* and *Enkhuizen* in North Holland, and also the largest of all the Zuiderzee towns, Amsterdam on the gulf of the IJ. Its much later counterpart in the Rhine estuary was Rotterdam. They both have in common their positions in pure fenland behind the dikes, as their names show, and at the mouths of small rivers, the Amstel and the Rotte. Almost all their streets are also canals (Grachten), i.e., waterways with dike banks. In contrast the well-known narrow Kalverstraat in Amsterdam is a former cattle lane running along plots of land between two canals.

Dam in Amsterdam

Building on marshy ground is difficult. Expensive grids of piles and tree-trunks must be driven deep into the ground down to the diluvial subsoil. Typical of the marshland towns are the canals, the narrow building plots of the gabled houses and the compact character of the construction even towards the fringes of the town. Nowhere can this be seen more clearly than in the capital **Amsterdam**. At the time of the North Sea and Baltic trade, which was also pursued by other Zuiderzee towns, Amsterdam was still very small and insignificant. It developed only in the era of discoveries and later when it became the seat of the East Indian Company and the largest trading city of the Low Countries and of the European continent. The famous 17th c. canal extensions all around the central medieval town bear witness to this expansion. For a long time, access to the port of Amsterdam was through the Zuiderzee. Only with the beginning of steam navigation did the city commission the building first of the North Holland Canal to Den Helder, and later the North Sea Canal right across the dunes to IJmuiden. The canal had to be subsequently enlarged several times. On the inland side it pushed through the construction of the Merwede Canal extending the sea route for the Amsterdam-Rhine shipping as far as Tiel on the Waal.

But **Rotterdam**, which took over the role of Dordrecht, is the real emporium in the Rhine estuary and the country's first port accessible from the interior by the Lower Rhine, the Lek, the Waal and the Merwede. It has the largest turnover of goods in the world, although in the 19th c. it also had to invest heavily when the estuary of the Maas became silted, and the threatened navigation had to be secured by an open canal leading into the sea at the Hook of Holland (the New Waterway).

Trade in the fen towns was followed by the processing of colonial products. Typical of these places are the "Zaanstreek" in the vicinity of Amsterdam, and Langstraat near Waalwijk in the area of the Rhine estuary.

Land in the fens in the vegetable-growing regions of the west country, on the Amstel and the "Streek" between Hoorn and Enkhuizen, is intensively farmed. It is worth noting that the soil particles of marl and dune sand are mixed to improve its quality. Only around Haarlem in the tulip country is the moorland covered with a thin, natural layer of wind-blown sand. The mild climate benefits the hot-house grown early vegetables. The production is sufficient to satisfy large home demand and also to supply London and the Ruhr area. The *Betuwe*, a river moor between the Waal and the Lower Rhine, is famous for its fruit. The industries of the fenland specialise mostly in processing overseas raw materials and half-finished products. The most important of these are metal, chemicals, electrical hardware, textiles and food.

The economic power and the cultural style of the fen country made its imprint imperceptibly upon the Geest country. Originally, the sandy regions knew only modest farming and sheep rearing. Only places where rivers could be crossed by a bridge or a ferry were important, as for example the ancient sister towns **Arnhem** and **Nijmegen**, developed on Roman foundations on the Lower Rhine and the Waal. Higher up the country are *Venlo*, *Roermond* and **Maastricht**. In certain parts of the Geest, cloth-making was typical, as in Twente around *Enschede* and *Almelo*, and in Brabant near Tilburg and Eindhoven.

On the whole the sandy outer provinces remained more or less uncultivated until the 19th c. Characteristically the influence of the fens began to show first in the most inacessible parts of the Geest: in the high moors which since the 17th c. were more and more cultivated, and today except for some small stretches in Peel in Brabant, are fully cultivated. The method was "fenning", i.e. removing of peat and farming on the subsoil (the Fen colonies of Groningen). The fuel requirements of the many fen towns made this method especially effective.

Since the 20th c. sandy heathlands have been cultivated by colonising communities using strong fertilisers. Manufacturing industries of all kinds, especially electrical, preferred to settle in the Geest towns with their low-cost land and, compared with the fens, less expensive construction and available labour. *Tilburg*, **Eindhoven** and *Helmond* thus expanded into sizable agglomerations, and the towns of Twente, Gelderland and Overijssel became important textile producers. On the Eems oil was found. The industrial development of the South Limburg tip around *Heerlen* was different because of the considerable coal deposits connected with those of Aix/Aachen and the Belgian Kempen. However, when the last coal mines were closed in 1975, a complete restructuring of the industries took place.

The way of life and the cultural landscape of the towns and villages in these parts of the country are more and more influenced by the fenlands. Canals were dug in the higher sand regions, and the entire country was thus linked to the central waterway network. Earlier, the main feature was the contrast between the fenlands with their well-to-do farms of the Frisian kind, and the poor Geest villages with Saxon-type buildings. Nowadays a general Dutch style has emerged, bearing the imprint of the country. This is particularly evident in the layout and construction of the towns. The modern Netherlands from Walcheren to *Groningen*, from Den Helder to Maastricht emerge as a geographical and cultural unit.

Luxembourg
Grand-Duché de Luxembourg
Grousherzogdem Lëtzebuerg
Grand Duchy of Luxembourg

——— District Frontiers
- - - Canton Frontiers

DISTRICT Canton	Area in sq. km (sq. miles)	Population	Main Town
LUXEMBURG	904 (349)	270,500	Luxembourg
1a Luxembourg (Stadt)	51 (20)	79,500	Luxembourg
1b Luxembourg (Umland)	187 (72)	34,300	Luxembourg
2 Esch-sur-Alzette	243 (94)	114,900	Esch-sur-Alzette
3 Capellen	199 (77)	25,800	Capellen
4 Mersch	224 (86)	16,000	Mersch
GREVENMACHER	525 (203)	37,900	Grevenmacher
5 Grevenmacher	211 (81)	15,800	Grevenmacher
6 Remich	128 (49)	11,500	Remich
7 Echternach	186 (72)	10,600	Echternach
DIEKIRCH	1157 (447)	53,300	Diekirch
8 Diekirch	239 (92)	21,400	Diekirch
9 Redange	268 (103)	10,300	Redange
10 Wiltz	294 (114)	10,000	Wiltz
11 Vianden	54 (21)	2,700	Vianden
12 Clervaux	302 (117)	8,900	Clervaux
Grand Duchy of Luxembourg	2586 (998)	360,000	Luxembourg

The **Grand Duchy of Luxembourg** (in French, *Grand-Duché de Luxembourg*; in Letzeburgish, *Grousherzogdem Lëtzebuerg*) is according to its constitution of 1868, a hereditary constitutional monarchy. The head of state is the Grand Duke (since 1964 Jean from the House of Nassau, born 1921). The country is divided into three districts, 12 cantons and 126 communes. The Parliament has one Chamber (Chambre des Députés) with 59 members elected for five years. The State Council (Conseil de l'Etat, with 21 members appointed for life by the Grand Duke), has a consultative function. The government, with at least three ministers, is appointed by the Grand Duke. One of them as Minister of State is the head of government.

The Luxembourgers are of Germanic stock descended from the Moselle Franks and are predominantly Catholic. Approximately one-quarter of all inhabitants of the Grand Duchy are foreigners (most of them Italians, Portuguese, French, Germans, Belgians and Spaniards). The official languages are French (predominant) and German. The colloquial language is Letzeburgish (= Moselle Frankish, a Middle Frankish dialect).

The capital city of Luxembourg is the seat of the European Court of Justice and of the Secretariat of the European Parliament.

The Grand Duchy of **LUXEMBOURG** is geographically divided into two characteristic regions, the Ardennes, here called Ösling or Islek, and part of the Uplands of Lorraine called Gutland (in French Pays Gaumais).

Ösling, although by nature rather infertile, has been developed to a considerable degree of agricultural productivity, corresponding to the high standards of this prosperous little country. The contrast with the economically backward German region of Western Eifel, which is similarly cursed by nature, is striking. The wooded mountain region is also a popular tourist country.

Gutland, which extends over shell-limestone, red marl and black jurassic soils is, on the other hand, very fertile. On the limestone slopes along the Moselle, between Schengen and Wasserbillig, grow the well-known grapes from which

Regions of the Benelux Countries

are produced the wines of the Belgian-Luxembourg customs area. The most important types are Rivaner, Riesling, Auxerrois, White Burgundy, Ruländer and Traminer. Across the middle of Gutland there is, however, a less fertile strip of Jurassic sandstone, separated north and south from the surrounding country by marked steps. The abbey town of *Echternach* on the Sûre is dominated by its steep slopes. This sandstone table is characterised by bizarre rock formations and drops almost vertically into the Valley of the Alzette and its tributaries. Upon it in the middle of the woods lies the capital city of **Luxembourg**. It was built in an impregnable position as a fortress controlling the route between France and Germany, but its fortifications were razed in 1866.

Luxembourg, and also Belgium, touch in the south on a layer of Brown Jura (Dogger), which contains one of the richest iron-ore deposits in Europe,

known as the Minette. When it was tapped after the invention of the Thomas process in the last quarter of the 19th c., the area quickly became one of the largest iron-working districts in Europe. The Luxembourg share of the ore deposits is minute compared with that of France. The mines in the tiny tip of Belgium have already been exhausted. The ore with its iron content of 20–35% is relatively poor, which is the reason why it is called Minette (= small ore). To avoid high transport costs, heavy industries were encouraged to settle next to the mines. Coke for fuelling the blast furnaces is imported from abroad. After the turn of the century, when a large part of Lorraine still belonged to Germany, industrialisation proceeded by leaps and bounds. Luxembourg became an industrialised country, its most important company being the Aciéries Réunies Burbach-Esch-Dudelange (ARBED).

Population

BELGIUM lies on the frontier between the Germanic and the Romance linguistic areas. The French-speaking **Walloons** live in the southern part of the Kingdom. The **Flemings**, speaking a Dutch dialect, inhabit the northern part of the country. The dividing line which has hardly changed since the Middle Ages is the linguistic frontier between Flemish and Walloon. It runs approximately from Visé on the Meuse east–west across Waremme, Halle and Ronse and Menen on the French border. Brussels is a Walloon enclave on Flemish territory and is officially bilingual (French/Dutch). Next to Flemings and Walloons, **Germans** around Eupen, St Vith and Arlon constitute the third linguistic and population group. Their share of the total population is only 0·6%. Conflicts between Flemings and Walloons have occurred again and again, mainly for economic reasons. Before the Second World War, the Walloon areas of Belgium were clearly privileged economically because of their coal deposits and the iron and steel industries based on them. Today, owing to the economic restructuring, the relationship has been reversed to the

disadvantage of the coal districts. On the other hand, the number of French-speaking Belgians has diminished because of their very low birth-rate. They number today only about 40% of the total population.

The population increase has slowed considerably since the Second World War. The birth-rate (14 per thousand) is among the lowest in Europe, and at the same time the death rate (12 per thousand) is relatively high. Generally speaking, the birth-rate in the Flemish parts of the country is above the national average.

The population density in Belgium is approximately 322 per sq. km (834 per sq. mile), which is exceeded only by Monaco and the Netherlands. It has to be kept in mind, however, that the regional population distribution can vary widely from the average. One extreme is the six large urban areas, Brussels, Antwerp, Liège, Ghent, Charleroi and Borinage. More than one-third of the total population live here and the density in some places is over 1000 per sq. km (2590 per sq. mile). Also large parts of the provinces of Antwerp, East and West Flanders, have a higher than average density (500 per sq. km –

Oostende
Brugge
Gent
Ieper
Ko-trijk
BRUSSELS
Turnhout
Antwerp
Mechelen
Leuven
Hasselt
St. Truiden
Tournai
Namur
Liège
Eupen
Mons
Huy
Charleroi
Malmédy
Dinant
Bastogne
Bouillon
Arlon

Linguistic Regions in Belgium

——— Linguistic Frontier

German

Dutch (Flemish)

French

Bilingual (French and Dutch/Flemish)

1295 per sq. mile). On the other hand, the density in the mountainous region of the Ardennes is only 50 per sq. km (130 per sq. mile) and in places even less.

The high population density in Belgium is a sympton of its high ratio of urban dwellers. Almost half of the population lives in towns, and a further 38% in urbanised communities. Rural communities account for only about 13% of the total. The occupational structure of the Belgian population reflects a very high degree of industrialisation and urbanisation. Before industrialisation agriculture was the most important sector of the economy, but now accounts for only about 6% of the working population. Industry, on the other hand, employs almost 46% and the number of people employed in the service sector is even higher (approximately 48%).

In the territory of the **NETHERLANDS**, several Germanic tribes intermingled between the 2nd millennium B.C. and the 5th c. A.D.: the **Frisians** in the north, the **Saxons** in the east, and the **Franks** in the south. The Frisians are the only group which has preserved a certain degree of independence up to the present; their

language is recognised as an official one along with Dutch. When the former Dutch colonies acquired their independence, further population groups such as the *Indonesians* and *Surinamese* and people from the Antilles came to the country, but their proportion of the population is less than 2%.

The population increase after 1945 was around 11%. This was the result of a high birth-rate (19 per thousand), and a relatively low death rate (8 per thousand) due to the favourable age structure of the population. Towards the end of the 1960s, the birth-rate dropped sharply for a time but is still around 15 per thousand, a comparatively high figure for Europe. The death rate remained unchanged. The population growth is, therefore, today some 8 per thousand, excluding the immigration of some 20,000 people.

The population density is approximately 412 per sq. km (1067 per sq. mile), which is, except for Monaco, the highest in the world. Although the area of the Netherlands is relatively small, there are still considerable regional differences as far as the distribution of the population is concerned. The highest density (more than 1000 per sq. km (2590 per sq. mile)) is reached in the so-called "Randstad Holland" (see map under "Economy") in the west of the country. This is the largest concentration in the Netherlands. Here, in only 10% of the country's territory, live more than 40% of its total population. To Randstad Holland belong to most important cities: Amsterdam, Haarlem, Leyden, The Hague, Delft, Rotterdam, Dordrecht, Utrecht, etc. Other concentrations are the so-called Brabant town line (Bergen op Zoom, Roosendaal, Breda, Tilburg, 's-Hertogenbosch and Eindhoven), and South and Middle Limburg. Between these three extends an area of predominantly rural character with a lower population density. Nevertheless, there are some larger cities in this area, such as Nijmegen, Arnhem, Apeldoorn, Enschede and Groningen. The intensity of urbanisation in the Netherlands becomes clear when we take into account that only about 20% of the total population live in rural communities.

The high urbanisation of the Netherlands is also clearly reflected in the occupational structure of its population. Agriculture, forestry and fisheries together account only for about 7% of the working population, while the industrial sector accounts for 36%. The service sector, by far the largest, employs 57% of all the working people. This kind of proportion between the industrial and service sectors of the economy is matched by very few industrialised countries in the world. It is a sign that the Dutch economy has reached an extraordinarily high degree of development which will be difficult to surpass.

LUXEMBOURG lies on the German side of the dividing line between the Romance and the Germanic populations (which runs further north across Belgium into French Flanders). The French/German linguistic frontier in the north-west of Luxembourg follows the Belgian frontier, moves west into Belgian territory at Arlon and touches between Athem and Esch on the Alzette several places on Luxembourg territory. The current language in the Grand Duchy is mostly "Letzeburgish", a branch of Moselle-Frankish, which is also to some extent spoken around Arlon in Belgian-Luxembourg. High German will also be understood everywhere. The administrative language in Luxembourg is French, the mother-tongue of the Counts and Dukes of Luxembourg. The territory, which used to be much larger, previously had a majority of French-speaking rather than German-speaking inhabitants.

The largest population group in the country is the **Luxembourgers**, numbering about 270,000. To this must be added some 90,000 foreigners who form around 25% of the total population and 30% of the working population. Most of them live in the capital city of Luxembourg and in the industrial districts in the south of the country. Their most important home countries are Italy, Portugal, France, Federal Germany, Belgium and Spain.

Compared with other EEC countries, the birth-rate in Luxembourg is very low (around 12 per thousand), and its death rate very high (also around 12 per thousand), owing to a topheavy age pyramid of the population. The result is a stagnating population growth. If it were not for the relatively high birth-rate of the foreigners, there would be a progressive decline in population.

The average population density in Luxembourg is approximately 139 per sq. km (360 per sq. mile). The capital city and the highly industrialised Canton Esch which together have only 18% of the territory, account for 63% of the total population. That means that the density here is much higher (more than 400 per sq. km (1063 per sq. mile)) than in the rest of the country. In Gutland there are only between 75 and 100 people per sq. km (194–259 people per sq. mile), and to the north in Ösling, the density sometimes drops to less than 50 per sq. km (130 per sq. mile). The occupation structure of the population is characterised by the high proportion of people employed in mining and industry (47%). The service sector accounts for 43% of the working population, a figure reflecting the importance of the capital city as an international administrative capital. Agriculture employs only about 10% of the working population.

History

Prehistory and Early History. – In the early Stone Age (about 4000 B.C.), the loess areas of Belgium and also the Dutch Geest were inhabited by **Celts**. The numerous megalithic tombs in the Dutch province of Drente bear witness to this. Since the fenlands were less suitable for settlements, it was only in about 1500 B.C. that the **Germans** advanced into them, building their homes on "warfts" (artificial mounds) to protect them against floods.

1st c. B.C.   The northern coastal areas were the land of the **Frisians**. The Rhine Delta was occupied by the Germanic **Batavians**.

58 B.C.–A.D. 500.   **Roman** domination. – 58–51 B.C. – **Julius Caesar** conquered Gaul, the northern part of which was inhabited by Celtic **Belgae**. From 12 B.C. to A.D. 9. the Romans tried unsuccessfully to subjugate the Germanic lands on the right bank of the Rhine. A.D. 69–71. – A great uprising of the Batavians under Iulius Civilis took place.

4th and 5th c.   The Salian **Franks** occupied the territory between the Meuse, the Schelde, and the Lower Rhine. Tongres became a Bishopric. About 440 Clovis (*Chlodio*), the ancestor of the Merovingians, made Tournai his capital.

About 481–843.   The Low Countries were incorporated in the Frankish Empire.

6th–8th c.   Christianity expanded. Utrecht and Liège became Bishoprics.

843.   The Carolingian empire was divided by the Treaty of Verdun. The territory west of the Schelde went to France (Charles the Bald); east of the Schelde to the Empire of Lothar (Lotharingia).

870.   By the Treaty of Mersen (Meerssen near Maastricht), Lotharingia was divided between France and Germany (Ludwig the German).

The Emergence of Counties, Duchies and Towns (10th–14th c.). After the disintegration of the Lotharingian Empire, numerous individual feudal domains emerged. These tried to join with each other in various forms, and to weaken the sovereignty of their large neighbours. The general term for these territories was coined for the first time in the 11th c. as the "Low Countries". Up to the end of the 18th c. it comprised also present-day Belgium.

Brabant: The territory originally known as Lower Lotharingia became a Duchy in 1006. – In 1288 it took over Limburg, in 1355 Luxembourg, and in 1430 joined with Burgundy. The so-called Golden Bull of Brabant from Emperor Charles IV (1349) exempted it from all foreign jurisdiction. In the 15th c. Brabant was the focal point of crafts, trade and learning in the Low Countries. In 1648 it was divided into North and South Brabant.

Breda: In 1404 the town and domain became the property by marriage of the Counts of Nassau-Dillenburg who acquired in 1530, again by marriage, the Duchy of Orange in Southern France.

Burgundy (Bourgogne): The Duchy, created in 884, became in the 14th–15th c. a powerful state between France and Germany. Between 1384 and 1473, the Dukes acquired almost all secular domains in the Low Countries. After the death of the last Duke the Burgundian Low Countries were acquired by the House of Habsburg (1477).

Flanders (*Vlaanderen*): In 864 a county was created in defence against the Norsemen. The Wallonian Flanders were mostly under the feudal sovereignty of France (Crown Flanders). During the Crusades, the Counts of Flanders became in 1204–61 the "Latin" emperors of Constantinople. In 1384 Flanders was acquired by Burgundy. The Flemish towns, especially Ghent, Ypres and Bruges, acquired in the 12th–14th c. because of their trade and cloth-making considerable economic power and increased freedoms. In 1302 the army of Flemish Guilds defeated the French knights in the "Battle of the Golden Spurs" near Kortrijk (Courtrai).

Friesland: Zuiderzee and the Eems was conquered by the Counts of Holland only after long fighting in the 13th–14th c.

Gelderland: The county, created in the 11th c., became a Duchy in 1339 and since 1379 has been ruled alternately by Jullich, the Counts Egmont, Cleve and Burgundy.

Hainaut: The county was created in the middle of the 9th c. as a defence against the Norsemen. In the 11th–13th c. it was united several times with Flanders; in 1299 it belonged to Holland; in 1345 it was acquired by the Dynasty of Wittelsbach, and in 1433 by Burgundy.

Holland: The County of Holland was created in the 11th c. within the Duchy of Lower Lotharingia. Count William II was in 1247–56 King of Germany against Frederick II. In 1299 Holland was united with Hainaut.

Limburg: The county created in 1060 became a Duchy at the beginning of the 12th c. as part of Lower Lotharingia. It was united in 1221–6 with Luxembourg and since 1288 with Brabant. It was divided in 1648.

Liège: The town became a bishopric in 721. Its territorial possessions had been since the 4th c. an ecclesiastical principality and part of Germany. Its citizens fought repeatedly for their freedom in the 15th and 17th c. The town was conquered by Charles the Bold in 1477, and thereafter was linked with Burgundy.

Namur: The county created in the 10th c. became about 1200 part of Hainaut, of Flanders in 1262, and of Burgundy in 1420.

Utrecht: The bishopric, founded in 696, acquired considerable territorial possessions in the 10th–11th c. The Bishop was for long the main representative of the imperial power in the Low Countries. In 1528 Emperor Charles V acquired secular authority by treaty. In 1577 the Princess of Orange introduced the Reformed religion. In 1579 the Union of Utrecht was signed here.

From the Unification of the Low Countries to the Spanish Domination (15th–16th c.). – The Duke of Burgundy, Philip the Good, who united several counties in his possession, initiated the separation of the Low Countries from the Holy Roman Empire. A little later the Low Countries were acquired by the Austrian Habsburgs who added other territories to them. Spain took over power by inheritance.

1384–1473   The Dukes of Burgundy united in their possessions almost the entire territory of the Low Countries.

1419–67   Under Duke *Philip the Good*, the Netherlands experienced their first period of economic prosperity. It was also the first period of importance for Dutch painting (Jan van Eyck was Philip's court painter).

1467–77   Duke *Charles the Bold*, the richest and most ambitious prince of his time, suppressed the nobles and towns. He was killed in 1477 at Nancy.

1477   *Maria*, daughter and heiress of Charles the Bold, married the Archduke Maximilian of Austria, the future Emperor *Maximilian I*. Thus the Burgundian Low Countries came into the possession of the **Habsburgs**.

1519–56:   Emperor **Charles V** (born 1500 in Ghent) brought under Habsburg domination, among others, Utrecht (1528) and Geldern (1583). His aim was to make the entire territory into a strong state and to reduce the ancient liberties which restricted the privileges of the Crown. After 1520 Luther's teaching penetrated into the country, but after 1550 **Calvinism** became the dominant creed in the northern provinces. Charles V fought the new religion (Inquisition Trials from 1522), because it endangered the cohesion of the state.

1556   When, after the abdication of Charles V, his world empire was divided, the Low Countries became the possession of **Spain**.

BELGIUM

The Subjection of the Southern Netherlands, the Future Belgium (1556–1648). – Spain wanted to impress its authority upon the Low Countries through political, economic and religious repression. The nobles and the Estates opposed it, and in the end the conflict culminated in a popular uprising and an armed clash. The Northern Netherlands (seven provinces), were able to liberate themselves from Spanish domination (Republic of the United Netherlands), while the Walloon provinces had to swear loyalty to the Spaniards (Union of Arras). This sealed the separation of the two parts of the country and laid to a large extent the territorial frontier between present-day Belgium and the Netherlands.

1556–98   **Philip II** of Spain (son of Charles V), a dominant figure of the **Counter Reformation**, wanted to impose his absolute authority upon the free Netherlands. He sent Spanish troops into the country, spurned the rights of the Estates and the nobles, and tried with fanatical intolerance to exterminate Protestantism.

1559–67   Under the governorship of *Margaret of Parma* (daughter of Charles V), unrest and opposition grew. *Cardinal Granvella*, Adviser to the Crown, was recalled by the King in 1564 at the insistence of the Princes of Orange.

1566   The Dutch nobles concluded an alliance in Breda, calling themselves **Geuze** ("beggars"). This was originally a nickname derived from a petition sent to the Governor. Later the armed uprising, especially the naval one, was called Geuze (Water-Geuze). The population rioted and devastated the Catholic churches.

1567–73   Under the Governor, the **Duke of Alba**, Philip II sent new troops to suppress the rebellion. Alba had thousands of people executed. In 1568 the Counts *Egmont* and *Hoorn* were beheaded in Brussels.

1568   The freedom fight began in the Northern Netherlands.

1579   The Union of Utrecht (Protective Alliance), was signed by the seven Protestant northern provinces.

1579–1604   The subjugation of the Southern Provinces. In 1604 the fortress of Ostend, the last Dutch base in the southern provinces, was taken by the Spaniards after a three-year siege. The split of the Low Countries into the Northern and the Southern parts was thus sealed except for a short interval in 1792–1830.

1598–1621   Under the regency of Archduke *Albrecht*, the husband of Isabella, daughter of Philip II, the country enjoyed an economic recovery. This was the peak period of Baroque art (Rubens, van Dyck, Jordaens, Brouwer).

1648   The Treaty of Westphalia brought an end to the 30 Years War. The southern provinces, the future Belgium, remained under Spain. Holland blocked the Schelde.

1667–97   During the wars of Louis XIV, the French armies fought several times in the Spanish Netherlands.

1701–14   In the War of the Spanish Succession, the French were defeated by the English under Marlborough, and by the Austrians under Prince Eugene. In the Spanish Netherlands they lost the battles of Ramillies (1706), Oudenaarde (1708) and Malplaquet (1709).

From the Austrian Assumption of Power to the Unification of Belgium and the Netherlands (1714–1830). – After the War of the Spanish Succession, the Southern Netherlands became the possession of Austria. A popular uprising demanding the creation of the United Belgian States was crushed. When Austria was defeated by France (Coalition War), the Northern and Southern Netherlands were united under French sovereignty underwritten by the Congress of Vienna.

1714   The Spanish Netherlands became **Austrian**.

1745–8   In the Austrian War of Succession, the French occupied almost the entire territory (Battle of Fontenoy, 1745), but the Peace Treaty returned it to Austria.

1765–90   Emperor *Joseph II* ruled in the spirit of Enlightenment. His well-meant but hasty reforms injured the religious feelings of the population.

1789–90   After a popular uprising inspired by the French Revolution, the Austrian Netherlands declared themselves an independent **republic** under the name of the **United Belgian States** (this was the first use of the name Belgium in modern times). When Emperor Leopold II reasserted his rights, the Austrian troops once again subjugated the country.

1792–4   Occupation of Belgium and the Netherlands by the French. In the First Coalition War, the French Revolutionary Army defeated the Austrians at Jemappes (1792) and Fleurus (1794).

1795–1813   As a consequence of the Austrian defeat, the entire Low Countries (Northern and Southern provinces) became **dependent on France**.

1815   Napoleon was decisively defeated in the Battle of Waterloo (south of Brussels).

1815–30   The Congress of Vienna decided to create the **Kingdom of the United Netherlands** (Eupen and Malmédy were given to Prussia). The Kingdom comprised the Northern Netherlands, Belgium and the former Bishopric of Liège. The Universities of Ghent (1816) and Liège (1817) were founded.

The Kingdom of Belgium (from 1830). – The economic, religious and linguistic conflicts between the northern and southern parts of the country, led to a popular uprising in Belgium. In the fight against the Dutch army, Belgium held the upper hand and became independent. After some initial growing pains, Belgium rose to become the leading industrial country on the European continent. It also became a successful colonial power (Belgian Congo). After the Second World War, Belgium gave up her rather unsuccessful policy of neutrality and joined the Western Defence Alliance (NATO) and the European Economic Community. In the 1960s the linguistic struggle developed into sharp conflicts between the Flemings and the Walloons.

1830   Belgium declared **independence**.

1831–65   *Leopold I*, Prince of Coburg, was elected King by the National Assembly.

1834   University of Brussels was founded.

1835   The first railway line on the European continent, running from Mechelen to Brussels, was opened.

1839   The great powers guaranteed the neutrality of Belgium. Belgium obtained the western part of Limburg and Luxembourg.

1863   The tolls of the Schelde were lifted. The Netherlands received compensation.

1865–1909   Belgium became an industrial state. Its development was dominated by the conflicts between the liberal and clerical opinions. After the Workers' Congress in Brussels (1886), socialism became increasingly important.

1908   The territory of the Congo, created as an independent state by Leopold II in 1881–5, became a Belgian colony (Congo Belge).

1840–1932   The **Flemish Movement** prevented the language and the way of life of the Flemish from becoming influenced by France, and obtained equality in public life. In 1930 the University of Ghent became Flemish. In 1932 all central administrative offices became bilingual.

1914–18   When the German ultimatum was rejected in the **First World War**, the German troops invaded Belgium and occupied the country despite the stubborn resistance of the Belgian army. The government fled to Le Havre in France.

1919   The Treaty of Versailles acknowledged Belgium's right of compensation for war damages. The districts of Eupen, Malmédy and Neutral-Moresnet became part of the country.

1921   Universal suffrage was introduced.

1935   Queen *Astrid*, wife of *Leopold III*, was killed in a car accident.

1939–45   In the **Second World War**, the German troops again occupied neutral Belgium (1940: Battle of the Ardennes 1944). The government escaped to England. The King signed the Capitulation document and was interned.

1944   The **Benelux Customs' Union** was formed. It entered into force gradually up to 1948.

1949   Belgium joined NATO.

1950   Leopold III abdicated. His son, **Baudouin** (*Boudewijn*, born 1930), became King in 1951.

1958   The Customs' and Economic Union of the Benelux countries was concluded by the Treaty of The Hague, initially for 50 years. The Economic Union came into force on 1 January 1960.

1960   The Belgian Congo became the independent Republic of the Congo (since 1971 Republic of Zaire). King *Baudouin I* married *Fabiola de Mora y Aragon*, from a Spanish noble family.

After 1960   the **linguistic struggles** between Dutch (Flemish) speaking Flemings and the French-speaking Walloons, became more acute.

1963   The *linguistic frontier* between the Flemings and the Walloons was fixed.

1970   Four linguistic regions were created: one Flemish, one French, one German and one bilingual Dutch/Flemish-French, in the capital city of Brussels. The Universities of Louvain and Brussels were each divided in two independent parts, one Flemish, one French.

After 1974   a world-wide energy crisis and economic recession affected the country owing to drastic increases in oil prices.

1974   Islam was put on equal terms with Christian churches and Jewish religious communities.

1975   Three regional parliaments were established in Brussels, in Mechelen (for Flanders), and in Namur (for Wallonia, including the German-speaking districts in East Belgium).

1976   Rapid increase in unemployment.

1977   Communal Reform.

1978   Agreement in principle about the Constitutional Reform ("Plan Egmont"). The country will be divided into **regions**, Flanders with eleven, Wallonia with thirteen sub-regions, and Brussels.

1979   Economic stagnation.

1980   Political difficulties because of continuing linguistic struggles.

THE NETHERLANDS

The Fight for Freedom and the Making of the State (1568–1648). – Seven Protestant northern provinces of the Low Countries (Union of Utrecht), under the leadership of William I, the Silent, rose against the Spanish. By the end of the 30 Years War, they had become independent. In the 17th c. the commerce of the young state flourished.

1568–84   *William I*, the Silent, *Prince of Orange*, became leader of the Freedom Fight against Spanish domination.

1568   Beginning of the armed resistance. William I collected troops, invaded the Netherlands in 1568, and soon became the leader of the rebels. He ordered the **Geuze** to take several coastal towns with their fleet. The Spaniards had to give up their siege of Leyden after a year when William ordered the dikes to be breached in 1574. Leyden was granted its University in 1575.

1579   The seven Protestant northern provinces (Friesland, Gelderland, Groningen, Holland, Overijssel, Utrecht and Zealand), formed an alliance, the **Union of Utrecht**. This served until 1795 as the constitutional basis of the Dutch Republic.

1581   The Northern Provinces declared their independence.

1584   William I was assassinated in Delft by a fanatical Catholic.

1585–1625   *Maurice of Orange*, the son of William and a governor, conquered numerous towns, and by his victory at Nieuwpoort (1600) forced the

Spaniards to retreat entirely from the Northern Provinces. Admiral *Jacob van Heemskerk* defeated the Spaniards at Gibraltar in 1607. Armistice from 1608 to 1621.

Economy and maritime trade began to flourish. Amsterdam became the most important merchant city in Europe. In 1612 the Dutch founded New Amsterdam, the future New York in North America. The East Indian and West Indian companies (founded 1602 and 1621) acquired territorial possessions in the Malayan Archipelago and in South America. In 1610 (or 1619) the founding of Batavia (Djakarta).

1609–19 Differences between the Province of Holland and the other Provinces, between the Republic supporters of the "Staaten" (Provincial Assemblies), and the partisans of the House of Orange and the Stadholders, led to internal struggles. The fight between the Gomarist (orthodox Calvinists) and the moderate Arminians represented by *Jan van Oldenbarnevelt* threatened internal stability. This 72-year-old leading statesman of the Province of Holland was executed in 1619 by the orders of Maurice of Orange.

1621–48 Admiral *Piet Hein* captured in 1628 during the 30 Years War the Silver Fleet arriving from Spanish South American territories. Dutch troops occupied North Brabant and Limburg.

The Peak of Power and Decline (1648–1792). – The Treaty of Westphalia (1648) recognised the independence of the Republic and acknowledged its conquests in North Brabant, Limburg and the colonies. The Republic became one of the leading trading nations and one of the strongest naval powers in the world. Painting reached its peak (Frans Hals, Rembrandt, Jan Steen, Vermeer van Delft) and the University of Leyden acquired European fame. The philosopher *Spinoza* (1632–77) lived from 1670 in The Hague. In the 18th c. struggles broke out between the opponents of the House of Orange and the Stadholders and led to the loss of the greater part of the fleet and brought about the decline of the country.

1648 **Independence** of the Netherlands.

1653–72 *Jan de Witt*, an opponent of the House of Orange, ran the affairs of State with an iron hand.

1652–4 and 1664–7 The Netherlands fought two navals wars against England. In the first they won several battles under their experienced Admirals *Michiel de Ruyter* and *Marten Tromp*, but in the end they were defeated. In the second war, de Ruyter blocked the Thames in 1667.

1668 De Witt concluded a triple alliance with England and Sweden, and thereby forced Louis XIV to give up his attack on the Spanish Netherlands.

1672 Popular uprising at the invasion of the French. The murder of de Witt.

1672–8 The war of Louis XIV against the Netherlands. The French conquered Geldern and Utrecht. Holland was saved by breaching the dikes. England, siding with France, was defeated by de Ruyter in several naval battles. Brandenburg and Austria supported the Netherlands which, under the Peace Treaty of Nijmegen, did not suffer any losses.

1672–1702 *William II*, **William of Orange**, the Stadholder of the Netherlands was also King of England from 1689 (William and Mary).

1702–92 Economy and arts did not reach the same levels as in the 17th c. European conflicts affected the Netherlands in many ways. The "patriots"

(opponents of the House of Orange), ruled the country until 1747 without Stadholders, and in 1786 forced the Stadholder, *William V* to leave the country. In 1787 he was brought back by Prussian troops.

1780–4 War against Britain in the American War of Independence. It cost the Netherlands the greater part of its fleet. This exacerbated a general decline of the country.

Vassal State of France (1792–1813). – In the period of the French Revolution, the Northern Netherlands, like the Southern Netherlands (Belgium), were conquered by France and afterwards incorporated into the French Empire.

1792–4 A French revolutionary army conquered Netherlands and Belgium in the First Coalition War.

1795–1808 Following the French example, both countries were united as the **Republic of Batavia**. The Dutch colonies were occupied by England in 1802.

1808–10 *Napoleon* created the **Kingdom of Holland**.

1810–13 The Kingdom of Holland was incorporated into the French Empire.

The Kingdom of the Netherlands (since 1813). – The French were forced to leave the country (1813). Prince William, the son of the last Stadholder, took over the government. – In 1814 England returned the colonial territories. An attempt to unite again Belgium and the Netherlands in one state (1815) failed. Belgium declared her independence in 1830.

1815 The **Kingdom of the United Netherlands** was created by the Congress of Vienna: *William I of Orange* was acknowledged as King.

1830 The Rebellion and secession of Belgium.

1839 Railway line, Haarlem–Amsterdam.

1840–90 During the rule of *William II* (died 1849), and *William III*, the conflicts between the liberals and the conservatives, the Catholics and the Calvinists, endangered the political stability of the Netherlands.

1840–53 The Haarlemmermeer was enclosed and 183 sq. km (71 sq. miles) of new land were reclaimed.

1890–1948 The government of *Queen Wilhelmina*, daughter of William III, introduced social legislation.

1917 Introduction of universal suffrage.

1914–18 In the **First World War** the Netherlands remained strictly **neutral**.

1920 The draining of the Zuiderzee (IJsselmeer) began.

1939–45 In the **Second World War**, the German army occupied the Netherlands. The government escaped to England. The country suffered heavily under the occupation.

1944 Belgium, the Netherlands and Luxembourg formed the **Benelux Customs' Union**. It was gradually put into effect up to 1948.

1948 Queen **Juliana**, born 1909, ascended to the Throne.

1949 The former colonial territories of the Dutch East Indies (Java, Sumatra, Borneo, Celebes, Moluccas Islands), formed the independent Republic of Indonesia with the capital Djakarta (former Batavia). In 1963 the new state annexed West New Guinea (West Irian).

1954 The Netherlands joined NATO.

1958 Customs' and Economic Union of the Benelux countries.

1966 Crown Princess *Beatrix*, born 1938, married *Claus von Amsberg*, a German aristocrat.

1967 The Crown Prince *Willem-Alexander* was born.

Since 1974 a worldwide energy crisis and economic recession have been caused by a sharp increase in oil prices.

1975 Dutch Guiana became independent as the Republic of Surinam. The Moluccan "Ambonese" staged terrorist attacks and took hostages.

1976 Prince *Bernhard* resigned all his public offices, having been involved in the "Lockheed Affair", but remained a member of the State Council. The Moluccans took hostages at Bovensmilde and strained relations between the coloured minority and the native Dutch population.

1978 Another hostage drama (train hijack at Assen by the Moluccans).

1979 Economic stagnation. "Plan 1981" to reduce unemployment.

1980 Queen Juliana abdicated because of age in favour of her eldest daughter, **Beatrix**.

LUXEMBOURG

The Middle Ages. – The little country of Luxembourg (Lützelburg) on the borders between Germany, Belgium and France, changed its rulers several times in the course of centuries. German and French influences continually opposed each other. By the Treaty of Verdun (843) it became part of Lotharingia, by the Treaty of Mersen (870) part of Germany.

10th–13th c. The **county** of Luxembourg was created and linked with Namur, Limburg and Brabant.

1308–1437 Four counts of Luxembourg became Emperors of Germany (Henry VII, Charles IV and his two sons, Wenzel and Sigismund).

1354–1477 Luxembourg became a **Duchy**. In 1443 it became part of Burgundy. In 1477 it was acquired by the Habsburgs.

Between the Great Powers. – Between 1555 and 1814 Luxembourg belonged successively to Spain, France, Austria and again to France.

1555–1700 Luxembourg was part of the Spanish Netherlands.

17th c. The 30 Years War and the wars of Louis XIV shattered the country.

1713–95 Luxembourg was part of the Austrian Netherlands.

1795–1814 Luxembourg was a **French Département**.

Luxembourg after the Congress of Vienna. The country became an independent Grand Duchy.

1815 The Congress of Vienna made Luxembourg a **Grand Duchy** and a part of the **German Bund**.

1815–91 A personal union with the Kings of the Netherlands.

1830–9 Belgium occupied the Walloon western part of the country, and the great powers acknowledged the annexation.

1867 After the disintegration of the German Bund, the great powers guaranteed Luxembourg's **independence** and neutrality.

1891 The crown passed to the Walram line of the House of Nassau-Weilburg.

1914–18 and 1939–45 In both **World Wars**, Luxembourg was occupied by the German Army.

1944 Belgium, the Netherlands and Luxembourg formed the **Benelux Customs' Union.** It was gradually put into effect until 1948.

1952 The **European Coal and Steel Union** entered into force; Luxembourg became the seat of the administration.

1954 Luxembourg joined NATO.

1958 The Customs' and Economic Union of the Benelux countries.

1964 The Grand Duchess, *Josephine-Charlotte* (Regent since 1919), abdicated in favour of her son, **Jean** (born 1921).

After 1974 A worldwide energy crisis and economic recession were caused by drastic increases in oil prices.

1976 The Prime Minister, *Gaston Thorn* became President of the EEC Council of Ministers.

1979 A coalition government of Christian Democrats and Liberals under *Pierre Werner* was formed.

Art

The Low Countries (until 1830 this included Belgium), have been inhabited since prehistoric times. Between 500 and 250 B.C., the Germans (above all the Batavians) began to penetrate further into the region on the left bank of the Rhine. Here they encountered the Celts, in particular the tribe of the Belgae. In 58 B.C., the country was conquered by Julius Caesar and came under Roman domination (see "De Bello Gallico"; the capital of the Belgian Tungri, Tongres, is the oldest town in the country; the capital of the Nervii was Tournai). An attempt to conquer the Germanic territories on the right bank failed.

There are many good collections of finds from prehistoric and Roman times. Among them, the Centraal Noordbrabants Museum in 's-Hertogenbosch and the National Museum of Archaeology in Leyden, the Gallo-Roman Provincial Museum in Tongres and the Bonnefanten Museum in Maastricht, should be mentioned.

After the fall of the West Roman Empire, the Salian Franks occupied the country. From about A.D. 480 the Low Countries belonged to the Frankish Empire. They were converted to Christianity probably in the 6th c. at the latest. Tongres was a bishopric as early as the 4th c. Utrecht and Liège became bishoprics in 696 and 721 respectively.

Under the Carolingians (751–814), the Frankish Empire consolidated, as is shown by various strongholds and monasteries. In Nijmegen, a castle chapel consecrated in 799 by Pope Leo III, and what is believed to be a Romanesque choir apse from 1155, can still be seen. Owing to the consequences of the Verdun Agreement of 843, the West Frankish Empire disintegrated. Tribal duchies and counties emerged and their capitals became the focal points of medieval civilisation: Brabant, Flanders, Geldern, Burgundy.

THE ROMANESQUE

Under the Carolingians, German influence was at first dominant. St Jean in Liège, built in 990 by Bishop Notger, had the Imperial chapel of Aix/Aachen as its model; in 1755 it was completely reconstructed. The Convent Church of St Gertrude in Nivelles, begun c. 1000, is one of the most significant early medieval buildings. Its patron was the daughter of Pippin the Elder.

The influence of the Rhineland was conspicuous above all in the Valley of the Meuse. Here famous goldsmiths' shops and ironworks appeared in the 12th c. and their products were in demand in the entire Christian West. One of the earliest existing examples is the reliquary of Pope Alexander, believed to be the work of Godefroy of Huy (c. 1145; Musées Royaux d'Art et d'Histoire in Brussels). The famous bronze font carried by ten bulls and ascribed to Rainier of Huy, was conceived in the traditions of the Carolingian-Ottonian Renaissance (1107–18; now in the early Romanesque Church of St Barthélemy in Liège). Other important objects are the silver Shrine of St Hadelinus (c. 1400, in the church in Visé near Liège), the Alexander Shrine of Stavelot (c. 1150; Musées Royaux d'Art et d'Histoire in Brussels), the reliquaries of Godefroy de Claire (c. 1170, in the Collegiate Church of Notre-Dame in Huy), and the Shrine of St Servatius (c. 1150, in the Church of St Servatius in Maastricht).

The most important Lotharingian master of the art of gold, enamel and jewellery, was Nicholas of Verdun (documented between 1181 and 1205). He was of particular importance for the development of this art, having already anticipated the noble beauty of the classical 13th c. Gothic forms (the shrine of the Virgin in the Cathedral of Tournai, 1205). His works or those of his school can also be seen in Vienna, Cologne and Milan. Another famous goldsmith was Hugo of Oignies (several reliquaries in the Treasury of the Convent of Notre-Dame in Namur).

In the field of book illumination, several Bibles must be mentioned. Above all, those from the independent Benedictine Abbey of Stavelot founded in 648, from the Premonstratensian Abbey of Park near Louvain, consecrated in 1129, and from the Abbey Floreffe, founded in 1121. Early examples of remarkable books with gold and ivory encrusted covers were produced in the Luxembourg town of Echternach, in the Benedictine Abbey founded in 689 by St Willibrord (Codex aureus, first half of the 11th c.).

Among the churches there are the early Romanesque Monastery Church of Soignies, begun in 965 and completed about 1150, the Church of Orp-le-Grand (c. 1150), and the Church of St Séverin-en-Condroz (baptismal fonts from the 11th c.); also the Churches of St Barthélemy and of the Holy Cross in Liège. The latter consecrated in 979 by Bishop Notger, has a Romanesque western choir dating from about 1175, and a Gothic east choir and nave from the 14th c.

The Church of St Servatius in Maastricht, the oldest church in the Netherlands (begun in the 6th c.; nave and east crypt much modernised) has a western portico believed to be Carolingian, a transept and choir from the early 11th c., while the south portal and the north cloisters are Gothic. The Church of Our Lady in Maastricht, built in the 11th c. on Roman foundations, still shows traces of the Rhine influence in its powerful western part which is built like a fortress with a massive front wall almost without openings, without any windows or gates.

GOTHIC

The magnificent Cathedral of Tournai, begun about 1140, is situated on the borderland between the French and German linguistic areas. Its austere structure with five towers above the transept, betrays a mixture of German (Romanesque) and French (Gothic) architectural ideas (11th–12th c.). The heightened and extended choir (end of the 13th c.) is purely French. The building had a decisive importance for the entire Gothic church architecture in Northern France.

The cathedral architecture of the Ile-de-France penetrated more and more into the Low Countries. First, in the wake of the Cluniac Reform, churches were built with three-aisled Benedictine choirs. Later, in the 12th–13th c. came large Cistercian monasteries, based on Cîteaux or Clairvaux, such as the Dune Abbey Ter Duinene near Koksijde-Bad, destroyed in the 16th–17th c. and the Abbey of Villers founded by Bernard of Clairvaux in 1146 and destroyed in 1794 (early Gothic church c. 1250, refectory). Their majestic ruins bear witness to their former importance. The Abbey of Orval, also destroyed by the French, in 1793, belongs to the same category. The common features of these Cistercian churches are usually a straight choir-end, no towers (turrets) and scanty interior decoration.

Surviving secular buildings from the Gothic era must be sought within the framework of feudal architecture. The most impressive of them are the Castle of Bouillon, built high on a rocky spur with foundations from the 11th c. from which Godefroy of Bouillon embarked in 1095 on the Crusade to the Holy Land, and the 's-Gravensteen in Ghent, a huge water fortress surrounded by the Leie and built (1180–1200) on foundations from the 9th c. The latter is a most remarkable specimen of medieval fortification technique with its outer wall and gallery, flanked by twenty-four wall towers, and a powerful keep (stronghold tower) in the main castle building which stands in the middle of a huge courtyard and houses the Palas (residence of the Lords) and innumerable halls. Gothic architecture in the Low Countries tended first to be sparing in its forms, and only at a later stage did more elaborate constructions begin to appear. St Gudula in Brussels (also called St Michael, begun 1220), with its massive western front of the 14th–15th c., is one of the masterpieces of that style (valuable stained glass of the 16th–17th c.). The Catholic Church of St John in 's-Hertogenbosch was built (1280–1412) on Romanesque foundations, and reconstructed in late Gothic in the 15th–16th c.; there are flying buttresses on the outer side of the choir, a bell tower with forty-eight bells, and interesting pews from 1480.

The enormous seven-nave Cathedral of Our Lady in Antwerp is famous because of its size. The north tower (carillon) is 123 m (404 feet) high. The construction, begun in 1352, continued until the 16th c. It had to be reconstructed many times due to frequent destruction (fire in 1533, Iconoclastic damages in 1566, and the aftermath of the French Revolution in 1794). Inside are famous paintings by Rubens, including the "Raising of the Cross", and the "Assumption" on the high altar. The Cathedral of St Bavon in Ghent (begun in the 10th c. crypt; choir of the 13th–14th c.; transept and nave 1539–59) is important mainly for its interior decoration: paintings by Pourbus the Elder and Rubens, and above all, the Altar of Ghent.

The Cathedral of Utrecht, built from 1254 onwards on the site of a 10th c. Romanesque church, has been only partly preserved. The five-aisled nave collapsed in a storm in 1674. The 112 m (367 feet) high tower (1321–82; carillon of forty-seven bells), free-standing since the catastrophe, was built by Jan van Henegouwen. Its typical two-stage construction has often been imitated.

In the same category are the former Dominican Church of Maastricht consecrated in 1294 (now a concert hall) and the pilgrim church in Halle built in 1341–1467, with a fine sculptural decor (particularly on the west portal, tower and choir), a Renaissance alabaster altar by Jehan Mone (1533) and the wooden statue of the Miraculous Virgin (known since the 13th c.).

St Rombout in Mechelen should have had the highest tower in Christendom. It was designed for a height of 168 m (551 feet), but it is actually only 97 m (318 feet) high. The carillon from the 15th–17th c. has forty-nine bells. Inside are some well-known masterpieces of art such as Van Dyck's "Crucifixion", and four Baroque tombstones. The massive Bovenkerk (St Nicholas) in Kampen was built by Rutger of Cologne in 1369–93. The Church of St Peter in Leyden, begun in 1339, has an especially ancient look to it. The Church of St Jacob in Liège, founded in the 11th c. was rebuilt in 1513–38 into a superb specimen of Gothic architecture. It still has its Romanesque portico (1170) on the west side and a Renaissance portal of 1560 in the west aisle (elaborate vaulting, stained glass from 1520 to 1540).

Unique are the secular Gothic buildings – gates, cloth halls, belfries, guildhalls, town halls and town houses, displaying the full range of late Gothic delight in sumptuous decoration. They express convincingly the burghers' consciousness of freedom, their spirit of economic enterprise and the quest for pomp of the wealthy Flemish cloth-makers.

Bruges: Town Hall (1376–1420); Oude Griffie (1535–7); Cloth Hall (1284–1364) with a leaning belfry, 83 m (272 feet) high (carillon).

Brussels: Town Hall (15th–18th c.) with a tower 96 m (315 feet) high (Archangel Michael at the top).

Louvain: Town Hall (1448–63 by M. de Layens).

Oudenaarde: Town Hall (1526–36 by H. van Peede) with a tower 40 m (131 feet) high.

Ghent: Town Hall (1518–35) with an elaborate north façade.

Ypres: Cloth Hall (original 13th c; destroyed 1914–18; reconstructed in original style), 132 m (433 feet) long.

These buildings no doubt showed the spirit of independence of the towns. As a contrast the early medieval feudal Castle 's Gravensteen in Ghent should be mentioned again as well as the Burg of Bruges, the second residence of the Counts of Flanders, demolished in 1434.

Apart from the remarkable products of the bronze casters from the Meuse Valley, the sculpture in the Middle Ages did not change much. Good sculptural decor can be seen in the Cathedral of Tournai, in the Churches of Our Lady and St Servatius in Maastricht (tympana and capitals from about 1170; west front, first half of the 14th c.) and in the Church of St Jacob in Liège. An excellent Romanesque statue of the Virgin from 1180 was preserved and is in the Archaeological Museum in Liège. On the whole, little of the Romanesque and Gothic periods survived the Iconoclastic storms.

The first sculptor whom we can identify as an individual was *Claus Sluter* (d. 1406), who was in the service of the Burgundian Court. His work was in the so-called "soft" Gothic style, but he anticipated the naturalism of the later period, for example in his statues for the Carthusian Monastery of Champmol in Dijon (the "Well of Moses", the "Calvary", the tomb of Philip the Bold). Late Gothic carved altars from Antwerp and Brussels were exported as far as Germany (the carver family Borman in Brussels).

In the field of medieval painting, the frescoes in the Cathedral of Tournai (12th c.), in St Gertrude of Nivelles (*c.* 1300), in the refectory of the former Abbey of Bijloke in Ghent (1323–30), and in the

Dominican church in Maastricht (1337) should be noted.

Outstanding book illuminations were produced in the Abbeys of Stavelot (Bible of 1093–7), and Park near Louvain (Bible of 1148). The Royal Library of Brussels possesses an "Alexandreis" from the first half of the 14th c.

Miniature painting, which should have stimulated the devotion of the aristocracy with sumptuous prayer books, reached its peak in the "Livre d'heures" of the Duke of Berry ("Les très riches heures du Duc de Berry"), by *Paul of Limburg* and his brothers *Jan* and *Hermann*, produced in Chantilly about 1416. Their uncle *Jean Malouel* (d. 1419) transferred the miniature technique to panels (altar panels for Champmol, now in the Louvre).

The work of the miniaturists, their new sense of reality and their new conception of perspective (landscapes) had great importance for the brothers **van Eyck**, who instigated the first great period of Dutch painting. Together with the Italian, the Dutch School became the leading one in Europe. Its main representatives were the brothers *Hubert van Eyck* (c. 1370–1426), and *Jan van Eyck* (c. 1390–1441), who possibly participated as miniaturists in the prayer book of Turin-Milan. They were also the creators of the Altar of Ghent, although it is not possible to determine their individual contributions.

The Altar of Ghent (St Bavon in Ghent) is a polyptych with a fixed central panel and movable wings. When open it shows the Adoration of the Mystic Lamb in a landscape among praying patriarchs, prophets, apostles and confessors, angels playing music, Christ in majesty, the Virgin, and St John the Baptist; when closed, there appear the portraits of the Donor and his wife, the two St Johns, and above them the Annunciation. The landscape painted with impressive precision shows a new treatment of reality, much different from the medieval one. The Donor pictures are the first portraits of real people. Adam and Eve are the first natural nudes of the modern era.

The Altar of Ghent has a curious history: it was rescued from the Iconoclasts in 1566 and from a fire in 1640. It was split into parts and came to Ghent via Paris, Berlin and Brussels in 1920. It was removed in the Second World War and re-installed after its end. The Predella (socle) and the panel of the left wing (now a copy) are missing.

Jan van Eyck, described by Vasari as the inventor of oil painting, also painted several pictures of the Virgin (Lucca Madonna, the Madonna of the Canon ver der Paele, 1436) and the famous "Giovanni Arnolfini and his Wife", with an intimate interior and charming details.

Besides the brothers van Eyck, a host of other outstanding artists worked in Flanders between 1400 and 1500. By an old classification they are sometimes called "primitives", but they were of towering importance to late Gothic Flemish painting. The **Master of Flémalle** ranks together with the van Eycks and Rogier van der Weyden, among the founders of **early Dutch painting**. He may well be identical with *Robert Campin* (d. 1444 in Tournai). He was the artist responsible for three altar panels of Flémalle (now in the Städelsches Institut in Frankfurt), of the "Annunciation" triptych, the "Mérode Altarpiece" and the "Nativity".

Rogier **van der Weyden** (c. 1400–64) was more interested in people, than in landscapes. He was the perfect master of the Gothic way of expression, full of tension and expressiveness. His main works are the "Descent from the Cross" (or "Lamentation of Christ"), the "Virgin and St Luke", the "Portrait of Philippe de Croy" and the "Altar with the Virgin" (triptych of Chancellor Rolin). *Dirk (Dierick) Bouts* (c. 1410–75) impresses with the dignity and solemnity of his presentation and his interest in depth and perspective ("Paradise"). His main work is the four-panel "Last Supper Altarpiece" in the Church of St Peter in Louvain.

Peter Christus (c. 1420–73) was strongly influenced by Jan van Eyck, but was not quite his peer ("St Elijah as a Goldsmith"). *Hugo van der Goes* (c. 1440–82) was one of the main personalities of the old Dutch School. He impresses most by his tendency toward the monumental, the warmth and beauty of his colours and his novel treatment of light ("Portinari Altarpiece", "Monforte Altarpiece", the "Fall of Man", with a charming representation of the snake as a half-human half-animal creature).

Hans **Memling** (1430–95) was of German origin and worked in Bruges from 1466. An unusually large number of his paintings (about 100) have been preserved, among them the "Last Judgment", "Man with a Medal", "Christ as a Source of Grace with Angel Musicians". His treatment of the legend of St Ursula in the excellent collection of the Groeninge Museum in Bruges is important for our understanding of the Middle Ages. After the death of Memling, *Gerard David* (*c.* 1460–1523) became the chief painter of the School of Bruges ("Virgin and Child with Saints"; "Annunciation").

Quentin Massys (Metsys and other spellings, 1466–1530) was a member of the St Luke's Guild in Antwerp. His work already shows a strong influence of the Renaissance, whose clarity and peace are again and again disturbed by Gothic restlessness (a number of good portraits: "Banker and his Wife", "Portrait of Canon", "Doctor Paracelsus").

Joos van Cleve (d. about 1540) on the other hand was still very much a product of the Middle Ages. He was the court painter of Francis I of France. Almost as many of his paintings have been preserved as those of Hans Memling. They consist mainly of biblical scenes and portraits (triptych with the "Death of the Virgin", "Portrait of the Emperor Maximilian I").

Geerten tot Sint Jans (*c.* 1460–90), was one of the freshest and most original among the old Dutch masters. His paintings contained a profusion of details: "Lamentation of Christ", "Burning of the Bones of St John the Baptist" and, above all, "St John the Baptist" sitting pensive and serene in a bright, expansive landscape.

Hieronymus **Bosch** (1453–1516) broke radically with all traditions and followed no existing school in either technique or style. He developed a specific type of allegory, swarming with extremely realistic creatures. His unbridled fantasy mixed sharp realism with mischievous satire and fascinating grotesque often bordering on the perverse. His mostly religious scenes are hard to interpret. They have a dreamlike and/or nightmarish character; yet their details would seem to have been lovingly and playfully drawn (the triptych "The Garden of Earthly Delights" (also known by many other names), the "Last Judgment", the "Hay Waggon").

THE RENAISSANCE

The Renaissance could make its way only slowly and gradually against the rich traditions of the earlier period. For example, the Gothic Grotekerk of St Bavo in Haarlem was built as late as the end of the 15th c. First only decorative elements were changed. The new Italian architectural ideas made their first appearance, still a little cumbersome, with the construction of the Antwerp Town Hall (1561–5; front 78 m (256 feet) long) by *Cornelis Floris*, also called *de Vriendt* (1514–75). The builder was also well known as a sculptor (Rood screen in the Cathedral of Tournai) and ornament designer. He created the Floris style, a continuation of Roman Grotesque.

Lieven de Key (*c.* 1560–1627) built the Stadhuis in Leyden and the Butchers' House in Haarlem, one of the most remarkable specimens of Dutch Renaissance (original 1603, partly restored in 1929 after a fire). *Hendrik de Keyser* was the architect of the Zuiderkerk in Amsterdam (1603–11) and of the detached Town Hall in Delft (1618).

In the realm of sculpture where Italian influence was also strong, the foremost talents, apart from Cornelis Floris, were *Guyot de Beaugrant, Jehan Mone, Jacques Dubroeuq* and *Lancelot Blondeel*. Most impressive are the twin marble tombs of Engelbrecht of Nassau (d. 1504) and his wife (probably by an Italian artist). The tradition of representative tombs continued into the 17th c.

The most important Mannerist sculptors, such as Giovanni da Bologna (Giambologna, 1529–1608), whose dynamic statues were very influential, worked elsewhere, mainly in Florence. Some bronze casters worked in Germany or at the Imperial Court in Prague, for example Hubert Gerhard (1550–1620; St Michael on St Michael's Church in Munich) and *Adrian de Vries* (*c.* 1560–1626), the court sculptor of Rudolph II (the Mercury fountain in Augsburg).

The art of faience arrived in Holland from Italy somewhat later. It became well established and reached its peak in the

17th c. with artists such as *A. de Kijser* and *Adam Pijnacker* (1621–73). Most famous was the **Delft porcelain** with a strong white tin glaze and often painted in cobalt-blue with motifs frequently taken from Japanese and Chinese models (Chinoiserie), but also with local genre scenes. Main items were vases, friezes, tiles and luxury plates.

In the field of painting, the influence of the Renaissance likewise increased in the 16th c. The "Romanists" were most affected by Italy, although they could not deny some expression of the late Gothic restlessness indicating a break-up of established traditions. The "Mannerists", naturally also indebted to the late Renaissance painting of Florence, interpreted the feeling of uneasiness and anxiety caused by the Counter-Reformation.

The founder of **Romanism** was *Jan Gossaert* called *Mabuse* (*c.* 1478–1532), who visited Rome and conveyed the impressions of his journey in the characters and Renaissance buildings in his paintings. He painted mainly Madonnas and portraits ("St Luke painting the Virgin"). *Jan van Scorel* (1495–1562) even became curator of the papal collection of antiquities in the Belvedere in Rome, then went to Utrecht and Haarlem (paintings of biblical history, portraits).

Anthonis Mor (1519 to *c.* 1577; also spelled Moor, Antonio Moro, etc.) was above all an influential portrait painter. *Frans Floris* (1516–70), the brother of Cornelis Floris, ran a workshop in Antwerp of almost Rubensian dimensions.

In the northern part of the Low Countries worked *Lucas van Leyden* (1494–1533). His main field of activity was etching ("Ecce Homo"). As a painter he was not quite original and was strongly influenced by Dürer. Among the **Mannerists** there was *Carel van Mander* (1548–1606) who was also an art historian ("Het Schilder-Boeck"), *Hendrik Goltzius* (1558–1617), and *Cornelis Cornelisz* (1562–1638), also called *Cornelis van Haarlem* whose "Slaughter of the Innocents" was important for the development of group painting.

The greatest Dutch painter of the second half of the 16th c. was without doubt *Pieter* **Breughel** (*c.* 1525–69, spelling varies), called the "Peasant Breughel". He was an artistic personality of Shakespearian proportions whose creative originality was second to none, although he was considerably influenced by Hieronymus Bosch. He discovered the world of the peasant, as an entirely new area of inspiration, and illustrated the seasons, the comedy and the tragedy of human life. Some forty paintings of his exist, half of them in the Museum of Fine Arts in Vienna.

Breughel's two sons were also well-known painters. *Pieter Breughel the Younger* (1564–1637), because of his paintings with scenes of nocturnal fires, earned the nickname "Hell Breughel". *Jan Breughel* (1568–1625), because of his still-life pictures is known as "Velvet Breughel" or "Flower Breughel".

The traditional and temperamental differences between north and south increasing since the Reformation, were exacerbated by the religious and political separation at the end of the 16th c. Since 1600 it became obvious that Flemish and Dutch art had embarked on different trends of development. Dutch painting in the 17th c. played a leading role north of the Alps as it had done before in the 15th c. Its two great representatives, Rubens in the Catholic south and Rembrandt in the Protestant north, personify the individual character of the now separate Flemish and Dutch art. An extremely limited area hosted an almost incredible number of outstanding painters whose influence extended in many ways up to the 19th c.

THE BAROQUE

The appearance of *Peter Paul* **Rubens** (1577–1640) marked the beginning of the Baroque age in Flanders. Rubens's genius, earthy by nature but restrained and groomed by his Italian training, was unimpeded by any Classical ambitions. His use of brilliant colours (especially red) created a corresponding atmosphere for his sensuous and sumptuous scenes. The influence of Titian was strong. His paintings showed increasing freedom, mobility and looseness of construction leading to an accomplished mastery in depicting powerful movements of man and beast. His treatment of flesh was equalled by none. He was also an outstanding draughtsman (collection of drawings in the Albertina graphic collection in

Rubens: the "Raising of the Cross" (detail).

peasants in inns, at games, and in brawls, dramatic scenes in soft-shaded colours.

David Teniers the Younger (1610–90) painted contemplative, narrative pictures, men smoking and drinking, country life, outdoor feasts, etc. He was also a highly valued landscape painter.

In the north there were several artists around the turn of the 16th–17th c. Next to Rembrandt, the foremost among them was *Frans* **Hals** (1580–1666), a disciple of Carel van Manders. His subjects were taken from everyday town life, genre pictures, portraits, civic guard group portraits. He developed the corporative or group portrait to a diversity and variety of characters previously unknown (Frans Hals Museum in Haarlem). He seized the reality of the moment and with his hasty-looking brush strokes achieved near Impressionist effects.

Vienna). He kept a large and busy studio. There are some 500–600 of his own paintings and a host of others signed by him, but only in part his own work. His masterpieces are: the "Raising of the Cross" in the Cathedral of Antwerp, the "Lion Hunt", and a set of twenty-one colossal paintings executed for Maria of Medici (in the Louvre); the "Portrait of Helena Fourment in a Fur Coat" and the "Ildefonso Altarpiece" (both in the Museum of Fine Arts in Vienna).

Rubens's disciple *Anthonis van Dyck* (1599–1641) was after 1632 the court painter in London. His religious scenes and his portraits showed a sensual and spiritual unity in form and colour (warm, dark tones). His people were depicted in elegant and distinguished poses; individuality seemed often to give way to a conventional desire to show only elegance and beauty.

Jacob **Jordaens** (1593–1678) was the master of genre pictures, exuding joy of life and a great appetite for food and drink ("The Bean King"). He was also an outstanding painter of female nudes with brilliant flesh tones, influenced by Rubens.

Only the genre painters could escape the overwhelming influence of Rubens. *Adriaen Brouwer* (1605–38) was a Dutchman who worked in Antwerp. He painted

The towering personality of Dutch Baroque was, nevertheless, **Rembrandt** *Harmenszoon van Rijn* (1606–69), who worked first in Leyden and later in Amsterdam. His life was full of conflicts and vicissitudes. He was the most powerful and versatile genius of the Baroque period and the undisputed leader of his time both as a painter and as a draughtsman. His landscape etchings followed in the footsteps of *Herkules Segher* (1589–1645). The subjects of his paintings were taken from all walks of life, but most were portraits and biblical scenes. The contrasts of light and shadow made his interiors dramatic. He brought the chiaroscuro painting, taken over by intermediaries from Caravaggio, to the peak of perfection. Inner conflicts are reflected in facial expressions. Stark naturalism and utmost spirituality alternate with periods of gentle clarity, moderation and self-control. All his life he was preoccupied with his self-portraiture to an extent unsurpassed by any other artist. Many drawings and over 300 etchings are known to exist. Rembrandt also brought to its peak the group portrait, that typical form of Dutch bourgeois pride (civic guard portrait), masterly developed by *B. van der Helst* (1613–70) and Frans Hals.

When he painted his "Night Watch", showing a company of guardsmen, his way of treating the light incensed his public and earned him hostility and anger.

When old he deviated so much from the contemporary taste that he had little appeal to the late 17th c. and also for the time that followed. Only the late 19th c. again began to appreciate his greatness and importance. (It was then that thorough research into Rembrandt began.)

The third Dutch 17th c. master of timeless fame was *Jan van der Meer* called **Vermeer van Delft** (1632–75). He left behind, compared with Rembrandt, only a relatively small number of works (some forty paintings). He was a genius of interior scenes, of the meticulously tidy burghers' house, with a few persons shown in insignificant domestic occupations, such as "Young Woman Reading a Letter", the "Lace-maker" or the "Kitchen Maid". Vermeer van Delft was an outstanding master of the technique of painting. His pictures were mostly small with soft, delicate colours (blue, lemon-yellow). Famous also are his only two landscapes, the "View of Delft" and "A Delft Street".

The well-known Vermeer forger *Hans van Meegeren* managed to deceive the foremost experts of the 20th c. ("Christ in Emmaus", in the Boymans-van Beuningen Musuem in Rotterdam, was proved in 1945 to have been painted in 1936.)

There were many more painters such as *Pieter de Hooch* (1629 to about 1683); *Jan Steen* (1626–79), a painter with an unerring eye for the comedy of man and a master of the Dutch genre scene; *Adriaen van Ostade* (1610–85), also a master of the genre with stark chiaroscuro effects, and of the etching; *Gerard ter Borch* (1617–81) a genre painter, too, who liked to place his scenes in elegant bourgeois surroundings. Last but not least there was *Jacob* **van Ruisdael** (1630–81) who painted vast open landscapes with heavy clouds and a grave feeling of loneliness and melancholy. He also influenced the painters of German Romanticism, especially by his etchings. The stream of great talents began to dry up towards the end of the 17th c. Other craftsmen pursued the great traditions in the 18th c., such as *Jan van Huysum* (1682–1749) with his intensely coloured flower pieces, but without any strength of their own to develop or to improve them.

In the field of 17th c. sculpture, the Flemings *Jerome Dusquesnoy the Elder* (*c.* 1570–1641) and *Jerome Dusquesnoy*

the Younger (1602–54), *Pieter Verbruggen the Elder* (1609–87) and *Artus Quellinus the Elder* (1609–68) worked in the shadow of Rubens. Flemish wood carving retained its significance in the Baroque age. Outstanding among the 18th c. sculptors were *Peter Anton de Verschaffelt* (1710–93) and *Augustin Ollivier* (1739–88).

In the Dutch part of the Low Countries, the architect *Hendrik de Keyser* (1565–1621), best known as a builder of towers, was also a sculptor. He created the impressive tomb of William the Silent in Delft.

Baroque architecture in Flanders – also under the overpowering influence of Rubens – was much more ostentatious (for example, the Jesuit church in Antwerp, 1614–21, burned down in 1718 and reconstructed in the original style) than the Dutch which tended more towards Palladio and was more classical and sober. Its main personality was *Jacob van Campen* (1595–1657), builder of the former Town Hall of Amsterdam (about 1650, now the Royal Palace) and the new Church in Haarlem 1645–9. Another outstanding architect was *Pieter Post* (1608–69) builder of the "House in the Woods", the royal country residence in Haagse Bos near The Hague. *Philip Vinckeboons* (1607–87) and the architect family *Husly* should also be mentioned. This building tradition continued throughout the 18th c., but the French Classical influence became increasingly penetrated by the Baroque.

18th–19th CENTURY

The 18th c. Flemish painting had mainly national significance. The impact of the Rubens's School began to fade. There were among others *P. J. Verhaghen* (1728–1811) and *Jaques-Louis David* (1748–1825), who was born in Paris but worked for a long time in Brussels. He managed at least to free himself from Baroque and helped to open the way for **Classicism** in painting. He was the painter of the French Revolution and the court painter of Napoleon, and his politically motivated paintings reflected the exciting events of his lifetime.

Dutch painting in the first half of the 19th c. still bore the signs of the decline that had set in after the flourish of the 17th c.

Outstanding personalities began to appear only towards the middle of the century, such as *Jozef Israëls* (1824–1911), close to the French Barbizon School, the Impressionist *Johan Barthold Jongkind* (1819–91) and members of the "School of The Hague" who combined pictures of nature and genre scenes with Classical reminiscences of the 17th c.

The Belgian painters of the 19th c. followed the current European trends. They were able but not outstanding professionals and included the Romanticist *Gustav Wappers* (1803–74), *Emile Wauters* (1846–1933), *Alfred Verhaeren* (1849–1924), *Fernand Khnopff* (1858–1921), *Antoine Wiertz* (1806–65) and others. The graphic art of the Symbolist *Felicien Rops* (1833–93) bore the mark of the so-called "Poor People's Pictures" School begun by Courbet and continued by the sculptor Constantin Meunier.

An outstanding personality was *James Ensor* (1860–1949), a painter and etcher of demoniac ghostliness and visionary nightmares who was indebted to Symbolism and paved the way to Expressionism.

The 19th c. brought about the definitive separation of Belgium and the Netherlands (1830). As elsewhere in Europe, **Historicism** was the dominant trend.

In Belgian architecture Baroque forms long continued to be fashionable. Their ostentation and wealth of decor corresponded to the taste of the wealthy Flemish burghers. The influences of France, of Rococo and later of Classicism made themselves felt. Brussels was given an entirely new face (Place Royale). Historicism brought about gigantic architectural projects such as the National Bank (built 1859–64, façade from 1952) and the monumental Law Courts (1866–83) by J. Poelaert, dominating the town panorama with the dome of its central part.

In Holland *P. J. H. Cuypers* (1827–1921), who built the Central Station and the Rijksmuseum in Amsterdam, must be mentioned; his work marks the dividing line between Historicism and modern architecture.

For sculptors Historicism was a fertile field. Good sculptors were *Toon Dupuis* (1877–1937), *J. Mendes da Costa* (1863–1939), and *Lambertus Zijl* (1866–1947). Monuments were much in favour in the 19th c. and many were produced by *Charles van der Stappen* (1843–1910), *Jules Dillens* (1849–1904), and in particular *Constantin Meunier* (1831–1905), who chose his subjects among the proletariat (miners, etc.) and treated them with evocative realism. *Georges Minne* (1867–1941) played a role in the development of Art Nouveau and is regarded as a forerunner of Expressionism.

19th–20th CENTURY

Around the turn of the century, the break with tradition became final. This was best demonstrated by the work of the Dutchman *Vincent* **van Gogh** (1853–90), who as an apostle of the Borinage mining district, started from the "Poor People's Pictures" to become one of the earliest representatives of **Expressionism**.

The Fauvists, too, found in him their inspiration. Out of his troubled personal life, Vincent van Gogh gave with his seemingly flickering brush-stroke a moving expression to his inner anxieties. His colours were frequently virulently glaring, thickly applied and betrayed passionate obsession and deep excitement (landscapes, mainly of Provence, portraits, still-life). Dutch painting managed yet again to win a leading role, but the number of modern trends and their internationalism, recognising no frontiers, worked against the formation of purely national goals.

Jan Sluijters (1881–1957) was close to Expressionism; *Kees van Dongen* (1877–1969) was, together with his compatriot *L. Zijl*, a member of the artist group "The Bridge" formed in Dresden in 1905. The French parallel to this group was the Fauvists who also claimed van Dongen as one of their members.

One of the pace-setters of modern painting was *Piet* **Mondrian** (1872–1944), who became acquainted with Cubism in Paris, and by his "neo-Plasticism" paved the way in Holland for abstract painting. He was also one of the founders of the journal "De Stijl" in 1917. He used almost exclusively primary colours and his aesthetic views influenced to the same extent painting, architecture, sculpture and design. He emigrated to New York in 1940 and found a great response there. North American painting after the Second World War was much influenced by him.

Willem de Kooning (b. 1904) went to the USA in 1926. He is a typical representative of abstract Expressionism and of Action Painting.

The graphic artist and painter *Hendrik Werkmann* (1882–1945) was shot by the Gestapo shortly before the end of the Second World War. His importance in the art of book design is now being acknowledged. An interesting artist also working as a designer is *M. C. Escher* (born 1898) who combined in his Mannerist work abstract sculpture, illusionist effects and an anticipation of Op Art.

René Magritte (1898–1967) and *Paul Delvaux* (born 1897) are two of the great names of Surrealism; the talented *Rik Wouters* (1882–1916) parted company with Cézanne. *Constant Permeke* (1886–1952) was heavily influenced by Expressionism. *Frans Masereel* (b. 1889) became known for his socially critical graphic art (wood carvings). Belgian painting looked more and more towards Paris. *Pierre Alechinsky* (b. 1927) and *Corneille* (real name Cornelis van Beverloo, b. 1922), the master of "opulent monotony" who worked in Amsterdam and Paris, formed in Paris in 1948, together with the Dane, *Asger Jorn* (real name A. Jorgensen, 1914–73), the Dutchmen *Constant* (C. A. Nieuwenhuys, b. 1920) and *Karel Appel* (b. 1921), the international art group "COBRA" (CO = Copenhagen, BR = Brussels, A = Amsterdam).

Op Art, which developed after the Second World War from abstract Constructivist movements derived, like Tachism, many of its ideas from Suprematism, from "De Stijl" and from Piet Mondrian. The painter *Edgar Ferhout* (b. 1921) moved from pure Realism to Tachist paintings. The COBRA group combined the restless and informal ways of painting of the post-war era with elements from folklore, primitive art and Art Brut.

The diverse currents of the present art scene with their constantly growing mixture of categories and increasingly strong impact of artists' personalities invoking actions, happenings, Flux-movements, process-art, etc., have had their numerous exponents in the Netherlands.

Dutch painting and architecture produced in the 20th c. a number of first-rate personalities. Sculpture in the first half of this century was less remarkable, but after the Second World War it became stimulated by a host of public commissions: *Hildo Krop, John Raedecker, M. S. Andriessen, Wessel Couzijn, V. P. Esser, G. Romijn*. Apart from these, the Japanese *S. Tajiri*, of US origin but working in Holland, should also be named. The moving memorial "Monument for a Devastated City" in Rotterdam is by the Russian-French sculptor *Ossip Zadkine* (1954). *Georges Vantongerloo* (also a member of "De Stijl"), who was a founder member of the group "Abstraction-Création", is regarded as a pioneer of the "concrete" art in Belgium. Other members were the Dutchman *Theo van Doesburg* (real name C. E. M. Kupper, 1883–1931), Naum Gabo and Antoine Pevsner.

Roel d'Haese (b. 1921), a talented metal sculptor, belongs to the younger generation. A collection of modern sculpture is on display in the Middelheim Open-Air Museum in the Nachtegalen Park near Antwerp.

The Belgian *Henry* van de Velde (1863–1957) played a decisive part in the development of modern architecture. He was one of the founders of the Art Nouveau style (in Belgium "style coup de fouet"), and worked also as a designer. He achieved his main success in Germany where he designed the College of Applied Art in Weimar. In Brussels he founded the Institut des Arts Décoratifs de la Cambre. Other well-known Belgian Art Nouveau architects were *Victor Horta* (1861–1947; Maison Tassel in Brussels) and *Paul Hankar* (Maison Kleyer in Brussels, 1898). Later, Belgian architecture drew closer to the trends currently prevailing in Holland.

The creations of the Dutch architect *Hendrick Petrus* Berlage represented the beginning of modern architecture. An excellent example of his style is the unfinished Amsterdam Stock Exchange (1898–1903). He founded the "Amsterdam School" (the Port Administration

Building in Amsterdam, 1914) which rid itself completely of the eclecticism of the 19th c. Art Nouveau architects were *Willem Kromhout, T. Sluyterman* and *L. A. H. Wolf.* The work of Berlage was continued by *M. de Klerk, P. L. Kramer* and *M. van der Mey.* The latter eventually broke away from Berlage and embraced the ideas of Expressionism.

The art group "De Stijl" attracted architects close to Cubism, such as *Jacobus Johannes Oud* (1890–1963), *Robert van 't Hoff, Jan Wils* and *Gerrit Thomas Rietveld* (1888–1964), who worked with Theo van Doesburg and took part in the foundation of the CIAM (Congrès Internationaux d'Architecture Moderne). Doesburg's ideas were taken over by the Paris group "Abstraction-Création". Next to J. J. P. Oud, a great number of outstanding Dutch architects subscribed to West-European **Functionalism**. The increasing worldwide impact of modern

Dutch architecture is mainly due to them. The essentially Romantic "Amsterdam School" has been definitely overcome.

A personality out of the ordinary was *Willem Marinus Dudok* (b. 1884) who preferred massive and ponderous brick buildings. The "Delft School" (Town Hall in Enschede, 1933) was a creation of *C. M. Granpré Molière.* It played a leading role in reconstruction after the Second World War. The destroyed city of Rotterdam became a focus of urbanist activity mainly due to *J. H. van den Broek, J. B. Bakema,* and others, who developed here a new Functionalism. The ideas of the CIAM were revived. The conception of the Delft School persisted in the Catholic church architecture. However, the great numbers of modern buildings resulted in a kind of routine aesthetics with few really significant features. The "Team X", *Aldo van Eijk,* and the "Forum Circle" have tried to find new solutions in urban building.

Literature

The dividing line between the Dutch and French linguistic areas runs across **BELGIUM**. In connection with this division, a bilingual literature has developed since the Middle Ages on the territory of the present Kingdom. What has been written in Dutch is commonly described as Flemish literature. French writing in the Walloon linguistic area represents a parallel and independent literary branch.

Flemish literature experienced its first flowering as early as the 12th–14th c. Famous were the minstrel love songs of **Henry of Veldeke** (*c.* 1170) which influenced German minstrel songs. Also well known were the names of *Hadewych* and *Jacob van Maerlant* (13th c.); the most important Middle Dutch romance of chivalry "Karel en de Elegast", and the best known animal story "Van den vos Reinaerde" originated in their lifetime. Other outstanding achievements were the mystic works of *Jan van Ruusbroec* (1293–1381) and the folk story "Elckerlyc" by *Petrus Dorlandus* (1454–1507).

Between the 16th and 19th c. Flemish literature was insignificant. New influences appeared only after 1815 when the Northern and Southern Provinces were reunited. At that time Flanders very slowly underwent the process of linguistic transition from Middle Dutch to High Dutch. The Romanticist *Hendrik* **Conscience** (1812–83), often called the "Flemish Walter Scott", brought to literature a new beginning. Another great literary name of that period was *August Snieders* (1825–1904).

The second half of the 19th c. was dominated by Realism, expounded mainly in the works of *Guido* **Gazelle** (1830–99) and his follower *Albrecht Rodenbach* (1856–80). Towards the end of the century a new group of writers appeared calling themselves "Van Nu en Straks" and fighting against Romanticism and the traditional historical awareness. Exceptional personalities of this movement were *August Vermeylen* (1872–1945), *Karel van de Woestijne* (1878–1929), *Stijn Streuvels* (1871–1919) and *Hermann Teirlinck* (1879–1967). *Cyriel Buysse* (1859–1932) belonged at first to the same group, but later turned to a new literary trend. He rates as the founder of Flemish Naturalism.

Events of the First World War led to the appearance of the "homeland novel", thanks mainly to *Felix* **Timmermans** (1886–1947). This trend lasted up to the Second World War. Among the best novels and stories by Timmermans are "Pallieter", "The Beautiful Hours of Symforosa, the Young Beguine", and "Child Jesus in Flanders".

Expressionism made its entry into Flemish literature at the same time. *Paul André van Ostaijen* (1896–1928; Essays), *Victor J. Brunclair* (1899–1944) and *Wies Moens* (b. 1898), were almost exclusively lyrical poets. However, international standards were set only after the Second World War. *Maurice* **Roelants** (1895–1966) began and developed the psychological novel. Flemish Realism reached its peak with *Marcel Matthijs* (1899–1964) and *Johan* **Daisne** (b. 1912). The latter was mainly inspired by *Pirandello* and *E. T. A. Hoffmann*, and was the first to develop a specifically Flemish literary trend. Similarly significant was *Maurice* **Gilliams** (b. 1900), creator of Flemish Individualism. *Ivo* **Michiels** (b. 1923) achieved so far the only international breakthrough of Flemish "nouveau réalisme" with his novels "The Book Alpha" (1963) and "Orclies Militaris" (1968). His third novel "Exit" (1972) was purely experimental.

Lyrical poetry was shaped by men such as *Hubert van Herreweghen* (b. 1920), *Jan Veulemans* (b. 1928), *Paul Snoek* (b. 1933) and *Pieter Aerts* (b. 1928). Their works followed in the traditions of the first half of the century and were part of the specifically Flemish literary expression. Although nowadays an increasing number of Flemish writers aim not only at domestic but also at international readership, none of them has approached the degree of fame and popularity enjoyed by Felix Timmermans.

The French language literature of Belgium was for centuries before the founding of the Kingdom, part and parcel of French literature. This applied to the medieval chroniclers *Jean Froissart* and *Philippe de Commynes*, as well as to the Prince *Charles Joseph* **de Ligne** (1735–1814). After the bilingual country became independent nothing really changed at first. Close contact between

Belgian writers and France, especially with Paris, went on and, unlike in Flanders, no specific literary trends developed. The breakthrough was achieved when *Charles* de Coster (1827–79) published in 1867 his novel "Tyll Ulenspiegel", a colourful picture of his Flemish home country. De Coster was inspired by French Realism, Classical German literature and English Romanticism.

Attempts to foster a literature specifically in "Belgian-French" led to the appearance of the journal "La Jeune Belgique", founded by *Max Waller* (1860–89). Among the best known names associated with this publication were the poet *Albert Giraud* (1860–1929) and *Emile* Verhaeren (1855–1916).

Another journal, "L'Art Moderne", also founded in 1881, had opposite aims, namely orientation towards France. Somewhere in between these two stood "La Wallonie" (founded in 1886), where writers of either persuasion could publish: Emile Verhaeren, *Maurice* Maeterlinck (1862–1949), *Charles van Leberghe* (1861–1907). *Grégoire Le Roy* (1862–1941) and *Max Elskamp* (1862–1931).

Recently, prose writers such as *Marie Gevers* (b. 1883) and Georges Simenon (b. 1903) have become internationally known. Simenon's "Commissaire Maigret", appearing since 1930, has been translated into many languages. *Jean Ray* (1887–1964) ranks high among the writers of horror stories. The triumph of Belgian French literature was the election of Marguerite Yourcenar, as the first woman member of the Académie Française (1980).

Symbolism and poetry are represented by *Géo Librecht* (b. 1891), *Pierre Nothomb* (1887–1966), *Robert Vivier* (b. 1894), *Edmond Vandercammen* (b. 1901) and others. *Fernand Crommelynck* (1885–1970) and *Michel* de Ghelderode (1898–1962) were successful dramatists. The Surrealist *Henri* Micheaux (b. 1899) who settled in Paris in the 1920s, provided powerful stimuli in modern French poetry. Of Belgian origin also are the world-famous authors of comics including *Hergé*, the creator of "Tintin", *René Goscinny* ("Asterix", "Lucky Luke") and *Remacle* ("Vieux Nick" and "Barbenoire").

Whereas the origins of Flemish and French literature on the territory of Belgium can be traced back to the 12th–13th c., the beginnings of Dutch literature specifically of the Netherlands, cannot be reliably reconstructed because the relevant manuscripts are lacking.

A genuine separation from Flemish literature came only when the Reformation began to spread. The present Dutch National Anthem "Wilhelmus" was based on the Geuze songs of that period which had for their subject the uprising against the Spaniards. In the wake of the Reformation appeared the so-called Pamphlet literature; its most remarkable work was the satire of the Catholic Church by *Philips van Heer van Sint Aldegonde* Marnix (1540–98).

When the Spaniards occupied Antwerp in 1585, most of the wealthy burghers fled to Holland, primarily to Amsterdam. As Flemish literature was losing its significance at that time, Renaissance literature began to emerge in Holland and reached its peak in the 17th c. (the Golden Century). The poet *Pieter Corneliszoon* Hooft (1581–1647) and his sonnets ("Emblemata Amatoria", 1611), *Gerbrand Adriaensz Bredero* (1585–1618) and *Joost* van der Vondel (1587–1679), the Dutch master of Baroque drama, were all well known. The poet and statesman *Jacob Cats* (1577–1600) was famous for his innumerable didactic and colloquially written poems. Even now the works of Cats enjoy a special place in the libraries of many homes in Holland.

In the second half of the 17th c. French Classicism made itself felt in Holland. Its most important representatives were the dramatist *L. Rotgans* (1663–1710) and the poet *H. K. Poot* (1689–1733). About 1720 several weekly journals ("spectatoriale geschriften") began to spread enlightening ideas. The outstanding literary figure of that time was *Jan* van Effen (1684–1735; "De Hollandsche Spectator").

Romantic literature had appeared in Holland since about 1770 under the simultaneous influence of French, English and German examples. Most significant among its representatives were *R. Feith* and *W. Bilderdijk*, while the poet *A. Staring* opposed their exuberant Romanticism with his sober coolness. Less exalted Romanticism was expressed in the works of *Everhardus Johannes* **Potgieter** (1808–75). He was also the best known literary critic of his time.

The most outstanding Dutch writer in the 19th c. was *Eduard Douwes-Dekker* (1820–87), known under his pen-name **Multatuli**. He did not follow any particular literary trend and could be compared to some extent with his Flemish contemporary, the poet Guido Gezelle.

About 1880, a group of young writers appeared calling themselves **"Bewegung van Tachtig"**. They tried to give Dutch literature international significance, being inspired by French Naturalism and Impressionism on the one hand, and by English Romanticism on the other. It can be compared with the Flemish movement "Van Nu en Straks". The main names were *W. J. T. Kloos* (1859–1938), *H. Gorter* (1864–1927), *A. Verwey* (1865–1937) and *J. van Eeden* (1860–1932).

In the first half of the 20th c. several new trends originated. The first among them was the New Romanticism with poets like *P. N. van Eyck* (1887–1954), *A. Roland Holst* (b. 1888), *J. C. Bloem* (1887–1966) and *M. Nijhoff* (1894–1953) who all experimented with new elements of style in their work. *A. van Schendel* (1874–1946) wrote neo-Romantic novels. Also well known were the ironic-realistic stories by the Belgian *Willem*

Elsschot (real name Alfons de Ridder), 1882–1960.

Expressionism reached Holland in 1914. Outstanding authors were *F. Bordewijk* (novels), *S. Vestdijk* and *M. Gijsen* (stories), *J. Daisne* (realism) and *L. P. A. Boom* (neo-Naturalism). *Simon Carmiggelt* (b. 1913) wrote humorous short stories, *Hella S. Haasse* (b. 1918) psychological novels and stories.

No Dutch book since the end of the Second World War has enjoyed such popularity as the "Het Achterhuis", the "Diary of *Anne* **Frank**" (1946). It tells of her experiences in an Amsterdam hideout where she was concealed from 1942 to 1944.

A new literary generation has come to the fore since the 1950s. They reject all formal principles of poetry and call themselves "atonaal". The best known writers of this new trend are *L. J. Swaanswijk* and *H. M. J. Claus*. Prose and drama veer towards neo-Naturalism, their characteristic feature being the use of shocking details. *C. K. van het Reve* (b. 1923), *H. Mulisch* (b. 1927) and *Jan Wolkers* (b. 1925), should also be mentioned.

The most important representative of the "Zeventigers" is *Heere Heeresma* (b. 1932). Others on the younger literary scene are the novelists *A. Burnier* (b. 1931, women's problems), *Jaap Harten* (b. 1930) and the poet *J. Bernlef* (b. 1937).

Music

The territory of the Benelux countries has always been exposed to the influences of their Romance and Germanic neighbours. This left its mark not only on their art but also on their music, which in the 15th–16th c. was of international repute.

The evolution began when most domains in the Low Countries were united under the Dukes of Burgundy. It reached its peak under Charles the Bold and Charles V and gradually declined after the separation of the Northern Provinces (the present Netherlands) and the Southern ones (the present Belgium). The Low Countries then were almost identical territorially with the present Benelux countries, so the term **Dutch music** can be applied to the music of all three at that period. This term would, therefore, cover not only the works of Dutch composers but those of Flanders, Wallonia and Northern France.

Dutch music brought the style already existing about 1400 to high perfection. Its dominant element was the four- and five-voice choir. Technically it created a vocal polyphony in which individual voice registers applied the same melody in a concerted way.

The first period of Dutch music was closely connected with the Burgundian Ducal Court in the 15th c. (Philip the Good, Charles the Bold). The most important composers of this Burgundian era were *J. Ciconia* who worked at the Courts of Venice and Padua, and *Guillaume* **Dufay** (*c.* 1400–74) who was also occasionally invited to Italy. His innovative treatment of the motet and the song composition of the 14th c. sparked off the first great period of Dutch music. Also important was *Gilles Binchois* who composed at the Burgundian Court at Dijon.

Towards the end of the 15th c. the tone was set by the famous Schools of Cambrai and Antwerp (Franco-Flemish School). Under their leadership Dutch music asserted itself against music from England and Italy, and set the trend for nearly all European composers. This leading role lasted until the end of the 16th c. The motets, secular songs and polyphonic masses by the composers *Pierre de la Rue,*

Nicolas Gombert, Johannes Ockeghem, Josquin Desprez, Adriaan Willaert, Henri Isaak and *Clemens non Papa* spread far and wide, especially since the invention of note printing at the beginning of the 16th c. *Johannes Tinctoris* was the leading theoretician of that time.

In the late period of Dutch music, the reputation of *Philippe de Monte, Jacob de Kerle* and above all, **Orlando di Lasso**, native of Mons, extended beyond the frontiers of the Low Countries. Next to Palestrina, Di Lasso (real name *Roland de Lassus*, born about 1532) was the most highly esteemed composer of the 16th c. He worked for a long time in Germany, conducting the court band in Munich from 1560 up to his death in 1594. The principle of Dutch polyphony was abandoned by *Jan Pieter Sweelinck*. He was highly significant in 17th c. organ music, but with him the supremacy of Dutch music came to its end.

Towards the end of the 17th c. the Dutch School, which up to then had been universal and European, disintegrated. Under various foreign influences different trends appeared in each region. Composers in the whole area became more and more mere imitators, unlike the trendsetters of the previous centuries. French Classical music strongly influenced Walloon composers who increasingly found their way to Paris, while the composers from Flanders and Holland stayed at home and, working in isolation from the great contemporary European currents, fell into oblivion. Only in the 19th c. did there appear in Holland a composer of significance, *Joseph Verhulst*. The Flemings woke from their long lethargy at the beginning of the 20th c.

Among the **Walloon composers** from present-day Belgium, several made a name for themselves in 18th c. Paris: *Jean-Noel Hamal* (Oratorio "In Exitu Israel"), *Jean-Baptiste Lœillet, Jean-François Gossec* ("Messe des Morts"), *Pierre van Maldere* and *André Ernest Modeste* **Grétry** (1742–1813), one of the founders of French Opéra Comique ("Zémire et Azor", "Richard Cœur de Lion", "Céphale et Procris").

In the 19th c. *César* **Franck** from Liège acquired an international reputation. He took French citizenship and moved to

Paris where he became a celebrated organ teacher, and composed his highly original Symphony in D Minor, several symphonic poems, an Oratorio, a violin sonata and a large amount of organ music. He successfully introduced German aesthetics into the French style and in this respect he had a far-reaching significance. Among his most talented followers were the Frenchman Vincent d'Indy and the Belgian *Guillaume Lekeu* who died very young, before his creative genius could fully develop. He left behind a beautiful violin sonata and a sensitive string adagio. *Charles de Bériot* and *Henri Vieuxtemps* were the founders of the still famous Belgian Violin School. Both composed several virtuoso violin concertos: Vieuxtemps's 4th and 5th have been performed relatively frequently, primarily in French- and English-speaking countries. *Eugène* **Ysaye** (1858–1931), one of the greatest violin virtuosos of his time, carried this tradition forward to the 20th c. His six sonatas for solo violin are ranked among the masterpieces of their kind. An important music teacher of that time was *Mathieu Crickboom* whose violin course is still among the best and most widely used.

The Belgian Romanticist *Peter* **Benoît** (1834–1901) was of considerable significance for the music of his country around the turn of the century. His music, often popular and frequently quite spectacular (notably, "La Pacification de Gand"), was a fitting expression of the national character. At the same time some of his compositions already anticipated new musical development.

At the beginning of the 20th c. Belgian music was dominated by *Paul* **Gilson** (1865–1942). Among his superbly orchestrated symphonic works was a highly original suite entitled "La Mer", which should have merited international fame equal to Debussy's composition of the same name. Gilson was the founder of the so-called School of Flemish Brabant to which *Auguste de Boeck*, *Gaston Brenta* and *Marcel* **Poot** (b. 1901) also belonged. The latter is the most popular Belgian composer of the 20th c. In his exclusively tonal music, colour, rhythm and melody combine in spectacular fireworks to reflect the Belgian taste for folklore, mass processions, festivals and fairs. The group around Poot also called themselves "Synthesists".

The School of Antwerp was much less exposed to Latin influence than the School of Flemish Brabant, and had a clearly Romantic character. Its members were *Marinus de Jong, Karel Candael, Louis Mortelmans, Flor Alpaerts* and also the well-known organist and composer *Flor Peeters*.

The School of Liège followed in the footsteps of César Franck and Vincent d'Indy and also of Gabriel Fauré and Gabriel Pierné. *Joseph Jongen* (Symphony for organ and orchestra, 1928) and his brother *Léon Jongen*, were the most significant exponents of this school. Composers such as *Armand Marsick, Jean Rogister* and *Albert Dupuis* are hardly known outside Belgium.
An individual difficult to place is *René* **Bernier** (b. 1905). Characteristic features of his music are Mediterranean spirit, elegance and clarity. Composers such as *Jean Absil, André Souris, Fernand Quinet, Victor Legley, Jean Louël, Jacques Stehmann, Pierre Bartholomée, Jacqueline Fontyn* and the Dutchman *Henk Badings*, follow various contemporary and avant garde currents.

The Benelux countries produced many great *interpreters of classical music*. Singers (Female): Claudine Boons, Clara Clairbert, Mina Bolotine, Suzanne Danco, Rita Gorr, Claudine Arnaud, Ely Ameling, Aafje Heynis, Erna Spoorenberg and Christina Deutekom. Singers (Male): Frédéric Anspach, Maurice de Groote, Georges Lens, José van Dam, Louis Devos, Jules Bastin, Camillo Meghor and Julien Haas. Piano: François Glorieux, Cor de Groot, Jenny Solheid and Naum Sluzny. Violin: Eugène Ysaye, Alfred Dubois, Arthur Grumiaux, Maurice Raskin, Georges Octors, Carlo van Neste, Rudolf Werthen, Hermann Krebbers, Theo Olof and André Gertler and also Rumanian-born Lola Bobesco. Cello: Tibor de Machula and Edmond Baeyens. Harpsichord: Aimée van de Wiele. Harp: Mireille Flour. Organ: Flor Peeters and Feike Asma. Trumpet: André Marchal and Theo Mertens. Flute: Frans Bruggen. Horn: Francis Orval. Conductors: Willem Mengelberg, Desiré Defauw, Eduard van Beinum, Willem van Otterloo, Franz André, André Cluytens, André Vandernoot, Bernard Haitink, Louis de Froment, René Defossez, Eduard van Remoortel, Daniel Sternefeld, Hans Vonk, Edo de Waart, Hubert Soudant and François Huybrechts.

The best *symphony orchestras* in the Benelux countries are the Concertgebouw Orchestra in Amsterdam and the Residentie Orchestra in The Hague. In Brussels the Radio Symphony Orchestra (Orchestra of the RTB and BRT), and the Belgian National Orchestra (ONB/NOB) have a good international reputation. Apart from these there are music ensembles of a high standard in Rotterdam, Hilversum, Antwerp, Liège and Luxembourg, ensuring a varied and lively musical life in these cities. The only opera house of international repute is the Théâtre Royal de la Monnaie in Brussels, famous particularly for its 20th c. ballet directed by Maurice Béjart. The modern "Nederlands Dans Theater" is watched with interest all over the world.

As for *music festivals*, the Festival of Flanders which takes place in Ghent and Bruges, and the Holland Festival, rank among the most significant events in Europe. The *music competition* "Concours Reine Elisabeth", held in Brussels, alternately for piano and violin, is among the most demanding. Its prizewinners range from David Oistrach, Leonid Kogan, Jaime Laredo, Michael Rabin, Vladimir Ashkenazy, Nicola Petrov to Philipp Hirschhorn, Stoika Milanova and Gidon Kremer.

In the field of **musical entertainment** the Benelux countries have provided little of importance, although some entertainers (Lou van Burg, Johannes Heesters, Rudi Carell) and dance orchestras scored successes outside their home countries. However, the contribution of some singers has been considerable, for example the Belgian *Jacques Brel* (1929–1978) and the Dutchman *Herman van Veen*.

In the world of jazz, the Belgian-born guitarist and virtuoso mouthorgan player *Jean "Toots" Thielemans* (b. 1922) achieved a reputation as a swing interpreter and composer. In Holland the musician *Peter Schilperoort* (b. 1919), an experienced player of several instruments (especially clarinet), founded in 1945 the world-famous Dixieland Group, "The Dutch Swing College Band".

Economy

In **BELGIUM** the most important economic factor is its highly developed **industry**. Industrialisation began early in the 19th c., based on deposits of coal and iron ore, and it then spread all over continental Europe. But the advantage of this early start turned into a drawback after the Second World War. Insufficient investment made the industrial plant quickly obsolete. State investment inducements, encouraged by the competition within the EEC reversed the situation in the early 1960s, and today Belgium is one of the most modern industrial countries in the world.

The starting point of Belgian industrialisation was the area along the Valley of the Meuse and the Sambre with the old Walloon districts of Borinage, Centre, Charleroi and Liège. The coal seams together with the iron ore deposits which in due course became exhausted, were the necessary prerequisites for an iron and steel industry which as early as the beginning of the 19th c. had become internationally important. The demand for raw materials soon exceeded the capacity of local production and in the last century both coal and iron ore had to be imported. The competition of cheaper imported coal mainly from the USA led, as in other European mining districts, to the closure of several large mines in the 1960s. The proportion of foreign coal now exceeds 35% of total consumption. About half of the domestic production comes from Kempen where the structure and location of deposits make it possible to use more economical mining methods than in the Sambre-Meuse Valley. The coal from Kempen is also of better quality.

The highly export-oriented metal processing industry that developed in the wake of iron and steel became the most important industrial development in Belgium. Its main locations are Namur, Liège and Antwerp and its products range from machines, industrial equipment and consumer goods, to enamelware, rolling stock construction, railway engines, small arms, textile machinery and ships.

Traditional locations of the textile industry are Flanders and Brabant. The linen industry was once the leader but is now in decline and has been overshadowed by cotton and synthetic fibres. Equally well known is the Belgian glass industry in Flanders, Hainaut, Liège and Namur. Its main products are plate glass and mirror glass. The export-oriented plants in these provinces supply approximately 25% of world demand.

After the Second World War, Belgian industry underwent deep structural changes and relocation. With increasing imports of raw materials, location around the ports showed considerable cost advantages. Antwerp in particular benefited from it and developed, together with its surroundings, into a massive industrial agglomeration. Large petro-chemical and chemical facilities dominated the area. In contrast, smaller enterprises are characteristic of the industrial region around the capital, Brussels, which accounts for approximately one-fifth of the country's total industrial output.

Owing to the high density of industry and of population in Belgium, and to its situation between the North Sea coast and the Central European hinterland, **communications** in the country were extremely well developed as early as the last century. The railway network, which is among the most highly developed in the world, must be mentioned first. About one-fifth of the transport capacity is taken by goods in transit. The road network is also excellent. The construction of motor-ways (highways), begun in 1941, is as good as complete. The system of water-ways forms a network of its own and has a total length of 1500 km (932 miles). The volume of goods transported by water exceeds by far that of the railways. The largest ports are Antwerp, Brussels, Bruges and Ghent, which are also accessible to sea-going vessels. Ostend is one of the most important ferry ports between the Continent and Great Britain.

In Belgium only a small fraction of the working population is employed in **agriculture**. Their number has decreased steadily since industrialisation. In 1920 it was 23%; today the farming population does not exceed 6%. One-third of all farms are worked as a second occupation, and yet the country's agriculture supplies the greater part of all basic foodstuffs that the population requires. Industrial raw materials such as flax and sugar-beet are also produced. Special products like grapes, chicory and flower bulbs are mostly exported. This has been made possible by the high technological level of agriculture combined with the most up-to-date farming methods.

Average yields per hectare (2·471 acres) of wheat, sugar-beet, potatoes and milk are considerably above the EEC average and are among the highest in the world. The area of farmland is over 1·6 million hectares (4 million acres), almost half of it being pastures and meadows. The rest is arable and special crop areas. Forestry has hardly any significance at all. The location

of agricultural production is decided basically by the natural diversity of the country. The position in relation to important consumer markets is often decisive. This applies first of all to special and high-intensity crops. These concentrate mainly in regions with light soil, in particular south of Brussels. Fruit growing is widespread south-east and south-west of Antwerp (Kempen and Waasland), around Sint-Truiden, Namur, Liège, Mons and Charleroi. The region of intensive farming is the fertile plain of Hainaut and Hesbaye; wheat and sugar-beet are the main crops; they can also be found in parts of the fenlands. The soil of Geest Flanders and of Kempen is ·especially suitable for potatoes and wheat. Pastures and meadows are found mainly in the Ardennes, in the Pays de Herve and in Famenne; to a lesser extent in parts of Kempen and in the fens.

In recent decades the **service sector** has much increased in importance. The number of people employed in it now exceeds those working in industry. The main locations of the service sector are quite naturally the large towns, primarily the capital Brussels.

Many **tourist** areas also show a high degree of service employment in their economy. The majority of people on vacation flock to the seaside resorts along the coast with Ostend as the mid point. Lagging far behind the coast is the recreation area of the Ardennes with its pleasant river valleys of the Semois, Maas, Ourthe and Lesse and vast stretches of woodland. The health resorts of this region, for example, Spa, have lately registered smaller increases of visitors than the seaside resorts. The third category of tourist attraction is the old historic towns, above all Brussels, Bruges and Ghent. The largest number of foreign visitors comes from Great Britain, followed by France, Federal Germany and the USA.

The NETHERLANDS is now, like Belgium, a modern industrial country with a high proportion of the working population employed in the service sector. After the Second World War their number exceeded those employed in industry. This phenomenon is characteristic of highly developed national economies. Although this was once an agricultural country and one of the world leaders in trade and shipping, its industry received its decisive inducement for growth only after the Second World War. It now accounts for 45% of the net national product and is its largest contributor. Agriculture produces only about 7%, although farmland takes about 60% of the total land surface of the country.

Raw materials for Dutch **industry** are almost wholly absent. Local resources are almost non-existent. Recently even the South Limburg coal-pits had to close because they could not compete with the enormous natural gas fields opened in the provinces of Groningen, Friesland and Drente, and on the North Sea shelf. Compared with natural gas, oil production plays only a minor role. Owing to the lack of raw materials in the country, no heavy industries developed as an economic basis during the industrialisation period, unlike Belgium, Germany or other typical industrial countries. A significant metallurgical industry was built up only in the last decades in a convenient location near IJmuiden on the North Sea Canal. Cargoes of ore and coal from overseas can be discharged right next to the blast furnaces. The same applies for the aluminium mill in Delfzijl at the mouth of the Eems. Traditional shipbuilding still exists with shipyards in Rotterdam, Schiedam and Amsterdam. Other branches of the metal industry are the manufacture of machines, motor cars, vehicles, earth-moving equipment, office machines, machine tools, metal furniture and household equipment.

However, the most important sector is the food industry and tobacco processing. Innumerable small and medium-sized enterprises process local and imported agricultural products, tobacco, brandy and beer.

The most significant growth sector is the relatively new chemical industry. Its capacity has more than quadrupled in the last fifteen years. Its leaders are the oil refineries and large petro-chemical plants in Rotterdam and Amsterdam, followed next by fertilisers, salt, dyes and detergents. A special place belongs to synthetic fibres, of which Holland is one of the world's leading producers.

Another important branch after traditional textiles, is the electrical industry, most notably Philips. The seat of this world combine is Eindhoven. The textile industry is based in Twente and Amsterdam.

The largest industrial agglomeration in the Netherlands is the so-called **Randstad Holland** (see map, opposite), the surface area of which occupies about 10% of the country's total. Approximately two-thirds of the economic potential and nearly half of the country's population are based in this limited area. The most important cities are Amsterdam, Haarlem, Leyden, The Hague, Delft, Rotterdam, Dordrecht and Utrecht. The advantages of the Randstad Holland lead to ever higher concentrations of industry and density of population. The country's planners have tried for the last twenty years to arrest or reduce the structural imbalance. The backward regions such as North Brabant, Limburg, Nijmegen, Arnhem, Terneuzen and Vlissingen/Flushing were given assistance, and some successes have already been registered.

Dutch **agriculture** as a whole has reached a degree of intensity unsurpassed by any other European country. It is, therefore, very much export-oriented. On the other hand some basic foodstuffs, such as wheat, must be imported because local production is not sufficient to feed the population. The most labour and capital intensive sector of agriculture is market gardening (truck farming). While occupying some 5% of farmland, it has the highest export surplus. About 7% of cultivation is under glass, mainly in the areas south of The Hague. Hot-houses are used for growing cucumbers, tomatoes, grapes and flowers. Vegetables, fruit, bulbs and flowers are grown mainly outside. The main distribution areas are Betuwe, South Limburg and South Beveland. Tulip, daffodil and hyacinth growing are concentrated in the polders around Haarlem and Aalsmeer.

Animal husbandry is also important. This is why the proportion of pasture reaches almost two-thirds of all farmland. Butter and cheese are the main products. Cattle breeding is concentrated mainly in two provinces, Friesland and North Holland. Apart from beef cattle, poultry farming also plays a role. The farms are mostly mixed, combining animal husbandry with crop growing. In addition many produce seeds, legumes, oil seeds, sugar-beet and potatoes.

The most important **communications** and transport installations in the Netherlands are the inland waterways and sea ports. The entire economy of the country is based on low-cost transport facilities in particular for bulk cargoes. Rotterdam is

Urban Regions in the Netherlands

Randstad Holland

Groningen
Leeuwarden
Harlingen
Sneek
Assen
Den Helder
Hoorn
Alkmaar
Meppel
Haarlem
Zwolle
AMSTERDAM
Deventer
Apeldoorn
Enschede
Leyden
Utrecht
THE HAGUE
Arnhem
Rotterdam
Nijmegen
Dordrecht
's-Hertogenbosch
Middelburg
Breda
Tilburg
Eindhoven
Roermond
Maastricht

not only the largest sea and inland port in Europe, but also ranks among the largest in the world. The Port of Amsterdam is much smaller but is still very important. The network of inland waterways provides a connection between the sea ports and the European hinterland, and has a combined length of 4350 km (2703 miles).

The road network carries a large part of the goods transported, and is in excellent condition. There are approximately 1250 km (777 miles) of highways. On the other hand, railway traffic is relatively insignificant, having suffered both from the high percentage of road transport and the competition of the oil and gas pipelines.

After the Second World War, the Netherlands became an important **tourist country**. Favourite vacation areas are the West Frisian Islands and the seaside resorts on the North Sea coast, such as Scheveningen, Noordwijk and Bergen. Very popular too are the towns and villages around the IJsselmeer. World

famous are the folk costumes of Volendam near Edam. Improved communications in connection with the Deltaplan have also helped the Zealand Islands to become popular tourist resorts. Interesting old cities and towns, such as Amsterdam, Delft, Leyden, Gouda, Haarlem and Middelburg attract many visitors. The same applies to the bulb fields when the flowers are in bloom. Large numbers of tourists visit the National Park "Hoge Veluwe" near Arnhem. Most foreign visitors come from Federal Germany, followed by the USA, Great Britain, France and the other Benelux countries, Belgium and Luxembourg.

In **LUXEMBOURG, metallurgy** is the basis of the economy. It developed relatively late, towards the end of the 19th c. handicapped at first by the total absence of fuel deposits. Coal could be imported at economically feasible rates only after the railway communications had been built up. Smelting of local iron ore (Minette), the deposits of which are among Europe's largest, only became possible with the invention of the Thomas process. Because of the economic links with the German Reich (Customs' Union 1843–1919), however, the necessary capital was available, and Luxembourg was able to catch up quickly with the traditional industrial countries. The company ARBED (Aciéries Réunies Burbach-Esch-Dudelange), which within a short timespan became the largest employer and the largest enterprise both in turnover and output in the Grand Duchy, made Luxembourg, together with the SMMR (Société Minière et Métallurgique de Rodange), an internationally significant producer of iron and steel. The tiny country is seventeenth in the world in the output of crude steel, and its per capita production is by far the highest in the world. The steel and pressed steel mills with their blast furnaces are all located in the south of the country between Dudelange and Rodange. Here also are the mining districts where iron ore is extracted from open-cast mines. Approximately 95% of the iron and steel production is exported.

In 1959 an Office for Industrial Development was created in Luxembourg with the aim of gradually restructuring the economy which was considered too one-sided and oriented exclusively to the production of iron and steel, and therefore vulnerable to crises. After the Goodyear tyre plant was founded in 1950 other industries eventually moved in. They were mainly synthetic fibres, plastics, pharmaceuticals, all considered to be growth industries. The high standard of living is due not only to the high degree of industrialisation, but also to a not inconsiderable extent, to the contribution of some 90,000 foreign workers, 78% of whom live either in the capital or in the industrial south. Several thousand workers daily cross the frontiers of Belgium, France and Federal Germany.

Compared with Belgium and the Netherlands, the ratio of people working in agriculture is relatively high, averaging some 10%. Almost 85% of farmland is devoted to animal husbandry. Given the geological character of the country, the proportion of pastureland is naturally higher in the less endowed Ösling than south of it in Gutland where the cultivation of feed plants plays an even greater role. Next to cattle breeding, only grape growing in the Valley of the Moselle is an economic factor of any significance. The average annual production is about 100,000 hectolitres (2,200,000 gallons).

Worth noting is the unusually high degree of mechanisation in Luxembourg agriculture, a sign of the high standard of the national economy. The production figures have increased correspondingly so that today the food requirements of the country can to a large extent be satisfied by home-grown supplies.

Forestry is also of considerable importance, especially in Ösling, large parts of which are densely wooded. Total forested area is 90,000 hectares (222,390 acres); more than half of it, 50,000 hectares (123,550 acres), consisting of deciduous trees, and 31,000 hectares (76,601 acres) are mixed and fast growing coniferous forests. The rest of the area is occupied by brushwood, formerly used for tanning bark.

The **communication** network of Luxembourg is, compared with other European countries, relatively young. The first railway line was opened only in 1859, and nine years later it was connected with the tracks of the neighbouring countries as a prerequisite for industrialisation. Since 1965 Luxembourg has been connected with the European waterway network by the Port of Mertert on the Moselle. The total turnover of goods is 1·5 million tons, 85% of which is bulk cargo destined for the steel industry. The road network is approximately 5000 km (3107 miles) long. Good roads connect the capital with long-distance highways in the neighbouring countries, Belgium, France and Federal Germany.

Tourism plays only a relatively modest role within the framework of the general economy. It is confined mostly to the capital city and to some smaller holiday resorts in Ösling. Here it has eventually become in addition to agriculture and forestry, a significant source of income for the local population. After the city of Luxembourg, the largest number of tourists visit the ancient abbey town of Echternach on the Sûre.

Holland, Belgium & Luxembourg A to Z

Atomium in Brussels

Aalst (Alost)

Country: Belgium. – Province: East Flanders.
Altitude: 7–29 m (23–95 feet). – Population: 80,000.
Postal code: B-9300.
Telephone code: 0 53.
ⓘ **Stedelijke Commissie voor Toerisme en Vremdelingenverkeer,**
Stadhuis;
tel. 21 57 51.

HOTELS. – *Molenhof*, Molenstraat 8, III, 12 r.; *Borse van Amsterdam*, Grote Markt 26, IV, 6 r.; *De la Gare*, Stationsplein 11, IV, 18 r.; *Cottem*, Molenstraat 12, IV, 6 r.; *Des Arcades* (no rest.), Stationsplein 8, V, 9 r.

RESTAURANTS. – *Hostellerie Ter Linden*, Oude Gentbaan 49; *Meiboom*, Korte Zoutstraat 58.

EVENTS. – *Carnival* with a traditional *throwing of onions* from the belfry; *carillon concerts* in the Grote Markt (Saturday 11 a.m.–12 noon; Sunday 11.30 a.m.–12 noon).

Belfry in the Market Place in Aalst

Aalst (in French, Alost), lies on the banks of the Dender in the Belgian province of East Flanders. The town is the seat of district administration and education for a wider area.

There are numerous industrial plants, mainly cotton processing, textile mills, engineering, etc.; hops cultivated in the neighbouring villages are marketed in Aalst. However, the town is basically part of the Greater Brussels commuter belt. The capital has many job opportunities and is only 28 km (17 miles) to the south-east.

HISTORY. – The Castle of Aalst is first mentioned in Chronicles in 866. The township received its charter in 1164 after it was granted as an imperial fief to the Counts of Flanders. In the Middle Ages, Aalst quickly developed into the capital of a county of the same name within Imperial Flanders. During the Dutch Liberation Wars, the town rapidly became the scene of fighting in which many inhabitants lost their lives, and numerous buildings were destroyed or damaged. The same destiny befell Aalst in the wars of Louis XIV, as well as in both World Wars. Fortunately, several valuable buildings survived.

SIGHTS. – On the west side of the Grote Markt stands the **Amsterdam Stock Exchange**, a brick and sandstone building in the Flemish late Renaissance style, erected in 1630–4. The façade is embellished with arcades; the structure is topped with four baroque round gables and a slender central tower. Opposite stands the former *Town Hall*. It is the oldest of its kind in the whole of Belgium; its special features are the rear and one of the side façades, which date from the first half of the 13th c. The beautiful *belfry* (carillon with 52 bells), dates from the 15th c. The *monument to Dirk Martens* of 1856, in front of the Town Hall, commemorates the first Belgian printer, born in Aalst in 1450. He developed his own lettering system and was the first in the Netherlands to print Greek and Hebrew texts.

East of the Grote Markt stretches the P. Daensplein, in the middle of which stands the **Church of St Martin**. The construction of the church was started about 1480 by the little-known builder Jan van der Wouwe. The most remarkable parts of it are the work of the famous architects D. and H. de Waghemakere, the builders of Antwerp Cathedral, and of the great master builder L. Keldermans from Mechelen. Because of the Religious Wars in the 16th c., the building remained unfinished.

Inside St Martin's Church, many first-rate works of art can be seen, among them, a painting by Peter Paul Rubens or one of his disciples (*"St Roch receiving from Christ the Gift of Healing the Plague-Stricken"*), a large fresco from the 16th c. in the Chapter Hall (the "Last Judgment"), a remarkable *tabernacle* by J. Duquesnoy the Elder (1604), etc. In the Treasury is a monstrance in three parts by the goldsmith Lestiens of Antwerp (1631).

Achterhoek

Country: The Netherlands. – Province: Gelderland.
ⓘ **VVV Gelderland,**
Stationsplein 45,
NL-6811 KL Arnhem;
tel. (0 85) 45 29 21.

The Dutch region of Achterhoek is also known as Gelderse Achterhoek or Graafschap. It lies south of the Twente and is in fact the eastern

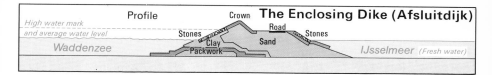

Profile   Crown   **The Enclosing Dike (Afsluitdijk)**
High water mark / and average water level — Road — Stones
Waddenzee   Stones   Clay / Packwork   Sand   IJsselmeer (Fresh water)

part of the province of Gelderland bordered by the IJssel, the Old IJssel, and the North German lowlands.

Achterhoek is a sandy flatland some 10–50 m (33–164 feet) above sea level, the surface of which, with its wide river valleys and marked morainal beds, was formed in the next to last Ice Age, when the glaciers pushing from the north covered this part of the Netherlands. Agriculture, especially the production of butter and poultry, is this region's most important occupation. Small villages and isolated individual farmsteads are the typical forms of settlements in the vast agricultural countryside. Industrial enterprises settled mainly on the banks of the **IJssel** and the **Old IJssel**; among them brickworks and iron foundries, stocking manufacturers, and cotton processing plants.

Afsluitdijk/ The Enclosing Dike

Country: The Netherlands.
ⓘ **VVV Den Helder-Julianadorp,**
Julianaplein,
NL-1780 AA Den Helder;
tel. (0 22 30) 1 35 97.
VVV Friesland-Leeuwarden,
Stationsplein 1,
NL-8911 AC Leeuwarden;
tel. (0 51 00) 3 22 24.

The *Afsluitdijk or Enclosing Dike of the IJsselmeer (30 km (19 miles) long and 90 km (56 miles) wide) connects the provinces of North Holland and Friesland. The dike was built in the years 1927–32 and made the former Zuiderzee into an inland lake – the present-day IJsselmeer.**

The *Zuiderzee* was an inland lake up to Roman times. During the Middle Ages the sea level in the North Sea rose and mighty tidal waves made it into a sea bay. Since then the Government and the inhabitants of the country have speculated on how to reclaim the flooded land. Only in the 19th c. did the technological means for such a reclamation become available. Because of considerable food shortages

in the Netherlands during the First World War and a tidal wave in 1916 (which again caused great damage), the Government approved and put into effect plans devised by Lely. The objective of the enterprise was not only to obtain agricultural land, but also to protect against flooding. The construction of the Enclosing Dike had the effect of reducing the length of dikes in the area of the IJsselmeer by nearly 300 km (186 miles). At the beginning of the dike in North Holland, large locks, *Stevin Sluizen*, were built to drain the enclosed area. On its outward side are several harbour docks protected by stone breakwaters.

Driving across the dike. – A good road (A7) starts at Den Oever in North Holland and runs a little below the crown of the dike. On the right there is an unobstructed view of the IJsselmeer; on the left the view of the North Sea is obstructed by the grassy dike. – After 6·5 km (4 miles) on the right there is a **monument** where the dike was completed (28 May 1932), with an observation tower, a small restaurant, a foot-bridge across the road and parking. From the platform there is an unobstructed view over the sea. – Continuing you reach *Breezanddijk*, an artificial island with a small harbour which was the starting point for the construction of the dike. – After 11 km (7 miles) you come to the large *Lorentzsluizen* installations with parking on the right, and a restaurant behind them on the left. It is 4 km (2 miles) further to the end of the dike (filling station) where the west coast of the province of Friesland begins.

Alkmaar

Country: The Netherlands. – Province: North Holland. Altitude: Below sea level. – Population: 67,000. Postal code: NL-1800 AA to 1899. Telephone code: 0 72.
ⓘ "Alcmaria" VVV,
Waagplein 3,
NL-1811 JP Alkmaar;
tel. 11 42 84.

HOTELS. – Motel *Alkmaar*, Arcadialaan 2, I, 183 b.; *Victory* (no rest.), van der Boschstraat 3, III, 34 b.; *Marktzicht*, Houttil 34, IV, 15 b.; *De Nachtegaal*, Langestraat 100, V, 29 b.; *Houtzicht*, Kennemerstraatweg 157–159, V, 15 b. – CAMPING.

RESTAURANTS. – *Koekenbier*, Kennemerstraatweg 16; *Rôtisserie Rue du Bois*, van den Boschstraat 3; *Gouden Dukaat*, 1er Etage, Fnidsen 107; *Kinheim*, Stationsweg 58.

EVENTS. – *Cheese Market every Friday from 10 a.m. to 12 noon, from the end of April until approximately mid-September. *Canal cruises* from the Mient Quay near the Cheese Market.

The Dutch town of Alkmaar in the province of North Holland lies 8 km (5 miles) from the North Sea coast on the North Holland Canal. Its charming townscape with many architectural monuments and beautiful old guild and burgher houses of the 16th and 18th c. has been preserved unspoiled. Together with the famous Cheese Market, it is one of the area's prime tourist attractions.

Alkmaar is in the midst of a large rural area. Many inhabitants of the province of North Holland come to its schools and shops. The most significant part of its economy is, however, the widely diversified industries which have settled in the northeast of Alkmaar, benefiting from the transport facilities provided by the North Holland Canal. Important branches are engineering, paper and textile mills, food industries (canneries and chocolates), as well as the building of organs.

HISTORY. – Alkmaar was founded in the 10th c. and received its charter in 1254. Its period of prosperity, however, came only after the Dutch Wars of Liberation against the Spanish occupation, in which Alkmaar played a special role. The town was the first that succeeded in defeating Frederick of Toledo, the son of the Duke of Alba, who besieged it. This was achieved by a special stratagem. On 8 October 1573, the sluices were opened and the area around the town flooded. This remarkable victory marked the beginning of the Spanish defeat.

SIGHTS. – In the west of the Old Town, which is surrounded by beautiful parks laid out on the site of the former fortifications, stands the **Grote Kerk** (*St Laurenskerk*; Reformed; carillon), a fine late Gothic construction erected in 1470–1520. Worth seeing are the pulpit (1665) and the Baroque pews, the tombstone of Count Floris V of Holland (d. 1296), in the choir left of the ambulatory, a late Gothic organ of 1511 and, in the southern transept, a brass tomb plaque from the 16th c. There is also a large organ of 1645 (organ recitals in July and August, Fridays at 11.15 a.m.– 12.15 p.m.).

The Langestraat, the main street of the town, leads from the Grote Kerk eastward to the Mient Quay. Right in the Langestraat (No. 46), stands the **Town Hall** (*Stadhuis*; 16th–17th c.). In the Doelenstraat (No. 3), is the interesting *Municipal Museum*. – At the end of the Langestraat go left across the Mient to the

Municipal *Weigh-house*, which was converted in 1582 from the former Church of the Holy Ghost. A beautiful tower was added in 1599; its carillon dates from 1688. In front of the Weigh-house, when the *Cheese Market takes place, the square is almost completely covered with round cheeses brought in on traditional racks by carriers dressed in guild costumes. The cheeses are then weighed in the Weigh-house and loaded on to carts.

Cheese Market in Alkmaar

In the picturesque part of the Old Town by the Mient, on the Canals "Luttik Oudorp" and "Verdronkenoord", as well as in the adjacent streets, many gabled houses, dating from the beginning of the 17th c. still stand. Among them is the elegant little *Customs House* (Accijnstoren, from 1622) at the end of the Verdronkenoord, by the North Holland Canal. From here runs the Bierkade to *Victoriepark* in which there is a monument commemorating the defence of the town against the Spanish in 1573.

SURROUNDINGS of Alkmaar. – To reach **Egmond aan Zee** leave the town by the road to Bergen. After 2·5 km (2 miles) turn left through the "Sea of Egmond", drained in 1556 and continue to *Egmond aan de Hoef* 8 km (5 miles) away. This used to be the family seat of the Counts Egmond who later settled in Southern Holland and whose castle was destroyed in 1573 by the Spanish. The ruins are well worth seeing. 3 km (2 miles) further south on the road to Castricum is *Egmond Binnen*, formerly famous for its Benedictine Abbey, destroyed in 1573 and rebuilt in 1935. In its church many of the Counts of Holland were buried. After 2 km (1 mile), you reach **Egmond aan Zee** (Hotel Bellevue, I, 78 b.; Frisia, IV, 55 b.; Atlantic, IV, 30 b.), a well-known seaside resort with a good beach.

From Alkmaar to Bergen aan Zee leave Alkmaar in a north-westerly direction; a good road passes near the railway station and then runs across flat pasture-land. After 6 km (4 miles) you reach **Bergen**, also called *Bergen Binnen* or *Bergen in het Bosch* (Hotel Marijke, II, 100 b.; Metamorphose, II, 38 b.; Elzenhof, II, 60 b.; Parkhotel, III, 50 b.; Het witte Huis, IV, 100 b.), a lively summer resort patronised by artists. Scattered in the woods are many charming country houses and numerous hotels and restaurants. In the middle of town are the ruins of a church which was burned down in 1574. Also worth seeing is a monument to the Russians who perished here in 1799. 5 km (3 miles) north of Bergen is the village of *Schoorl*, and a further 5 km (3 miles) north-west, between *Camperduin* and *Petten* (nuclear research facility and European School), are the large dikes of the *Hondsbosse Zeewering*. – The route continues from Bergen partly through wooded dunes; after 5 km (3 miles) you reach **Bergen aan Zee** (Hotel Nassau-Bergen, II, 63 b.; Prins Maurits, II, 60 b.), a quiet place, popular as a seaside resort, with a beautiful wide beach.

From Alkmaar to Den Oever the road continues first eastward across the North Holland Canal and then to the village of *Omval*. Beyond it the road turns left on the N99 (right to Edam) and north-east through vegetable-growing country with an extensive network of canals. To the left is the picturesque village of *Broek op Langendijk*, known for its vegetable auctions. 15 km (9 miles) from Alkmaar you cross the road running from Schagen to Hoorn. Near *Aartswoud*, on the right, is the Wieringermeer Polder, and 15 km (9 miles) beyond, on the left is the *Middenmeer*. From here it is another 15 km (9 miles) to **Den Oever** at the beginning of the Enclosing Dike of the IJsselmeer.

Amersfoort

Country: The Netherlands. – Province: Utrecht.
Altitude: 4–49 m (13–160 feet). – Population: 87,000.
Postal code: NL-3800 AA to 3839.
Telephone code: 0 33.
ⓘ **VVV Amersfoort-Eemland,**
  Stationsplein 8,
  NL-3813 LE Amersfoort;
  tel. 3 51 51.

HOTELS. – *De Witte*, Utrechtseweg 2, II, 23 b.; *Berghotel Amersfoort*, Utrechtseweg 225, II, 38 b.; *'t Oude Raedthuys*, Hof 15, V, 10 b. YOUTH HOSTEL: de Genestetlaan 9, 130 b.

RESTAURANTS. – *Lamme Goetsack*, Lieve Vrouwe-straat 8; *Oude Tram*, Stationsplein 4.

EVENTS. – Performance by the *town trumpeters* every Saturday morning in summer.

The lively and friendly town of Amersfoort in the Dutch province of Utrecht is surrounded by a vast area of forest and heath. It lies at the confluence of several small rivers, which, further downstream, form the Eem. This well-preserved old town contains a number of interesting historic buildings and is surrounded by a double ring of canals.

Amersfoort is the commercial and cultural capital of the Eem area, and the part of the country called Geldersche Vallei. It has several institutions of higher education, large markets and important industrial plants – electrical engineering, motor industry, machines and chemicals. Apart from this, agricultural produce from the surrounding area is mainly processed in the city. Nevertheless, many of its inhabitants work in the nearby provincial capital of Utrecht and even in Amsterdam 50 km (31 miles) away.

HISTORY. – Amersfoort is first mentioned in Chronicles in 1028. It received its charter in 1259 and developed quickly due to its cloth-manufacturing and well-known breweries. It soon became a member of the North German Hanse. In the first half of the 15th c. the town extended beyond its ramparts and the construction of new fortifications was started about 1450 and completed in 1561. Within the confines of the original inner moat there lies today a well-preserved medieval town with only a few gabled houses from the later Renaissance period.

SIGHTS. – In the Hof, the main square of the Old Town, stands the Gothic **Church of St George** (*St Joriskerk* or *Grote Kerk*). The building was started in 1243 and completed in 1534. Inside is a beautiful Gothic rood-screen from the 15th c. The tomb of the famous Dutch builder Jacob van Campen should not be missed. South-west of here stands *St Mary's Tower* (Onze Lieve Vrouwen-toren), 100 m (328 feet) high, it is an imposing late Gothic structure with a carillon by the famous F. Hemony, which is among the best of its kind in the Netherlands. The Tower originally belonged to St Mary's Church, destroyed in 1787 by a gunpowder explosion.

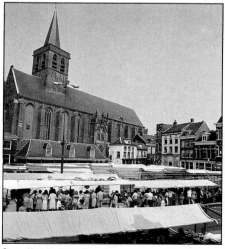

Grote Kerk in Amersfoort

From the O. L. Vrouwekerkhof you follow the adjacent outer canal northward and, on the other side of the Eem, you come to the **Koppelpoort** (15th c.), a former gate in the second city wall. In the street called Westsingel, which runs on the far side of the outer canal, is the *Fléhite Museum* (house No. 50). Displayed there is a historic collection, including souvenirs of the statesman Jan van Oldenbarnevelt, who was born in Amersfoort in 1547 and whose bust stands near the grammar school. The Westsingel then follows the outer canal and after a few yards it crosses the Utrechtsestraat and becomes the Zuidsingel. On the right is the *Marienhof* of 1480, a former monastery which now houses the National Office of Archaeology.

If you then cross the canal by a bridge, and turn to the right on the other side you come to the *Monnikendam* flood-gate, dating from the 15th c. Pass the picturesque circle of old houses, the **Muurhuizen**, built on and against the Old City wall when it became obsolete after the city boundaries were extended. You then arrive at the *Kamperbinnenpoort* on the other side of the canal, which is the oldest city gate in Amersfoort (13th c.). Worth seeing also is the *Exhibition Hall* at Zonnehof dating from 1959 and built by the architect G. Rietveld.

South-west of the city on the *Amersfoortse Berg*, 49 m (161 feet) high, and offering a good view, stands the *Belgenmonument* in memory of the Belgian refugees from the First World War.

SURROUNDINGS of Amersfoort. – **Excursion to Hilversum via Soestdijk.** – The road to Hilversum leaves Amersfoort to the north-west, and goes first via *Soest*, a town with a population of 38,000 to **Soestdijk** (8·5 km – 5 miles). At the end of the town stands the extensive Palace of the same name, with a beautiful park, now the residence of the Queen Mother. Queen Beatrix now lives in the *Palace of Drakestein* south-west of here. – The road then leads through the delightful wooded area of *Baarnse Bos* which stretches as far as Hilversum. 4 km (2 miles) beyond Soestdijk; you reach a fork in the road, to the south of which is *Baarn* (population 24,000; Hotel de Prom, III, 49 b.), a favourite summer resort of the people of Amsterdam. The University Botanical Garden (Cantonpark) is located here. Turn left and proceed through the woods to the *Kasteel de Hooge Vuursche*, which is now a hotel. 6 km (4 miles) further you reach **Hilversum** (see page 179).

Amsterdam

Country: The Netherlands. – Province: North Holland. Altitude: Below sea level. – Population: 987,000.
Postal code: NL-1000 AA to 1129.
Telephone code: 0 20.

ⓘ **VVV Amsterdam e.o.,**
Rokin 5,
NL-1012 KK Amsterdam;
tel. 26 64 44.
VVV Amsterdam,
Stationsplein (by the railway station),
NL-1012 AB Amsterdam;
tel. 22 10 16.
VVV Amsterdam,
Utrechtseweg (open from Easter to 15 September).

THE AIRPORT. – The **Central Airport of Schiphol** near Amsterdam is one of the largest and most modern airports in Western Europe and connects with the city of Amsterdam by a railway (Station Zuid). The airport area lies 4 m (13 feet) below sea level.

HOTELS. – *Amstel Hotel*, Prof. Tulpplein 1, L, 183 b.; *Amsterdam Hilton*, Apollolaan 138, L, 507 b.; *Sonesta Amsterdam*, Kattegat 1, L, 720 b.; *De l'Europe*, Nieuwe Doelenstraat 2–4, L, 119 b.; *Marriott Amsterdam*, Stadhouderskade 21, L, 635 b.; *Okura Intercontinental*, Ferd. Bolstraat 175, L, 754 b.; *Apollo*, Apollolaan 2, L, 400 b.; *Schiphol Airport Hilton*, Schiphol Centrum, L, 290 b.

Grand Hotel Krasnapolsky, Dam, I, 548 b.; *Memphishotel Ramada*, De Lairessestraat 87, I, 160 b.; *Caransa*, Rembrandtsplein 19, I, 132 b.; *Doelen Hotel*, Nieuwe Doelenstraat 24, I, 180 b.; *Alexander-Dikker en Thijs*, Prinsengracht 444, I, 50 b.; *Novotel Alpha Amsterdam*, Europaboulevard 10, I, 1200 b.; *Die Port van Cleve*, N.Z. Voorburgwal 178, I, 211 b.; *EuroCrest Hotel Amsterdam*, De Boelelaan 2, I, 520 b.; *Carlton* (no rest.), Vijzelstraat 2–18, I, 280 b.; *American*, Leidsekade 97, I, 324 b.; *Pulitzer*, Prinsengracht 315–331, I, 340 b.; *Schiller*, Rembrandtsplein 26–36, I, 170 b.; *Amster Centre*, Herengracht 255, I, 220 b.; *Adda Parkhotel*, Stadhouderskade 25, I, 350 b.; *Victoria*, Damrak 1–5, I, 240 b.; *Apollofirst*, Apollolaan 123–125, I, 72 b.; *Golden Tulip Centraal Hotel*, Stadhouderskade 7, I, 210 b.; *Delphi*, Apollolaan 101–105, I, 100 b.; *Piet Hein* (no rest.), Vossiusstraat 53, I, 60 b.; *Jan Luyken*, Jan Luykenstraat 54–58, I, 130 b.; *Arthur Frommer*, Noorderstraat 46, I, 180 b.; *Casa 400*, James Wattstraat 75, I, 800 b.; *Atlas*, Rembrandtsplein 8–10, I, 60 b.; *Euromotel Amsterdam Schiphol*, Oude Haagseweg 20, I, 341 b.; *Rijnders*, Wanningstraat 1–7, I, 100 b.; *Napoleon*, Valkenburgerstraat 72, I, 90 b.; *Euromotel E9*, Joan Muyskenweg 10, I, 270 b.

Choura, Marnixstraat 372, II, 40 b.; *Damrak*, Damrak 49, II, 54 b.; *Dikker en Thijs Garden Hotel* (no rest.), Dijsselhofplantsoen 7, II, 180 b.; *De Roode Leuw*, Damrak 93–94, II, 138 b.; *AMS Hotel Terdam v.h. De Haas*, Tesselschadestraat 23–29, II, 150 b.; *Trianon*, J. W. Brouwersstraat 3–7, II, 130 b.; *Beethoven*, Beethovenstraat 43–51, II, 140 b.; *Estherea*, Singel 305–307, II, 135 b.; *Borgmann* (no rest.), Koningslaan 48, II, 35 b.; *Owl*, Roemer Visscherstraat 1–3, II, 71 b.

AMS Hotel Holland, P. C. Hooftstraat 162–168, III, 150 b.; *Museum Hotel*, P. C. Hooftstraat 2–10, III, 360 b.; *Atlanta*, Rembrandtsplein 8–10, III, 60 b.; *Vondel*

Amsterdam – illumination of the canals

(no rest.), Vondelstraat 28–30, III, 52 b.; *Vondelhof* (no rest.), Vondelstraat 24, II, 28 b.; *Marianne*, Nicolaas Maesstraat 107, III, 30 b.; *Toledo* (no rest.), Willemsparkweg 205, III, 32 b.; *Engeland*, Roemer Visscherstraat 30, III, 60 b.; *Parkzicht* (no rest.), Roemer Visscherstraat 33, III, 28 b.; *Imperial* (no rest.), Thorbeckeplein 9, III, 40 b.; *Eden*, Amstel 142–144, III, 135 b.; *Cynthia*, Vondelstraat 44–46, III, 65 b.; *Belfort*, Surinameplein 53, III, 40 b.; *Slotania*, Slotermeerlaan 133, III, 148 b.; *Westropa 1*, Eerste C. Huygensstr. 105, III, 53 b.; *Sipermann*, Roemer Visscherstraat 35, III, 20 b.; *Parklane* (no rest.), Plantage Parklaan 16, III, 15 b.; *De Stadhouder* (no rest.), Stadhouderskade 76, III, 50 b.; *Nicolaas Witsen* (no rest.), Nicolaas Witsenstraat 4–8, III, 56 b.; *D'Huifkar* (no rest.), Weteringschans 82, III, 45 b.; *Koningshof* (no rest.), Koninginneweg 167–169, III, 30 b.; *De IJ-Tunnel*, Prins Hendrikkade 144–145, III, 120 b.; *Monopole* (no rest.), Amstel 60, III, 31 b.; *De Lantaerne* (no rest.), Leidsegracht 111, III, 67 b.; *Flipper*, Borssenburgstraat, III, 30 b.; *Amber*, Koningslaan 56, III, 35 b.; *Eureka* (no rest.), 's Gravelandseveer 4, III, 30 b.; *Heemskerk* (no rest.), J. W. Brouwersstraat 25, III, 22 b.

Cordial, Rokin 62, IV, 90 b.; *Hotel de Amstel* (no rest.), Weesperzijde 28, IV, 42 b.; *Toro* (no rest.), Koningslaan 64, IV, 20 b.; *Armada* (no rest.), Keizersgracht 713, IV, 54 b.; *Terminus* (no rest.), Beursstraat 19, IV, 100 b.; *Washington* (no rest.), Frans van Mierisstraat 10, IV, 38 b.; *Savoy* (no rest.), Michelangelostraat 39, IV, 37 b.; *Canal House* (no rest.), Keizersgracht 148, IV, 35 b.; *Arsenal* (no rest.), Frans van Mierisstraat 97, IV, 20 b.; *Hestia* (no rest.), Roemer Visscherstraat 7, IV, 34 b.; *Westropa 2* (no rest.), Nassaukade 389–390, IV, 54 b.; *De Rijk* (no rest.), Leidsekade 91, IV, 57 b.; *Van Rooyen* (no rest.), Tweede Helmersstraat 6, IV, 28 b.; *Hegra* (no rest.), Herengracht 269, IV, 22 b.; *Kennedy Park* (no rest.), Van Eeghenlaan 24, IV, 33 b.; *Paap* (no rest.), Keizersgracht 39, IV, 41 b.; *Vincent van Gogh* (no rest.), V.d. Veldestraat 5, IV, 38 b.; *De la Poste* (no rest.), Reguliersgracht 5, IV, 38 b.; *Asterisk* (no rest.), Den Textstraat 16, IV, 30 b.; *Weichmann*, Prinsengracht 328, IV, 70 b.; *Pierre* (no rest.), Valeriusstraat 24, IV, 29 b.; *Aalders* (no rest.), Jan Luykenstraat 13–15, IV, 53 b.; *Belga* (no rest.), Hartenstraat 8, IV, 25 b.; *Rokin* (no rest.), Rokin 73, IV, 60 b.; *Prinsen* (no rest.), Vondelstraat 38, IV, 54 b.; *Hotel "Z"* (no rest.), Van Eeghenstraat 6, IV, 16 b.; *City* (no rest.), Utrechtsestraat 2, IV, 47 b.; *Fantasia* (no rest.), Nieuwe Keizersgracht 16, IV, 50 b.; *Kooyk* (no rest.), Leidsekade 82, IV, 40 b.; *Sangam* (no rest.), Marnixstraat 388, IV, 50 b.; *Mondial* (no rest.), Leidsekade 89, IV, 29 b.; *Casa Cara* (no rest.), Emmastraat 24, IV, 23 b.; *Van Haalen*, Prinsengracht 520, IV, 40 b.; *Welvaart* (no rest.), Koninginneweg 149, IV, 26 b.; *Hooft P. C.* (no rest.), P. C. Hooftstraat 63, IV, 35 b.; *Hans Brinker Hotel*, Kerkstraat 136, IV, 225 b.; *Oiszewski*, Plantage Muidergr. 87–91, IV, 32 b.; *Koning* (no rest.), Tweede Helmersstraat 14, IV, 33 b.; *Courbet* (no rest.), Courbetstraat 34, IV, 21 b.; *Kap* (no rest.), Den Textstraat 5B, IV, 26 b.; *De Stern*, Utrechtsestraat 18, IV, 22 b.; *Du Commerce*, Beursstraat 5, IV, 14 b.; *Tabu* (no rest.),

Marnixstraat 386, IV, 42 b.; *Museumzicht* (no rest.), Jan Luykenstraat 22, IV, 25 b.; *Pax* (no rest.), Raadhuisstraat 37, IV, 22 b.; *Groot*, Herengracht 135–137, IV, 40 b.; *Groenendael* (no rest.), Nieuwendijk 15, IV, 24 b.; *Anco* (no rest.), O. Z. Voorburgwal 55, IV, 37 b.

Aalborg (no rest.), Sarphatipark 106–108, V, 70 b.; *Ambassade* (no rest.), Herengracht 341, V, 66 b.; *De Gerstekorrel*, Damstraat 22–24, V, 53 b.; *Sander*, Jacob Obrechtstraat 69, IV, 30 b.; *De Korenaer*, Damrak 50, IV, 27 b.; *Toren*, Keizersgracht 164, V, 80 b.; *Wienerwald*, Kleine Gertmanplantsoen 5, V, 32 b.; *Mikado* (no rest.), Amstel 107–111, V, 25 b.; *Linda* (no rest.), Stadhouderskade 131, V, 40 b.; *Verdi* (no rest.), Wanningstraat 9, V, 30 b.; *Damhotel*, Damrak 31, V, 40 b.; *Albatros* (no rest.), Nieuwendijk 100, V, 45 b.; *Alcor* (no rest.), Gerrit vd Veenstraat 90, V, 12 b.; *Perseverance* (no rest.), Overtoom 78–80, V, 28 b.; *De Pool* (no rest.), Damrak 42–43, V, 58 b.; *Cuhfus* (no rest.), Overtoom 122, V, 24 b.; *Metro* (no rest.), Van Eeglenlaan 19, V, 13 b.; *De Leydsche Hof* (no rest.), Leidsegracht 14, V, 29 b.; *l'Espérance*, Stadhouderskade 49, V, 15 b.; *Thorbecke* (no rest.), Thorbeckeplein 3, V, 24 b.; *Hemonyhof*, Hemonystraat 7, V, 39 b.; *Wijnnobel* (no rest.), Vossiusstraat 9, V, 27 b.; *House of Marjos* (no rest.), Van Baerlestraat 71, V, 27 b.; *Granada*, Leidsekruisstraat 13, V, 24 b.; *Cok Young Budget*, Koninginneweg 30–32, V, 400 b.; *Peters* (no rest.), Nicolaas Maesstraat 72, V, 10 b.; *Torenzicht* (no rest.), O. Z. Achterburgwal 93, V, 46 b.; *Young Budget Hotel Kabul*, Warmoesstraat 38–42, V, 257 b.; *Bierenbroodspot* (no rest.), Michelangelostraat 28, V, 14 b.; *Van de Kasteleen* (no rest.), Frans van Mierisstraat 34, V, 26 b.; *Smit* (no rest.), P. C. Hooftstraat 24–26, V, 70 b.; *De Munck* (no rest.), Achtergracht 3, V, 24 b.; *King* (no rest.), Leidsekade 84–86, V, 60 b.; *Holbein* (no rest.), Holbeinstraat 5, V, 12 b.; *De Moor* (no rest.), Prinsengracht 1015–1017, V, 59 b.; *Continental* (no rest.), Damrak 40–41, V, 35 b.; *Keizershof*, Keizersgracht 630, V, 24 b.; *Titus* (no rest.), Leidsekade 74, V, 22 b.; *Van Acker* (no rest.), J. W. Brouwersstraat 14, V, 21 b.; *Van Gelder* (no rest.), Damrak 34, V, 33 b.; *Albany* (no rest.), Pieter de Hoochstraat 86, V, 12 b.; *Florence* (no rest.), Van Eeghenstraat 44, V, 11 b.; *Oecumene Hotel San Luchesio* (no rest.), Waldeck Pyrmontlaan 9–11, V, 42 b.; *Clemens* (no rest.), Raadhuisstraat, V, 16 b.; *The Flying Dutchman* (no rest.), Scheldestraat 30, V, 10 b.; *Golden Gate*, Warmoesstraat 7, V, 33 b.; *Van Hulssen* (no rest.), Bloemgracht 108, V, 17 b.; *Huize Bakker-Stoit* (no rest.), Nicolaas Maesstraat 81, V, 14 b.; *Van Onna* (no rest.), Bloemgracht 102, V, 20 b.; *Biervliet* (no rest.), Nassaukade 368, V, 17 b.; *Van Lennep* (no rest.), Jac. van Lennepkade 1, V, 19 b.; *Albert* (no rest.), Sarphatipark 58, V, 31 b.; *Huize Gregoire* (no rest.), Nicolaas Maesstraat 77, V, 16 b.; *Ardina* (no rest.), Keizersgracht 268–284, V, 65 b.; *Galerij* (no rest.), Raadhuisstraat 43, V, 20 b.; *Astoria*, Martelaarsgracht 15, V, 32 b.; *'t Centrum van Amsterdam*, Geldersekade 77, V, 36 b.; *Van Ostade* (no rest.), Van Ostadestraat 123, V, 35 b.; *Heuvel's Private Home* (no rest.), Nieuwe Kerkstraat 147, V, 12 b.; *Ronnie* (no rest.), Raadhuisstraat 41, V, 18 b.

YOUTH HOSTELS. – *Stadsdoelen*, Kloveniersburgwal 97, 220 b.; *Vondelpark*, Zandpad 5, 290 b.

CAMP SITES. – *Amsterdamse Bos*; *Vliegenbos Amsterdam Noord*; *Amsterdamse IJsclub*; *Zeeburg*; *De Badhoeve*.

RESTAURANTS. – *Dikker en Thijs*, Prinsengracht 444, Ecke Leidsestraat; *Boederij*, Korte Leidsedwarsstraat 69, *'t Swarte Schaep*, Korte Leidsedwarsstraat 24, old Dutch; *Auberge*, Leidseplein 8; *Neptunus*,

Rokin 87; *Molen De Dikkert*, Amsterdamseweg 104; u. a. – Many Indonesian, Chinese and Indian restaurants, among them *Bali*, Leidsestraat 89, *Indonesia*, Singel 550, both Indonesian; *Fong Lie*, P. C. Hooftstraat 85, Chinese. – *Nachtrestaurant 66* (open 10 p.m. to 4 a.m.), Reguliersgracht 26.

CAFÉS. – In the Kalverstraat and the Keizersgracht, the Damrak and the Rembrandtsplein. – BRANDY AND LIQUEUR TASTING: *C. V. Wijnand Fockink* (*D'Gekroonde Wildeman*; house of 1679), near the Dam, Pijlsteg 31 (you empty your glass without touching it with your hand).

EVENTS. – The *Hotel Fair Horecava* (January); *Boat Exhibition Hiswa* (March); *Home and Household Fair* (April); *World Press Photo Exhibition* (April); *Indian Market Pasar Malam* (May); *Holland Festival* (June); *Vondelpark Festival* (June–August); *Flower Show* (first Saturday in September); *Harbour Exhibition Europort* (November); *Caravan (Trailer/Camper) Exhibition* (December); *International Windjammer Regatta* **"Sail Amsterdam"** (August).

MARKETS. – *Flea Market*, Waterlooplein between Valkenburgerstraat and Rapenburgerstraat (Monday to Saturday) as well as the Noordermarkt (Monday, 8 a.m.–1 p.m.); *Antique Market* (Thursday, 10 a.m.–10 p.m.; Friday/Saturday, 10 a.m.–6 p.m.); *Flower Market*, Singel (Monday to Saturday, 9 a.m.–5 p.m.); *Stamp Market* (Wednesday and Saturday, 1–4 p.m.); *Rare Books* (Monday to Saturday, 10 a.m.–4 p.m.); *General Market* (Monday to Saturday, 10 a.m.–4 p.m.).

CANAL CRUISES. – One-hour *canal cruises*; *city round trip and canal cruise* (half-day); the *House of Anne Frank, Van Gogh Museum and Canal Cruise* (half-day); bookings at Transport Office VVV Amsterdam.

The Dutch capital city of **Amsterdam (which is not the permanent royal residence nor the seat of the Government, however; both are in The Hague) lies in the province of North Holland at the junction of the Amstel and the IJ, an arm of the IJsselmeer. Together with its ten outer suburbs, the population of

Inside the Concertgebouw of Amsterdam

Amsterdam numbers more than 1 million, and represents the largest urban concentration in the "Randstad Holland".

The Municipal University, the Free University based on Protestant reform, the Royal Dutch Academy of Sciences, numerous other research institutes and Academies of Music make Amsterdam the most important cultural area of the country. In the same context, more than forty museums, as well as the world-famous *Concertgebouw Orchestra*, must be mentioned.

At the same time Amsterdam is the focal point and cornerstone of Dutch economy. The city owes its reputation primarily to its harbour and its commerce. Powerful financial institutions (among others, the Bank of the Netherlands) and large shipping lines have their headquarters here. The port, which is the second largest in the Netherlands, lags considerably behind Rotterdam (approximately 20 million tons annual turnover vs. 280 million tons), but is still an important transshipping point for various goods such as mineral oils, ores and grain, as well as, to a lesser extent, coal, general cargo, oil-seed and animal feed.

Apart from the service sector of the economy, industries also play an important role. Amsterdam lies in the middle of an enormous industrial belt which stretches between IJmuiden at the opening of the North Sea Canal into the sea, and Hilversum to the south-east of Amsterdam. Especially important is the harbour industry which developed after the Second World War, stimulated by a giant petro-chemical and chemical complex partly supplied by a pipeline from the oil port of Rotterdam. Other industries are shipbuilding, steel, engineering, motor, and aircraft manufacturing; as well as textiles and breweries. One should not forget diamond-cutting, which came here after the sacking of Antwerp in 1576 and developed into a specialised industry.

The Old City has been built on a pattern of concentric segments. Its houses are built on piles driven through the layers of mud and swamp into the firm sandy bottom up to 18 m (59 feet) deep. In an area of about 800 hectares (1977 acres) are crammed some 6,750 architectural monuments. On the canals, or Grachten, which are about

2 m (7 feet) deep, are moored more than 2,000 houseboats. Several hundred bridges give the city a picturesque character. The oldest part of the city as far as the Singelgracht is encircled by extensions of the 16th and 17th c. The most influential builders of that period were H. de Keyser, J. van Campen and Ph. Vingboons. Beyond the Singelgracht new districts have developed since 1870, and these have expanded even further in the 20th c., particularly through the influence of the founder of the Amsterdam School of Architecture, H. P. Berlage.

HISTORY. – Amsterdam was founded about 1270, and in the course of the 13th c. with the opening of the Zuiderzee became connected to the sea. The city experienced some prosperity in the Middle Ages. In 1368 it became a member of the Hanse, and in 1489 the future German Emperor Maximilian I gave his crown to its coat of arms. Amsterdam's real period of prosperity began with the Dutch Wars of Independence. It gained its freedom in 1578 and, after the devastation of Ghent and the decline of Antwerp, began to attract merchants, manufacturers and artists from the Spanish Netherlands. In the years 1585–95, it nearly doubled in size and at the beginning of the 17th c. was already the most important commercial capital in Europe. Rembrandt, F. Bol, G. Flinck and J. van Ruisdael were active in Amsterdam about the middle of that century. – In the 18th c. the city lost a large part of its fleet because of the participation of Holland in the American War of Independence against England. Its alliance with France in 1797, as well as the Napoleonic Continental blockade in 1806–13, completely destroyed its commerce. Moreover, the construction of the North Holland Canal (1819–25), which should have avoided the difficult passage into the Zuiderzee, did not have the expected effect. It was only the construction of three more canals – first the North Sea Canal in 1873, then the Merwede Canal in 1892 which connected the two Rhine branches, the Waal and the Lek, and most recently the new Amsterdam-Rhine Canal – which made it possible for Amsterdam to become the second largest sea and inland harbour in the country.

Places of Interest

Allard-Pierson Museum
Oude Turfmarkt 127,
Tuesday to Friday 10 a.m.–4.30 p.m.
Saturday and Sunday 1.15–4.30 p.m.
Archaeological collection of the University.

Amstelkring Museum
Oudezijds Voorburgwal 40,
Monday to Saturday 10 a.m.–5 p.m.
Sunday 1–5 p.m.
Collection of paintings and books and ecclesiastical objects.

Amsterdam History Museum
Kalverstraat 92,
Monday to Saturday 9.30 a.m.–5 p.m.
Sunday 1–5 p.m.

Anne Frank House
Prinsengracht 263,
Monday to Saturday 9 a.m.–5 p.m.
Sunday 10 a.m.–5 p.m.

Begijnhof (*Nunnery*)
Spui.

Botanical Gardens (*Hortus Botanicus of the University of Amsterdam*)
Plantage Middenlaan 2,
Monday to Friday 10 a.m.–12.30 p.m.
Saturday and Sunday 1–4 p.m.

Botanical Garden of the Free University
Boeckhorststraat 8,
Buitenveldert,
Monday to Friday 8 a.m.–4.30 p.m.
Closed Saturday and Sunday.

Film Museum
Paviljoen Vondelpark,
Tuesday to Friday 10 a.m.–12.30 p.m. and 1.30–5 p.m.

Flower Auction Aalsmeer
Legmeerdijk 313, Aalsmeer,
Monday to Thursday and Saturday 7.30 a.m.–1.30 p.m.
Bus service from Central Station.

Fodor Museum
Keizersgracht 609,
Monday to Saturday 9.30 a.m.–5 p.m.
Sunday 1–5 p.m.
Paintings.

Jewish History Museum
Nieuwmarkt 4,
Monday to Saturday 9.30 a.m.–5 p.m.
Sunday 1–5 p.m.

t'Kromhout
Hoogte Kadijk 147,
Monday to Saturday 10 a.m.–4 p.m.
Sunday 1–4 p.m.
19th c. shipyard.

Madame Tussaud
Kalverstraat 156,
June to September: Monday to Sunday 10 a.m.–10 p.m.

September to June: Monday to Sunday 10 a.m.–6 p.m.
Saturdays until 10 p.m.

Medical/Pharmaceutical Museum
Nieuwmarkt 4,
Monday to Saturday 9.30 a.m.–5 p.m.
Sunday 1–5 p.m.

Municipal Museum
Paulus Potterstraat 13,
Monday to Saturday 9.30 a.m.–5 p.m.
Sunday 1–5 p.m.

Museum of Architecture
Droogbak 1a,
Monday to Friday 10 a.m.–5 p.m.
Open only for exhibitions.

Museum of Biblical Antiquities
Herengracht 366,
Tuesday to Saturday 10 a.m.–5 p.m.
First Sunday in every month 1–5 p.m.

Museum of Geology
Nieuwe Prinsengracht 130,
Wednesday 1.30–5 p.m.

National Museum (*Rijksmuseum*)
Stadhouderskade 42,
Monday to Saturday 10 a.m.–5 p.m.
Sunday 1–5 p.m.

National Museum of Aeronautics "Avidome"
Schiphol Airport,
April to October: Monday to Sunday 10 a.m.–5 p.m.
November to March: Tuesday to Sunday 10 a.m.–5 p.m.
Closed Christmas and New Year's Eve.

Netherlands Industrial and Technical Institute
Rozengracht 224,
Monday to Friday 10 a.m.–4 p.m.
Saturday 1–4 p.m.
Sunday 12 noon–5 p.m.
Closed Bank Holidays.

Netherlands Maritime Museum
Kattenburgerplein 1,
Monday to Saturday 10 a.m.–5 p.m.
Sunday 1–5 p.m.

Amsterdam – bird's-eye view of the Royal Palace

Old Church (*Oude Kerk*)
Oudekerksplein,
Tower can be visited June to September.

Portuguese Synagogue
Jones Daniel Meijerplein,
Daily 10 a.m.–1 p.m.
Closed Saturdays and Jewish holidays.

Rembrandt's House
Jodenbreestraat 4–6,
Monday to Saturday 10 a.m.–5 p.m.
Sunday 1–5 p.m.

Royal Palace
Dam,
June, July, August, Monday to Friday.

Six's Picture Gallery
Amstel 218,
Accessible only with letter of introduction from the Rijksmuseum.

Theatre Museum
Herengracht 168,
Monday to Saturday 10 a.m.–5 p.m.
Sunday 1–5 p.m.

Tobacco Museum
Amstel 57,
Monday to Friday 10 a.m.–5 p.m.

Tropical Museum
Linnaeusstraat 2a,
Monday to Friday 10 a.m.–5 p.m.

Sunday 12 noon–5 p.m.
Collection of specimens from the tropics and sub-tropics.

Van Gogh Museum
Paulus Potterstraat 7–11,
Monday to Saturday 10 a.m.–5 p.m.
Sunday 1–5 p.m.

Van Loon Foundation
Keizersgracht 672,
Daily except Wednesdays 1–4 p.m.

Westerkerk (*Western Church*)
Prinsengracht, Corner of Raadhuisstraat,
Tower can be visited June to September.

Willet-Holthuysen Museum
Herengracht 605,
Monday to Saturday 9.30 a.m.–5 p.m.
Sunday 1–5 p.m.
Collection of furniture, china, glass, etc.

Wine Merchants' Guildhall
Koestraat 10–12,
Tuesday to Saturday 10 a.m.–12 noon and 2–4 p.m.

Zoological Garden "Artis"
Plantage Kerklaan 40,
Monday to Sunday 9 a.m. until dusk.

Zoological Museum
Plantage Middenlaan 53,
Monday to Saturday 9 a.m.–4.30 p.m.
Sunday 1–4.30 p.m.

Amsterdam – City of the Diamonds

A lively diamond trade had already developed in Amsterdam in the 16th c. and quickly expanded. Diamonds discovered in South Africa in 1867 were mostly cut in Amsterdam and the city became the most important diamond centre in the world. The supreme skill of the diamond cutters and polishers of Amsterdam played a decisive role. To an expert, the description *"Amsterdam Cut"* is synonymous with perfectly produced work.

The value of a gem diamond depends not only on its **cut**, but also on its **colour**, the degree of its **purity**, as well as the **weight** of the stone. These four factors determining the value are described after their English initials as the four "Cs" of a diamond (*c*olour, *c*larity, *c*ut and *c*arat weight).

The **brilliant cut** is the best known and most favoured type of cutting. Therefore cut and polished diamonds are usually called brilliants, but strictly speaking, brilliants are only those where the full cut is in 58 facets. Other cuts, **Marquise/Navette, Oval, Emerald, Drop and Heart** also have 58 facets each. Apart from these there are also cuts called *Baguette* (simple cut with 24 facets); *Octahedrons* (16 facets); and *Carré* (a square cut). – Facets are the surfaces created by cutting, which must be arranged at certain angles to each other in order to obtain the optimum refraction of light (sparkle or fire). The largest horizontal facet is called "table". The following shades of colours are distinguished:

River	*Pure white* (Blue-white)
Top Wesselton	*Clear white*
Wesselton	*White*
Top Crystal	*Slightly tinted white*
Crystal	*Tinted white*
Top Cape	*Considerably tinted white*
Cape	*Yellowish*

Diamonds with pure strong colours such as *yellow, brandy-brown, rose, green* or *blue*, are most highly valued.

The degree of **purity** (recognisable under 10× magnification):
Internally Flawless
V.V.S.I.
(*Very, Very Small Inclusions*)
S.I.
(*Small Inclusions*)
I. Piqué
II. Piqué
III. Piqué

The **weight** of a diamond is measured in **carats** (1 ct=0·2 g). The word "carat" came originally from Arabic and meant "dried red currant seed", with which, in earlier times, diamonds were weighed in India and with gold in Africa. Via Dutch the word carat became adopted in international trade jargon as a jeweller's measure. Carats, abbreviated as "ct", are used to express the weight of precious stones (1 metric carat=200 mg); also the purity of gold, i.e. the content of gold in alloys (24 carat gold=pure gold; 18 ct=750/1000; 14 ct=585/1000 parts of gold).

Usual Kinds of Cuts of Gem Diamonds

| Brilliant | Marquise/Navette | Oval | Emerald | Pear/Drop | Heart |

Famous Diamonds

The largest brilliant is the *Cullinan* (530 ct) in the British crown; it was part of the largest rough diamond ever found ("Cullinan" 3106 ct), which was cut into 105 parts.

Other well-known large diamonds or brilliants are the *Excelsior* (rough 955 ct; divided into 22 brilliants weighing together 374 ct); the *Jonker* (rough 726 ct; divided into 12 brilliants); the *Nizam of Hyderabad* (polished 340 ct); the *Great Mogul* (polished 280 ct); the *Jubilee* (rough 651 ct; polished 245 ct); the *Star of Yakutia* (232 ct); the *Orloff* (polished 200 ct); the *Victoria* (rough 469 ct; polished 184 ct); the *Koh-i-nor* ("Mountain of Light", rough 191 ct; polished 186 ct); the *Regent* (rough 410 ct; polished 140 ct); the *Florentine* (137 ct); the *Southern Star* (rough 362 ct; polished 129 ct); the *Shah* (116 ct); the *Hope* (rough 112 ct; polished 44 ct).

Guided tours for individual visitors and groups are arranged in the following diamond cutting and polishing shops in Amsterdam:

Amsterdam Diamond Centre
Rokin 1,
tel. 27 98 59.
Monday, Tuesday, Wednesday, Friday and Saturday 9 a.m.–6 p.m.
Thursday 9 a.m.–9 p.m.
April to October, also Sunday 10 a.m.–6 p.m.

Gassan Diamond House
Nieuwe Achtergracht 17–23,
tel. 22 53 33.
Monday to Saturday 9 a.m.–5.30 p.m.
April to October, also Sunday 10 a.m.–5 p.m.

Holshuysen-Stoeltie B.V.
Wagenstraat 13–17,
tel. 23 76 01.
Monday to Saturday 9 a.m.–5.30 p.m.
April to October, also Sunday 10 a.m.–5 p.m.

Individual visitors and small groups can visit the following:

C. Slijper
Diamantbeurs,
Weesperplein 4, 4th floor, room 107,
tel. 22 50 33.
Monday to Friday 9 a.m.–5 p.m.
Group tours to be arranged.

Tax Free Diamond Centre
Damstraat 6,
tel. 26 75 47.
Monday to Saturday 9 a.m.–6 p.m.

Jewellers' shops with diamond polishing:

Diamonds Direct
(*Herman Schipper B.V.*),
Heiligeweg 3,
(polishing: Rokin 9–11),
tel. 23 65 72, 24 96 16, 23 78 69.
Monday to Saturday 9 a.m.–6 p.m.

Bernard Schipper B.V.
Kalverstraat 38,
tel. 22 69 29.
Monday, Tuesday, Wednesday, Friday, Saturday 9 a.m.–6 p.m.
Sunday 9 a.m.–9 p.m.

Jewellers:

As Bonebakker & Zoon B.V.
Rokin 88–90,
tel. 23 22 94.
Monday to Friday 9 a.m.–5.30 p.m.
Saturday 9 a.m.–5 p.m.

Diamonds Direct
(*Herman Schipper B.V.*),
Amsterdam Sonesta Hotel,
Kattengat 1,
tel. 25 75 32.
Daily 9.30 a.m.–9.30 p.m.

Carel van Pampus B.V.
Kalverstraat 56,
tel. 23 39 79.
Monday to Saturday 8.45 a.m.–5.30 p.m.

John van der Vet B.V.
Koningsplein 13,
tel. 24 30 26.
Tuesday to Friday 9 a.m.–5.30 p.m.
Saturday 9 a.m.–5 p.m.

Description of the City

Inner City

The traffic hub of the inner city is the **Dam** on the western edge of the oldest part of Amsterdam. It is a large square in which stands the massive *national monument* erected after the Second World War to commemorate those who lost their lives in 1940–5. On the western side of the square, on the site of the former town hall, stands the **Royal Palace** (*Het Paleis*), erected on 13,659 piles, a major work of the Dutch Classicism of the 17th c., built by the architect Jacob van Campen from Haarlem. Its tower (carillon) is 51 m (167 feet) high. The *Royal Apartments* which the Queen uses when in Amsterdam, are richly decorated with marble statues. The most outstanding room is the Council Hall, one of the most beautiful banquet halls in Europe. In the Throne Room is an important painting by Ferdinand Bol. In the ante-room ("Vierschaar") are four marble caryatids (figures used as pillars) by A. Quellinus the Elder. – In the north-west corner of the Dam is the **New Church** (*Nieuwe Kerk*; Reformed), built in the 15th c. but later rebuilt several times. Inside the church, which is the scene of royal proclamations, are a number of tombstones of famous naval heroes; among them the Baroque tomb of Admiral M. A. de Ruyter (d. 1676) by R. Verhulst. The choir screen and the pulpit (1649) are also worth seeing, as well as a plaque commemorating the Dutch poet J. van den Vondel, who was buried here in 1679.

North-east of the Dam, towards the Central Station, runs the wide Damrak, one of the main thoroughfares of the inner city. On the right is the **Stock Exchange** (*Koopmansbeurs*), a brick structure built by the architect H. P. Berlage in 1899–1903, which became the model of modern Dutch architecture. – At the northern end of the Damrak, where it meets the Prins-Hendrik-Kade, a large bridge crosses the *Open Havenfront*, one of the departure points for the interesting cruises of Amsterdam's canals and harbour; on the other side of the bridge is the Stationsplein and the **Central Station** (*Centraal Spoorweg Station*), which was built on an artificial island in the IJ and opened in 1889. On its northern side, overlooking the harbour (de Ruyterkade) are the mooring places ("Steiger") of many motor boats and ferries.

The **harbour installations** were begun in 1872 in conjunction with the construction of the North Sea Canal, the objective being to restore the former importance of the capital city, which was being overtaken by Rotterdam. A *cruise of the canals and harbours* runs continually in summer and intermittently in winter, and is especially impressive in the evening when the houses and bridges are illuminated.

The entire harbour area was reclaimed from the IJ. The canal was deepened and artificial islands with landing berths were created. On the southern side of the IJ is a series of large docks, including the *Westerdok* (on the outer side of the quay of the Holland-America line, Stenenhoofd), the *Oosterdok* and the *IJhaven*, as well as important dockyards. West of the Westerdok lie the *Houthaven* (timber port), the *Minervahaven*, the *Coenhaven* and the impressive *Petroleumhaven*, which gives access to the North Sea Canal. To the west are the installations of the *Westhaven* which are still partly under construction, with loading facilities for coal, oil, ores and grain, and with oil storage tanks, refineries and chemical plants. On the north bank of the IJ lie several smaller docks and the locks of the North Holland Canal. Not far west from the Central Station, by the harbour, stands the 13-storey *Port Administration building* (Havengebouw), built in 1958–60 by Dudok van Heel, which is some 60 m (198 feet) high and has a restaurant with a panoramic *view*. At the Oosterdok is the *Dutch Maritime Museum*.

On the southern side of the Open Haven-front and the Oosterdok runs the Prins-Hendrik-Kade, the former "Buitenkant". To the east on the other side of the inner harbour stands the church of *St Nicholas* (1885–6, Catholic). Still further east is the "Weeping tower" ("Schreierstoren"), built in 1487. It was here that lamenting fishermen's wives and children used to gather to see their menfolk off to sea. On the corner of the "Binnenkant" stands the *Shipping House* (Scheepvaarthuis; 1913), an interesting example of the Dutch Art Nouveau, and headquarters of several shipping companies. A little further on (No. 131 Prins-Hendrik-Kade) is the former residence of *Admiral de Ruyter*.

Near St Nicholas's Church, the Zeedijk forks off from the Prins-Hendrik-Kade leading to the Nieuwe Markt. This is one of the oldest, yet most notorious, streets in Amsterdam with a number of leaning houses. No. 1, dating from the 15th c., is the oldest existing house in the city. Not far south-west is the Oudezijds Voorburg-wal, a street with a charming atmosphere. Here in No. 40 is the *Amstelkring Museum* with a collection of church antiquities, paintings and engravings.

Haarlem, Alkmaar   Zaandam

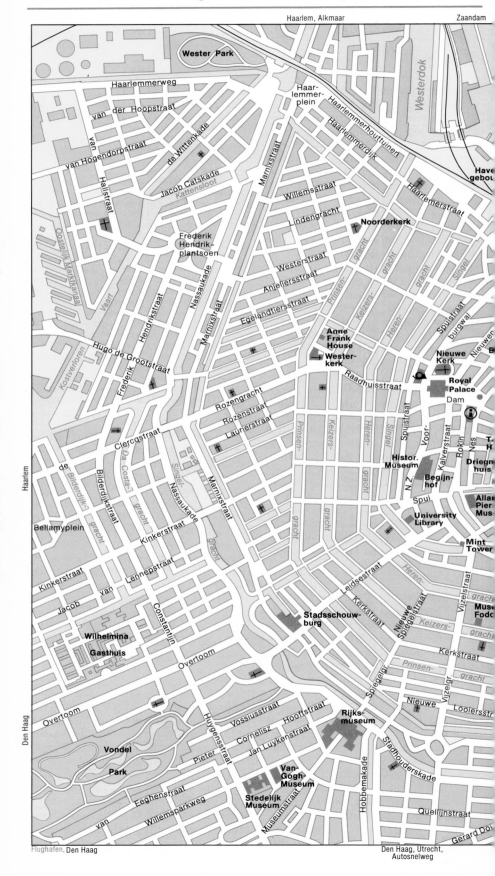

Wester Park

Haarlemmerweg

van der Hoopstraat

Haar-
lemmer-
plein

Haarlemmerhouttuinen

Haarlemmerdijk

van Hogendorpstraat

de Wittenkade

Marnixstraat

Haarlemerstraat

Have
gebou

Halstraat

Jacob Catskade

Kattensloot

Willemsstraat

Lindengracht

Noorderkerk

Oostelijk Marktkanaal

Frederik
Hendrik-
plantsoen

Westerstraat

Anjeliersstraat

Egelandtiersstraat

Nassaukade

Marnixstraat

Prinsen-

Keizers-

Heren-

Singel

Vaart

Hendrikstraat

Anne
Frank
House

Wester-
kerk

Nieuwe
Kerk

Nieuwer

B

Hugo de Grootstraat

Frederik

Raadhuisstraat

Royal
Palace

Dam

Rozengracht

Rozenstraat

Laurierstraat

Clercqstraat

Da Costa

Prinsen-

Keizers-

Heren-

Singel

Spuistraat

Voor-

Kalverstraat

Rokin

Nes

T
H

Histor.
Museum

Driegn
huis

de Bilderdijk-

Bilderdijkstraat

Sinjel-

Nassaukade

Marnixstraat

Begijn-
hof

Spui

N.Z.

Alla
Pier
Mus

Bellamyplein

gracht

gracht

University
Library

Mint
Tower

Kinkerstraat

Lennepstraat

gracht

Leidsestraat

Heren-

Vizelstraat

grach

Kinkerstraat

Jacob

van

Constantijn

Kerkstraat

Nieuwe
Spiegelstraat

Keizers-

Mus
Fodo

Wilhelmina
Gasthuis

Overtoom

Stadsschouw-
burg

grach

Kerkstraat

Prinsen-

gracht

Overtoom

Vossiusstraat

Hoofstraat

Huygensstraat

Cornelisz

Jan Luykenstraat

Rijks-
museum

Spiegel

Vizelgr.

Nieuwe

Loolersstr

Vondel

Pieter

Stadhouderskade

Park

Van-
Gogh-
Museum

Eeghenstraat

Stedelijk
Museum

Willemsparkweg

van

Museumstraat

Hobbemakade

Quellijnstraat

Gerard Dou

Haarlem

Den Haag

Edam, Afsluitdijk

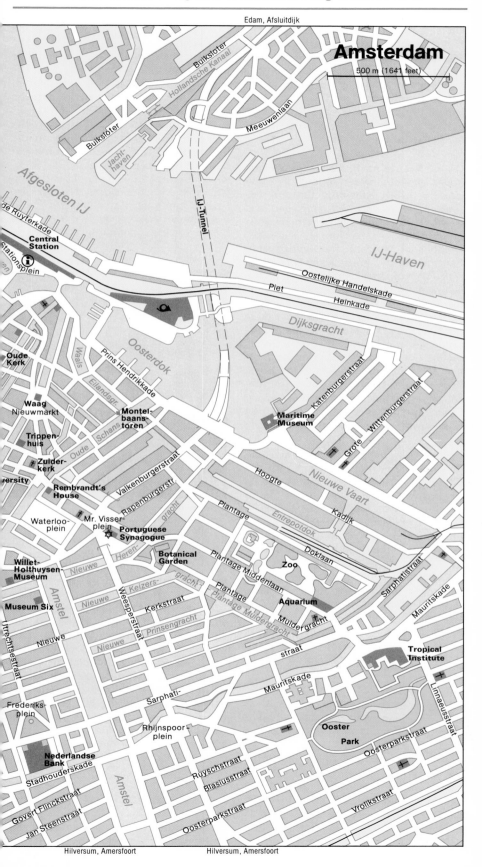

Amsterdam

500 m (1641 feet)

Buiksloter
Hollandsche Kanaal
Meeuwenlaan
Buiksloter
Jacht-haven
IJ-Tunnel
Afgesloten IJ
de Ruyterkade
Central Station
Stationsplein
IJ-Haven
Oostelijke Handelskade
Piet Heinkade
Dijksgracht
Oude Kerk
Waals
Prins Hendrikkade
Eilandsgr.
Oosterdok
Katenburgerstraat
Wittenburgerstraat
Maritime Museum
Waag
Nieuwmarkt
Montel-baans-toren
Schans
Grote
Trippen-huis
Oude
Zuider-kerk
Nieuwe Vaart
Hoogte
University
Rembrandt's House
Valkenburgerstraat
Rapenburgerstr.
gracht
Plantage
Entrepoldok
Kadijk
Doklaan
Waterloo-plein
Mr. Visser-plein
Portuguese Synagogue
Heren-
Botanical Garden
Plantage Middenlaan
Zoo
Sarphatistraat
Mauritskade
Willet-Holthuysen-Museum
Nieuwe
Keizers-gracht
Plantage Kerklaan
Plantage Muldergracht
Aquarium
Amstel
Museum Six
Nieuwe
Weesperstraat
Kerkstraat
Prinsengracht
Muldergracht
Nieuwe
straat
Tropical Institute
Utrechtsestraat
Mauritskade
Linnaeusstraat
Frederiks-plein
Sarphati-
Rhijnspoor-plein
Ooster Park
Oosterparkstraat
Nederlandse Bank
Stadhouderskade
Ruyschstraat
Blasiusstraat
Amstel
Govert Flinckstraat
Jan Steenstraat
Oosterparkstraat
Vrolikstraat

Under its roof is a hidden Catholic church. Further south stands the **Old Church** (*Oude Kerk*; Reformed), built in the 13th c. with a high western steeple dating from the 15th and 16th c., offering a beautiful view. Magnificent stained glass from the Dutch High Renaissance (1555), as well as the tombstones of well-known admirals can be seen inside.

On the **Nieuwmarkt** stands the Weighhouse, *St Anthonieswaag*, built as a city gate in 1488, and now housing the *Amsterdam History Museum* and the Jewish History Museum (temporary exhibitions also in the former Municipal Orphanage). Not far to the south-west in Koestraat is the *Wine Merchants Guild Hall* (Wijnkopersgildehuis). East of the Nieuwmarkt on the Oudeschans stands the *Montelbaanstoren*, the remains of the 15th c. fortifications. The southern side of the Nieuwmarkt opens on to the picturesque canal Kloveniersburgwal. On its eastern side, at No. 29, is the *Trippenhuis*, built in 1662, now the seat of the Royal Academy of Sciences. South on the Zandstraat stands the former *Southern Church* (Zuiderkerk), built in 1603–11 by H. de Keyser, who is buried here.

Further west, between Oudezijds Voorburgwal and Achterburgwal, stands the **City Hall** (*Raadhuis*), the former Admiralty building which used to be the seat of the Stadhouders. South of the City Hall, between Oudezijds Achterburgwal and Kloveniersburgwal is the **Municipal University**, founded in 1632, with over 17,000 students (entrance through the Passage Oudenmanhuisportje). It occupies the former Old People's Home (Oudemannenhuis), built in 1754. Diagonally opposite the University, where Oudezijds Voorburgwal, Oudezijds Achterburgwal and Grimburgwal meet, stands the famous *Driegrachtenhuis* (1610).

West of here, passing through the Langebrug, you can reach the lively **Rokin** leading from the Dam to the Muntplein. When this street was built, the River Amstel had to be partly filled in. To the west, parallel to the Rokin, and also running from the Dam to Muntplein, is the narrow *Kalverstraat, the main shopping street of the city (pedestrian). On its western side the beautiful portal (1581) of No. 92 belongs to the former *Municipal

Orphanage, which was originally the Monastery of St Lucia. Adjacent, to the south, is the *Begijnhof*, a charming little precinct dating from the 14th–17th c. The main entrance today is at the end of the Begijnensteegs, which forks off to the right from Kalverstraat. In No. 156 Kalverstraat is the *Madame Tussaud Wax Museum*. Not far to the south on the Singel (No. 423), is the **Municipal University Library** (enlarged in 1966), which has over 2 million books and is the largest library in the country. It possesses, apart from valuable manuscripts and incunabula, the well-known *Rosenthal Library* (Jewish literature).

The Westerkerk in Amsterdam

In the western part of the inner city, there are two churches on the **Prinsengracht** worth visiting: to the north, the *Noorderkerk*, built in 1622 by H. de Keyser; and to the south on the Westermarkt, the *Westerkerk* built in 1620–31 by the same architect. Rembrandt is buried in this church (commemorative stone). Its steeple, which is 85 m (279 feet) high, is the highest in the city (carillon; view). Nearby on the Rozengracht stood the house in which Rembrandt died (No. 184, plaque). Prinsengracht, No. 263, is the **House of Anne Frank**, the Jewish girl who became famous through her Diary. She and her family hid here during the German Occupation.

Southern Parts of the City

On the **Muntplein** at the south-east end of the Rokin and the Kalverstraat, stands the Munttoren (*Mint tower*; 15th c.), the remains of an old city gate, which is the focal point of a picturesque area. East of here lies the busy **Rembrandtsplein**, with a statue of Rembrandt. Nearby is the *Tobacco Museum Niemeijer* (Amstel 57). Across the Thorbeckeplein you reach the **Herengracht**, which has preserved the appearance of elegant and fashionable Amsterdam in the 17th and 18th c. In house No. 605, built in 1672, is the *Willet-Holthuysen Museum* with furniture from the 16th–18th c., a rich collection of china and glass, as well as a fine library. No. 168 is a beautiful canal mansion housing the *Theatre Museum*. Near the eastern end of this tree-lined canal (Amstel 218), is the *Six's Picture Gallery, one of the most important private collections in the country (among others, Rembrandt: "**Jan Six", 1654). Further south on the Keizersgracht, No. 609, is the **Municipal Fodor Museum**, founded by the merchant Ch. J. Fodor (died 1860), containing paintings particularly from the middle of the 19th c.

The Rijksmuseum in Amsterdam

The world-famous *Rijksmuseum* (**National Museum**) is situated at Stadhouderskade No. 42, a vast brick building by P. J. H. Cuypers (1877–85). It offers, apart from its unique collection of masterpieces, an extensive survey of the artistic and cultural developments of the Netherlands. It possesses large collections of old Dutch crafts, medieval Dutch sculpture and modern Dutch paintings.

Rijksmuseum Amsterdam

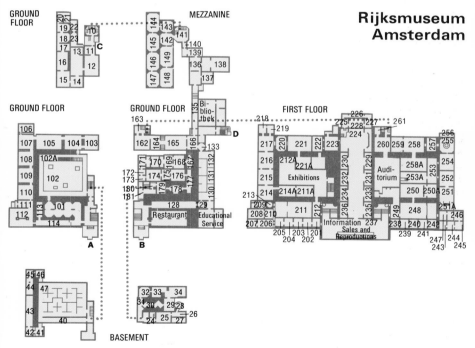

A   Entrance Stadhouderskade Ost
B   Entrance Stadhouderskade West
C   Entrance Hobbemastraat
D   Entrance Luykenstraat (to the Print Room, Reading Room and Library)

FIRST FLOOR
Paintings
201–02   Dutch painters of the 15th c: Gerrtgen tot Sint Jans, Jan Mostaert (biblical subjects)
203–09   Dutch painters of the 16th c. (Renaissance)

204   Lucas van Leyden
205   Jan van Scorel, Maerten van Heemskerck
206   Pieter Aertsz, Joachim Bueckelaer (subjects from peasant life and still life)
209   Joose de Momper (landscapes)
210–28   Dutch painters of the 17th c.
210   Werner van den Valckert (group portraits)
211   Thomas de Keyser, Pieter Saenredam
211/212A Frans Hals (portraits)
212   Sale of reproductions and catalogues
214A   Jan van Goyen, Hendrik Averkamp, Esaias van de Velde (landscapes)

BASEMENT
Sculpture and Decorative Art

24	Dutch and foreign glassware from the 18th c. (different techniques of glass-making)
25	Dutch furniture in the style of Louis XVI
27	Original furnishing from a house in Haarlem
28	Dutch porcelain: Weesp, Loosdrecht, Amstel and The Hague
29	Furniture from the Empire period, gilded silverware
30	French and Dutch clothing of the 18th c.
31	Lace from the 18th to 19th c.
32	Dutch porcelain
33	Empire
34	Art Nouveau

Study Collection

40	Sculpture and decorative arts
43	Dutch history, sculpture and decorative arts
47	Paintings

In the eastern half of the **ground floor** is the *Dutch History Museum* with a collection of articles concerning the army, navy and the colonies. Worth a special mention is the art of the mariner of the 17th c. – In the western half of the ground floor is the *Print Room* (Pretenkabinet), and the *Library*. Next to it is a section for older sculpture (12th–16th c.), stained glass, a collection of textiles, implements and furniture. – On the **first floor** is a * *collection of older paintings*, one of the most important galleries of Dutch painting, as well as the collection of *sculpture and decorative art* (*faiences, etc.).

Only the most important of the great number of masterpieces can be mentioned here. Among them, above all: the "Night Watch" by *Rembrandt*, which was restored after a knife attack in 1975. It is one of the largest and most famous compositions of the master and dates from 1642. Also by Rembrandt, the "Anatomy Lesson of Dr Deyman", the "Staalmeesters", and the "Jewish Bride". – *Frans Hals* is represented by several impressive portraits, among them the "Merry Drinker" and a Civic Guard picture completed by Pieter Codde. – *Jan Steen* is shown here not only as a humorist, with several successful paintings, but also as a religious painter with his "Christ in Emmaus" and the "Adoration of the Shepherds". – *Gerhard ter Borch* and *Gabriel Metsu* are also represented, as is *Pieter de Hooch* with his most outstanding works. – One of the most precious treasures of the museum are the works of *Jan Vermeer van Delft*, among them, the "Straatje" (Little Street in Delft). – Among the landscapes, the "Mill near Wijk bij Duurstede" by *Jacob Ruisdael* is outstanding. – From Flemish painters of the 17th c. there are *Rubens* (sketch for the "Crucifixion"), and *Anthonie van Dyck* (several portraits). *Crivelli, Bellini* and *Mantegna, Veronese, Tintoretto* and *Bassano* are among the Italians; *Velazquez* ("Still Life"), *Murillo* ("Annunciation", "Virgin with Child"), *Cano* and *Cerezo* among the Spaniards.

In the **south-west annex** of the Rijkmuseum is a *collection of modern Dutch paintings* which, together with those in the Municipal Museum, provide an opportunity of becoming thoroughly acquainted with Dutch painting of the 19th c. – Also in the south-west annex is a *collection of Asian art*.

South-west of the Rijkmuseum in the Paulus Potterstraat (Nos. 7–9), stands the *Van Gogh Museum* (*Rijkmuseum Vincent van Gogh*) built in 1968–73 by Rietveld, Van Dillen and Van Tricht. It is filled to capacity with 200 paintings, 500 drawings and 700 letters by the artist, as well as the works of his contemporaries (among others, Gauguin and Toulouse-Lautrec). In the neighbouring building (No. 13) is the *Municipal Museum* (*Stedelijk Museum*), which possesses a choice collection of mainly Dutch and French paintings of the 19th–20th c. South of the Municipal Museum on the van-Berle-Straat stands the massive **Concertgebouw**. Here the Concert Orchestra (Concertgebouworkest), founded in 1888, gives its concerts. Remarkable examples of the Dutch Art Nouveau architecture can be found in the streets south of the great museums, especially in Apollo and Churchilllaan. South of Churchilllaan on the Europaplein stands the **Conference Centre R.A.I.** (over 45,000 sq. m (484,200 sq. feet), built in 1959–65). The *Olympic Stadium* (60,000 seats) lies south-west of the Vondelpark.

Eastern Parts of the City

The St Antoniesbreestraat runs south from the Nieuwmarkt to the Zwanenburgwal. Beyond it, between the Houtkoopersburgwal in the north and the Binnen-Amstel in the south, extends the former **Jewish quarter**. More than 70% of the Jewish population of Amsterdam was deported in the Second World War during the German occupation. The middle of the Jewish quarter is the Waterlooplein. Even today there is a lively trade in clothes and bric-à-brac (flea market). The philosopher Baruch Spinoza was allegedly born here in 1632 in No. 41. The main street of the Jewish quarter is Jodenbreestraat. Here, in No. 4, is the *Rembrandt House* (1606; since 1911 a museum with drawings and etchings). The great painter lived here from 1639 to 1658. Nearby, on the north side of the Meijerplein stands the *Portuguese Synagogue* (1671–75).

East of the Jewish quarter and beyond the canal Nieuwe Herengracht in the part of the city called PLANTAGE, lies the **Botanical Garden** ("Hortus Botanicus", entrance Middenlaan 2). Still further east is the **Zoo** ("Natura Artis Magistra"; entrance Kerklaan 40), with an *Aquarium, Zoological Museum* (Middenlaan 53), a

The Zaanse Schans near Amsterdam

voluminous library and a café/restaurant. From the east end of Middenlaan, crossing a canal, you reach the *Muiderpoort*, which dates from the 18th c., and further on, across the Singelgracht, the world-famous *Tropical Museum which is well worth visiting (entrance Linnaeusstraat 2A).

SURROUNDINGS of Amsterdam. – **Excursions by motor boat** (only in summer; departures from Stationsplein or from de Ruyterkade): through the *North Holland Canal* or through the *IJsselmeer* to *Monnikendam* and *Volendam* (with an option to visit the former island of Marken); from de Ruyterkade to *Harderwijk* as well as from No. 162 Sloterkade across the *Aalsmeer* to the *Brassemer Meer* and to the *bird sanctuary Avifauna*. Very popular is an outing from Stadthouderskade upstream on the Amstel past the Beer Garden *'t Kalfje* to the village of *Ouderkerk* where, by the church, is a cemetery of Portuguese Jews, with a number of interesting tombstones.

Another interesting trip is an excursion to *Zaandam*, north-west of Amsterdam. Zaandam, which lies on both banks of the River *Zaan*, is part of the sprawling industrial town of **Zaanstad**. It is the main focal point of the Dutch timber trade. There is an Open-Air Museum *Zaanse Schans (houses and windmills of traditional timber construction, narrow canals). On the Dam is a monument of Tsar Peter the Great who studied the craft of shipbuilding here in 1697. (In an inn, in the old part of the town call Krimp, "Czaar Peterhuisje" can be seen.)

Antwerp (Antwerpen, Anvers)

Country: Belgium. – Province: Antwerp.
Altitude: 329 m (1079 feet). – Population: 666,000.
Postal code: B-2000.
Telephone code: 0 31.

ⓘ **Dienst voor Toerisme,**
Suikerrui 19;
tel. 32 01 03 and 32 22 84.
Information Office,
Koningin Astridplein (in front of the railway station);
tel. 33 05 70.

HOTELS. – *De Keyser*, De Keyserlei 66–70, L, 117 r.; *Plaza*, Charlottalei 43, L, 78 r.: *Empire*, Appelmansstraat 31, I, 70 r.; *Theater*, Arenbergstraat 30, I, 83 r.; *Antwerpen Crest*, Gerard Legrellelaan 10, I, 306 r.; *Waldorf*, Belgiëlei 36, I, 95 r.; *Eurohotel Antwerpen*, Copernicuslaan 2, II, 350 r.; *Quality Inn*, Luitenant Lippenslaar 66, II, 179 r.; *Horex Antwerp Tower Hotel*, Van Ertbornstraat 10, II, 56 r.; *Congresshotel*, Plantin en Moretuslei 136, II, 173 r.; *Novotel-Antwerpen Noord*, Luithagensteenweg 2, III, 119 r.; *Drugstore-Inn*, Koningin Astridplein 43, III, 26 r.; *Tourist*, Pelikaanstraat 20–22, III, 146 r.; *Terminus*, Franklin Rooseveltplein 9, IV, 45 r.; *Columbus*, Frankrijklei 4, IV, 29 r.; *Old Tom*, De Keyserlei 53, IV, 31 r.; *Métropole*, Handschoenmarkt 3–7, IV, 15 r.; *Smaragdion*, Koningin Astridplein 44, IV, 17 r.; *Florida*, De Keyserlei 59, IV, 38 r.; *Billard Palace*, Koningin Astridplein 40, IV, 68 r.; *Résidence Rubens*, Amerikalei 115, IV, 25 r.; *Canterbury* (no rest.), Van Maerlanstraat 46, IV, 20 r.; *Hansa*, Noorderlaan 97, IV, 30 r.; *Vredehof*, De Keyserhoeve 14, V, 15 r.; *Cécil*, van Arteveldestraat 8, V, 12 r.

IN DEURNE: *Rivierenhof*, Turnhotsebaan 244, IV, 15 r. – IN KRUISSCHANS (13 km (8 miles) north-west): *Nautilus*, Scheldelaan 301, IV, 20 r. – IN LILLO (20 km (12 miles) north-west): *Scaldis*, Tolhuisstraat 8, IV, 8 r. – IN AARTESELAAR: *GB Motor Hotel*, Boomsesteenweg 13, II, 128 r. – IN MIDDELHEIM: *Esso Motor Hotel*, Wilrijkse Plein, on the motorway (highway) junction of E3 and E10.

YOUTH HOSTELS. – Erich Sasselaan, 127 b.

CAMP SITES. – St-Anna Strand, on the left bank of the Schelde; by the Wezenberg swimming pool, north of the Nachtegalenpark between Jan Van Rijwijcklaan and Gérard Le Grellelaan.

RESTAURANTS. – *La Pérouse* (floating), Pontoon bridge on the Steenplein; *La Rade*, Ernest Van Dijckaai 8, first floor, with beautiful view over the Schelde; *Critérium*, De Keyserlei 25; *Cigogne d'Alsace*, Wiegstraat 7; *Le Relais*, Kelderstraat 1; *St. Jacob in Galicië*, Braderijstraat 12–16; *Sir Anthony Van Dijck*, Oude Koornmarkt 16; *China Garden*, De Keyserlei 17; *Vateli*, Kipdorpvest 50, and many others, among them several exotic ones. – IN AARTSELAAR (some 10 km (6 miles) outside the city): *Lindenbos*, Boomsesteenweg 139.

CAFÉS. – Several on Keyserlei and on Koningin Astridplein.

EVENTS. – *Flower and Plant Show* in the International Cultural Centre (September). *International Fair of Flower Growers* (beginning of September); several exhibitions in the Royal Museum of Fine Arts; *Carillon concerts* from the spire of the Cathedral (Monday 9–10 p.m. – June to September); *Concerts* in the Cathedral (Friday 8.30 p.m. – June and July); the *Kirmes Week of Antwerp* (August); *Celebration of the Liberation*, as well as *Archers' and Guilds' Feasts* on the Market Place (beginning of September).

MARKETS. – *Flea Market*, Blauwtorenplein (Sunday 9 a.m.–1 p.m.); *Antique Market*, Hendrik Conscienceplein (from Easter until September, Saturdays 10 a.m.–6 p.m.); *Bird Market*.

SIGHTSEEING. – *Canal cruise*: the Schelde and the harbour (approximately 3 hours); *River cruise on the Schelde* (upstream only). Further excursions to Ostend, Flushing, Zierikzee (information at the shipping company, Flandria, Steenplein, B-2000 Antwerp, tel. 031/33 74 22 and 33 49 27).

The Belgian city of *Antwerp (in Flemish: Antwerpen; in French: Anvers), the capital of the province of the same name, enjoys a favourable position on the right bank of the Schelde (Escaut) which here is up to 500 m (1640 feet) wide. It lies 88 km (55 miles) from the estuary of the Schelde and the North Sea, and is not only one of the largest sea ports in the world, but also one of the most interesting cities in Belgium. Thanks to its harbour, Antwerp has been for centuries an important commercial city. Banking and insurance, as well as crafts and industry quickly became established here.

Nowadays, the most important branches of industry are shipbuilding and ship repairing, as well as the petro-chemical and motor industries. A special role is played by diamond dealing and the diamond industry, and the world fame of Antwerp is mainly due to this. In the area of Greater Antwerp there are more than 250 diamond cutting and polishing shops. The prosperity of earlier centuries can be seen in the superb Cathedral, the Town Hall, and other outstanding buildings; it is also attested by the masterpieces of painting, now in the possession of the city and which date mainly from the 15th

Antwerp: Panorama with the Cathedral of Our Lady

to 17th c. when the lively and relaxed school of the Southern Netherlands flourished here. Quentin Massys, "Velvet Breughel", Rubens, van Dyck, Jordaens, Corn, de Vos and others all lived in Antwerp. – The city has the largest community of Orthodox Jews in Europe.

HISTORY. – According to a legend, the name of the city is derived from "Handwerpen" (literally: "hand thrown"); in the Roman era there was allegedly on the site of the present-day Antwerp the castle of a giant, Druon Antigonus, who levied tolls on the passing sailors, and if these were refused, he cut off one of their hands and threw it into the Schelde. Historic references to the city go back to the 7th c. In 1031, Antwerp is mentioned as a harbour, and in 1313 it became the first city of the Hanse. Its wealth increased when it took over, at the end of the 15th c., the commerce of Bruges. Under the protection of Charles V, Antwerp developed into the busiest and wealthiest commercial city in Christendom, and by about 1560 had a population of 100,000. More than 100 ships sailed in and out of its harbour daily, and more than 1000 foreign merchants had their headquarters in

Antwerp. Also the diligence of its workers resulted in increasing development from the 16th c. The products of Antwerp went as far as Arabia, Persia and India.

This prosperity began to decline in the reign of Philip II, however, and when the Duke of Alba started his trials of the heretics, thousands of burghers left the city. The Spaniards sacked the city in 1576, when 7000 people are said to have lost their lives. The fate of Antwerp was sealed in 1585 when it was taken by Duke Alexander Farnese, and its commerce was lost to Amsterdam and Rotterdam. Another heavy blow was the loss of the shipping on the Schelde, which fell into the hands of the Dutch upon the unification of the seven provinces, as well as the complete closure of the river after the Treaty of Westphalia in 1648. The population steadily declined, and in 1790 numbered only 40,000. A turn for the better came only at the end of the 18th c. In 1800–3, Napoleon ordered the building of the quays on the Schelde and the construction of the Old Harbour docks, after which trade and industry began to develop rapidly. Prosperity increased considerably under Dutch rule, and in 1830 the population had increased to 73,500. The main reason was trade with the Dutch colonies, but later this moved to Rotterdam and Amsterdam. The shelling and siege of the city in 1830 and 1832

The Cathedral of Our Lady, Antwerp

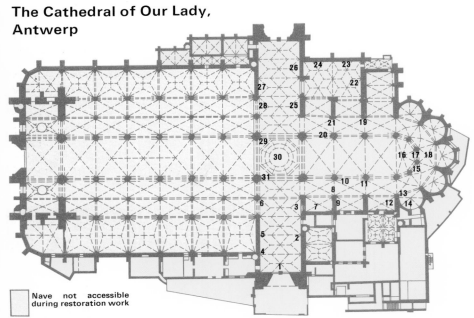

Nave not accessible during restoration work

1 Meridian of Antwerp (brass strip in the floor)
2 B. E. Murillo: St Francis of Assisi (17th c.)
3 P. P. Rubens: "Descent from the Cross"; "Visitation" and "Presentation in the Temple" (1612; side panels)
4 M. de Vos: "Marriage at Cana" (1597)
5 O. van Veen: "The Last Supper" (17th c.)
6 M. de Vos: "The Birth of Christ" (1577)
7 Leonardo da Vinci (?): "Head of Christ" (16th c.)
8 O. van Veen: "Resuscitation of the Young Man from Naim" (1604)
9 P. P. Rubens: "Resurrection" (1612); Tomb of the Printer Jan Meretus
10 Unknown German Master: "Ordination of a Bishop" (1571)
11 A. Francken: "The Coming of the Holy Ghost" (16th c.)
12 A. Quellin the Younger: Tomb of Ambrosius Capello (7th Bishop of Antwerp, 1676)
13 O. van Veen: "Resurrection of Lazarus" (17th c.)
14 Tomb of the printer Christopher Plantin
15 A. Quellin the Younger: "Virgin and Child" (marble, c. 1700)
16 P. P. Rubens: Assumption (1626)

17 A. Matthijssens: Death of the Virgin (1633)
18 Tomb of Isabella of Bourbon, the second wife of Charles the Bold, Duke of Burgundy (1478)
19 School of Rogier van der Weyden: Marriage of the Virgin (15th c.)
20 L. de Heere: Descent from the Cross (16th c.)
21 O. van Veen: Entombment of Christ (16th c.)
22 The Shrine of Our Lady of Antwerp (16th c.)
23 Stained glass window, Henry VII, King of England and his wife, Elizabeth of York, 1503
24 Stained glass window, Philip the Handsome, Duke of Burgundy and his wife, Joanna of Castille.
25 P. P. Rubens: Raising of the Cross (1610)
26 M. Pepijn: St. Norbert Praying (1637)
27 F. Francken: Jesus and the Doctors (1586)
28 M. de Vos: Descent from the Cross (16th c.)
29 M. Pepijn: High Priest Aaron (17th c.)
30 C. Schut: Assumption (painting in the dome, 47 m (155 feet) high, 1647)
31 M. Pepijn: St. Francis of Assisi (17th c.)

"Head of Christ" in the Cathedral of Antwerp

caused great damage, and it was only in 1863, when the Belgians bought back the Schelde toll, which they had conceded in 1839 to the Dutch, that conditions were created for a new upsurge of commerce. After the First World War the volume of goods handled increased steadily (in 1937 over 28 million tons), and this upward trend continued after the Second World War (1977 over 100 million tons). The main imported items are grain, minerals, coal, crude oil, phosphate, cotton and furs.

From 1859 Antwerp was systematically built up into one of the strongest fortresses in Europe. But on 4 October 1914 when the British First Lord of the Admiralty, Winston Churchill, arrived with Royal Marine and Royal Navy reinforcements, the Germans had already pushed within bombardment range of the city. Antwerp surrendered on 10 October, and some 25,000 British troops were forced across the border into prison camps. The outer rampart was removed only after the Second World War, and nowadays only some moats ("Vestingwater") remain.

Description of the City

The Inner City

In the middle of the inner city, the oldest part of which extends east of the Schelde as far as St Katelijnevest and south to Lombaardvest, stands the *Cathedral (Onze Lieve Vrouwekatedraal), the largest Gothic church in Belgium (117 m (384 feet) long, 55 m (180 feet) wide, and 40 m (131 feet) high). The northern spire is 123 m (404 feet) high, and has a fine carillon. The construction of the

church was begun in 1352, and lasted well into the 16th c. The church was heavily damaged by fire in 1533 and then by the Iconoclastic riots in 1556, as well as by the French Republicans in 1794. It was restored in the 19th c. (all the sculptures on the outer side are modern).

The spaciousness of the INTERIOR and the grand perspective of its seven aisles are noteworthy. In the transept hang the world-famous masterpieces of Rubens: left the *"Raising of the Cross", from 1610; right, the *"Descent from the Cross", both painted shortly after the artist returned from Italy. The painting of the *"Assumption" on the high altar in the choir, is also by Rubens, and is perhaps the finest of his ten versions on this subject (1626). Other works of art in the Cathedral, some of which are modern, are also well worth seeing.

West of the church go through the narrow Maalderijstraat to the Grote Markt, in the middle of which is the large **Brabo Fountain** of 1887 by Jef Lambeaux, showing the Roman Governor Silvius Brabo in the act of throwing the hand of the giant Antigonus into the Schelde.

The west side of the Grote Markt is occupied by the **Town Hall** (*Stadhuis*) built in 1561–5 by Cornelis de Vriendt. Its façade is 78 m (256 feet) long; inside it is richly decorated, including tapestries by H. Leys illustrating the history of Antwerp. Most of the other buildings at the Market are former guild houses (Gildehuizen) from the 16th–17th c. On the north side are the *Coopers' Guild Hall*, No. 5; the *Archers' Guild Hall*, No. 7; and the *Grocers'*

The Brabo Fountain and the Spire of the Cathedral

House, No. 11; south-east are the *Tailors' Guild Hall*, No. 38 and the *Carpenters' House*, No. 40. The *Cityrama* in No. 29 gives an idea of the development of the city. The streets behind the Town Hall (Gildekamerstraat) and north of it (Zilversmid, Braderij, and Kuipersstraat), create a good impression of old Antwerp.

Through Braderijstraat you can reach Vleeshouwerstraat in which, left, stands the *old Butchers' House* (Vleeshuis, built 1501–3), now housing the Museum for Applied Art and Local History. Not far to the north on the Veemarkt, stands the former *Dominican Church of St Paul* built in 1533–71. It was damaged by fire in 1968. Near the church are various picturesque little corners such as the *Potagie-poort* (No. 15 St Paulusplaats), leading to a small quiet square surrounded by the remains of the old Dominican Monastery, or the *Old Exchange* (No. 15 Hofstraat), built in 1515, with a charming arcaded courtyard.

Not far west of the Cathedral, on the Conscienceplaats, stands the former *Jesuit Church* (Sint Carolus Borromeus-kerk) built in 1614–21 by Huyssens and Aguilon. The church was burned down in 1718 and was restored in the 18th–19th c., its original style slightly simplified. Only the beautiful spire behind the choir, the façade, two side chapels of the choir and three large altar paintings by the School of Rubens, have been preserved.

South of the Cathedral is the busy Groenplaats with a statue of Rubens dated 1840. To the east, the Meirbrug can be reached via the long Schoenmarkt which is partially lined with beautiful old houses.

From the south-west corner of the Groen-plaats, south of the Cathedral, you can reach, via Reyndersstraat and Leeuwen-straat (second street on the left), the small Friday Market (Vrijdagmarkt). On its western side in No. 22 is the *Plantin Moretus Museum*, the house of the famous printer Christoph Plantin. It is one of the finest specimens of Flemish Renaissance architecture (16th–17th c.; front house 18th c.). The well-preserved interior, an old Flemish patrician dwelling, with its business premises, is second to none.

The **Plantin Printing Works** were founded in 1549 by Christoph Plantin (*c.* 1520–89), and from 1576 were located in this building. The family of Plantin's son-in-law, Johann Moerentorf or Moretus (d. 1610), preserved it in its original state. Rubens often painted, between 1613 and 1637, for the leading member of this family, Balthasar Moerentorf (d. 1641), son of Johann. From the middle of the 17th c. the Printing Works were limited to the production of Mass and Prayer Books, for which Plantin received from Philip II in 1570 exclusive production rights for all Spanish lands. When this privilege was recalled by the Spanish Governor in 1800, the work was stopped and only occasionally resumed.

On the ground floor of the Museum, in rooms Nos. 1–3 are portraits of the members of the family and important personalities of the 15th–16th c., some of them by Rubens. There are also manuscripts from the 10th to 16th c. Under the arcades of the picturesque courtyard is the Sales Office (No. 4). Room No. 7 illustrates the processes involved in the making of a book in the 15th–18th centuries; beautiful incunabula, among them a 36-line Bible from 1450 attributed to Gutenberg, are shown here. Old galley proofs are displayed in the Proof Readers' Room, No. 9. Room No. 13 is the Type Room and Room No. 14 the Composing and Printing Room, with seven old presses. On the first floor is the Library and the Print Gallery; on the second floor the Type Foundry with its old equipment (17th–18th c.), and the well-known collection of Max Horn of rare bindings and valuable books.

Adjacent to the Plantin Moretus Museum on the northern side of the Friday Market, No. 23, is the *Print Collection*, the most valuable of its kind in Belgium; it can be visited only for research purposes.

The North-eastern Part of the Old City

The districts lying between the inner city and the ring of avenues are split into a northern and a southern half by the **Meir**, a long and busy artery which was formed by bridging a canal. The Meir, together with its eastern continuation, the Leys-straat, the Huidevettersstraat in the south, and the streets leading from the Meirbrug to the Groenplaats, are the commercial heart of the city. By the Meirbrug at the western end of the Meir, between the Eiermarkt and the Schoenmarkt, stands the high-rise *Torengebouw*. Further to the right, on the Meir, is the **Royal Palace**, built in 1745 as a patrician house, and the *Municipal Banqueting Hall*. Behind it, to the right, the Rubensstraat leads to the **Rubens House** nearby (Nos. 9–11; Museum), standing on the site of a house built by Rubens in 1613–17, where he lived until his death in 1640. (Only a gate in the courtyard and a garden pavilion remain from the original building.)

From the north side of the Meir, the short Twaalfmaandenstraat leads to the *Exchange (Handelsbeurs), built in 1868–72 by J. Schadde in the style of the old Stock Exchange of 1531, which was destroyed by fire in 1858. It has a vast glass-covered vestibule with a public passage on all four sides.

North of the Exchange runs the Lange Nieuwstraat. Immediately left is the picturesque St Niklaasplaats, surrounded by the buildings of a former hospital dating from the 15th c., with an attractive late Gothic chapel. Further east on the northern side of the Lange Nieuwstraat, stands the Church of *St Jacob (Sint Jacobskerk) dating from the 15th–16th c. with rich Baroque decoration. Here, the leading families of the city had their tombs, private chapels and altars. The most remarkable is the Rubens Chapel behind the high altar, with the tomb of the artist (d. 1640), and the **Altarpiece with the Virgin, Infant and Saints (St George has the face of the artist). Rubens painted it in the last years of his life. Shortly before his death he willed that it be placed in his burial chapel. Other paintings in the church are by de Vos, Seghers, Jordaens, and the "Last Judgment" by Bernaert van Orley. Nearby in the National Security Institute is a permanent exhibition of diamonds.

North-west of the Church of St Jacob in the Keizerstraat, on the right-hand side, is the Chapel of St Anne, begun in 1513. At the end of the street on the left-hand side in No. 10 is the former residence of the Burgomaster, N. Rockox (17th c.; Museum). Further north are the Academy of Arts (a former Franciscan monastery) founded in 1663, the Museum of Flemish Culture in Minderbroederstraat (No. 22), and north-east on the Paardenmarkt, the Capuchin Church with paintings by van Dyck and Rubens (right and left in the transept). The most interesting return route to the Meir is southward through Rodestraat, where the Begijnhof dating from 1542–6 can be seen, past the Ossenmarkt and the St Jacobsmarkt.

South-western and South-eastern Parts of the Old City

South of the Friday Market the Sint Andrieskerk, or Church of St Andrew, consecrated in 1529, contains interesting paintings. On one of the columns in the southern transept there is a small medallion portrait, placed there in memory of Mary Queen of Scots, by two of her Maids of Honour, who took refuge in Antwerp after Mary's execution. *The Royal Museum of Fine Arts (Koninklijk Museum van Schone Kunsten, 1879–90, closed Mondays) on the large Leopold de Waelplaats contains, on the ground floor, works by modern artists, some 1500 paintings and sculptures from the 19th to 20th c. These provide a good survey of the development of the fine arts in Belgium since 1830. On the first floor is a *Collection of old masters consisting of more than 1000 works almost exclusively belonging to the Flemish and Dutch Schools. The twelve most important rooms are numbered as well as labelled with letters.

The Old Dutch masters of the 15th c. are well represented. There is, among others, the triptych "Calvary and the Seven Sacraments" by Rogier van der Weyden, two smaller paintings by Jan van Eyck (one Madonna and a St Barbara), as well as a large triptych by Hans Memling. From the 16th c. is the triptych "Entombment", a masterpiece by Quentin Massys. There are some excellent religious paintings by Rubens, including the "Last Communion of St Francis", "Adoration of the Magi", "Education of the Virgin", and "Virgin with Parrot". The predecessors, disciples and followers of Rubens are represented by a number of works. Paintings by Jordaens and van Dyck are of good quality but do not represent the best achievements of either artist. Worth seeing also are some characteristic examples of Flemish paintings of the 16th–17th c., as well as paintings of animals and still-life of the 17th c. To the Dutch School of the 17th c. belong the "Young Fisherman" by Frans Hals and a portrait by Rembrandt. Among the Italian paintings are three notable works, a series of small panels by Simone Martini, a "Calvary" by Antonello da Messina, and a Titian.

The Huidevetterstraat, which forks off the Meir, connects to the south with Lange Gasthuisstraat, No. 19 of which houses the Museum Mayer van den Bergh (closed Mondays). It contains an excellent collection of furniture, sculpture, paintings, etc. There are, among others, important paintings by P. Breughel the Elder, and Quentin Massys. In the former Chapel of the Maagdenhuis (No. 33, originally a girls' orphanage, 16th c.), is a

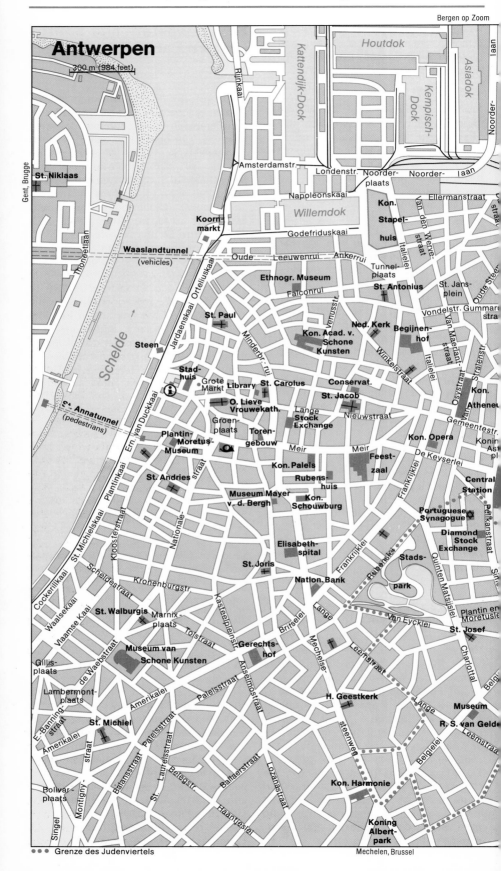

Bergen op Zoom

Antwerpen

300 m (984 feet)

Kattendijk-Dock

Houtdok

Asiadok

Kempisch-Dock

Noorder- laan

Gent, Brugge

St. Niklaas

Rijnkaai

Amsterdamstr.

Londenstr. Noorder- Noorder- laan
plaats

Napoleonskaai

Ellermanstraat

Koorn- markt

Willemdok

Kon.
Stapel- huis

Godefriduskaai

Van den Werve straat

Italielei

Waaslandtunnel
(vehicles)

Oude Leeuwenrui Ankerrui

Tunnel- plaats

Thoneetlaan

Ortelluskaai

Ethnogr. Museum

Falconrui

St. Antonius

St. Jans- plein

Oude Steer

Jardaenskaat

St. Paul

Venusstr.

Vondelstr. Gummare stra

Steen

Minderbr. rui

Kon. Acad. v.
Schone
Kunsten

Ned. Kerk

Begijnen- hof

Van Maerlant straat

Schelde

Winkelstraat

Italielei

Stratenstr

Stad- huis

Grote Markt

Library St. Carolus

Conservat.

Kon.
Atheneu

St. Annatunnel
(pedestrians)

Ern. van Duckkaai

O. Lieve
Vrouwekath.

St. Jacob

Lange
Stock
Exchange

Nieuwstraat

Oysterstr

Gemeentestr.

Plantin- Moretus- Museum

Groen- plaats

Toren- gebouw

Meir

Meir

Kon. Opera

De Keyserlei

Konin Ast pl

Plantinkaai

St. Andries

straat

Kon. Paleis

Feest- zaal

Frankrijklei

Central
Station

St. Michielskaai

Nationale-

Museum Mayer
v. d. Bergh

Rubens- huis

Kon.
Schouwburg

Portuguese
Synagogue

Pelikanstraat

Klooster straat

Elisabeth- spital

Diamond
Stock
Exchange

Cockerillkaai

Scheldestraat

Kronenburgstr.

St. Joris

Nation. Bank

Frankrijklei

Rubenslei

Stads- park

Quinten Matsislei

Waalsekaai

St. Walburgis

Marnix- plaats

Kasteelpleinstr.

Briselei

Lange

Van Eycklei

Plantin en Moretusle

Vlaamse Kaai

Tolstraat

Mechelse

Leemstraat

St. Josef

Gillis- plaats

de Waebsstraat

Museum van
Schone Kunsten

Gerechts- hof

Anselmostraat

Chariottal

Belgi

Lambermont- plaats

Amerikalei

Paleisstraat

H. Geestkerk

Lange

Museum
R. S. van Gelde

Leemstraa

E-Banning- straat

St. Michiel

Paleisstraat

Amerikalei

straat

Laureisstraat

Steenweg

Belgielei

Bolivar- plaats

Montigny-

Batanssstraat

St.

Belegstr.

Ballaerstraat

Lozanastraat

Kon. Harmonie

Singel

Haantjeslei

Koning
Albert- park

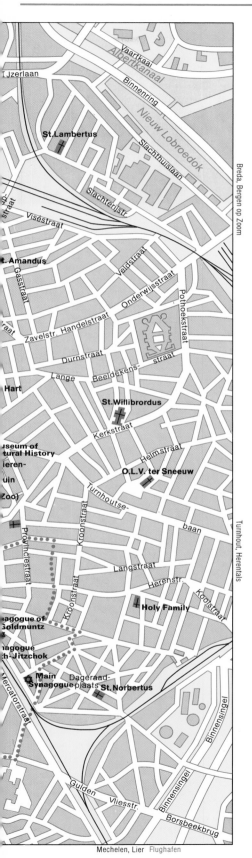

Mechelen, Lier Flughafen

Museum of Pottery, Furniture and Paintings. Further south is the hospice of *St Elisabeth*, founded in the 13th c. In its church is a richly carved high altar by A. Quellinus the Younger (1682).

At the northern end of Leopoldstraat, which runs parallel to the east of Lange Gasthuisstraat, is the **Royal Dutch Theatre** (*Koninklijke Nederlandse Schouwburg*, 19th c.). To the south is the **Botanical Garden** (*Plantentuin*).

The Avenues and the New Town

The ramparts, built in 1540–3 and razed in 1859, were replaced by wide **avenues** (in Flemish *Leien*) which now enclose the Old City to the east. From the North Harbour, Italielei leads to the Tunnelplaats, into which the *Schelde Road Tunnel* opens. It then continues to Rooseveltsplaats with the *Koninklijk Atheneum* (grammar school) on the north-east corner. Italielei then becomes Frankrijklei. On the left stands the *Royal Flemish Opera* (Koninklijke Vlaamse Opera); then the Teniersplaats, from where Leysstraat leads right to the Meir and De Keyserlei left to the Central Station. At the end of Frankrijklei on the right is the *National Bank* (1875–80); then Britselei, at the end of which, left, are the **Law Courts** (*Justitiepaleis* or *Gerechtshof*) built in 1871–5. Amerikalei, which is next, runs not far from the Royal Museum and the *Church of St Michael and St Peter* to the *Bolivar Square*.

From Teniersplaats, the wide Keyserlei runs eastwards to the **Central Station**. It is lined with hotels, cafés and shops, and becomes especially lively on summer evenings. North of the Station is the vast and busy Koningin Astridplein. East of the Station (entrance from Koningin Astridplein next to the Station building) is the well-known *Zoo (Dierentuin)* with an Aquarium, Dolphinarium, Reptile House, Nocturnal House and Planetarium. To the north is a *Festival Centre* with a Concert Hall and the *Museum of Natural History*.

Between Frankrijklei, the Zoo and Koning Albertpark, lies the **Jewish quarter**, the largest and most important Jewish community in Europe, inhabited mostly by Orthodox Jews and containing numerous synagogues, as well as one of the Diamond Stock Exchanges.

East of Frankrijkei on the north-west edge of the Jewish quarter is the **Park**, with picturesque ornamental lakes and several monuments. Further south, along the road to Mechelen, there is the pretty **Koning Albertpark**, also called *Pépinière* or *Warande*. South-west of here extends an elegant new district, the main artery of which is Jan van Rijswijcklaan.

The Steen

The Quays of the Schelde and the Harbour

The tidal zone of the **Schelde** extends far beyond Antwerp (the average difference 4·20 m (14 feet)). The depth of the river allows passage for sea-going vessels of up to 8 m (26 feet) draught, even at low tide. Along a 5·5 km (3 miles) stretch of the river bank, **quays** 100 m (328 feet) wide were laid out at the end of the 19th c., which allow even the largest ships to dock (short cruise, one hour, departure by the Steen). At the Ernest van Dijckkaai and the Jordaenskaai, above the warehouses, lie two *elevated pedestrian terraces** with cafés, offering a magnificent view over the busy river area as well as of the Cathedral and the Steen. – Opposite the south end of the southern terrace at St Jansvliet is the access to the pedestrian *tunnel under the Schelde*, which leads to the left bank of the river. It is 572 m (1877 feet) long and runs 31·5 m (103 feet) below the water line (elevators and escalators). – Not far west from Bolivar Square begins the new *J. F. Kennedy Tunnel*, divided between rail and road, under the Schelde.

A remnant of old times is the **Steen**, a part of the former castle of Antwerp. In its present form it dates mainly from 1521. It houses the *National Maritime Museum** (*Nationaal Scheepvaartsmuseum*), with numerous models of ships, among them a Flemish man-of-war of the 15th c., some 150 junks and other Asian vessels, and a rich collection of nautical instruments, old land and sea charts, etc. South of the Steen is the mooring place from which leaves the ferry to the suburb of St Anna, as well as the boats for the Schelde and harbour cruises, and for excursions on the Schelde. – Further north on Ortelius-kaai on the right is the stately *customs house* (Tolhuis) of 1896, and at the

northern end of Van Meterankaai, the *Pilot House* (Loodswezen) which, among other things houses the School of Navigation.

North-east of the Pilot House, the main part of the harbour and the huge **Northern Docks** can be reached.

The oldest docks are the *Bonaparte-* and *Willemdok*, the former built by Napoleon in 1803–13 for war purposes. At the east end of the WIllemdok is the mighty *Koninklijk Stapelhuis*. Further north is the *Kattendijkdok*, founded in 1853–60, which connects directly with the Schelde through the *Kattendijk Lock*. It is linked north and east with other smaller docks such as the *Straatsburgdok*, into which opens the

Port of Antwerp

--- Harbour cruise
1 Asiadok
2 Kempischdok
3 Houtdok
4 Kattendijkdok
5 Straatsburgdok
6 Lefebvredok
7 Amerikadok
8 1st Havendok
9 Schuildok Lichters
10 2nd Havendok

—— Schelde cruise
11 3rd Havendok
12 Albertdok
13 Leopolddok
14 4th Havendok
15 5th Havendok
16 Industriedok
17 Hansadok
18 Marshalldok
19 6th Havendok
20 Churchilldok

Albert Canal and the *Lefebredok*, and connected with the Schelde through the *Royers Lock*. North again are the newer docks, the large *Albertdok* with four spacious lateral docks. From here runs a 5 km (3 miles) long canal (*Leopold-* and *Hansadok*) with some other large lateral docks, to the *Van Cauwelaert* and *Boudewijn Lock*, and thus provides a direct connection with the Schelde, 12 km (7 miles) upstream from the quays of the Old City. – Toward the north stretches for more than 10 km (6 miles) the *Kanaaldok*, under which runs the *Frans-Tijmans Tunnel*. By the *Zandvliet Lock, the largest sea-lock in the world, it connects with the Schelde and with the new 37 km (23 miles) long *Rhine-Schelde Canal*.

SURROUNDINGS of Antwerp. – the *Riveirenhof in Duerne (3 km (2 miles) east of Koningin Astridplein by the Turnhoutsebaan exit) lies on the banks of the *Schijn*, a small tributary of the Schelde. On its western edge is a palace of the 18th c. housing the Sterckshof Museum (decorative arts; closed in winter). – Also worth seeing is the small *Park te Boelaer* in Borgerhout, 3 km (2 miles) south-east of the Central Station, and nearby to the east the *Park von Boekenberg*, with a palace of 1752 (now a café). In the south of the city, beyond Koning Albertpark, is the vast *Nachtegalenpark with the former Palace of Middelheim (café-restaurant). What used to be the Palace Gardens is now an outdoor "Museum of Modern Sculpture", displaying the works of famous artists, among them Rodin, Maillol, Moore, Giacometti, Manzù and others.

11 km (7 miles) north-east of Antwerp (exit in the direction of Breda, turn right at Merksen) is the popular summer resort of *Schotenhof*. 42 km (26 miles) north-east of Antwerp the industrial town of **Turnhout** has a population of 38,000 (Hotel Kempen, IV, 25 r.; Terminus, IV, 16 r.). It can be reached by an interesting drive through the changing scenery of northern *Kempen*. Turnhout was formerly the seat of the Burgundian and Austrian royal households. There still remains the former palace of the Dukes of Brabant, nowadays the Law Courts. This was built by Jan Keldermans and Dominikus Waghemakere in 1525. The Begijnhof, dating from 1665, with its beautiful Baroque church houses an interesting Museum of Playing Cards and Antiquities. Inside the Gothic Church of St Peter (carillon) are several works of art well worth seeing: an "Ecce Homo" from the beginning of the 15th c., a stone statue of the Saviour, beautiful confessionals and a high altar dating from 1740.

From Antwerp interesting CRUISES can be made (departure from the Steen) downstream to *Lillo* (Museum of the Polder) and *Doel*. On both sides is the alluvial area of the Schelde, lying below sea level. There are other cruises to *Rotterdam, Zierikzee, Veere, Flushing, Middelburg, Bergen op Zoom* (see page 101), *Zeebrugge* and *Ostend* (see page 229). Upstream, past the *South Harbour* and the suburb of *Hoboken* (large shipyards) via *Rupelmonde*, birthplace of the famous geographer Mercator (Gerhard Kremer, 1512–94; Mercator Museum), to the industrial town of **Temse** (population 15,000; Hotel Belle Vue, IV, 14 r.), where there is a Gothic church.

Apeldoorn

Country: The Netherlands. – Province: Gelderland. Altitude: 20–60 m (66–197 feet). – Population: 135,000.
Postal code: NL–7300 AA to 7399.
Telephone code: 0 55.

ⓘ **VVV Apeldoorn,**
Stationsplein 6,
NL-7311 NZ Apeldoorn;
tel. 21 22 49.

HOTELS. – *Bloemink,* Loolaan 56, I, 56b.; *De Keizerskroon,* Koningstraat 7, II, 100 b.; *Suisse,* Stationsplein 15, II, 24 b.; *Nieland,* Soerenseweg 73, III, 87 b.; *Sprengenhorst,* Wieselse Enkweg 35, IV, 40 b.; *Huize Haytink,* Loolaan 25, V, 18 b. – Several BOARDING HOUSES.

YOUTH HOSTEL. – Asselsestraat 330, 130 b.

RESTAURANTS. – *Euridice,* Churchillplein 3; *Echoput,* Amersfoortseweg 86 (about 4 km (2 miles)). In Beekbergen (5 km – 3 miles): *Woeste Hoeve,* Arnhemseweg 792.

The town of Apeldoorn in the Dutch province of Gelderland, first mentioned in the Chronicles in 793, lies on the eastern edge of the Veluwe, a region of sandy woods and heath which rises to 110 m (361 feet) between the rivers Rhine, IJssel and Eem.

Apeldoorn has become a fashionable residential town with superb parks. There is a School of Theology, a Roman Catholic Seminary as well as schools of engineering and machine construction. The town is also the commercial heart of a wider area. Its varied economy is based on a wide range of industries such as metal, paper, textiles and chemicals, and also the manufacture of fishing nets and the building of computers.

SIGHTS. – The most beautiful part of Apeldoorn, *Berg en Bos*, lies on the Wilslaan. In summer it is superbly illuminated. Also worth seeing are the *Oranjepark*, the *Wilhelminapark*, and other parks. The Royal Country Residence **Het Loo** (1685–92) is 2 km (1 mile) north of the town. It was once the favourite home of King William I and King William III, and of Queen Wilhelmina. Now part of the building is occupied by an interesting museum. In its park is the Castle *Oude Loo* (14th–15th c.), and the *Royal Stables* with a collection of fine old coaches.

SURROUNDINGS of Apeldoorn. – To the *National Park, De Hoge Veluwe (to Hoenderloo 13 km

(8 miles)), first take the road leading south-west to Ede through pleasant wooded countryside. 12 km (7 miles) from Apeldoorn is a fork at the edge of the National Park. To the right the road continues to Ede, and 3 km (2 miles) further passes the entrance to the Park St Hubert; after a further 5 km (3 miles) in the village of *Otterlo* is the western entrance to the park. Straight on from the fork in 1 km (about ½ mile) lies the village of *Hoenderlo* and the eastern entrance to the National Park.

This large nature reserve, with an area of over 5400 hectares (13,343 acres), includes a *game park* in the south. Adjoining it to the north is the *Museumspark* with the highly interesting *National Museum Kröller-Müller* best reached by car from Otterlo. It houses primarily collections of modern art, among them many outstanding works by Vincent Van Gogh. The sculptures in the Park should not be missed. The *Hunting Lodge St Hubertus* can also be visited.

A typical landscape in the Belgian Ardennes

Ardennes

Country: Belgium.

(i) Union des Syndicats d'Initiative des Cantons de l'Est,
Avenue Blonden 33,
B-4000 Liège;
tel. (0 41) 52 20 60.
Amblève et Affluents,
Avenue Blonden 33,
B-4000 Liège;
tel (0 41) 52 20 60.
Cœur de l'Ardenne,
Pavillon du Tourisme,
Place MacAuliffe,
B-6650 Bastogne;
tel. (0 62) 21 27 11.
Forêts d'Ardenne et Haute-Lesse,
Rue de Luxembourg 52,
B-5400 Marche-en-Famenne;
tel. (0 84) 31 10 54.
Haute Meuse Dinantaise,
Avenue Franchet d'Esperey 17,
B-5500 Dinant;
tel. (0 82) 22 27 65.
Lesse et Lomme,
B-5430 Rochefort;
tel. (0 84) 21 27 37.
Ourthe et Aisne,
Rue du Baty 8,
B-5450 Hotton;
tel. (0 84) 46 62 04.
Ourthe-Néblon,
Avenue Blonden 33,
b-4000 Liège;
tel. (0 41) 52 20 60.
Semois et Vierre,
Bureau du Château Fort,
B-6830 Bouillon;
tel. (0 61) 46 62 57.
Semois Namuroise,
Mont des Champs,
B-6868 Bohan-sur-Semois;
tel. (0 61) 50 02 01.
Sud-Ardenne et Gaume,
Pavillon du Tourisme,
B-6700 Arlon;
Tel. (0 63) 21 17 97.

The Ardennes (in French, Les Ardennes; in Luxembourg called Ösling, and in dialect Islek), form a high plateau covered partly with moor and heath, and partly with woods, fields and pastureland intersected by numerous narrow valleys. The subsoil is sandstone (greywacke), slaty clay and limestone. It is, in fact, a continuation of the Rhine slate uplands stretching from the border of Federal Germany right across southern Belgium and northern Luxembourg as far as northern France. The rivers Meuse and Sambre form its northern boundary.

In the north-east corner of this area lies the **Hautes Fagnes**, a highland moor with only very few roads, the summit of which, the *Signal de Botrange* (694 m – 2277) is the highest point in the country. The highest point of the Ardennes themselves is the *Baraque de Fraiture* (652 m – 2139) on the uplands between the valleys of the Ourthe and the Amblève. In the north and south foothills of the Hautes Fagnes the rivers *Vesdre, Gileppe* and *Warche* were dammed and the artificial lakes became picturesque and popular tourist attractions. The characteristic features of the limestone areas are the superb grottoes (Rochefort, Dinant, Ramioul, Remouchamps, Furfooz), as well as copious springs and underground rivers, for example the River Lesse which flows through the **Grottes de Han** (see page 172).

The climate of the Ardennes is relatively harsh for Central Europe. The average annual temperature is fairly low (January 0°C (32°F); July 15·4°C (60°F)) and the precipitation reaches considerably high levels (1000–1300 mm (39–51 inches) p.a.). Snow is abundant in winter. As a result of these circumstances, the dairy industry and cattle breeding are the most important branches of agriculture. Farming (rye, oats and forage crops) plays only a very subordinate role. Next to agriculture, forestry is also of importance. Approximately one-third of the area of the Ardennes is covered with woods, mostly deciduous. Conifers appear only in the north-east. Because of the remoteness of the area, there is not much industrialisation. This is why there has been a high degree of emigration and, especially since 1950, a marked decrease in population.

On the other hand, the tourist industry has steadily increased in importance. In particular, the small towns in the deep river valleys have become more and more popular for excursions and summer vacations. Most attractive is the *Valley of the Upper Meuse** with its wooded slopes, bizarre rock formations, often with castles or ruins towering above the picturesque villages. Among the towns, Namur and Dinant are well worth visiting. Quiet summer resorts and little towns with good fishing or hunting in equally attractive countryside can be found in the valleys of the rivers Semois, Lesse, Ourthe, Amblève, Vesdre and Sûre, and in their side valleys. Among the best known tourist areas to be mentioned is the health resort Spa (see page 249), at the northern edge of the Ardennes; and the small towns of Malmédy, Stavelot, La Roche (see page 233), Bouillon (see page 103), Bastogne (see page 99 and Saint-Hubert.

Arlon (Aarlen)

Country: Belgium. – Province: Luxembourg.
Altitude: 450 m (1476 feet). – Population: 23,000.
Postal code: B 6700.
Telephone code: 0 63.

ⓘ **Syndicat d'Initiative,**
Pavillon du Tourisme,
Place Léopold;
tel. 21 63 60.

HOTELS. – Arly, Avenue du Luxembourg 81–83, II, 27 r.; Du Nord (no rest.), Rue des Fauborgs 2, III, 25 r.; Des Druides, Rue Neufchâteau 106, IV, 25 r.; A l'Écu de Bourgogne (no rest.), Place Léopold 9, IV, 18 r.; Paris, Avenue du Luxembourg 75, IV, 29 r.; Courtois, Avenue de la Gare 45, IV, 12 r.; Du Stade (no rest.), Avenue du Luxembourg 79, IV, 16 r.; Cosmopolite (no rest.), Rue de la Gare 33, IV, 8 r.; Grand Hôtel du Luxembourg, Avenue de la Gare, V, 17, r.; Bristol, Marché-au-Beurre 15, V, 5 r.; Maison Blanche, Route de Toernich 210, V, 13 r – Hostellerie du Pfeiffeschof, 3 km north-east, III, 9.

YOUTH HOSTELS. – Rue Z. Gramme 35–37, 80 b.

CAMPING SITE. – Terrain des Quatre-Vents, Route de Bastogne 304.

RESTAURANTS. – Relais du Nord, Rue Fauborgs 2; Toit Doré, Grand Rue 13; Métropole, Marché-aux-Légumes 19.

EVENTS. – Maitrank with traditional performances.

SPORTS and LEISURE. – Soccer, basketball, volleyball, tennis, judo, water sports, etc. in the Centre Sportif et Récréatif du Beau Site, Avenue de Luxembourg; also athletics, billiards, cycling, bowling, skiing, etc.

The town of Arlon (Flemish: Aarlen), which the Romans called Orolaunum, now capital of the Belgian province of Luxembourg, lies on a high plateau in the Ardennes on the slopes of a hill at the top of which stood the former fortress of the Counts of Arlon. In the course of its history, the town has been frequently destroyed, so that now there are hardly any monuments of the past.

SIGHTS. – The middle of the modern part of the town is Place Léopold, which is overlooked by the steeple of St Martin's Church (1914, 97 m (318 feet) high). In the square is the building of the Law Courts (Palais de Justice) and of the Provincial Government. North-west from here through the Rue du 25 Août, you come to the Rue des Martyrs, in which is the interesting **Provincial Museum** (Musée Luxembourgeois) with antiquities from the surrounding countryside

Lipperscheid in the Luxembourg Ardennes

A Roman relief in the Museum of Arlon

now runs through the *Forest of Transinne*, 12 km (7 miles) to the village of **Halma**, and then into the Province of Namur. 12 km (7 miles) beyond Halma there is a fork in the road to Rochefort and Han (13 and 19 km (8 and 12 miles) respectively). – Continue on road No. 48 down into the Valley of the Meuse, and by the Rocher Bayard you reach the Meuse Valley Road, 19 km (12 miles) from **Dinant** (98 m (322 feet); see page 136).

From Arlon via Redange to Ettelbruck (39 km – 24 miles). – Leave Arlon by road No. 483 in a northerly direction. 4 km (2 miles) beyond the town there is a small road forking to the right up to the village of *Guirsch* (2 km – 1 mile). From the church is a magnificent view. You then cross the *Belgian/Luxembourg border* by road No. 22, which forks after 14 km (9 miles), and can go north via the villages of *Menzig and Nieder-Feulen* to Ettelbruck (roads Nos. 12, 21, 15; 18 km (11 miles)), but it is perhaps preferable to use road No. 22, which is 2 km (1 mile) longer, but follows the beautiful bends of the Atterttal past a ruined castle and a Gothic chapel in the village of *Useldange*. 12·5 km (8 miles) after Useldange, you meet road No. 7 coming from Luxembourg via Mersch. 4·5 km (3 miles) to **Ettelbruck** (198 m (650 feet); see page 144).

(*Roman tomb reliefs, old chimney plates, the "Monument of a Traveller", etc.).

The Old Town stretches east of Place Léopold up the hill. At the bottom, near the Grand' Place is the *Roman Tower* (Tour Romaine), a remnant of the Roman Wall of the 4th c. (Museum). At the top of the hill (450 m (1476 feet), extensive view), stands the *Church of St Donatus*, which was built in the 17th c. and later enlarged. Next to it, to the north-east, are the gardens of the former Capuchin Monastery, now a public park.

SURROUNDINGS of Arlon. – **Via Neufchâteau to Dinant** (107 km (66 miles), road No 48). – The well-built and interesting road leaves Arlon by Rue des Faubourgs towards the north-west. After 14 km (9 miles) you reach *Habay-la-Neuve* (400 m – 1312 feet). 2 km (1 mile) to the east on the road to Martelange, by a lake surrounded by woods, stands the *Palace Pont d'Oye*. Beyond Habay you cross the large *forest of Anlier* to **Neufchâteau** 22 km (14 miles) away (427 m (1401 feet), Hotel La Potinière, IV, 6 r.), a small town with a population of 3000. The "Tour Griffon" is the remains of a fortress destroyed in 1555. 11 km (7 miles) further comes the hamlet *Recogne*. 14 km (9 miles) to the north is the little town of **St Hubert**, a well-known place of pilgrimage (434 m (1424 feet), population 3000, Hotel du Luxembourg, IV, 10 r.). The former Benedictine Abbey, founded in 687, was rebuilt in 1729 and now houses the Royal Archives. The church dates from 1526–68 and 1700. In a chapel next to the choir is the cenotaph of St Hubert (d. 727), the missionary of the Ardennes. The Game Park of 15 hectares (37 acres) is also worth seeing. – After Recogne, the road to Dinant runs across hilly and wooded countryside. 17 km (11 miles) from here at the *Barrière de Transinne* (high dam), cross the road from Sedan and Bouillon to Liège. A picturesque and winding stretch of the road

Arnhem

Country: The Netherlands. – Province: Gelderland. Altitude: 20–60 m (66–197 feet). – Population: 281,000.
Postal code: NL-6800 AA to 6879.
Telephone code: 0 85.
ⓘ **VVV Arnhem,** Stationsplein 45, NL-6811 KL Arnhem; tel. 45 29 21.

HOTELS. – *Rijnhotel*, Onderlangs 10, i, 52 b.; *Haarhuis*, Stationsplein 1, I, 200 b.; *Postiljon Motel Arnhem*, Europaweg 25, I, 58 b.; *De Leeren Doedel*, Amsterdamseweg 467, III, 22 b.; *Rembrandt* (no rest.), Paterstraat 1–3, IV, 32 b.; *Hendriks*, Korenmarkt 39–40, V, 50 b.; *Groot Warnsborn DMP*, Bakenbergseweg 277, I, 44 b. (6 km – 4 miles to the north-west). – Several BOARDING HOUSES.

YOUTH HOSTELS. – Diepenbrocklaan 27, 200 b. – Several CAMP SITES.

RESTAURANTS. – *Retonde*, Velperplein 22; *Boerderij*, Parkweg 2; *Begijnemolen*, Zijpendaalseweg 28a; *Sonsbeek Paviljoen*, Zijpendaalseweg 30; *Smidse*, Duizelsteeg 12; *Dorsviegel*, Hoogstraat 1.

FLEA MARKET. – Kerkplein: Friday 8.30 a.m.–1 p.m.

Arnhem, the capital of the province of Gelderland, lies predominantly on the right bank of the Lower Rhine, some kilometres below the point where the IJssel separates from the Rhine. Part of the city lies in the hills at the edge of the Veluwe, a vast area of woods and moorland.

The importance of Arnhem exceeds its regional significance. It is the seat of the Law Courts, of several government agencies and of the Provincial Government of Gelderland, as well as of a number of higher educational institutions such as a School of Drama, a School of Music and a School of Forestry.

Industry plays an important role in the economy of the town. Especially important is the tin-smelting plant founded in 1929, which processes ores from the Dutch Antilles. This plant produces approximately one-fifth of the total world output of tin. Apart from this, there are several chemical and engineering plants and other industrial enterprises.

HISTORY. – The first mention of Arnhem in Chronicles dates from 893, but it is believed that it was built on the site of the Roman settlement *Arenacum* mentioned by Tacitus. It received its charter in 1233 from Otto III, Count of Geldern. Because of its favourable position on the Rhine, trade flourished throughout the Middle Ages. In the 15th c. Arnhem became a member of the Hanse, to which it belonged until the beginning of the 17th c. Emperor Charles V raised the town's status and it became the most important place in Gelderland. In the course of centuries Arnhem fell twice into the hands of the French, who occupied it in 1672–4 and 1795–1813.

In November 1813 the town was conquered by the Prussian troops. Arnhem was heavily damaged in the Second World War, especially in the fighting between the German occupational forces and the British paratroopers in September 1944, and again when it was taken by the Allies in April 1945. Less than 150 houses remained habitable, but the town was quickly and skilfully rebuilt.

SIGHTS. – The traffic hub of Arnhem is Willemsplein, not far east from the Central Station. Adjacent, to the south is Nieuwe Plein. South of Nieuwe Plein a line of narrow shopping streets, Rijn-, Vijzel-, Ketel- and Roggestraat lead through the Old City eastwards to Velperplein. The oldest part of the town can be reached by any one of the side streets going south. Here near the Rhine extends the vast Market Place, at the north end of which stands the **Grote Kerk** dating from the 15th c. (Reformed). It was badly damaged in the Second World War, but has been rebuilt. From its tower (carillon) there is a beautiful view. In the choir is the fine marble tomb of the last Duke of Geldern, Charles of Egmond (d. 1538), the rival of Charles V. To the east, opposite the choir of the church, is the **old Town Hall**, called the *Duivelshuis* after the three devils above its entrance. It was built

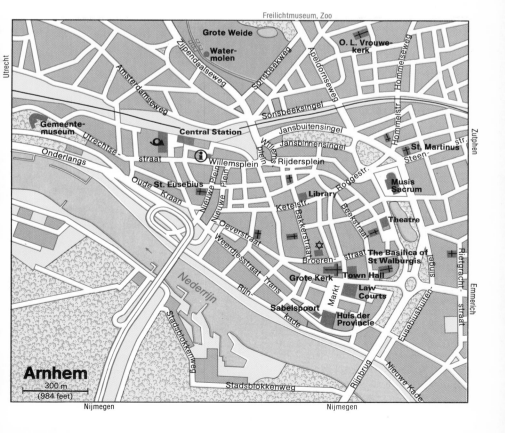

Arnhem
300 m
(984 feet)

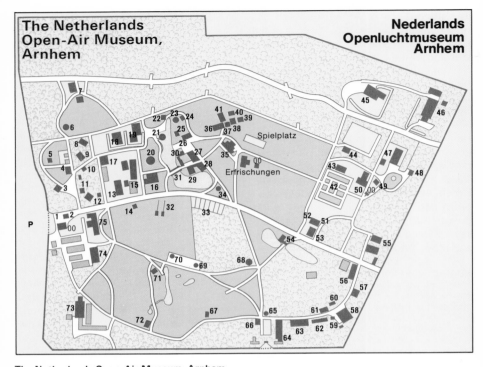

The Netherlands Open-Air Museum, Arnhem

Nederlands Openluchtmuseum Arnhem

The Netherlands Open-Air Museum, Arnhem

1 Entrance
2 Information
3 Horse-driven Oil Mill – Zieuwent (Gelderland)
4 Small Veluwe Farmhouse – Vierhouten (Gelderland)
5 Fowler's Hut – Aerdenhout (North Holland)
6 Exhibition of Bee-keeping
7 Betuwe Farmhouse – Varik (Gelderland)
8 Sheeppen – Ederveen (Gelderland)
9 Day Labourer's Cottage – Nunspeet (Gelderland)
10 Pebble Floor – Geesteren (Gelderland)
11 Achternoek Wheelwright's Shop – Woold (Gelderland)
12 Small Achterhoek Farmhouse – Harreveld (Gelderland)
13 Farmhouse from the Vollenhove District – Kadoelen (Overijssel)
14 Dovecote – Hamersveld (Utrecht)
15 Farmhouse – Staphorst (Overijssel)
16 Farmhouse with Pyramid Roof – Zuid-Scharwoude (North Holland)
17 Small Achterhoek Farmhouse – Beltrum (Gelderland)
18 Farmhouse – Giethoorn (Overijssel)
19 Large Farmhouse – Oud-Beijerland (South Holland)

20 Drainage Mill – Noordlaren (Gronigen)
21 Sawmill – Numansdorp (South Holland)
22 Eelmonger's Hut – Amsterdam (North Holland)
23 Small Drainage Mill (fantail type) – Gouda (South Holland)
24 Sheeppen – Texel (North Holland)
25 Fisherman's Cottage – Marken (North Holland)
26 Boatyard – Marken (North Holland)
27 Building for temporary exhibitions
28 Middle-class House – Zaandam (North Holland) (souvenir shop and exhibition)
29 Merchant's House – Koog on the Zaan (North Holland)
30 Coach-house with living accommodation – Zaan region (North Holland)
31 Double Drawbridge – Ouderkerk on the Amstel (North Holland)
32 Shooting Range
33 Plots with various old-fashioned crops
34 Post Mill – Huizen (North Holland)
35 Laundry – Overveen (North Holland)
36 Cottage – Bedum (Groningen)

37 Outhouse – Woold (Gelderland)
38 Farrier's Shed – Scherpenzeel (Gelderland)
39 Workman's Cottage – Zanderweer (Groningen); Farm Labourer's Cottage – Beemster (North Holland)
40 Clogmaker's Workshop
41 Workmen's Terrace Houses – Tilburg (North Brabant)
42 Herb Garden
43 Herb Garden Exhibition Building
44 Sheeppen – Daarle (Overijssel)
45 Frisian Farmstead – Midlum (Friesland)
46 Groningen Farmstead – Beerta (Groningen)
47 Drenth Farmhouse – Zeijen (Drenthe)
48 Day Labourer's Hut – Onstwedde (Groningen)
49 Village School – Lhee (Drenthe)
50 Farmhouse-Inn, "De Hanekamp" – Zwolle (Overijssel)
51 Horse Mill for crushing grain – Wormerveer (North Holland)
52 Parlour – Hindeoopen (Freisland)
53 Gelderland Farmhouse – Arnhem (Gelderland)
54 Paper Mill – Veluwe (Gelderland)
55 Farmstead – Etten en Leur (North Brabant)

56 Kempen Farmhouse – Budel (North Brabant)
57 Brewery and Bakehouse – Ulvenhout (North Brabant)
58 South Limburg Farmstead – Krawinkel (Limburg)
59 Limburg Wayside Shrine – Margraten (Limburg)
60 Boundary Post – Roosteren-Susteren (Limburg)
61 South Limburg Outhouse – Terstraeten (Limburg)
62 Archery Butts – Roermond (Limburg)
63 Exhibition
64 Lecture Room and Exhibition
65 Summer-House – Meppel (Drenthe)
66 Toll Collector's House – Zuidlaren (Drenthe)
67 Boundary Post of a Hunting Ground – Arnhem (Gelderland)
68 Tower Mill – Delft (South Holland)
69 Small Drainage Mill – Wouterswoude (Friesland)
70 Small Drainage Mill – Gorredijk (Friesland)
71 Twente Bakehouse – Denekamp (Overijssel)
72 Small Twente Farmhouse – Beuningen (Overijssel)
73 Exhibition of Regional Costumes
74 Shed for Drying Wood – Haarlem (North Holland)
75 Restaurant

c. 1540 for Maarten van Rossem, the military commander of Duke Charles of Geldern.

Opposite to the north-east, stand the *Law Courts*, built in 1958–63, and the *Rijksar-*

chief Gelderland dating from 1880. On the south side of the square stands the imposing **Huis der Provincie**, reconstructed in 1954, the seat of the Provincial Government, with a beautiful courtyard. Next to it rises the *Sabelspoort*, built in the

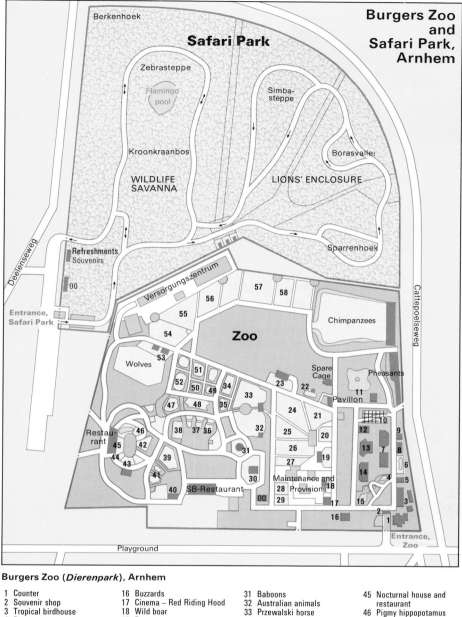

Burgers Zoo
and
Safari Park,
Arnhem

Safari Park

Berkenhoek

Zebrasteppe

Flamingo
pool

Simba-
steppe

Kroonkraanbos

Borasvallei

WILDLIFE
SAVANNA

LIONS' ENCLOSURE

Deelenseweg

Refreshments
Souvenirs

Sparrenhoek

00

Versorgungszentrum

Entrance,
Safari Park

57   58

56

55

Chimpanzees

54

Zoo

53

Wolves

51

52   50   49   34

47   48   35

33

23   22

Spare
Cage

Pheasants

11
Pavillon

10

Cattepoelseweg

Restau-
rant

46

45   42

44   43

38   37   36

39

32

31

24

25

26

27

21

20

19

12

13   7

14

9

8

6

41

40   SB-Restaurant

30

00

28   Provisions
29

Maintenance and
18

17

15

16

2

1

5

4

3

Entrance,
Zoo

Playground

Burgers Zoo (*Dierenpark*), Arnhem

1 Counter	16 Buzzards	31 Baboons	45 Nocturnal house and
2 Souvenir shop	17 Cinema – Red Riding Hood	32 Australian animals	restaurant
3 Tropical birdhouse	18 Wild boar	33 Przewalski horse	46 Pigmy hippopotamus
4 Parrots	19 Bears	34 Emus	47 Polar bears
5 Guinea pigs	20 Barbary sheep	35 Alpacas	48 Tigers
6 Water fowl	21 Aurochs	36 Leopards	49 Pecarry
7 Pheasants	22 Parrots	37 Lions	50 Hyenas
8 Small birds of prey	23 Small monkeys	38 Elephants	51 Malayan bears
9 Owls	24 Bison	39 Giraffes	52 Sealions
10 European birds	25 Watusi cattle	40 Tigers	53 Wolves, foxes, raccoons
11 Flamingos	26 Zebu	41 Hippopotamus	54 Red deer
12 Large birds of prey	27 Gayals, water buffalo	42 Rhinoceros	55 Nilgai antelopes
13 Peacocks	28 Moufflon	43 Primates	56 Lamas
14 Birds of prey	29 Fallow deer	44 Tapirs	57 Camels
15 Pelicans, ducks	30 Panther		58 Dromedaries

14th c. (the market front dating from 1642), which is a remnant of the city wall.

Further south is the **bridge across the Rhine**, which was the target of much fighting in the Second World War. On the town side stands a monument commemorating the British paratroopers. From the bridge runs a belt of wide avenues on the site of the former fortifications along the eastern edge of the Old Town. On the left-hand side is the

Peasant's house in the Open-air Museum of Arnhem

St Walburgisbasiliek (Catholic), the oldest church in the town (consecrated in 1422; beautiful pulpit), and the **Municipal Theatre**. On the Velperplein is the Concert Hall, *Musis Sacrum* with exhibition rooms.

West of the Central Station at No. 87 Utrechtseweg, in the grounds of the *Reeberg* (beautiful view over the Rhine countryside), is the **Municipal Museum** (*Gemeentemuseum*), housing a collection of paintings, antiquities and decorative art. Particularly interesting is the Chinese and Delft porcelain, as well as a collection of glass. On the west side of the town at Heijenoordseweg, No. 150, is the Model Housing Estate for Handicapped People (*Het Dorp*). North from the railway station extends the wooded Municipal Park **Sonsbeek**, covering 500 hectares (1236 acres), with a *Belvedere*, from which there is an extensive view over the Betuwe.

North of the town is the ****Dutch Open-air Museum** (*Nederlands Open-luchtmuseum*). It can be reached by Zijpendaalse or Apeldoornseweg then by turning respectively left or right into Schelmseweg (4 km – 2 miles). It lies in beautiful wooded countryside and occupies an area of 33 hectares (82 acres). It is open from 1 April to 31 October. It was founded in 1912 to preserve the Dutch folk art and country way of life, and it offers a unique insight into Dutch peasant handicrafts and village architecture. The tour takes about 2 hours.

A number of typical buildings, such as the peasant and fishermen's houses, windmills of all kinds, all sorts of workshops, an entire group of houses from the region of the Zaan, etc., were transferred intact with all their implements from the original sites and arranged here according to province. In the main exhibition building, temporary *Exhibitions of National Costumes take place. In the coach-house various types of coaches and carts are shown. Some 500 m (1641 feet) to the west of the Open-air Museum is the ***Zoo** (Burgers Dierenpark), open all year, where a great variety of birds is exhibited. It encloses impressive rocky grounds as well as a **Safari Park**. Some 2 km (1 mile) east of the middle of the town, stands the recently constructed and popular shopping area, *Presikhaaf*. It lies south of the IJ, and is much patronised by visiting foreigners. In the suburb of BRONBEEK is the *Museum of the Dutch-Indian Army* (Indisch Legermuseum). It lies between Arnhem and Velp at No. 147 Velperweg.

Assen

Country: The Netherlands. – Province: Drenthe.
Altitude: 20 m (66 feet). – Population: 44,000.
Postal code: NL-9400AA to 9499.
Telephone code: 0 59 20.
(i) **VVV Assen,**
   Brink 42,
   NL-9401 HV Assen;
   tel. 1 43 24.

HOTELS. – *Overcingel*, Stationsplein 10, II, 70 b.; *De Brink*, Singelpassage 2, II, 32 b.; *De Jonge*, Brink-straat 85, V, 41 b.; etc.

CAMP SITE. – Witterzomer 7.

RESTAURANTS. – *Bistro La Belle Epoque*, Markt 6; *China*, Groningerstraat 7.

EVENTS. – *Ice Speedway Competition* (beginning of February); *Grand Prix of the Netherlands*, on the Motorcycle Racing Track (last Saturday in June); *Motorcycle racing, 750 cc* (first Sunday in September).

Assen, the capital of the Dutch province of Drenthe, lies at the confluence of two inland waterways, Drentse Hoofdvaart and Noord-Willemskanaal, in attractive wooded surroundings. It became an independent community only in 1807 and received its charter in 1809 from King Louis Bonaparte. It quickly developed into the capital of Drenthe and an important junction for inland shipping. The population, which in 1809 was only 600, increased rapidly, numbering 13,000 at the beginning of the 20th c. and tripling in the following 65 years.

SIGHTS. – Unlike other provincial capitals in the Netherlands, Assen has no historic monuments, having been an insignificant village until well into the last century; nor is its past particularly noteworthy. Nevertheless, a visit to the **Provincial Museum**, Aan de Brink, should not be missed. It houses a unique collection of weapons, tools, pottery, and other finds from the Stone and Bronze Ages, such as mummified corpses found in bog. All the finds come from nearby sites. Next to the Museum stands the *Gouvernement*, a neo-Gothic building constructed on the site of a former convent which was abolished in the Reformation, and of which only the church and part of the cloisters from the 13th c. remain. The church now forms part of the Town Hall. The superb period rooms of the *Ontvanger* (House of the Tax Collector), give a good picture of the way of life of a provincial official in the 17th–18th c.

SURROUNDINGS of Assen. – A worthwhile excursion can be made to the east and south-east of the town to a region called **Hondsrug**. More than fifty megalithic tombs from the Stone and Bronze Ages were found here. A visit to the prehistoric graves *de Papeloze Kerk* between the villages of *Sleen* and *Schoonoord* is recommended. Most of them have been restored to their original condition and made accessible to visitors. The largest megalithic tomb in Drenthe, known since 1685, lies between *Bronneger* and *Borger*.

Bastogne (Bastenaken)

Country: Belgium. – Province: Luxembourg.
Altitude: 515 m (1690 feet). – Population: 11,000.
Postal code: B-6650.
Telephone code: 0 62.
ⓘ **Syndicat d'Initiative,**
Hôtel de Ville (Town Hall),
Pavillon du Tourisme,
Place MacAuliffe;
tel. 21 27 11.

HOTELS. – *Lebrun*, Rue de Marche 8, III, 27 r.; *Le Borgés*, Place MacAuliffe 10–11, III, 18 r.; *The Bulge Hotel*, Rue de Marche 14, IV, 15 r.; *Au Luxembourg*, Place MacAuliffe 25, V, 9 r.; *L'Europe*, Place MacAuliffe 35, V, 7 r.; *Du Sud*, Rue de Marche 39, V, 14 r. – IN WARDIN 5 km (3 miles) east on the road to Diekirch): *Du Chalet de Marenwez*, V, 11 r.

CAMP SITE.

Bastogne (in Flemish Bastenaken), on a high plateau in the Ardennes is a small Belgian town on the River

Wiltz, which has its source not far to the south-west. The town was badly damaged by heavy fighting during the "Battle of the Bulge" in 1944. Local specialities are the tasty Ardennes ham and nuts.

SIGHTS. – The *church* in the Place Saint Pierre was originally Romanesque. The present structure dates from the 15th c. and the tower from the 12th c. Inside are some old ceiling paintings as well as a 12th c. altar. Behind the church stands the *Porte de Trèves*, dating from the 14th c., a relic of the city wall razed in 1688. In the Place MacAuliffe is the *"Nuts" Museum* with souvenirs of the Second World War. In the square stands an American tank as well as a bust of the American commander, General MacAuliffe, the defender of the town.

Memorial to US soldiers near Bastogne

SURROUNDINGS of Bastogne. – The Route de Clervaux runs north-east (2 km – 1 mile) to a large star-shaped **memorial** on the *Mardasson* hill. It was built in 1950 to commemorate the 77,000 US soldiers who lost their lives in the Battle of the Bulge, the last German offensive of the Second World War. In the crypt there are three mosaics by Fernand Léger. Next to it is a *Museum* ("Bastogne Historical Center"), with souvenirs of the Battle.

Some 15 km (9 miles) south of Bastogne on the Upper Sûre and on the Belgian-Luxembourg border lies the village **Martelange** (Hôtel Martinot, IV, 16 r.) with slate quarries. South-west from here is the forest of Anlier (Forêt d'Anlier). – 2 km (1 mile) to the north of Martelange stands the *monument to the Chasseurs Ardennais* (the Regiment of Ardennes Rifles). East of Martelange a road runs along the Belgian-Luxembourg border to **Wiltz** (see page 267), and **Ettelbruck** (see page 144). An excursion to the north in the attractive valley of the **Ourthe** (see page 233) is recommended.

The Belgian North Sea Coast (Polders)

Country: Belgium. – Province: West Flanders.
ⓘ **Westtoerisme,**
Vlaamingstraat 55,
B-8000 Brugge 1;
tel. (0 50) 3 73 33.

Sea food

The area of Belgium known as the Polders is situated in the province of West Flanders and comprises a coastal stretch some 15 km (9 miles) wide. It is part of the fenlands which begin in northern France near Calais and border the entire North Sea coast as far as Denmark as a more or less narrow margin of land. In the north the Polders extend along the Wester Schelde in the Dutch part of Flanders, close to the city of Antwerp. Inland, these marshy strips are bordered by the somewhat higher elevation of the Flemish Geest. They are separated from the sea by a band of dunes running parallel to the coastline.

Beach on the Belgian North Sea Coast

The surface of the Polders is not only below the high-water mark of the North Sea, which is a characteristic of all marshy regions, but in some places even below the normal sea level. These marshes were uninhabitable before people began to construct dikes in the 8th c. to protect the threatened territories against frequent flooding. The only exceptions were the so-called Wurts or Warfts, artificial mounds rising above the high-water mark

on which human settlements already existed in Roman times.

The soil of the fens consists of fertile mud which the North Sea deposited on top of extensive layers of peat, before the construction of the dikes began. The flooding of the former peat bogs started about the beginning of our era, and the danger of this increased with the rise of the sea level from the 3rd c. A.D. onwards. The natural barrier of the dunes lining the coast could not resist the increasing impact of the waves; it was broken in several places and the sea began to penetrate inland.

The swamps were drained when this coastal area was enclosed by dikes. However, the draining of the low-lying marshes presented serious problems. The rivers, fed by innumerable canals and ditches, had to have locks built at their estuaries to prevent the sea from flooding the land at high tide. In many cases the dikes were not strong enough and in the Middle Ages catastrophic floods often cost the lives of thousands of people. On 29 October 1914, the marshes of the Yser were intentionally flooded when the locks were opened to block the advance of the German troops.

When the marshes were drained, large stretches of rich pastures and fertile farmland were created. Wheat, barley, sugar-beet and fodder are the most important crops. The entirely flat country-side is dotted with huge farmsteads, either isolated or in small groups. There are only a few towns and all of them are on the coast, with the exception of *Veurne* (see page 263), *Diksmuide, Nieuwpoort* (see page 224), and **Bruges** (see page 106). When the marshes were enclosed with dikes, the old sea inlets became silted, as for example the Zwin. This led from the estuary of the Schelde to Bruges, the largest Flemish port in the Middle Ages but silting caused its decline. Today harbours and industry requiring water transport facilities must be located directly on the coast (e.g., the coking plants and glass industries in Zeebrugge and the chemical industries in Ostend).

Extremely important economically is tourism, which is concentrated on the fine sandy beaches. The coast is lined with a continuous stretch of dunes with only very few breaks to the sea. This strip varies in width, and rises in the vicinity of De Panne to a height of some 30 m (98 feet). The beaches stretching on both sides of the ferry terminal of **Ostend** (see page 229), are among the best-known and most visited seaside resorts in Europe. Next to Ostend the most important resorts are *Knokke-Heist* (see page 184), *Blankenberge* (see page 102) and *De Panne* (see page 234).

Bergen op Zoom

Country: The Netherlands. – Province: North Brabant.
Altitude: 0–5 m (0–16 feet). – Population: 42,000.
Postal code: NL-4600AA to 4699.
Telephone code: 0 16 40.

ⓘ **VVV Bergen op Zoom,**
Grote Markt/Hoogstraat;
tel. 3 56 60.

HOTELS. – *De Gouden Leeuw*, Fortuinstraat 14, II, 36 b.; *De Draak*, Grote Markt 37–38, IV, 50 b.; *De Schelde*, Antwerpsestraat 56, IV, 30 b.; *Old Dutch*, Stationsstraat 31, IV, 15 b.; *De Blauwe Vogel*, Stationsplein 5, V, 18 b.

YOUTH HOSTEL. – Klaverveldenweg 25, 80 b.

RESTAURANTS. – *Moby Dick*, Kremerstraat 33; *Bistro La Pucelle*, St Josephstraat 9; *Bloemkool*, Wouwsestraatweg 146.

EVENTS. – *Carnival Procession* (Monday before Lent); *Flower Market* (every Saturday from Easter to October).

The former fortress town of Bergen lies in the west of the Dutch province of North Brabant. To distinguish it from Bergen Binnen, Bergen in het Bosch and Bergen aan Zee, it became known as Bergen op Zoom, which means "on the edge".

It is connected by a canal to the sea inlet of Oosterschelde, once one of the estuaries of the Schelde, and through this it connects to the North Sea. Through the centuries the town has often been besieged. Although in earlier times its economy was based on trade with England, today it is the capital of oyster and lobster farming, sardine fishing, and the growing of asparagus and strawberries. Apart from this, there are important industrial plants such as metal, timber and textile, as well as food processing.

The Town Hall on the Markt in Bergen op Zoom

HISTORY. – Bergen op Zoom received its charter in the 13th c. In the following century it developed into one of the most important commercial cities of the Netherlands. During the Dutch Liberation Wars, the Duke of Alba turned the town into a strong fortress. In 1577 it was abandoned by the Spaniards, and between then and 1605 besieged by them three times without success. In 1662 the Marquess of Spinola failed to storm its fortifications. In 1747 the French Army, commanded by Count Loevendals, for the first time in history conquered the town.

SIGHTS. – On the Grote Markt stands the 15th c. **Town Hall**. Its beautiful façade dates from 1611; the vestibule is decorated with the coast of arms of the former leading families of burghers. Among the most important treasures inside the building is a superb late-Gothic chimneypiece of 1521, from the Markiezenhof. The Gothic **Grote Kerk** of the 13th–15th c. contains numerous tombstones from the 16th–18th c. From its tower (carillon), there is a beautiful view as far as Antwerp. In the Steenbergsestraat stands the *Markiezenhof*, a mansion with a fine façade, built in 1475 as a palace for the Margrave. At the western end of the Lieve Vrouwestraat rises the quaint 15th c. *Gevangenpoort*, a relic of the former fortifications.

Betuwe

Country: The Netherlands. – Province: Gelderland.
ⓘ **Prov. VVV Gelderland
en VVV Arnhem an de Zuid-Veluwe,**
Stationsplein 45,
NL-6811 KL Arnhem;
tel. (0 85) 45 29 21.

The region of Betuwe in eastern Holland is a flat alluvial land bordered in the north by the Lower Rhine and its continuation, the Lek, in the south by the Rhine branch, the Waal, and in the west by the Linge, a small river in the Rhine Delta.

Betuwe, with approximately 100 inhabitants per sq. km (259 per sq. mile) is among the least populated areas of Holland. The most important occupation on this flat land, which is protected by dikes against flooding by the rivers, is agriculture, with industry playing only a minor role. In its lowest parts meadows predominate; on the higher river terraces farming is possible. Towards the German border fruit is intensively grown.

In the past Betuwe has always been an extremely inaccessible region like the neighbouring plains of *Tielerwaard*, *Maas en Waal* and *Rijk van Nijmegen*. It helped the northern Netherlands in their efforts in the 16th–17th c. to rid themselves of the Spanish overlordship, by functioning as a barrier between the north and south routes.

Blankenberge

Country: Belgium. – Province: West Flanders.
Altitude: 4 m (13 feet). – Population: 14,000.
Postal code: B-8370.
Telephone code: 0 50.
ⓘ **Dienst voor Toerisme,**
Leopold III plein;
tel. 41 22 27.

HOTELS. – *Albatros*, Consciencestraat 47, I, 18 r; *Petit Rouge*, Zeedijk 127, II, 60 r; *Strandhotel*, Zeedijk 86, II, 22 r; *Poseidon* (no rest.), Ruzettelaan 157, III, 21 r; *Laforce*, Zeedijk 180–181, III, 38 r.; *Idéal*, Zeedijk 244, III, 50 r.; *Azaert*, Molenstraat 31, III, 43 r.; *Du Commerce*, Weststraat 64, III, 30 r.; *Le Berkeley*, Zeedijk 93, III, 22 r.; *Riant Séjour*, Zeedijk 188, III, 20

r.; *Impérial*, Kerkstraat 26, III, 72 r.; *Marie-José*, Marie Josélaan 2, IV, 38 r.; *Thonnon*, De Smet de Naeyerlaan 54, IV, 27 r.; *Du Littoral*, Verweehelling 6, IV, 45 r.; *Miramar*, Zeedijk 169, IV, 34 r.; *Oud Belgie*, IV, A. Ruzettelaan 2, 22 r.; *Lion d'Or*, Kerkstraat 17, IV, 86 r.; *Suisse*, J. de Troozlaan 33, IV, 27 r.; *Laetitia*, Zeedijk 238, IV, 25 r.; *Nismes et Tongres*, De Smet de Naeyerlaan 97, IV, 19 r.; *Centrum* (no. rest.), Kerkstraat 59, IV, 22 r.; *St Jean*, Descampstraat 44, IV, 39 r.; *Rosemary*, G. de Troozlaan 46, IV, 20 r.; *Comte de Flandre*, Kerkstraat 149, IV, 24 r.; *José*, Visserstraat 18, IV, 42 r.; *Des Colonies*, Kerkstraat 95, IV, 16 r.; *Belgica*, Kerkstraat 97, IV, 39 r.; *Malecot*, Langestraat 89–91, IV, 40 r.; *Gordon's Hotel*, Weststraat 88, IV, 15 r.; *Parc-Cygne*, De Smet de Naeyerlaan 133, IV, 29 R.; *Au Singe d'Or*, Zeedijk 184, IV, 20 r.; *Conscience*, Grote Markt 32, V, 27 r.; *Eden*, Zeedijk 149, V, 25 r.; *De Bruxelles*, Kerkstraat 96, V, 24 r.; *Mistral*, Zeedijk 228, V, 24 r.; *Aquarium*, De Smet de Naeyerlaan 33c, V, 24 r.; *St Michel*, J. de Troozlaan 13, V, 25 r.; *D'Orange*, Kerkstraat 92, V, 58 r.; *Leopold II*, Onderwijsstraat 23, V, 21 r. – Numerous BOARDING HOUSES. – Two CAMP SITES near the beach.

RESTAURANTS. – *L'Huîtrière*, De Smet de Naeyerlaan 1; *Colonies*, Kerkstraat 95; *St-Hubert*, Manitobaplein 15; *Auberge Joinville*, J. de Troozlaan 5; *Malbeck*, Hoogstraat 4; *Grande Marée*, Bakkersstraat 6.

EVENTS. – *Prinsenball* (February); *Carnival Procession*; International two-day *Rambling Contest for tourists* (May); Traditional *Harbour Feast* (May); *Day of the Tourist* (June); *Consecration of the Sea* (July); *Municipal Small Arts Theatre* (July/August, daily); the *Great Flower Show* (August).

Casino with gambling tables on the dike promenade.

SPORTS and LEISURE. – Angling, riding, swimming, sailing, tennis. In the *sports stadium*, football, basketball, volleyball, squash, badminton and mini-football pitches; dancing studio. Tennis and judo. Athletic tracks and equipment, small indoor swimming pool with sauna.

The little town of Blankenberge lies on the Belgian North Sea coast and thanks to its 3 km (2 miles) long beach has been a seaside resort since 1860. It still rates among the best in Belgium although today it has been overtaken by Knokke-Heist. It is very popular as a place for family vacations. Tourism has remained its main source of income, whereas the tiny fishing harbour plays only a modest role.

SIGHTS. – The main street is Kerkstraat, passing by the railway station, at the north end of which there are steps up to the dike. Opposite the railway station is the Gothic *Church of St Antonius*, consecrated in 1358 and restored in the 17th c., and again recently. West from Kerkstraat, the Grote Markt can be reached via Langestraat or Molenstraat. In the square is a monument to the Flemish writer Hendrik Conscience and a war memorial. In the west is the *harbour* (yachting and deep-sea fishing). The entrance to the harbour is protected against silting by a 300 m (984 feet) long Estacade or Pilework. Here, the 2-km (1-mile) long **dike promenade** begins (**Zeedijk**, 10 m (33 feet) above sea level), lined with hotels and villas. The *Casino* is approximately in the middle of the promenade. From the north-east end of the dike, a *pier* extends 350 m (1148 feet) out into the sea, and offers a beautiful view. There is a café/restaurant, and in a pavilion, the *Aquarama*, an interesting sea aquarium.

Bouillon

Country: Belgium. – Province: Luxembourg.
Altitude: 221 m (725 feet). Population: 3,000.
Postal code: B-6830.
Telephone code: 0 61.

ⓘ **Syndicat d'Initiative et de Tourisme,** Burg;
tel. 46 62 57 and 46 62 89.

HOTELS. – *Hostellerie aux Armes de Bouillon – Le Luxembourg*, Rue de la Station 13, III, 60 r.; *De France*, Faubourg de France 1, IV, 19 r.; *Hostellerie du Cerf*, Route de Florenville, IV, 9 r.; *Au Vieux Prieure*, Rue de la Gare 17, IV, 10 r.; *Auberge d'Alsace*, Faubourg de France 3, IV, 12 r.; *Du Château Fort*, Rue du Brutz 18, IV, 15 r.; *Au Vieux Moulin*, Porte de France 1, IV, 16 r.; *Central au Duc de Bouillon*, Rue des Hautes-Voies 2, V, 18 r.; *Roi Albert*, Quai des Remparts 6, V, 10 r.; *Le Castel*, Quai de la Maladrerie 8, V, 4 r. – Above the town: *Ardennes*, Rue Abattis 45, III, 32 r.; *Saule*, Rue VIllage 39, III, 12 r.; *Le Tyrol*, Rue au-dessus de la Ville 23, IV, 12 r.; *Du Panorama*, IV, 42 r.; *Gai Repos*, V, 12 r. – Numerous BOARDING HOUSES.

YOUTH HOSTEL. – CAMP SITE.

RESTAURANTS. – *La Vielle Ardenne*, Grand-Rue 9; *Les Sports*, Quai du Rempart 28; *Le Pourquoi-Pas?*, Voi Jocquée 1; *Aux Oeillets*, Quai du Rempart 34; *La Petite Marmite*, Grand-Rue 16; *Windsor*, Boulevard Heynen 1, *Le Chalet*, Rue du Petit.

EVENTS. – From March to September numerous exhibitions, concerts, fireworks, dancing, etc.

SPORTS and LEISURE. – Tennis, swimming pool, water sports, horseback riding and fishing.

Bouillon is a small town in the south of the Belgian province of Luxembourg near the French border. Attractively situated in a bend of the River Semois, surrounded by the wooded hills of the Southern Ardennes and dominated by a monu-

mental castle, it is a popular summer resort and excursion spot.

SIGHTS. – The Castle Square can be reached from the lower bridge, the *Pont de Liège*, or the *Vieux-Pont*, past the church on the left bank of the river and about 1 km (about ½-mile) up the hill (parking). On the right is the entrance to the *Castle, situated on an isolated rocky

Castle of Bouillon

promontory almost enclosed by the Semois. It is one of the oldest and best preserved specimens of medieval feudal architecture. Godefroy of Bouillon (*c.* 1060–1100), who was one of the leaders of the First Crusade, ceded the castle to the Bishop of Liège just before he left the country for the Holy Land in 1095. The nobles of the region disputed for centuries the Bishop's possession. Under Louis XIV, the castle and the town were taken by the French and fortified by Vauban. The interior of the castle offers some impressive sights. From the balcony there are beautiful views over the town and river. – On the north side of the Castle Square is the **Ducal Museum** (*Musée Ducal*), consisting of two sections: a charming townhouse of the 18th c. houses a historical collection from the neighbouring area, and in the annex, named after Godefroy of Bouillon, there is a section about the history of the Crusades. In two neighbouring rooms are paintings by Albert Raty.

Brabant

Country: Belgium. – Province: Brabant.
ⓘ **Federation du Tourisme du Brabant,**
Rue Marché aux Herbeš 61,
B-1000 Bruxelles;
tel. (02) 5 13 07 50.
Region de Nivelles,
Hôtel de Ville,
B-1400 Nivelles;
tel. (0 67) 22 21 61.
Est du Brabant Wallon,
Hôtel de Ville,
B-1300 Wavre;
tel (0 10) 22 39 01.
Noord-Westbrabant,
Gemeentehuis
B-1703 Kobbegem;
tel. (02) 4 52 82 28.
Midden-Brabant,
Tiensevest 170,
B-3000 Leuven;
tel (0 16) 22 09 61.
Hageland en Haspengouw,
Stadhuis,
B-3300 Tienen;
tel. (0 16) 81 10 07.
Zuid-Westbrabant,
Basiliekstraat 136,
B-1500 Halle;
tel (02) 3 56 46 66.

The boundaries of the Belgian province of Brabant in the heart of Belgium correspond roughly to the central part of the country bearing the same name. Across the south of Brabant, 30 km (19 miles) from Brussels, runs the linguistic frontier between the Walloons and the Flemish. The region which extends between the River Dender in the west and the Gete in the east is a rolling country rising gently southward toward the plateaux of Hainaut and Hesbaye and reaching some 100–160 m (328–525 feet) above sea level. The Dender separates its northern part from the lower Belgian region of Kempen. This part of Brabant is divided between Little Brabant and Hageland east of it. To the south lies Central Brabant, sometimes called the Brabant Region.

Brabant is the northern part of the Central Belgian plain, which is formed by cretaceous and tertiary formations. Although it is lower than South Central Belgium, the rivers Gete, Dijle, Senne and Dender have cut their valleys deep into the soft rock strata. These valleys divide the **area of Brabant** into several plateaux which, further to the north in *Little Brabant* and in

Hageland, have eroded into many isolated hills. The latest top layer in this hilly country is formed by hard late-tertiary conglomerate rock which resists erosion exceptionally well. Protected by them, even occasional isolated hills were able to escape destruction, such as the *Pellenberg* near Louvain, on the edge of Hageland.

In the extreme north of Brabant, clay and sand soil predominates. It is considerably more fertile than the Geest-type sands in Flemish Kempen. Further south on the slopes and on the heights, it is replaced by the extremely fertile loess.

The utilisation of the land follows a similar pattern. In the areas with loess topsoil, the main crops are wheat and sugar-beet. Stock raising, especially horse breeding, also plays a part. Large rectangular farmsteads are a dominant feature of the small hamlet-type villages. Often individual farmhouses stand alone in the middle of tree-lined fields and meadows. Where the fertile loess cover is missing, there are large forests, such as the *Forêt de Soignes* south of Brussels. Near the important consumer markets of **Brussels** and **Louvain** (see pages 113 and 200) extend enormous vegetable fields and orchards. In the south they give way to thousands of greenhouses in which tasty grapes are grown. Next to market gardening, dairy, pig and poultry farming are also important.

Compared with other parts of the country industry in Brabant plays a relatively minor role, except of course in the heavily

Horse Market in Hedel (North Brabant)

In the Forêt de Soignes (Brabant)

industrialised urban region of Brussels. A compact industrial zone exists only in the Valley of the *Senne* between Vilvoorde and Clabecq along the canal from Charleroi to Wilbroek. The major industries are steel, chemicals, textiles, paper and food processing. Other important towns in Brabant are *Tienen* and *Nivelles* (see pages 252 and 226).

North Brabant (Netherlands; see page 227).

Breda

Country: The Netherlands. – Province: North Brabant.
Altitude: 5 m (16 feet). – Population: 119,000.
Postal code: NL-4800AA to 4899.
Telephone code: 0 76.
ⓘ **VVV Breda,**
Willemstraat 17,
NL-4811 AJ Breda;
tel. 22 57 33.

HOTELS. – *Mostbosch*, Burg Kerstenslaan 20, I, 83 b., *Euromotel Breda,* Roskam 20, I, 170 B.; *Euromotel Brabant*, Heerbaan 4, I, 170 b.; *Novotel Breda*, Dr Batenburglaan 74, II, 163 b.; *Huis Den Deyl,* Marellenweg 8, IV, 17 b.; *De Gouden Leeuw*, Korte Boschstraat 1, V, 12 b.; *Du Lion d'Or*, Stationsweg 5, V, 35 b. – CAMP SITE.

RESTAURANTS. – *Turfschip*, Chasséveld; *Asia-China Garden*, Grote Markt 45; *Auberge Arent,* Schoolstr. 2; *Walliser Stube*, Grobe Markt 44; *Withof*, Hoofstraat 86; *Heestermans*, A. Oomenstraat 1a; *Mirabelle*, Dr Batenburglaan 76.

The Dutch city of Breda in the province of North Brabant lies near the Belgian border on the confluence of the Mark and the Aa. It is not only of cultural importance, being the seat of a Catholic Bishop, and headquarters of numerous research and educational institutes, but is also one of the most important industrial capitals of the country. The many industries include engineering, synthetic fibres, food

processing, the manufacture of matches and brewing. Breda is also an important tourist attraction.

HISTORY. – Breda, protected by a castle, developed in the 12th c., obtained its charter in the middle of the 13th c. and has played an important role in the history of the Netherlands since the end of the Middle Ages. The town was fortified in 1534 by Count Henry of Nassau and survived numerous sieges. The Agreement of Breda in February 1566 marked the beginning of the Dutch uprising against the Spanish. Well known is the surprise attack and defeat of the Spanish by Maurice of Orange, who, in March 1590, secretly brought seventy men into the town hidden in Adriaan van Bergen's peat boat. The Peace Treaty of Breda ended, in 1667, the second naval war against England, and secured for the Dutch the possession of the East Indies. The fortifications were renewed in 1682 and were used until the wars against the French in 1793–5 and 1813, but have since been pulled down. With the silting of the navigable River Mark in the 18th c. Breda lost for some time the importance it had in trading, but after it became connected to the Dutch railway system, it quickly developed into a major industrial city.

Town Hall in Breda

SIGHTS. – In the middle of the town, which is surrounded by concentric canals, the "Singels", lies the Grote Markt with the **Town Hall** (*Stadhuis*), dating from the 18th c. The former *Vlees-* and *Boterhal*, with a sandstone portal of the 17th c. and gables of 1733, houses the *Stedelijk and Bischoppelijk Museum* which has a collection of town and church antiquities. In the north-west corner of the Markt stands the **Grote Kerk** (*Lieve Vrouwekerk;* Reformed), a Gothic building begun before 1290. In the choir, apart from rich late Gothic, influences of the Renaissance can be discerned. The superb tower, 96 m (315 feet) high, was built in 1468–1509, and received its crown after a fire in 1694. In the Prince's Chapel, to the left of the choir, behind a richly carved grille, stands a monumental *Renaissance tomb of Count Engelbrecht II of Nassau who was Governor General of the Netherlands under

Emperor Maximilian I (d. 1504) and of his wife Cimburgis of Baden (d. 1510). It is an alabaster masterpiece of the 16th c., possibly by Tommaso Vincitore from Bologna, or by the Florentine Pietro Forrigiano (1472–1522). In the ambulatory are several other tombstones, among them on the same side behind an attractive iron grille the wall tomb of Count Engelbrecht I (d. 1443), his son Jan of Nassau (d. 1475), and their spouses. Interesting also are the late Gothic pews, beautifully carved, with scenes satirising the clergy. Equally well carved is the pulpit c. 1600. In the baptistry off the right side aisle is a copper font made in 1540 in Mechelen by Joos de Backer from Antwerp. On the left, next to the organ, is a large wall painting of St Christopher (c. 1500), and in the north transept a wall painting of the Annunciation c. 1450.

Not so far to the north-east of the Grote Kerk stretches the Kasteelplein with an *equestrian statue of William III of Orange* (1921). On the west side of the square is the *Ethnographic Museum*. At the north end of the Kasteelplein stands the former **Kasteel**, mentioned as early as the 12th c., which was the family residence of the Counts of Nassau-Orange. The present building was built in the 16th–17th c. and now houses the *Royal Military Academy* (open on Saturdays for visitors). East of here extends the Valkenbergpark, at the north entrance of which stands, since 1905, a monument commemorating the 500th anniversary of the unification of the domain of Breda with the House of Nassau (1404). At the southern exit is the *Begijnhof*, built in the 17th c., which is still inhabited by the beguines (lay sisters).

SURROUNDINGS of Breda. – **Via Baarle-Nassau to Turnhout** (36 km – 22 miles). Leave Breda in a southerly direction by the Ginnekenstraat which at the edge of the town crosses the road leading from 's-Hertogenbosch to Bergen op Zoom and Middelburg. After 3 km (2 miles) you come to **Ginneken**, a large village now part of Breda, with the beautiful moated 17th c. Château Bouvigne. South-west extends an attractive wooded park, the Mastbos, with an area of over 500 hectares (1236 acres). 3 km (2 miles) beyond it, you reach a fork in the road. To the right runs the road to Lier, described below; the road to Turnhout then passes through the beautiful forest of *Ulvenhoutse* to **Baarle-Nassau**. 16 km (10 miles) further the neighbouring community, *Baarle-Hertog*, is a Belgian enclave within Dutch territory (Baerle-Duc, population 1500) which has been separated from Baarle-Nassau since the 15th c. 6 km (4 miles) further at the border station Baarle-Nassau, you cross the *Dutch/Belgian frontier* (customs) and after 8 km (5 miles) arrive at **Turnhout** (see page 91).

From Breda to Lier (58 km (36 miles); on Belgian territory; road No. 51). You follow first the road via *Ginneken* and *Ulvenhout*, described above, and after 6 km (4 miles) fork to the right. After the village of *Strijbeek* cross the *Dutch-Belgian border* (customs) into the flat sandy countryside of Kempen, partly covered with pine woods. After 12 km (7 miles) you reach **Hoogstraten**, a township with a population of 4500, with the Church of St Katherine in late-Gothic style (1524–46; tower 102 m (335 feet) high). In the choir is the *tomb of the founder Antoine de Lalaing (d. 1540) and his wife Elisabeth van Kuilenberg (d. 1555), by Jehan Mone (1527–9). It is one of the best Renaissance monuments in Belgium. Also interesting are the stained-glass windows (1528–41), the pews dating from the 15th–16th c, the pulpit of 1735 and the tomb of Count Leopold van Salm-Salm (1770). Next to the church stands the Town Hall, a small brick building copied from the original 16th c. structure which was destroyed in the Second World War. Nearby is the Baroque church of the beguines. East of the town on the banks of the Mark stands the Old Palace, a picturesque Baroque building (1525), now housing a penitentiary. – The road to Lier crosses the *Mark* after Hoogstraten, and a little further, the canal from Antwerp to Turnhout. 12 km (7 miles) further on, at **Oostmalle**, with a 16th c. church, you cross road No. 4 and the E3 leading from Antwerp via Turnhout to Tilburg and to Eindhoven respectively. Later the road crosses the *Albert Canal* and the highway from Antwerp to Liège: after 23 km (14 miles) comes **Lier** (see page 197).

Bruges/Brugge

Country: Belgium. – Province: West Flanders.
Altitude: 9 m (30 feet). – Population: 120,000.
Postal code: B-8000.
Telephone code: 0 50.
(i) **Dienst voor Toerisme,**
Markt 7;
tel. 33 07 11.

HOTELS. – *Holiday Inn*, Beoveriestraat 2, II, 128 r.; *Duc de Bourgogne*, Huidevettersplein 12, II, 10 r.; *Parkhotel*, Vrijkdagmarkt 6, III, 37 r.; *Bourgoensch Hof* (no rest.), Wollestraat 39, III, 12 r.; *Portinari*, Garenmarkt 15, III, 50 r.; *Bryghia* (no rest.), Vosterlingenplaats 4, III, 18 r.; *Europ* (no rest.), Augustijnenrei 18, III, 29 r.; *Jacobs* (no rest.), Baliestraat 1, III, 34 r.; *Grand Hôtel du Sablon*, Noordzandstraat 21, III, 47 r.; *De Pauw* (no rest.), St-Gilliskerkhof 8, III, 9 r.; *Comte de Flandre*, 't Zand 19, IV, 13 r.; *De Londres*, 't Zand 15, IV, 25 r.; *De Barge* (no rest.), Katelijnepoort, IV, 24 r.; *Lodewijk van Maele*, Malseweg 488, IV, 16 r.; *Central*, Markt 30, IV, 8 r.; *Princess*, Korte Zilverstraat 7, IV, 8 r.; *Rembrandt-Rubens* (no rest.), Walplaats 38, IV, 26 r.; *Fevery* (no rest.), Collaert Mansionstraat 3, IV, 12 r.; *Minnewater*, Minnewater 2c, IV, 10 r.; *Lybeer*, Korte Vulderstraat 31, IV, 26 r.; *St Christophe*, Nieuwe Gentweg 76, IV, 20 r.; *Du Singe d'Or*, 't Zand 18, IV, 19 r.; *Spinola*, Krom Genthof 1, IV, 35 r.; *Rome*, Zuidzandstraat 56, IV, 11 r.; *Normandie* (no rest.), Vrijdagmarkt 16, IV, 7 r.; *De Krakele*, St-Pieterskaai 71, IV, 15 r.; *De Sneeuwberg*, Hallestraat 2, V, 18 r.

Procession of the Holy Blood

YOUTH HOSTEL. – Baron Ruzettelaan 143, 208 b. – CAMP SITES: St Kruis, St Michiels and Loppem.

RESTAURANT. – *Weinebrugge*, outside the city to the south-east, Konig Albertlaan 242.

EVENTS. – *The Procession of the Holy Blood (every year on Ascension Day); *Festival of Flanders – International Music Days* (end of July–early August); *The Triennial Festival of Belgian Art* (every third year: summer 1983, etc.); *The Pageant of the Golden Tree* (every fifth year: 1985, etc.); *carillon concerts* (15 October–14 June, on Sunday, Wednesday, Saturday, 11.45 a.m.–12.30 p.m.; from 15 June to September, Monday, Wednesday, Saturday, 9–10 p.m., Sunday, 11.45 a.m.–12.30 p.m.

FLEA MARKET. – Sunday, 9 a.m.–1 p.m.

SPORTS and LEISURE. – Sailing and water-skiing on the Brugge-Damme Canal, in the Boudewijnpark and in Zeebrugge (Quay); rowing on the canals.

*Bruges (in Flemish Brugge), the old capital of Flanders, now capital of West Flanders, has been a bishopric since 1559. It lies on the little River Reye or Roya, 12 km (7 miles) south of the sea port of Zeebrugge, with which it is connected by the Boudewijn Canal. Other canals connect Bruges with Ostend, Nieuwpoort, Veurne, Ghent and Sluis.

Bruges with its many interesting old buildings and picturesque canals has preserved its medieval **townscape, the best of all Belgian cities, despite some restoration work and the destruction of the old city wall. This had to give way to the needs of traffic in the middle of the 19th c. and only four gates have been preserved. Industries include steel, cotton, furniture, brewing and the manufacture of yeast and gin, as well as the manufacture of precast concrete, paints, television sets and outboard motors. Lace making is also important. Next to industry the service sector plays an important part.

Bruges is the headquarters of the College of Europe, an Academy of Arts and a Chamber of Commerce and Industry. The city is also significant in commerce and tourism. The principal goods handled by its port (approximately 10 million tons), are crude oil (57%), coal, iron ore, general cargo, and fish.

HISTORY. – Bruges was mentioned as *Municipium Brugense* as early as the 7th c. The Norsemen who landed in the estuary of the Reye called it "Bruggja", which means "Mooring Place". The Margrave Balduin I (called the Iron Arm; d. *c.* 879), who was a prince of the Holy Roman Empire, founded a powerful dynasty of Flemish counts in Bruges. He was a son-in-law of Charles the Bald of France and he built his castle here. Later Robert the Friese (d. 1093) established his residence in this prosperous trading city. During the 12th–13th c., Bruges became one of the most important European merchant towns. It was then still connected to the North Sea by the sea inlet Zwin, into which flowed the Reye. As a capital of the "Flemish Hanse in London", Bruges controlled almost the entire English trade, especially the wool trade, which was important for the Belgian cloth industry. At the same time it was a commercial hub for the cities of the German Hanseatic League.

In the 14th c. Bruges reached the pinnacle of its prosperity. When Joanna of Navarre, the wife of Philip the Handsome of France, entered Bruges in the year 1301 and saw the pomp and sumptuous clothes of the women of Bruges, she indignantly exclaimed: "I thought I alone was Queen, but here I see hundreds of others around me." The Governor of Flanders appointed by Philip, Jacques de Châtillon, oppressed the guilds of Bruges to such an extent that the population of the city, led by Pieter de Coninck and Jan Breydel, rose and massacred the French ("The Bruges Matins," 1302). The victory over the French nobility achieved by the Flemish burghers in the same year at Kortrijk ("Battle of the Spurs"), secured the continuing independence and prosperity of the towns. However, the destructive competition between Bruges and Ghent deprived them of the full fruits of their victory. The decline of Bruges began in the 15th c., mainly due to the silting of the Zwin. But this did not become apparent for a considerable time owing to the resplendent appearance of the city under the Dukes of Burgundy, who had ruled Flanders since 1384. About the turn of the century, the more important merchants began to leave Bruges and settle in Antwerp, and the religious disturbances in the second half of the 16th c. completely destroyed the prosperity of the city.

Only in recent times has Bruges regained some of its importance, thanks to its industry and to lively tourism. Bruges is frequently mentioned by Chaucer and other early English writers. Later, Wordsworth praised its quiet streets, and Longfellow its belfry. Caxton was in Bruges some time after 1441, becoming acting governor of the Merchant Defenders in the Low Countries. Here he "practised and learned at great charge and dispense" the art of printing. The exiled Charles II established his court in Bruges in 1656. He was elected King of the Archers' Guild and in the same year he founded the Royal Regiment of Guards, thus making Bruges the birthplace of the Grenadier Guards.

Description of the City

Inner City

The main square and the central focus of traffic in Bruges is the ancient Markt in the middle of the inner city. Here stands the 1887 memorial of the Guild Masters *Jan Breydel* and *Pieter de Coninck* who led the uprising against the French. On the south side of the square are the *Halle, built in the 13th–14th c., a rectangle 18 m (59 feet) long and 43·5 m (143 feet) wide, with a *belfry of the 13th–15th c., 83 m (272 feet) high, which leans a little towards the south-east. In its picturesque courtyard is the entrance to the tower. There are 366 steps and from the top is a magnificent view of the city and its surroundings. Its carillon dates from 1743, has 47 bells, and is one of the largest and most beautiful in Belgium. Next to the entrance to the tower is the *Folklore Museum* which houses local antiquities.

The Town Hall in Bruges

View of the Belfry in Bruges

On the eastern side of the Markt stands the neo-Gothic building of the **Provincial Government** (*Provinciaal Hof*), which is the seat of the Provincial Administration of West Flanders. Adjacent to it on the south is the *Post Office*, on the third floor of which are the *Municipal Archives* (entrance No. 3 Breidelstraat). On the west side of the Markt, at the corner of St Amandstraat, is an attractive 15th c. brick building, the

Bouchoute House. Opposite is the *Cranenburg*, now completely renovated, where in 1488 the burghers of Bruges, incited by those of Ghent, held prisoner the then Romano-German King Maximilian (son of Emperor Frederick III) for eleven weeks until he acknowledged under oath the Estates as the ruling council and ordered the withdrawal of all foreign troops.

Towards the east of the Markt, through the short Breidelstraat, you reach the picturesque **Burg**, a square named after the Castle of the Counts. The castle was demolished in 1434 and was the oldest residence of the Counts of Flanders. On the left, at the corner of Breidelstraat, is the lovely *Landshuis* of 1622, the former Priory. Next to it, in the tree-lined northern part of the square, stands the monument (1887) to the painter Jan van Eyck. The former *Cathedral Church* of St Donatian or St Donaas, founded about 900 and demolished by the French in 1799, also stood here. Its foundations were excavated in 1955, and a model of the church is on display.

On the south side of the square stands the *Town Hall (*Stadhuis*), an elegant Gothic building dating from 1376–1420, its façade decorated with statues. In its large Gothic Hall is a beautiful vaulted timber ceiling, and murals (1895–1900) of A. and J. De Vriendt illustrating the history of Bruges. On the left of the Town Hall stands the former **Recorder's House** (*Oude Griffie*) built in 1535-7, now used as part of the Law Courts. Its richly gilded façade is adorned with

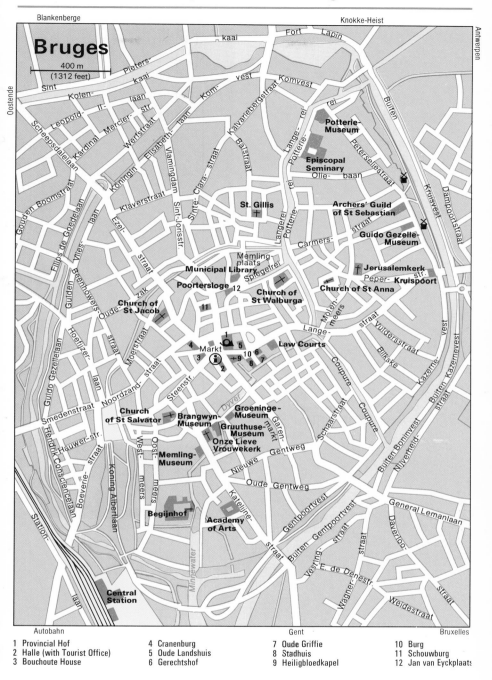

Bruges

400 m
(1312 feet)

Blankenberge

Knokke-Heist

Antwerpen

Oostende

Fort Lapin

Kaai

Pieters-kaai

Sint

Kolen-laan

Leopold-II-laan

Scheepsdalelaan

Kardinaal Mercier-str.

Wertstraat

Elisabeth-laan

Vlamingdam

Koningin

Klaverstraat

Sinte-Clara-straat

Sint-Jorisstr.

Ezel

Vlies

Filip de Goedelaan

Gouden Boomstraat

Beenhouwers-

Oude Zak

Gulden

Vest

straat

Moerstraat

Hoefizer-laan

Guido Gezellelaan

Smedenstraat

Noordzand-straat

Steenstr.

Hauwer-str.

Hendrik Consciencelaan

Boeverie-

West

Oost

meers

Koning Albertlaan

Station-laan

vest

Komvest

Kalvariebergstraat

Kom-laan

Balstraat

Langerei

Potterie

Peterseliestraat

Krusvest

Dampoortstraat

rei

Carmers-

Langerei

Potterie

Peper-str.

straat

Kruispoort

Molen-meers

Lange-straat

Yuldersstraat

Blikste

Coupure

Scharsstraat

Coupure

Buten-Kazernevest

vest

Kazerne-straat

Buten Boninvest

Nijverheid-

Buiten Boninvest

General Lemanlaan

Daverloo-

straat

Gentpoortvest

Buiten Gentpoortstraat

Vesting-straat

E. de Denestr.

Wagner-straat

straat

Weidestraat

Potterie-Museum

Episcopal Seminary
Olie-baan

St. Gillis

Archers' Guild of St Sebastian

Guido Gezelle-Museum

Memling-plaats

Municipal Library
Spiegelrei

Poortersloge 12

Church of St Jacob 11

Church of St Walburga

Jerusalemkerk

Church of St Anna

1
4 **Markt** 5
3 +9 10 6
2 8 7

Law Courts

Church of St Salvator

Brangwyn-Museum

Groeninge-Museum

Gruuthuse-Museum

Onze Lieve Vrouwekerk

Memling-Museum

Dyver

Garen-markt

Gentweg

Nieuwe

Oude Gentweg

Kateljine-straat

Begijnhof

Academy of Arts

Minnewater

Central Station

Autobahn

Gent

Bruxelles

1 Provincial Hof	4 Cranenburg	7 Oude Griffie	10 Burg	
2 Halle (with Tourist Office)	5 Oude Landshuis	8 Stadhuis	11 Schouwburg	
3 Bouchoute House	6 Gerechtshof	9 Heiligbloedkapel	12 Jan van Eyckplaats	

statues. A picturesque vaulted passage leads across the Reye to Huidenvetters-plaats and Steenbouwersdijk. Next to the Oude Griffie are the **Law Courts** built in 1722–7 on the site of the so-called Free Office of Bruges, the town hall of the free peasantry. The back of the Law Courts dates from the 16th c. In the Aldermen's Hall ("Vierschaar") is a superb *chimney-piece from the Free Office, designed in 1529 by the painter Lanceloot Blondeel

and executed by Guyot de Beaugrant in black marble. On it are the Legend of Suzanna in alabaster, and statues carved in wood of the Emperor Charles V and his grandparents. There are also medallions of his parents. In the southern corner of the Burg to the right of the Town Hall, stands the two-storey building of the ***Chapel of the Holy Blood** (*Heilig-bloedkapel*). According to tradition the name commemorates the gift to the city in

1150 of a few drops of Christ's blood, which had been brought from the Holy Land by Dietrich of Alsace, Count of Flanders. The Lower Church dates from about 1150. The Upper Church, where the Holy Blood is shown in one of the side chapels (closed on Wednesday afternoon), was restored in the 15th c. Next to the Upper Church is a small Museum with ecclesiastical antiquities, precious reliquaries of 1614–17 and several paintings from the 15th–16th c.

Southern Parts of the City

From the passage between the Town Hall and the Oude Griffie, the **City Canal** or **Rei** can be reached (beautiful view over the canal). Here are the docks for the motor boats which operate the *canal cruises. The cruises run during the day, and from June to September in the evening, when the city is floodlit and offers some spectacular views. The duration of the cruise is approximately 45 minutes. On the other side of the *Blindenezelbrug* to the left, are the Steenhowersdijk and the Groene Rei with picturesque views of the ancient buildings of the inner city, especially of the belfry and the back of the Law Courts. To the right of the Blindenezelbrug is the Huidenvettersplaats, in which stands the former *Tanners Guildhall* of 1630. Behind it to the right, the Rozenhoedkaai leads to the beautiful tree-lined **Dyver**. At its beginning on the right is the *bridge of St John of Nepomuk*, from which the Markt can be reached in a north-westerly direction through the Wollestraat.

Some 200 m (656 feet) south-west on the left of the Dyver is the entrance to the ****Groeninge Museum** (*Municipal Museum*), which is set back off the street. It houses an excellent collection of old Flemish paintings as well as a modern gallery and a collection of Bruges townscapes. Among the most important paintings of the old Flemish period, the following should not be missed: Jan van Eyck, "Madonna with the Donor, Canon van der Paele" (1436) and a portrait of van Eyck's wife (1439); Petrus Christus, "Portrait of a Lady Donor"; Hugo van der Goes, "Death of the Virgin"; Hans Memling, "Triptych of St Christopher" (1484) and an altar panel of the Annunciation;

"Virgin and Child" by Michelangelo in Bruges

Gerard David, "The Judgment of Cambyses", and a triptych with the "Baptism of Christ"; Pieter Pourbus, "Portrait of Jan Fernaguut and his Wife" from 1551; Hieronymus Bosch, "Last Judgment"; an unknown master of the 15th c., "The Legend of St Ursula" (side panels of a triptych).

At the south-west end of the Dyver a quaint little passage leads to the Groeninge-Museum. Next to it is the former **Gruuthuse Palace**, an attractive group of buildings from the 15th c. in which King Edward IV of England took refuge when he was exiled in 1471. On summer evenings Son-et-Lumière performances take place in its courtyard. Inside is the *Gruuthuse Museum* with extensive collections of antiquities and applied arts. Especially valuable are the collection of lace, the prehistoric collection, and the lapidary collection. In an annex of the 18th c. is the *Brangwyn Museum*, named after the British painter Brangwyn (1867–1956), whose works are shown here.

Immediately behind the Gruuthuse Palace stands the *Church of Our Lady (Onze-Lieve-Vrouwekerk)*, built in the 12th–13th c. In the 14th–15th c., side aisles and a series of chapels were added together with the tower, 122 m (400 feet) in height. Inside the church are numerous works of art, among them Michelangelo's **Virgin and Child (1503–4). This stands on the altar of a chapel at the end of the outer right aisle at the place where Dürer admired it in 1521. In a chapel in the ambulatory on the right are the *Tombs of Charles the Bold of Burgundy (d. 1477) and his daughter Mary of Burgundy, the consort of the future Emperor Maximilian. She died in 1482, aged 25, after a fall from a horse. The tombs date from 1559 and 1495–1502 respectively. The tomb of Mary is still in Gothic style and is more significant as a work of art. The life-sized effigies of father and daughter in gilded copper lie on black sarcophagi. In the same chapel are also several important paintings, among them A. Isenbrants' *"Mater Dolorosa" of 1530.

To the west, opposite the Church of Our Lady, stands the **Hospital of St John** (*Sint Janshospitaal*), which was founded in the 12th c. Left of the entrance in Mariastraat is a walled-in gate with interesting sculptures from the 13th c. In one of the former hospital wards is the **Memling Museum** displaying the paintings by Hans Memling (*c.* 1413–94), considered to be gems of old Flemish art. Especially worth noting is the shrine of St Ursula (1489), one of the most important works of the artist, with six paintings illustrating the Legend of the Saint. There is also the equally famous St John's Altar of 1479 with the "Mystic Marriage of St Catherine", and a diptych, dating from 1487, of the "Virgin with an Apple"; in the other wing is an impressive portrait of the donor. There are also paintings by other old Flemish masters, as well as objects of applied arts. Well worth seeing is also the ancient *dispensary* of the hospital.

To the south of St John's Hospital are several picturesque lanes where in summer lacemakers sit and work in front of their houses. Through these lanes the Wijngaardplaats can be reached. On the right a bridge, from which there is a pleasant view, leads to the entrance into the 13th c. *Begijnhof, still inhabited by Benedictine Sisters. Its white cottages surround a tree-lined courtyard. On the left between the entrance gate and the church, which was founded in 1245 and restored in 1605, is a small *Museum* where lace can be bought and which gives a good impression of the life of the beguines.

South of the Begijnhof extends the *Minnewater ("Sea of Love"), the former inner dock of the harbour, dating from the 13th c., which has a Gothic lockhouse. The best view is from the bridge on the shorter north side. On the south side of the bridge, to the right, a 1398 tower has been preserved. From here interesting walks can be taken along the former moat; to the east by the Katelijne and Gentpoortvest to the massive 15th c. *Gentpoort*; to the west by the Begijnenvest which runs not far north of the *Central Station* (built in 1939, paintings in the hall by René de Pauw), and its continuation the Hendrik Consciencelaan to the *Smedenpoort* (1368). East from the Smedenpoort through the Smedenstraat, you reach the old Vrijdagmarkt (Friday Market) and the adjacent Square 't Zand; further on you come through Zuidzandstraat to the Church of St Salvator. You can return to the Markt in a north-easterly direction, via the Steenstraat with beautiful gabled houses of the 16th and 17th c.

From the Church of Our Lady, the **Church of St Salvator** can be reached in a north-westerly direction via the short Greetstraat. It has been the Cathedral church since 1834, and is the oldest parish church in the city. It was originally erected in the 10th c. and in its present form dates partly from the 12th–13th c., and partly from the 14th–16th c. Its fortress-like western tower was built in several stages. The lower part is Romanesque (1116–27); it was continued in brick in 1183–1228 and a further part added in the 15th c. It was then rebuilt in neo-Romanesque style in 1844–6, and received its central spire in 1871.

The *INTERIOR of the church, which is 101 m (331 feet) long, has simple harmonious proportions and contains several outstanding works of art. The best of them can be seen in the *Church Museum, the entrance to which is in the south transept. In the ambulatory are six beautiful memorial brasses of the 14th–16th c. In the Museum is a good collection of old Flemish paintings by Dirk Bouts, Pieter Pourbus and others.

Northern Parts of the City

From the north-western corner of the Markt you come via the Egg Market and the adjacent St Jacobstraat, to the Church of St Jacob, built in the 13th–15th c. Inside are numerous paintings by local artists from the 16th–17th c. Further to the north-west, at the end of the Ezelstraat stands the *Enzelpoort*, originally built in the 14th c., beyond which extend new city districts.

The Vlamingstraat, one of the main shopping streets of the city, starts in the north-eastern corner of the Markt. In the middle part, beyond the *Schouwburg* (Municipal Theatre, 1868), stands the old *Natiehuis van Genua* (the House of the Genoese merchants) of 1399. Opposite and a short way to the east, the Academiestraat leads to the Jan van Eyckplaats. On the right corner, the 14th c. *Poortersloge* now houses the State Archives. On the north side of the square, in the former Customs' House (1477) is the Municipal Library with 100,000 books and 600 manuscripts, among them several missals from the 13th–14th c.

Not far north of Van Eyck Square lies the Hans Memlingplaats, with a statue of the painter Hans Memling (1871). On the north side of the square stands the *Convent of the Black Sisters*, founded in 1561, and now a hospital. In the tiny Oosterlingenplaats adjacent to the north, stands a house built in 1478 which was formerly the seat of the German Hanse. From here you come to the *Torenbrug* with a pleasant view to the left over the Augustijnenrei. Crossing the canal by the bridge, the road continues by Gouden Handstraat and St Gilliskerkstraat as far as the *Church of St Gillis*, which dates from the 13th and 15th c. From here you follow the Lange Rei eastward, cross the canal not far to the north-east and continue on its right bank along the Potterierei. Beyond the next bridge on the right is the Episcopal Seminary, now occupying the premises of the former *Abbey Terduinen* which was transferred to Bruges in 1623. Further north is the Hospice De Potterie, founded in 1276, with a church dating from the 14th and 16th c. Inside the present-day Hospice is the *Potterie Museum*, which contains a substantial collection of ecclesiastical gold and silverware, furniture, tapestries and paintings.

On the east side of the Potterie Museum the Peterseliestraat leads to the north-east districts of Bruges which were reconstructed in 1970. Two old *windmills* are still standing on the Kruisvest; there is a beautiful view over the spires of the city and the nearby Kruispoort. Turn right into Carmersstraat and on the left at No. 164 is the picturesque *House of the Archers' Guild of St Sebastian*, built in 1573. There is a collection of portraits on the ground floor. No. 85 on the right is the *English Nunnery* (girls' school), with a beautiful domed church (1736–9). It is not open to visitors. Further on at No. 54 Rolweg is the house where the Flemish poet and priest, *Guido Gezelle* was born (1830–99). It is now a museum. At the end of the Kruisvest stands the stately Kruispoort, built in the 14th–15th c. and now a *history museum*.

West from the Kruispoort, the Peperstraat leads to the late Gothic Jerusalemkerk founded in 1428, with stained glass from the 15th–16th c. and an interesting crypt. Nearby, the *Church of St Anna*, built in the 16th–17th c., is rich in Baroque decoration. To the west, beyond the canal, is the *Church of St Walburga*, formerly a Jesuit church, dating from 1619–42. From here going south-west via Ridders-, St Walburga- and Philipstockstraat, you can return to the Markt.

SURROUNDINGS of Bruges. There is a worthwhile drive of 7 km (4 miles) north-east along the eastern side of the Brugge-Sluis Canal to the little old town of Damme (see p. 131).

A number of excellent roads connect Bruges with the North Sea resorts. Zeebrugge (16 km (10 miles) north); Knokke-Heist (17 km (11 miles) north-east, see p. 184); Blankenberge (14 km (9 miles) north-west, see p. 102); Wenduine (16 km (10 miles) north-west); De Haan (17 km (11 miles) north-west); and Ostend (24 km (15 miles) west, see p. 229).

Brussels/ Bruxelles/Brussel

Country: Belgium. – Province: Brabant.
Altitude: 15–100 m (49–328 feet).
Population: 1,055,000.
Postal code: B-1000 to 1200.
Telephone code: 02.

(i) **Commissariat-Général au Tourisme/ Commissariaat-Generaal voor Toerisme,** Rue du Marché aux Herbes/Grasmarkt 61; tel. 6 32 45.

Tourisme Information Bruxelles, Rue du Marché aux Herbes/Grasmarkt 61; tel. 5 13 89 40.

DIPLOMATIC REPRESENTATIONS: Embassies: *Australia*, 52 Avenue des Arts; *Canada*, 6B Rue de Loxum; *New Zealand*, 47–48 Boulevard du Régent; *United Kingdom*, Britannia House, 28 Rue Joseph II; *USA*, 27 Boulevard du Régent; *Republic of Ireland*, 19 Rue du Luxembourg.

AIRPORT. – The **Airport**, *Brussels National*, is connected to the city by a separate railway line (journey takes about 15 minutes).

Taxi stands are at the railway stations and in all main squares, near theatres, concert halls and hospitals.

HOTELS. – IN THE UPPER TOWN: **Président-Centre* (no rest.), Rue Royale 160, 1, 73 r.; **Astoria*, Rue Royale 103, 1, 112 r.; **Westbury*, Rue Cardinal Mercier 6, II, 252 r.; *International* (no rest.), Rue Royale 344, III, 23 r.; *Du Congrès* (no rest.), Rue de Congrès 42, IV, 38 r.; *Résidence du Jardin Botanique*, Rue Royale 171, IV, 33 r.; *Ballon Nord* (no rest.), Rue de Brabant 24, V, 16 r.

IN THE LOWER TOWN. – Near the Gare du Nord: **Hyatt Regency Brussels*, Rue Royale 250, L, 325 r.; **Brussels Sheraton*, Place Rogier 3, L, 474 r.; **Palace* (no rest.), Place Rogier 22, I, 356 r.; *Siru*, Rue des Croisades 2, III, 103 r.; *Galaxy* (no rest.), Vooruit- gangstraat 7, III, 36 r.; *Des Colonies*, Rue des Croisades 8–10, III, 100 r.; *Albert 1er et Terminus*, Place Rogier 20, IV, 253 r.; *Départ Nord*, Rue du Progrès 15, V, 19 r.; *Le Renard* (no rest.), Rue du Progrès 25, V, 18 r.

ON THE INNER BOULEVARDS AND IN THE OLD TOWN: **Amigo*, Rue de l'Amigo 1–3, L, 183 r.; **Atlanta*, Boulevard A. Max 7, I, 244 r.; **Royal Windsor*, Rue Duquesnoy 5–7, I, 264 r.; **Métropole*, Place de Brouckère 31, I, 339 r.; *Bedford*, Rue du Midi 135, II, 220 r.; *Président-Nord* (no rest.), Boulevard A. Max 107, II, 63 r.; *Plaza*, Boulevard A. Max 118–126, II, 230 r.; *Queen Anne* (no rest.), Boulevard E. Jacqmain 110, III, 57 r.; *Elysée* (no rest.), Rue de La Montagne 4, III, 18 r.; *Grand Hôtel G. Scheers*, Boulevard A. Max 132–142, III, 62 r.; *Mirabeau* (no rest.), Place Fontainas 18–20, III, 29 r.; *Windsor*, Place Rouppe 13, IV, 25 r.; *Central* (no rest.), Rue A. Orts 3, IV, 150 r.; *Vendôme* (no rest.), Boulevard A. Max 98, IV, 38 r.; *St James* (no rest.), Rue de la Concorde 40, IV, 28 r.; *Anspach* (no rest.), Boulevard Anspach 48, IV, 39 r.; *A la Grande Cloche*, Place Rouppe 10, IV, 45 r.; *Aux Arcades* (no rest.), Rue des Bouchers 36, IV, 17 r.; *Auberge Autrichienne* (no rest.), Avenue de Stalin- grad 122, IV, 23 r.; *Du Grand Colombier*, Rue du Colombier 10, IV, 15 r.; *Le Béarn* (no rest.), Rue des Bouchers 37, V, 17 r.

NEAR THE GARE DU MIDI: *De France* (no rest.), Boulevard Jamar 21, III, 27 r.; *Résidence Jamar* (no rest.), Boulevard Jamar 1, IV, 28 r.; *Les Acacias*, Avenue Fonsny 6, IV, 43 r.; *Du Merlo*, Avenue Fonsny 2, V, 19 r.

NEAR AVENUE LOUISE: **Brussels Hilton*, Boulevard de Waterloo 38, L, 373 r., roof-garden restaurant En Plein Ciel, 27th floor; **Ramada Brussels*, Chausée de Charleroi 38, L, 20 r.; **Mayfair*, Avenue Louise 381, L, 95 r.; *Brussels Hôtel Résidence*, Avenue Louise 319, II, 46 r.; *Concorde Louise*, Rue de la Concorde 59, IV, 26 r.; *Richmond Résidence*, Rue de la Concorde 21, IV, 26 r.; *Astor*, Rue Capitaine Crespel 4, IV, 13 r.

NEAR THE PALAIS DU CINQUANTENAIRE: *Park Hotel*, Avenue de l'Yser 21, I, 46 r.; *Léopold III* (no rest.), Square Joséphine-Charlotte 11, IV, 15 r.

IN THE SOUTH AND WEST OF THE CITY: *Du Midi*, Boulevard du Midi 19, IV, 9 r.; *King Charles Résidence*, Chaussée de Charleroi 22, IV, 20 r.; *Stella*, Avenue W. Churchill 8, V, 11 r.

IN THE EAST OF THE CITY: *Plasky*, Avenue E. Plasky 212, III 30 r.; *Résidence Acacias*, Rue Marie-Thérèse 41, IV, 27 r.; *Lambeau*, Avenue Lambeau 150, IV, 12 r.

NEAR LUXEMBOURG STATION *Grand Veneur*, Rue du Luxembourg 66, IV, 15 r.; *Du Grand Laboureur* (no rest.), Place du Luxembourg 6, V, 13 r.

BY THE AIRPORT (10 km (6 miles) north-east, in Diegem): **Holiday Inn*, Holidaystraat, I, 288 r.; *Novotel Brussels Airport*, III, 162 r.

Further numerous BOARDING HOUSES, mostly in the Upper Town near the Boulevards. – YOUTH HOSTELS: Poststraat 911, 240 b.; Centeurope, Rue Verte 124, 216 b.; *Hôtel de Jeunes*, Rue des Etudiants 14, 75 b. – CAMP SITE: Huizingen.

RESTAURANTS. – Brussels restaurants are plentiful and well known for their excellent and varied cuisine. Some of the best around the Grand' Place (especially in the Rue Grétry and the Fish Market, St Catherine), hide their proficiency in the culinary arts behind an unpretentious façade.

IN THE CITY: **Aux Armes de Bruxelles*, Rue des Bouchers 13; **Le Londres*, Rue de l'Écuyer 23; **Maison du Cygne*, Grand' Place 9; *Chez Léon*, Rue Dominicains 2; *Ravenstein*, Rue Ravenstein 1; *Comme Chez Soi*, Place Rouppe 23; *Carlton*, Boulevard de Waterloo 28–29; *Filet de Bœuf*, Rue Harengs 8; *En Provence*, Place du Petit Sablons 1; *Bernard*, Rue de Namur 93; *Eperon d'Or*, Rue des Eperonniers 8; *Au Bon Vieux Temps*, Impasse St Nicholas 4; *Couronne*, Grand' Place 28; *La Tête d'Or*, Rue de la Tête d'Or 9. IN THE SUBURBS: **Villa Lorraine*, Chaussée de la Hulpe 28; *Prince d'Orange*, in Uccle; *Ancienne Barrière*, Chaussée de Charleroi 172, in St- Gilles; *Chez Marcel*, Rue Wayez 84, in Anderlecht; *Parc Savoy*, Place Marie-Jose 9, im Südosten; *Moulin de Lindekernale*, Avenue Debecker 6, in Woluwé-St- Lambert.

CAFÉS are numerous in Brussels, especially on the Inner Boulevards, in the neighbourhood of the Opera, the Stock Exchange, and the Porte de Namur.

EVENTS. – The *Cultural Festival* ("Europalia", end of September/October); *Brussels Commercial Fair* (in spring in the Palais du Centenaire); *Son et Lumière* in the Grand' Place (Monday, Tuesday, Thursday and

Sunday, from 2 April–13 May at 9.30 p.m. and 10.30 p.m.; from 14 May–31 July at 10.30 p.m.; from 1 August–30 September at 9.30 p.m. and 10.30 p.m.); *Ommegang* (traditional entertainment performed every year in July); Concerts of the Festivals of Flanders and Wallonia as well as the Music Competition "Concours Reine Elisabeth"; *Brussels Motor Show* (January/February).

MARKETS. – *Bird Market* on the Grand' Place (every Sunday morning); *Flower Market*, Grand' Place (every Sunday morning); *Antiques and Old Books* on the Place du Grand-Sablon (Saturday 10 a.m.–6 p.m., Sunday 10 a.m.–1 p.m.); *Flea Market* (Vieux Marché), Place du Jeu de Balle (daily 9 a.m.–1 p.m.); *Fruit and Vegetable Market*, Place St Catherine; *Horse Market,* Place de la Vaillance, Anderlecht (every Friday morning); *"Marché du Midi"* by the Gare du Midi (every Sunday morning – clothing and a wide range of exotic foods); *Kermesse* (traditional fair) on Boulevard du Midi (from 21 July, the National Day (commemorating the accession of King Leopold I, 1831), until approximately 20 August).

The Flea Market, Brussels

Brussels, the capital of Belgium (Flemish, Brussel; French, Bruxelles), is the seat of the Government and, together with Mechelen, the seat of the Archbishop; it is also the capital of the province of Brabant and the headquarters of the European Communities, NATO, and numerous other international organisations. It lies at the geographical midpoint of the country where the last hills of the valley of the Senne, a tributary of the Schelde, merge into the Flemish plain.

The actual city area is enclosed by a pentagon of boulevards on the site of the former fortifications. It is divided into the Lower Town, intersected by several branches of the Senne now vaulted over or filled in, and the smaller Upper Town, set on the crest of the hills to the east of it, as well as several districts adjacent in the east and north. In 1921 some other communities were incorporated into Brussels, including Laeken where the Royal residence is located, Neder-Over-Heembeek and Haren. Around the Inner City are eighteen suburbs which are connected to it but have an independent administration. Nowhere in Belgium do the Flemish and the Walloons come so close to each other as in Brussels, where the linguistic frontier runs only a few miles south of the city. Officially, Brussels is bilingual, but in the central section French predominates, whereas most of the suburbs are Flemish.

The townscape of Brussels is essentially modern, especially since considerable reconstruction was undertaken in the middle of the city at the beginning of the 20th c. The road connections between the Lower and Upper Town have been levelled and completely modified, and even today, important alterations to the street system, especially numerous underpasses, are still being built. The character of the old Brabant capital has thus substantially changed, and has now only been preserved in a few isolated places. The underground railway network begun in 1969 is being currently extended.

Brussels is the important cultural and educational capital of Belgium, with its universities, technical colleges, the Royal Academy, many other schools and cultural institutions. The fact that it is situated at the cross-roads of several main commercial arteries of Western Europe and that it is the headquarters of the country's most important financial institutions, make it the economic hub of the country. Labour-intensive industries predominate, including the manufacture of Brussels lace, of wool, cotton and silk garments, and of carpets and porcelain. There are also engineering, motor and chemical industries, as well as breweries. More important than industry is the business and service sector, where – especially since the city was linked to the sea by the Willebroek Canal – more than 60% of the workforce is employed. Also important is the Canal of Charleroi, linking Brussels with the coal-mining area of southern Belgium.

HISTORY. – The founding of Brussels is attributed, according to legend, to St Gaugerich or St Géry, the

Bishop of Cambrai, who is believed to have brought Christianity to Belgium. He is supposed to have founded the earliest settlement, which was named after him, about 580 on an island in the Senne. In the Chronicles of the 10th c. the settlement is named as *Bruocsella* (from Bruoc=Break, and Sele=settlement?). In 977 Duke Charles of Lower Lotharingia built a stronghold on the Island of St Géry. In the 11th c. the warlike Counts of Louvain, the future Dukes of Brabant, settled on the hill of Coudenberg. The town, being on the important commercial highway midway between Bruges and Cologne, developed rapidly, and by 1455 already had a population of 43,500. The fortifications, which were extended in 1357–79 and reinforced in 1530, enclosed by that time the entire area within the present-day Boulevards. These fortifications remained in existence until the 19th c.

The Dukes of Burgundy on occasion held their court in Brussels and attracted many members of the French nobility. The French language became, therefore, fashionable and was adopted by the nobles from the Low Countries. When the country was acquired by the Habsburgs in 1477, and especially in the reign of Charles V, a glittering court life developed in Brussels. Mary of Hungary moved in 1546 from Mechelen to the Coudenberg, and Philip II transferred there the Governor Generalship under Margaret of Parma. In 1566 the first rebellion of the Dutch against the Spanish domination started in Brussels, but in spite of this, after much fighting, the city was held by the Spanish. During the wars of Louis XIV it suffered much damage when Marshall Villeroi burned down the Lower Town in 1695. It suffered also intermittently at the beginning of the 18th c. because of its opposition to the Austrians, but peace came under Maria Theresa and her Governor, Prince Charles of Lorraine (1744–80), when the population reached 74,000. After the storms of the revolutionary period and the French occupation, a new period of expansion began; first slowly during the union of the country with the Netherlands, and then much faster after the revolution of 1830 when Brussels became the capital of the new Kingdom of Belgium.

Places of Interest

Albert I Royal Library,
4 Bd de l'Empereur,
Mont des Arts,
Brussels.
Weekdays.

Atomium,
Heysel,
Laeken.
9.30 a.m.–5.30 p.m.
Panorama 9.30 a.m.–8.30 p.m. (1 May–31 August).

Breughel's House,
132 Rue Haute,
Brussels.
2–6 p.m. (Tuesday–Friday).

Centre Public d'Aide Sociale,
Saint Pierre Hospital,
298a Rue Haute,
Brussels.
2–5 p.m. on Wednesdays.

Charlier Museum,
16 Ave des Arts,
Saint-Josse.
9.30 a.m.–12.30 p.m. (Sundays).
By appointment other days.

Children's Museum,
32 Rue Tenbosch,
Ixelles.
Weekdays, by appointment, 9.30–11.30 a.m. and 1.30–3.30 p.m. Wednesday, Saturday, Sunday 2.30–5 p.m.

Chinese Pavilion,
44 Ave Van Praet,
Brussels (Laeken).
9.30 a.m.–12.30 p.m. and 1.30–4.50 p.m.
Closed Mondays.

Cinema Museum,
9 Rue Baron Horta,
Brussels.
5.30–10.30 p.m.

Communal Museum of the City of Brussels,
Grand' Place (1 Rue du Poivre),
Brussels.
10 a.m.–noon and 1–5 p.m. (from 1 April–30 September);
10 a.m.–noon and 1–4 p.m. (from 1 September–31 March)
Weekends and holidays 10 a.m.–noon.

Communal Museum of Woluwe-Saint-Lambert,
40 Rue de la Charette,
Woluwe-Saint-Lambert.
2–4 p.m.
(Wednesday, Saturday, 1st and 3rd Sunday of each month)
2–6 p.m.

Constantine Meunier Museum,
59 Rue de l'Abbaye,
Ixelles.
9 a.m.–noon and 2–5 p.m.
Sundays 9.30 a.m.–12.30 p.m. (closed Tuesday and Thursday).

Costume and Lace Museum,
4–6 Rue de la Violette,
Brussels.
10 a.m.–noon and 1–5 p.m. (1 April–30 September).
10 a.m.–noon and 1–4 p.m. (from 1 October–31 March).
Weekends and public holidays 10 a.m.–noon.

Design Centre,
51 Galerie Ravenstein,
Brussels.
10 a.m.–6 p.m.
Saturday 10 a.m.–1 p.m. and 2–6 p.m.

Erasmus's House,
31 Rue du Chapitre,
Anderlecht.
10 a.m.–noon and 2–5 p.m. (closed Tuesdays and Fridays except by appointment).

Exotarium of Brussels,
Manhattan Centre,
Place Rogier, St-Josse.
2–6 p.m.
Saturday 10 a.m.–7 p.m.
Sunday 10 a.m.–6 p.m.

Horta Museum,
25 Rue Americaine,
Saint-Gilles.
2–5.30 p.m. (closed Mondays).

Hôtel de Ville,
Grand' Place,
Brussels.
9 a.m.–4.30 p.m. (from 1 April–30 September).
9 a.m.–3.30 p.m. (from 1 October–31 March).
Weekends and holidays 10–11.30 a.m.

Institut Royal des Sciences Naturelles de Belgique,
31 Rue Vautier,
Ixelles.
9.30 a.m.–12.30 p.m. and 2–5 p.m. (1 March–30 September).
9.30 a.m.–12.30 p.m. and 2–4 p.m (1 October–28 February).
Closed Fridays.

Instrument Museum of the Royal School of Music,
17 Petit Sablon and 37 Grand Sablon,
Brussels.
Petit Sablon: 2.30–4.30 p.m. (Tuesday, Thursday, Saturday).
5–7 p.m. (Wednesday).
10.30 a.m.–12.30 p.m. (Sunday).

International Museum of the Press (Mondaneum),
696 Chaussée de Louvain,
Schaerbeek.
9 a.m.–noon and 2–5 p.m. (weekdays).

Lemonnier Camille Museum,
(House of the Writers),
150 Ch. de Wavre,
Ixelles.
1–3 p.m. on Wednesdays and by appointment.

Locks Museum,
70 Rue des Bouchers,
Brussels.
7 a.m.–8 p.m. (Monday–Friday).

Musée Bruxellois de la Gueuze,
Brasserie Cantillon,
56 Rue Gheude,
Anderlecht.
Wednesday 1–5 p.m.
Saturday 10 a.m.–5 p.m.

Musée de Dynastie,
21 Rue Brederode,
Brussels.
2–5 p.m. (Wednesday and Saturday).
10 a.m.–noon and 2–5 p.m. (Sundays and public holidays).

Musée des Beaux-Arts d'Ixelles,
71 Rue J. Van Volseem,
Ixelles.
1–7.30 p.m.
Saturday 10 a.m.–5 p.m.
Sunday 10 a.m.–1 p.m.

Musées Royaux des Beaux Arts,
3 Rue de la Régence,
Brussels.
10 a.m.–noon and 1–4.45 p.m. (17th, 18th, 19th c.).
10 a.m.–1 p.m. and 2–5 p.m. (15th–16th c.).

Museum of Air and Space,
Parc du Cinquantenaire,
Brussels.
9.30 a.m.–noon and 1.15–4.45 p.m.

Museum of Belgian Railways,
North Station,
Rue du Progrès,
Saint-Josse.
9 a.m.–5 p.m. (weekdays).

Museum of Private Brewery,
10 Grand' Place,
Brussels.
10 a.m.–noon and 2–5 p.m.
Saturday 10 a.m.–noon.

Museum of Carriages,
Parc du Cinquantenaire.
Temporarily closed.

Museum of Modern Art,
1 Place Royale and 3 Rue de la Régence,
Brussels.

Museum of Porte de Hal,
Bd de Waterloo,
Brussels.
Temporarily closed.

Museum of Resistance,
14 Rue Van Linth,
Anderlecht.
Weekdays and holidays – only by appointment.

Museum of Spectacles,
33 Rue Royale,
Brussels.
9 a.m.–6 p.m. weekdays.

Museum of the Hotel de Belle-Vue,
7 Place des Palais,
Brussels.
10 a.m.–4.45 p.m.

National Botanical Gardens,
Palais des Plants,
236 Rue Royale,
Schaerbeek.
Domaine de Bouchout,
8 Brusselsestwg,
1860 Meise.
Palais des Plants: 2–5 p.m. from Easter to end of October; Sundays and holidays 2–6 p.m.
Park: every day from 9 a.m. to sunset.

Planetarium,
10 Ave de Bouchout,
In French: Wednesday, 2–3.30 p.m.; Thursday 10.30 a.m. and 2 p.m.; Friday 10.30 a.m.
In Dutch: Tuesday and Wednesday 2 p.m.; Thursday 10.30 a.m.

Post and Communications Museum,
40 Place du Grand Sablon,
Brussels.
10 a.m.–4 p.m. (Tuesday–Saturday).
10 a.m.–12.30 p.m. (Sundays and holidays).

Royal Museum of Army and Military History,
3 Parc du Cinquantenaire,
Etterbeek.
9.30 a.m.–noon and 1.15–4.45 p.m.
Weekends and public holidays 9.30 a.m.–4 p.m.

Royal Museum of Art and History,
50 Parc du Cinquantenaire,
Etterbeek.
9.30 a.m.–12.25 p.m. and 1.30–4.50 p.m.
Weekends 9.30 a.m.–3.30 p.m.

Schott Museum,
27 Rue du Chêne,
Brussels.
2–5 p.m. (Tuesday and Thursday).

Tram Museum,
184 Ninovesestwg,
1750 Schepdaal.
2–6 p.m. (weekends and holidays from Easter to 30 September).

Van Buuren Museum,
41 Ave Leo Errera,
Uccle.
2–4 p.m. (Mondays except public holidays).
Other days by appointment.

Wardrobe of Manneken-Pis,
King's House,
Grand' Place,
Brussels.
10 a.m.–noon and 1–5 p.m. (1 April–30 September).
10 a.m.–noon and 1–4 p.m. (1 October–31 March).
Weekends and holidays 10 a.m.–noon.

Wiertz Museum,
62 Rue Vautier,
Ixelles.
10 a.m.–5 p.m. (16 February–15 November).
10 a.m.–4 p.m. (16 November–15 February).
Weekends 10 a.m.–noon and 1–5 p.m.
Closed Mondays.

Description of the City

The Market Place and the North-eastern Parts of the Lower Town

Town Hall, Brussels

In the middle of the OLD TOWN is the ****Grand' Place**, 110 m (361 feet) long and 68 m (223 feet) wide, around which stand the Town Hall and the former Guildhalls. In its medieval compact shape, it is one of the most harmonious squares in the world, and is extraordinarily attractive, especially in the evening. Most of the buildings were reconstructed in 1695 in Baroque style, but despite this the square has still preserved its splendid character and represents a happy mix of Gothic and Baroque elements. The Grand' Place has played an important role not only on various festival occasions, but also in political events ranging from the 14th and 15th c. to the Revolution of 1830. The Counts Egmont and Hoorn were beheaded here in 1568.

The ***Town Hall** (*Hôtel de Ville*, 60 m (197 feet) long and 50 m (164 feet)

Brussels – Illuminated Grand' Place

wide), is one of the largest and most beautiful of its kind in Belgium. The front part of the building dates from the 15th c., and the rear from the beginning of the 18th c. The splendid *tower, 96 m (315 feet) high, built by Jan van Ruysbroek in 1455, has a pierced spire crowned by the statue of St Michael, the Patron Saint of the City. From the tower there is a superb view. Inside the Town Hall are several remarkable rooms; especially worth mentioning is the large Salle du Conseil with a painted ceiling and tapestries designed by Victor Janssens (d. 1736), the large Salle Gothique, and the Salle des Mariages, both with exquisite wood panelling, and the Escalier d'Honneur with allegorical wall paintings (1893) by Lalaing. Opposite the Town Hall is the **Broodhuis** or **Maison du Roi**, a building erected in 1875–85 in the style of the 15th–16th c. It was originally the Bakers' Guildhall, but is now the *Museum of the City of Brussels* (Musée Communal), with collections illustrating the history of the city, etc. North of it, in a tiny cul-de-sac (Schnud-develde) opening into the Petite Rue des Bouchers, is the *Toone Puppet Theatre*.

Manneken Pis, Brussels

The former **Guildhouses** (*Maisons des Corporations*) date primarily from the end of the 17th c., and with their picturesque gables, pillars and balconies, as well as their sculptural decor and rich gilding, contribute to the special character of the square.

Starting in the north-west corner, on the right of the Town Hall at the Rue de la Tête d'Or, the Guildhouses are situated in the following order: The *Haberdashers* (No. 7); the *Boatmen* (No. 6, with a gable in the shape of a prow); the *Archers* (No. 5, with a gilded phoenix on the gable), the *Joiners and Coopers* (No. 4, façade from 1644); the *Tallow Merchants* (No. 3, from 1644); and at the corner of the Rue au Beurre, the massive *Baker's House* (Nos. 2–1); on the northern side to the right of the Broodhuis, the former *Painters' House* (Nos. 26–27), and the *Tailors' House* (Nos. 24–25); on the other side of the street (Rue de la Colline No. 24) is the old *Weighhouse* from 1704. Next to this, taking up the entire south-east side of the Square, is the so-called *House of the Dukes of Brabant* (Nos. 13–19), which belonged to several Guilds. Further left from the Town Hall on the south-west side of the square, is the *Brewers' House* (No. 10, now housing the Brewery Museum; on its gable is an equestrian statue of Charles of Lorraine); then follow the *Butchers' House* (No. 9), usually referred to as the House of the Swan, and the *House of the Star* (L'Etoile, No. 8), reconstructed in 1897.

Not far south-west of the Town Hall, on the corner of the Rue de l'Etuve and Rue du Chêne, is the famous **Manneken Pis*. It is a fountain with a bronze statue of a little boy relieving himself which was created in 1619 by Jérôme Duquesnoy the Elder as the replacement for an earlier statue.

The origin of the "Little Man", called in the popular tradition "The Oldest Citizen of Brussels", is unknown. It is mentioned in the Chronicles as early as the 15th c. Several legends and a turbulent history surround this figure. It was stolen several times, but each time retrieved. In the War of the Austrian Succession in the years 1741 –5, it was taken away and broken up, but the pieces were found and it was restored and returned to its original place. Even in recent times there have been attempts to steal it. On important holidays, the figure is dressed in one of the numerous costumes reflecting the various periods of its lifetime, which are kept in the Musée Communal.

From the Grand' Place you come via the short Rue au Beurre to *St Nicholas' Church* (14th–15th c.), reconstructed after the bombardment of 1695. Opposite is the back of the Stock Exchange. Here begins, on the right, a succession of ancient streets crossing the entire city from the Gare du Nord to the Gare du Midi. Beyond the crossroads and a series of streets leading to the Place de l'Albertine, you arrive via the Rue des Fripiers at the **Place de la Monnaie**, named after the former Mint, on the site of which were erected the high-rise buildings of the *Central Post Office* and the *City Administration Offices* (Centre Administratif), and an underground car park constructed. Opposite stands the **National Opera** (*Opéra National*, also called *Théâtre Royal de la Monnaie*) dating from the 19th c.

From the Place de la Monnaie runs the busy shopping street, the **Rue Neuve**. On the left is the *Passage du Nord* leading to Boulevard Adolphe Max, and not far north of it, on the right, the *Galerie de l'Etoile*. Further right, around the corner in the Place des Martyrs stands a memorial to the Patriots who lost their lives in the fighting against the Dutch in 1830. To the left is the *Eglise du Finistère* (1713–30). The Rue Neuve leads north into the Boulevard du Jardin Botanique, behind which extends the Place Rogier, a square surrounded by hotels and restaurants, and the nucleus of the northern part of the city. On the north side of the square towers the *Centre International Rogier*, completed in 1960, which contains on 30 floors, 85 companies, offices for 2500 people, 120 apartments, 2 theatres and parking for 1000 cars. Further to the north comes the **Gare du Nord** with an interesting *Museum of the Belgian Railways* (entrance Rue du Progrès).

The oldest connection between the heart of the Lower Town and the Upper Town is the line of streets consisting of the Rue du Marché aux Poulets, the Rue du Marché aux Herbes and the Rue de la Madeleine, which runs a little to the north of the Church of St Nicholas and the Grand' Place. The lower part of this area has partly preserved its old picturesque character. At the end of the Marché aux Herbes, on the left, are the **Galeries St-Hubert**, one of the oldest glass-covered shopping arcades in Europe. It was built in 1847 and is 213 m (699 feet) long. It is intersected by the quaint Rue des Bouchers with its popular restaurants, and divided into two halves, the *Galerie de la Reine* and the *Galerie du Roi*, with the smaller *Galerie des Princes* next to it. The Rue de la Madeleine lost its importance when it ceased to be the main access road to the Upper Town. On the left is the 15th c. *Chapel of St Madeleine*. At its upper end, the Rue de la Madeleine opens into the Place de l'Albertine. Not far to the north is the **Gare Centrale** (the central station, not the main station), built below ground-level in 1953 according to the designs of architect V. Horta. Next to it stands the massive office block of the Belgian Airline *Sabena*, built in 1954, as well as the highrise building now occupied by the State Lottery. North-east of the Place de l'Albertine, the Rue Cantersteen leads towards the Cathedral.

Above the Place de l'Albertine to the south-east rises the *Mont des Arts, the layout of which was completely changed in 1956–8. Under its garden terraces is a three-storey underground car park with entrances from the Place de la Justice and the Rue des Sols. The Mont des Arts leads to the Montagne de la Cour, a little below the Place Royale. At the foot of it is an *equestrian statue of King Albert I* (1951). To the right is the main entrance to the **Royal Library** (*Bibliothèque Royale de Belgique*). Most of this building was reconstructed in 1956–8. It now has 17 floors, six of which are below ground, and contains some two million books, as well as a *Collection of prints* (Cabinet des Estampes) with 650,000 items and 28,000 valuable manuscripts. The nucleus of the library was the famous ''Bibliothèque de Bourgogne'', a collection belonging to Philip the Good of Burgundy. Left of the statue of King Albert stands the new *Palais de la Dynastie* with a Banqueting Hall. The modern *Congress Hall* which can accommodate 1500 people, is situated on the left of the upper terrace, from which there is a good view of the Lower Town and the Town Hall spire. To the right are the offices of the Belgian Protestant Church. Adjacent to it, to the south-west, with an entrance from the Place du Musée, is the former Chapel, built in 1760, which is all that remains of the so-called *Old Court* (Ancienne Cour). The Court was built in 1750 as a residence for the Austrian Governors of the Low Countries.

Not far east from the Mont des Arts on Rue Ravenstein stands the massive **Palais des Beaux-Arts** by V. Horta, built in 1921–8, with exhibition and concert halls, and movie (cinema) theatres. Opposite is the upper exit of the *Galerie Ravenstein* leading to the Gare Centrale. South, next to the Palais des Beaux Arts, stands the *Hotel Ravenstein** (15th–16th c.). It is the last surviving mansion from the Burgundy period in Brussels. In the Rue Baron Horta, next to the Palais des Beaux Arts, there once stood the Pensionnat Heger. Charlotte Brontë stayed here in 1842 and 1843, first as a pupil then as a teacher, and fell in love with Mr Heger. Her stay provided the background for "Villette" and "The Professor".

The Inner Boulevards and the Western and Southern Parts of the Lower Town

The so-called **Inner Boulevards** constructed over the covered river-bed of the Senne in 1867–74, cut across the whole length of the Old City from the Gare du Nord to the Gare du Midi, and run parallel to the oldest line of streets formed by the Rue Neuve and the Rue du Midi. The most lively sector is in the northern and middle parts of the Boulevards where fashionable shops, cafés and restaurants abound and where the population of the surrounding districts gathers in the evening. The Boulevards Adolphe Max and Emile Jacqmain, which start from the Boulevard du Jardin Botanique, converge in the elongated **Place de Brouckère**. In the middle of this square there stood until recently the *Monument Anspach*, a fountain 20 m (66 feet) high commemorating Burgomaster Jules Anspach (1863–79), who was the principal instigator of these Boulevards. The monument has been removed and will eventually be placed in the Fishmarket.

The **Boulevard Anspach**, which connects the Place de Brouckère with the Stock Exchange, is, together with the Boulevard Adolphe Max, one of the liveliest and busiest streets in the city. The **Stock Exchange** (*Bourse*), constructed in 1871–3 in neo-Classical style, is a bit overloaded with decoration. It contains a domed hall, the best view of which can be obtained from the gallery. On the other side of the Stock Exchange, opposite the Rue des Pierres (the Flemish name of which, "Steenstraat", stems from a medieval castle), the Rue du Borgval ("Burgwall") leads on the right towards the Place St Géry, in which there is a covered market. Here is the site of the former Island St Géry, the ancient heart of the city. Not far south is the *Church of Notre-Dame aux Riches-Claires*, begun in 1665, with a 19th c. side aisle. Further to the southeast on the other side of the Boulevard Anspach is the *Church* of *Notre-Dame de Bon-Secours* (1664–94) which has an interesting interior.

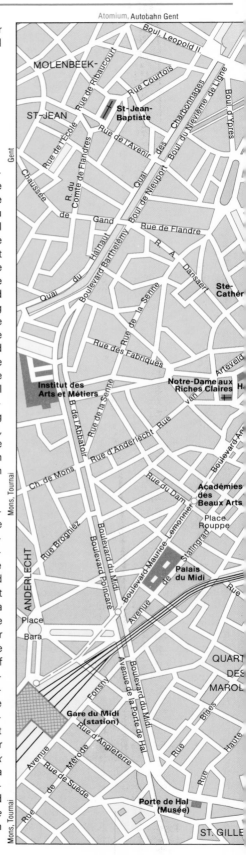

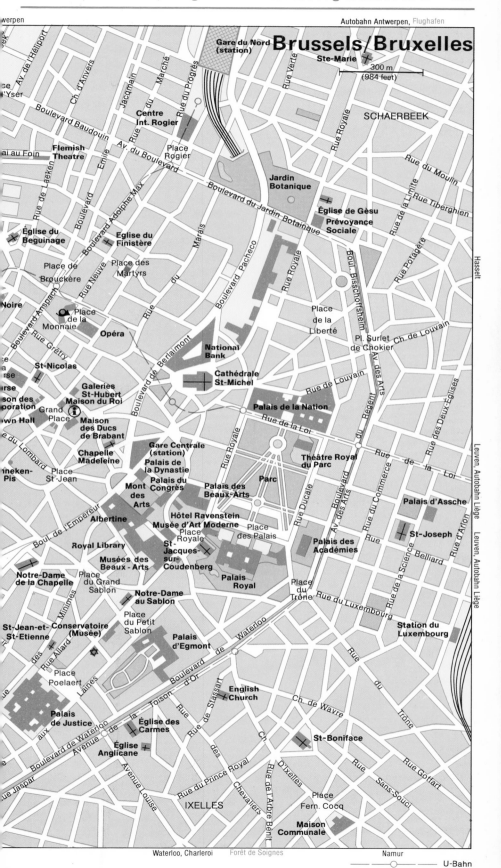

werpen

Autobahn Antwerpen, Flughafen

Av. de l'Héliport

Ch. d'Anvers

Jacqmain

Marché

Rue du Progrès

Gare du Nord (station)

Ste-Marie

Brussels/Bruxelles

300 m
(984 feet)

Boulevard Baudouin

'Yser

Rue du

Marché

Centre
Int. Rogier

Rue Verte

Rue Royale

SCHAERBEEK

Rue du Moulin

Flemish
Theatre

Emile

Av. du Boulevard

Place
Rogier

Boulevard Adolphe Max

ai au Foin

Rue de Laeken

Boulevard

Jardin
Botanique

Rue de la Limite

Rue Tiberghien

Boulevard du Jardin Botanique

Église de Gèsu

Prévoyance
Sociale

Rue du Moulin

Église du
Beguinage

Église du
Finistère

Marais

Boulevard Pacheco

Rue Royale

Rue Potagère

Hasselt

Place de
Brouckère

Rue Neuve

Place des
Martyrs

Rue du

Place
de la
Liberté

Boul. Bisschofsheim

Noire

Place
de la
Monnaie

Opéra

Pl. Surlet
de Chokier

Ch. de Louvain

Boulevard Anspach

Rue Grétry

National
Bank

Av. des Arts

St-Nicolas

Boulevard de Berlaimont

Cathédrale
St-Michel

Rue de Louvain

Régent

Rue des Deux-Églises

rse

Galeries
St-Hubert
Maison du Roi

Palais de la Nation

son des
poration

Grand
Place

Rue de la Loi

wn Hall

Maison
des Ducs
de Brabant

Leuven, Autobahn Liège

e du Lombard

Chapelle
Madeleine

Gare Centrale
(station)
Palais de
la Dynastie

Théâtre Royal
du Parc

Rue de la Loi

neken-
Pis

Place
St-Jean

Palais du
Congrès

Parc

Rue Ducale

Av. des Arts

Rue du Commerce

Palais d'Assche

Leuven, Autobahn Liège

Mont
des
Arts

Palais des
Beaux-Arts

Albertine

Hôtel Ravenstein
Musée d'Art Moderne

Place
des Palais

Rue

St-Joseph

Rue de la Science

Belliard

Royal Library

Place
Royale

Musées des
Beaux-Arts

St-
Jacques-
sur-
Coudenberg

Palais des
Académies

Rue d'Arlon

Notre-Dame
de la Chapelle

Place
du Grand
Sablon

Palais
Royal

Place
du
Trône

Rue du Luxembourg

Station du
Luxembourg

Notre-Dame
au Sablon

Minimes

St-Jean-et-
St-Etienne

Conservatoire
(Musée)

Place
du Petit
Sablon

Palais
d'Egmont

Waterloo

Rue du

Rue Allard

Place
Poelaert

Laines

Boulevard
d'Or

Rue de Stassart

English
Church

Ch. de Wavre

Rue du Trône

Palais
de Justice

aux

Boulevard de Waterloo

Avenue de Waterloo

Église des
Carmes

Toison

Rue des

St-Boniface

Église
Anglicane

Avenue Louise

Rue du Prince Royal

Chevaliers

Rue de l'Arbre Bénit

D'Ixelles

IXELLES

Place
Fern. Cocq

Rue Sans-Souci

Rue Goffart

ue Jaspar

Maison
Communale

Waterloo, Charleroi

Forêt de Soignes

Namur

U-Bahn

The Boulevard Anspach continues as the Boulevard Maurice Lemonnier which ends just before the **Gare du Midi** on the Place de la Constitution. North of the Gare du Midi at No. 56 Rue Gheude, is the **Gueuze-Museum** (*Musée Bruxellois de la Gueuze*). It is housed in the only Brussels brewery which still produces Gueuze beer in the traditional way.

Gueuze Beer is a speciality of the Brussels region. Its brewing is based on the use of the *Lambic*, which is made of roughly one-third crude wheat, two-thirds malt barley, and of three-year-old hops. The various phases of the brewing procedure can be seen in the Museum. The Lambic belongs to the so-called "wild" or natural beers, the fermenting of which is not induced by the addition of yeast into the fermenting vat, but is later triggered off spontaneously in the barrels. Yeast cells, *Brettanomyces lambicus* and *B. brucelensis*, live in the sides of these barrels. After two or three days of fermenting, the Lambic is made and is afterwards kept for several years in the barrel. By mixing several kinds of Lambic the actual Gueuze is obtained, and is then bottled like champagne, closed with cork and wire. Then follow fermenting in the bottle and a process of ripening lasting some two years. Gueuze beer is brownish in colour, a little fizzy, and somewhat bitter in taste. It is served chilled at 7–10°C (44–50°F). Sometimes the beer is unfiltered, in which case it is necessary to ensure that the sediment is left in the bottle.

Parallel to the Boulevard Maurice Lemonnier runs the Rue du Midi, with the Academy of Arts (*Académie des Beaux-Arts*), and the Municipal Art Library, and the Avenue de Stalingrad, which begins on the other side of the Place Rouppe. Between the latter and the Boulevard Lemonnier is the *Palais du Midi*, housing offices and an industrial college.

From the beginning of the Boulevard Anspach at the Place Brouckère, you proceed west along the Rue de l'Evêque and, leaving a large car park on the left, you pass the *Black Tower* (Tour Noire), which is a relic of the first city wall of the 12th c. Then you come to the **Church of St Katharine**, reconstructed in 1854, with some paintings from the earlier church. The tower of that church, dating from the 17th c., stands on the southern side, opposite the west door. In the streets to the west of the church, in the Rue St Catherine and the Rue de Flandre, there still stand some **gabled houses** from the 16th–18th c. (e.g. in the courtyard of No. 46 Rue de Flandre, the so-called *Bellona*

House (Hôtel de Bellone), with sculptures by J. B. Cosyn (1698)). The part of the town to the west of here has preserved its Flemish character to a considerable extent.

North-east of the Church of St Katharine stands the former **Eglise du Beguinage** (1657–76), with a remarkably spacious interior. Further to the north in the Rue de Laeken, is the *Flemish Theatre* of 1887.

From the southern corner of the Grand' Place you come through a number of quaint old lanes with interesting gabled houses dating from the 17th–18th c., into the southern part of the Old Town. In the Place de la Chapelle stands the **Church of Notre-Dame de la Chapelle** (begun *c.* 1210), which has a 15th c. nave. The interior is architecturally very attractive, and contains not only some remains of 15th c. frescoes but also the tomb of the painter Pieter Breughel the Elder, erected by the artist's son Jan, "The Velvet Breughel". Nearby, west of the church, is a little railway station which marks the point where the surface railway from the Gare du Midi enters a tunnel running beneath the entire area of the central city as far as the Gare du Nord.

South of the Place de la Chapelle begins the busy Rue Haute, the high street of the densely populated district called LES MAROLLES. This district is inhabited by a mixed Flemish/Walloon population, and its name is derived from a former Convent. Pieter Breughel the Elder lived in No. 135 Rue Haute. Parallel, to the east, below the Law Courts, runs the Rue des Minimes with the *Franciscan Church* (St Jean and St Etienne) of 1700–15. To the west of the Rue Haute is the Rue Blaes, which leads to the Place du Jeu de Balle, the Flea Market.

At the southern end of the Rue Haute and of the Old City, where the western and the upper outer boulevards meet, stands the *Porte de Hal*. It is the only relic of the 14th c. fortification and was completely rebuilt in 1868–70. Inside is the *Royal Museum of Arms and Armour* (Musée Royal d'Armes et d'Armures). From here the Boulevard du Midi leads to the Place de la Constitution in front of the Gare du Midi, where the inner boulevards terminate.

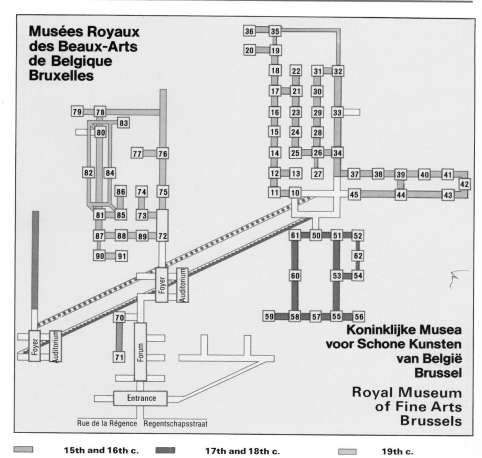

Musées Royaux des Beaux-Arts de Belgique Bruxelles

Koninklijke Musea voor Schone Kunsten van België Brussel

Royal Museum of Fine Arts Brussels

15th and 16th c.		17th and 18th c.		19th c.	
10–17, 21–34	Old Dutch School		Flemish School	72–86	Belgian School
10–17	Flemish Primitives		Spanish School	72–77	Realism
	11 Van der Weyden		French School		72 J. Stevens, 72, 75
	13 Bouts, 14 Memling		Dutch School		Meunier
	17 Bosch		Italian School		75 Artan 76 Boulenger
21–34	Flemish School		della Faille Donation		77 A. Stevens
	22 Metsys, 24 Mostaert		Drawings and Sculptures	78, 80	Impressionism
	25 Gossart				"Luminism"
	26 Van Orley		**19th c.**		79 Meunier
	31 Breughel, 32 Moro		Neo-Classicism		80 De Braekeler and
	34 Bril		Romanticism	85	Vogels
17, 24, 25	Dutch School		In Preparation		Symbolism
18–20	German School				Khnopff
	20 Cranach			86	Historic Hall
11, 12, 15, 16	French School		**Temporary Exhibitions**	87–89	French School
37–45	Delporte Bequest				87 Gauguin, 88 Courbet,
					89 Delacroix and David
				78, 79, 82–84	Water Colours, Drawings
					and Sculptures

The Older Parts of the Upper Town

The boundary of the higher ground on which the Upper Town is built is marked by the line of streets some 2 km (1 mile) long consisting of the Rue Royale and its south-western continuation, the Rue de la Régence. Its midpoint is the *Place Royale on the Coudenberg (Cold Hill), not far above the terraces of the Mont des Arts where the old residence of the sovereigns used to be. This square, as well

as the Rue Royale and the other streets around the Park, bear the imprint of the French architect B. Guimard who, in the 1770s, erected here a number of buildings in the Classical style. – In the Place Royale, which offers a superb view over the Lower Town, stands the impressive *equestrian statue of Godefroy de Bouillon*, the Duke of Lower Lotharingia and leader of the First Crusade in 1097. The monument dates from 1848. The south-eastern side of the Place Royale is occupied by the Royal Church, **St-Jacques-sur-Coudenberg** (1776–85), with a copper-covered dome. On the north-western side in No. 1 is the *Museum of Modern Art (Musée d'Art Moderne), where temporary exhibitions are mounted, and which houses an important collection of sculpture, almost exclusively of works by modern Belgian artists. In the western corner of the Place Royale (entrance No. 3 Rue de la Régence) is the building, erected in 1875–81, of the Royal Museum of Fine Arts (Musées Royaux des Beaux-Arts), with a rich collection of old paintings, especially of the Flemish and Dutch Schools.

Royal Palace, Brussels

The *Picture Gallery offers a good survey of the development of Flemish paintings from the 15th–17th c. It contains a substantial collection of works by old Dutch masters of the 15th c., among them a beautiful Pietà by Petrus Christus, a "Calvary", and some important portraits by Rogier van der Weyden, two large characteristic panels of the "Judgment of the Emperor Otto", by Dierick Bouts, excellent portraits by Memling, as well as a fine "Adoration of the Magi" by Gerard David. The greatest painter of the transition period from the 15th to the 16th c., Quentin Massys, is represented by one of his masterpieces, a triptych of the "Legend of St Anne". Bernaert van Orley is the creator of a triptych of "The Trials of Job" and an "Entombment". From the Flemish School of the 16th c., the Museum possesses a number of large altar paintings from the School of Rubens. Jordaens is represented by several of his best works, among them an allegory of "Fecundity". There are several paintings by van Dyck and many others by the disciples and followers of Rubens. Among the works by Teniers the most remarkable is "The Flemish Kermesse". From the Dutch School of the 17th c. there are some well-known names but not always represented by their best works. Especially worth seeing are the portraits by Frans Hals, Rembrandt, van der Helst, T. de Keyser and N. Maes; genre paintings by Jan Steen and G. Metsu; landscapes by Hobbema, Jan van der Meer, van Haarlem, Van Goyen, and others. Many foreign schools, especially painters from Italy, Spain and France are represented. The extension built in 1974 houses pictures of the 14th–16th c., as well as the Delporte Bequest.

By the northern side of the Fine Arts Museum, where it overlooks the square, the short Rue du Musée, accessible through an arch, leads to the Place du Musée. In it stands a bronze statue of Prince Charles of Lorraine of 1846. On the left is the Cabinet des Médailles (collection of 55,000 coins and medals), which belongs to the Royal Library.

On the north side of the Place Royale begins the Rue Royale, which forms one side of the Park. At its far end, the beautiful cupola of the Church of St Mary of Schaerbeek can be seen. On the right-hand side of the Place des Palais stands

the Royal Palace (Palais Royal), built on the site of the Ducal Palace, destroyed by fire in 1731. The Palace dates from 1827–9 and was completely rebuilt in 1905. In the 14th c. the Park opposite the Palace was a hunting preserve of the Dukes, and was laid out in its present form in 1776–80. Popular afternoon concerts are given here. In the north-east corner of the Park is the Théâtre Royal du Parc dating from 1782.

Opposite the north side of the Park, across the Rue de la Loi stands the Palais de la Nation (1779–83), the seat of the Senate and of the Lower House. The adjacent buildings house several Ministries. On the west side of the Palace, the Rue des Colonies and the old Rue Treurenberg lead left from the Rue Royale to the Cathedral. On the left-hand side of Rue Royale is a terrace with the Congress Column, 45 m (148 feet) high, erected here in 1850–9 to commemorate the Congress of 1830. From the column, which is surmounted by the statue of Leopold I, there is a superb view over the Lower Town. In front of the statue the Tomb of the Belgian Unknown Soldier bears an eternal flame. Behind the terrace extends the massive complex of the Cité Administrative, consisting of several high-rise office buildings.

On the western slope of the Upper Town stands the majestic *Cathedral (St Michel and St Gudule, the Patron Saints of the city), dating from the 13th–15th c. with an impressive façade and two truncated towers 65 m (213 feet) high.

The interior of the Cathedral is remarkable for its harmonious proportions (length 108 m (354 feet), width 50 m (164 feet)). There are some outstanding *stained glass windows* from the 16th–17th c.; those by the painter Bernaert van Orley can be seen in the transept (1537–8), and in the northern chapel, left of the choir (1540–7). Excellent *paintings*, works of the School of Rubens, are in and in front of the southern chapel, to the right of the choir. The carved *pulpit* is by H. Verbruggen (1699), and some *Brussels tapestries* by van de Borght (1785), are exhibited in the choir between mid-July and mid-August.

Opposite the north side of the Cathedral stands the **National Bank**, built in 1859–64 and enlarged in 1905 and 1948. Its façade on to the Boulevard de Berlaimont dates from 1952.

The Rue de la Régence, which runs from the Place Royale to the south-west, passes the Museum of Fine Arts on the way to the Church **Notre-Dame au Sablon**, also called *Notre-Dame des Victoires*. This late Gothic building, begun about 1400 and completed in the 16th c., has an interesting interior containing in the choir murals of 1435. West of the church is the Place du Grand Sablon, sloping downhill towards the Place de la Chapelle.

South-east of the Rue de la Régence lies the picturesque **Place du Petit Sablon**, constructed in 1890 and encircled by an original *railing: there are forty-eight short pillars linked by wrought-iron grilles bearing bronze statuettes representing various guilds of the 16th c. In the upper part of the square stands the *monument of Counts Egmont and Hoorn* (1864), surrounded by ten marble statues of their famous contemporaries. Opposite the upper exit of the Petit Sablon is the **Palais d'Egmont** with reception rooms of the Ministry of External Affairs. The building dates from the 19th c., and has beautiful gardens. It occupies the site of a 16th c. palace, the first owner of which was Count Egmont. It was here that Great Britain, Ireland and Denmark signed the agreements of 22 January 1972 under which they became members of the Common Market.

Beyond the Petit Sablon on the left of the Rue de la Régence stands the **Royal School of Music**, built in 1876–7 (entrance Place du Petit Sablon). Inside is the *Museum of Musical Instruments* (Musée Instrumental du Conservatoire Royal), which has one of the most outstanding collections in the world, and also a beautiful concert hall. The Rue de la Régence opens into the Place Poelaert in

which are located the massive Law Courts. From the square is another beautiful view.

*The Law Courts** (*Palais de Justice*) dominate the Brussels townscape. The building, designed by J. Poelart (d. 1879), dates from 1866–83 and cost over 50 million Belgian francs. It is the largest building of the 19th c., with an area of 26,000 sq. m (279,760 sq. feet) (St Peter's in Rome is 15,160 sq. m (163,122 sq. feet)). Above the massive building the central dome soars to a height of 104 m (341 feet) above the level of the square. Inside are numerous meeting rooms of the highest tribunals of the country, as well as an enormous vestibule (Salle des Pas Perdus). South-east of the Law Courts the wide Rue des Quatre Bras leads into the Boulevard de Waterloo opposite the entrance into the Avenue Louise, which can also be reached by an underpass 500 m (1640 feet) long.

The Boulevards of the Upper Town

The Boulevards which enclose the pentagon of the Old City of Brussels and which are 8 km (5 miles) long, are called "Boulevards Extérieurs" or "Ceinture" to distinguish them from the Inner Boulevards. They were built between 1818 and 1840 on the site of the former 14th c. fortifications. The Upper Boulevards are far larger than those in the west of the city and have an average width of 80 m (262 feet). To help accommodate the heavy traffic, underpasses were built at the most important crossings, as well as a number of tunnels and a flyover (overpass) 1.5 km (1 mile) long.

In the northern part of the Boulevards, the Boulevard du Jardin Botanique runs past the Place Rogier near the Gare du Nord, towards the Upper Town. On the left are the attractive **Botanical Gardens** dating from 1826–30. Most of the plants from the hothouses have been transferred to the Estate of Bouchout. In a building accessible from the Rue Royale is the *Museum of Forestry*. After the junction with the Rue Royale (on the left there is a high-rise building of the insurance company, Prévoyance Sociale) comes the Boulevard Bischoffsheim. At the Place Madou, marked by a 31-storey building,

Buildings of the European Communities on the Rond-Point Robert-Schuman

begins the busy Boulevard du Régent. This crosses the Rue de la Loi not far from the Palais de la Nation, and then skirts the fashionable parts of the city near the Park and the Quartier Léopold on the left. On the right between the Boulevard and the Park, stands the **Palais des Académies**, constructed in 1823–9 for the Prince of Orange. It is now the headquarters of the *Académie Royale des Sciences, des Lettres et des Beaux-Arts*, and the *Académie de Médicine*, both with valuable libraries. Further on to the right is the Place du Trône with an equestrian statue of Leopold II (1925). Behind are the gardens of the Royal Palace. The Boulevard du Régent ends at the square called the Porte de Namur, where it is crossed by a line of streets leading from the Inner City towards Ixelles. Then comes the Boulevard de Waterloo, beginning as a tunnel 300 m (948 feet) long beneath the busy Place Louise. The Rue des Quatre Bras leads to the right towards the Law Courts, the Avenue Louise to the left towards the Bois de la Cambre. The Boulevard then slopes down past several University Institutes towards the Porte de Hal.

The Outer Districts and the Suburbs

The Rue Royale continues beyond the Boulevards into the suburb of SCHAER-BEEK. In the Place de la Reine stands the *Church of St Mary*, dating from 1845–53,

a domed structure in Romanesque Byzantine style which can be seen from a distance. The continuation of the street, the Rue Royale Ste Marie crosses the Place Colignon, in the middle of which stands the *Town Hall* of Schaerbeek, built in 1885–7 in the style of old Flemish town halls. About 1 km (about a $\frac{1}{2}$ mile) to the south-east we came to the pretty **Parc Josaphat**, with several lakes, garden restaurants and a banqueting hall. The Boulevards Lambermont and General Wahis border it on the east. They form part of an imposing ring road which surrounds the eastern suburbs from the Bois de la Cambre as far as the exhibition grounds near Laeken.

The Rue de la Loi, which begins at the Palais de la Nation, runs eastward past the Quartier Leopold and the Quartier Nord-Est on the north side. In the middle of the QUARTIER NORD-EST lies the Square Ambiorix, a charming sloping square with garden terraces. At the end of the Rue de la Loi is the Rond-Point Robert-Schuman with, on the left, the massive building of the **European Communities**, the seat of the European Commission. East of the Rond-Point extends the *Parc du Cinquantenaire*, named after the exhibition of 1880, held on the occasion of the 50th anniversary of the independence of the Kingdom. The **Palais du Cinquantenaire**, erected in 1879–80, was completed in 1905 by a massive *Triumphal Arch* (Arcades du Cinquantenaire). The two wings of the Palace, as well as its more recent annexes, house the *Royal Museum of Arts and History (*Musées Royaux d'Art et d'Histoire*, entrance from the Avenue des Nerviens).

The Museum contains a *collection of plaster casts* which illustrate the development of sculpture in Belgium as well as an important *Collection of Antiquities* of which the Egyptian and the Greco-Roman Sections are especially worth a visit (they were rearranged after a fire in 1946). There is also a *Museum of Carriages* and an excellent **Collection of Applied Arts*. The latter offers a unique survey of medieval and modern arts and crafts in Belgium, especially of carpet weaving, gold and silverware, furniture-making and wood carving. There is also a section containing Belgian and foreign lace, textiles and costumes, and a large collection of ceramics, with Delft pottery and East Asian porcelain. In the north wing of the building is the interesting **Royal Military Museum** with collections illustrating the history of the Belgian Armed Forces from the end of the 18th c. to the present time.

South of the Rue de la Loi extends the fashionable QUARTIER LÉOPOLD with a regular grid of rather monotonous streets. The most important buildings are grouped around the Place Frère Orban: to the south, the *Church of St Joseph* (1842–9); and to the east the *Palais d'Assche* (1880). In the southern part of the Quartier Léopold lies the Square de Meeus, half of which belongs to Ixelles. It is crossed by the Rue du Luxembourg leading to the square in front of the Gare du Quartier Léopold. – To the east, on the other side of the railway, is the **Parc Léopold**, built in 1852. The upper part of the park encloses the **Royal Institute of Natural History** (1898; entrance No. 31 Rue Vautier). The Museum has ten sections, among them a zoological collection with a highly interesting Palaeontological Department containing among other exhibits ten large **skeletons of the iguanodon (on the average 4·5 m (15 feet) high and 8·5 m (28 feet) long), an enormous saurian, a lizard-like creature which walked like a kangaroo on its hind legs and tail. (These skeletons were found in 1877–80 in the chalk layers of the coal deposits of Bernissart.) Opposite is the entrance to the *Musée Wiertz*, a former studio of the painter (1806–65), in which his works are exhibited.

South-east of the Quartier Léopold extends the suburb of IXELLES, the main artery of which is the busy shopping street the Chaussée d'Ixelles. It starts at the Porte de Namur and runs past the *Town Hall of Ixelles*. A short way to the east in the Rue Jean van Volsem, is the **Musée des Beaux Arts d'Ixelles**, which contains valuable examples of modern, mainly Belgian, art, especially from the period of the Impressionists. The Chaussée d'Ixelles then runs downhill into *Bas-Ixelles* where, next to the attractive lakes (*Etangs d'Ixelles*), is the old *Broadcasting House* (RTB). Here stands the monument of the Belgian poet *Charles De Coster*, who lived from 1827 to 1879 and who is buried in the cemetery of Ixelles. The monument shows the character of his main work, "Thyl Ulenspiegel" (1867). On the southern side of the lakes stands the former **Abbaye de la Cambre**, dating from the 17th–18th c., with a 14th–15th c. Gothic church. It now houses the *School of Architecture and Decorative Arts*. Further south, on the Plateau de Solbosch stand the buildings of the **Free University**. This is an independent institution founded in 1834 by the Freemasons in opposition to the Catholic University of Louvain. It has about 7000 students. Below the Plateau stretches the suburb of BOENDAEL with the Church of St Adrien. Inside are two interesting carved altars dating from the 15th–16th c. South-east of Boendael is the village of *Boitsfort*, neatly situated at the northern edge of the Forêt de Soignes, with several picturesque lakes. To the north of it on the Hillock of Three Lime Trees (Trois Tilleuls) extends a modern residential area famous for its blossoming trees, especially Japanese cherries.

The wide *Avenue Louise, which starts at the Boulevard Waterloo, is lined on both sides by houses in different styles, the most modern at the far end of the street. At the beginning, on the left, is the fashionable *Galerie Louise*. On the Rond-Point where the Avenue curves towards the south, there is a good view on the left over Bas-Ixelles. At the end of the street begins the *Bois de la Cambre (some 2 km (1 mile) long and 500 m (1640 feet) wide) and which since 1860 has been turned into a superb wooded park. It is the most popular promenade in the immediate neighbourhood of Brussels. There is an attractive lake and several restaurants.

South of the Old Town of Brussels lies the suburb of ST GILLES, with a massive *Town Hall* and the interesting *Horta Museum* (No. 25 Rue Américaine), devoted to the leading architect of Belgian Art Nouveau. On the slope of the Senne Valley in FOREST are the *Parc de Forest* and the *Parc Duden*. The Chaussée de Bruxelles which runs along the edge of the latter, leads to the interesting Parish Church of *St Denis* dating from the 12th–13th c., with the tomb of St Alène (d. *c.* 640), and sculptures from the 13th c. The suburb of UCCLE lying to the south contains the pretty *Parc Wolvendael* as well as the **Observatory**, standing on a hillock to the east and offering a panoramic view. The suburb of St Gilles is associated with Nurse Edith Cavell (1865–1915). She founded and headéd a large school for nurses in the present Rue Edith Cavell. When war broke out in 1914, she actively helped fugitive soldiers to escape to Holland. Arrested, she was held at the Prison of St Gilles before being sentenced to death and shot.

House of Erasmus, Brussels-Anderlecht

The suburb of ANDERLECHT lies to the south-west of Brussels on both sides of the Canal of Charleroi. In the Square Jan Dillen stands the Parish Church of **St Pierre** (15th–16th c.). Inside are frescoes from the period of construction. The crypt dates from the 11th c. On the eastern side of the square is the **House of Erasmus** (entrance No. 31 Rue du Chapitre). The great humanist Erasmus of Rotterdam lived here in 1521. The house, furnished in the period style, contains many mementoes of him. Not far to the west is a charming *Beguinage*.

The suburb of KOEKELBERG to the north-west of Brussels can be reached from the western end of the Boulevard du Jardin Botanique, first by the flyover (overpass), which runs above the Place

de l'Yser and the Boulevard Léopold II, then slightly uphill through the *Parc Elisabeth*. On the plateau of Koekelberg stands the enormous **Basilique Nationale du Sacré Cœur**, designed by Huffels, begun in 1926 and consecrated in 1951, but not yet completed. Inside are some valuable *stained-glass windows by Jean Huet. From the Basilique there is a beautiful view. The Quai de Willebroek leads from the Place de l'Yser to the **port of Brussels** in the north of the city. The harbour was constructed in 1895–1922 when the 16th c. *Willebroek Canal*, which links Brussels with the Rupel, a tributary of the Schelde, was widened. It is accessible to medium-sized ships. The main dock, the **Bassin Vergote** to the west of the Allée Verte, was in the 18th c. the most popular promenade of the people of Brussels. To the south of it the *Charleroi Canal* opens into several smaller side docks. Further north-east is the Foreport of **Avant-Port**. At the north end of the Bassin Vergote stands the large *Monument du Travail* by Constantin Meunier.

The suburb of LAEKEN, lying north of the harbour, is the favourite residence of the Royal Family. Leopold I and Leopold II died here. From the north end of the Bassin Vergote you can reach the Avenue de la Reine via the *Pont de Laeken*; from here there is a good view of the harbour area. At the end of the Avenue stands the **Church of Notre-Dame** of Laeken, in Gothic style, erected in 1854–72, by J. Poelaert. Behind the choir is the Royal Vault. North-west of the church in the *cemetery* of Laeken are several tombs of patrician Belgian families. The choir of the *Old Church of Laeken* is well preserved, and is the purest specimen of early Gothic in Brussels (13th c.). The Avenue du Parc Royal leads from the Church of Notre-Dame towards the north along the Royal Park. In the park on the right stands the *Royal Palace*, built in 1782–4 for the then Governor, Duke Albert von Sachsen-Teschen. It can be seen from the street and the superb hot-houses can be visited from the end of April to the middle of May. To the left of the Avenue extends the **Park of Laeken**, public property since 1903. In it is a *monument to Léopold I* in the form of a "Gothic pyramid", dating from 1880. From it in the evening there is a beautiful view. At the north end of the Avenue du Parc Royal, where it merges with the eastern ring road by the Rondell Gros Tilleul, you will find on the right the *Chinese Pavilion* (1906–10), with collections of Far-Eastern art, and the *Japanese Tower* brought from the Paris World Exhibition in 1900.

Not far west from the Park of Laeken are the **Brussels Exhibition Grounds** in which stands the **Palais du Centenaire**, with exhibition rooms, restaurants, etc., and a park with a restaurant. This is the site of the *World Exhibition of 1958*, which was visited by 42 million people. There remains only the *"**Atomium**", some 110 m (361 feet) high, weighing 2500 tons. It was built as a model of an atom of iron; inside is an observation gallery and a restaurant. In its central sphere there is a Euratom Exhibition. There is also an architecturally interesting *Pavillon du Génie Civil*, displaying a panorama of Belgium on the scale of 1:3500.

SURROUNDINGS of Brussels. – There are several rewarding excursions around Brussels, for example to the village of **Grimbergen**, 12 km (7 miles) north of the central part of the city. (Exit via Laeken, turn right after 7 km (4 miles) at the Rondell "Gros Tilleul".) At the village of Grimbergen an Abbey was founded in the 12th c. and there remains an interesting * church (1660–1700). Its Baroque decoration is the richest in Belgium. – 14 km (9 miles) south-west of Brussels is the medieval **Castle of Gaasbeek** dating from the 13th–16th c., now public property. It can be reached via the Porte d'Anderlecht in the direction of Mons. (5 km (3 miles) from the middle of the city, turn right at the "Het Rad" (group of houses), and continue in the direction of Lennik.) The castle now houses a museum with numerous works of art, among them some excellent Brussels tapestries. There is also a beautiful park (40 hectares – 99 acres). – 10 km (6 miles) south of the city, leaving via the suburb of Uccle, you can reach the village of **Beersel** (Hôtel du Centre, III, 12 r.), with an interesting moated * castle of the 14th c. A little further to the south-west lies the Estate of *Huizingen* (92 hectares – 227 acres), containing playgrounds, camp sites, an open-air swimming pool, a youth hostel, etc. A short drive further east is *Alsemberg*, with a 15th c. church. From here via the Lion Mound of **Waterloo** (10 km (6

Castle of Beersel, near Brussels

miles), see page 265), you come to the motorway (highway) from Charleroi to Brussels.

South-east of Brussels beyond the Bois de la Cambre extends the * **Forêt de Soignes**, some 4000 hectares (9884 acres) of mainly beech trees, which ranks among the most beautiful forests in Belgium. In the middle of it, at a crossroads some 13 km (8 miles) south-east from the city, lies the village of **Groenendael** in a beautiful valley. It can be reached from the Porte de Namur via Ixelles and Boitsfort, and then by road No. 430. Here stood the famous **Augustinian Abbey** founded in 1343 by the mystic Ruysbroek. The only remaining building dates from the 18th c. and now houses the fashionable restaurant Château de Groenendael. On the northern slope of the valley lies the *Arboretum de Groenendael* in which there are more than 500 exotic species of trees and shrubs and a Forestry Museum. – 5 km (3 miles) south-east of Groenendael, beyond the Forêt de Soignes, is the pretty summer resort of *Genval* (Hostellerie la Lagune, III, 6 r.), with a medicinal spring and several lakes. 3 km (2 miles) further east lies *Rixensart* with the Palace of the Counts of Mérode (1631–62). – From Groenendael you can drive via the Route de Mont-Saint-Jean, north-east to Tervuren or south-west to *Waterloo* (see page 265). – South-east of Brussels near Wavre is the Amusement Park of *Walibi*, with a Dolphinarium, etc.

From Brussels via Tervuren to Louvain (28 km (17 miles), Road No. 3.). – The * Avenue de Tervuren, laid out in 1895–7 by King Leopold II, leads from the Palais du Cinquantenaire towards the eastern boundary of the city past the attractive lakes of *Woluwe-St-Pierre* (Etangs Mellaerts, with restaurant and canoeing). To the right of the Avenue de Tervuren, in the direction of Auderghem, you can reach the * **Abbaye du Rouge Cloître**, then across the north-eastern tip of the Forêt de Soignes you arrive at the links of the Royal Golf Club of Belgium. 13 km (8 miles) further, not far to the right from the main road, lies the village of Tervuren. North-east of this ancient village, stretches the vast * **Park of Tervuren** with 234 hectares (578 acres), old trees and beautiful lakes. In the 17th–18th c. it was a favourite place for Court festivities. At the edge of the lake (restaurant and canoeing), stands the Chapel of St Hubert, built in 1617. North-east from here, across a French-style terraced garden you reach the * **Museum of Central Africa** (*Musée Royale de l'Afrique Centrale*), containing exhibits from Zaire (formerly the Belgian Congo). Especially interesting are the collections of

Museum of Central Africa in Tervuren, near Brussels

masks and African sculpture. – The road to Louvain runs past the northern entrance to the Park and the Museum. On the left, opposite the Museum, is an impressive sculpture (1935), representing an elephant with three African riders, by A. Colin. 15 km (9 miles) further the road reaches **Louvain** (Flemish: *Leuven*; see page 200).

From Brussels via Ninove to Kortrijk (90 km – 56 miles). – Leaving Brussels in a westerly direction on the Chaussée de Ninove, you follow the straight road N9, across the rolling farmland of Brabant. After 19 km (12 miles) comes the village of *Lombeek*, 2 km (1 mile) to the left. In its church is a beautiful carved *altar of the 16th c. The N9 crosses the border of the Province of East Flanders, some 5 km (3 miles) before Ninove. – **Ninove**, which lies 1 km (about a ½ mile) to the right of the main road, is an old town with a population of 12,000. There is a Premonstratensian (religious order founded at Prémontré in 1119) abbey there. Some of its buildings date from the 16th–17th c., but most interesting is a beautiful church built in 1635–1723, with some 18th c. wood carvings. – Beyond Ninove the road crosses the *Dender* (French: Dendre), and after 11 km (7 miles) you reach the crossroads, with road No. 56 going from Mons to Ghent. 7 km (4 miles) to the south on this road, near the linguistic frontier, lies the old township of **Geraardsbergen** (French: *Grammont*), with a population of 18,000. It has a beautiful 14th c. Town Hall and a Gothic Church of St Barthélemy. The town is overlooked by the *Oudenberg* (La Vieille-Montagne); the chapel on the hill, is a place of pilgrimage and has a beautiful view. 9 km (6 miles) beyond the crossroads mentioned above, comes the village of *Nederbrakel*, at the end of which the road forks. If you turn right and follow road No. 9 for 15 km (9 miles) you will reach the charming little old town of **Oudenaarde** (see page 232). From there the road extends another 12 km (7 miles) on the left bank of the *Schelde* upstream as far as Kerkhove. Or you can continue straight on after Nederbraken on road No. 62. This is a better road and 3 km (2 miles) shorter, across the wooded and undulating countryside and extending into the Province of Hainaut. – 13 km (8 miles) past the village of **Ronse** (French: *Renaix*; Hotel Alfa, IV, 7 r.; Savoy, IV, 13 r.), there is an especially pretty stretch of road No. 57 along the foot of the *Mont de l'Hootond* (150 m (492 feet), good view). On the left is the *Mont de l'Enclus* (141 m – 463 feet). – The road crosses the *Schelde* before Kerkhove. Here the river forms the border between the provinces of East and West Flanders. After 11 km (7 miles) comes *Kerkhove* where the road meets the other route coming from the right via Oudenaarde. In *Harelbeke* or *Harlebeke* on the River Leie (French: *Lys*), 17 km (11 miles) further on you reach road No. 14 coming from Ghent. This runs to the left for 5 km (3 miles) along the river to the town of **Kortrijk** (see page 186).

Clervaux

Country: Luxembourg. – Canton: Clervaux.
Altitude: 360–520 m (1181–1706 feet). – Population: 1500.

ⓘ **Syndicat d'Initiative,**
Place Bénélux (Easter to 15 September);
tel. 9 20 72.

HOTELS. – *De l'Abbaye*, Grand'rue 80, II, 45 r.; *Central*, Grand'rue 9, II, 33 r.; *Du Parc*, Rue du Parc, II, 12 r.; *International*, Grand'rue 10, II, 12 r.; *Koener*, Grand'rue 14, III, 22 r.; *Du Commerce*, Rue de Marnach 2, III, 44 r.; *Des Nations*, Rue de la Gare 29, III, 47 r.; *Kremer*, Rue de la Gare 33, IV, 45 r. – YOUTH HOSTEL, 96 b. – CAMP SITE.

SPORTS and LEISURE. – Tennis, angling.

The Luxembourg health resort of Clervaux lies in the north of the country on a hill surrounded by the River Clerf. On the top of the hill is the castle and the church. Clervaux is a very popular place for excursions in summer because of its superb *location and beautiful wooded surroundings.

Clervaux in the Valley of the Clerf

SIGHTS. – The old **Castle** of the Lords of Lannoy is a picturesque group of buildings with massive towers dating from the 12th–17th c. It was burned down in the Second World War, but has been restored since, and now serves occasionally as an exhibition ground; there is also a restaurant. On the other bank of the Clerf is a *game park*. Further north-west up the valley, on a rocky promontory near the railway station, stands the *Loretto Chapel*, which has been a place of pilgrimage since 1786. Inside are beautiful wood carvings.

On the high plateau to the west above Clervaux, on the road toward Eselborn, stands an imposing **Benedictine Abbey** towering 100 m (328 feet) above the valley and visible from afar. It dates from 1910 and has a fine neo-Romanesque church and crypt. Nearby in the lane leading straight downhill toward the village is a *monument* to the peasants who rebelled against being drafted into the French Revolutionary Army in 1798. From here there is a good view left into the valley of the Clerf. The best *view* of the village and the Abbey is, however, from a hill 1 km (about a ½ mile) to the south on the road towards Marnach.

SURROUNDINGS of Clervaux. – **Via the Clerf Valley to Wiltz** (21 km – 13 miles). Cross the *Clerf* in Clervaux and then follow the river upstream on the left bank with a view of the Benedictine Abbey high above the village on the right bank. The *Valley* now becomes narrower and more winding with wooded slopes on both sides. The road follows the railway line, which sometimes passes through tunnels and so avoids the river bends. 11 km (7 miles) further comes *Wilwerwiltz* where the road crosses the Clerf and winds away from the valley. After 10 km (6 miles) the road reaches **Wiltz** (see page 267).

Condroz

Country: Belgium. – Province: Namur.
ⓘ **Hesbaye-Meuse-Condroz,**
Avenue Blonden 33,
B-4000 Liège;
tel. (0 41) 52 20 60.
Meuse Namuroise,
Ancienne Chaussée de Ciney,
B-5220 Andenne;
tel. (0 85) 22 10 77.

The undulating plateau of Condroz, 180–340 m (591–1116 feet) above sea level, is a part of Belgium which is often described as the foothills of the Ardennes. It stretches south of the rivers Sambre and Meuse. Its southern border is formed by the lowlands of Fagne and Famenne. In the east the region ends at the foot of the Hautes Fagnes, the highest part of the Ardennes.

The subsoil of Condroz consists of sandstone of the upper devonian period and of younger limestone of the carboniferous period. The rock layers of different hardness were, during earlier formation phases, pushed into a sloping position. In a later geological period the forces of erosion brought them to the surface and made them clearly discernible. The sandstone layers form the crests of the hills running from east to west, which alternate from north to south with parallel

limestone troughs. The rivers Meuse and Ourthe penetrate the hard sandstone and create picturesque and deeply cut valleys.

Condroz lacks important industries as well as an efficient transportation network. There is, therefore, only one sizeable township, the well-known tourist resort **Dinant** (see page 136). Agriculture and the tourist industry are the most important sources of employment. Correspondingly, the population density, which is about 100 per sq. km (259 per sq. mile), is relatively low for Belgium. Agricultural development is limited in essence to the limestone troughs filled with clayish soils, whereas the sandstone hills are densely wooded for the most part. The main crops are wheat, barley, potatoes, flax and animal fodder. Dairy farming and cattle breeding have recently become increasingly important. In the villages and hamlets, typical dwellings are large rectangular farmsteads surrounded by limestone walls. Most of these farms are over 100 hectares (247 acres) in size.

Damme

Country: Belgium. – Province: West Flanders.
Altitude: 8 m (26 feet). – Population: 1000.
Postal code: B8351.
Telephone code: 0 50.
ⓘ **Dienst voor Toerisme,**
Stadhuis,
Burgstraat 4;
tel. 35 55 19.

HOTELS. – *De Gulden Kogge*, Kanaalweg 5, IV, 6 r. – IN SIJSELE (Damme): *Hotel Clio*, Gensesteenweg 82, IV, 15 r. – BOARDING HOUSES. – *Kazemat*, Kerkstraat 28; *Hungenaert*, Kerkstraat 37.

RESTAURANTS. – *Kasteel van Moerkerke*, Dorpsstraat 7, Damme-Moerkerke; *De Damsche Poort*, Kerkstreet 6; *De 3 Zilveren Kannen*, Kerkstraat 9; *De Lieve*, Hoogstraat 8; *Den Heerd*, Hoogstraat 3; *'t Galjoen*, Natielaan 10 A; *Lamme Goedzak*, Markt 13; *Maeriant*, Kerkstraat 21; *Napoleon*, Kanaalweg 11.

CAFÉS. – *St. Pietershoeve*, Slekstraat 12; *'t Wapen van Damme*, Kerkstraat 23; *Pub Kazemat*, Kerkstraat 28; *'t Hemeltje*, Kerkstraat 44; *Hertog van Brabant*, Kerkstraat 36.

EVENTS. – *The International Ulenspiegel Festival* (May–September).

SPORTS and LEISURE. – Bowling and skittles, Ter Polders, Waterstraat 3.

The charming little Belgian town of Damme lies on the Zwin, 7 km (4 miles) north-east of Bruges, for

which it served as the outer port until the beginning of the 15th c. In that period, the continuing silting of the harbour of Bruges affected also the harbour of Damme and rapidly caused the decline of what was then the largest wine port of northern Europe.

The prosperity of Damme lasted only some 200 years, but there are still several interesting buildings from that period. They give a friendly atmosphere to the "birthplace" of Thyl Ulenspiegel, the famous character from the work of Charles De Costers (1827–79).

SIGHTS. – The **Church of Our Lady** is a brick building in the style of the Schelde Gothic. It was begun in 1230; the choir was completed in 1250, and at the beginning of the 14th c. was transformed into an interesting nave-shaped choir. Inside can be seen some figures of apostles from the year 1400 carved from oak. The altar of St Anne dates from 1555, and the Baroque altar of the Holy Cross from 1636. Worth seeing also is the

Burgundian houses in Damme

beautiful **Town Hall** with four corner turrets. Its basement was built in 1464–8 by Godefroy de Bosschere. Also very attractive is the patrician house *De Grote Sterre* of the 15th c. The *Huis St Jan*, also dating from the 15th c., houses the **Museum van Maerlant** with good collections of antiquities.

SURROUNDINGS of Damme. – A boat excursion to *Bruges (see page 106) on the *Napoleon Canal*, built in 1812, can be thoroughly recommended.

Delft

Country: The Netherlands. – Province: South Holland.
Altitude: below sea level. – Population: 86,000.
Postal code: NL-2600 AA to 2699.
Telephone code: 0 15.
ⓘ **VVV Delft,**
Markt 85,
NL-2611 GS Delft;
tel. 12 61 00.

HOTELS. – *De Ark*, Koornmarkt 59–65, III, 36 b.; *De Vlaming*, Vlamingstraat 52, III, 14 b.; *Juliana*, Maerten Trompstraat 33, III, 45 b.; *Central*, Wijnhaven 6–8, III, 80 b.; *'t Raedthuijs*, Markt 38–40–42, III, 30 b.

RESTAURANTS. – *Le Chavalier*, Oude Delft 125; *De Prinsenkelder*, Schoolstraat 11; *Rotiss. Het Fornuis*, Bestenmarkt 30; *Straatje van Vermeer*, Molslaan 18; *Solmar*, Verwersdijk 124; *Bastille*, Havenstraat 6; *Vieux Jean*, Heilige Geest Kerkhof 3; *Oranjehof*, Hyppolytusbuurt 8.

EVENTS. – A three-week-long *Fair of Arts and Antiques* in summer; *Delft Tattoo* ("Taptoe-Delft", end August–early September, every evening 9–11 p.m., on the Market Place); *Boat cruises* on the canals.

Delft, with its picturesque Old Town encircled by canals, lies on the River Schie in the Dutch province of South Holland between Rotterdam and The Hague. In the town is a Technical University and several research institutes. The town is also the site of several industrial enterprises, mainly vehicle and machine construction, electrical engineering, production of building materials, paper and cardboard. The manufacture of porcelain, which was world-famous from the 17th to the middle of the 18th c., has been recently revived. Delft is the birthplace of the scholar and statesman Hugo de Groot (Grotius; 1583–1645), of the painter Jan Vermeer, whose famous "View of Delft" hangs in the Mauritshuis in The Hague, and of the natural scientist Anthoni van Leeuwenhoek (1632–1723), inventor of the microscope.

HISTORY. – It is believed that in the 11th c. there was a slave colony on the site of Delft, from which the town developed. It received its charter in the 13th c., and afterwards carpet making and brewing flourished within its walls. Commerce also expanded rapidly. To be able to compete with Dordrecht, Schiedam and even Rotterdam, the outer port Delfthaven was constructed in the 15th c. on the River Maas. Delft reached its peak of prosperity in the 17th c., thanks to the rapid growth of the manufacture of porcelain. The majority of magnificent buildings still preserved in the Old Town also date from this period.

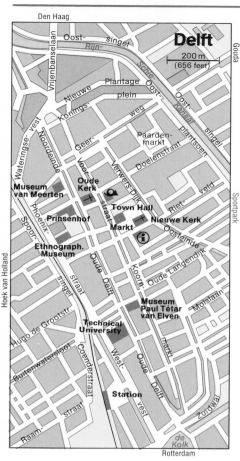

Den Haag

Delft

200 m
(656 feet)

Oost-Singel
Rijn-
Vrienbanselaan
Plantage
plein
Nieuwe
Konings-
Geer-
Noordeinde
Waterlingse- vest
Phoenix-
Spoor-
Museum
van Meerten
Oude
Kerk
Prinsenhof
Ethnograph.
Museum
Paarden-
markt
Verwers-Dijk
Doelenstraat
Town Hall
Markt
straat
Nieuwe Kerk
Riet-
Oosteinde
Koorn-
Oude Langendijk
singel
straat
Oude Delft
Museum
Paul Tétar
van Elven
Technical
University
West-
Oude Delft
vest
Station
straat
Zuidwal
Raam-
de
Kolk
Rotterdam

Scbie-Oost-Kanaal
weg
Oost-Kanaal
plantsoen
singel
veld
Paardenmarkt
Molslaan
markt
Coenderstraat

Gouda
Sportpark

Hoek van Holland
Hugo de Grootstr.
Buitenwatersloot

buried. In front of the church on the left stands his bronze statue (1886).

Set apart on the west side of the Markt stands the **Town Hall** (*Stadhuis*). It was rebuilt in the Renaissance style and its façade was restored in 1966. Inside are several interesting paintings from the 16th–18th c.

Going in a north-westerly direction from the Town Hall you reach, via the Hippolytusbuurt, the **Oude Kerk** (Reformed), built about 1250. It has a slightly leaning tower and beautiful wooden vaulting dating from 1574. In the interior are several important works of art: a carved pulpit from 1548, several tombstones, among them in a niche in the choir the marble tomb of Admiral Piet Hein (d. 1629) who, in 1628, captured the Spanish Silver Fleet; in a chapel to the left of the choir, the tomb of Admiral Maarten Harpertszoon Tromp who commanded the Dutch Navy in thirty-two naval battles, and in the narthex (western porch) of the church, in the wall, the tomb of Leeuwenhoek. Several interesting old houses have been preserved around the Oude Kerk in the Voorstraat and to the south, in the Hippolytusbuurt, Wijnhaven and Koornmarkt.

SIGHTS. – The town is intersected by many picturesque canals. Its central point is the spacious Markt; on its east side stands the *Nieuw Kerk (formerly the Church of St Ursula; Dutch Reformed; organ concerts in summer). It is a Gothic building dating from 1396–1496, with a tower 108 m (354 feet) high (carillon from 1663; view). In the choir is the magnificent *tomb of William the Silent from 1614–21, one of the masterpieces of Dutch Baroque sculpture. In the vault beneath it are buried forty-one princes and princesses from the House of Nassau-Orange, as well as Queen Wilhelmina. In the ambulatory on the right stands a monument of King William I (d. 1843 in Berlin), and above it on the wall is a memorial relief of Prince Frederick William of Orange who died in 1799. The relief is by Canova, dates from 1806, and was brought here in 1896 from Padua where the Prince was originally buried. On the northern wall of the choir is the marble memorial to Hugo Grotius, and to its right, in the floor, the place where he is

View towards the Oude Kerk in Delft

The Oude Delft, a canal which crosses the city from north to south, passes to the west of the Oude Kerk and is lined with picturesque old houses, Just opposite the Oude Kerk stands the *Prinsenhof. It was originally the Monastery of St Agatha and after 1575 it served for a long time as the Residence of the Princes of Orange. In the country's history the Prinsenhof is tragically well known, for here the founder of Dutch independence, Prince William of Orange (William the Silent), was assassinated in 1584. Inside this picturesque complex is an interesting museum devoted mainly to the eighty-year war of the Dutch against the Spanish (1568–1648). The *Oranje-Nassau Museum*, which was transferred here from The Hague in 1962, forms a part of it. This has a collection of pictures and other mementoes illustrating the history of the House of Nassau-Orange. In the oldest part of the Monastery, dating from about 1430, there is an ambulatory with a double gallery which is unique in Holland. To the south behind the Prinsenhof at No. 4 Agathaplein, is the small *Ethnographic Museum.* Not far north of the Prinsenhof, also on the Oude Delft, is the *Museum Huis Lambert van Meerten* with an important collection of applied arts, old furniture and paintings, and a good selection of Delft pottery, imaginatively displayed on two floors.

In the southern part of the Oude Delft stands the administrative building of the *Technical University* which was founded in 1863 and has approximately 10,000 students. The modern premises of the university are in the south-east of the city beyond the Provinciaal Canal. Further south you reach, on the left, the Koornmarkt via the Breestraat. Here at No. 68 is the *Museum Paul Tétar van Elven,* which has a painter's studio of the time of Vermeer, old furniture, Delft pottery, etc. At No. 196 Rotterdamseweg is the firm *De Porceleyne Fles,* a manufacturer of ceramics, which still produces the famous Delft pottery. There is an exhibition room in the building.

Travelling south-east from the Nieuwe Kerk along the Canal Oosteinde the road reaches the 14th c. *Oostpoort,* which stands in the south-eastern corner of the Old Town at the junction of several canals and offers a beautiful view of the town.

Deventer

Country: The Netherlands. – Province: Overijssel.
Altitude: 4–11 m (13–36 feet). – Population: 65,000.
Postal code: NL-7400 AA to 7439.
Telephone code: 0 57 00.
ⓘ **VVV Deventer,**
Stationsplein 2,
NL-7411 HB Deventer;
tel. 1 62 00.

HOTELS. – *Postiljon Motel Deventer,* Deventerweg 121, I, 210 b.; *De Keizerskroon,* Stroomarkt 10, II, 21 b.; *Royal,* Brink 94, V, 26 b.

RESTAURANTS. – *'t Arsenaal,* Nieuwe Markt 33; *IJsselhotel,* Worp 2.

EVENTS. – *Carnival Procession* (Monday before Lent); *Annual Fair* (Good Friday), and *Kermis* (first week in June).

Deventer is a town on the right bank of the IJssel in the Dutch province of Overijssel. Although there are several beautiful old houses, the inner city has a predominantly modern character. It is a lively industrial town. Important are carpet-making and bicycle production. It is also well known for its pastries (honey cakes called "Koek"). A famous son of the city was the theologian Geert Groote (1340–84), who founded the association "Brotherhood of Common Life" here about 1376.

SIGHTS. – In the Brink, the vast main square of Deventer, stands the late Gothic **Weigh-house** (1528–31) with an imposing outside staircase of 1643–4. Inside, and also in the *House of Three Golden Herrings* (1575) behind the Weigh-house, is the *Municipal Museum of Antiquities.* On the west side of the square stands the *Penninckshuis* (1588), a former Mennonite Church.

South-west of the Brink, on the Grote Kerkhof, stands the ***Grote Kerk** (St Lebuinus,* Dutch Reformed). It is a massive Gothic structure built in the 14th–16th c. with interesting bas-reliefs and frescoes, as well as a Romanesque crypt of the 11th c. The massive south tower dates from the 15th c. and has a Baroque spire with a carillon. On the south-east side of the Grote Kerkhof, stands the **Town Hall** with a façade of 1694. Inside is a fine painting of the Council Chamber with all the mayors and aldermen, a work of ter Borch (1667). The artist himself was, towards the end of his life, alderman of Deventer. On the first floor is the *Athenaeum Library* founded in the 14th c., with 120,000 books, over 500 manuscripts and incunabula. Next to it stands the former *Landshuis* with a façade dating from 1632. It is now the police headquarters.

East of the Brink, you arrive, via the Bergstraat, at a strange and somewhat gloomy part of the Old City stretching not far from the banks of the IJssel and overlooked by the **Bergkerk** (Church of *St Nicolaas*) (12th–15th c.). The church has two late Romanesque towers. Inside are frescoes of the 13th–16th c. From the opposite bank of the IJssel there is a beautiful view of the town.

SURROUNDINGS of Deventer. – Drive east on the E8 and after 20 km (12 miles) turn right to **Markelo** (Hotel de Haverkamp, IV, 12 b.), well known for its exhibitions and festivities.

Diekirch

Country: Luxembourg. – Canton: Diekirch.
Altitude: 200 m (656 feet). – Population: 5600.
ⓘ **Syndicat d'Initiative,**
Place Guillaume,
L-Diekirch;
tel. 8 30 23.

HOTELS. – *Hiertz*, Rue Clairefontaine 1, II, 7 r.; *Du Parc*, Avenue de la Gare 28, II, 50 r.; *Au Beau Séjour*, Rue de l'Esplanade 12, III, 38 r.; *De la Paix* (no rest.), Place Guillaume 7, III, 8 r.; *Au Bon Accueil*, Avenue de la Gare 77, IV, 11 r.; *Europe*, Place de l'Étoile 1, IV, 35 r.; *De la Gare*, Avenue de la Gare 13, IV, 12 r. – Two CAMP SITES.

The Luxembourg town of Diekirch is a popular holiday resort. It is situated on the left bank of the Sûre on the border between the region of Gutland and the Ösling, which is part of the Ardennes. The township, surrounded by wooded hills, is the administrative capital of a canton of the same name.

"Devil's Altar" near Diekirch

Diekirch developed on the site of a former Roman settlement. It received its charter in 1260. Economically important, apart from the tourist industry, are a large brewery and an iron foundry.

SIGHTS. – Near the Place d'Armes stands the old **Parish Church** dating from the 10th and 15th–16th c. In the north-western part of the Old Town, on the spacious Place Guillaume stand the *Church of St Laurent*, built in 1868 in a neo-Romanesque style, the *District Court* in Classical style, and the **Municipal Museum**, housing interesting Roman objects, among them beautiful mosaics.

SURROUNDINGS of Diekirch. – The charming surroundings of the town can be explored on well-marked footpaths. Path "D" runs some 2·5 km (about 1 mile) south through the woods to the **Deiwelselter** (*Devil's Altar*), which is a striking stone monument.

Diest

Country: Belgium. – Province: Brabant.
Altitude: 23 m (75 feet). – Population: 20,000.
Postal code: B-3290.
Telephone code: 0 13.
ⓘ **Vereniging voor Vreemdelingenverkeer,**
Molenbergstraat 28;
tel. 33 23 62.

HOTELS. – *De Haan*, Grote Markt 19, IV, 8 r.; *Carine*, Leuvenseweg 284, V, 7 r.; *Modern*, Leuvenseweg 4, V, 14 r.; *Falstaff*, E. Robeynslaan 2, V, 8 r. – YOUTH HOSTEL: St Janstraat 2, 130 b.

RESTAURANTS. – *Gulden Valk*, Demerstraat 2; *Empereur*, Grote Markt 24; *Modern*, Leuvensesteen-weg 93; *Gasthof 1618*, Begijnhof-Kerkstraat 18.

The Belgian town of Diest in the province of Brabant, situated on both banks of the Demer in the transition zone between the fertile Haveland and the wooded Kempen, is a market town in an intensively farmed area. The main products grown here are asparagus, early potatoes and other vegetables. Since the second half of the 13th c., when Diest received its charter, it ranked among the most important towns in Brabant because of its famous cloth-making, but this has long since disappeared. Its place was taken by large flour-mills and other branches of the food industry. Diest is best known in the country as the city of beer.

SIGHTS. – The Grote Markt in the middle of the Old Town is framed by several beautiful *patrician houses* of the 16th–18th c. In the south-west of the square is the pre-Classical **Town Hall** (*Stadhuis*) dating from 1726, housing the *Municipal Museum* (Stedelijk Museum), with a collection of rare works of art. In the midst of the Markt stands the **Church of St Sulpitius**, one of the best examples of Brabant Gothic. It was built in 1417–1534, and in its tower is a carillon of forty-three bells. In the choir are some superb pews (1491) and the tomb of Philip of Nassau-Orange (d. 1618). Other interesting buildings are the early Gothic *Church of Our Lady*, consecrated in 1253, and the former *Cloth Hall* (Lakenhalle) in the Ketelstraat, dating from 1346.

At the end of the Begijnenstraat in the north-east part of the Old Town is the **Begijnhof**, founded in 1252. In the middle stands the 14th c. Gothic *Church of St Katherine*. The Begijnhof of Diest is one of the oldest in Flanders. Its well-preserved 17th c. houses are separated from the street by a magnificent *Baroque portal*. Behind the Begijnhof extend the former 19th c. fortifications, now a park in which some remains of the old city wall can still be seen.

SURROUNDINGS of Diest. – An excursion to the picturesque *Premonstratensian Abbey Averbode, 6 km (4 miles) to the west is well worth while. The monastery was founded in the 12th c. The oldest part of the building, which dates from the 14th–18th c., is the entrance gate standing at the point where the three provinces, Brabant, Limburg and Antwerp meet. The Baroque church, built by Jan van Eynde in 1664 has rich interior furnishing, pews dating from 1672, a high altar (1758) and a beautiful organ, as well as noteworthy pictures by P. J. Verhaghen. The monastery building possesses several works of art and a large library, parts of which can be visited on written request, but only by men.

Scherpenheuvel (French: *Montaigu* – Hotel de Zwaan, IV, 8 b.; de Valk, IV, 7 r.), 6 km (4 miles) west of Diest, is a popular place of pilgrimage. Worth seeing is the *Church of Our Lady, standing on high ground. It was built in 1609–27 by W. Coebergher, and although it shows strong Italian influence, it is nevertheless the most important Baroque building in Belgium. In the interior are good paintings by T. van Loon, a marble relief by F. Duquesnoy and a rich treasury.

Dinant

Country: Belgium. – Province: Namur.
Altitude: 90 m (295 feet). – Population: 12,000.
Postal code: B-5500.
Telephone code: 0 82.

ⓘ **Syndicat d'Initiative,**
Rue Grande 37;
tel. 22 28 70.

HOTELS. – *De la Couronne*, IV, 25 r.; *Grand Hôtel des Postes*, IV, 62 r.; *Henroteaux*, IV, 30 r.; *Hostellerie du Thermidor*, IV, 5 r.; *De la Citadelle*, IV, 19 r.; *Belle Vue*, IV, 7 r.; *De la Gare*, IV, 22 r.; *Du Plateau*, IV, 11 r.; *De la Collégiale*, IV, 14 r.; *De l'Etoile*, V, 8 r.; *Des Grottes*, V, 7 r. – CAMP SITE.

RESTAURANTS. – *Baguettes du Mandarin*, Avenue Churchill; *Rôtisserie Javaux*, Rue du Velodrome 2; *La Strada*, Rue Grande 24.

CAFÉ. – *Taverne Wiertz*, Place Roi Albert Ier.

EVENTS. – Several concerts and theatre performances all year round.

SPORTS and LEISURE. – Swimming, canoeing on the Meuse, water-skiing, angling, tennis, riding, Alpine climbing, hunting, golf (18 holes).

Dinant is the second largest city in the Belgian region of Condroz. It nestles in the upper valley of the Meuse, under precipitous limestone rocks crowned by a powerful citadel. Thanks to this favourable *location it has become a very lively tourist resort, especially at week-ends.

From the time of the Hohenstaufen Dynasty the town belonged to the Diocese of Liège and was highly prosperous as early as the 13th–15th c. It was famous throughout the Middle Ages for its brass

Dinant in the Valley of the Upper Meuse

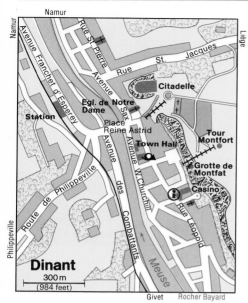

Dinant
300 m
(984 feet)

and copperware, the so-called dinan-deries, the manufacture of which has been recently revived. The town was con-quered and destroyed in 1466 by Philip the Good, when 800 of its inhabitants are said to have been drowned in the Meuse. In the First World War, Dinant was an important bridgehead on the Meuse and, therefore, the focus of heavy fighting, in which 674 of its citizens perished. It also suffered heavy damage in the Second World War but has since been rebuilt.

SIGHTS. – The main street in the southern part of the elongated town is the Rue Grande, which runs parallel to the right bank of the Meuse as far as the Place Reine Astrid where a bridge crosses the river. Through traffic, however, is con-centrated on the left bank. In the Place Reine Astrid, at the foot of the citadel hill, stands the **Church of Notre-Dame**, a beautiful early Gothic structure from the 13th c. Originally there was a Romanes-que basilica but it was destroyed in 1227 by falling rocks. The central tower with an onion-shaped dome (1566) provides a harmonious contrast to the citadel soaring high above the town. Further south in the Rue Grande stands the *Town Hall* (Hôtel de Ville), with a monument to the citizens who lost their lives in 1914. The Rue Grande continues southward as the Rue Léopold and, at the end of the town, passes between the rocks of the high plateau and the famous *Rocher Bayard. This is a rocky needle some 40 m (131 feet) high, rising steeply up from the

river. Bayard was the name of the horse of the legendary four sons of Aymon. Fleeing from Charlemagne they all rode on the same horse and crossed the river here in one mighty jump.

The northern continuation of the Rue Grande is the Rue Adolphe Sax, named after the inventor of the saxophone, who was born here in No. 31. Further north the road passes through the rocky cleft, the *Fonds de Leffe*, which is the beginning of the suburb of LEFFE. There is a former **Premonstratensian Abbey** dating from the 17th–18th c.

From the promenade on the right river bank, a footpath leads to the *Grotte de Mont-Fat* and further on to the *Tour de Montfort*, high above the river. It can also be reached by a chair-lift. The path then continues to the **citadel** some 100 m (328 feet) above the river. It was built by the Dutch government in 1821 on the site of the former dilapidated fortress which had belonged to the Bishops of Liège. The citadel can also be reached from the Grand' Place behind the church, either by a series of 408 steps cut out of the rock, by a cableway, or by a road (1 km – about a ½ mile) via the Rue Adolphe Sax and then to the right by the Rue St Jacques. From the terrace is a *pictur-esque view over the river valley.

On the left bank of the Meuse is the suburb of ST MÉDARD which has a *rail-way station* and several hotels. West of the bridge, on the road to Philippeville, is the entrance to the **Grotte de Raim-paine** ("La Merveilleuse"), which is about 500 m (1641 feet) long with beautiful stalactite formations.

SURROUNDINGS of Dinant. – 11 km (7 miles) to the north-east is the village of **Spontin** (Hotel Cheval Blanc, IV, 12 b.), with a moated castle dating from the 11th–12th c. The present building, one of the finest in Belgium, is regarded as a perfect example of a medieval castle.

The village of **Celles** (Hostellerie Val Joli, III, 7 r.; des Ardennes, IV, 6 r.), 10 km (6 miles) south-east of Dinant, is famous for its Church of St Hadelinus, built in the Mosan Romanesque style with a beautiful 9th c. crypt and squat fortress-like towers. Inside is a stone pulpit and early Gothic pews of the 13th c.

The Church of Notre-Dame in **Hastière**, upstream on the left bank of the Meuse, is an interesting 11th c. basilica. Worth seeing is its western façade and the western portico of the tower with handsome arcades.

Opposite Dinant is the village of *Bouvignes* with the castle **Crèvecœur**. This was built between 1320 and

1382, and destroyed in 1554. Also worth seeing is the Church of St Lambert, with an early Romanesque crypt, and the Maison de Baillage with a stepped gable.

Near **Annevoie** (Auberge de la Poste, IV, 8 r.), 12 km (7 miles) downstream from Dinant, left of the river, is a palace of the same name built in 1627 in the style of Louis XIV and enlarged in 1771. Especially interesting are its *gardens with lakes and fountains.

Dordrecht

Country: The Netherlands. – Province: South Holland. Altitude: 3 m (10 feet) below and 5 m (16 feet) above sea level. – Population: 188,000. Postal code: NL-3300AA to 3329. Telephone code: 0 78.

(i) **VVV Dordrecht,**
Stationsweg 1,
NL-3311 JW Dordrecht;
tel. 3 28 00.
Paviljoen "De Molenhoeck";
tel. (0 18 59) 27 55.

HOTELS. – *Bellevue-Groothoofdspoort,* Boomstraat 37, II, 49 b.; *Statenhof,* Steegoverssloot 57, IV, 50 b.; *Ponsen,* Stationsweg 7, IV, 49 b.; *Blauwpoort,* Blauwpoortsplein 9, V. 17 b.; *Van der Brankke,* Wolwevershaven 42, V, 52 b. – IN ZWIJNDRECHT: *Swindregt,* Pieter Zeemanstraat 47, III, 12 b.; *Meerdervoort,* Karel Doormanlaan 77–79, IV, 20 b. – YOUTH HOSTEL: Noordendijk 382, 88 b. – CAMP SITE.

RESTAURANTS. – *Camelot,* Singel 389; *Wantij-paviljoen,* Wantijpark; *Het Napolitaensche Peerdt,* Nieuwstraat 30.

EVENTS. – *Days of the Windmills* (July/August, Saturday afternoons).

The ancient town of Dordrecht, known in its shorter form as Dordt, lies in the province of South Holland near Rotterdam between the Oude Maas, which is here accessible to large sea-going vessels, the Merwede and the two branches of the Maas, the Noord and the Dordtse Kil. There are shipyards, shipping companies, engineering plants and chemical industries; it is also popular for water sports. Thanks to its favourable location as a port it was once the wealthiest commercial town of the Netherlands, but it was overtaken in the 18th c. by Antwerp and Rotterdam. Today, Dordrecht is a river port as well as a sea port, and the turnover of goods which it handles, especially of goods in transit, is over five million tons.

HISTORY. – According to the Chronicle of Ghent, Dordrecht was destroyed by the Norsemen as early as 937. It was mentioned in the Chronicles for the first

The Grote Kerk in Dordrecht

time about 1138 when it was called Thuredrit. When it received its charter in 1220 it was already an important commercial port trading with England, the Rhineland and Flanders. However, in 1421 the entire area south of the town was flooded in the so-called "Elizabeth Flood", and the economic development of Dordrecht came to a standstill, as its land communications were largely severed. The sea port regained its importance only at the end of the 19th c.

SIGHTS. – The Voorstraats Haven is the main canal of the city. On the Visbrug stands the monument of the statesmen Johan and Cornelis de Witt, who were born in Dordrecht, the latter being the Mayor of the town. Further west stands the *Town Hall* (Stadhuis), built in heavy Classical style. From here you reach, via the Grotekerksbuurt, the **Grote Kerk** (Reformed), begun about 1300 and rebuilt in the 15th–16th c. It has a massive tower 70 m (230 feet) high, with a carillon. In the well-proportioned interior is a superb choir grille from 1744, and also magnificent *pews (1538–41), the most important specimens of their kind in Holland.

North-east of the Grote Kerk at No. 27 Nieuwe Haven, is the **Museum van Gijn**, with the collection of antiques of Simon van Gijn (d. 1922), housed in his former residence (built in 1792). From here a footbridge crosses the Nieuwe Haven to the Vleeshouwersstraat. This leads back to the Visbrug, and further east via the Groenmarkt to the Scheffersplein. In the latter stands the statue of the painter and builder Arij Scheffer, who was born in Dordrecht in 1795. At the end of the Wijnstraat, which leads in a north-easterly direction from the Scheffersplein, stands the **Groothoofdspoort**, a Gothic city gate reconstructed in 1618, with a fine relief and a domed tower. From its northern side there is a beautiful view over the Oude Maas, the Noord and the Merwede.

In the Museumsstraat not far from the Spuihaven, stands the **Dordrecht Museum** with a good collection of paintings by Dordrecht masters of the 17th–19th c., and by other more recent Dutch artists.

The best view of the city and the wide expanses of water with many ships can be obtained from the dikes near *Zwijndrecht*, on the right bank of the Oude Maas (ferry from Hooikade not far west of Nieuwe Haven); or from *Papendrecht* at the opening of the Noord into the Merwede (ferry from the Merwekade at the northern end of the Riedijkshaven). East of the city, a road crosses the Merwede and skirts Papendrecht to the north-east.

SURROUNDINGS of Dordrecht. – In summer it is possible to travel to **Rotterdam** (see page 236) and back by motor boat in 4$\frac{1}{2}$ hours (including a harbour cruise).

Drente/Drenthe

Country: The Netherlands. – Province: Drente (Drenthe).

(i) **Prov. VVV Drenthe,**
Brink 42,
NL-9401 HV Assen;
tel. (0 59 20) 1 43 24.

The Dutch region of Drente (Drenthe) is mostly flat and lies some 10–20 m (33–66 feet) above sea level. It is situated in the extreme north-east of the wide Geest plains of the country. Its borders mostly coincide with those of the province of the same name.

The most conspicuous heights of Drente are the moraines of Hondsrug rising to 32 m (105 feet). The Hondsrug is a range of hills some 50 km (31 miles) long stretching from Emmen in the south-east to Groningen in the north-west, and formed in the next to last Ice Age (the Saale Ice Age). From here the surface of Drente slopes slightly and almost imperceptibly westwards. It consists of marly detritus from the same period, later overlaid by enormous sediments of sand.

After the Ice Ages, large flat moors developed in the lower parts of Drente and covered the layers of sand. In the troughs in the more elevated parts of the country, vast high moors developed. They have now been completely drained. To cultivate them the "Fenning technique" was used, particularly in the Groningen area. The fen colonies in Drente are primarily in the south of the province around *Beilen* and *Hoogeveen*.

THE FEN COLONIES. – Fen, in Dutch "Venn", means swamp or moor. The fen colonies are therefore settlements situated in moorlands. In the Netherlands, mainly in the high moor areas of Groningen and Drente, the colonisation of the moors began early in the 17th c. A few years later this novel land-reclaiming method was employed also in north-west Germany.

The moors were first drained by man-made ditches, the so-called "wieks" which opened into a navigable canal. The main wiek functioned as a collecting canal; it was then linked to several "inwieks" or side canals and in a further phase of colonisation still smaller "achterwieks" were added. The settlements of the "fehntjes" often stretched for miles along the drainage canals, which were at that time the only means of communication. The plots of land belonging to the individual farmsteads and called "hides" were long strips between 50 and 130 m (164–427 feet) wide, laid at right angles to the wieks, and which extended into the dried-out moorland. Such villages are described as "hide settlements of the moors".

The conversion of the moor soils into fertile land required a special method. First the topsoil, a layer of peat some 50 cm (20 inches) deep, was cut and put aside. Then the remaining layers of peat were removed and ferried by boat on the wieks and canals to the towns to be used mainly as fuel. The mineral subsoil was then mixed with the topsoil which had been removed in the first place.

The farming villages of Drente located off, the moors, were formerly separated by vast stretches of heath. However, in the last eighty years these have been replaced partly by plantations of pine trees, but mainly by rye, oats and potato fields. The arable area of most farmsteads is generally below 20 hectares (49 acres), but on the high moors farms of up to 50 hectares (124 acres) are not uncommon.

Compared with agriculture, industry plays only a subordinate role in the economy of Drente. There are a few works in the south-east, mainly because there was a considerable potential of unused labour in that area after the cutting of peat was

The Communal Building in Slaen (Drente)

given up. Apart from that, drilling for oil near Schoonebeek and Meppel has become increasingly important in recent years.

The average density of population in the area is 100 per sq. km (259 per sq. mile), which is very low; the only important township in Drente is **Assen** (see page 98) which lies in the middle of the region. *Emmen*, near the frontier of the Federal Republic of Germany, is also of some importance.

A special feature of Drente is the numerous prehistoric megalithic tombs, the so-called Hunebedden, made of enormous boulders of rock. These rocks originated in Scandinavia and were deposited here mainly in the area of Hondsrug by the glaciers of the Saale Ice Age. Anyone who is interested in the prehistory of the Netherlands should not miss a visit to this moraine country. The most famous tombs can be seen some 3 km (2 miles) north of the village of *Havelte* not far from the road to *Frederiksoort*.

Echternach

Country: Luxembourg. – Canton: Echternach.
Altitude: 158 m (518 feet). – Population: 4200.
ⓘ **Bureau Officiel de Renseignements,**
Porte St Willibrord;
tel. 7 22 30.

HOTELS. – **Bel-Air*, Route de Berdorf 1. L, 44 r.; *Grand Hôtel*, Route de Diekirch 27, I, 40 r.; *Du Parc*, Rue de l'Hôpital 9, I, 35 r.; *St Hubert*, Rue de la Gare 21, II, 36 r.; *Petite Marquise*, Place du Marché 18, II, 41 r.; *Des Ardennes*, Rue de la Gare 38, II, 37 r.; *Du Commerce*, Place du Marché, 16, III, 42 r.; *De la Sûre,*

Rue de la Gare 49, III, 35 r.; *Universel*, Rue de Luxembourg 40, III, 32 r.; *De l'Etoile d'Or*, Rue de la Gare 39, III, 37 r.; *Régine*, Rue de la Gare 53, III, 11 r.; *Au Soleil*, Rue des Remparts 20, III, 21 r.; *Conzemius* (no rest.), Rue Maximilien 30, III, 10 r.; *De Luxembourg* (no rest.), Rue de Luxembourg 36, IV, 12 r.; *Bon Accueil* (no rest.), Rue des Merciers, IV, 11 r.; *De l'Abbaye*, Rue des Merciers 2, IV, 11 r.; *Prince Henri et Terminus*, Rue de la Gare 51, IV, 14 r.; *Wagener-Hartmann* (no rest.), Rue de Luxembourg 29, IV, 15 r.; *Petite Suisse* (no rest.), Rue A. Duschcher 56, V, 22 r. – YOUTH HOSTEL, 190 b. – Numerous CAMP SITES.

RESTAURANTS. – *Auberge de l'Aiglon*, Rue Maximilien 2a. – IN GEYERSHOF (7 km (4 miles) to the southeast): *La Bergerie*.

EVENTS. – The **Dancing Procession** commemorating St Willibrord (on Whit Tuesday).

The ancient Luxembourg township of Echternach on the Sûre is situated on the frontier between Luxembourg and the Federal Republic of Germany, 30 km (19 miles) northeast of the capital Luxembourg.

It is a market town and a very popular tourist resort in the so-called Swiss Luxembourg. It developed around a Benedictine Abbey which was founded in 698 by the Northumbrian monk St Willibrord, the missionary of the Frisians, and dissolved in 1795. The monastery was famous in the Middle Ages for its manuscript writing and copying as well as its school of book illumination.

SIGHTS. – In the Market Place stands the **Town Hall** (*Denzelt*) with interesting late Gothic arcades (1520–30) on the ground floor. Nearby stands the early

The Market Place in Echternach

Romanesque Basilica of **St Willibrord**, dating from the 11th–13th c., which even today is the destination of numerous pilgrims. During excavations in the crypt after the First World War an 8th c. altar was uncovered and behind it the tomb of St Willibrord.

The upper part of the altar had been found at the beginning of the 20th c. in the neighbouring village of Rosport, but only recently could it be proved that this was the oldest altar crown ever found. Since 1915 it has been in the State Museum in Luxembourg under the name of "the **Stone Relief of Echternach**".

On high ground behind the basilica stands the 13th c. Parish Church of *St Peter and St Paul* built on the foundations of a Roman castellum (excavations). Fifteen minutes to the west, above the town, is the pavilion *Trosskneppchen*, with a superb view. Fifteen minutes further is the entrance to the **Wolfs-schlucht*, an interesting cleft in the rocks 50 m (164 feet) high and 150 m (492 feet) long.

Edam

Country: The Netherlands. – Province: North Holland.
Altitude: below sea level. – Population: 22,000.
Postal code: NL-1135 AA.
Telephone code: 0 29 93.
ⓘ **VVV Edam,**
Kleine Kerkstraat 5,
NL-1135 AT Edam;
tel. 7 15 43.

HOTELS. – *Damhotel*, Keizersgracht 1, IV, 21 b.; *De Harmonie*, Voorhaven 92, V, 10 b. – CAMP SITE.

The Dutch town of Edam in the province of North Holland lies in the reclaimed area (Polders) on the IJsselmeer to which it is connected by a canal. The most important part of the town's economy, apart from tourism, textiles and ceramics, is the dairy industry which produces the famous cheese, also called Edam. The town was founded in the 13th c. as a customs post, and the cheese trade was the source of its prosperity in the 16th–17th c.

SIGHTS. – The *Grote Kerk* dating from the 14th c. was burned down in 1602 and restored later in the 17th c. It has some valuable stained-glass windows. The *Town Hall* on the Domplein dates from the 18th c. and houses a small collection of paintings, to be seen in the beautiful

Edam Cheeses

Council Hall. Opposite is the *Municipal Museum* with a fine façade from 1737. The oldest carillon in Holland, dating from 1560, can be heard from the old *tower* which remains from the demolished St Mary's Church.

SURROUNDINGS of Edam. – 5 km (3 miles) south-east of the town is the popular fishing village of **Volendam* (Hotel van Diepen, III, 37 b.; Spannder, IV, 104 b.), with a picturesque harbour. It was formerly a resort favoured by artists and it is well known for its folk costumes, but these are nowadays worn mostly for the tourists.

Eindhoven

Country: The Netherlands. – Province: North Brabant.
Altitude: 20 m (66 feet). – Population: 193,000.
Postal code: NL-5600AA to 5699.
Telephone code: 0 40.
ⓘ **VVV Eindhoven,**
Stationsplein 24 (at the station),
NL-5611 AC Eindhoven;
tel. 44 92 31.

HOTELS. – **Cocagne*, Vestdijk 47, I, 276 b.; *Holiday Inn*, Veldm. Montgomerylaan 1, I, 400 b.; *Motel Eindhoven*, Aalsterweg 322, I, 300 b.; *Astor*, Prins Hendrikstraat 4, III, 29 b.; *De Bijenkorf*, Markt 35, III, 35 b.; *Dommelhotel*, Jonckbloetlaan 13, III, 70 b.; *Parkhotel*, Alberdinck Thijmlaan 18, IV, 64 b.; *Eikenburg*, Aalsterweg 281, V, 20 b.; *De Sport*, Kleine Berg 16, V, 16 b.; *De Ridder* (no rest.), Hertogstraat 15, V, 16 b. – *Sheraton Inn Geldrop*, an der Autobahn E 3, Bogardeind 219, II, 200 b.

RESTAURANTS. – *De Vest*, Stationsplein 7; *Du Théâtre*, Lesage ten Broeklaan 2a; *Blauwe Lotus*, Limburglaan 20; *Mei-Ling*, Geldropseweg 17; *Van Turnhout*, St Trudoplein 7. – 2 km (1 mile) north-east by the swimming pool De IJzeren Man: *Karpendonkse Hoeve*, Sumatralaan 3.

The modern industrial town of Eindhoven, situated on the River Dommel in the Dutch province of

Eindhoven, a sectional model of the Technical Museum "Evoluon"

North Brabant, was until the second half of the 19th c. an unknown and insignificant little town. The increase in its population began after the foundation of the Philips Works in 1891, and by 1918 the town had 64,000 inhabitants. In the following decades it became the largest city in southern Netherlands, and the fifth largest in the country. In addition to the Philips combine, the DAF Motor Works are important. Other industries are engineering and the manufacture of consumer hardware, glass, man-made fibres, paper, textiles and tobacco.

Although the commuter belt of Eindhoven reaches as far as Belgium, it is not exclusively an industrial town. Since 1956 it has had a Technical University, two colleges of social sciences, a school of industrial design, several scientific libraries, and a Chamber of Commerce.

SIGHTS. – Near the station stands the monument to *A. F. Philips* (d. 1951), a son of the founder of the firm. In the Jacob-Oppenheim-Straat rises a steel-framed tower 45 m (148 feet) high with the largest **carillon** in Holland, consisting of sixty-one bells donated in 1966 by the staff of Philips.

The *Church of St Katherine* in neo-Gothic style was designed in 1867 by the well-known architect P. J. H. Cuypers. The *Van-Abbe-Museum* in Bilderdijklaan

exhibits mainly works of modern artists. A visit to the Philips Museum *Evoluon specialising in technology and science, is also recommended. It is in the Noord Brabantlaan, not far from the Rondweg (ring road).

In the southern district of STRATUM is the interesting *Zoo "Animali"*.

Eisch Valley / Vallée de l'Eisch

Country: Luxembourg. – Cantons: Capellen and Mersch.

ⓘ **Syndicat d'Initiative,**
Rue Jean Majerus,
L-Mersch;
tel. 32 80 81.

HOTELS. – IN MERSCH: *Marisca*, Place de l'Etoile 1, II, 19 r.; *Des 7 Châteaux*, Route d'Arlon 3, III, 23 r. – IN SEPTFONTAINES: *Des Roches*, Rue de l'Eglise 12, IV, 8 r. – IN SIMMERSCHMELZ: *Simmerschmelz*, IV, 15 r.

YOUTH HOSTEL at Castle Hollenfels. – Several CAMP SITES.

The Eisch is a little river in northern Lorraine. It has its source on the frontier of Belgium and Luxembourg some 20 km (12 miles) west of the capital of the Grand Duchy. For a short stretch it forms the border between the two countries then turns east, crosses the western part of the Luxembourg Gutland in a picturesque *valley known as the "Valley of the Seven Castles", and then joins the Alzette near Mersch.

The little town of **Mersch** with its well-restored palace and a beautiful belfry (1707) is a suitable starting point for a drive into the "Valley of the Seven Castles" to see its unusual sandstone formations and enjoy its woods. 8 km (5 miles) from the town you reach a fork from which, on the right 2 km (1 mile) up the hill, you come to the village of *Hollenfels*. It is overlooked by the **Castle of Hollenfels** standing high on a weathered rock and now a youth hostel. The newer part of the building dates from the 16th c. Of the oldest part only a large tower with two vaulted halls built one above the other remains.

Some 4 km (2 miles) further upstream on the Eisch is **Ansembourg**, with a ruined castle towering above it. At the entrance to the village on the right, is the new Palace of Ansembourg dating from the 17th c., with gardens laid out in the French style. Also worth seeing is the ruined *Nunnery of Marienthal*, founded in 1237. Next to it is the Monastery of the Pères Blancs d'Afrique (1886), now housing a missionary school and a small museum of African ethnography.

The next village of interest is 8 km (5 miles) further on. It is **Septfontaines**, a quiet little summer resort with a fine church of the 16th c. and a ruined castle on a wooded hill.

Further upstream comes *Hobscheid*, a small Luxembourg village and the last one in this most charming part of the valley. From here the Belgian town of Arlon can be easily reached. On the way, lying to the left above the valley, is *Koerich*, which has an interesting church and the ruins of another castle.

Enkhuizen

Country: The Netherlands. – Province: North Holland.
Altitude: sea level. – Population: 14,000.
Postal code: NL-1600 AA to 1699.
Telephone code: 0 22 80.
(i) **VVV Enkhuizen,**
Meidenmarkt 2,
NL-1601 HL Enkhuizen;
tel. 3164.

HOTELS. – *Het Wapen von Enkhuizen*, Breedstraat 59, II, 54 b.; *Du Passage*, Paktuinen 8, IV, 22 b.; *Die Port van Cleve*, Dijk 74–76, V, 10 b. – CAMP SITE.

RESTAURANTS. – *Die Drie Haringhe*, Dijk 28; *Markerwaard*, Dijk 62; *Lotus*, Westerstraat 95.

EVENTS. – *Bulb Show* (second half of February, approximately ten days); *Jazz Festival* (beginning May); *Fair* (Mid-June, five days); *Holiday Market* in *Sprookjesstad* (July/August, every Thursday); *Sailing Regatta* (August); *Fair* (mid-September); *Riding Competition and Trotting Races* (third Thursday in September).

Enkhuizen, birthplace of the painter Paulus Potter (1625–54), lies on the IJsselmeer in the province of North Holland, and is intersected by several canals. It ranks as one of the prettiest towns in Holland. Many thousands of tourists visit it every year to see its well-preserved buildings of the 15th–17th c. In those days, Enkhuizen was a wealthy and prosperous port with a population of some 40,000, owing initially to its trade with the Baltic countries and later also to herring fishing.

Its decline came when most of the merchants moved to Amsterdam, and it reached its lowest point when the herring fleet, numbering some 400 boats, was destroyed by the French in 1703 and the harbour silted up. At present, the most important sectors of the town's economy, after tourism, are the paper industry, metal works, fishing and bulb growing.

In the Harbour of Enkhuizen

SIGHTS. – From the *station* there is a good view of the lively **harbour** dominated at the entrance to the town by the *Drommedaris Tower*, a remnant of the former fortifications of 1540. It contains a *carillon* by Hemony, ranking among the best in Holland. Beyond the canal a street forks off left from the Spoorstraat and follows the water towards the Gothic **Westerkerk** (15th c.). Inside is one of the most beautiful choir screens in the north of Holland. In front of the church is the former *mint* of the 16th c. with an impressive gabled façade.

The Westerstraat runs from here to the *Zuiderkerk* built in 1625–54 with an onion-shaped tower and a splendid carillon. Nearby on the Kaasmarkt, left, stands the *Weigh-house* of 1559. Inside is an interesting 17th c. surgery (doctor's office). The Westerstraat then continues towards the Breedstraat where, on the right, stands the **Town Hall** (*Stadhuis*). Built in 1688, it resembles the Royal Palace in Amsterdam. Inside hang precious tapestries (1705). The council chamber is decorated with Utrecht velvet dating from 1609 and is well worth seeing. On the second floor is a small *Museum of Antiquities*.

The *Koeport* on the western edge of the town was built between 1649 and 1730, and is another remnant of the former fortifications.

Enschede

Country: The Netherlands. – Province: Overijssel.
Altitude: 50 m (164 feet). – Population: 141,000.
Postal code: NL-7500 AA to 7549.
Telephone code: 0 53.
(i) **VVV Enschede,**
    Markt 31,
    NL-7511 GB Enschede;
    tel. 32 32 00.

HOTELS. – *Memphis*, M. H. Tromplaan 55, I, 61 b.; *Parkhotel*, Hengeloesetraat 200, III, 23 b.; *Atlanta*, Markt 12, III, 42 b.; *Industrie*, Haaksbergerstraat 4, IV, 37 b.; *Raedthuijs*, Raadhuisstraat 12, IV, 16 b.

CAMP SITES. – *Aamsveen*, Lappenpad 250; *Boekelo*, Oude Deldenerweg; *Klein Zandvoort*, Keppelerdijk 200; *Twente*, Oude Deldenerweg.

RESTAURANTS. – *Koetshuis*, Walstraat 48; *Marmite*, Oliemolensingel 40.

EVENTS. – *Household Exhibition* (end March); *Fair* (first week after Easter); *Tattoo* (June); *Holiday Entertainment for Young People* (mid-June–mid-August); *Autumn walks around Enschede* (October); *International Military Contest* (mid-October); *Flower and Art Show* (ten days mid-October); *International Marathon* (every two years in August – 1981 onwards).

SPORTS and LEISURE. – Riding, tennis, golf, water sports, bowling and skittles.

The Dutch town of Enschede, situated on the Twente Canal in the province of Overijssel near the West German frontier, is the focal point of the Dutch cotton industry and at the same time plays an important part in the cultural life of the eastern part of the country. There is a specialised textile school, a technical university, founded in 1961, and an art college, as well as three famous museums.

Enschede received its charter in 1325. The industrialisation of what was, until then, an insignificant little town began in the 1830s, and brought with it a swift increase in population. To the traditional cotton and wool industries comprising numerous spinning, weaving and bleaching establishments, must be added the manufacture of artificial silk and of ready-made clothes. Textile machinery and allied equipment are also produced here. Other industries were recently introduced, such as chemicals and electrical engineering, in order to diversify the economic structure, thought to be too restricted and therefore vulnerable.

SIGHTS. – The best known of the three museums of Enschede is the **Rijksmuseum Twenthe**, at No. 129 Lasondersingel, in the north of the town. It houses an important collection of antiquities and paintings, manuscripts, wooden sculptures, Delft pottery and valuable tapestries.

West of the central area, in No. 2 De Ruyterlaan, is the *Natuurmuseum*, with a collection of rare birds, insects, reptiles and mammals, minerals and fossils. Nearby stands the *Synagogue*, topped by a somewhat oriental copper dome. It dates from the year 1928. East of here is Boulevard 1945, from which the Langestraat branches off on the left, leading into a street called De Klomp. On the left of this is the *Elderinkshuis* (1783), the only historic building in the town to survive the Great Fire of 1862. Further south-east in a little park by the Espoortstraat, is the *Twents-Gelders Textielmuseum* which illustrates the development of the whole of the textile industry from the old craftsmanship to the modern plants.

Ettelbruck

Country: Luxembourg. – Canton: Diekirch.
Altitude: 185 m (279 feet). – Population: 6000.
ⓘ **Syndicat d'Initiative,**
Grand'Rue 13;
tel. 8 20 68.

HOTELS. – *Herckmans,* Grand' Rue 36, II, 17 r.; *Central,* Rue de Bastogne 25, III, 21 r.; *De Luxembourg,* Rue Prince Henri 7–9, III, 22 r.; *Cames,* Rue Prince Henri 45, III, 13 r.; *De la Place du Marché* (no rest.), Rue de Bastogne 5, V, 9 r. – CAMP SITE.

The friendly little Luxembourg town of Ettelbruck nestles at the confluence of the Wark and the Alzette with the Sûre, at the border between Gutland and Ösling, which is the local name for the Luxembourg part of the Ardennes. The township is popular as a vacation resort, thanks to its pretty wooded surroundings. It is a good starting point for tours in the "Switzerland of Luxembourg", in Gutland and in the Ardennes and is also a popular tourist attraction. Apart from tourism, the dairy industry plays an important role in the economy of the region.

SIGHTS. – At the entrance to the town stands a *monument to the American General Patton* who successfully attacked the Germans here in December 1944 during the "Battle of the Bulge". The town was then almost completely destroyed, but has since been rebuilt. There are unfortunately no buildings of any artistic or historic merit. Above the town, to the east, rises the *Nouck,* a hill 310 m (1017 feet) high, with a beautiful view over Ettelbruck.

SURROUNDINGS. – Ettelbruck lies approximately in the middle of Luxembourg. Interesting excursions can be made into any part of the country. Recommended are outings into the **Valley of the Sûre** (see page 250), the *Valley of the Black Ernz (Mullerthal),* and to **Wiltz** (see page 267), as well as to the capital **Luxembourg** (see page 203), nearby.

Eupen

Country: Belgium. – Province: Liège.
Altitude: 300 m (984 feet). – Population: 185,000.
Postal code: B-4700.
Telephone code: 0 87.
ⓘ **Syndicat d'Initiative,**
Marktplatz 8;
tel. 55 34 50.

HOTELS. – *Chapeau Rouge,* Aachener Straße 38, III, 6 r.; *A. Boston,* Vervierser Str. 2–4, IV, 14 r.; *H. Bosten,* Haasstr. 81, V, 13 r.; *Schmitz-Roth,* Rathausplatz 3, V, 28 r.; *Europe,* Schilsweg 65, V, 10 r. – BOARDING HOUSES: *Kirfel,* Klötzerbahn 22; *De Lamboy,* Aachener Str. 117; *Zum goldenen Anker,* Marktplatz 13. – YOUTH HOSTEL: Judenstr. 79, 169 b.

CAMP SITE. – *Camping Hertogenwald,* Oestraße; *Camping à la Ferme,* Baelen.

RESTAURANTS. – *Gourmet,* Haasstr. 81; *Le Brasier,* Aachener Str. 57; *Vier Jahreszeiten,* Haasstr. 38.

EVENTS. – *Carnival* (famous procession, last Monday before Lent); *International Flea Market* (end May); *Fair in the Upper Town* (from Saturday to Tuesday in the week before 24 June); *Fair in the Lower Town* (from Saturday to Tuesday in the week after 22 September); *Christmas Market* (Sunday before Christmas).

SPORTS and LEISURE. – The Eupen Sports Complex, Stockberger Weg (indoor sports stadium); sports stadium of Eupen, Judenstrasse (gymnasium, football and handball, dirt track, basketball), pin bowling, billiards, tennis, swimming (covered and open-air pools), riding, shooting. WINTER SPORTS: Skiing school, tobogganing, ski lift and cross-country skiing. WATER SPORTS: Sailing on the reservoir of the Vesdre.

Eupen is the largest town in the German-speaking part of Belgium. It lies at the confluence of the Vesdre and the Hill. In the south and southwest the wooded hills of the Hautes Fagnes, of which the Signal de Botrange (694 m – 2277 feet) is the highest point in the Ardennes, reach almost to the edge of the town, whereas in the north and west the green carpet of a continuous belt of meadows and pastures stretches from the hills of the Aachener Wald to the banks of the Meuse.

Eupen has, despite its modest altitude of 300 m (984 feet), a fairly cool highland climate. This is very healthy, and thanks to it the town has acquired a reputation as a popular health resort. Visitors can among other things enjoy the Kneipp water-cure. Most of the inhabitants are employed in the textile industry and the manufacture of man-made fibres. Some 25% of its workforce commute from the surrounding countryside.

HISTORY. – Eupen, which once belonged to the Duchy of Limburg, is first mentioned in the Chronicles in 1213 as a prosperous township. The Duchy's border location proved frequently to be a drawback for the town. After the Battle of Worringen in 1288, Limburg (and therefore Eupen) became part of the Duchy of Brabant, but in 1387 Joanna of Brabant handed over Limburg to Burgundy. Only ninety years later, in 1477, the Duchy of Limburg was acquired by the Austrian Habsburgs. Their domination, however, lasted only until 1555 when the Duchies of Limburg and Brabant were taken over by Spain. The Dutch Wars of Independence against the Spaniards and the Thirty Years War of 1618–48 did not leave the population in peace. In 1674 Eupen received its city charter. After the Peace Treaty of Utrecht in 1713 the Austrian Habsburgs became its rulers for the second time. This was a period of prosperity for Eupen, which in 1721 had a population of 13,000. The famous cloth industry of Eupen exported its products to the whole world. In 1795 the district of Eupen was annexed by France, but after the defeat of Napoleon it became part of Prussia (The Congress of Vienna 1815). Until 1921 Eupen was the westernmost district of Germany. By the Treaty of Versailles the town was given to the Kingdom of Belgium, but between 1940 and 1944 it was once again reintegrated into Germany.

SIGHTS. – The town is characterised by the buildings from Eupen's period of prosperity (18th c.). As well as the superb *patrician houses* in the Market Place, in the Gospertstrasse and the Werthplatz, the *Parish Church of St Nicholas* is especially worth seeing. It was built in 1721–6 to the plans of the city architect of Aachen, Mefferdatis. Inside is a Baroque high altar by Couven of 1744, and an attractive baptistry with a Baroque altar. Also of interest are the pulpit and the wrought-iron choir screen. Until the French Revolution the *Town Hall* was part of a *Capuchin Monastery*. The former Baroque church of this monastery is also worth visiting.

In the district of NISPERT is the Chapel of St John (*Johanneskapelle*) built by Couven in 1747, with beautiful stucco decoration inside.

SURROUNDINGS of Eupen. – The **Barrage d'Eupen** on the Vesdre, the largest reservoir in Belgium, with a capacity of 25 million cu. m (883 million cu. feet) is a good place for an outing.

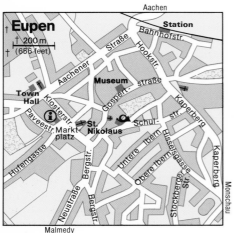

Fagne and Famenne

Country: Belgium. – Province: Namur.
ⓘ **Entre-Sambre-et-Meuse,**
Place de Damvillers,
B-6338 Ligny;
tel. (0 71) 88 80 57.
Lesse et Lomme,
B-5430 Rochefort;
tel. (0 84) 21 27 37.

The two Belgian regions, Fagne and Famenne, together form a depression running from east to west between the Ardennes in the south and the Condroz in the north, separated by the valley of the Meuse. Their average altitude is 180 m (591 feet) above sea level, except the divide between the rivers Lesse and Ourthe, which north-east of Han-sur-Lesse reaches an altitude of 300 m (984 feet).

Like the Condroz (see page 131) both regions are characterised by patterns of high ridges and troughs. These hilly ranges running from east to west consist of hard slates with valleys of limestone running parallel. Typical of the limestone troughs are numerous stalactite caves and other karst formations, for example the famous **Grottoes of Han (see page 172) or of *Rochefort* (see page 173).

Agriculture is practised primarily in the southern part of the region where clay soil on limestone permits the cultivation of crops including grain and vegetables. Further north pastures and meadows predominate.

Large industries are almost completely non-existent in either region. The population density is very low, averaging only some 50 per sq. km (130 per sq. mile). The Most important townships are *Marche-en-Famenne*, *Rochefort* and *Durbuy*, well-known tourist resorts in the Famenne, and also *Chimay* and *Philippeville*.

Flanders/ Vlaanderen (Flandre)

Country: Belgium. – Provinces: West Flanders, East Flanders.

ⓘ **Federatie voor Toerisme in Oost-Vlaanderen,**
Koningin Maria-Hendrikaplein 27,
B-9000 Gent;
tel. (0 91) 22 16 37.
Westtoerisme,
Vlamingstraat 55,
B-8000 Brugge;
tel. (0 50) 33 73 44.

The Brugge-Damme Canal in West Flanders

Flanders (in Dutch Vlaanderen, in French Flandre), is a historic region covering the territory of the former County of Flanders. It stretches from the far north of France across Western Belgium as far as the Westerschelde in the south-west of Holland. Its eastern border is formed by the rivers Schelde and Dender, while in the south it merges imperceptibly into the border areas of Hainaut.

The territory of Flanders is geographically not one single unit but consists of three different areas. Along the coast stretches a narrow *band of dunes* and behind it follows a stretch of marsh some 15 km (9 miles) wide, the so-called *Polders* (see page 100); still further inland lies Inner Flanders, called *Houtland*, sometimes also described as *Geest Flanders*. Its flat northern part consists, below ground, of tertiary and quaternary sands which are replaced in the hilly southern part, rising up to 156 m (512 feet) (Kemmelberg), by a layer of loess. The border between these two formations runs approximately along the line Aalst–Roeselare.

The agriculture of Flanders is characterised by a large number of small-holdings with widely scattered ownership. However, this applies less to the marshes than to the sand-and-clay areas of Geest Flanders. The characteristic forms of rural settlements are small farmsteads either in groups or in rows. Hedges and lines of poplars surround individual fields. The main crops are wheat, sugar-beet, oats, barley and potatoes, and certain industrial plants such as flax, chicory, tobacco and hops, the growing of which is very labour intensive.

Flanders is not only an intensively farmed country, but also, apart from the marshes, a densely populated industrial one, averaging 400 people per sq. km (1036 per sq. mile). The traditional textile industries still play a dominant role. The production of linen and wool which reached its peak in the Middle Ages still exists, but has been overtaken by cotton processing, primarily around Ghent. In recent years, however, the introduction of other industries has been encouraged to avoid a restricted and therefore considerably vulnerable structure. An important factor in the location of new industries is the *canal zone of Ghent,* extending north of the city in the direction of Terneuzen. The favourable transport conditions benefit especially the heavy petro-chemical and motor industries. Among the most important towns in Flanders are **Bruges** (see page 106), **Ghent** (see page 152), **Sint-Niklaas** (see page 246), **Ypres** (see page 268), **Aalst** (see page 64) and **Ronse.**

Flevoland

Country: The Netherlands. – Region: Southern IJsselmeerpolder.

ⓘ **Informatiecentrum Nieuw Land,**
Houtribhoogte,
NL-Lelystad;
tel. (0 32 00) 2 77 99.

Flevoland is a very new Dutch polder in the southern IJsselmeer, consisting of two parts and lying 4–5 m (13–16 feet) below sea level. It is separated from the mainland by a broad stretch of water, the so-called

Veluwemeer. This was necessary because the water table in the higher lying coastal areas would have otherwise dropped unacceptably low. The older part of the polder, drained between 1950 and 1957, covers 54,000 hectares (133,000 acres) and is called Oostelijk-Flevoland (East Flevoland). Adjacent to it, to the south, is the more recent polder Zuidelijk-Flevoland (South Flevoland), won from the sea in 1968, covering 43,000 hectares (106,250 acres).

The reclamation and cultivation of East Flevoland was carried out in the mid-1960s. Some 2000 agricultural enterprises were founded here, growing at first mainly rape-seed, oats, and barley, followed by wheat, fruit and vegetables. The cultivation of the more recent South Flevoland is not yet quite completed. All phases of soil preparation can still be seen here, starting with the pre-cultivation undertaken by the State, followed by barley and then wheat sowing.

From Elburg to Nijkerk (110 km – 68 miles). – From Elburg (population 5000, Hotel De Bonte Os, IV, 18 b.), East Flevoland can be reached by a bridge crossing the Veluwemeer. The road forks immediately after the bridge. To the south-west some 4 km (2 miles) away, is *Flevohof, a combination of an agricultural exhibition and a seaside resort. There are temporary exhibitions of all kinds mainly about farm life, model farms, children's playgrounds, etc. South of the Veluwemeer is an extended recreation area with yacht harbours, beaches, water sports facilities, camp sites, etc.

5 km (3 miles) further on the road turns south-west and in another 12 km (7 miles), past Biddinghuizen, arrives at Dronten (population 7500; Hotel 't Galjoen, 14 b.; camp site). This is used for shopping by the people of the rural polder area. The town square, the Agora De Meerpaal, constructed on the lines of an ancient prototype is worth seeing not only because of its architecture but also because it is a multi-purpose complex where several events can take place, such as exhibitions, weekly markets or sporting activities. There are also a theatre and a café/restaurant.

5 km (3 miles) north on the shore of the Ketelmeer is the archaeological Maritime Museum Ketelhaven, where you can see, among other exhibits, finds from the excavation of the Roman "Castellum Nigrum Pullum". From here the road going west passes Swifterbant, and after 24 km (15 miles) reaches Lelystad (Hotel De Eerste Aanleg, V, 20 b.), the administrative centre of the two Flevoland polders, which has only existed since 1967 and already has a population of 20,000. It has a somewhat controversial urban design, attempting to realise modern concepts of urban planning, for example, roads segregated by the type of traffic, and services concentrated in the central part of the town. In the northern part of the town tower the 143 m (469 feet) high chimneys of a power station fuelled by natural gas. The Information Bureau (Expositiegebouw) of the government services Zuiderzeewerke and IJsselmeerpolder is near the harbour. Nearby at the Houtrib Locks is the end of the dike between Lelystad and Enkhuizen which was completed in 1975 and is an essential part of the future polder Markerwaard. This polder is still in the planning stage and will eventually be situated in the south-west of the IJsselmeer.

The Oostvaardersdijk which begins south-west of the port of Lelystad belongs to the polder SOUTH-FLEVOLAND. – On the way to Hollandse Brug in the south-west (37 km – 23 miles), you can see an extensive nature reserve and relatively new polderland in various stages of cultivation. 4 km (2 miles) east a settlement called Almere has been established since 1975 on the Gooimeer. It is planned as an overspill area for the urban concentration of Randstad Holland, and should reach a population of 200,000 by the year 2000. 6 km (4 miles) beyond Almere, turn left across an area still under government pre-cultivation. After a further 6 km (4 miles) along the south bank of the Canal Hoge Vaart, turn right to the Nijkerk Lock in the south. Not far from here, on the shores of the Eemmeer and Wolderwijd, extensive recreation grounds and water sports facilities are planned. After 5 km you reach Nijkerk where the direct road from Elburg comes in.

Flushing/Vlissingen

Country: The Netherlands. – Province: Zealand.
Altitude: sea level. – Population: 44,000.
Postal code: NL-4380 AA to 4399.
Telephone code: 0 11 84.
(i) VVV Vlissingen,
Walstraat 91,
NL-4381 GG Vlissingen;
tel. 1 23 45.

HOTELS. – *Grand Hôtel Britannia*, Boulevard Evertsen 44, I, 60 b.; *Strandhotel*, Boulevard Evertsen 4, I, 76 b.; *Riche*, Boulevard Bankert 26, IV, 20 b.; *Piccard*, Badhuisstraat 178, IV, 60 b.; *Tromp*, Paul Krugerstraat 76–82, V, 32 b. – YOUTH HOSTEL: Breewaterstraat 14, 130 b.

RESTAURANT. – *Beursgebouw*, Beursplein 11.

Flushing (in Dutch, Vlissingen) is an important port on the southern coast of the former Island of Walcheren, part of the province of Zealand. It is located at the mouth of the Schelde, which here is over 4 km (2 miles) wide. Flushing is after IJmuiden the only large port directly on the North Sea. It is the departure point for ferries to Breskens.

The sea port, 12 m (39 feet) deep, is separated by locks from two interior docks. These are connected to Middelburg by the Walcheren Canal. Several industries are located in the harbour area and on the canal, among them shipbuilding, machinery and vehicle construction, leather and fish processing plants. More recently some chemical and petrochemical works were added. When the project, known as the "Delta Plan", is completed the industrial zone of Flushing will be extended by approximately 30,000 hectares (74,000 acres). A conventional and a nuclear power station have sufficient capacity to provide the necessary energy.

HISTORY. – Flushing is first mentioned in the Chronicles of 1247. Because of its harbour, which was already important in the Middle Ages, it received town status in 1315. It played an important part in the Dutch uprising against the Spanish. After the Geuze had taken Brielle, Flushing was the first Dutch town to fly the flag of freedom in 1572. Flushing is the birthplace of the famous Admiral Michiel Adriaanszoon de Ruyter (1607–76) and of the poet Jacobus Bellamy (1557–86).

SIGHTS. – In the Oude Markt stands the *Grote* or *St Jakobskerk* dating from the 14th c., burned down in 1911 and restored in its original style. The **Town Hall** (Stadhuis) in Houtkade dates from 1733. At the Bellamy Park is the *Municipal Museum* with antiquities and memorabilia of the famous naval hero Admiral de Ruyter.

In the Beursplein stands the *Old Exchange* of 1672. Next to it is the Rotunda on which rises the *statue of Admiral de Ruyter*. From here there is a good view of the port and the sea. The coast of Zealand Flanders can be seen opposite. From the Rotunda the Boulevard de Ruyter with the *Gevangentoren* (1563) and the Boulevard Bankert lead north-west to a seaside resort which has a beautiful beach facing south.

Admiral de Ruyter in Flushing

Friesland

Country: The Netherlands. – Province: Friesland.
(i) VVV Friesland-Leeuwarden,
Stationsplein 1,
NL-8911 AC Leeuwarden;
tel. (0 51 00) 3 22 24.

The province of Friesland in the north-east of the Netherlands lies close to the Dutch-German border next to East Friesland. The name

Boats in Sloten

"West Frisian Islands", used for the islands off the Dutch coast, stresses their geographical connection with the mainland provinces. In the south-west and the north, Friesland borders on the IJsselmeer and the Waddenzee, whereas in the south and the south-east its boundary is the Wouden, an area of sandy ridges with a transition to the morainic plateau of Drente. In the east, it merges into the marshland of Groningen.

Friesland, which has its own language and literature, consists of two parts. In the west are extensive marshlands along the North Sea coast which have been partly reclaimed from the sea and partly developed from the inland fresh-water lakes. In the Frisian lake district, a popular recreation area for water sports not far from the town of Sneek, several of these lakes still remain. In the east of Friesland extend several moors, the greater part of which are cultivated. In some areas peat cutting took place and, because the terrain was difficult to drain, lakes formed here.

Agriculture is the main economic activity in Friesland. There is a narrow strip of fertile farmland along the coast of the Waddenzee where sugar-beet, grain, flax and seed potatoes are grown, but apart from this the entire area is used as pastureland since the heavy marshy clay soil does not lend itself to any intensive cultivation. The farms, usually with 20–50 hectares (49–124 acres), specialise in the production of butter and the breeding of Frisian cattle.

Originally the characteristic form of settlement in this country was the so-called warft village. The Frisian farmsteads with their pyramid-shaped roofs, were once

Repairing of nets in Winsum, Friesland

mainly clustered on artificial mounds called warft or wurt where they were protected from flooding by tidal waves or when the dikes burst. Such warft villages are seldom seen today. They were in most cases replaced by scattered settlements which had the advantage that the farmhouses could be nearer their fields.

Milk produced by the farms is made into butter and cheese by numerous dairies in the neighbourhood. Of some importance are several food processing plants, as well as small shipyards which build boats mostly under 50 tons for use on the innumerable Frisian canals. The most important towns in Friesland are the administrative capital **Leeuwarden** (see p. 188) **Sneek** (see p. 248), **Harlingen** (see p. 173), **Dokkum** and **Bolsward** (see p. 249).

Hautes Fagnes in winter.

represent an enormous natural reservoir of water. Several rivers have their sources here, and on many of them dams were built, forming large man-made lakes. The remote moorland is crossed only by very few footpaths. The best views can be had from either the *Signal de Botrange* northeast of Malmédy (see page 210) or from the *Mont Rigi* (672 m – 2205 feet) near the Baraque-Michel.

The German-Belgian Nature Reserve

Countries: Belgium and the Federal Republic of Germany.

ⓘ **Syndicat d'Initiative d'Eupen,**
   Marktplatz 8,
   B-4700 Eupen;
   tel. (0 87) 55 34 50.
   Fremdenverkehrsamt Monschau,
   Austrasse 5,
   D-5108 Monschau;
   tel. (0 24 72) 33 00.

The German-Belgian Nature Reserve was created in 1971 by the amalgamation of the German Nature Reserve "Nordeifel" with the Belgian Nature Reserve "Parc Natural 'Hautes Fagnes'". The area, which comprises approximately 244,000 hectares (603,000 acres), extends east of the line Eupen–Malmédy.

The characteristic landscape of this undulating range of rounded hills is that of the **Hautes Fagnes** (the word "Fagnes" corresponds to the English "Fens" = marshland). Its average altitude is around 400 m (1312 feet), and its highest point is the Signal de Botrange, 694 m (2277 feet) above sea level, which is also the highest point in Belgium.

The area consists of extensive moor and heath, which give it its name and which

German-Dutch Nature Reserve

Countries: The Netherlands and the Federal Republic of Germany.

ⓘ **VVV Roermond,**
   Kloosterwandstraat 12,
   NL-6041 Roermond;
   tel. (0 47 50) 1 32 05.
   Städtisches Verkehrsamt Mönchengladbach,
   Am Hauptbahnhof,
   D-4050 Mönchengladbach;
   tel. (0 21 61) 2 20 01.

The Dutch-German Nature Reserve extends south-east of the Maas (Meuse) between the Dutch towns Venlo and Roermond. It was created in 1976 as an extension of the German Nature Reserve "Schwalm-Nette".

The flat landscape of the Lower Rhine with river meadows, moors, and farmland is a popular recreation area for the inhabitants of the nearby urban regions of Eindhoven and Krefeld-Duisburg. Some of the footpaths of the park straddle the frontier (no border controls).

Roermond and **Venlo** (see pages 235, 262 respectively).

German-Luxembourg Nature Reserve

Countries: Luxembourg and the Federal Republic of Germany.

ⓘ **Office National du Tourisme,**
Place d'Armes (Cercle),
L-Luxembourg;
tel. 48 79 99.
Vereinigung Deutsch-Luxemburgischer Naturpark
D-552 Irrel

The German-Luxembourg Nature Reserve extends along both banks of the River Our and the Lower Sûre. It con-sists of high plateaux and hills, with wooded valleys deeply cut into the slate rocks of the Luxembourg Ardennes. In the river valleys nestle pictur-esque villages and towns with interesting histories. On the Luxem-bourg side the Nature Reserve ex-tends from Echternach in the south as far as Clervaux in the north.

Deutsch-Luxemburgischer
Naturpark

The German Nature Reserve "Südeifel" was created in 1958. In the adjacent border region of Luxembourg existed similar landscapes with valleys, meadows and woods, near-extinct species of birds and brilliant orchids. German and Luxem-bourg conservationists wanted to expand this Nature Reserve across the border into Luxembourg. Five years later, in May 1963, several local organisations created the German-Luxembourg Nature Reserve Association. The German-Luxembourg Nature Reserve was the first of its kind in Western Europe to be jointly administered by two countries (Europapark No. 1).

In the Luxembourg part of the Nature Reserve there are, especially in the so-called "Suisse Luxembourgeoise", beautiful walks and vistas, medieval buildings of considerable cultural signifi-cance and finds from the Roman period. **Echternach** (see page 140), which is in the middle of this popular tourist area, can be reached easily by the E42 from the capital Luxembourg.

In the northern part of this reserve mighty rocks tower above the roads. In **Cons-dorf** there are remains of a castle once used as a place of refuge and of what once was a Roman camp. **Berdorf**, which is one of the most important vacation resorts on the high plateau, dominates the valley of the Black Ernz, the Sûre and the Aesbach. An excursion to **Beaufort**, immediately next to the picturesque Hallerbachtal is worthwhile because of the well-preserved 17th c. palace and a ruined 12th c. castle which is floodlit in the vacation season. Well-marked foot-paths run from here to unique rock formations. Apart from the usual leisure facilities, refreshment places for visitors on horseback are situated in **Bourscheid** and in Beaufort.

At the confluence of the Wiltz and the Clerf lies *Kautenbach*, a typical Ardennes settlement nestling in a deep valley between wooded heights. In the neigh-bourhood are a ruined 13th c. castle and a monument to St Donatus. From **Vianden** (see page 264), the *Centrale Hydro-Electrique de Pompage* can be reached; this is the largest pumping station and reservoir in Europe. It is open to visitors. *Hosingen* is a holiday resort with a restored church and a water tower with a Belvedere. Nearby is a game reserve. North of beautifully situated **Clervaux** (see page 130). In *Troisvierges* is an interesting parish church with a remark-ably elaborate high altar. In the north of the Nature Reserve, on the high plateau of the Ardennes, there are wide stretches of deciduous and coniferous woods. *Weiswampach* is the starting point for walks in the Valley of the Our.

Ghent

Country: Belgium. – Province: East Flanders.
Altitude: 5–29 m (16–95 feet). – Population: 220,000.
Postal code: B-9000.
Telephone code: 0 91.
ⓘ **Dienst voor Toerisme,**
Borluutstraat 9;
tel 25 36 41 and 23 36 41.

HOTELS. – *St. Jorishof* (protected monument), Botermarkt 1, I, 73 r.; *Parkhotel*, Wilsonplein 1, II, 37 r.; *Eden*, Stationstraat 24, II, 27 r.; *Carlton*, Koningin Astridlaan 62, II, 29 r.; *Ascona*, Vooskenslaan 105, II, 38 r.; *Europahotel*, Gordunakaai 59, II, 40 r.; *Terminus*, Koningin Maria Hendrikalaan 6, IV, 16 r.; *Benelux*, Recollettenlei 1, IV, 15 r.; *Trianon* (no rest.), St-Denijslaan 203–205, IV, 17 r.; *Des Alliés*, Antwerp-seweg 1, IV, 15 r.; *Britannia*, St-Baafsplein 18, IV, 20 r.; *De IJzer* (no rest.), Vlaanderenstraat 93, IV, 16 r.; *Maldegem*, Antwerpseweg 7, IV, 8 r.; *De Karper*,

Ghent – Panorama of the central part of the City

Kortrijkseweg 2, V, 15 r.; *La Lanterne*, Prinses Clementinalaan 118, V, 16 r.; *Pullman*, Koningin Maria Hendrikaplein 12, V, 15 r.; *Du Progrès*, Koornmarkt 9 V, 15 r.; *Cosmopolite*, Koningin Astridlaan 102, V, 12 r.; *L'Azalee-Azalea* (no rest.), Prinses Clementinalaan 61, V, 16 r. – *Holiday Inn*, 5 km (3 miles) south-east, II, 120 r. – YOUTH HOSTEL: Sint Pietersplein 12, 200 b.

RESTAURANTS. – *Le Vieux Strasbourg*, Vogelmarkt 25–27; *The Horse Shoe*, Lievekaai 8; *Patijntje*, Gordunakaai 94; *Chez Jean*, Cataloniestraat 3; *Ter Toren*, St-Bernadettestraat 564. – In Beervelde: *Renardeau*, Dendermondesesteenweg 16. – Several good CAFÉS in the inner city.

EVENTS. – *Clothing and Textile Fair* (February/ March); *Spring Fair of Flanders*, Leisure Activities (February/March); *Antiques Fair* (April/May); *International Fair of Ghent* (September); *International Gardening Exhibition* (every two years; next in 1983); *Carnival* (February/March); *Communal Feast* (July); *Organ Concerts* (July/August); *The Festival of Flanders* (August/September); *Flower Show* (every five years; next in September 1984); *International Poultry Show "Het Neerhof"* (November); *International Flower Pageant* (every five years; next in April–May 1985); *International Dog Show* (every two years: next in 1982); *Classical Bicycle Races* ("Omloop Het Volk", March); *International Canoeing Regatta* (May); *International Rambling Contest* (August and November); *Horse Market* in St Amandsberg (May); *Onion Market* and Procession with Lights, Ledeberg (August).

FLEA MARKET. – Beverhoutsplein (Friday 7 a.m.– 1 p.m., Saturday 7 a.m.–6 p.m.).

The beautiful old Belgian city of *Ghent (in Flemish, Gent; in French, Gand), is the capital of the province of East Flanders, and the seat of a university. It lies at the confluence of the Schelde (Escaut) and the Leie (Lys), the many branches of which intersect the city. With its five suburbs, Ghent is the third largest urban region in Belgium.

There are important industries in the city, among them spinning and weaving mills employing over 10,000 people and producing the world-famous Flemish linen. Being the second largest port of Belgium after Antwerp, Ghent also ranks as an important commercial city. The harbour is connected by several canals to the Westerschelde (Ghent-Terneuzen Canal), and with the North Sea (Brugge-Ghent Canal, as well as the Brugge-Ostende Canal and the Brugge-Zeebrugge Canal), and is being steadily enlarged. It can accommodate ships of up to 60,000 tons, and its annual turnover of goods is some 10 million tons. On the Ghent-Terneuzen Canal is a steel mill as well as numerous other industrial plants which make use of this waterway. Ghent is also the focus of Belgian horticulture.

HISTORY. – Ghent is mentioned in the Chronicles as far back as the 7th c. In the 12th c. its cloth industry was already well developed and its 13th c. expansion was not equalled until the 19th c. In the 14th–15th c. Ghent was one of the most important cities in Europe. Its citizens, organised in powerful guilds and possessing a strong sense of independence, opposed for centuries the Counts of Flanders who were backed by France. One of the most significant personalities of that period was the patrician Jacob van Artevelde (born about 1287), who ruled the city for years with near-dictatorial powers and fostered an alliance of Flemish cities, but who was murdered in a 1345 rebellion. He entered into a pact with England's Edward III, whose third son John of Gaunt (Ghent) was born here in 1340. The marriage of the heiress of Count Louis II with Duke Philip the Bold of Burgundy brought Flanders under Burgundian domination, and Ghent had to submit. After the Battle of Gavere on the Schelde on 23 July 1453, when thousands of Ghent's citizens lost their lives, the most prominent burghers and the City Council had to come out from within the walls wearing only their shirts, begging the victor for mercy. The Burgundian period in the 15th c. was a time of prosperity for Ghent when culture and the arts flourished. The brothers van Eyck (the Altar of Ghent), were active here then. The city remained one of the largest in Europe during the 16th c. under the Emperor Charles V, who was born in 1500 in the Prinsenhof. Ghent saw its cloth industry decline as river navigation developed. After Alexander Farnese, the Spanish Governor of the Netherlands, brought Ghent back under Spanish domination (1584), the decline of the city became irreversible. A revival began in the 18th c. when the cotton industry was introduced, but it was not until the 19th c. that industry and commerce brought about real prosperity and wealth. The Belgian/French poet and Nobel Prize winner, Maurice Maeterlinck, was born in Ghent in 1862 (d. 1949).

Description of the City

Inner City

The Inner City is surrounded by the River Leie and the western branch of the Schelde, the *Upper Schelde*. The central point of Old Ghent is the **Sint Baafs-plein**. On its eastern side stands the *Cathedral of **St Bavon** (*Sint Baafs*), a majestic building begun in the 10th c. It has a crypt from that date, a 13th–14th c. choir and a 15th–16th c. tower (carillon and an extensive view). The transepts and the nave were completed only in 1539–59.

Inside the Cathedral three of the many paintings are of particular merit; in the southern part of the ambulatory in the first chapel *"Christ among the Doctors" by F. Pourbus the Elder (1571); in the sixth chapel the Altar of Ghent (entrance fee), and in the tenth chapel *"St Baaf Entering the Abbey of St Amand" (or the "Conversion of St Baaf") by Rubens (1624). **The **Altar of Ghent** is the greatest masterpiece of old Flemish painting, allegedly begun by Herbert van Eyck (*c.* 1370–1426) in the year 1420 and completed by his brother Jan van Eyck (*c.* 1390–1441) in 1431–32. This large polyptych, perhaps the most monumental work of medieval altar painting in existence, illustrates in sequential panels the story of Salvation from the Fall of Man to the Redemption. The work became famous shortly after its completion and has had a checkered history. It was narrowly saved from the Iconoclasts in 1566 and from a fire in 1640. The central panels were taken to Paris in 1794, and when they were returned in 1816 they were shown alone because the wings had been sold to the Berlin Museum. "Adam and Eve" was later acquired by the Brussels Museum (1861). In 1920, however, the entire work was reassembled and installed in the Cathedral (with the exception of the "Predella" (Socle), which had been lost in 1550). In 1934 the panel of the left wing ("The Just Judges") was stolen. The outer panel was recovered, but the inner one was never found. The copy is by Van der Veken. In the Second World War, the paintings were hidden in Pau in Southern France, but were found there in 1942 and taken to Germany. After the end of the war they were returned to the Cathedral. – In the *crypt* (entrance fee, closed in winter), is a rich *Treasury.

On the north side of Sint Baafsplein stands the *Royal Flemish Theatre* dating from 1897 to 1899. On the west side is the **Cloth Hall** (*Lakenhalle*) built in 1426–41 and restored in 1900–3. Inside is an audio-visual display and a café/restaurant (Raadskeler). Next to it is a **belfry** 95 m (312 feet) high (entrance through the Cloth Hall). It dates from 1320 to 1339 and houses a small Museum of Antiquities. It also has a fine carillon. From its galleries there is a beautiful view. South-east of the Cathedral is the so-called *Geeraard de Duivelsteen* (the castle of Gerard the Devil), a 13th c. mansion now housing the provincial archives. It has an interesting crypt. In front of it stands a large monument to the brothers van Eyck, dating from 1913.

Town Hall in Ghent

North-west of Sint Baafsplein on the Botermarkt (Buttermarket), stands the *Town Hall* (*Stadhuis*) of the 15th–17th c. Its picturesque northern façade on the Hoogpoort by D. De Waghemakere and R. Keldermans is one of the best examples of Gothic architecture in Belgium. Its interior (entrance fee) was restored in 1870 and contains several beautiful halls and a decorative Gothic staircase. North of the Town Hall on the Hoogpoort, are several fine old mansions: the *Goldsmith's Hall* (1481); on the corner of the Botermarkt, the *St Jorishof* (Cour St Georges), now a hotel, parts of which date from the 13th c. and which has a pleasant courtyard; further on the *Grote* and *Zwarte Moor* from the end of the 15th c. and the *Sikkel* ("Sickle"; now a School of Music). Behind them is the picturesque Achtersikkel.

West of the belfry rises the impressive 13th–15th c. **Church of St Nicholas**. Behind it is the Koornmarkt on the west side of which stand the impressive *Post Office* building and several attractive gabled houses of the 17th–18th c. Other notable old gabled houses can also be seen on the Graslei, which runs along the Leie behind the Post Office. Among them are, No. 16, the *House of Free Boatmen* (Gildehuis der Vrije Schippers) (1531), the most beautiful Gothic guildhall in Belgium, Nos. 13–15, the *Grainweighers' House* (Gildehuis der Graanmeters) (1698), No. 11, the *Grain Warehouse* (Koornstapelhuis *c.* 1200), and No. 8, the *House of the Masons* (Gildehuis van de Metsers of 1526). West of the Church of St Nicholas from *St Michael's Bridge* which crosses the Leie to the large **Church of St Michael** there is an excellent *view looking backwards. St Michael's was begun in 1440 and completed in the 17th c., but its majestic tower remains unfinished. The impressive *interior of the church houses a number of altar paintings, mainly of the 19th c. In the north transept is a *"Crucifixion" by A. van Dyck and his disciples (1630).

North of St Michael's Church, a walk along the Koornlei affords a fine view of the houses on the Graslei; right across the *Grasbrug* and left via the Pensmarkt, is the Vegetable Market or Groentenmarkt and the former *Meat Market Hall* (Groot Vleehuis) (1408–17). It contains an old chapel.

North beyond the Leie is the ancient St Veerleplein where, from the 15th to the 18th c., executions were carried out. In the time of the Inquisition (1545–76) it was where the Lutheran heretics were burned. The sentence was solemnly proclaimed and carried out in the presence of secular and church authorities with a service and a procession. On the north side of the square stands the castle of *'s Gravensteen, which is surrounded by the River Lieve and is one of the strongest moated fortresses in Western Europe. It was built in 1180–1200 on the foundation of a 9th c. structure. Together with the Castle of Bruges, it was the residence of the Counts of Flanders and

Castle 's Gravensteen in Ghent

still remains an almost unique specimen of medieval fortress architecture. A visit to it should not be missed. Behind the gatehouse is a large courtyard surrounded by the outer wall with a defence gallery and 24 half-towers. In the courtyard stands the main building consisting of a massive keep or "Meestentoren" (from its roof is an excellent view of the castle and the city), and the residence (Palas) with several halls. In one of them is a collection of instruments of torture. South-west of the Gravensteen, in No. 7 Jan Breydelstraat, is the *Museum of Decorative Arts* (Museum voor Sierkunsten en Industriele Vormgeving).

In a north-easterly direction from the St Veerleplein is the Kraanlei. There, at No. 4, *Alijns Godhuis*, is a children's hospital founded in 1363 and extremely well restored in 1962. It has a picturesque courtyard and an old chapel, and now houses the ***Museum voor Volkskunde** (Folklore Museum). It contains a unique collection of tools and implements as well as several workshops, and provides a vivid picture of the lives of the Flemish people. East of the museum, across the *Zuivelbrug*, is the Vrijdagmarkt (Friday Market), in which stands a bronze statue of Jacob van Aetevelde. He made himself master of the town in 1338, and his clever policies secured the independence of Flanders. Between the Zuivelbrug and the Friday Market stands an iron cannon over 5 m (16 feet) long, called *De dulle Griet* (Mad Meg), dating from the mid-15th c. Adjacent to the Friday Market in the south-east, is the Square Bij St Jacobs with the **Church of St Jacob** of the 12th, 13th and 17th c. Nearby to the north, in the former Monastery of Baudeloo, is the *Athenaeum* (grammar school)

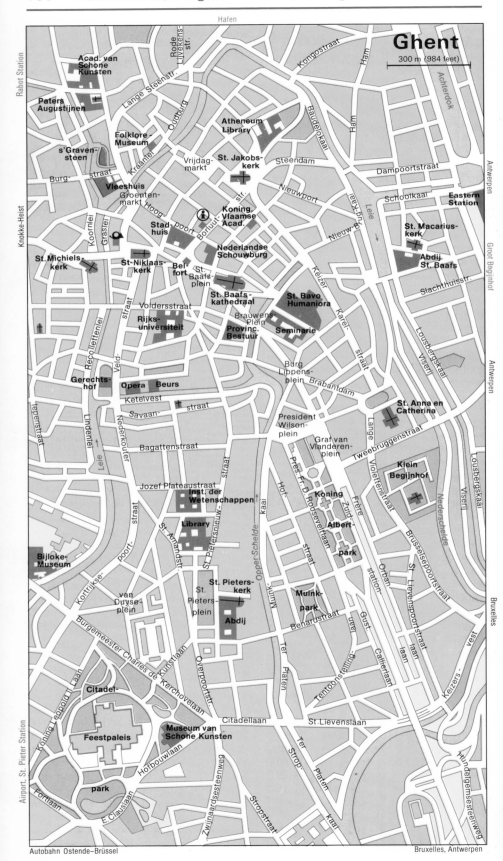

and the *Municipal Library*. South-west of here, via the Koningstraat and leaving the building of the *Royal Flemish Academy* on the left, you return to the Sint Baafsplein.

To the south-west of the Sint Baafsplein, in the Volderstraat, stands the **University** (*Rijksuniversiteit*), founded in 1816 with 12,000 students. Lectures are given in Flemish. South of it runs the long Kouter (formerly the flower market) with the *Stock Exchange;* its entrance is in the former guardhouse (1739). In the south corner of the square is the *Royal Opera,* built in 1837–40. West of this, between the Leie and one branch of the Schelde, stand the **Law Courts** (*Gerechtshof*), completely rebuilt after a fire in 1926.

Western and Southern Parts of the City

West of the Gravensteen via the Gewad, is a street called the Prinsenhof, so named because there once stood a palace here in which the Counts of Flanders resided from 1353, and where Charles V was born. The only part that remains is the *Donkere Poort*, a vaulted archway leading to the Bachten Walle. This leads further west to the so-called **Rabot**, a small fortification dating from the end of the 15th c. The railway station, *Rabotstation,* is next to it on the north-east. Here begins the Begijnhoflaan, named after the former *Great Begijnhof* (or nunnery), *St Eliza-beth*, which lies east of it and which still partly preserves its characteristic 17th c. features.

From the Begijnhoflaan you follow the *Coupure Canal* southwards to its con-fluence with the Leie, where, on the right, are several university institutes. Further south on the Bijlokekaai is the large *Municipal Hospital*, the modern premises of which incorporate part of the former *Abbey Bijloke* (founded in 1228). In the remaining premises of the former Abbey is the **Bijloke Museum** (the *Municipal Museum of Antiquities*, entrance Gods-huizenlaan 2). In its 35 m (115 feet) long *Refectory* is an exhibition of 14th c. murals. About 1 km (about a ½ mile) west is the 2·2 km (1 mile) long *National Watersportbaan* for sailing boats.

South-east of the Museum of Antiquities, beyond the Leie, the **Citadel Park**

occupies the site of the former for-tifications. At its midpoint stands the **Floralia Palace** (*Feestpaleis*), built in 1913 for the World Exhibition; it contains a Concert Hall, Exhibition Rooms, a restaurant, etc. The Flower Festival of Ghent takes place here. On the east side of the Park stands the *Museum of Fine Arts (Museum voor Schone Kunsten);* the entrance is on the north-west side. Although it does not contain the master-pieces of Flemish art seen in the museums of Brussels, Antwerp or Bruges, it houses a large number of interesting old and modern paintings (by Hieronymus Bosch, Rubens, van Dyck, Jordaens, Poubus, Frans Hals, Verhaghen, and Meunier among others). There are also tapestries and sculptures. Further south on the K. L. Ledgeganckstraat is the *Botanical In-stitute of the University* with a *botanical garden* (Plantentuin). 1 km (about a ½ mile) west is the *main station* (St Pietersstation).

North-east of the Citadel Park on a hill called the *Blandijnberg* stands the **Church of St Peter**, originally the Ora-torium of the Benedictine Abbey, founded about 630 by St Amandus, the missionary of Flanders. It was built in 1578 and re-placed between 1629 and 1719 by a domed structure 57 m (187 feet) high. The building adjacent to the former Abbey to the south now houses a youth hostel, a school museum of natural history and an exhibition of applied arts, and contains among other things, beautiful 16th c. Gothic *cloisters*. From the Church of St Peter you can return to the central part of the city either via the Muinkkaai or north via the St Pietersnieuwstraat, passing on the left the large building of the *University Library* with a tower 64 m (210 feet) high. The Library has 3 million books and 4000 manuscripts.

Eastern Parts of the City and the Suburbs

East from the northern end of the Muink-kaai is the President Wilsonplein, the central point of the south-eastern part of the city. To the south of it lies the **Koning Albertpark** on the site of the former Southern Station. North-east of the Park, on the Arteveldeplein, stands the *Church of St Anna* (1856). From here the Lange Violettenstraat branches off to the south. In No. 59 is the **Little Begijnhof** (*Klein*

Begijnhof van Onze Lieve Vrouw ter Hooie), the origins of which go back to the year 1234. The present Begijnhof has remained unaltered since the 17th c. The church dates from the 17th–18th c. and some 40 beguines still live in tiny cottages around a tree-lined lawn.

Going north from the Arteveldeplein via the Koepoortkaai, and then right across the *Slachthuisbrug* you come to the Gandastraat. Here on the left are the remains of the *Abbey of St Bavon (St Baafsabdij)*. According to legend it was founded in 642 by St Amandus and since the 10th c. has been restored several times. It now houses a lapidary collection. In the 12th c. Romanesque refectory several old tombstones can be seen, among them, by the eastern wall, the severely damaged tomb of Hubert van Eyck. The cloisters date from 1177 and were rebuilt in 1495.

At the eastern end of the Gandastraat comes the Kasteellaan. From the north end of this street, going to the right across the Antwerpenplein, you reach the suburb of ST AMANDSBERG. In the Oostakkerstraat stands the **Great Begijnhof** (*Groot Begijnhof*), founded in 1242 and transferred here in 1873 from its original site. There are more than 80 houses inhabited by some 85 beguines, 14 communal rooms, and a large church in the middle. They make a picturesque scene. In the Arenbergstraat is the *Museum of the Beguines* (open on Sundays and holidays from 1 April to 30 September, otherwise upon request).

In the north of the city is the **harbour area** with several large docks. Nearby in the suburb of OOSTAKKER stands the *Pilgrim Church, Onze Lieve Vrouw van Lourdes in Vlaanderen*, built in 1873–7, with a cave which attracts many visitors.

SURROUNDINGS of Ghent. – North-east via Oostakker to **Lochristi** (10 km – 6 miles); there is an interesting *chateau and extensive begonia plantations (in blossom from mid-July to mid-September).

Gouda

Country: The Netherlands. – Province: South Holland.
Altitude: 5 m (16 feet). – Population: 54,000.
Postal code: NL-2800 AA to 2899.
Telephone code: 0 18 20.

ⓘ VVV Gouda,
Waag, Markt 36,
NL-2801 JK Gouda;
tel. 1 32 98.

HOTELS. – *De Zalm*, Markt 34, III, 52 b.; *Het Blauwe Kruis*, Westhaven 4, IV, 24 b.; *De Utrechtse Dom*, V, 30 b.

RESTAURANTS. – *Mallemolen*, Oosthaven 72; *Rotiss. Etoile*, Blekerssingel 1; *Julien*, Hoge Gouwe 23; *Old Dutch*, Markt 25; *Zes Sterren*, Achter de Kerk 14. – IN REEUWIJK: *D'Ouwe Stee*, 's Gravenbroekseweg 80; *Elfhoeven*, Ree 2.

EVENTS. – *The Holland Festival*: Concert of the Dutch Bach Society (June, in the Church of St John); *Potters' Feast* (mid-August); *Cheese and Wine Feast* (end August); *Cheese Market* (Thursday, 9–10 a.m.).

The old Dutch market town of Gouda lies in a fertile polder area in the province of South Holland between Utrecht, Rotterdam and The Hague, at the confluence of the Gouwe and the IJssel. It is a typical Dutch town, well known for its cheeses ("Goudse Kaas"), which weigh up to 5–10 kg (11–22 lb). It also manufactures stoneware, candles and clay pipes, and its syrup waffles are delicious.

HISTORY. – Gouda's prosperity dates from the 13th c., when it received its charter from Count Floris V of Holland. Afterwards it quickly developed into an important commercial town. The city was taken in 1572 by the Geuze and later on played a major role in the State Council of the Low Countries. In the 17th c. the decline began. When the traditional cloth making was replaced by the manufacture of pipes, however, increasing industrialisation began to take its effect and Gouda regained its economic importance.

SIGHTS. – In the middle of the spacious Markt stands the massive *Town Hall (Stadhuis)*, a late Gothic building (1449–59), once surrounded by a moat. It has a Renaissance staircase (1603) and an interesting interior (entrance fee). On its eastern side is an astronomical clock

Begonia Show in Lochristi, near Ghent

with moving figures and a carillon. On the north-east side of the Markt stands a fine *weigh-house*, a typical example of Dutch Renaissance architecture, built by Pieter Post in 1668.

A stained-glass window in the Grote Kerk in Gouda

Not far south of the Markt is the **St Janskerk** or **Grote Kerk** (Dutch Reformed), dating from the 15th–16th c. Measuring 115 m (377 feet) long and 45 m (148 feet) wide, it is the largest church in the Netherlands (carillon). Inside (entrance fee, closed Sunday), are a number of superb and colourful ****stained glass windows**. Donated by princes and prelates and later by sister towns, they illustrate the transition from ecclesiastical to the heraldic-allegorical popular style in stained glass. The best among them were painted by Wouter and Dirck Crabeth in 1555–77 (Nos. 5–8, 12, 14–16, 18, 22–24). Behind the church in the former Catharini-Gasthuis (Hospital) at No. 10 Oosthaven and at No. 14 Achter de Kerk,

is the **Municipal Museum** with an old dispensary, surgical instruments, a torture chamber, etc. Further south, at No. 29 Westhaven in a 17th c. merchant's house, the *Pijpenmuseum de Moriaan* has an interesting collection of Gouda clay pipes, pottery and tiles.

SURROUNDINGS of Gouda. – Not far north of the town are the **Reeuwijkse Plassen** (*lakes of Reeuwijk*), formed as a result of peat cutting. This is a popular spot for water sports and there are several hotels and restaurants. East of Gouda (13 km – 8 miles), is the little town of **Oudewater** (population 7000) which lies on the River IJssel and is the birthplace of the painter Gerard David (*c.* 1460–1523). There are some beautiful gabled houses from the classic period of Dutch architecture (1600–20), especially in the Market Place, by the harbour, and in the Leeuwerik and the Wijtstraat. In the Town Hall, built in 1588, is a painting showing the atrocities committed here by the Spaniards in 1575. Next to it the weigh-house of 1595 has interesting medieval scales which were used to weigh people suspected of witchcraft. 15 km (9 miles) south-east of Gouda on the road to Gorinchem (34 km – 21 miles) and to Dordrecht (49 km – 30 miles) is the little town of **Schoonhoven** on the *River Lek*. It has a population of 11,000 and is the home of many goldsmiths and silversmiths. Near the harbour stands the Gothic Church of St Bartholomaeus, with pews and a pulpit dating from the 17th c. There is also a former grain warehouse (1556), a weigh-house restored in 1616, and a late Gothic Town Hall (15th–16th c.; carillon). By the river is the Veerpoort, an imposing Renaissance gate. North-west of Gouda (10 km – 6 miles) on the road to Leyden (see page 189) is the village of **Boskoop** (Hotel Florida, III, 15 b.; Neuf, IV, 30 b.) on the *River Gouwe* which lies in the middle of an important agricultural and fruit-producing area. ("Boskoop" is the well-known name of an apple.) Here in large nurseries roses, rhododendrons, azaleas, clematis, yews, etc. are grown. A visit here is particularly recommended at blossom time.

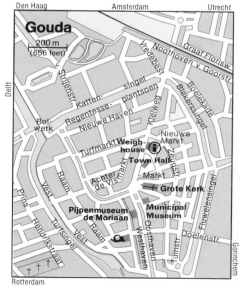

Groningen

Country: The Netherlands. – Province: Groningen.
Altitude: sea level. – Population: 202,000.
Postal code: NL-9700 AA to 9799.
Telephone code: 0 50.
(i) **Prov. Groninger VVV,**
Grote Markt 23,
NL-9712 HR Groningen;
tel. 13 97 00.

HOTELS. – *Euromotel Groningen*, Expositielaan 7, I, 218 b.; *Helvetia*, Hereplein 51, II, 50 b.; *Grand Hôtel Frigge*, Heerestraat 72, II, 132 b.; *Motel Terminus Noord*, Donderslaan 156, III, 114 b.; *De Doelen*, Grote Markt 36, III, 70 b.; *Maison Cassée*, Vismarkt 10, IV, 19 b.; *Weeva*, Gedempte Zuiderdiep 8, V, 132 b. – CAMP SITE: In the town park.

RESTAURANTS. – *Porte de l'Est*, Veemarktstraat 96; *Crémaillère*, Gedempte Zuiderdiep 58; *La Bâfre*, Kruissingel 1; *Rôtiss. Le Mérinos d'Or*, Astraat 1; *Bij Koos Kerstholt*, Vismarkt 50; *Bali*, Rademarkt 15; *Bistro La Coquille*, Oosterstraat 39.

EVENTS. – *Indoor Athletic Championship* (January), Martinihallen Complex; *Caravan Show* (February); *Exhibition of Gardening and Leisure Activities* (March/April); *Building Exhibition Onderdak* (April); *Trotting Races* in the Town Park (March and November); *Fair* (May); *International Rowing Regatta* on the Eems Canal (June); *Gronings Ontzet* (Liberation of Groningen, 28 August); *International Fair* (August/September); *Voor Anker Water Sports Exhibition* (November); *Snuffelmarkt* (small gifts for the holidays) (November).

FLEA MARKET. – Grote Markt.

Groningen is the capital of the Dutch province of the same name. It lies on the confluence of the Drentse Aa, here called Hoornse Diep, and the Winschoter Diep. Its harbour is accessible to small coastal boats and can be reached either by the Reit-diep, which opens into the North Sea 20 km (12 miles) north-west of here, or by the Damsterdiep and the Eems Canal.

Groningen is the seat of a University and several research institutions, and the see of a Catholic Bishop. It is the most important town in the north of the Netherlands, and not only the capital of the province of Groningen but also the focal point of parts of the neighbouring provinces of Drente and Friesland. It has one of the largest markets in the whole country, dealing in cattle, vegetables, fruit and flowers from the surrounding countryside. Groningen is also the head-quarters of the Dutch Grain Exchange. The town is connected to its outer port

Delfzijl by the Eems Canal. The most important industries are shipbuilding, chemicals, electrical equipment, paper and furniture manufacturing. The waterways are used to export industrial as well as agricultural products.

HISTORY. – Groningen was founded in Roman times. It is not, however, mentioned in the Chronicles until the early 11th c., when the Emperor Henry III bestowed here a fief on the Bishop of Utrecht. In 1284 the town was already prosperous enough to become a member of the Hanse, and it soon became one of the most important commercial centres in Northern Europe. In 1579 it joined the Union of Utrecht. A year later it was occupied by the Spanish, who, however, were besieged here in 1594 by the army of Maurice of Nassau. After another siege in 1672, which the city successfully withstood, the defence installations of Groningen were reinforced in 1698 by the famous Dutch fortification specialist Coehoorn. The ramparts of the citadel were later converted into promenades. In the Second World War the Inner City, with its 16th–18th c. gabled houses, suffered considerable damage, but this has since been repaired.

SIGHTS. – The main shopping street of Groningen is the Herestraat, which opens into the Grote Markt in the middle of the town. On the west side of the Market Place stands the **Town Hall** (*Stadhuis*), built in 1777–1810 in neo-Classical style, and behind it to the west its annex, completed in 1962. Next to it is the *Goudkantoor*, an elegant structure of 1635. In the north-east corner of the Grote Markt stands the **Martinikerk**, a 13th–15th c. Gothic brick building. It contains an old organ built by the humanist and musician Agricola (1442–85), who was born near Groningen. In the choir are 16th c. murals. The *tower of the Martinikerk is 96 m (315 feet) high and dates from 1464. It was burned down several times and each time was rebuilt. Together with its carillon it represents the distinctive landmark of the town and there is a beautiful view from its top. Behind the church, on the Martini-kerkhof, stands the Renaissance building

Town Hall in Groningen

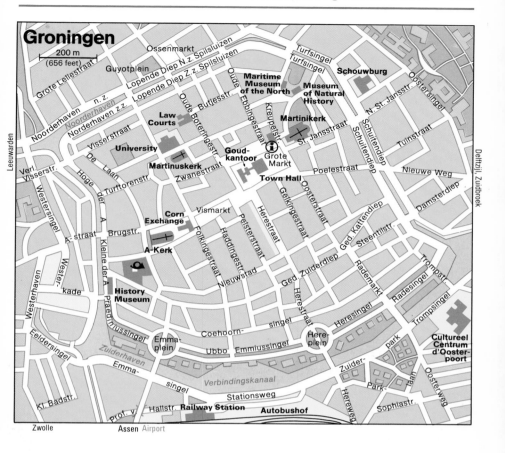

of the *Provincial Government* (Provinciehuis) and the *Prinsenhof*, the former
residence of the Stadholder. It now
houses the *Museum of Natural History*
(closed Sunday). North of the Prinsenhof
at No. 9 St Walburgstraat is the *Maritime
Museum of the North* (Noordelijk
Scheepvaartmuseum, closed Monday).

North-west of the Grote Markt in the
Oude Boteringestraat stand the elegant
Law Courts (Gerechtsgebouw) dating
from the 15th–17th c. In the Broerstraat is
the **University**, with some 10,000 stu-
dents, which was founded in 1614. The
present building dates from 1906–9.
Opposite, to the south, stands the neo-
Gothic *Martinuskerk*, built by P. J. H.
Cuypers. Behind it is the *University
Library*.

Not far north of the University are, next to
each other, the Ossenmarkt with two
charming gabled houses (17th–18th c.)
and the Guyotplein, named after the
founder of the oldest Institute for the Deaf
and Dumb in the country. The Institute,
which was inaugurated in 1790, is

nearby. Further north is the *Nieuwe Kerk*
or *Noorderkerk*, built in 1660–5, a copy of
the church of the same name in Amsterdam. Going south via the Nieuwe and
Oude Kijk in't Jatstraat, you come to the
Vismarkt, now the Flower Market, in the
middle of the town immediately to the
west of the Grote Markt. On the west side
of the Vismarkt stands the *Corn Exchange*
(Korenbeurs; 1865). Behind it is the
Gothic *A-Church* (13th and 15th c.), with
an interesting interior, a Baroque tower
and a Bible Museum. Not far to the south-
west at No. 59 Praediniussingel is the
History Museum (closed Monday),
with a collection of antiques, applied art,
Chinese and Japanese porcelain and
paintings, including works by the painters
Josef Israëls (1824–1911) and Hendrik
Willem Mesdag (1831–1915), who were
born in Groningen.

In the north-west of Groningen lies the
beautiful Park *Noorderplantsoen*, occupying the site of the former fortifications. In the south of the town lies the
small wooded Park *Sterrebos*, with a
garden restaurant and in the south-west

the large *Stadspark*, with a restaurant, a race track, various sports grounds and a large camp site.

SURROUNDINGS of Groningen. – 15 km (9 miles) to the south-west on the road to Heerenveen is the village of *Midwolde*. In its small 13th c. church is the fine *marble tomb of Rombout Verhulst, dating from 1664. 2 km (1 mile) further south near the pretty village of *Leek* the Château *Nienoord* houses a Museum of Coaches (closed in winter). In the gardens is a curious shell grotto. Leaving Groningen by the E35 and proceeding south you arrive in 10 km (6 miles) at the Station of *Tinaarloo*, near which is a well-preserved megalithic tomb. 35 km (22 miles) north of Groningen, near the village of *Uithuizen*, not far from the Waddenzee, stands the beautiful 15th c. *Menkemaborg* which is well worth a visit. 25 km (16 miles) north-east of Groningen is the little town of *Appingedam*, with an interesting Town Hall dating from 1630, and the Church of St Nicholas (13th c.). 5 km (3 miles) further east is the industrial town and port of **Delfzijl** (Eems Hotel, III, 12 b.), with a population of 22,000 and a well-known salt-water aquarium.

Delfzijl is also important as a harbour for the **marshland of Groningen**. This marshland extends along the Dutch coast of the Wattenmeer between Friesland and the estuary of the Eems. Agriculture is the most important occupation of its inhabitants. The soil is fertile and wheat, sugar-beet, barley and rapeseed are grown here. Characteristic landmarks are the massive farmsteads of the old warft villages, with unusually large barns. A large proportion of the agricultural produce is exported, mostly by sea. The harbour of Delfzijl lies on the estuary of the Eems and is linked with Groningen by the Eems Canal, navigable by ships of up to 2000 tons. On the banks of the canal are numerous natural gas fields. Other canals which can be used by ships of up to 1350 tons lead via the capital of Friesland, **Leeuwarden** (see page 188), to *Harlingen* (see page 173) on the Waddenzee and to *De Lemmer* on the IJsselmeer. From thence, the big cities in the south, with their important markets for agricultural products, can quickly be reached.

Haarlem

Country: The Netherlands. – Province: North Holland.
Altitude: sea level. – Population: 232,000.
Postal code: NL-2000AA to 2099.
Telephone Code: 0 23.
ⓘ **VVV Haarlem,**
Stationsplein 1,
NL-2011 LR Haarlem;
tel. 31 90 59.

HOTELS. – *Golden Tulip Hotel Lion d'Or*, Kruisweg 34, I, 80 b.; *Gouwenberg*, Kenaupark 33, II, 20 b.; *Van Aken*, Baan 1, III, 65 b.; *Fehres* (no rest.), Zijlweg 299, III, 20 b.; *Gouwenberg*, Grote Markt 27, III, 38 b.; *Die Raeckse*, Raaks 1–3, IV, 65 b.; *Wienerwald*, Grote Markt 10, IV, 29 b.; *Huize Beatrix*, Zijlweg 196, IV, 50 b.; *Faasse*, Jansweg 40, IV, 20 r.; *Roeland*, Amsterdamsevaart 86, IV, 17 b. – YOUTH HOSTEL: Jan Gijzenpad 3, 110 b.

RESTAURANTS. – *Coninckshoek*, Koningstraat 1–5; *Royal*, Kleine Houtstraat 44; *Bolwerk*, Kennemerplein 5; *Visrestaurant Haarlem*, Kruisstraat 9; *Lantaern*, Frankestraat 33.

EVENTS. – *Flowering time of the bulb fields* (beginning of April–mid-May); *traditional Flower Market* (Friday and Saturday before Whitsun – the seventh Sunday after Easter).

Haarlem, the capital of the Dutch province of North Holland, lies between Amsterdam and the North Sea, approximately 7 km (4 miles) from the coast, on the little River Spaarne. It is part of the "Randstad Holland", and architecturally is closely linked with its neighbouring townships of Heemstede, Bloemendaal and Zandvoort.

Haarlem is the cultural capital of southern Kennemerland. It is the seat of a Roman Catholic and an Old Catholic Bishop, and boasts a number of research institutes, colleges and libraries. It is also important as an industrial city. Shipyards, railways works, machine and car-body works, as well as food processing are the most important industries.

However, the town has become famous through the growing and sale of bulbs (tulips, hyacinths, crocuses, daffodils, etc.), which are exported all over the world. The tulip came here at the end of the 15th c. from Asia Minor via South Germany and in the 17th c. became a fashionable plant for which enormous prices were paid. A century later the trade in hyacinths was of similar proportions.

HISTORY. – From the 11th to the 13th c. Haarlem was the seat of the Counts of Holland, who granted it town status in 1245. After the rebellion of the Low Countries against the Spanish domination, the prosperous city was conquered by the Spanish in July 1573 despite its heroic resistance. Its commander, the entire garrison, Protestant clergy, and 2000 citizens were then executed. In the 17th c. Haarlem was the scene of considerable artistic activity, and the painters Frans Hals, Jacob van Ruisdael, P. Wouverman, Adr. van Ostade and many others lived here. The architect Lieven de Key (c. 1560–1627) founded a school of building here, and the public buildings and numerous gabled houses in the Old Town bear witness to its achievements.

SIGHTS. – In the middle of the Old Town lies the Grote Markt, where ten streets converge. In it stands the statue of I. J. Coster, a contemporary of Gutenberg, to whom the Dutch attribute the invention of printing. Here also are important old buildings of the city, including the former *Meat Market** on the south side, now an exhibition hall. It was built in 1602–3 by

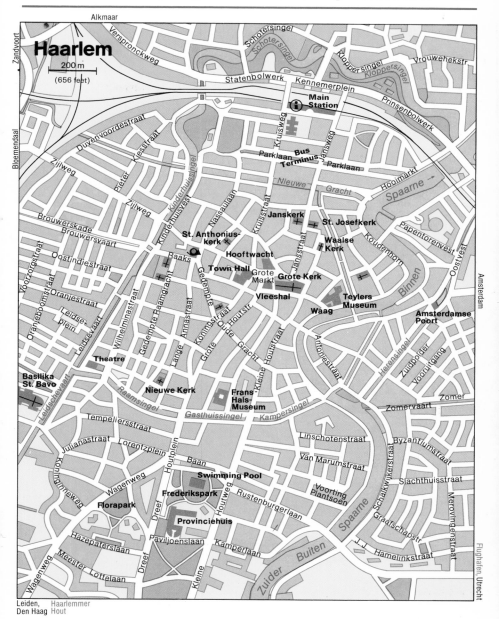

Lieven de Key, and ranks among the most important works of the northern Renaissance. Opposite, on the corner of the Smedestraat, stands the *Old Town Hall* (guardhouse, rebuilt *c.* 1650). – Next to the Meat Market stands the **Grote Kerk** or *St Bavokerk* (Dutch Reformed), built towards the end of the 15th c., with a tower 80 m (262 feet) high and a fine carillon. In the *interior of the church is the tomb of Frans Hals (d. 1666), in the choir a beautiful choir-screen (1510) and 'an organ built in 1735–8 by C. Muller, one of the most outstanding in the world. It has 5000 pipes, 68 stops and 3 manuals. –

On the west side of the market is the **Town Hall**, dating from the 13th–17th c., with an ancient council hall. It now houses the Municipal Archives. Behind it is the *Municipal Library* with a comprehensive record of the history of printing.

Not far north-east of the Markt at No. 79 Janstraat, is the Episcopal Museum (*Bisschoppelijk Museum*) which houses an important collection of ecclesiastical antiquities. – East of the Grote Kerk, on the corner of the Damstraat and the Spaarne, stands the old *Municipal Weigh-house*, built in 1598, now a

restaurant. From here you can enjoy a view of the boats on the River Spaarne, and the old gabled houses lining its banks. Next to it, No. 16 Spaarne, is the *Teyler Museum, with an outstanding collection of minerals, fossils, physical instruments, an organ, and a number of drawings and paintings by Dutch masters. – On the other side of the Spaarne, at the north-east end of the Spaarwouderstraat, stands the medieval *Amsterdam Gate*.

At the southern edge of the Old Town at No. 62 Groot Heiligland, is the **Municipal Frans Hals Museum**. The building, dating from 1608, was originally a *Hospice for old men*. The museum ranks among the foremost picture galleries in the country. There are numerous works by important artists, paintings of the Haarlem School of the 16th–17th c., and, above all, eleven portraits by Frans Hals, the liveliest and most striking of all Dutch portrait painters. The museum is sometimes open in the evening, with candlelight and music. – Not far west of the Frans Hals Museum is the *Nieuwe Kerk* or *St Annakerk* (Dutch Reformed) of 1648, with a fine tower. – Further south-west, beyond the Leidsevaart, is the *Basilica St Bavo*, built in Byzantine neo-Romanesque style in 1895–1906 (Catholic).

South of the town lies the beautiful **Frederikspark**, and, to the south of the park, the *Pavilion*, built in 1788 as a country residence. In 1806–10 it was the palace of King Louis Bonaparte and in 1817–20 the residence of the widow of Prince William V of Orange. South-west of the Frederikspark in the *Florapark* is a monument to the painter Frans Hals. – South of the Pavilion stretches the *Hout, a pleasant wood with old trees and the curious *Hildebrand fountain* (1962). There is a café/restaurant in the park.

SURROUNDINGS of Haarlem. – **To Zandvoort** (10 km – 6 miles); a round trip via Bloemendaal aan Zee and back to Haarlem (21 km – 13 miles). First drive south on the N99 towards The Hague. 3 km (2 miles) beyond Haarlem turn right into the *Aerdenhout* and then on through the woods. After 7 km (4 miles) comes **Zandvoort** (population 16,000, Hotel Bouwes, I, 113 b.; Bouwes Palace, I, 200 b.; Hoogland, I, 51 b.; Zeemotel, II, 51 b.; Astoria, III, 25 b.; Zuiderbad, 64 b.), which is, after *Scheveningen* (see page 243) and *Noordwijk aan Zee*, the leading seaside resort in Holland. It has a magnificent beach lined with dunes. There is an observation tower 60 m (197 feet) high with a lift (elevator) and a café, a dolphinarium and a casino. Nearby is a golf course. North-east of Zandvoort is the 4·2 km (3 miles) long

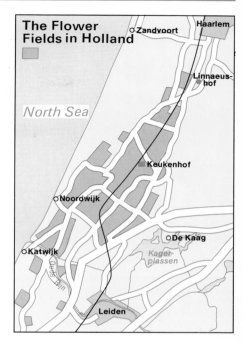

The Flower Fields in Holland
North Sea
Zandvoort
Haarlem
Linnaeus-hof
Keukenhof
Noordwijk
De Kaag
Katwijk
Kager-plassen
Oude Rijn
Leiden

motor race track of Zandvoort where the Grand Prix of the Netherlands (Formula I) takes place. Return to Haarlem along the North Sea coast (11 km – 7 miles). After 4 km (2 miles) you reach *Bloemendaal aan Zee*, a group of houses near the popular holiday resort **Bloemendaal** (Hotel Rusthoek, III, 40 b.), where the road leaves the coast. Continue eastwards across the dunes of the Kennemerland (nature reserve with several lakes, camp sites), past *Overveen Station*. From here it is 7 km (4 miles) to **Haarlem**.

Round tour from Haarlem through the *flower fields (68 km – 42 miles); with a trip to the seaside resorts Noordwijk aan Zee and Katwijk aan Zee and to Keukenhof, 78 km – 48 miles). Leave Haarlem in a southerly direction on the road to Hilversum via Aalsmeer. After 4 km (2 miles) comes Heemstede (population 26,000, Museum of Land Reclamation) on the edge of the Haarlemmermeer-Polder. Continue straight on where the road to Hilversum branches off to the left. On the left is the "flora" flower exhibition ground. 3·5 km (2 miles) further is *Bennebroek* with the "Linnaeushof" where flower shows and a children's flower procession take place in summer. After a further 3 km (2 miles) you arrive at *Vogelenzang*. Then as far as *Noordwijk Binnen* (13·5 km – 8 miles), where from April to mid-May you drive along roads through never-ending *fields of flowers. In Noordwijk Binnen you may branch off to the popular seaside resort **Noordwijk aan Zee**, 2 km (1 mile) west (Hotel Palace, I, 255 b.; de Baak, I, 186 b.; Noordzee, II, 220 b.; Badhotel Zeerust, II, 70 b.; Zee en Duin, II, 50 b.; Clarenwyck, II, 48 b.; de Zeeleeuw, III, 92 b.). – From Noordwijk Binnen you drive via Katwijk a.d. Rijn (from here 3 km (2 miles) to the west is the North Sea resort *Katwijk aan Zee*) and *Valkenburg*, part of the way along the banks of the *Old Rhine*, as far as **Leyden** (see p. 189). From here you can take the road north-west to *Oegstgeest*, and west again to the N99 from The Hague to Haarlem (the first section of which is a highway), which can be followed to the right via *Sassenheim, Lisse* and *Hillegom* to **Haarlem** (31 km – 19 miles).

Dutch tulip fields near Haarlem

Keukenhof near Lisse

1 km (¼ mile) north-west of Lisse is **Keukenhof, the former "kitchen yard" of a medieval castle, where the largest "open-air flower show" in the world can be seen. (Opening times from early April daily, 8 a.m.– 8 p.m.) Every year 700 different kinds of tulips bloom in the fields here. The attraction is the variety of plants and colours. Apart from tulips, there are hyacinths, daffodils and other plants. The park, with its lakes, canal-like waterways and old trees, is also very beautiful.

The Hague/ Den Haag/ 's-Gravenhage

Country: The Netherlands. – Province: South Holland. Altitude: sea level. – Population: 682,000. Postal code: NL-2500 AA to 2599. Telephone code: 0 70.

ⓘ **National Bureau voor Toerisme,** Bezuidenhoutseweg 2, NL-2594 AV Den Haag; tel. 81 41 91. **VVV Den Haag/Scheveningen,** Nassauplein 31, NL-2585 EC Den Haag; tel. 65 89 10. *Information,* Kon. Julianaplein 8 (at the Central Station), NL-2595 AA Den Haag. *Gemeentelijke Informatiecentrum,* Groenmarkt.

DIPLOMATIC REPRESENTATION. – *American Embassy,* Lange Voorhout 102; *Australia,* Koninginnegr. 23; *Canada,* Sophialn. 7; *Great Britain,* Lange Voorhout 10; *Ireland,* Dr Kuyperstr. 9; *New Zealand,* Lange Voorhout 18.

HOTELS. – *Promenade* Van Stolkweg 1, L, 194 b.; *Des Indes,* Lange Voorhout 56, I, 160 b.; *Babylon,* Kon. Julianaplein 35, I, 250 b.; *Bel Air,* Johan de Wittlaan 30, I, 700 b.; *Grand Hotel Central,* Lange Poten 6, I, 229 b.; *Parkhotel De Zalm* (no rest.), Molenstraat 53, II, 200 b.; *Corona,* Buitenhof 41–42,

II, 45 .; *The New Corner,* Van Merlenstraat 132, III, 25 b.; *Du Commerce,* Stationsplein 64, III, 31 b.; *Excelsior,* Stationsweg 131–133, III, 64 b.; *Savion,* Prinsestraat 85, IV, 16 b.; *Eripe,* Laan van Meerdervoort 223, IV, 28 b.; *Forest,* Adelheidstraat 37–39, IV, 14 b.; *Het Spinnewiel,* Laan van N. O. Indie 279, IV, 25 b.; *Sweelinck* (no rest.), Sweelinckplein 78, V, 22 b.; *Bristol,* Stationsweg 126–130, V, 58 b.; *Stationsbodega,* Stationsplein 43–44, V, 11 b.; *Mont-Blanc,* Stevinstraat 66, V, 12 b.; *Petit,* Groot Hertoginnelaan 42, V, 30 b.; *'t Sonnehuys,* Renbaanstraat 2, V, 55 b.; *Rondeel,* Stationsplein 38–40, V, 34 b.; *Mem* (no rest.), Anna Paulownastraat 8, V, 21 b.; – IN KIJKDUIN: *Atlantic,* Deltaplein 200, I, 300 b. – IN RIJSWIJK: *Hoornwyck* (Motel), Jan Thyssenweg 2, I, 149 b.; *Piet v. d. Valk,* Geestbrugweg 18, V, 19 b. – IN VOORBURG: *Canterbury,* Parkweg 2, V, 11 b. – IN WASSENAAR: *Bianca,* Gravestraat 1, III, 25 b.; *Auberge de Kieviet,* Stoeplaan 27, II, 12 b.; *Duinoord,* Wassenaarse Slag 26, IV, 35 b. – IN SCHEVENINGEN: see page 243.

YOUTH HOSTEL. – Monsterseweg 4, 375 b. – CAMP SITE.

RESTAURANTS. – *Royal,* Lange Voorhout 44; *Saur,* Lange Voorhout 51; *Bajazzo,* Vos in Tuinstraat 2a; *House of Lords,* Hofstraat 4; *Hof van Brederode,* Grote Halstraat 3; *Raden Ajoe,* Lange Poten 31; *Garoeda,* Kneuterdijk 18a; *Hoogwerf,* Zijdelaan 20 (3 km (2 miles) on the road to Wassenaar). – IN MARIAHOEVE: *Les Compagnons,* Denenburg 47. – IN KIJKDUIN: *Bretagne,* Deltaplein 510; *Turpin,* Deltaplein 616; *Golden Hill,* Deltaplein 506. – IN VOORBURG: *Canterbury,* Parkweg 2. – IN RIJSWIJK: *Tropic Paradise,* Steenwoordelaan P 14.

EVENTS. – *International Poultry Show "Avicultura"* (January); *Antique Market* (May–September, every Thursday); *Geranium Market* (April/May); *Flag Day* (the Day of Dutch Fishermen), at the harbour of Scheveningen (May); *The International Kite Flying Day,* on the beach of Scheveningen (June); *Festival of Holland:* Concerts, Operas, Ballet, Dancing (early June); *International Rose Exhibition* (June– September); *International Choir Festival* (end of June); *Summer Feast* (end of June); *The Hague Horse Show* (end of June); *Indonesian Market,* Pasar Malam Besar (June/July); *International Tennis Championship* (early July); *North Sea Jazz Festival* (mid-July); *The Day of the Horse* (mid-July); *The Hague Flower Show* (every Saturday in August); *Prinsjesdag* (18 September); *Rekreade* (early September); *Fair for Woman* (end of September); *International Dog Show* (October).

FLEA MARKET. – Herman-Costerstraat (Monday, Friday and Saturday 8 a.m.–6 p.m.).

SPORTS and LEISURE. – Billiards, bowling, golf, skittles, riding, ice skating, tennis, squash, angling, water sports.

The Hague, which is officially called 's-Gravenhage, is the third largest city in the Netherlands. It is part of "Randstad Holland", the seat of the Dutch Government and the capital of the province of South Holland. It lies near the North Sea, on the coast of which is the seaside resort of Scheveningen.

The Hague is a residential city favoured by retired people who appreciate its situation and its well-cared-for appearance. It bears the imprint of a cultural, political and administrative city. Ministries, embassies, several international organisations, the International Court of Justice and the Permanent Court of Arbitration have their headquarters in the city. There are also several colleges, research institutes and societies, as well as institutions of higher education. Banks, businesses and industrial companies have selected The Hague for their administrative headquarters.

Industry plays only a subordinate role in The Hague, employing less than 30% of its working population. Nevertheless its structure is very varied, including textiles, electrical equipment, hardware, and furniture manufacturing, printing works, rubber, pharmaceuticals, and food processing. Most of the plants have been established by the harbour and in Scheveningen (see page 243), the largest seaside resort in the Netherlands, taking advantage of more favourable transport facilities in these locations. Fishing is also important in Scheveningen.

The Hague also has a favourable reputation as the "City of Arts". Many Dutch painters live here and it has an important position in international art dealing. Other crafts, including furniture, gold and silverware, pottery, etc., are well established here.

HISTORY. – The Hague was originally a hunting preserve of the Counts of Holland (the "Count's Hedge"), and from the middle of the 13th c. was their habitual residence. From 1593 it was the headquarters of the General States, and in the 17th and early 18th c. it was the focal point of important diplomatic negotiations. It developed fast and became a focus for luxury and recreation. However, jealousy on the part of the other cities with voting rights excluded The Hague from the State Council and it remained the "largest village in Europe", until Louis Bonaparte as King of Holland gave it its municipal charter. At the same time he transferred his residence to Amsterdam and therefore deprived the city of much of its importance. Only in the mid-19th c., when the population exceeded 100,000, did the city experience more vigorous development. Today, with the substantial damage of the Second World War repaired, The Hague's wide straight streets, spacious squares, shady promenades and extensive residential districts, give an impression of distinction, elegance and, above all, friendliness.

Description of the City

The Old Town

In the middle of the Old Town stands the *Binnenhof, an irregular group of buildings, some old and some more recent, surrounding an open space. Count William II of Holland built a castle here (1250), which his son Floris V enlarged and where he took up residence in 1291. The Stadholders resided here from the time of Maurice of Nassau-Orange. At present both chambers of the Dutch Parliament have their meetings in the Binnenhof and it is also the location of several ministries.

On the east side of the Square is the *Ridderzaal*, a hall of the time of Floris V used for audiences, conferences, and on the third Thursday in September, for the Opening of Parliament by the Queen. (The Queen arrives in a gilded coach.) Next to it, on the east, is the oldest group of buildings. Since the time of Philip the Good these have been used as *Law Courts*. The northern wing of the former Binnenhof contains the former *meeting rooms of the General States*. The former *assembly hall of the States of the United Netherlands*, built in 1652 by Pieter Post, is now the First Chamber of the Parliament. The former *ballroom* (1790) on the south side of the courtyard is now the Second Chamber.

Adjoining the Binnenhof on the west is the **Buitenhof** with an equestrian statue of King William II (d. 1849). On the northern side of the Square stands the *Gevangenpoort*, with a collection of medieval instruments of torture. The brothers Cornelis and Johan de Witt were murdered here in 1672 after being accused of an attempted assassination of Prince William III. In the Square stands the monument of Johan de Witt. In the adjacent Square to the east, at No. 14 Lange Vijverberg, is the *Museum of*

The Parliament Building in The Hague

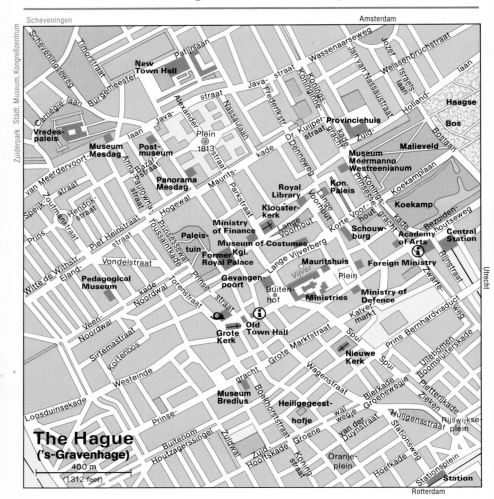

Costumes which has rooms furnished with antique furniture. From here there is a beautiful view of the ***Vijver**, the picturesque old ornamental lake reflecting the long façade of the Binnenhof buildings.

On the east side of the lake, the street called Korte Vijverberg leads to the elegant **Mauritshuis** on the east of the Binnenhof between the Vijver and the Plein. It was built in 1633–44 by Pieter Post for Count John Maurice of Nassau, the governor of Brazil. It now houses the famous ****Picture Gallery** (*Koninklijk Kabinet van Schilderijen*), which was formed from the collections of the Princes of Nassau-Orange.

The collection of the Mauritshuis, although relatively small, overshadows other galleries in Holland by the high standard of its exhibits. Among the early Dutch painters, the "Lamentation of Christ" by *Rogier van der Weyden* is especially important. German painters of the classic period are represented, among others, by three masterpieces by *Hans Holbein*. Paintings of the

Flemish School include examples by *Rubens* ("Portrait of Bishop Michiel Ophovius") and *Anthonie van Dyck*.

However, the Dutch masters of the 17th c. are the most valued part of the collection. There are several magnificent portraits by *Frans Hals* and fifteen paintings by *Rembrandt* (among them the "Anatomical lesson of Dr Nicholaas Tulp", "Simeon in the Temple", "Homer", "David and Saul", and three self-portraits). Other famous masterpieces are the "Golden Fleece" by *Karel Fabritius*; three most important paintings by *Jan Vermeer van Delft* ("View of Delft", "Head of Girl" (also known as "Girl with the Pearl") and "Diana"); *Jan Steen* is represented by thirteen of his realistic paintings. There are also the "Young Bull" by *Paulus Potter* and miniatures by *Gerrit Dou, Gerard ter Borch* and *Gabriel Metsu*.

In the middle of the Plein stands a bronze statue of Prince William the Silent. On the west side are the *Ministry of the Interior*, the *Hoge Raad* (Supreme Court of the Netherlands) and the *Ministry of Justice*. On the south side is the *Ministry of Defence*, and on the east side the *Ministry of Foreign Affairs*.

From the north-east corner of the square, the Lange Houtstraat leads north to Tournooiveld; going east along the Korte Voorhout you pass the *Royal Theatre* (Schouwburg) and arrive at the Prinsessegracht, on the south side of which are the **Academy of Arts** (*Academie van Beeldende Kunsten*) and the *Museum of Applied Arts* (*Museum van Kunstnijverheid*, entrance by the Academy).

Further north at No. 30 Prinsessegracht, we find the **Museum Meermanno-Westreenianum**, a bequest of the Baron A. H. J. van Westreenen van Tiellandt (d. 1848). The collection consists primarily of a large library of manuscripts and early prints, but there are also some antique vases and statues as well as Chinese and Japanese curios. It gives a good impression of the interests of an art lover in the first half of the 19th c. Koningskade runs east parallel to Prinsessegracht and in Nos. 1–2 is the modern *Provinciehuis*, the offices of the Provincial Government of South Holland.

To the north of the Korte Voorhout and the Tournooiveld is the Square Lange Voorhout, which together with Kneuterdijk, Vijverberg and Willemspark, forms the most prestigious part of the city. On the east side of the square stands the former *palace of the Queen Mother*, now the *Royal Palace*, where foreign diplomats are received. On the north side of the Lange Voorhout, in No. 34, is the **Royal Library**, one of the largest libraries in the country, with over 1 million books, and many valuable manuscripts. Further west on the corner of the Parkstraat stands the *Kloosterkerk*, dating from about 1400. Opposite, to the west, is the *Ministry of Finance*, housed in the former residence of the Oldenbarneveldts.

In the south-west corner of the Plein is the beginning of the Street Lange Poten; with its continuation, the busy Spuistraat, it is the main business artery of the city. To the south the Spui leads to the 17th c. **Nieuwe Kerk** in which the brothers de Witt and Spinoza are buried.

In the middle of the Spuistraat, the shopping arcade *"Passage"* leads on the right to the Buitenhof and the Groenmarkt, west of which is the Vismarkt. Between those two markets stands the 16th c. **Old Town Hall** with annexes from the 18th–19th c. West of it stands

the **Grote Kerk** (*St Jacob*, Reformed) dating from the 15th–16th c. and well restored in 1961–3.

In the finely vaulted *interior of the Grote Kerk with its high, light choir, are several tombstones and memorial plaques, among them, on the rear choir wall, those of the poet and statesman Constantijn Huyghens (d. 1687) and of his son, the physicist and astronomer Christiaan Huyghens (d. 1695). Also worth seeing are the carved pulpit (1550), the arms of the Knights of the Golden Fleece, the large organ (1881), and the windows in the choir and in the northern transept.

The tower is 96 m (315 feet) high and has a carillon (open to the public in July and August).

South of the Grote Kerk extends the Grote Markt. On the corner of the Prinsegracht stands the former *weigh-house* of 1681. Diagonally opposite in No. 6 Prinsegracht is the **Museum Bredius** which houses the large collection of paintings and drawings, furniture and china of the art historian Dr Abraham Bredius. Further south at Nos. 72–74 Paviljoensgracht is *Spinoza's House*, where the philosopher Baruch Spinoza (1632–77) lived from 1671 until his death, and where he completed his "Ethic". The house is now a museum. Opposite is the pretty almshouse, *Heilige Geesthofje* (1616). At the south end of the Paviljoensgracht stands a statue of Spinoza (1880).

The Northern Parts of the City

North of the Groenmarkt and the Buitenhof in the Noordeinde, stands the former **Royal Palace** (*'t Oude Hof*), built by Pieter Post in 1640. After the royal residence was transferred to the Soestdijk Palace, it became the headquarters of the *International Institute of Social Studies*. In front of the palace stands an equestrian statue of William the Silent (1845). Beyond the *palace gardens* (Prinsessetuin), at No. 2e Hemsterhuisstraat, is the *Museum voor het Onderwijs* (Pedagogical Museum). On the right at No. 65b Zeestraat, which is the northern continuation of the Noordeide, is the *Panorama Mesdag*. This is a gigantic painting of Scheveningen in the year 1880 by the painter H. W. Mesdag. In No. 71 is the *Royal Numismatic Cabinet*, an important collection of coins, medals and cameos. At No. 82 is the *Dutch Postal Museum*.

East of the Zeestraat extends the fashion-able residential district of Willemspark. At its central point in the "Plein 1813" stands the **National Monument** de-signed by W. C. van der Waaijen-Pietersen and Koelman, and erected in 1869 to commemorate the restoration of independence to the Low Countries in November 1813. Further north on the former Alexander-Veld stands the **New Town Hall**, built in 1953.

Going westward from the Javastraat you arrive at Laan van Meerdervoort. In the garden pavilion, No. 7F, is the interesting *Mesdag Museum, with a collection of 19th c. French, Dutch and Italian paint-ings presented to the city by the painter H. W. Mesdag (1831–1915).

Not far north of here stands the **Peace Palace** (*Vredespaleis*), a massive red brick building (1907–13); the American millionaire Andrew Carnegie (d. 1919) donated 1·5 million dollars for its con-struction. It is the seat of the *International Court of Justice* and the *Academy of International Law*. Almost all countries in the world contributed to its interior decoration and furnishing. A visit to the *Great Hall of International Justice* is recommended.

West of the Peace Palace lies the modern residential district of DUINOORD, built in the style of the old Dutch architecture of the Hofjes. Here on the edge of the Park *Zorgvliet* (No. 41 Stadhouderslaan) is the *Municipal Museum* (*Gemeente-museum*). It contains a collection of municipal antiquities, ceramics and draw-ings, some good paintings and an excel-lent display of musical instruments. It also has a *section of modern art (Mondrian, Klee and others). Not far north in Johan de Wittlaan is the **Nederlands Congres-gebouw** (*Conference Hall*, 1969).

Haagse Bos

From the Korte Voorhout the Leidse-straatweg runs between *Malieveld* and the deer park called *Koekamp* eastward into the *Haagse Bos (Het Bos)*, a wooded park some 2 km (1 mile) long with beautiful tree-lined avenues. At its eastern end stands the moated Palace **Huis ten Bos**, formerly a royal country retreat. It was built in 1644–6, with two wings added in 1748. The first In-ternational Peace Conference took place here in 1899 and after restoration it will become the residence of Queen Beatrix. Also worth seeing is the octagonal *Oraniensaal* with walls 15 m (49 feet) high, completely covered with murals painted in the years 1648–53.

Scheveningen (see page 243).

SURROUNDINGS of The Hague. – Take road N99 to the north-east. After a few miles there is a fork (3 km – 2 miles) to the *Castle Duivenvoorde, originally a medieval building, restored in 1631 by Johan Van Wassenaer. Continuing on the N99 further north you reach Den Deijl, part of **Wassenaar** (which lies 1 km (about a ½ mile) to the left). It is an old residential district, built in modern Dutch style and surrounded by well-kept parks and beautiful woods, with a zoo (aviary, café/restaurant), and a recreation and amusement park.

Hainaut (Henegouwen)

Country: Belgium. – Province: Hainaut.
ⓘ **Fédération Touristique de la Province de Hainaut,**
Rue des Clercs 31,
B-7000 Mons;
tel. (0 65) 31 61 01.

The region called Hainaut in French, and Henegouwen in Dutch, cor-responds to the Belgian province of the same name. In the north Hainaut merges gradually into the hilly country of Brabant. In the south it is bordered by the Valley of the Sambre, and generally by the French frontier. In the west it reaches only a little beyond the Schelde, whereas in the east it merges imperceptibly into the region of Hesbaye. South of the Haine depression, near the bor-der of France and Condroz, lie the two important industrial districts Borinage and Centre.

Hainaut is the western part of a wide open plain covered with a thick layer of loess. It is divided into several large plateaux by the rivers Schelde, Dender and Senne. Toward the north, the tableland (average altitude 160–200 m – 525–656 feet) gradually slopes into the lower lying hilly areas of South Brabant. In the valleys lie large closely built-up villages, whereas the high plateaux are covered with vast, treeless expanses of fields of wheat and sugar-beet. The character of the land is in many ways similar to the rich fertile plains of Picardy and the Rhineland, but there are certain differences. Where there are tertiary clays beneath the loess, the land is richer in water and the proportion of meadowland is higher. This applies to approximately 45% of the agricultural land. On the other hand areas where the subsoil consists of chalk and lime are drier and more fertile.

The area of Mons, Charleroi and La Louvière (Borinage and Centre), is a large industrial region. There are blast furnaces and steelworks, petro-chemical installations, machinery manufacture, electrical industries, and numerous other plants. In addition, large limestone and porphyry quarries (cement and brickworks) are also important. The heavy industry was originally based on coal, and innumerable coal mines, slag heaps and mining villages are characteristic features of the country. The ore for smelting comes mainly from Lorraine. Coal mining has steadily decreased since 1957, dropping from 4 million tons to approximately 1 million tons. The entire region has thus become economically depressed.

Apart from the industrial zone in the south, the population density is fairly low by Belgian standards (less than 200 per sq. km – 518 per sq. mile). The largest towns are **Mons**, capital of the province (see page 217), **Charleroi**, **Fournai**, **Ath** and **Soignies**.

Halle (Hal)

Country: Belgium. – Province : North Brabant.
Altitude: 35 m (115 feet). – Population: 32,000.
Postal code: B-1500.
Telephone code: 02.
(i) **Dienst voor Toerisme,**
Stadhuis,
Grote Markt;
tel. 3 56 37 74.

HOTEL. – *Des Eleveurs*, Baziliekstraat 134, III, 14 r.

RESTAURANT. – *Willy Borghmans*, Theunckensstraat 8.

EVENTS. – At Whitsun (the seventh Sunday after Easter), and on the first Sundays in September and October, a large *procession of pilgrims*.

The Belgian town of Halle (in French: Hal) is a well-known place

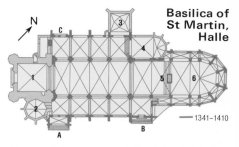

Basilica of St Martin, Halle

—— 1341–1410

A Large south door
B Small south door
C North door

1 Belfry (before 1300, carillon and Museum of Bells)
2 Baptistry (c. 1440; font of 1446)
3 Trazegnies Chapel (1467, alabaster altar by J. Mone, 1533)
4 Chapel of Our Lady (before 1335, marble tomb of the Dauphin Joachim, died 1460)
5 High altar (above the Black Madonna of Halle)
6 Choir (consecrated 1409; below – crypt with treasury)

of pilgrimage in the province of Brabant. It is a lively town, 15 km (9 miles) from Brussels, lying on the River Senne and on the canal linking Brussels and Charleroi, not far from the linguistic border between Flanders and Wallonia. Halle is also an industrial town with blast furnaces, textile, leather and food processing plants.

SIGHTS. – On the Grote Markt stands the *Town Hall*, a brick building (1616). To the left rises the *Basilica of Our Lady (St Martinus Basiliek)*, a notable building in Brabant Gothic dating from the 14th–15th c. Its elegant architecture shows French influence. Worth seeing is the sculptured decoration. The oldest (14th c.) statues are on the west portal, on the tower and in the choir. Particularly beautiful are the statues of the apostles above the arches which are believed to date from the same period and reveal similarities to the work of Claus Sluter. Somewhat later is the 15th c. decoration on the south door and inside the chapel north of the choir, where a beautiful alabaster altar by Jehan Mone can be seen. It is a Renaissance work (1533), with reliefs of the Seven Sacraments, and other statues. There is also a marble memorial with the effigy of the Dauphin Joachim (d. 1460), the son of Louis XI of France. Above the modern high altar is the wooden statuette of the Virgin, which was known to have been in Halle in the 13th c. There is also a rich treasury. In the belfry is a *museum* which includes, among others, bells from the period of Charles V.

SURROUNDINGS of Halle. – An interesting excursion can be made to **Braine-le-Château**, 6·5 km (4 miles) south-east, where there is a beautiful old palace. From here, you can continue to **Waterloo** (see page 265), with its famous *Lion Mound.

Grottoes of Han/ Grottes de Han

Country: Belgium. – Province: Namur.

ⓘ **Office du Tourisme**
(Syndicat d'Initiative),
B-5432 Han-sur-Lesse;
tel. (0 84) 37 75 96.
Bureau des Grottes,
B-5432 Han-sur-Lesse;
tel. (0 84) 3 72 13.

HOTELS (Some closed in winter). – IN HAN-SUR-LESSE: *Des Voyageurs,* Route de Rochefort 1, IV, 32 r.; *De la Lesse,* Rue des Grottes 1, IV; 10 r.; *Des Ardennes,* Rue des Grottes 2, IV, 26 r.; *Du Parc,* Rue Joseph Lamotte 4, V, 10 r.; *l'Escale,* Rue d'Hamptay 47, V, 7 r. – YOUTH HOSTEL: *Le Gîte d'Etape,* 150 b. – CAMP SITE.

RESTAURANTS. – IN HAN-SUR-LESSE: *L'Ardena,* Rue des Grottes 14; *Belle-Vue et de la Grotte,* Rue Joseph Lamotte 1; *Pavillon des Grottes,* Sortie des Grottes; *La Taverne Ardennaise,* Rue d'Hamptay 36; *Taverne du Centre,* Rue des Grottes 3.

CAFÉS. – IN HAN-SUR-LESSE: *Bus Stop,* Rue des Grottes 1 b; *Le Châlet,* Rue des Grottes 10; *La Clé d'Or,* Rue d'Hamptay 38; *Le Square,* Rue d'Hamptay 40; *Taverne des Grottes,* Rue des Grottes 20; *Taverne du Stade,* Rue de Charleville; *Le Benelux,* Rue des Grottes 19; *Gîte d'Etape,* Rue du Gîte 8.

The world-famous ****Grottoes of Han** are in the south-east of the Belgian province of Namur. The little River Lesse flows through stalactite caverns which have an amazing variety of rock formations.

Their origin is due to the porosity of the limestone in this area. A visit takes about two hours. The village of Han-sur-Lesse nearby is a popular base for excursions.

Take the narrow-gauge Grotto light railway from the church opposite the Grotto Office. The line is approximately 3 km (2 miles) long and runs only in summer. In winter the tour starts at the exit of the Grottoes. Tickets for both the visit to the Grottoes and the railway can be purchased at the office. The line runs in a wide arc across the wooded crest of the *Rochers de Faule,* from which you can see the enormous meandering loops of the valley created by the Lesse before it bored out its subterranean bed. Not far east below the railway terminus is the *Perte de la Lesse* (Gouffre de Belvaux; 159 km (99 miles)), where the roaring river disappears into the cave. Only a short stretch of its underground course is known. 10 minutes' walk north, below the station, is the entrance to the Grottoes, the so-called *Trou du Salpêtre* (175 m – 574 feet).

The Grottoes have been known since 1771. They consist of an intricate sequence of caverns, totalling 5 km (3 miles) in length of which only 3 km (2 miles) are accessible; some caverns were not discovered until 1962. They are surprisingly impressive, thanks to cleverly arranged illumination. Especially striking are the *Salle des Scarabées,* the *Salle des Renards,* the *Salle du Vigneron,* the *Grotte du Précipice,* Le *Trophée,* Le *Styx* and the *Salle des Mystérieuses,* all with superb

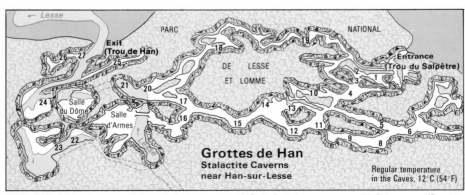

Grottes de Han
Stalactite Caverns
near Han-sur-Lesse

Regular temperature
in the Caves, 12°C (54°F)

1 Salle des Scarabées	9 Grotte du Cocyte	16 Grotte Centrale	24 Embarquement (Departure
2 Salle des Renards	10 Grotte du Précipice	17 Le Trophée	of boats)
3 Grotte de la Grenouille	11 Salle d'Antiparos	18 Salle des Mystérieuses	25 Grotte des Petites
4 Salle du Vigneron	12 Salle des Priapes	19 Grotte des Aventuriers	Fontaines
5 Grande Rue	13 Grotte de l'Hirondelle	20 Le Capitoie	26 Grotte de la Grande
6 Petite Rue	14 Labyrinthe	21 Le Styx	Fontaine
7 Salle de l'Escarpement	15 Salle des Mamelons	22 La Tamise	27 Débarquement (Arrival of
8 Salle Blanche		23 Salle des Draperies	boats)

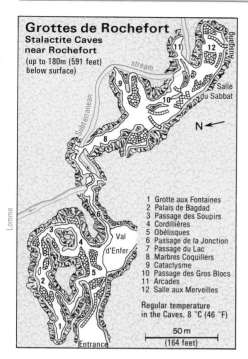

Grottes de Rochefort
Stalactite Caves
near Rochefort
(up to 180m (591 feet)
below surface)

Subterranean
stream
Lomme
Salle du Sabbat
Ausgang
N←
Val d'Enfer

1 Grotte aux Fontaines
2 Palais de Bagdad
3 Passage des Soupirs
4 Cordillières
5 Obélisques
6 Passage de la Jonction
7 Passage du Lac
8 Marbres Coquillers
9 Cataclysme
10 Passage des Gros Blocs
11 Arcades
12 Salle aux Merveilles

Regular temperature
in the Caves, 8 °C (46 °F)

50 m
(164 feet)

Entrance

Above the Grottoes at the end of the avenue is a 17th c. *Loretto Chapel* (view). Nearby, to the east, is the *Palace of Beauregard*.

Harlingen

Country: The Netherlands. – Province: Friesland.
Altitude: sea level. – Population: 15,000.
Postal code: NL-8860 to 8862.
Telephone code: 0 51 78.

ⓘ **VVV Harlingen,**
Voorstraat 47,
NL-8861 BD Harlingen;
tel. 22 76.

HOTELS. – *Hofstee*, Franekereind 23–25, IV, 61 b.; *Zeezicht*, Zuiderhaven 1, IV, 35 b.; *Anna Caspari*, Noorderhaven 67–69, 29 b. – CAMP SITE.

RESTAURANT. – *Neptunus*, Oude Ringmuur 3.

EVENTS. – *Lanenkaatsen* (third week in June), a unique ball game in the street; *Sailing Regatta* (June); *July Festival Week* (first week in July); *Fishermen's Festival* with Fireworks (end of August/beginning of September).

The town of Harlingen (in Frisian: Harns), in the Dutch province of Friesland, lies on the coast of the Waddenzee opposite the North Sea islands of Vlieland and Terschelling. It was founded in 1243 near a place where, in 1134, a village was swept away by high tides.

stalactite formations. The *Salle d'Armes* is a beautiful round cave where the Lesse reappears (refreshments are available). The *Salle du Dôme* is one of the widest (154 m (505 feet) long, 140 m (459 feet) wide and 129 m (423 feet) high), and is viewed by a light carried by an attendant.

The exit from the Grottoes is by boat through the *Trou de Han*. The gradual emergence of daylight reflected in the subterranean stream is quite impressive. A museum with a restaurant is situated at the exit. From here the walk back to Han takes approximately three minutes.

SURROUNDINGS of Han-sur-Lesse. – To the east, in the Valley of the Lesse, is a *Safari Park* (round-trip 10 km (6 miles), 1½ hours).

6 km (4 miles) north-east of Han-sur-Lesse is the little town of **Rochefort** with a population of 5000 (Hotel Central, III, 7 r.; Bristol, III, 6 r.; la Favette, IV, 22 r.); it is dominated in the south by a ruined castle. Formerly the capital of a county, it is now a popular summer resort and a starting point for visits to the caves of Rochefort.

The *Caves of Rochefort (Grottes de Rochefort)*, are not as impressive or as popular as those of Han. They can be reached from the Market Place, by first following the road towards Bouillon for about 300 m (328 yards), and then by turning left and going uphill through an old avenue of lime trees. The visit lasts about 1 hour. Most interesting is the *Salle aux Merveilles*, the *Salle du Sabbat*, 90 m (295 feet) high (son et lumière), as well as the *Val d'Enfer* and *Les Arcades*.

Harlingen is the home port of an important lobster fishing fleet. Imported goods are mainly coal, timber and other industrial raw materials needed in Friesland. The

At the harbour of Harlingen

harbour is linked with Leeuwarden by the Van-Harinxma Canal. Ferries to Vlieland and Terschelling depart from here. Shipyards, fish processing plants, timber industries and the production of building materials are all located around the harbour.

SIGHTS. – The **Town Hall** at No. 86 Norderhafen dates from 1736 and was designed by the architect Hendrik Norel. Its council chamber is worth visiting. The building was restored in 1956. In its vicinity are several beautiful *patrician houses* (16th–18th c.). In the north-eastern part of the town is the *English Park*, laid out on the site of the former fortifications, the remains of which can still be seen. The *Grote Kerk* (Nieuwe Kerk; Dutch Reformed; 1775), was built on a warft (artificial mound) and has an excellent organ of 1776. In front of the church stands a 12th c. tower. The **Municipal Museum** (open April– October) at No. 56 Voorstraat is housed in one of the many surviving gabled houses, and contains valuable antiquities of silver and porcelain, paintings, friezes, old town plans and interesting ship models. On *Westerzeedijk* in the south of the town stands the "Steenen Man", a monument erected in 1774 to commemorate the Spanish Governor Caspar de Robles who repaired the dikes after the tidal wave in 1570.

SURROUNDINGS of Harlingen. – A motor boat (no car-loading facilities) connects Harlingen daily with the small North Sea island of **Vlieland**. The crossing takes two hours. On the island, the village *Oost Vlieland* (Badhotel Bruin, III, 70 b.; Strandhotel, III, 180 b.; Kap Oost, IV, 70 b.), is a popular quiet seaside resort. The island has an excellent beach 2 km (1 mile) east of the village, and pleasant wooded dunes. There is a nature reserve with interesting birds.

The large North Sea island of **Terschelling** can be reached from Harlingen by motor boat in two hours. (Car ferry facilities, reservations recommended.) On the island are several villages with a total population of about 4000. The most important is **West Terschelling** (Hotel Nap, III, 54 b.; Lutine, III, 20 b.; Paal 8, IV, 94 b.; Oepkes, IV, 43 b.), with a large dock and a 15th c. lighthouse "Brandaris". 6 km (4 miles) north-east of West Terschelling in the partly wooded interior of the island is the village of *Midsland* with beautiful gabled houses. On the north coast there are good beaches and bathing. The north-east of the island is occupied by the nature reserve *Boschplaat* (4400 hectares – 10,872 acres).

Hasselt

Country: Belgium. – Province: Limburg.
Altitude: 39 m (128 feet). – Population: 64,000.
Postal code: B-3500.
Telephone code: 0 11.

ⓘ **Dienst voor Toerisme,**
Lombaardstraat 3;
tel. 22 59 61.

HOTELS. – *Parkhotel*, Genkerweg 350, III, 11 r.; *Century*, Leopoldplein 1, IV, 10 r.; *Memling*, Kempischeweg 103, IV, 15 r.; *Schoofs*, Stationsplein 7, IV, 15 r.; *Royal*, Havermarkt 17, V, 12 r.

RESTAURANTS. – *Van Dijck*, Kiezelweg 19; *t'Claeverblat*, Lombaardstraat 34; *Figaro*, Mombeekdreef; *Diana*, Kiewitstraat 239; *Savarin*, Dorpstraat 34.

EVENTS. – Theatre performances, concerts and operas all year in the *Cultural Complex; Exhibitions* in the Begijnhof; *Motor racing* at the Zolder Race Track (north of the town).

Hasselt is the lively capital of the Belgian province of Limburg. It lies between Liège and Antwerp on the Demer, a tributary of the Dijle. South of it extend fertile fields and orchards. To the north is the coalfield of Limburg. In addition to Hasselt's importance as a market and focal point for trade, it is also a significant industrial town. The most important branches of industry are food processing, chemical and electrical engineering.

HISTORY. – Hasselt was already a market town in the early Middle Ages, when it belonged to the County of Loon. It received its town status in the 12th c. In 1366 Hasselt was acquired, together with County Loon, by the Diocese of Liège and became the seat of local administration. In 1795 it was annexed by France and became the capital of the Département of Meuse-Inférieure, and later, in 1813, the capital of the Dutch province of Limburg. In 1839 Limburg was divided between Belgium and Holland and Hasselt became the capital of the Belgian province of Limburg.

SIGHTS. – The Grote Markt in the middle of the town is surrounded by a number of interesting patrician houses from the 17th and 18th c. Via the Kortstraat you reach the Gothic Cathedral of **St Quintin** (*St Quintinuskathedraal*), built in the 13th– 14th c. on Romanesque foundations. Its choir was enlarged in the 15th–16th c.; the beautiful pews were made in 1549; and the wooden statues in the interior date from the 15th–16th c. In the tower is a fine carillon of forty-two bells.

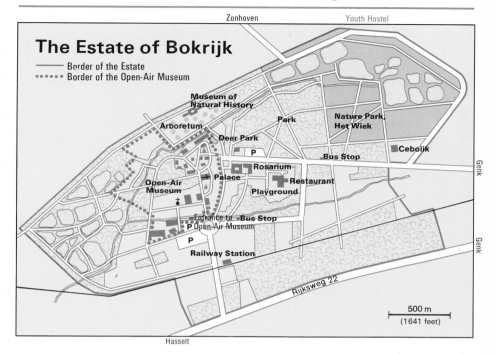

The Estate of Bokrijk

—————— Border of the Estate
•••••• Border of the Open-Air Museum

Zonhoven   Youth Hostel

Museum of Natural History

Arboretum   Park   Nature Park, Het Wiek

Deer Park

P   Cebolik

Bus Stop

Rosarium

Open-Air Museum   Palace   Restaurant

Playground

Entrance to Open-Air Museum   Bus Stop
P

P

Railway Station

Rijksweg 22

Genk

Genk

500 m
(1641 feet)

Hasselt

Not far west from the Grote Markt stands the *Church of Our Lady* (1726–31, restored in 1951). Inside is the tomb of Anne-Catherine Lamboy, the Abbess of Hasselt. The tomb, as well as the high altar with a 14th c. statue of the Virgin, is believed to be the work of the sculptor Jean Delcour from Liège. North of the Grote Markt on Groenplaats stands the **Town Hall**, an attractive patrician house (1675). It was rebuilt in the 18th–19th c. in the Classical style. Going from the Cathedral via the Zuivelmarkt you come to the *Begijnhof*, built in 1707–62 in Renaissance style.

SURROUNDINGS of Hasselt. – **To Genk** (13 km – 8 miles). – Leave Hasselt in a northerly direction via Hoogstraat and Demerstraat, cross the *Albert Canal* and turn right about 1·5 km (1 mile) from the middle of town. Continue on road No. 22 across pretty heathland with dunes, pine forests and many lakes. 5 km (3 miles) further, a little lane forks to the left into the *Estate of* **Bokrijk**, 540 hectares (1334 acres) of heath and woods. In it is an interesting manor house dating from the 18th–19th c. with a Museum of Natural History and an *Open-Air Museum extending over 30 hectares (74 acres). It contains farmsteads, windmills, a Romanesque church, etc.

6·5 km (4 miles) beyond the fork mentioned above, you reach the industrial town of **Genk** (Hotel Atlantis, III, 29 r.; Hotel Majestic, IV, 14 r.; Drive-Inn, IV, 8 r.; Ulenspiegel, IV, 14 r.), which lies on the edge of the coal-mining district in the region of Kempen. Interesting events in Genk are its Carnival Procession, Torchlight Procession on St Martin's Day, and the Procession of the May Queen.

In the Open-Air Museum of Bokrijk

Den Helder

Country: The Netherlands. – Province: North Holland. Altitude: sea level. – Population: 61,000. Postal code: NL-1780 AA to 1799. Telephone code: 0 22 30.

ⓘ **VVV Den Helder/Julianadorp,** Julianaplein; tel. 1 35 97.

HOTELS. – *Motel Bethlehem*, Marsdiepstraat 2, II, 141 b.; *Forest*, Julianaplein 43, III, 35 b.; *Het Wapen van Den Helder*, Spoorgracht 43–44, IV, 54 b. – IN HUISDUINEN: *De Branding*, 20 b. – CAMP SITE.

The Ferry Den Helder – Texel

RESTAURANTS. – *Land's End*, Havenplein 1; *Prinsenkelder*, Prins Hendriklaan 1; *Visrestaurant Kalkman*, Het Nieuwe Diep 27b.

EVENTS. – In summer there are various shows and entertainment for tourists. One of the most interesting is *National Navy Day* (end of July/early August), when naval vessels stationed in the area can be visited.

SPORTS and LEISURE. – Water-skiing, sailing (a modern Yacht Harbour), deep sea fishing.

The Dutch port of Den Helder is situated on the northern tip of West Friesland in the province of North Holland between the Waddenzee and the open North Sea opposite the Island of Texel. It is connected with Amsterdam by the North Holland Canal. Den Helder became known as the largest naval port of the Netherlands and one of the country's prime bulb growing areas. Fishing and textiles are the most important industries.

HISTORY. – Den Helder came into being about 1500, and up to the end of the 18th c. was only a fishing village. In 1811, however, it was strongly fortified by Napoleon as the "Gibraltar of the North". The fortifications were continued later by the Dutch government. Since the construction of the North Sea Canal, the town has lost its former role as the outer port of the Dutch capital, now taken over principally by IJmuiden. In 1673, the Dutch fleet under Admiral de Ruyter defeated the English and French fleets off the coast of Den Helder. In 1799, 10,000 English and 13,000 Russians, under the command of the Duke of York, landed here. The Duke manœuvred the Russians behind the French, but they got lost in the dunes and most of them were captured in the Battle of Bergen. The English, after an unlucky skirmish near Castricum, had to yield to the superior forces of General Brune and re-embarked.

SIGHTS. – Not far east of the town on the other side of the North Holland Canal, is the Port of **Nieuwediep**, which, together with the arsenal, the shipyards of the Royal Naval College and the Zoological Research Station of the Dutch Zoological Society, is called *Willemsoord*. – In the harbour square stands the *monument* to members of the Dutch navy who lost their lives in the First and Second World Wars. Further west is another monument to Dutch seamen. Near the harbour square is the dock for the ferries to the Island of Texel.

From the harbour runs a **dike** built entirely of Norwegian granite, and extending 60 m (197 feet) below sea level ("Zeepromenade", view over the Marsdiep to the Island of Texel). It protects the coastline against high tides for some 10 km (6 miles) and leads to the village of **Huisduinen** where there is a *lighthouse* 69 m (226 feet) high ("Vuurtoren", with a good view over the sea). South of Huisduinen an excellent beach stretches along the North Sea coast; inland is the nature park *De Donkere Duinen*. – South of the town are the residential areas *Nieuw Den Helder* and *De Schooten*.

SURROUNDINGS of Den Helder. – 6 km (4 miles) south on the North Sea coast, near *Julianadorp aan Zee* is the bungalow village "De Zandloper", with a good beach. (*Julianadorp* is 2 km (1 mile) inland.)

From Den Helder to the Island of Texel (departure from the harbour square; car ferry facilities). The North Sea Island of *Texel is 24 km (15 miles) long, up to 10 km (6 miles) wide and covers 18,600 hectares (45,960 acres). Its population is 11,000. The land is mostly pasture on which graze some 10,000 sheep. (The local green ewe cheese is excellent.) It is a popular place for excursions. On its southern shore is the harbour 't Horntje, completed in 1962. 7 km (4 miles) north of it lies the main township **Den Burg** (Hotel den Burg, IV, 72 b.) with a Museum of Antiquities. 6 km (4 miles) north-west of here, on the west coast of the island, is the small fishing village *De Koog* (Hotel Opduin, III, 104 b.; Gouden Boltje, IV, 28 b.) which is popular as an unspoiled resort and has a good sandy beach. Between Den Burg and De Koog in "De Dennen" (The Firs), is the *Museum of Texel* with a large collection of birds. It is worth while to continue north of Den Burg via the villages of *Zuideijerland* or *Waal* to *de Cocksdorp*, situated in one of the bays of the *Eijerlandse Gat* (13–15 km (8–9 miles) according to route chosen). North-west of here innumerable sea birds nest on the northern tip of the island, the so-called Eijerland. The area is partly a nature reserve; the birds' eggs are collected and sold in Amsterdam. There are daily tours from the warden's house in De Koog to the nesting places. Advance booking is recommended.

's-Hertogenbosch

Country: The Netherlands. – Province: North Brabant.
Altitude: 5 m (16 feet). – Population: 87,000.
Postal code: NL-5200 AA to 5259.
Telephone code: 0 73.

ⓘ VVV 's-Hertogenbosch,
Markt 77,
NL-5211 JX 's-Hertogenbosch;
tel. 12 30 71.

HOTELS. – *Eurohotel*, Hinthamerstraat 63, I, 78 b.;
Golden Tulip Hotel Central, Mr. Loeffplein 98, II, 152
b.; *Chalet Royal*, Wilhelminapark 1, III, 6 b.; *Nieuwe
Meierijsche Kar*, Oude Engelseweg 14, IV, 21 b.;
Royal, Visstraat 26, IV, 22 b.; *Terminus*, Stationsplein
19, V, 20 b.; *Markzicht*, Oude Engelseweg 22a, V,
22 b.

RESTAURANTS. – *Rôtisserie 't Misverstant*; Snelle-
straat 28; *Raadskelder*, Markt 1a; *Aub. De Koets*, Korte
Putstraat 21; *Bistro Bois-Le-Duc*, Kerkstraat 54;
Kikvorsch, Parade 6. – IN ST MICHIELSGESTEL: *Pettelaar*,
Pettelaarseschans 1. – IN HINTHAM: *Zeuve Zinnen*,
Hintham 104.

FLEA MARKET. – First Sunday in every month,
noon–5 p.m.

**'s-Hertogenbosch (in short Den
Bosch), in French Bois-le-Duc, is
the capital of the Dutch province of
North Brabant. It lies at the confluence of the Dommel and the Aa as
well as on the Zuid Willemsvaart in
flat pasture land which is flooded
every year in winter. It is a busy
commercial town (important cattle
markets), and the home of diversified industries which include the
manufacture of cigars and hardware, food processing and brewing.**

HISTORY. – 's-Hertogenbosch probably owes its
name to Duke (Hertog) Henry I of Brabant, who gave
the town its charter in 1185 in order to protect the
northern borders of his Duchy from Geldern and
Holland. Because of its favourable transport facilities
the original fortress town quickly developed into a
trading city. In 1559 's-Hertogenbosch became the
seat of a Bishop. Its fortifications were destroyed in
1856. The town is the birthplace of the famous painter
Hieronymus Bosch (1450–1516), and of Theodor
van Thulden (1606–69), a friend and disciple of
Rubens.

SIGHTS. – The Inner City, which lies
between the Dommel and the Zuid
Willemsvaart, is triangular in shape, and
its central area is a triangular Markt, from
which three main streets, the Hinthamerstraat, Vughterstraat and Hoge Steenweg, lead to the three points of the
triangle. In the Markt stands a statue of
Hieronymus Bosch. On the south side of
the square is the **Town Hall** (*Stadhuis*),
originally Gothic but rebuilt in late

Baroque style with elements of Classicism. It has an astronomical clock
(showing an equestrian tournament) in
the gable, and a carillon (Wednesday, 10
a.m.–11 a.m.) in the tower which dates
from 1650. In the vestibule are two
notable murals by A. Derkindern
(1892–7), and on the first floor are 18th c.
Gobelin tapestries. In the 16th c. Gothic
cellar is a café/restaurant.

From the east side of the market you can
go along either the Hinthamerstraat or the
Kerkstraat to the *Cathedral (St Jans-
kathedraal*; Catholic) which is the most
important medieval church in the country.
The building was originally Romanesque,
but was rebuilt in 1280–1312, and then
again in late Gothic style in the 15th–16th
c. The flying buttresses on the outer side
of the choir are especially striking. The
lower part of the *belfry* (48 bells) dates
from the Romanesque period (*c.* 1200).
From its top is an excellent view (carillon,
Wednesday, noon until 1 p.m.).

Among the treasures in the lofty INTERIOR of the
Cathedral are a carved *Renaissance pulpit* by C.
Bloemaert (1566–70), and the large organ
(1617–35); in the baptistry stands the *bronze font* by
Art van Tricht (1492). In the Chapel of Our Lady
dating from 1268 is a much venerated figure of the
Virgin ("de Zoete Moeder van den Bosch"; late 13th
c.). The most beautiful part of the church is the well-
proportioned choir which is surrounded by chapels.
The *carved pews* (1480) are considered to be the
best examples in Holland. There is a rear rood screen
with wooden reliefs in High Renaissance style. At the
beginning of the ambulatory, on the right, is a fresco
(1444); in the first chapel on the left is a 15th c. high
altar.

Opposite the Cathedral, north-east at No.
94 Hinthamerstraat, is the building of the
Confraternity of Our Lady, also called the
"Confraternity of Swans", believed to
have been founded in 1318, the members
of which include the Princes of Orange
and the Dutch Queen Mother. Inside are
mementoes of some of its famous
members (closed in August). Not far
south-west in St Jacobskerkhof is the
Provincial Museum (*Central Noordbrabants Museum*) with antiquities from
Roman, German and Frankish periods,
manuscripts, paintings, drawings, maps
and coins from the province of North
Brabant, local antiquities and a good
library.

South of the Cathedral extends the wide
Parade Ground with the *Episcopal Palace*.
Not far west at No. 20 Waterstraat are the

Provinciehuis on the outskirts of 's-Hertogenbosch

state archives of North Brabant. From here via the Keizerstraat you arrive at the Church of *St Catherine* or *Kruiskerk*, consecrated in 1533 and rebuilt in 1916–17, with notable paintings by P. J. Verhaghen (1728–1811) and others.

South-east of the town on the banks of the Zuiderplas, stands the new **Provinciehuis**, a high-rise building over 100 m (328 feet) high, the seat of the Provincial Government. Inside is a collection of modern art, tapestries and statues.

Pays de Herve (Land van Herve)

Country: Belgium. – Province: Liège.
ⓘ **Bureau du Tourisme,**
Hôtel de Ville,
B-4800 Verviers;
tel. (0 87) 33 61 61.

The region called Pays de Herve in French, and Land van Herve in Flemish, is situated east of the Belgian town of Liège between the rivers Meuse and Vesdre. Eastwards it extends into the district of Eupen.

The soil in the entire area is unusually clayish and therefore water-resistant despite the fact that the subsoil is entirely

composed of porous chalk and lime. Rainfall is very high (900–1000 mm; 35–39 inches). These are the reasons why this highly distinctive area, reaching an altitude of 354 m (1161 feet), is used mostly for pasture and orchards; it is framed with hedges which resemble the French "bocage" (copse). The main source of income is the sale of butter and cheese; occasionally also of fruit.

Industries play only a subordinate role in this border region of Belgium. The only one worth mentioning is the textile industry in Verviers. In the western part there are also coal mines, around which several large industrial plants have been built using coal as raw material for their products.

Hesbaye/ Haspengouw

Country: Belgium. – Province: Limburg.
ⓘ **Haspengouw,**
Stadhuis,
B-3840 Borgloon;
tel. (0 12) 74 10 38.
Hageland/Haspengouw,
Stadhuis,
B-3300 Tienen;
tel. (0 16) 81 10 07.

The part of East Belgium called Hesbaye in French, and Haspengouw in Flemish, is a vast plateau which in the west at the watershed between the Dijle and the Grote Gete, merges into the similar landscape of Hainaut. The Valley of the Meuse forms its southern and eastern boundaries; in the north it reaches as far as the Demer, which divides it from Kempen.

South of the line Tienen–St Truiden–Tongeren–Maastricht, Hesbaye consists of chalk and lime strata, covered by extensive layers of loess. The latter also cover the northern part of the area, but here they are overlaid by tertiary sands. In the southern part the annual precipitation is absorbed more quickly by the subsoil rocks than in the north, and therefore this area is described as Dry Hesbaye. The north is Wet Hesbaye.

The difference in the wetness of the two areas is clearly reflected in their agriculture. Dry Hesbaye is characterised by intensive wheat, fodder and sugar-beet cultivation. Dairy cattle and other livestock are widely bred. The farms, sometimes as large as 50–100 hectares (124–247 acres), stand within large compact villages.

In the less fertile Wet Hesbaye settlements are more widely dispersed. Crops which are easier to grow are cultivated, and to a large extent pastureland and meadows prevail. The countryside, which in the south is open and monotonous, is here enlivened by hedgerows and trees.

Industry plays only a minor role in Hesbaye, with the exception of some sugar refineries in the south. On the other hand, the main agricultural production areas are surrounded by important towns which provide markets for the region's products and at the same time possess a wide range of food processing plants. The most important among them are **Tienen** (see page 252), **Sint-Truiden** (see page 247), and **Tongeren** (see page 253). Further away are **Liège** (see page 192), **Maastricht** (see page 208), **Hasselt** (see page 174), **Namur** (see page 222) and **Huy** (see page 182).

Hilversum

Country: The Netherlands. – Province: North Holland.
Altitude: 5 m (16 feet). – Population: 94,000.
Postal code: NL-1200 AA to 1249.
Telephone code: 0 35.

ⓘ **VVV Hilversum,**
Stationsplein 2,
NL-1211 EX Hilversum;
tel. 1 16 51.

HOTELS. – *Het Hof van Holland*, Kerkbrink 1–7, I, 110 b.; *Hilfertsom*, Koninginneweg 28–30, II, 107 b.; *Haags Koffiehuis*, Naarderstraat 7, V, 16 b.; *Dennenhof*, Eikenlaan 44, V, 13 b.; *Frans Hals*, Frans Halslaan 80, V, 18 b.

RESTAURANTS. – *Palace Résidence*, 's-Gravelandseweg 86; *Carrousel*, Emmastraat 2; *Spandershoeve*, Bussumergrintweg 46.

The town of Hilversum situated in the extreme south-east of the Dutch province of North Holland in the pleasant region of Gooiland, became famous for its radio and television stations. Hilversum is one of the fashionable residential and commuter districts of Amsterdam. The numerous residences of wealthy citizens of Amsterdam and the large

parks contribute to the character of the town. There are also many modern buildings designed by famous architects. Industry, mainly textile, leather, electrical engineering and pharmaceuticals, plays only a subordinate role. Hilversum developed from a poor village after the railway line Amsterdam–Amersfoort was built in 1874.

The **new Town Hall**, complete with tower, was built in 1928–30 to the design of the architect W. M. Dudok and is considered one of the most important modern buildings in the country. The carillon was installed in the tower in 1958. There are also other buildings, including schools, by the same architect. Apart from these *Broadcasting House*, the *Hotel Gooiland*, the Catholic *St Vituskerk* built by Cuypers, with a tower 98 m (322 feet) high, and the *Noorderkerk* are also of interest. The *old Town Hall* in Kerkbrink houses the *Goois Museum*.

SURROUNDINGS of Hilversum. – An interesting excursion can be made across **Gooiland**, the so-called "garden of Amsterdam". From Hilversum take the road to Laren (5 km – 3 miles), *Blaricum* (7 km – 4 miles), *Huizen* on the Gooimeer (10 km – 6 miles), Naarden (16 km – 10 miles), and *Bussum* (19 km – 12 miles); this is a very attractive, scenic route. From Bussum back to Hilversum is 27 km (17 miles). – In the little town of *Laren* with a population of 14,000, a visit to the artists' colony and the Singer Memorial Museum, which includes modern paintings, sculpture and East Asian art, is recommended. *Naarden* (see page 220), is also worth a visit.

On the edge of the Gooi extend the **Loosdrechtse Plassen (the lakes of Loosdrecht)**, a stretch of shallow lakes forming a popular water sports area. In **Nieuw Loosdrecht**, 6 km (4 miles) south-west of Hilversum, stands the *Kasteel Sijpestein*, a mansion built in imitation 16th c. style, with beautiful gardens and a good art collection. 7 km (4 miles) west of Hilversum comes **Oud Loosdrecht**, and 5 km (3 miles) north-west of the town, the village of *'s-Graveland* (Hotel Wapen van Amsterdam, IV, 18 b.), with the interesting *Trompenburg Palace*.

Holland

Country: The Netherlands. – Provinces: North Holland, South Holland.

ⓘ VVV Amsterdam e. o.,
Rokin 5,
NL-1012 KK Amsterdam;
tel. (0 20) 26 64 44.
VVV het Gooi,
Stationsplein 1–3,
NL-1211 EX Hilversum;
tel. (0 35) 1 16 51.
VVV Kennemer-Amstelland,
Stationsplein 1,
NL-2011 LR Haarlem;
tel. (0 23) 31 90 59.
VVV Den Haag e. o.,
Postfach 85973,
NL-2508 CR Den Haag;
tel. (0 70) 54 62 00.
VVV Rotterdam e. o.,
Stadhuisplein 19,
NL-3012 AR Rotterdam;
tel. (0 10) 13 60 00.

The fen region of Holland lies in the north-west of the Netherlands and comprises two provinces, North and South Holland. It extends between Haringvliet, Hollandsch Diep and Merwede in the south, the North Sea in the west, the Waddenzee in the north, the IJsselmeer and a line between Hilversum, Utrecht and Gorinchem in the east. Holland, the drained marshes of which lie consistently below sea level, is protected from the North Sea by an almost uninterrupted stretch of dunes.

Its geological subsoil consists of layers of clay, created by the North Sea after the Ice Age glaciers melted. The North Sea, slowly advancing from the Doggerbank, deposited them behind mighty coastal dikes thrown up by tides and made of flotsam, debris and sand. Later vast moors and thick layers of peat formed over them. These were preserved only in central Holland; in the extreme north and south of the area, the moors were re-covered by a new layer of clay when the North Sea advanced again after the beginning of the present era. The lakes in central Holland were created by peat cutting, which caused the sinking of the surface. Such depressions then quickly filled with water. Most of these lakes have since been drained and turned into farmland.

The history of the colonisation of Holland is closely connected with dike-building. In the 12th–13th c. the technique was already sufficiently developed to turn the marshes which originally lay within the tidal area into habitable and fertile polders. These marshes, which had sunk below sea level because of peat cutting, had to be drained. This was a task just as difficult as protecting them from possible flooding. The sinking of Holland extended over long periods. At the beginning all incoming water drained away at low tide, but as the sinking continued drainage installations had to be devised and were powered by the well-known Dutch windmills. Because of the high technical expense the large lakes of Holland were drained only very late, in 1612 (Beemster) and 1852 (Haarlemmermeer). These areas are now called "droogmakerijen".

There is a striking difference in the character of their settlements between the older marshes and the newer "droogmakerijen". In the older polders villages prevail. The farms line both sides of the canals and ditches and their fields are laid out at right angles to them. The "droogmakerijen", on the contrary, are characterised by scattered settlements. Instead of villages there are individual farmsteads.

The diversification of farmland is conditioned by the age, origin and quality of the soil On the sandy soils just inland of the coastal dunes vegetables are grown. Bulb growing is also important. The old polders are pastureland, interspersed with relatively small horticultural areas producing flowers and ornamental plants. Farmland prevails in the more recent fens, where grain, potatoes, vegetables and plants necessary for industrial purposes are grown, but pasturing still has a role to play.

A typical Dutch landscape near Rijpwetering

Holland is the economic and cultural heartland of the entire Netherlands. This has brought about an enormous concentration of industries of all kinds, and one of the highest population densities in the world. Cities such as **Amsterdam, Rotterdam, Haarlem, Leyden, The Hague, Delft, Gouda, Utrecht** and **Hilversum** (see the respective pages), to name only the largest, form, together with some others, an urban region which is known as "**Randstad Holland**". More than 3·5 million people live here.

HOLLAND🌷

Although strictly speaking the name Holland means only the fen region described above, it is currently used for the entire Netherlands.

So, for example, the Dutch Tourist Office uses in their printed matter the emblem which is reproduced here, consisting of the word "Holland" with 2 symbolic tulips.

Hoorn

Country: The Netherlands. – Province: North Holland.
Altitude: below sea level. – Population: 26,000.
Postal code: NL-1620 AA to 1699.
Telephone code: 0 22 90.
ⓘ **VVV Hoorn,**
   Rode Steen 2,
   NL-1621 CV Hoorn;
   tel. 1 81 93.

HOTELS. – *Petit Nord*, Kleine Noord 55, III, 55 b.; *De Vale Hen*, Vale Hen 8–10, III, 18 b.; *De Keizerskroon*, Breed 31–33, IV, 46 b.; *De Posthoorn*, Breed 27, V, 30 b. – *Het Gouden Hoofd*, V, 8 b. (3½ km (2 miles) in Wester Blokker).

RESTAURANTS. – *Oude Rosmolen*, Duinsteeg 1; *In de Oude Zaadmarkt*, Grote Noord 115; *Bonte Koe*, Nieuwendam 1; *Kod Nikole*, Nieuwendam 2.

EVENTS. – *Street Festival* "Hoorn Can Cope" (every Wednesday from mid-June to mid-August).

Hoorn, situated in the Dutch province of North Holland in a bay of the IJsselmeer, is the former capital of West Friesland. Today it is an important market for cattle and cheese and at the same time the chief town of a wide rural area. Its industries are food processing, metal and timber; tourism is also economically important. There are two yacht harbours in Hoorn, and its many beautiful

gabled 17th c. houses provide a very attractive *townscape.

The town is the birthplace of the navigator Willem Schouten (1580–1625), who rounded the southern tip of America in 1616, and called it "Cap Hoorn" (Cape Horn) after his home town. Jan Pieterszoon Coen (1587–1629), one of the founders of the Dutch Colonial Empire in the East Indies, was also born here.

HISTORY. – Hoorn was founded in the 14th c. as a trading settlement. It received its charter in 1356. Its time of prosperity was in the 16th c. when the town was the most important port on the Zuidersee. On 11 October 1573 a naval battle took place off the coast of Hoorn between the Spaniards and the citizens of Enkhuizen, Edam, Monnikendam and Hoorn. The Spanish Admiral du Bossu was captured by the Dutch. From the 17th c. Hoorn steadily lost its importance and many merchants moved to Amsterdam. When the Markerwaard was enclosed with dikes, the harbour was cut off from the sea.

SIGHTS. – In the Nieuwstraat stands the **Town Hall** dating from 1613. Inside is the Council Chamber, built into the chapel of a former 15th c. monastery. In the chamber is a painting by Blanderhoff (1633) of the naval battle of 1573. At the end of the Nieuwstraat, in the Kerkplein, stands the **Grote Kerk**, rebuilt in 1883, and the former *St Jansgasthuis* (1563). Kerkstraat leads from here to Rodesteen Square, where there is a statue of J. P. Coen. In the Rodesteen stands the old *Weigh-house* (1609) and the former *Proostenhuis* (1632) which was the assembly hall of the Council of West Friesland. It now houses the **West Frisian Museum** with a collection of antiquities and paintings.

North-west of Rodesteen stands the *Noorderkerk* (1441–1529). – In the Grote Oost is the former *Oosterkerk*, dating from the 15th c. East of here at the end of Kleine Oost, on the left stands the 16th c.

The Harbour of Hoorn

Oosterport which is all that remains of the city wall. In the south of the town is the picturesque **harbour** with the *Hoofdtoren*, a 16th–17th c. tower, and the *dike* (good view of the IJsselmeer).

SURROUNDINGS of Hoorn. – **To Enkhuizen and Medemblik.** The road runs through the most prosperous area of North Holland where the farmhouses are as neat as patrician villas. Most of them are surrounded by water-filled ditches, and bridges link them to the road. – You can go to Enkhuizen either by a direct road (18 km – 11 miles) which passes through only a few villages, or you can drive approximately the same distance via the villages of *Westblokker, Oostblokker, Westwoud, Hoogkarspel, Grootebroek* and *Bovenkarspel*. These villages are part of the "Streek". Most interesting, however, is a drive on the dike along the IJsselmeer. After 18 or 24 km (11 or 15 miles) depending on the route chosen, you reach **Enkhuizen** (see page 143), a small town situated at the east end of a peninsula jutting into the IJsselmeer.

To reach Medemblik you can drive either directly from Hoorn (23 km – 14 miles) by a road which runs in long straight stretches across fertile farmland and pastureland, or follow the coastal road along the IJsselmeer from Enkhuizen across the experimental polder *Andijk*, which was created when the draining of the Zuiderzee was begun. After 22 km (14 miles) you reach **Medemblik** (Hotel Wapen van Medemblik, V, 55 b.), a little old town with a population of 5000 and a small harbour on the IJsselmeer. Worth seeing is the 13th c. Kasteel Radboud, the lofty tower of the Church of St Bonifatius and the modern Town Hall. Outside the church is the tomb of Lord George Murray (1695–1760), the commander of the Jacobites at Culloden, who died in exile at Medemblik.

Huy (Hoei)

Country: Belgium. – Province: Namur.
Altitude: 77 m (253 feet). – Population: 18,000.
Postal code: B-5200.
Telephone code: 0 85.

ⓘ **Syndicat d'Initiative,**
Quai de Namur 1;
tel. 21 29 15.

HOTELS. – *De l'Aigle Noir*, Quai Dautrebande 8, III, 13 r.; *Du Fort*, Chaussée Napoléon 5–6, IV, 22 r.; *La Renaissance*, Rue des Sœurs Grises 18, IV, 6 r.; *Du Mouton Bleu*, Rue Entre Deux Portes 2, IV, 11 r. – YOUTH HOSTEL: Promenade de l'Ile, 50 b.

RESTAURANT. – *Plat d'Etaing*, Quai de Namur 15.

SPORTS and LEISURE. – Sailing and water-skiing on the Meuse.

The Belgian town of Huy (in Flemish Hoei), is pleasantly set in an undulating landscape at the confluence of the Meuse and the Hoyoux, approximately half-way between Namur and Liège.

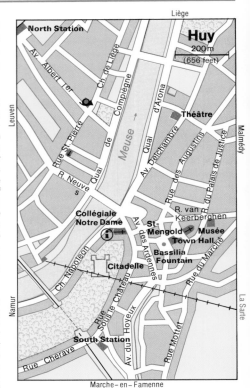

Huy received its freedom charter in 1066 from Prince Bishop Theoduin and had reached a high degree of prosperity by the late Middle Ages because of its famous brassworks and wool industry. Its most important architectural monuments date from that period. The impressive citadel which dominates the town was blasted out of the rocks in 1822. Today, iron foundries, sugar refineries and paper mills are the most important factors in the economy of Huy.

SIGHTS. – On the right bank of the Meuse stands the massive *Collegiate Church of Notre-Dame**, the most significant High Gothic building of its kind in Belgium. It was begun in 1311 on the foundations of an earlier Romanesque basilica and completed in 1377. In its west tower is a superb rose window. Especially worth seeing is the Bethlehem portal on the east side of the church, above which fine 14th c. sculptures have been preserved. Inside is an interesting treasury.

Nearby, to the east of the church, is the Grand' Place, with an attractive *Bassilia fountain* from 1406, the only Gothic fountain with a bronze basin still existing in Belgium. Here also stands the **Town Hall** (*Hôtel de Ville*), a superb building in

Louis XV style dating from 1766. Inside is a small collection of paintings. Behind the Town Hall in the quaint Place Verte, stands the Gothic *Church of St Mengold*, the interior of which was restored in the 17th c. Behind the church, a lane leads to the former Franciscan Monastery in the Rue van Keerberghen, now housing a *Municipal Museum*.

In the north of the town is the **Peace University** (*Université de Paix*), founded in 1964 by the Dominican priest, Father Pire, the 1958 Nobel Peace Prize winner. From the left bank of the Meuse a 3·5 km (2 miles) long scenic cableway leads over the **citadel** to the hamlet of *La Sarte*.

Kampen

Country: The Netherlands. – Province: Overijssel.
Altitude: sea level. – Population: 30,000.
Postal code: NL-8250 AA to 8299.
Telephone code: 0 52 02.
ⓘ **VVV Kampen,**
Ouderstraat 160,
NL-8261 CZ Kampen;
tel. 1 35 00.

HOTELS. – *De Stadsherberg*, IJsselkade 48, I, 40 b.; *Van Dijk* (no rest.), IJsselkade 30–31, III, 50 b.; *De Steur*, Oudestraat 8, V, 18 b.

RESTAURANT. – *Zuiderzee Lido*, 5 km (3 miles) from the town at the Roggebotsluis lock.

EVENTS. – In summer, several *sailing regattas*; *Organ recitals* in the Bovenkerk (July–August, Thursday, 8 p.m.–9 p.m.); *Cruise on the IJsselmeer* (last Saturday in August).

SPORTS and LEISURE. – Sailing, fishing, hunting.

The former Hanseatic town of Kampen in the Dutch province of Overijssel has a pleasant setting on the left bank of the IJssel, 4 km (3 miles) upstream from its estuary into the **IJsselmeer. Kampen is the main town and also the trading hub of a wider rural area. It has a Theological College with a long tradition, a Military College, and a School of Agriculture.**

The most important source of employment is in industry. There are plants processing agricultural products from the area, shipbuilding, timber (lumber) yards, and the manufacture of agricultural machinery and building materials. Tourism, mostly associated with the yacht harbour, is also important. Many tourists are attracted by the picturesque Old Town.

SIGHTS. – In Oudestraat stands the *Town Hall, restored in 1543, with good sculptural decoration on the façade, and an interesting Council Chamber. Opposite the Town Hall, to the west, rises the *New tower*, also called the *Tower of the Holy Ghost* (1649–64; carillon). From here, going west via the Broederstraat and the Broederweg, you arrive at the former *Franciscan Church Broederkerk*, built between 1473 and 1490. Crossing a bridge over the moat, you then come to the impressive *Broederpoort*, a gate in the Old Town moat which is now a museum. South of it, nearby, is another gate, the *Cellebroederspoort*. Both gates date from 1465. In the Muntplein in the southern part of the town stands the large *Church of St Nicholas* (Bovenkerk), with a lofty interior. Most of the church was built in the 14th–16th c. East of here on the IJssel, stands the white 14th c. *Koornmarktspoort*. In the north of the town is the 14th c. *Church of Our Lady* (Buitenkerk).

Kempen (Campine)

Country: Belgium and the Netherlands.
ⓘ **Toeristische Federatie van de Province Antwerpen,**
Kon. Elisabethei 22,
B-2000 Antwerpen;
tel. (03) 37 28 00.
Provinciaal Verband voor Toerisme In Limburg,
Domein Bokrijk,
B-3600 Genk;
tel. (0 11) 2 26 99.
VVV Kempenland,
Stationsplein 24,
NL-5611 AC Eindhoven;
tel. (0 40) 44 92 31.

Kampen on the IJssel

The region called Kempen extends from the north-east of Belgium into the southern part of Holland. Historically, it stretches from the marshy grounds of the Lower Schelde in the west to the Valley of the Meuse in the east. Its southern border is formed by the rivers Rupel, Dijle and Demer. The transition into the plain of South Holland is so gradual as to be almost imperceptible. The region comprises large parts of the Belgian provinces of Limburg and Antwerp and the southern part of the Dutch province of North Brabant.

The surface formation of Kempen is very uniform. The region lies mostly 5–35 m (16–115 feet) above sea level and reaches its highest elevation in the south-east. Only the plateau of Limburg Kempen rises to between 60 and 100 m (197–328 feet) above sea level. The geological subsoil of Kempen consists of cretaceous and tertiary sedimentary rocks overlaid by gravels and sands from the Ice Age. The material was brought here by rivers fed with melted snow and ice. Such landscape is usually described as "geest".

The Grote Peel in Dutch Kempen

The infertile soil is only suitable for growing very frugal field plants. Only rye, oats, potatoes and some undemanding feed plants prosper here. Because agriculture is not very profitable here, Kempen was until a few decades ago among the regions of Belgium with the lowest population density. Heath and banks of quicksand, occasionally planted with pines, are partly used as army training grounds. There are a few scattered villages and farms on the poor soil and some small towns. Even now these conditions apply to considerable areas of the region. Industrialisation has been very rapid during recent years and has made deep inroads into the traditionally agrarian outlook of the country.

The beginning of industrialisation goes back about a hundred years. In those days heavy industry settled along the old Meuse-Schelde Canal: zinc and copper foundries, metal and glass industries as well as large brickworks, to name only the most important branches. After the First World War when large deposits were discovered deep below the covering rocks, coalmining began. There were in all seven mines connected with the waterway network by the Albert Canal. The primary coal-mining district of Kempen is around Genk. The output, as in other countries, has dropped sharply in recent years and several pits have closed. It was, however, possible to compensate economically for the decline of coalmining by the introduction of new industries or the expansion of existing ones.

Despite important industries, larger towns are still rare in Kempen. The most important are *Turnhout, Herentals*, **Hasselt** (see page 174), **Mechelen** (see page 211), and **Lier** (see page 197). More significant for the country are the many workers' settlements and urbanised villages.

Knokke-Heist

Country: Belgium. – Province: West Flanders.
Altitude: 0–3 m (10 feet) – Population: 29,000.
Postal code: B-8300.
Telephone code: 0 50.
ⓘ **Initiatief V.Z.W.**,
Meerlaan 30a;
tel. 6002 15.
Dienst voor Toerisme,
Stadhuis;
tel. 60 16 16.

HOTELS (Most closed in winter). – IN KNOKKE: *Majestic*, Zeedijk 688, II, 61 r.; *Grand Hôtel Motke*, Zeedijk 645, III, 84 r.; *Britannia*, Elisabethlaan 75, III, 35 r.; *Eden* (no rest.), Zandstraat 16, III, 19 r.; *Britannique* (no rest.), Van Bunnenlaan 31, III, 24 r.; *Malibu*, Kustlaan 47, III, 27 r.; *Aquilon*, Lippenslaan 266, 7 r.; *Prince's* (no rest.), Lippenslaan 113, IV, 38 r.; *Sélect* (no rest.), Koniginnenlaan 27, IV, 18 r.; *Prins Boudewijn*, Lippenslaan 25, IV, 30 r.; *Wellington*, Elisabethlaan 92, IV, 76 r.; *Rogier*, Lippenslaan 171, IV, 13 r.; *Epsom*, Marie-Joséstraat 2, IV, 18 r.; *De la Gare*, M. Lippensplein 10, IV, 6 r.; *Mayfair*, Kustlaan 10, IV, 39 r.; *Prince de Liège*, Lippenslaan 24, IV, 13 r.; *Le Nouvel Hôtel*, Van Bunnenplein 1c, IV, 52 r.; *Les Heures Claires*,

Congostraat 9, IV, 20 r.; *Le Fouquet's* (no rest.), Dumortierlaan 26, IV, 18 r.; *Grand Hôtel Dorchester*, Kustlaan 6, IV, 80 r.; *De Londres*, Van Bunnenplein 12, IV, 36 r.; *Westland* (no rest.), Lippenslaan 175, IV, 15 r.; *Welvaart*, Zoutelaan 6, IV, 20 r.; *Le Chapon Fin*, Kustlaan 12, IV, 6 r.; *Elisabeth*, Burg. F. Desmidtplein 2, V, 23 r.; *Réal*, M. Lippensplein 6, V, 17 r.; *Sambre et Meuse*, Lippenslaan 184, V, 22 r.; *Hanna*, Seb. Nachtegaelestraat 15, V, 15 r.; *Du Nord* (no rest.), Lippenslaan 54, V, 10 r.; *Rust aan Zee*, Lippenslaan 2, V, 54 r.; *Coventry*, Ieperstraat 19, V, 15 r.; *St. Margaret*, Seb. Nachtegaelestraat 1, V, 35 r.; *Au Grand Chef*, Lippenslaan 137, V, 115 r. – Numerous BOARDING HOUSES. – CAMP SITES.

IN HET ZOUTE: *Memling Palace*, Albert Square, L, 86 r.; *Elysée*, Elisabethlaan 17, I, 15 r.; *Lugano*, Villapad 8, II, 25 r.; *Charls* (no rest.), Albert I plein 9, II, 24 r.; *Les Hirondelles*, II, Elisabethlaan 4, 11 r.; *Claridge's* Zeedijk 798, II, 90 r.; *Aux Ducs de Bourgogne*, Zoutelaan 175, III, 28 r.; *Auberge St Pol* (no rest.), Bronlaan 31, III, 16 r.; *Ascot* (no rest.), Zoutelaan 116, III, 19 r.; *Eldorado*, Elisabethlaan 3, III, 34 r.; *Norfolk*, Elisabethlaan 6, III, 15 r.; *Pavillon du Zoute*, Bronlaan 4, III, 39 r.; *Eden* (no rest.), Zandstraat 16, III, 19 r.; *Balmoral*, Kustlaan 84, III, 28 r.; *Katelijne*, Kustlaan 100, III, 15 r.; *Si Versailles*, Kustlaan 199, III, 7 r.; *Shakespeare*, Zeedijk 786, III, 36 r.; *Belle Vue*, Kustlaan 98, III, 5 r.; *The Links* (no rest.), Elisabethlaan 41, III, 36 r.; *Excelsior*, Zeedijk 714, III, 49 r.; *Victoria* (no rest.), Golvenstraat 2, IV, 34 r.; *Cécil*, Elisabethlaan 20, IV, 12 r.; *Windsor (no rest.)*, Kustlaan 54, IV, 26 r.; *Les Loris*, Elisabethlaan 8, IV, 10 r.; *Les Arcades* (no rest.), Elisabethlaan 46, IV, 12 r.; *Des Nations*, Zeedijk 704, IV, 32 r.; *Florida*, A. Bréartstraat 9, IV, 21 r.; *Chalet Tinnel*, Elisabethlaan 73, IV, 27 r.; *Good Luck*, Elisabethlaan 8, IV, 8 r.; *Le Rayon Vert*, Brits Pad 32, IV, 6 r.; *Marie-Siska*, Zoutelaan 177, V, 6 r.; *St Christophe*, A. Bréartstraat 8, V, 17 r. – Numerous BOARDING HOUSES.

IN ALBERTSTRAND: *Sofitel Thalassa la Réserve*, Elisabethlaan 132, I, 120 r.; *Résidence Albert* (no rest.), Zeedijk 482, III, 24 r.; *Du Soleil*, Zeedijk 495, III, 29 r.; *De la Digue*, Zeedijk 21, III, 36 r.; *Lido*, Zwaluwenlaan 16, IV, 37 r.; *Des Ardennes*, Bayauxlaan 55, IV, 24 r.; *Astoria*, Zeedijk 44, IV, 58 r.; *Simoens*, Zonnelaan 5, IV, 45 r.; *Nelson*, Meerminlaan 34, IV, 47 r.; *Derby*, Bayauxlaan 44, IV, 40 r.; *Midan*, Zeedijk 543, IV, 36 r.; *Atlanta*, J. Nellenslaan 172, IV, 32 r.; *Albert Plage*, Meerminlaan 22, IV, 16 r.; *Rally*, Bayauxlaan 68, IV, 12 r.; *Trianon*, Zeedijk 17, IV, 42 r.; *L'Avenir*, J. Nellenslaan 217, IV, 12 r.; *Kismet*, Canadaplaan 26, IV, 11 r.; *Mary*, J. Hostestraat 2, V, 14 r.; *Caroline*, P. Parmentierlaan 272, V, 15 r.; *Miramar*, Meerminlaan 19, V, 36 r. – Numerous BOARDING HOUSES.

IN DUINBERGEN: *Du Soleil*, Patriottenstraat 19, III, 29 c.; *Pierre et Gabriel*, Patriottenstraat 32–34, III, 25 r.; *La Dunette*, De Wandelaar 7, IV, 8 r.; *Edelweiss*, Patriottenstraat 28–30, IV, 30 r.; *Bel Air*, Patriottenstraat 24, IV, 33 r.; *Les Sables d'Or*, Elisabethlaan 95, IV, 8 r.; *La Pré Feuillet*, Leeuwerikenlaan 5, IV, 9 r.

IN HEIST: *Les Hirondelles*, Zeedijk 218, II, 10 r.; *Square*, De Kinkhoorn 21, IV, 32 r.; *Bristol*, Zeedijk 294, IV, 30 r.; *Royal*, Zeedijk 228–229, IV, 41 r.; *Old Fischer*, Heldenplein 33, V, 6 r.; *Beau Séjour*, Duinenstraat 11, V, 23 r.; *Windsor*, Elisabethlaan 351, V, 16 r.; *St-Yves*, Zeedijk 222, V, 17 r. – Numerous BOARDING HOUSES. – YOUTH HOSTEL: Noordstraat 15, 70 b. – CAMP SITES.

Beach Life in Duinbergen (Knokke-Heist)

RESTAURANTS. – IN KNOKKE: *Aquilon*, Lippensalaan 266; *Toison d'Or*, Kustlaan 33; *Hippocampus*, Kragendijk 160; *Alexandra*, Van Bunnenplein 2a; *Le Frison*, Dumortierlaan 89; *Panier d'Or*, Zeedijk 656; *Uilenspiegel*, De Judestraat 65; *P'tit Bedon*, Zeedijk 667. – IN HET ZOUTE: *Belle Vue*, Kustlaan 98; *Chalet du Zwin*, im Naturschutzgebiet (entrance fee). – IN ALBERTSTRAND: *Olivier*, J. Nellenslaan 159; *Esmeralda*, J. Nellenslaan 48; *Flots Bleus*, Zeedijk 509. – IN DUINBERGEN: *Wielingen*, De Wandelaar 7. – IN HEIST: *Old Fisher*, Heldenplein 33; *Rôtisserie Boerenhof*, Koudekerkelaan 30 (Stationsplein).

EVENTS. – *Children's Carnival Procession* (Carnival Sunday); *Carnival Procession* (Tuesday before Lent); *"Poetry at the Seaside"* (Weekends, first half of June); *Festival of Majorettes* (June); *Golden Tern* (June); *Ornamental Garden Competition* (June–August); *Summer Festival* (July–August); *World Cartoon Festival* (July–August); *Traditional Market* (Thursdays, July and August); *Festival of Humour* (second half of July); *Consecration of the Sea* (15 August); *Tennis and Riding Tournaments* (August); *Floral Procession and Festival of Light* (second half of August); *International Firework Festival* (second half of August); *Winter Festival, Weekend, Christmas and New Year's Festivals*; *Biennial Festival of Poetry* (beginning of September); *International Grand Prix for Pictorial Arts*.

Casino (roulette, bridge) on the Albertstrand.

SPORTS and LEISURE. – Almost every form of sport is possible in Knokke-Heist, from water sports to skiing on artificial slopes; from archery to skating.

Knokke-Heist is, after Ostend, the most fashionable seaside resort in Belgium. It lies near the Dutch border in an attractive landscape of dunes.

The present tourist resort developed very rapidly after 1880, when the fishing village of Knokke merged with the residential suburb of Het Zoute and the more recent settlement of Albertstrand to

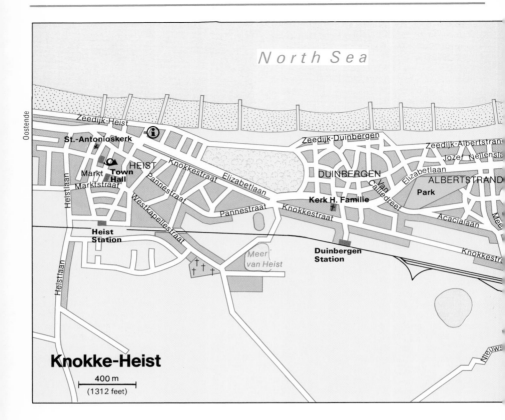

Knokke-Heist

400 m
(1312 feet)

the west. Later some other coastal settlements were absorbed into the growing built-up area. Today Knokke can accommodate 150,000 guests, up to five times its population, in some 13,000 apartments, 120 hotels and boarding houses, as well as in several camp sites. Its excellent wide beach is 12 km (7 miles) long, a distance of approximately one-fifth of the entire Belgian coast. To the large amount of accommodation available in the town can be added an unusually wide range of entertainments and recreational facilities catering to every taste.

SIGHTS. – The area around the station was the original village of KNOKKE. Several roads connect it with the dike about 1 km (about a ½ mile) away. The busy Lippenslaan is its main street. To the right of Lippenslaan is the Verwéeplein with the *Town Hall* and the monument of A. Verwée (1896), the painter of animals. East of the Lippenslaan, the Elisabethlaan leads to the *golf course which is one of the largest in Europe.

West of here is the new district of ALBERTSTRAND with a **casino** by the dike and in the dunes, an artificial lake, the Zegemeer (Victory lake).

The **dike** (**Zeedijk**), which stretches for some 7 km (4 miles) from the district of HEIST across DUINBERGEN to HET ZOUTE, overlooks the wide beach and is lined with many hotels and villas. Its eastern end is approximately 4 km (2 miles) away from the Belgian-Dutch frontier. There is an indoor swimming pool with sea water and artificial waves. Between here and the frontier a salt-water meadow ("schorre") is all that remains of the estuary of the *Zwin*. This was formerly a sea inlet which became silted up and has recently been turned into a large nature reserve.

Kortrijk (Courtrai)

Country: Belgium. – Province: West Flanders.
Altitude: 19 m (62 feet). – Population: 77,000.
Postal code: B 8500.
Telephone code: 0 56.

ⓘ **Dienst voor Toerisme en Feestelijkheden,**
    Stadhuis;
    tel. 220033.

HOTELS. – *Broel*, Broekaai 8, III, 49 r.; *Du Damier*, Grote Markt 41, IV, 40 r.; *Du Nord*, Stationsplein 2, IV, 30 r.; *Du Centre*, Graanmarkt 6, V, 28 r. – YOUTH HOSTEL: Passionistenlaan, 83 b.

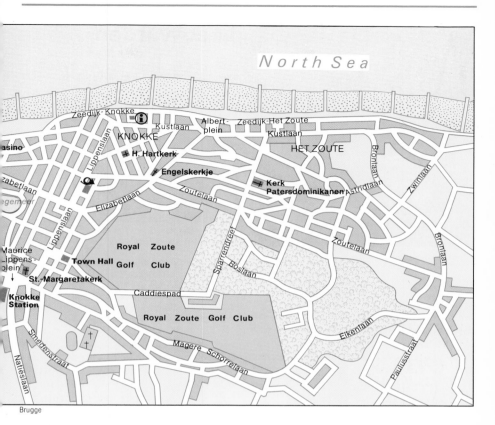

North Sea

Zeedijk-Knokke
KNOKKE
Kustlaan
Albert-plein
Zeedijk-Het Zoute
Kustlaan
HET ZOUTE
asino
H. Hartkerk
Lippenslaan
Engelskerkje
Kerk
Patersdominikanen
Astridlaan
Bronlaan
Zwinlaan
zabetlaan
egemeer
Elizabetlaan
Zoutelaan
Maurice
Lippens-
plein
St.-Margaretakerk
Town Hall
Royal   Zoute
Golf   Club
Lippenslaan
Sparrendreef
Boslaan
Zoutelaan
Bronlaan
Knokke
Station
Caddiespad
Royal   Zoute   Golf   Club
Eikenlaan
Smedenstraat
Natieslaan
Magere Schorrelaan
Paulusstraat

Brugge

RESTAURANTS. – *Boerenhof*, Walle 168; *Oud Walle*, Walle 199; *Périgord*, Lange Steenstraat 23.

EVENTS. – *Festival of Flanders* with International Choir Singing (end April–early June); *Easter Fair*; *International People's Procession* (two days second half of May); *Carillon Concerts* (Sundays, 12.30 p.m.–1 p.m., Mondays 5 p.m.–6 p.m.); *Memorial Feast of the Famous Battle of the Golden Spurs of 1302* (11 July).

The Belgian town of Kortrijk, in French Courtrai, lies in the province of West Flanders on the River Leie, which is connected by a canal to the Schelde. The economy of Kortrijk has been based on the textile industry since the beginning of the 14th c.

Flax, grown in the surrounding districts of Flanders, is still the most important raw material and is used in numerous spinning and weaving mills and processing plants. Kortrijk also has some synthetic fibre plants, large flax treatment plants and textile finishing factories involved in the manufacture of clothing, linen, carpets and canvas. There have been attempts recently to diversify the economy of Kortrijk, in order to compensate for the vulnerability of the single textile industry.

Machinery manufacture, electrical engineering, rubber, furniture, building materials and printing have all been introduced here. Polishing of precious stones is also a well-known and economically important activity.

HISTORY. – Kortrijk was an important road junction in Roman days, when it was known as Cortoriacum. In Merovingian times the settlement had the right to mint coins. It became the seat of a Flemish burgrave (lord of a "burg") and in 1189 received town status. Its period of prosperity began in the late Middle Ages when Kortrijk developed into the headquarters of the Flemish cloth-making industry. When this declined in the 16th c. it was replaced by linen weaving associated with the local cultivation of flax which has prevailed until the present day. The prosperous trading and industrial town was heavily damaged during the wars of Louis XIV; and also in both world wars. Despite this several architectural monuments have survived as evidence of Kortrijk's great past.

SIGHTS. – The central area of Kortrijk is the Grote Market, with a monument commemorating the victims of the First World War. In the middle stands a 14th c. *belfry*. In the north-western corner of the Markt is the Gothic **Town Hall** (*Stadhuis*), rebuilt in 1418–20, enlarged in 1519–26, and again in the 19th c., and restored in 1962. Inside are frescoes by G. Guffens and Jan Swerts (1875), and two

Begijnhof in Kortrijk

Leeuwarden

Country: The Netherlands. – Province: Friesland.
Altitude: 1 m (3 feet). – Population: 85,000.
Postal code: NL-9800 AA to 9099.
Telephone code: 0 51 00.
ⓘ VVV Friesland-Leeuwarden,
Stationsplein 1,
NL-8911 AC Leeuwarden;
tel. 3 22 24.

HOTELS. – *Eurohotel*, Europaplein 19, I, 96 b.; *Oranje Hotel*, Stationsweg 4, II, 74 b.; *De Kroon*, Van Swietenstraat 17, IV, 31 b.; *De Pauw*, Stationsweg 10, V, 65 b. – CAMP SITE.

RESTAURANTS. – *Sa Spunta*, Eewal 50; *Kota Radja*, Groot Schavernek 5. – IN ROODKERK: *Herberge De Trochreed*, Bosweg 25.

EVENTS. – *Four-day Walk* in the surroundings of the town (mid-June); *Household Exhibition* (September); *Market* for the exchange of goods (bartering) (end of October); *Camping Exhibition "Recreana"* (November); *Organ recitals, chamber music* and *theatre performances* take place regularly.

late Gothic chimney-pieces (1527), lavishly decorated with statuettes. Nearby, east of the Markt, stands the **Church of St Martin** which has three naves and was built in the 14th–16th c. In the central nave is a carved late Renaissance pulpit and in the choir a stone tabernacle (1587).

Just north of St Martin's Church is the picturesque *Begijnhof*, founded in 1241, now occupying 17th c. buildings. Further north on the Begijnhofstraat stands the **Church of Our Lady** (*O. L. Vrouwkerk*), founded by Baldwin IX, and completed in 1211. In its north transept is the *"Raising of the Cross" by van Dyck. Also worth seeing is the 14th c. statue of St Catherine. In front of the church stands a marble bust of the Flemish poet Guido Gezelle. From the Church of Our Lady, the Gezellestraat leads to the *Broelbrug* which has two squat and massive towers (*Broeltorens*, 13th–14th c.). Not far to the north-west on the north bank of the Leie on the Broelkaai is the **Municipal Museum** containing the *Arts Museum* (paintings) and an *archaeological collection*.

In the east of the town on the "Groeninghe Veld" (Groeningelaan), stands a monument erected in 1906, commemorating the Battle of the Golden Spurs.

Leeuwarden, the old capital of the Dutch province of Friesland, lies in a fertile fen district of the former Middelzee, enclosed by dikes in the 18th c. Leeuwarden is the economic and cultural capital of Friesland, and the location of several government offices and institutes of higher education. Its cattle market is the largest in the northern Netherlands. The most important source of employment is the food industry, processing agricultural products from the surrounding area. Tourism is also important.

HISTORY. – Leeuwarden was created by the amalgamation of three former "Wurt" settlements, which merged in 1435 when they received their town charters. The settlement soon became a prosperous trading place. When the Middelzee was enclosed and drained, the town lost its sea harbour and became instead an agricultural market and commercial capital of the Ostergos. Between 1524 and 1580 Leeuwarden was the seat of the Habsburg governor, and from 1584 to 1747 the place of residence of the Stadholders of the House of Nassau-Diez. In the 16th–18th c. the town was known for its fine gold- and silverware. The world-famous dancer and spy Mata Hari was born here in 1876.

SIGHTS. – The Inner City is laid out in the form of a star and is surrounded by canals. In its southern part is the main shopping street, the Wirdumerdijk. At its northern end, on the left, is the wide Waagplein, in the middle of which stands the attractive *old Weigh-house*, built in 1598. To the right along the canal (nearby in the Herestraat is the *Museum of Natural*

History), you reach Koningstraat, where, in an 18th c. former patrician house, you find the ***Frisian Museum**, the most important provincial museum in the Netherlands. Its well-endowed collections offer a very good general view of the entire Frisian civilisation. Especially worth seeing, among other things, is the Popta silver treasure, the Hindeloopen series of rooms, the Bisschop collection and a large collection of porcelain.

To the east, opposite the museum at No. 13 Turfmarkt is the **Kanselarij** housing the *Provincial Archives*. It was built in 1566–71 and has a staircase dating from 1621. North-west of here in the Grote Kerkhof stands the **Grote Kerk** or **Jacobijnerkerk** (Dutch Reformed) which was formerly the church of the Dominican monastery. Inside is the mausoleum of the Stadholders of Friesland of the House of Nassau-Diez.

Going south-west from the Grote Kerk you come via the Grote Kerkstraat and on the left the Beijerstraat to the Hoofplein. In it stands the 18th c. **Town Hall** (*Stadhuis*), a former *Royal Palace* ("Hof"). Between 1587 and 1747 this was the residence of the Stadholders. In the square is the monument of Count William Louis of Nassau-Diez (d. 1620), who was the Stadholder of Friesland.

The Grote Kerkstraat runs west past the *St Anthony Gasthuis* (on the left, 15th c.), and the *Buma Library* (on the right, No. 29, only classical literature) to the **Museum Het Prinsessehof**, housed in a rambling 17th c. mansion ("Oude Prinsessehof"). The museum possesses a good collection of Malayan copperwork, arms and textiles, and Chinese and Japanese ceramics.

The Grote Kerkstraat leads in a westerly direction to Oldehoofster Kerkhof, a large square, on the west side of which stands the unfinished tower **Oldehove**. It is a small leaning brick structure some 40 m (131 feet) high, built in 1529–32; from its top there is an extensive view. It was originally intended that the tower should form part of a church, but the latter could not be built because the ground was not solid enough. On the north side of the square (Boterhoek) is the building of the *Provincial Library*. Nearby to the northwest is a line of parks, *Noorderplantage*, in which stands the *Pier Pander Temple*.

This was built in 1924 to commemorate the Frisian sculptor Pier Pander (1864–1919). There are five marble statues by the artist. Further north-east extends the attractive park *Prinsen* or *Stadstuin* with the *Pier Pander Museum*.

SURROUNDINGS of Leeuwarden. – 5 km (3 miles) west is the village of **Marssum** with a manor house, *Heringa State* (the Popta Palace, 16th c.). It once belonged to the Mayor, Dr Henricus Popta (d. 1712), who commissioned the Popta silver which is exhibited in the Frisian Museum of Leeuwarden. – 15 km (9 miles) north-west of Leeuwarden is the village of *St Annaparochie*. It lies in the fertile polderland called Bildt, which was drained and cultivated in the 16th c. by people of non-Frisian stock, and where Frisian is not spoken even today. In the parish church of *St Annaparochie*, Rembrandt van Rijn and Saskia van Uilenburgh were married in June 1634. 11 km (7 miles) north-east of Leeuwarden, near the village of *Oenkerk*, you can visit the museum in the *Palace of Stania State*, which is part of the Frisian Museum in Leeuwarden and houses an agricultural collection.

Leyden (Leiden)

Country: The Netherlands. – Province: South Holland. Altitude: below sea level. – Population: 102,000. Postal code: NL-2300 AA to 2399. Telephone code 0 71.

ⓘ **VVV Leiden,**
  Stationsplein 210,
  NL-2312 AR Leiden;
  tel. 14 68 46.

HOTELS. – *Holiday Inn*, Haagse Schouwweg 10, I, 370 b.; *Nieuw Minerva*, Vrouwensteeg 11, III, 142 b.; *'t Karrewiel*, Steenstraat 55, III, 22 b.; *Huize de Wekker*, Herengracht 100, IV, 25 b.; *De Witte Singel*, Witte Singel 93, V, 18 b.

RESTAURANTS. – *Rôtisserie Oudt Leyden*, Steenstraat 53; *De Doelen*, Rapenburg 2.

EVENTS. – *Easter Fair; Floral Procession Rijnsburg* (first Saturday in August); *Liberation Day Festival* (3 October).

The university town of Leyden (in Dutch Leiden) is one of the oldest and most picturesque towns in Holland. It lies in the province of South Holland on the Oude Rijn. The river divides here into several branches linked by canals which flow quietly through the city.

Culturally, Leyden is one of the most important places in the country. The University has a library containing more than 1·5 million books and there are several other research institutes, including the Royal Institute for East Indian Languages and the Royal Society of Dutch Literature, as well as several important museums, in particular the National

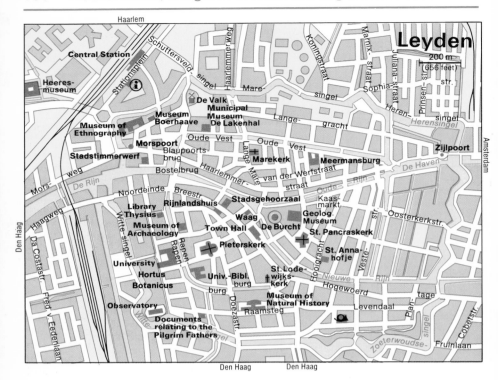

Den Haag   Den Haag

Museum of Antiquities and the National Museum of Ethnology.

Leyden is situated in the middle of a large market gardening area, the products of which are sold and to some extent are processed in the town. More important, however, are the hardware industry, machinery manufacture and the world-famous printing industry. From the textile industry, which was once very important, only a few spinning and weaving mills and finishing plants remain.

HISTORY. – In the 11th c. Leyden developed around the castle of the Counts of Holland. It received its charter in 1266 and in the 14th–15th c. became widely known for Dutch weaving. In the 16th c. it made history when the siege of the town by the Spaniards in the years 1573–4 was successfully turned back by William the Silent who gave the order for the dikes in South Holland to be breached. As a reward for their valiant defence the citizens are said to have been offered a choice between the remission of taxes for several years and the founding of a University. The University, which soon became famous throughout Europe, was founded in 1575. The greatest scholars of their time were active here: Justus Scaliger (d. 1609), Hugo Grotius (d. 1645), and in the 18th c. H. Boerhaave, who made famous its medical faculty. Several painters of the 16th–17th c. were also born in Leyden, among them Lucas van Leyden, Rembrandt, Jan Steen, Gerard Dou, Gabriel Metsu, Jan van Goyen, Frans van Mieris and both Willems van de Velde. A characteristic feature of Leyden is the so-called "Hofjes", alms-houses (houses founded by charities, especially for the aged poor) usually consisting of 10–30 cottages, of which some 35 were founded in the 16th–17th c.

SIGHTS. – In the oldest part of the town, which is also its central point, on a hill overlooking the confluence of the Old and New Rhine, stands the massive **fort** (*Burcht*). Its foundations go back to the early Middle Ages (good view). East of the fort is the *Geological and Mineralogical Museum* (Rijksmuseum van Geologie en Mineralogie, entrance No. 17 Hooglandse Kerkgracht). It possesses many valuable exhibits, some of them from the former Dutch colonies. Not far south-east of the fort stands the 15th c. **Church of St Pancras** (*Hooglandse Kerk*, Reformed), built in late Gothic style. In its spacious interior is the tomb of Mayor van der Werf (d. 1604) who was the defender of the town in the siege of 1574. In the choir are the twin tombs of Admiral Justinus of Nassau (d. 1630) and his wife. – Further south-east at No. 9 Hooigracht is the *St Annahofje*, with a little chapel (1492; open to visitors) in the courtyard.

Going south-west from the fort, you cross the New Rhine by the *Korenbeursbrug* to the Vismarkt; then north past the *Visbrug* (good view over the canals) to Aalmarkt in which stands the *Weigh-house* built by Pieter Post in 1658. The Maarsmansteeg leads south-west from the Visbrug to the Breestraat, the main shopping street of the town which, together with its extensions, the Noordeinde in the west and the Hogewoerd in the east, traverses the entire town in a large S-shaped bend. It is flanked by a number of gabled houses in Dutch Renaissance and Baroque styles. In the southern part of the Breestraat stands the 17th c. **Town Hall** (carillon), once one of the most striking examples of Dutch Renaissance architecture. Unfortunately it was burned down in 1929 and has since been partly restored in the old style. In the northern part of the Breestraat, on the right, stands the *Stadsgehoorzaal* (concert hall and theatre). On the other side stands the *Gemeenlandshuis van Rijnland*, built in the 16th c.

Not far west of the Town Hall stands the ancient **Church of St Peter** (St Pieterskerk, Reformed), dating from about 1315. Inside are several wall tombs of eminent professors and in one side chapel the tomb of John Robinson, the leader of the Pilgrim Fathers. In 1611 he founded in Leyden the first community of Independents, the Puritans exiled from England. – In the north-west corner of the Pieterskerkhof the Classical façade of the *Gravensteen* can be seen. The building was mentioned as early as 1392 and its oldest parts are the two towers in the middle. It was long used as a prison and now houses the Law Faculty of the University.

From St Pieterskerk the Nieuwsteeg leads past several recent University buildings southwards to the Steenschuur and to the small *van der Werf Park*. In it stands a monument to van der Werf, the Mayor of Leyden. On the south side of the park is the **Museum of Natural History** (*Museum van Natuurlijke Historie*; entrance Raamsteeg; accessible only to scholars and students by special permis-

sion of the museum authorities). It houses a rich collection of animals from the former Dutch colonies and a collection of *birds provided by the eminent ornithologist C. J. Temminck (d. 1858). There is also a Section of Comparative Anatomy.

On the left bank of the wide Gracht Rapenburg, not far east of the Church of St Pieterskerk, is the historic **University** (over 15,000 students), whose Faculties of Medicine and Sciences have been famous for centuries. Since 1581 the former chapel of the Convent of the White Nuns has been used as the old University building. Behind the University extends the *Botanical Garden (Akademietuin or Hortus Botanicus) founded in 1587. South of it is the *Observatory* (Sterrenwacht).

On the other side of the Rapenburggracht is the **University Library**, the oldest and one of the largest in the country with 1·5 million books and 20,000 manuscripts. Further north in No. 28, on the corner of Houtstraat, is the *National Museum of Antiquities, founded in 1818, with Greek, Etruscan and Roman sculpture, a collection of ancient vases and smaller items, a large collection of Egyptian antiquities and prehistoric and Roman finds primarily from the Netherlands. Near the museum are several interesting Baroque buildings, among them the small *Thysius Library* (No. 25 Rapenburg; 1655), the gate of the former *Georgdoelen* (1645), the *Hofje van Broukhoven* (1640) (No. 16 Papengracht), and the former *Law Courts* (1655) which are part of the old "Gravensteen", the prison at the time of the Counts of Holland.

Proceeding to the left of the Rapenburg Canal via the Noordeinde, you arrive at the Witte Singel where there is a bronze bust of Rembrandt. On the right, half-way along the Waddesteeg, there once stood the house in which Rembrandt was born.

At the north end of the Rapenburg, you come to the Rhine, here called "Galgewater". Cross it by the *Bostelbrug*, and a little further on the right you reach the beginning of the Haarlemmerstraat, another main shopping street of Leyden, some 1 km (1 mile) long. On the left, the *Blauwpoortsbrug* crosses the Oude Vest; a little further on is the departure point for cruises on Leyden's canals and surrounding lakes. From the Blauwpoortsbrug,

On the Oude Vest in Leyden

west via the Morsstraat, you come to the domed *Morspoort*, the former fortress gate (1699). About half-way along this street the short Smidsteeg leads south to the attractive *Stadstimmerwerf* ("Town carpenters' shop"; 1612).

North of the Blauwpoort the large Bestenmarkt opens out; not far east, at Nos. 28–30 Oude Singel, is the **Municipal Museum** (*Stedelijk Museum*) in the *Lakenhal*, a former Cloth Hall built in 1639–40. It contains some valuable paintings from the 17th–18th c., including works by Corn, Engelbrechtsz, Lucas van Leyden, Rembrandt and Jan Steen, as well as collections of applied arts and local antiquities.

East of the Municipal Museum beyond the canal Oude Vest is the *Marekerk*, a graceful domed edifice (1648). Further, at No. 159 Oude Vest, is the *Meermansburg*, the largest of the Hofjes of Leyden, built in 1681. In the Regents' Room are some valuable portraits. At the end of the Oude Vest is the colourful **harbour**. Nearby stands the *Zijlpoort*, built in 1666.

On the left of the Steenstraat, leading north from the Beestenmarkt, is the *National Museum Boerhaave* (History of Science) with many souvenirs of the great scholars, including C. Huygens, Leeuwenhoek and Boerhaave. The **National Museum of Ethnology** (*Rijksmuseum voor Volkenkunde*) which adjoins it has large collections of ethnographic material from all parts of the world but primarily from Indonesia.

From the *Rijnsburgerbrug* there is a good view, to the right, of the *Valk*, a flour mill built in 1743, now a Museum of Mills. Further north near the *station*, in the former Pesthuis (hospital for plague victims; 1658), is the *Dutch Museum of Army and Arms* (Nederlands Legermuseum "Generaal Hoefer").

SURROUNDINGS of Leyden. – A worthwhile excursion can be made by boat **across the Kager Meer to Schiphol** (from mid-June to the end of August, daily, 7½ hours return, departure from the harbour). You reach the **Kager Meer** (water sports) via *Leiderdorp*, pass through the *Zijl*, then across the *Braassemer Meer* via *Aalsmeer* to **Schiphol** (the Central Airport, see under Amsterdam) and from here back to Leyden. Also in summer there are daily boat excursions from 2 p.m. to 6 p.m. to the Kager and the Braassemer Meer.

From Leyden via Alphen aan den Rijn to Gouda or Utrecht (33/49 km – 21/30 miles respectively). Leave Leyden by the Levendaal in an easterly direction and then along the left bank of the *Old Rhine*. Many villages with brickworks, old fishermen's houses and windmills line both banks of the busy river. After 3 km (2 miles) you reach *Leiderdorp*, and 5 km (3 miles) further on *Koudekerk*, with the old mill in which Rembrandt's father lived. From here you can either bear right via Hazerswoude and Boskoop directly to Gouda (21 km – 13 miles), or go straight on in the direction of Alphen, 4 km (2 miles) beyond Koudekerk on the right is the entrance to the interesting *Bird Sanctuary* ("Avifauna"; open all year) where a large number of rare birds from all parts of the world can be seen (restaurant with terraces). 2 km (1 mile) further, you reach **Alphen aan den Rijn** (Hotel Toor, I, 45 b.), a little manufacturing town with a population of 37,000, which has a signal tower 85 m (279 feet) high (1963). 9 km (6 miles) from here is *Bodegraven*, well known for the production of local cheese (Tuesday Cheese Market). From here you can continue either along the other bank of the river to Woerden (10 km – 6 miles) and then via *Harmelen* (excursion to the manor house "De Haar") to **Utrecht** (26 km (16 miles); see page 257) or turn right in Bodegraven, cross the railway line and then take the autoroute. In 10 km (6 miles) you arrive at **Gouda** (see page 158).

Liège (Luik)

Country: Belgium. – Province: Liège.
Altitude: 70 m (230 feet). – Population: 436,000.
Postal code: B-4000.
Telephone code: 0 41.
ⓘ **Office du Tourisme,**
En Féronstrée 92;
tel. 32 24 56.

HOTELS. – *Ramada*, Boulevard de la Sauvenière 100–108, I, 105 r.; *Holiday Inn*, Esplanade de l'Europe 2, II, 200 r.; *Le Clou Doré* (no rest.), Mont Saint-Martin 33, III, 8 r.; *De la Couronne*, Place des Guillemins 11–13, III, 70 r.; *Les Terrasses*, Avenue Rogier 1, III, 20 r.; *Du Midi*, Place des Guillemins 1, IV, 24 r.; *Résidence du Cygne d'Argent*, Rue Beeckman 49, IV, 19 r.; *Métropole*, Rue des Guillemins 141, IV, 27 r.; *De l'Univers*, Rue des Guillemins 116, V, 54 r.; *Le Vénitien* (no rest.), Rue Hamal 2, V, 15 r.; *De Bavière*, Rue des Bonnes Villes 8, V, 16 r.; *Au Rail*, Place des Guillemins 15, V, 11 r.; *Résidence Albert Ier*, Rue Général-Jacques 6, V, 10 r.; *Au Duc d'Anjou*, Rue des Guillemins 127, V, 30 r.; *Monico*, Rue Général-Jacques 10, V, 15 r.; *Concordia*, Rue des Guillemins 114, V, 15 r.

RESTAURANTS. – *Au Vieux Liège*, Quai de la Goffe 41, with view over the Maas; *Rôtisserie de l'Empereur*, Place du 20-Août 15. – IN NEUVILLE-EN-CONDROZ: *Chéne Madame*, Avenue de la Chevauchée 70.

EVENTS. – *The Spring Industrial Fair* (April); *International Festival of Music* (September); *International Festival of the Youth Theatre* (October); *Autumn Industrial Fair* (September).

FLEA MARKET. – Quai de la Batte (on the Meuse, Sunday, 9 a.m.–1 p.m.).

Liège, in Flemish Luik, is the fourth largest Belgian city. It lies at the confluence of the Ourthe and the Meuse (Maas). It is the capital of the province of the same name and also of Wallonia, seat of a University and of a Bishop and, thanks to a long tradition of offering various financial advantages, also an important industrial area. Liège was the first place in Europe to start mining coal and is one of the largest river ports in Europe.

Industry employs well over 200,000 workers and includes blast furnaces, metal and construction works, textile, food, electronics and chemical factories, glass and arms (small arms of the "Fabrique National") manufacture. Liège is the home of the author Georges Simenon, born 1903 ("Inspector Maigret"), and enjoys increasing importance in research and science (University, technical colleges and institutes). The main urban districts with public buildings are on the left bank of the Meuse; residential and industrial districts are concentrated on the right bank. Liège is the junction of important international roads and railway lines. Supplies of iron ore for heavy industries are brought in primarily by water. The port can accommodate vessels of up to 2000 tons.

On the Meuse in Liège

HISTORY. – According to legend, Liège was founded in the 7th c. by St Lambert, Bishop of Maastricht, and has been a Bishopric since 721. It began to prosper only in the 10th–11th c. Since the 14th c. it has been the capital of a Duchy belonging to the Holy Roman Empire, with far-reaching ramifications. In contrast to the Flemish cities its citizens always had to share power with the Bishop. Internal feuding in the 13th–14th c. ended with the victory of the guilds. In the 15th c. the Dukes of Burgundy, who had already acquired the rest of Belgium, tried to take over the Duchy of Liège, but ran into heavy opposition from

the population. In 1467 the troops of Charles the Bold managed to take the city and its fortifications were razed. The city rose again, but not even the heroic courage of 600 Franchimontois who tried to break the siege could prevent another sacking and plundering in 1468. The city burned for seven weeks and only churches and monasteries survived the fire. Not until 1475 were the citizens permitted to rebuild. When Charles the Bold died in 1477 they regained their independence. In the 16th c., under the Prince-Bishop Eberhard von der Marck (1505–38), Liège experienced a new period of prosperity. In the same century, as well as later, there was new progress, thanks to coalmining and to the development of the arms industry. Repeated power struggles between the guilds – made powerful by industry – and the Prince-Bishops ended this time in the victory of the bishops. Several mayors were sent to the scaffold in the 17th c. Only 100 years later the French Revolution put an end to the ecclesiastical domination. In the 19th c. in particular, after the founding of Belgium as an independent country, Liège steadily expanded.

SIGHTS. – The central area of the city is formed by three connected squares, the Place St Lambert, the Place du Maréchal Foch and the Place de la République Française. On their south-western side stands the **Théâtre Royal** built in 1818–22 and modelled after the Odeon of Paris, with red marble columns taken from the destroyed Carthusian Church. Nearby, to the west of the theatre, at the end of the short Rue Hamel, stands the **Church of St John** (*St-Jean*), founded in 980 by Bishop Notger, and completely rebuilt in 1754–7. It has a 12th c. tower (carillon), built on foundations of 997, and 16th c. cloisters.

North-west of the Place de la République Française, at the end of the Rue Haute Sauvenière, stands the **Church of the Holy Cross** (*Ste-Croix*), consecrated in 979 by Bishop Notger and rebuilt several times; it has a Romanesque west choir (*c.* 1175) and a 14th c. Gothic east choir and nave. The church treasury is worth seeing. To the south-west on the Mont St Martin, stands the **Basilique St Martin**, visible from afar; it was originally built in the 13th c., but was burned down in 1312 during a fight between the burghers and the nobles when 1200 nobles were killed. It was again rebuilt in late Gothic style in the 16th c. The church has stained glass (1526–36) and in the first side chapel on the right fourteen marble plaques by J. Delcourt, commemorating the initiation of the Feast of Corpus Christi (Fête-Dieu). This was celebrated for the first time in 1246 following a vision by St Juliana, a Liège nun. In 1264 Pope Urban IV, who was once an Archdeacon of the Cathedral of Liège, proclaimed the date a church

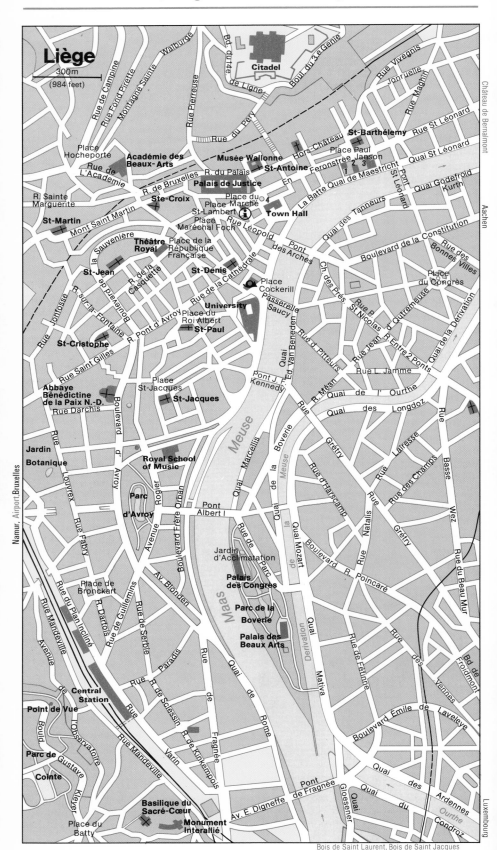

1 Musée d'Ansembourg   2 Musée d'Armes   3 Musée Curtius   4 Fontaine du Perron

holiday throughout Christendom. From the tower of the church there is a beautiful view.

Not far north of the Mont St Martin are the premises of the *Académie des Beaux Arts* (19th c.), the southern annex of which (Rue de l'Académie 34) houses the **Musée des Beaux-Arts** with a collection of modern paintings and sculpture. Among the pictures is a *portrait of Napoleon by Ingres which Napoleon donated to the city as a token of his favour.

The busy streets Rue de la Régence and Rue de l'Université, lead from the Place de la République south-eastwards to the University and to the banks of the Meuse. On the left of the former stands the **Church of St Denis**, founded in 987 by Bishop Notger but largely rebuilt in the 15th c. and again in the 18th c.; it has a Romanesque tower. On the left of the Place Cockerill at the end of the Rue de la Régence stands the neo-Gothic *Post Office* building and on the right the **State University**, founded in 1817 (approximately 10,000 students); part of its buildings belonged to an old Jesuit Monastery and part are extensions dating from 1889 to 1893. In the University are the *University Library*, containing over 1 million books, and the *Museum of Natural History* with a good palaeontological section.

From the Place Cockerill, the Rue Charles Magnette runs west to the Place du Roi Albert. There stands the former **Convent Church of St Paul**, originally founded in 971 by Bishop Heraclius, rebuilt in Gothic style in the 13th–14th c. and completed in the 16th c. It has been, since 1802, the Cathedral Church of the diocese and has a tower 90 m (295 feet) high with a carillon. In the spacious interior (85 m (279 feet) long, 34 m (112 feet) wide, and 24 m (79 feet) high), there is in the second chapel of the south aisle the beautiful reliquary of St Lambert. In the south transept there is a large stained-glass window (1530) with the Coronation of the Holy Virgin. And in the choir apse, there is a stained-glass window of 1557–87. On the south side of the church are the 14th c. *cloisters* (entrance in the Rue Bonne-Fortune), providing access to the church treasury and to the *Diocesan Museum* (open Saturdays and Sundays only).

South of the Cathedral, you arrive by the Rue St Rémy at the Place St Jacques, and at the *Church of St Jacob (St Jacques). It was founded in the 11th c. and rebuilt in 1513–38 into a splendid flamboyant Gothic structure with a Romanesque portico (1170) in the west, and a Renaissance portal (1558–60) in the northern aisle. In the beautiful lofty interior (80 m (262 feet) long, 30 m (98 feet) wide, 23 m (75 feet) high), is strikingly elaborate roof vaulting, and an interesting *stained-glass window (1620–40).

From the Place du Roi Albert via the short Rue du Pont d'Avroy in the west, you come to the southern end of the Boulevard de la Sauvenière which is constructed over an old branch of the Meuse and runs in an arc from the Place de la République Française. Nearby to the west, set slightly back, is the early Gothic *Church of St Christophe* originally belonging to a beguinage, and which was restored in 1890–2; it has a lofty vault. Further south is the Baroque *Church of the Benedictine Nuns* (1677–92).

The Boulevard de la Sauvenière continues to the south as the Boulevard d'Avroy, and its southern part skirts the beautiful *Parc d'Avroy** which was laid out on the site of an old harbour and which is bordered on the east by the Avenue Rogier. In the north of the park stands the *equestrian statue of Charlemagne* by L. Jehotte (1868). The earliest special privileges of the city are connected with the name of Charlemagne. A few yards to the east in Boulevard Piercot stands the *Royal School of Music*, built in 1881–6. In the middle of the Parc d'Avroy is a pond, a café/restaurant and a music pavilion featuring summer concerts. East of here in the Avenue Rogier is an elevated terrace surrounded by a wall with four groups of bronze statues, among them the *Bull-tamer by L. Mignon. Proceeding further east along the river you come to the Boulevard Frère Orban which is connected to the Island in the Meuse by the *Pont Albert I*. From the southern end of the Parc d'Avroy you arrive via the Rue des Guillemins at the *Central Station* (Station des Guillemins). Further on is the Plateau de Cointe. To the west of the Parc d'Avroy are the *Botanical Gardens* of the University.

Near the north-east of the Place de la République Française are the busiest squares of Liège, the Place du Maréchal Foch and the large Place St Lambert. In the Lambert Square stood the original episcopal cathedral of St Lambert, destroyed in 1794 by the French Revolutionaries and their Liège comrades. The ruins were removed in 1808. The excavated foundations of the church and a hypocaust (under-floor space for heating) of a Roman villa can be seen beneath the square (access by a staircase). On the north side of the square stand the *Law Courts (Palais des Princes-Evêques) built in 1526–40 by the Cardinal Bishop von der Marck as the palace of the Prince-Bishops. Its façade was restored in 1736–40. There are two picturesque inner courtyards. The west wing, added in 1848–56, now houses the Provincial Government. Adjacent to Lambert Square in the north-east is the Place du Marché (Market Place) with two Baroque fountains. The Fontaine du Perron is the symbol of the city. On the south side of the Market Place stands the Town Hall (Hôtel de Ville; 1714–18), and on the north side the domed structure of the former Church of St André (1772), now the Stock Exchange. North of the Market Place stands the Church of St Antoine (13th, 17th and 18th c.) which was heavily damaged in the Second World War and then rebuilt. Behind the church lies the remarkable Cour des Mineurs, the remains of a former monastery now housing the Walloon Museum (Musée de la Vie Wallone), an ethnographic museum showing all aspects of Walloon life.

The street En Féronstrée leads north-east from the Market Place to the Place Paul Janson. Here stands the early Romanesque Church of St Barthélemy (11th–12th c.). The interior was completely rebuilt in the 18th c. It has two towers, in one of them a carillon (1774). In the baptistry to the left of the choir stands a *font, cast between 1107 and 1118 by Renier de Huy. It rests upon ten half-figures of bulls and has five excellent high reliefs. There is also an ancient crypt.

In the block of houses south of the Place Paul Janson, between En Féronstrée and the Quai de Maestricht, are three interesting museums. On the corner of En Féronstrée and the Rue Hongrée, at No.

Cover of a Gospel in Musée Curtius

114, a patrician house dating from 1735 to 1740, is the Musée d'Ansembourg. The old furnishings have been preserved, together with a collection of decorative art and furniture. At No. 13 Quai de Maestricht is the Maison Curtius, a brick building with interesting sculptural decor, erected in 1600 for the patrician Jean Curtius. It houses the Archaeological Museum (Musée Curtius), with collections of Prehistoric, Roman and Frankish antiquities, furniture and applied art, especially glass. Also in the Quai de Maestricht in the former préfecture (No. 8), is the Arms Museum (Musée d'Armes) with a magnificent collection of small arms.

From the Quai de Maestricht going upstream via the Quai de la Batte and the Quai de la Goffe, you reach the Pont des Arches, built in 1858–62 on the site of the oldest bridge of Liège which dated from the 11th c. From here there is a good view. On the other bank, between the Meuse and a canal, lies the so-called Island of the Meuse (Outremeuse). The old district here of EN ROUTURE is interesting with its colourful life, to which the Puppet Theatre in the Tchantches Museum contributes. In the southern part of the island is the Jardin d'Acclimatation with the Congress Palace (Palais des Congrès, built in 1952–8; in summer, son et lumière (sound and light) performances, seats for spectators on the other bank of the Meuse). Also to be seen here is the *Tour spatiodynamique et cyberné-tique*, a 52 m (171 feet) high bizarre steel structure. In the *Parc de la Boverie* is the *Palais des Beaux Arts* with the *Museum of Walloon Art* and a *collection of prints*.

The best view of Liège is from the **Plateau de Cointe** in the south-west, which can be reached by the Avenue de l'Observatoire behind the Central Station. From the crossroads at the bus terminal (café/restaurant), the Avenue de Cointe runs south to the nearby *University Observatory* (Observatoire); to the north the Boulevard Gustave Kleyer crosses the *Parc de Cointe* towards the **Pointe de Vue* (orientation table). From here there is a view over the entire city, the Meuse Valley, and the side valleys of the Ourthe and the Vesdre with their many industrial plants. The best view is in late afternoon. From the aforementioned crossroads steps lead down to the **Basilique du Sacré-Coeur** (1936) and an impressive **monument to the Victims of the First World War** (*Monument interallié*). This was erected in 1937, and has an 83 m (272 feet) high tower.

Above the city to the north is the **Parc de la Citadelle** (alt. 158 m (518 feet)), which incorporates the grounds and bastions of the former 18th c. *citadel* (now barracks), and offers a good view. You can reach it either by car via the Rue de l'Académie and the Rue Montagne St Walburge (some 2 km (1 mile) from Place St-Lambert), or on foot from the Law Courts via the steep Rue Pierreuse, then to the right via the narrow Rue du Péry. This walk takes 20–25 minutes; a quicker route is via the Montagne du Bueren, 407 steps, starting not far east of the Church of St Antoine.

On a hill above the right bank of the Meuse beyond the district Outremeuse, stands the former fortress **Chartreuse**. Below this, from the garden of the *Hospice de la Chartreuse*, is another beautiful view of the town, especially in the morning.

Lier (Lierre)

Country: Belgium. – Province: Antwerp.
Altitude: 4–13 m (13–43 feet). – Population: 33,000.
Postal code: B-2500.
Telephone code: 0 31.

(i) **Zimmertorencomité,**
Stadhuis,
Grote Market;
tel. 80 22 33.

HOTELS. – *Handelshof*, Leopoldsplein 39–41, IV, 10 r.; *Du Commerce*, V, 10 r.

RESTAURANTS. – *De Fortuin*, Félix Timmermansplein 7; *Marnixhoeve*, Kesselsesteenweg 79.

The Belgian town of Lier (in French, Lierre) is the birthplace of the popular Flemish author Felix Timmermans (1886–1947). The town lies 17 km (11 miles) south-east of Antwerp at the confluence of the Grote and the Kleine Nete. It is the gateway to the region of Kempen.

The economy of the town is based on the textile industry with its old and well-known tradition of silk spinning, lace-making and embroidery. Also important are some more recently introduced industries including brewing, the manufacture of synthetic fibres, and the production of building materials near the Nete Canal. Lier has boat connections with Antwerp via this canal which is used by ships of up to 1350 tons. Many people commute daily between Lier and Antwerp.

HISTORY. – The origins of the town can be traced to a hermitage founded here in 760. In the early Middle

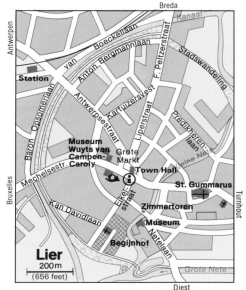

Ages the place was already well known for its cloth-making, and received its town charter as early as 1195. It was fortified in the late Middle Ages and its fortifications resisted all enemy attacks until 1784. They were then destroyed, but were rebuilt in 1830. During the First World War the town held a key strategic position and was often heavily shelled.

SIGHTS. – The Grote Markt in the middle of the town was heavily damaged during the shelling of Antwerp in 1914 but its main buildings survived. On its eastern side stands the *Town Hall* (18th c.; fine Rococo staircase). Attached to the Town Hall is the Gothic *belfry* (1369). Behind the Town Hall is the *Butchers' House*, built in 1418, and several interesting guildhouses from the 18th c., such as the Bakkershuis (1717), and D'Eykkenboom (1721). Not far west of the Markt at No. 12 Cauwenberghstraat, is the *Museum Wuyts van Campen-Caroly*, which contains paintings by Dutch Flemish masters and works by contemporary artists. From the Grote Markt across the Kleine Nete is the Church of **St Gommarus** (St Gommaire), built in 1425–1557, one of the masterpieces of Belgian late Gothic. Inside are several beautiful stained-glass windows and a ˙rood screen by F. Mynscheeren and J. Wischavens of Mechelen (1530–40). In one of the chapels in the ambulatory is a beautiful 16th c. triptych. The *church museum* is also worth visiting. Opposite the Church of St Gommarus stands the Romanesque *Chapel of St Peter*, the oldest building in the town (*c.* 1225).

South of the Grote Markt, the Eikelstraat passes through the *Gevangenenpoort* (14th c.) and continues by the wall promenade (former moat) to the *Begijnhof, one of the most picturesque in Belgium, with a Baroque church.

South-east of the Gevangenenpoort, in the Zimmerplein, stands the so-called *Zimmertoren* (Zimmer Tower), named after the astronomer and clock-maker Louis Zimmer (1888–1970); his centenary clock (1930) has thirteen dials (open to visitors; also, on the first floor an interesting astronomical studio). Next to the tower is the *Zimmer Pavilion* with the astronomical "wonder clock", which was one of the features at the New York World Fair in 1939.

SURROUNDINGS of Lier. – An interesting excursion can be made to the town of **Herentals**, 21 km (13 miles) away (population 19,000; Hotel Golf, IV, 14 r.;

de Zalm, IV, 11 r.). It lies on the Kleine Nete and on the Kempen Canal beyond the highway Antwerp–Liège. Its 14th c. Town Hall was built originally as a Drapers' Hall and has a tower (1534; carillon). In it is the small Fraikin Museum with a collection of sculptures by C. A. Fraikin (1817–93). In the Church of St Waldetrudis is a remarkable 16th c. carved altar by Borremans. Also worth seeing are several paintings and the stained-glass windows.

Limburg (Limbourg)

Country: Belgium and the Netherlands.

ⓘ VVV Hasselt,
Lombaardstraat 3,
B-3500 Hasselt;
tel. (0 11) 22 59 61.
VVV Noord-Limburg,
Keulsepoort 3,
NL-5911 BX Venlo;
tel. (0 77) 1 12 41.
Provinciale VVV in Limburg,
Kasteel "Den Halder",
Kerkstraat 31,
NL-6301 BX Valkenburg;
tel. (0 44 06) 1 39 93.

In the north-east of Belgium lies the province of Limburg with an area of 2400 sq. km (927 sq. miles), and less than 700,000 inhabitants. Beyond the eastern and north-eastern frontiers of the country is the Dutch province of Limburg, covering 2200 sq. km (849 sq. miles), and with over 1 million inhabitants.

The former county of Limburg, east of the Meuse, which later became a Duchy, was, by the Congress of Vienna in 1815, declared a province of the Kingdom of the United Netherlands; it then comprised

The dunes near Hechtel (Belgian Limburg)

the Northern Netherlands, Belgium and the former Bishopric of Liège. In 1830 for economic and linguistic reasons, the southern provinces rose against the northern ones. The southern provinces emerged from the conflict as an independent state, the present-day Belgium. In 1839 Limburg was divided into the Belgian province and the Dutch province, the latter being part of the German Bund until 1866.

The **Belgian Province of Limburg** is a flat area, only rising in the south, where the foreland of the Ardennes begins, to an altitude of about 200 m (656 feet). In this widely diversified region, the main town of which is **Hasselt** (see page 174), there are ponds, lakes, woods, heath and nature reserves. It offers to the vacationer all kinds of sports facilities including water sports and riding. Near *Houthalen*, north of Hasselt, the estates of *Hengelhoef* and *Kelchterhoef* are worth visiting. Near *Helchteren*, the game park "Molenheide" is ideal for walking. An excursion to the nature reserve of *Bokrijk* (see page 175), should not be missed. North-east of *Sint Truiden* (see page 247), is the little town of *Zoutleeuw* with the *Gothic Church of St Leonard. In the south, the province of Limburg merges into *Hainaut and Hesbaye* which are French oriented, while *Kempen* (see page 183) in the north provides a transition to the Netherlands.

The **Dutch Province of Limburg**, through which flows the Meuse (Maas), is the southernmost part of the Netherlands. *South Limburg* (Zuid-Limburg) is part of the province. It is a high plateau rising to between 50 and 250 m (164–820 feet), with a subsoil of lime, chalk, tertiary sands and massive layers of gravel, overlaid by a fertile layer of loess of Ice Age origin. The tributaries of the Maas cut deeply into the ground and split the district into several parts.

Apart from the towns the majority of the area is agricultural, although since the end of the last century industry has acquired a prominent role in its economy. Typical of the region are the large groups of villages with medium or small-sized farms in the surrounding open plain. Apart from these enclosed settlements there are numerous large farmsteads with an acreage of between 50 and 100 hectares (124–247 acres). The most important crops are wheat and sugar-beet. In certain places fruit and dairy farming are also pursued.

The economic structure of the South Limburg industrial area around the towns of **Maastricht** (see page 208), *Sittard*, *Heerlen* and *Kerkrade* was, until about ten years ago, almost exclusively focused on stone quarries and the mining of lignite. There were twelve coal mines, among them the largest pit in Europe, but the last of them closed in 1975. The annual output declined from approximately 10 million tons in 1966 to about 4·3 million tons in 1970. Today coal is imported. When the pits closed a systematic restructuring of allied industries began. One of the best known examples was the construction of a branch factory of the Dutch car manufacturers, DAF, which absorbed most of the workforce of the closed Maurits coal mine. Other industrial plants are textile, paper, ceramics, chemicals, leather and glass.

The "Three-Country Corner" (Belgium, Netherlands, W. Germany) in South Limburg

The little town of **Valkenburg**, a vacation resort with a large monastery, is a lively tourist attraction. The *Dwingelrots* (rock tower), with the ruins of the 13th c. castle of the Lords of Valkenburg on the top, overlook it in the south. Well worth seeing is the underground Mining Museum in a disused coal mine. The *Abbey Rolduc* near *Kerkrade* (founded 1104) has an interesting Romanesque church and another mining museum. North-east of Kerkrade in *Heerlen* are the remains of Roman Baths (Thermae), which were part of a Roman fort, and a Thermae Museum. South of *Vaals* is the "Three-

Country Corner" where the borders of Belgium, Holland and Federal Germany meet.

Downstream on the Maas lies the northern part of Dutch Limburg, around *Roermond* (see page 235) and **Venlo** (see page 262). The countryside here is mostly flat and monotonous, crisscrossed with canals and rivers, and many large farms. *Peel* in the west, which is part of North Brabant, contains vast areas of heath and moor. *Tegelen*, south of Venlo, has several plants producing ceramics, as well as a *Museum of Pottery.*

Uplands of Lorraine

Country: Belgium and Luxembourg.
ⓘ **Sud Ardenne et Gaume,**
Pavilion du Tourisme,
B-6700 Arlon;
tel. (0 63) 21 17 97.
Office National du Tourisme,
Avenue de la Gare 51,
L-Luxembourg;
tel. 48 79 99.

The largest part of the Uplands of Lorraine belongs to France, but they include also the southern half of the Grand Duchy of Luxembourg, here called Gutland, and the southernmost tip of Belgium (Pays Gaumais). The geographical boundary with the Ardennes in the north nearly parallels the line from Vianden in Luxembourg to Beaumont in France. In the east the Uplands of Lorraine jut into the Eifel (Bitburger Land). In the south and west, the region gradually merges into the French plateau of Lorraine.

Geographically, the Uplands of Lorraine belong to the so-called Paris Basin. This vast super-region can be compared to a giant bowl with Paris in the middle. It consists of several superimposed layers of rock rising gradually toward the outer rim of the basin. These layers are alternately hard and soft and therefore eroded into a step-like formation, the soft layers forming extensive plains arranged in concentric circles around the basin. These plains are separated from each other by steep terraces of hard rock. The steep face of these terraces is turned toward the outer edge of the basin.

In the Belgian and Luxembourg part of this terraced country, triassic and jurassic rocks overlie each other step-wise toward the inner side of the basin. In parts valuable arable land has formed over them. Across the middle of the Luxembourg Gutland runs a strip of Luxembourg jurassic sandstone, less fertile and deposited north and south to form a conspicuous terrace. From the town and Abbey of *Echternach* (see page 140) on the Sûre, you can look up at its steep slopes. This sandstone plain is characterised by bizarre rock formations and drops almost vertically into the Valley of the Alzette and its tributaries. There, crowning the terrace, in the middle of the forests, lies the capital city of Luxembourg. A natural fortress in an impregnable position blocking the road between France and Germany, its fortifications were nevertheless destroyed in 1866.

Luxembourg and Belgium join in the extreme south of both countries on a terrace of Brown Jura ("Dogger"), which conceals one of the richest deposits in Europe of the iron ore called Minette. Since this deposit was opened up for exploitation after the invention of an improved ore extraction technique in the last quarter of the 19th c., important iron works have developed in the area. The ore, with an iron content of only 30%, is relatively low grade and transporting it over long distances would have been extremely expensive. Therefore heavy industries settled around the ironworks which brought in coke from the outside. This process accelerated rapidly after the turn of the century. The share of Luxembourg in the ore deposits is fairly limited (the tiny tip of Belgium has long been exhausted as a mining district), but it nevertheless sparked the development of the Grand Duchy into an industrial state. The most important works are the Aciéries Réunies Burbach-Esch-Dudelange (ARBED).

Louvain (Leuven)

Country: Belgium. – Province: Brabant.
Altitude: 20–40 m (66–131 feet). – Population: 113,000.
Postal code: B-3000.
Telephone code: 0 16.
ⓘ **Dienst voor Toerisme,**
Stadhuis,
Naamsestraat 3;
tel. 23 49 41.

HOTELS. – *Binnenhof*, Maria-Theresia-Straat 65, III, 57 r.; *La Royale*, Martelarenplein 6, IV, 28 r.; *Mille Colonnes*, Martelarenplein 5, IV, 10 r.; *University Inn*, Naamsestraat 20, IV, 13 r.; *De la Gare*, Martelarenplein 15, IV, 14 r.

RESTAURANTS. – *Aende 7 Hoecken*, M.-de-Layensplein 9; *Astoria*, Martelarenplein 8; *Brouwershuis*, Margarethaplein 12; *Lion d'Or*, Krakenstraat 6; *Salons Georges*, Hogeschoolplein 15.

Louvain (in Flemish Leuven), lies on both banks of the Dijle at the western fringe of Hageland in the Belgian province of Brabant. The town, together with its suburbs (incorporated in 1977), contains over 100,000 inhabitants, and is the commercial, cultural and administrative capital of East Brabant and southern Kempen.

Its Catholic University (19,000 students) is world-famous. Erasmus of Rotterdam and Justus Lipsius once taught here.

Because of the linguistic quarrels between the Flemish and the Walloons, the University was divided in 1968. The independent "Université Catholique de Louvain" with 12,000 French-speaking students is now based on the new campus *Louvain-la-Neuve*, 35 km (22 miles) south of Louvain.

Industrial plants in Louvain are concentrated mainly in the north of the town along the canal linking the Dijle with the Rupel. The most important industry is brewing, with an annual output of over 4 million hectolitres (88 million gallons). A great number of historic buildings and several museums make the town an interesting place to visit.

HISTORY. – The ancient settlement derived its name from the Dutch words "Loo" (bushy hill) and "Veen" (marsh). In the 11th c. a town grew around the castle of the Counts of Louvain who, in 1106, became Dukes of Lower Lotharingia, and from 1190 onwards called

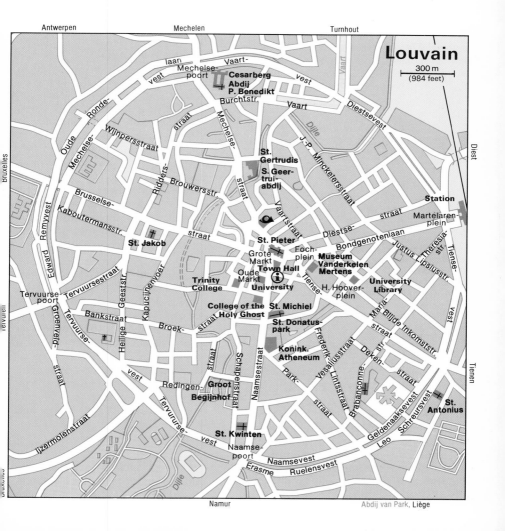

themselves the Dukes of Brabant. The town developed rapidly, owing to its situation on the trade route from Cologne to Bruges; in the 12th c. it became the capital of Brabant and was widely known for its cloth-making. It is said to have had, in the 14th c., 2500 looms and was, with its population of 100,000, one of the largest cities in Europe. Internal disputes, such as the uprising of the artisans against the merchants in 1379, and the general shifting of trade routes brought about the decline of commerce and crafts. But the University, which was founded in 1425 and became the bulwark of orthodoxy, provided an impetus for a revival. A new period of progress began in the 19th c. under Belgian administration. The town was heavily damaged in both World Wars. In the Second World War the churches in particular suffered, but all the damage has now been repaired.

SIGHTS. – The town is circular in shape and was once surrounded by moats. In the middle is the Grote Markt, a traffic junction where all the main streets converge. At the south side of the square stands the *Town Hall (*Stadhuis*). Built by Mathys de Layens in 1448–63, it is one of the most beautiful buildings of the late Gothic period and is decorated more lavishly than the town halls of Bruges, Brussels, and Oudenaarde. The three façades are adorned with numerous statues. Those in the niches represent eminent citizens from the town's history, while on the bases are relief carvings illustrating scenes from the Old and New Testaments, some of them with medieval coarseness. Inside the Town Hall is the Council Chamber with a carved domed ceiling (15th c.) and a Gothic chimney-piece. The *Church of St Peter (15th–16th c.) stands opposite the Town Hall. It has two west towers which remained unfinished because the ground was not solid enough to support them.

The INTERIOR of the Church of St Peter houses numerous art treasures, among them the late Gothic *brass font* in the chapel to the left of the west door, a carved pulpit by J. Berge (1742), a *rood screen* enclosing the choir (1488), and a magnificent tabernacle by M. de Layens (1450) in the ambulatory. Among the valuable paintings in the side chapels is the "**Last Supper**", a well-preserved masterpiece by Dierick Bouts (1464–8). Beneath the choir is the octagonal Romanesque crypt of the original 10th c. church; this was rediscovered during restoration work.

On the west side of the Town Hall, the Naamsestraat, lined with a number of old buildings, runs southward. On the right are the main buildings of the **Catholic University**, founded in 1425, which since 1835 has been independent of the state. The former *Drapers' Hall* (1317) was the seat of the University from 1432, but was burned down in 1914. The present buildings were erected after the First World War and later enlarged. The famous institution is said to have had 3000 students in the 16th c., divided among 52 colleges. Nobody could hold a public office in the then Austrian Netherlands without having a degree from Louvain.

Where the Naamsestraat widens stands the *Church of St Michael, built in 1650–6 by Willem Hesius. It has a splendid Baroque façade, one of the finest of its kind in Belgium. Further south is the *Royal Athenaeum* (grammar school) and the 15th c. *Church of St Kwinten* with some paintings from the School of Rubens. The picturesque *Grote Begijnhof* in the Schapenstraat was founded in the 13th c. Its buildings, which now house various University institutes, date from the 14th–18th c.

In the pretty *Park of St Donatus* behind the Athenaeum are two towers, the remains of the oldest *city wall*. In the spacious Mgr Ladeuzeplein stands the *University Library*, built in 1921–8 in Dutch Renaissance style. It was designed by the American architect Whitney Warren and financed primarily by American donations. It has a tower 85 m (279 feet) high with a carillon. The most valuable books in this library were lost in a fire in 1914 and still more in another fire in 1940. Despite this the library now contains more than one million books. The *Museum Vanderkelen-Mertens (*Municipal Museum*) in the Savoyestraat, has a collection of paintings from the 16th–20th c., a numismatic and print collection, and a library.

The elongated Old Market (Oude Markt), with its brick houses mostly renovated, presents a colourful picture. On its shorter southern side is the *Collegium Vauxianum* (Trinity College) with a 1567 façade. To the west, in the Brusselsestraat, standing back slightly from the road, is the *Church of St Jacob*, built in the 15th–16th c. with a choir (1785) and a Romanesque tower. In its sacristy are embroidered vestments from the Abbey of St Gertrude and 14th–15th c. reliquaries of St Jacob, St Margaret and St Hubertus.

North of the Oude Markt, standing somewhat to one side, is the old *Benedictine Abbey of St Gertrude*, which was heavily damaged in the Second World War. The Gothic *Church of St Gertrude* (13th–15th c.) was almost completely destroyed apart from the tower, built by Jan van Ruybrock in 1453, and one chapel. It was, however, reconstructed in 1953. The beautiful late Gothic choir-stalls, which rank among the best in Belgium, were made by M. de Wayer (*c.* 1550). They were badly damaged in an air-raid and buried under the debris, but have since been restored. Nearby rises the *Keizersberg* (Cesarberg) with a Benedictine Abbey at the top, built on the site of the castle of the Counts and Dukes of Brabant. According to legend the first fort here was constructed in the time of Caesar. There is a 14 m (46 feet) high statue of the Virgin.

South-east of the city is the *Premonstratensian Abbey of the Park* (*Abdij van Park*), one of the most remarkable monasteries in Belgium. Founded in 1129 the present buildings, which date from the 17th–18th c., house a large library and valuable archives. Its church was constructed in the 12th–13th c. and rebuilt in the 17th–18th c.

SURROUNDINGS of Louvain. – 2 km (1 mile) south-west of the city in **Heverlee** by the River Dijle, stands the 16th c. *Château Arenberg*. It now belongs to the University and has beautiful grounds, well worth a visit. Opposite the château stands an old farmhouse.

Luxembourg/ Luxemburg

Country: Luxembourg. – Canton: Luxembourg. Altitude: 230–380 m (755–1247 feet). – Population: 78,000.

(i) **Office National du Tourisme,**
Avenue de la Gare 51,
tel. 48 79 99.
Syndicat d'Initiative et de Tourisme de la Ville de Luxembourg,
Cercle,
Place d'Armes;
tel. 2 28 09 and 2 75 65.

EMBASSIES: *British*, Boulevard Franklin Roosevelt; *USA*, Boulevard E. Servaes.

HOTELS. – *Cravat*, Boulevard Roosevelt 29, L, 60 r.; *Holiday Inn*, on the Kirchberg, north, opposite the EEC building, L, 260 r.; *Novotel*, Route d'Echternach-Dommeldange, L, 151 r.; *Kons*, Place de la Gare 24, I, 141 r.; *Rix*, Boulevard Royal 20, I, 20 r.; *Alfa*, Place de la Gare 16, I, 100 r.; *Central Molitor*, Avenue de la Liberté 28, I, 36 r.; *Des Ducs*, Rue d'Anvers 12, I, 11 r.; *Eldorado*, Place de la Gare 7, I, 47 r.; *Continental*, Grand'Rue 86, I, 39 r.; *Alvisse Parc*,

Route d'Echternach-Dommeldange, II, 36 r.; *Gran Vatel*, Route d'Esch 406, II, 22 r.; *Terminus*, Place de la Gare 32, II, 47 r.; *Ancre d'Or*, Rue du Fossé 21, II, 15 r.; *International*, Place de la Gare 20–22, II, 67 r.; *Français*, Place d'Armes 14, II, 21 r.; *Cheminée de Paris*, Rue d'Anvers 10, II, 24 r.; *Dauphin*, Avenue de la Gare 42, II, 37 r.; *Delta* (no rest.), Rue Adolphe Fischer 76, II, 10 r.; *Schintgen*, Rue Notre-Dame 6, II, 36 r.; *Senator*, Rue Jos. Junck 38, II, 29 r.; *Euro*, Route d'Arlon 114, III, 21 r.; *City* (no rest.), Rue de Strasbourg 1, III, 28 r.; *Weyrich*, Route de Thionville 274, III, 20 r.; *Empire*, Place de la Gare 34, III, 42 r.; *Beaumont* (no rest.), Rue Beaumont 11–13, III, 12 r.; *Du Théâtre*, Rue Beaumont 3, III, 21 r.; *Carlton* (no rest.), Rue de Strasbourg 9, III, 46 r.; *Walsheim*, Place de la Gare 28, III, 20 r.; *Italia*, Rue d'Anvers 15–17, III, 23 r.; *Windsor*, Rue de Strasbourg 7, III, 23 r.; *A.B.C.*, Rue Zithe 39, III, 23 r.; *Graas* (no rest.), Avenue de la Liberté 78, III, 32 r.; *Elisabeth*, Rue du Fort Elisabeth 17, IV, 9 r.; *Vitali-Pax*, Route de Thionville 121, IV, 13 r.; *Mertens* (no rest.), Rue de Hollerich 16, IV, 10 r.; *Century* (no rest.), Rue J. Junck 6, IV, 23 r.; *Régina* (no rest.), Rue J. Junck 34, IV, 22 r.; *Becker*, Rue de la Station 5 – Dommeldange, IV, 14 r.; *Des Rochers*, Rue de Pulvermuhl 5 – Pulvermuhltal, IV, 14 r.; *De la Place* (no rest.), Place du Fort Wallis 11a, V, 15 r.; *Des Ardennes* (no rest.), Avenue de la Liberté 59, V, 12 r.; *Baezel* (no rest.), Rue du Fort Neipperg 30, V, 15 r. – Numerous BOARDING HOUSES. – At the Airport (5 km (3 miles) north-east, Route de Trèves-Findel): *Aérogolf-Sheraton*, L, 150 r.; *Air-Field*, Route de Trèves 6 – Findel, III, 10 r.

YOUTH HOSTELS. – Pfaffenthal, 308 b. – CAMP SITES, Dommeldange and Itzinger Sté.

RESTAURANTS. – *St-Michel*, Rue Eau 32; *Empereurs*, Av. Porte-Neuve 11; *Gourmet*, Rue Chimay 8; *Astoria*, Av. du 10-Septembre 14; *Alsacien*, Rue du Curé 24; *Rotiss. Ardennaise*, Av. du 10-Septembre 1; *La Poêle d'Or*, Marché-aux-Herbes 20; *Cordial*, Pl. Paris 1; *The President*, Pl. Gare 32; *Le Grimpereau*, Rue Cents 140.

EVENTS. – *Popular Feast* "Die E'Maischen" (Easter Monday); *International Fair* (second half of May); *National Holiday* (23 June); *Theatre in the Casemates* (July); *Barn Fair* (2 weeks, beginning on the last Sunday but one in August); *Pilgrimages* and *Processions* to the Statue of the Virgin in the Cathedral (7 days after Christmas, Easter and Whitsun); *Flea Market* (the second and fourth Saturday of each month).

Luxembourg is the capital of the Grand Duchy of Luxembourg, seat of the Grand Duke and the administrative headquarters of the district of the same name. It lies in the southern part of the country which borders on the Belgian province of the same name to the west. It is situated on a rocky upland, surrounded in the east and south by two deep valleys. One is the winding Valley of the Alzette in which lie the districts of Pfaffenthal, Clausen and Grund. The other is the Valley of the Pétrusse, which separates the old town from the modern districts around the railway station. The

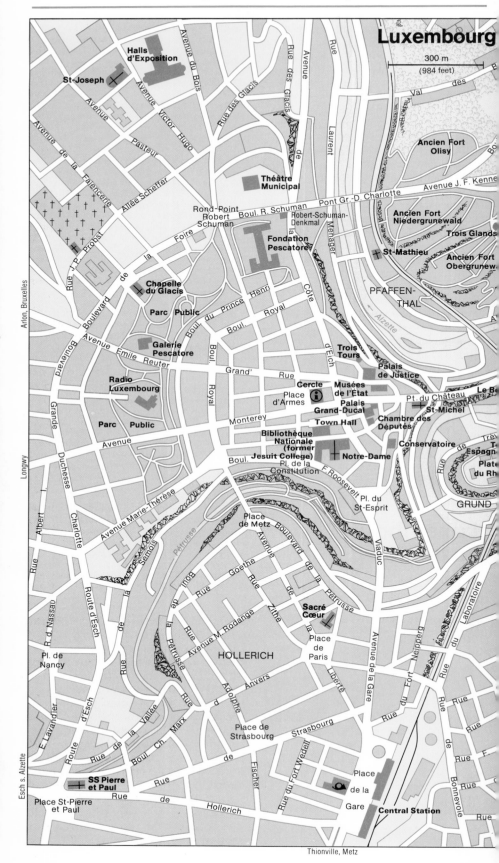

Luxembourg

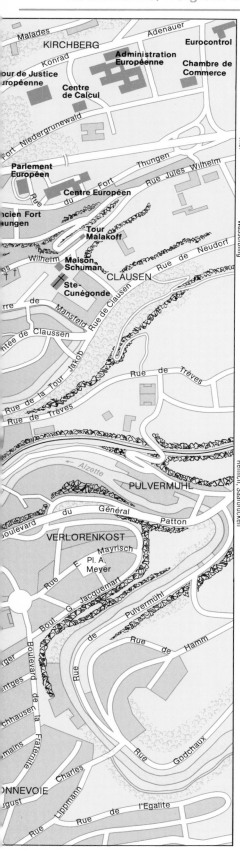

*panorama of Luxembourg is strikingly beautiful, with its hills and valleys, its bleached sandstone rocks, garden terraces and huge viaducts.

Luxembourg is one of the most exclusively administrative cities of Europe. This function largely overshadows all others. The town is the official residence of the Grand Duke and of the Luxembourg Government, as well as of numerous embassies and important national and European authorities. The most important international institutions and organisations include the headquarters of the Coal and Steel Union, the European Court of Justice and the European Investment Bank.

Educational institutes, a well-known institute of forestry, a medical faculty, numerous large libraries, archives, museums, a theatre, as well as a broadcasting and television station also have their headquarters in the city.

Owing to its strategic location (and airport) between Central and Western Europe, Luxembourg developed into a key commercial and financial city for more than just the Grand Duchy. It is the administrative headquarters of numerous national and international companies – financial, commercial and industrial. Large industrial enterprises have settled primarily in the lower-town districts and the suburbs. The widely diversified industrial spectrum ranges from steel mills, rolling mills and foundries, to machinery, chemicals, textiles and the food industry.

HISTORY. – The Romans built a settlement as early as the 4th c. on the site of an earlier Celtic town. About 926 Luxembourg is believed to have been protected by a fort and after 963 it passed into the possession of Count Sigefroi. He built here a castle which later became the family seat of the rulers of Luxembourg, and it was called *Lucilinburhuc*. Soon afterwards the uplands around the castle and the Valley of the Alzette were densely populated. The upper and lower towns received civic status in 1224.

The history of Luxembourg in the following centuries was checkered, and the town frequently changed hands. Every new overlord reinforced the fortress, which, in the 15th c., ranked among the most impregnable in Europe. Under Louis XIV it was largely rebuilt by Vauban. Between 1815 and 1866 Luxembourg was a fortress of the German Bund, but in 1867 the fortifications were pulled down and extensive parks were laid out in their place. The town assumed its modern role as an administrative capital in 1926 when it became the headquarters of the European Steel Cartel. It became even more prominent when the European Coal and Steel Union was founded in 1952 and later when the EEC steadily expanded. The town

The Capital City of Luxembourg – general view

today competes with Brussels and Strasbourg, which also contain many key European offices and institutions.

SIGHTS. – The modern part of the city is in the south, where the **railway station** (*Gare Centrale*) and busy shopping streets are situated. North of here the old town can be reached across the Valley of the Pétrusse either by the *Passerelle* viaduct, 308 m (1011 feet) long and 44 m (144 feet) high, or via the **Pont Adolphe**, a massive sandstone arch with a span of 85 m (279 feet). On the southern edge of the OLD TOWN the wide Boulevard Roosevelt, high above the Pétrusse, offers a beautiful view of the valley. In the middle of the street to the south is the Place de la Constitution, also with a *view. In it stands the Monument commemorating the victims of both World Wars. In the north-east corner of the square is the entrance to the *casemates* (vaulted chambers in the thickness of the walls) *of the Pétrusse* (open to visitors).

Parallel to the Boulevard Roosevelt runs the Rue Notre-Dame, also called Enneschtgaass; in this street is the *National Library* (until 1773 a Jesuit college). Next to it stands the **Cathedral of Notre-Dame**, formerly a Jesuit church built in the 17th c. and enlarged in 1935–8. It has an interesting late Renaissance doorway and a Baroque organ gallery. North of here is the spacious Place Guillaume with an equestrian statue of the Grand Duke and King William II. On the south side of

the square stands the impressive **Town Hall** (*Hôtel de Ville*, built in 1830–8).

East of the Place Guillaume is the **Grand Ducal Palace** (*Palais Grand-Ducal*), a former Town Hall. It is a Renaissance building, dating from 1572, which was enlarged in 1891. Next to it, on the southeast, is the *Chamber of Deputies* (1858). From here the Rue du St-Esprit runs south past the *School of Music* to the Place du St-Esprit. On the east side of the square is a terrace with a magnificent view over the Lower Valley of the Alzette. To the west is the *War Memorial* (Monument de la Solidarité Nationale). From the terrace on the left the scenic Corniche road follows the line of the old town wall to the **Church of St Michel** (11th and 16th c.). From here to the right across the old *Castle bridge* (Pont du Château; 1737), you reach the **Bock**, a steep rocky spur jutting into the loop of the little River Alzette. On it the excavated remains of the old castle and a gate tower from the former fortification can be seen. Next to the Castle bridge is the entrance to the old *casemates of Bock*.

From the Church of St Michel, you reach, via the Rue Sigefroi, the Fishmarket (Marché aux Poissons). On the right is the *State Museum (Musées de l'Etat) with Roman and Frankish antiquities, among them the stone relief of Echternach, the oldest existing altar crown ever found (8th c.). There are also collections of local and natural history, in particular an important zoological section. Behind the museum to the north are the **Law Courts** (*Palais de Justice*; 16th–19th c.).

To the west is the **Grand' Rue**, the main shopping street of the city. To its south extends the Place d'Armes, the east side of which is occupied by the **Town Hall** (*Cercle*) and the offices of the Municipal Transport Association. If you follow the Avenue Emile Reuter west from the Grand' Rue, you arrive at the ***Municipal Park**, laid out in 1872 in the west of the city on the site of the former fortifications and designed by the Paris garden architect E. André. In its southern part are the offices and studios of *Radio-Télé-Luxembourg*. To the north in the Villa Vauban is the *Municipal Pescatore Picture Gallery*. At the north end of the park near the *Pescatore foundation* (Municipal Old People's Home) is the best view over the Pfaffenthal. Nearby to the north-west is the busy Rond-Point Robert Schuman. From here the Boulevard Robert Schuman leads past the *New Theatre* on the left (1961–4) to the **Grand Duchess Charlotte Bridge** (*Pont Grande-Duchesse Charlotte*) opened in 1966. The bridge, which is 355 m (1165 feet) long with piers 234 m (768 feet) apart, crosses the Alzette 85 m (279 feet) above the valley in a single bold arch. The *Monument* to the right of the bridge is made of steel girders and was erected in 1966; it commemorates the French statesman *Robert Schuman* (1886–1963) who was born in Luxembourg and who was the moving spirit behind European integration.

The Trois Glands Fort in Luxembourg

J. F. Kennedy, the building of the **European Parliament** and further north-east the **European Court of Justice**, the **European Administrative Building**, a computer complex (*Centre de Calcul*), the *Chamber of Commerce* and the *Eurocontrol Institute*.

The suburb of PFAFFENTHAL lies on both banks of the Alzette to the north-west beneath the Bock. Here are four well-preserved *fortification towers* and the *Church of St Matthew*. East and above Pfaffenthal on a hill with a panoramic view extend the parks of the former forts, the *Lower* and *Upper Grunewald, Olizy* and *Thüngen*, the latter also known as the **Trois Glands** (*Three Acorns*).

East of Pfaffenthal is the suburb of CLAUSEN where the Spanish governor Duke Peter Ernst von Mansfeld (1517–1604) had a sumptuous palace. Only two *gates* with Roman sculptures in the walls are preserved. General George Patton (1885–1945), commander of the US Third Army, is buried in the American Military Cemetery at Hamm near the airport. On a rock on the park hill stands the statue of St Joseph, visible from afar.

The suburb of GRUND which lies on the right bank of the Alzette to the south beneath the Bock, is dominated by the Plateau of Rham were once stood a large Roman villa. On its fringe stands the third city wall (wall of Wenceslas; 14th c.) with massive towers. Continuing upstream you come to the *Valley of Pulvermühl* which has some bizarre rock formations. West of Grund is the beginning of the pretty Valley of the Pétrusse, which separates the old town from the area around the station.

The European Parliament Building in Luxembourg

The Grand Duchess Charlotte Bridge leads east to the PLATEAU OF KIRCHBERG, where the headquarters of several international organisations have recently been built, including the 24-storey **Centre Européen** (1966), south of Avenue

SURROUNDINGS of Luxembourg. – **To Mondorf-les-Bains** (19 km – 12 miles). Leave in a southerly direction past the station and then on the N3 (E9) into the narrow Valley of the *Alzette*. After 5 km (3 miles)

Thermal Baths in Mondorf-les-Bains

feet), population 2200, Hotel Beau Séjour, III, 10 r.; St Nicolas, III, 17 r.; Ardennes, III, 14 r.), with remains of fortifications and an interesting Church of the Deanery, the tower of which was originally a Roman watch tower. A visit to the Champagne Wine Cellars of St Martin (in summer) should not be missed.

Boat on the Moselle in Remich

you reach *Hesperange*, charmingly situated and overlooked by a ruined castle (1483). After 7 km (4 miles) at *Frisange* turn left on the N13. 3 km (2 miles) further the road reaches *Aspelt*, and some 3 km (2 miles) north-east of here on a hill south of *Dalheim* is an interesting Roman milestone marked by the effigy of an eagle. 3 km (2 miles) further comes *Mondorf*, a Luxembourg village with a church (1764). On the other side of the border is the French village of Mondorff. 1 km (about a ½ mile) beyond the Luxembourg village is *Mondorf-les-Bains* (194 m (637 feet), Hôtel du Grand Chef, I, 46 r.; Welcome, II, 18 r.; de la Gare, II, 19 r.; Windsor, III, 19 r.; International, III, 44 r.; Beau Séjour, III, 16 r.), a popular spa with sulphur springs. In the park is a pump room, thermal baths, a rose garden and, near the casino, a large open-air swimming pool.

22 km (14 miles) south-east of Luxembourg, situated on the River Moselle near the Luxembourg-German border, is the little old town of **Remich** (145 m (476

Maastricht

Country: The Netherlands. – Province: Limburg.
Altitude: 46–111 m (151–364 feet). – Population: 110,000.
Postal code: NL-6200 AA to 6299.
Telephone code: 0 43.

(i) **VVV Maastricht,**
Vissersmaas 4-5,
NL-6211 EV Maastricht;
tel. 1 28 14.

Maastricht, bird's-eye view of the City

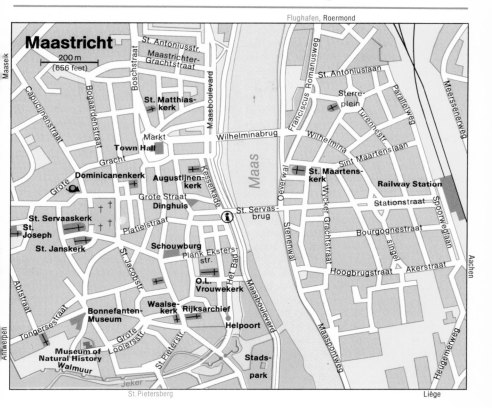

HOTELS. – *Grand Hotel de l'Empereur*, Stationsstraat 2, I, 60 b.; *Hotel Maastricht*, I, De Ruiterij 1, 220 b.; *Derlon*, Onze Lieve Vrouweplein 6, II, 50 b.; *Du Casque*, Vrijthof 52/Helmstraat 14, II, 80 b.; *Beaumont*, Stationsstraat, III, 139 b.; *Dominicain*, Helmstraat 16, III, 18 b.; *Du Chêne*, Boschstraat 104–106, IV, 40 b.; *Stijns*, Stationstraat 40, IV, 34 b.; *Moderne*, Markt 34, IV, 50 b.; *In de Posthoorn*, Stationstraat 47, IV, 24 b.; *Wijker Central*, Wijker Brugstraat 54, IV, 23 b.; *Old Hickory*, Meerssenerweg 372, V, 17 b.

RESTAURANTS. – *Coin des Bons Enfants*, Ezelmarkt 4; *Chez Jacques*, Brusselsestraat 15; *Château Neer-Canne*, Cannerweg 800 (5 km (3 miles) south-west).

Maastricht, the capital of the Dutch province of Limburg, lies on both banks of the Maas (Meuse). Its many interesting buildings have long been an attraction to art lovers. The town is strategically located for communication between Holland, Belgium and Germany, and between the industrial zones of Aix/Aachen, Liège, Kempen and Limburg. This became a distinct advantage after the foundation of the European Economic Community.

Maastricht fulfils not only an important cultural role as its numerous institutions of higher education show; it is also the commercial hub of a wider area extending beyond the national boundary well into Belgium. Its large vegetable and butter markets are increasingly frequented by foreign traders. Industry, too, plays an important part in the economic life of the town and includes paper-making, leather processing, brewing, printing, ceramics and glass manufacture. Tourism is also significant in the economy.

HISTORY. – Maastricht, which was known to the Romans as *Traiectum ad Mosam* or *Traiectum Tungorum*, is one of the oldest towns in the country. A Roman settlement already existed here about 50 B.C., and it was fortified in the 3rd century. In 382, the Bishopric of Tongres was transferred to Maastricht, which was then one of the main capitals of the Merovingian and Carolingian empires. From 1284 until the end of the 18th c. the town belonged alternately to the Dukes of Brabant and the Prince-Bishops of Liège. After 1621 it was one of the most important fortresses in the wars of the Dutch against the Spanish. When the Kingdom of Belgium was created in 1830, the economic development of the town was much restricted. The frontier line cut it off from a large part of its hinterland, and placed it in a peripheral position within the Netherlands.

SIGHTS. – On the right bank of the Maas extends the suburb of Wijk with the *main station* and the *Church of St Martin* (by Cuypers, 1859). Three bridges connect it with the left bank of the river on which lies the largest part of the city. From the

Wilhelminabrug dating from 1930–2 there is a *superb view of the town. This bridge leads directly to the vast Markt in which stands the **Town Hall** (*Stadhuis*) built by Pieter Post in 1658–64. In its tower is a carillon; the interior of the building is also worth visiting. North of the Town Hall is the Catholic *Church of St Matthew* (late 15th c.).

The *bridge of St Servatius* (St Servaasbrug) with seven arches was originally built in the 13th c.; from it there is a *good view of the town. This bridge leads from the Wijk to the Burgstraat. From the end of this street going to the right via the Kleine Straat you arrive at the 15th c. **Old Town Hall**, the former Law Courts, also called *Dinghuise*. Nearby to the north is the former *Augustinian Church of St Joseph*, (17th c.) with a beautiful Baroque façade overlooking the river. From the Old Town Hall, the Grote Straat, the main shopping street of Maastricht, runs west to the Vrijthof. On the right in the Grote Straat is the Gothic building of the former *Dominican Church*, now a concert hall, with murals (1337). In the lovely Vrijthof, which is planted with lime trees, stands the Church of St Servatius and the Church of St Jan.

The *Church of St Servatius** (*St Servaaskerk*, Catholic), is the oldest church in the Netherlands. The original structure was erected in the 6th c. over the tomb of St Servatius. Of this nothing remains except the extensively modernised nave and the east crypt. The narthex (the west porch) seems to be Carolingian. The west crypt, the transept, and the choir are from the beginning of the 11th c.; the south door is 13th c., and the cloisters on the north side of the church date from the 15th c. In the porch gallery is the famous *Keizersaal. Inside the church at the west end of the nave is a statue of Charlemagne (1843). In its base the remains of a 12th c. altar of St Mary can be seen. In the west crypt is the late Romanesque *reliquary of St Servatius (d. 384), a 12th c. masterpiece by Godefroid de Claire. The church treasury is well worth seeing. The Gothic **St Janskerk** (*Protestant*) has a tower 78 m (256 feet) high and was built in the 15th c.

The Bredestraat runs from the Vrijthof south-east to the Onze Lieve Vrouweplein. On the east side of this square stands the *Church of Our Lady** (*O. L.* *Vrouwekerk*, Catholic). It was built in the 11th c. on Roman foundations and has a massive west front obviously built for defence purposes. The most interesting features of the interior are the late Romanesque choir dating from the beginning of the 13th c. and the large crypt. The west crypt is all that remains of the earliest building. There is also a treasury and splendid 16th c. cloisters. Nearby to the south-east in the St Pieterstraat is the former Franciscan Church (Minderbroederskerk; 13th c.) now housing the *State Archives*. South of the Church of Our Lady are the remains of the former 13th c. *city wall* with the *Hell Gate* (*Helpoort*) and the *Pater-Vink Tower*. A few yards to the south, from a spot between two 16th c. bastions surrounded by the River *Jeker*, there is a picturesque view of the Helpoort, the principal churches of the city and the Villapark. – East of the Church of Our Lady, you can cross the canal by a bridge into the *Municipal Park* and enjoy a view of the river from its restaurant.

In the Ezelmarkt, in a 17th c. building, is the **Museum of Art and Archaeology** (*"Bonnefanten"* Museum) with a picture gallery and collections of Prehistoric, Roman and medieval antiquities.

Malmédy

Country: Belgium. – Province: Liège.
Altitude: 300–500 m (984–1641 feet). – Population: 6700.
Postal code: B 4890.
Telephone code: 0 80.

ⓘ **Syndicat d'Initiative et de Tourisme,**
  Place Albert 1er;
  tel. 7 72 50.

HOTELS. – *Bristol*, Place Albert Ier 47, IV, 9 r.; *International*, Place de Rome 1, IV, 10 r.; *Albert Ier*, Place Albert Ier 40, IV, 6 r.; *Au Rocher de Falize*, Route de Falize 100, IV, 6 r.; *Relais Sportif*, Av. du Pont de la Warche 4, IV, 7 r.; *Du Globe* (no rest.), Rue Devant l'Etang 4, V, 8 r.; *Des Ardennes*, Place de la Gare V, 6 r.; *Du Centre* (no rest.), Place Albert Ier 36, V, 8 r.; *Hostellerie des Trôs Marets*, B-4891 Bévercé (Malmédy), Rue du Mont 1, I, 7 r. (5 km (3 miles) north on the N28). – CAMP SITE: *Mon Repos*, Avenue de la Libération 3. – HOLIDAY VILLAGE: *Val d'Arimont*, Bévercé (Malmédy).

RESTAURANTS. – *Coloniaux*, Place de Rome 6; *Le Petit Louvain*, Chemin Rue 47; *La Truite Argentée*, Bellevue 3.

EVENTS. – A famous *Carnival Procession* on the last Monday before Lent.

The little district town of Malmédy belongs to the Belgian province of Liège. It lies at the confluence of the Warche and Warchenne on the southern slope of the densely wooded and very scenic Hautes Fagnes. Some 90% of its inhabitants are Walloons; about 10% of them speak German.

The checkered history of Malmédy is chiefly due to its situation in the border area of Belgium. Because of this the economic development of the area was long neglected. After the Second World War, however, several new industries settled here. The town has also acquired a reputation for its fine schools. Its well-cared-for-appearance and wooded surroundings helped to make it popular with tourists. This has contributed considerably to its prosperity.

Motor Racing Circuit of Francorchamps

(*Circuit National de Francorchamps*), 14·1 km (9 miles) long. The circuit has many bends and gradients and international motor races are held here every year. You can follow this circuit for a distance of 5 km (3 miles). Near the *Hôtel de l'Eau Rouge* (Route de Malmédy, IV, 6 r.), by the river of the same name, there are the grandstands on the right and opposite the starting and finishing lines of the races.

HISTORY. – Malmédy was for a long time a bone of contention between France, Holland and the German Empire. In the last 200 years it switched its allegiance from one country to another several times. The town developed around a monastery founded in 648 by St Remaclus, the Bishop of Malmédy, and until 1795 it was the main town of a principality under the lordship of a powerful line of Abbots owing allegiance only to the Holy Roman Empire. Afterwards it became French but after the defeat of Napoleon it was annexed by Prussia. After the First World War it became Belgian, but during the Second World War it was temporarily under German administration again.

SIGHTS. – In the north of the town stands the former **Abbey Church** built in 1775–84; it has two towers and contains several art treasures. In the buildings of the former monastery are a grammar school and the Law Courts. South of this in the middle of the town in the **Place Albert I**er, are several beautiful 18th c. patrician houses. Many were destroyed during the "Battle of the Bulge" in 1944 but have since been rebuilt in the old style.

SURROUNDINGS of Malmédy. – 9 km (6 miles) south-west on the River Amblève lies the little town of **Stavelot** with a population of 7000 (Hotel Val d'Amblève, IV, 15 r.; Orange, IV, 25 r.). Until the French Revolution it was, together with Malmédy, the seat of the Benedictine Abbey founded in 651 by St Remaclus, of which only the tower of the church and some other buildings remain (small museum). In the Parish Church of 1750 is the *shrine of St Remaclus, made of gilt and enamelled copperplate studded with precious stones. 2 km (1 mile) east above the city stands a ruined 15th c. castle from which there is a good view. An excursion can be made into the nature reserve of the Hautes Fagnes to the *Signal de Botrange* (694 m (2277 feet), observation tower), the highest summit in Belgium. Not far west of Malmédy is the **Motor Racing Circuit of Francorchamps**

Mechelen (Malines)

Country: Belgium. – Province: Antwerp.
Altitude: 7 m (23 feet). – Population: 65,000.
Postal code: B-2800.
Telephone code: 0 15.
ⓘ **Dienst voor Toerisme,**
 Stadhuis;
 tel. 21 30 37.

HOTELS. – *Egmond*, Oude Brusselstraat 50, III, 19 r.; *De Drie Paardekens*, Begijnenstraat 3–5, IV, 33 r.; *De Kroon*, Koning Albertplein 1, IV, 6 r.; *Claes*, Onze Liewe Vrouwstraat 51, IV, 16 r.; *De l'Europe*, Koning Albertplein 9, V, 9 r.

RESTAURANTS. – *Groene Lantaarn*, Steenwegstraat 2. – IN HOFSTADE: *Ambrooshoeve*, Wielendreef 3. – IN RUMST: *Potaerde*, Antwerpsesteenweg 76.

EVENTS. – A *Famous *Carillon Concert* every Monday from June to mid-September at 8.30 p.m.

The Belgian town of Mechelen (in French Malines), is a railway junction between Brussels and Antwerp on the tidal waters of the River Dijle. Since the 16th c. it has been the religious capital of the country and is, together with Brussels, the seat of the Archbishop Primate. It has an Archiepiscopal Seminary and a Carillon School.

The industries of the town comprise furniture-making, food canning, lace-making, carpet-manufacture, wool-processing, and railway workshops. In addition, many factories were founded here within the framework of the European Community by the member states. Mechelen is also well known for market gardening (asparagus, peas, etc.).

HISTORY. – In the Middle Ages Mechelen was called *Machlina* (in Latin *Mechlinia*). In 915 it was already part of the Bishopric of Liège and after 1213 it acquired an almost independent position, until Bishop Adolf von der Marck sold the town in 1332 to the Counts of Flanders. After 1369 the town belonged to Burgundy, and in 1473 was the seat of the Grand Council, the highest law court of the Low Countries. After the death of Charles the Bold, Margaret of York, his 3rd wife, resided here. The governorship of Margaret of Austria (1507–30) was the peak period of the town's prosperity. When Margaret's successor, Mary of Hungary, moved her residence to Brussels in 1546, Mechelen was compensated in 1555 by the foundation of the Archbishopric and became the seat of the Primate of the Low Countries. The first Archbishop was A. Perrenot de Granvella, the adviser to Charles V and Philip II (d. 1568). In the Religious Wars of the 16th c. the town joined the Union of Utrecht in 1579, and in the years 1580–5 it belonged to the Protestants. In the First and Second World Wars it was heavily damaged but has since been rebuilt.

SIGHTS. – The OLD TOWN is circular and ringed with wide boulevards on the site of the former ramparts. Its medieval appearance has in parts been well preserved. In the middle lies the Grote Markt with beautiful 16th–18th c. *gabled houses*. In the square stands the statue of *Margaret of Austria*. On the pavement around the monument are circles showing the sizes of the clock dials which were once on the Cathedral tower. On the south-east side of the Markt is the **Town Hall** (*Stadhuis*), part of which was the former *Cloth Hall*, built in 1320–6 and modelled after the Hall of Bruges. It was rebuilt after a fire in 1342. The north wing (1529) was built by Rombout Keldermans of Mechelen, and a

further wing was added in the 20th c. in accordance with Keldermans' original plans. On the north-east side of the square is the *Post Office*, a former Town Hall dating from the 14th–18th c., with a restored Gothic façade. On the south side, somewhat set back, is the former **Aldermen's House** (*Schepenhuis*) (1374), the first Town Hall of the city. It was also called the Old Palace, for from 1424 to 1616 it was the seat of the Grand Council. It now accommodates the *Town Library* and *Archives*.

In the north of the Grote Markt stands the *Cathedral Church of St Rombout, built in the 13th–16th c., with a late Gothic *western tower 97 m (318 feet) high. It was begun in 1452 and was intended to be 168 m (551 feet) high, which would have made it the highest tower in Christendom. It offers a beautiful view. The dials of the tower clock date from 1708 and have a diameter of 13·7 m (45 feet). The carillon, which dates from the 16th–17th c., has 49 bells, and, together with that of the Bruges belfry, is the most famous in Belgium.

Inside the lofty church are several remarkable works of art; the *statues of the Apostles* (1774) in the nave; in the north aisle next to the Chapel of Our Lady the tomb of Cardinal Mercier, 1851–1926. He was the spokesman for Belgium in the First World War. In the transept are several paintings of the Flemish School (15th–16th c.), among them the superb *"Crucifixion" by Anthony van Dyck (1627). In the choir is a Baroque high altar (1665) and four Baroque tombs of 17th–18th c. Archbishops. In the ambulatory, paintings illustrating the life of St Rombout by P. J. Verhaghen and others are to be seen, and in the second chapel, on the right, is the Coat of Arms of the Knights of the Golden Fleece who, in 1491, held a chapter meeting of their order in St Rombout.

Nearby, to the west of the Cathedral, is the *Academy of Fine Arts*. Many temporary exhibitions are held here.

North-west of the Cathedral, the St Katelijnestraat leads to the Gothic Church of St Catherine (1336–42). Not far to the west is the Baroque **Church of the Begijnhof** (1629–47), with a number of paintings by De Crayer and other artists as well as two statues by the wood carver L. Faid'Herbe, a disciple of Rubens (Benediction of Christ and Mater Dolorosa).

North-east of the Cathedral stands the **St Janskerk** (15th c.) with a vault (1722). The high altar is adorned by **a triptych by Rubens ("Adoration of the Magi"), one of his best works (1617–19). There

Town Hall in Mechelen

after the iron rail, which once ran along the now covered canal (1531–4). The **Hoogbrug**, which can be reached from here, is a bridge with three arches (13th–16th c.), and is the middle bridge on the Dijle. On the left bank in Zoutwerf there are some interesting 16th c. buildings, among them (No. 5) the *House de Zalm* (Salmon), a former Fishmongers' Guildhouse. It is now a *Museum of Applied Art* (Museum "De Zalm") with a beautiful Renaissance façade (1530–4). North-west in the Haverwerf, on the corner of the Kraanstraat, stands the so-called *Paradise* of the 16th c. and next to it, on the left, the beautiful *Duivelshuis*, another 16th c. wooden building, and (No. 20) *St Joseph's House* (1669). From the Dijle bridge, straight on via the Korenmarkt, with its former *Crossbowmen's House* (16th c.), and the Hoogstraat, you reach the **Brusselpoort** with two large towers. Here is the Brussels Gate or "Overste Poort", rebuilt in the 18th c., the only one of the twelve medieval town gates that remains.

are also several fine 17th c. wood carvings by T. Verhaghen on the pulpit, in the choir and on the pews in the transept. Not far east of the church, on the corner of the St Jansstraat and F. de Merodestraat, stands the *Hof van Busleyden*, an old and gracious Gothic building (1507) which was restored after the First World War. It now houses the *Municipal Museum* and contains paintings, sculptures and antiquities.

South-east of the St Jansstraat, the Biest leads to the Veemarkt. In it stands the former Jesuit **Church of St Peter and Paul** (1670–77), with a massive façade (1709) and an interesting interior. Next to it, on the left, in the Keizerstraat, is the late Gothic building of the former **Keizerhof**, now a *theatre*. It was built in 1480 by Margaret of York, the widow of Charles the Bold, and was a residence of Philip the Handsome and until 1516 of Charles V. Opposite are the *Law Courts* (*Gerechtshof*), a vast group of buildings around a large courtyard. It was once the "Hôtel de Savoie", the palace of Margaret of Austria, and later of Cardinal A. P. de Granvella, the first Archbishop of Mechelen and adviser to Charles V and Philip II. From 1616 to 1794, it was the seat of the Grand Council. The oldest parts were built by R. Keldermans in 1503–7. He was also responsible for the façade (1517–26). These were among the earliest Renaissance buildings in Belgium. Inside are several good chimney-pieces.

The long IJzerenleen joins the Grote Markt in the south-west. It was named

East of the Hoogstraat stands the **Church of Our Lady** (Onze Lieve Vrouw over de Dijle), founded in 1255 and mostly rebuilt in the 15th–17th c. in Flamboyant Gothic. In the chapel behind the Baroque high altar (1690) is the *"Miraculous Draught of Fishes"* by Rubens (1618) and several other paintings. From the Church of Our Lady you go south-east via Onze Lieve Vrouwstraat and Hanswijkstraat, to the beautiful Baroque Church **Onze Lieve Vrouw van Hanswijk** (1633–78) by L. Faid'Herbe). It contains the much venerated statue of the Virgin (988). Adjacent, to the east, is the Raghenoplaats, which lies on the ring boulevard. Nearby, to the west, is the Kardinal Mercierplaats. It is on a line of wide streets running from the *station* (on the left) to the Grote Markt. From the Dijle bridge there is a beautiful view upstream. Behind the bridge, on the right, is the *Royal Athenaeum* (Pitsenburg), the former house of the Teutonic Order (17th c.), and the *Botanical Gardens* (public park).

SURROUNDINGS of Mechelen. – Some 5 km (3 miles) south-east near *Muizen* on the road to Louvain, is the *Plankendael Zoo*. 13 km (8 miles) to the west is *Fort Breendonck* (a concentration camp 1940–4, now a museum).

19 km (12 miles) west on the right bank of the Schelde, where the River Dender joins it, lies the town of **Dendermonde** with a population of 22,000

(Hotel het Gulden Hoofd, IV, 5 r.; Wets, V, 5 r.), and with several interesting architectural monuments and art treasures. In the Grote Markt stands the beautiful Town Hall, formerly the 14th c. Cloth Hall, rebuilt after a fire in 1914. The former Butchers' Guildhall (1416) now houses an Archaeological Museum. Next to the Town Hall stand the massive Law Courts of 1924 and further west the Gothic Church of Our Lady, dating from the 14th–15th c. The church contains two remarkable *paintings by van Dyck ("Crucifixion", c. 1630; and "Adoration of the Shepherds", c. 1632), a superb high altar (1638), and a 12th c. Romanesque font.

Valley of the Meuse/ Vallée de la Meuse

The Meuse near Profondeville

Country: Belgium.

(i) Union des Syndicats d'Initiative des Cantons de l'Est, Avenue Blonden 33, B-4000 Liège; tel. (0 41) 52 20 60. Haute Meuse Dinantaise, Avenue Franchet d'Esperey 17, B-5500 Dinant; tel. (0 82) 22 27 65.

HOTELS. – IN ANDENNE: *Le Barcelone*, Rue Brun 14, V, 6 r.; *Du Condroz*, Rue Léon Simon 1, V, 6 r. – IN ANNEVOLE-ROUILLON: *Auberge de la Poste*, Rue du Rivage 12, V, 8 r.; *Belle-Vue*, Rivages 11, V, 6 r. – IN HASTIÈRE-PAR-DELA: *De l'Abbaye*, Rue de Blaimont 3, V, 14 r.; *Le Valmeuse*, Route des Ardennes 8–9, V, 10 r. – IN PROFONDEVILLE: *Auberge d'Alsace*, Avenue Gén.-Garcia 42, IV, 6 r.; *Pont de Lustin*, Chaussée de Dinant 106, V, 8 r.; *Hostellerie du Parc*, Chaussée de Dinant 26, V, 8 r. – IN RIVIÈRE: *Safari*, Point de Vue des 7 Meuses 10, IV, 16 r.; *Meuse et Ardenne*, Chaussée de Dinant 23, V, 6 r. – IN WAULSORT: *Grand Hôtel Régnier*, IV, 50 r.; *Grand Hôtel de la Meuse*, IV, 15 r. – IN WÉPION: *Sofitel*, Chaussée de Dinant 195, II, 122 r.; *Jacques Borel*, II, 122 r.; *Le Wépion* (no rest.), Chaussée de Dinant 354, IV, 6 r.; *Frisia*, Chaussée de Dinant 311, V, 10 r.; *Le Néviau*, Chaussée de Dinant 232, V, 6 r.

The River Meuse (in Dutch, Maas) rises in France 456 m (1496 feet) above sea level on the high Plateau of Langres. It flows for 450 km (280 miles) on French territory, 192 km (119 miles) on Belgian territory and 258 km (160 miles) on Dutch territory, and finally flows into the North Sea.

If you visit the **lower part of the Valley of the Meuse** in Belgium, start in Liège and proceed upstream past the many blast furnaces, iron foundries and various factories. The valley here is fairly wide and much industrialised, but occasionally a ruined castle, a château or picturesque rock formations give it a certain charm.

Beyond **Huy** (see page 182), you travel through several attractive villages with old churches. Just before Namur there are beautiful limestone cliffs. Upstream from **Namur** (see page 222), which is overlooked by a massive citadel, the scenic *Upper Valley begins. It is lined with beautiful wooded slopes, sometimes bare rocks, and cuts deeply into the Plateau of the Ardennes. In July and August it is possible to make the journey by boat. In contrast to the lower part of the valley, there are very few factories. Villages and country villas nestle among steep hills and are very popular as vacation resorts. Among them should be mentioned *Profondeville*, beautifully set on the left bank opposite the *Rochers de Frênes*, and **Annevoie** with a château built in 1627 and enlarged in 1775. Here there is a superb French park with fountains and illuminations. On the right bank the principal place is the large village of *Yvoir* with a church dating from the 16th–18th c. as well as the former palace, now the Town Hall; both are worth a visit.

Château de Freyr on the Meuse

On the left bank lies *Bouvignes sur Meuse*, a village with a population of 1000. Before becoming a village it was one of the oldest towns in the area. It has an interesting church with a twin choir, built in the 13th c. To the north, on a steep rock above the village are the remains of the castle of *Crèvecœur*, built in 1320 and destroyed in 1554. Upstream is the town of **Dinant** (see page 136), and beyond it, 1 km (about a ½ mile) to the south on the right bank, the **Rocher Bayard*, a steep rock. According to the legend, the horse Bayard fleeing Charlemagne is said to have split the rock with a single kick of his hoof. Upstream on the left bank is *Freyr* with a **château* (16th–18th c.) and beautiful French gardens. Opposite are the *Rochers de Freyr*, rocks popular with climbers, and a cave.

Climbing on the Freyr rocks

Koudekerkseweg 200 (2 km (1 mile) on the road to Koudekerke).

EVENTS. – *Market* (every Thursday), and *Fair* (first week in August). On both occasions it is possible to see beautiful local costumes (still worn by the countryfolk).

Middelburg lies in the middle of the former Island of Walcheren on the Canal Veere-Vlissingen (Flushing). It is in the shape of a star and is surrounded by canals. As the capital of the province of Zealand, it is an important market town for the surrounding rural area. Tourism and industry, including electrical, chemical and metal processing plants, are important economic factors.

HISTORY. – Middelburg received its town charter in 1217, and developed in the Middle Ages into an important commercial city. It became famous through its cloth-making, and also as a depot for French goods. It has been the seat of a Bishop since 1561. At about that time its economic decline began. The silting of the Arne made the use of its harbour more and more difficult. In the 17th c., however, many merchants from Antwerp came to settle in Middelburg and the town found itself in competition with Amsterdam. This second period of prosperity of Middelburg came to an end under French occupation. The decline could not be arrested nor reversed even when in 1817 a new harbour dock was built. The old central portion of Middelburg was heavily damaged in the Second World War, but almost all its unique architectural monuments have since been restored.

SIGHTS. – In the Markt stands the **Town Hall* (*Stadhuis*), built by A. Keldermans the Elder in the 16th c. It is one of the most beautiful secular Gothic buildings in the country. It was almost

Middelburg

Country: The Netherlands. – Province: Zealand.
Altitude: sea level. – Population: 37,000.
Postal code: NL-4330 AA to 4379.
Telephone code: 0 11 80.
ⓘ **VVV Middelburg,**
Lange Delft 23,
NL-4331 AK Middelburg;
tel. 1 21 12.
VVV Zeeland,
Stroopoortgang 3,
NL-4331 AV Middelburg;
tel. 2 80 51.

HOTELS. – *Nieuwe Doelen*, Loskade 3–7, II, 55 b.; *Du Commerce* (no rest.), Loskade 1, II, 60 b.; *De Huifkar*, Markt 19, V, 20 b.; *Court Oxhooft*, Singelstraat 14, V, 35 b. – CAMP SITE: *Het Zand*, Koninginnelaan 55.

RESTAURANTS. – *'t Oude Coffijhuijs*, Markt 49; *Michel*, Korte Geere 19; *Visrestaurant Bij het Stadhuis*, Lange Noordstraat 8; *La Castelière*, Vlasmarkt 18; *Abdij*, Abdij 5; *Host. Kasteel Ter Hooge*,

The Town Hall in Middelburg

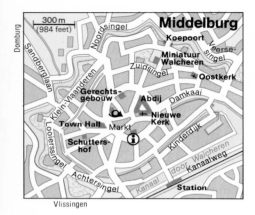

Middelburg

Vlissingen

the former Abbey is the **Zealand Museum** (*Zeeuws Museum*, open in summer only), with collections of antiquities, local costumes and natural history. The Gothic *Gistpoort*, an impressive gateway in the St Pieterstraat, also belonged to the Abbey.

From the St Pieterstraat via the ancient Balans Square, the former courtyard of the Crossbowmen's Guild (1582), you arrive at the Wagenaarstraat. Next to it, on the left of the Hofplein, are the *Law Courts* (1765) with wrought-iron window grilles.

In the north of the town on the Molenwater lies the **Miniatuur Walcheren** a model of the former Island of Walcheren with over 200 buildings in an area of some 7000 sq. m (8372 sq. yards). Nearby stands the *Koepoort* (Cowgate; restored in 1735), the only town gate remaining out of eight. To the south-east is the Baroque *Oostkerk* (1647–67, Dutch Reformed).

entirely destroyed in 1940, but has been restored and enlarged. Its façade (1512–13), most of which was preserved, is adorned with the statues of twenty-five Counts and Countesses of Zealand and Holland. Inside is an impressive Council Chamber with old paintings and tapestries by Flemish artists. West of the Town Hall, at the end of the Vlasmarkt at No. 5 Beddewijkstraat, stands the *Schuttershof*, which is the former Guildhall of the Corporation of Archers of St Sebastian. It was built in 1590 and now houses a Museum of Modern Art. Further southwest, beyond the Binnengracht is the *Kloveniersdoelen* (Hall of the Corporation of Arquebusiers), a Renaissance building dating from 1607–11 and restored in 1969.

North-east of the Markt lies the oldest part of the town, laid out in a circular plan. In the Groenmarkt stands the **Nieuwe Kerk** (former Abbey Church, Reformed), with a tower 85 m (279 feet) high ("de lange Jan", carillon), from which there is a surprisingly extensive view. Inside the church, the choir of which is detached (known as a *Koorkerk*), are the twin tombs of the Admirals C. and J. Evertsen (d. 1666), and the memorial plaques to the German King Count William of Holland (d. 1256) and his brother Floris (d. 1258). Adjacent to the church, on its northern side, is the *Abbey (Abdij)*, founded in the 12th c. The present picturesque buildings, adorned with a tower, date from the 13th–16th c. They were heavily damaged in the Second World War but have since been restored and are now occupied by the Provincial Government. They are grouped around the Abdijplein. In the north-west wing of

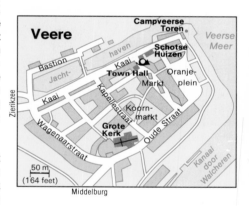

Veere

Middelburg

SURROUNDINGS of Middelburg. – 7 km (4 miles) north is **Veere** (Hotel De Campveerse Toren, IV, 40 b.), a colourful "little town on the north-east coast of the former Island of Walcheren. It is very popular with artists. Once a sizeable trading post, several beautiful old patrician houses testify to its period of prosperity in the early 16th c. The most impressive are the Scottish Houses (Schotse Huizen), which now contain a sizeable collection of antiquities. The Town Hall (c. 1470), has a superb façade adorned with statues and a tower. Inside is a small museum with interesting exhibits, among them the so-called Maximilian Cup (1551). There is an excellent view from the high tower of the large Church of Our Lady (15th–16th c.) Next to the church is a fine covered draw-well (1551).

Mons (Bergen)

Country: Belgium. – Province: Hainaut.
Altitude: 29–105 m (95–345 feet). – Population: 97,000.
Postal code: B-7000.
Telephone code: 0 65.

(i) **Office du Tourisme,**
Grand'Place 20;
tel. 33 55 80.
Fédération Provinciale de Tourisme,
Rue des Clercs 31;
tel. 31 61 01.

HOTELS. – *Europe* (no rest.), Rue Léopold II 7–9, IV, 22 r.; *Métropole*, Rue Léopold II 20, IV, 10 r.; *Résidence* (no rest.), Rue A. Masquelier 4, IV, 6 r.; *St Georges* (no rest.), Rue des Clercs 15, IV, 9 r.; *Du Parc* (no rest.), Rue Fétis 9, IV, 11 r.; *De la Cloche*, Place Léopold 9, V, 18 r. – 7 km (4 miles) north IN CASTEAU: *Eurocrest*, Chausseé de Bruxelles 38, III, 71 r. – IN MASNUY-ST-JEAN: *Amigo*, Chausseé Brunehault 4, II, 60 r. – YOUTH HOSTEL: Rue des Tuileries 7, 62 b.

RESTAURANTS. – *Devos*, Rue Coupe 7; *Le Vannes*, Rue Nimy 10; *Robert*, Boulevard Albert-Elisabeth 12; *Cuisine des Anges*, Rue Miroir 9; *Saey*, Grand'Place 12. – IN CUESMES: *Aquila*, Rue Frameries 74.

EVENTS. – *The Fight of the Knight Gille de Chin with a dragon* (a dramatised legend performed on Trinity Sunday).

The south Belgian town of Mons (in Flemish Bergen), lies on the crest of low hills between the rivers Haine and Trouille; it is the seat of the Provincial Government of Hainaut and the commercial and supply capital of the Borinage, one of the largest coal-mining and industrial districts in Belgium.

Mons is an important railway junction on the Brussels–Paris line. It has important cultural institutions, including the University, founded in 1965, the Royal College of Music, the Academy of Fine Arts, the Mining College, and other institutions of higher education, several first-class museums and a number of large libraries.

Industry plays only a modest role in the economic life of Mons. As well as textile and leather industries, there are also smaller pharmaceutical and metal-processing plants. The inland town-harbour, which is connected to the Schelde and to the Charleroi–Brussels Canal, handles mostly coal mined in the Borinage.

HISTORY. – Mons owes its origin to a monastery founded in the 7th c. by the Patron Saint of the town, St Waudru. The monastery and the castle of the

Counts on a hill formed the heart of the town. Mons is first mentioned in the Chronicles in 642. It was then called *Castri Locus*, and kept the name until the 12th c. Its peak period of prosperity was between the 13th and 15th c., but afterwards the town suffered heavily, particularly during the wars of the 17th and 18th c. From the end of the 17th c. it was held successively by the French, the Spanish and the Austrians and it came under siege repeatedly.

SIGHTS. – The town is surrounded by a ring of wide boulevards. Its central area, where all traffic converges, is the **Grand'Place**, still surrounded by several old houses. On its western side stands the **Town Hall** (*Hôtel de Ville*; 1459–67). Inside, on the ground floor, is a hall with Brussels tapestries (1707), the Salle de Mariages with old wooden panelling and a Gothic hall called the "Salle des Saquieaux" after the old name of the constabulary. Through the Town Hall you can enter the *Jardins du Mayeur*, where, in a former pawn shop (1622), is the **Municipal Museum** (*Musées du Centenaire*). It consists of a War Museum (1914–18 and 1940–5), a good collection of ceramics, an Archaeological Museum and a coin collection.

Nearby, to the west of the Grand'Place, at the highest point of the town and on the site of the old castle, is the **Square du Château** (*Castle Square*), with a good view over the surrounding area. On its south-western side stands the *belfry*, 84 m (276 feet) high, built in 1662–72, with a fine carillon of forty-seven bells (the oldest one dating from 1390). There is an elevator to the top. The British and Canadian War Memorial stands on the edge of the park. Designed by Lutyens it was unveiled in 1952 by Field Marshal Lord Alexander. To the north, opposite the belfry, in a former 17th c. Jesuit monastery, is the *public library* with 140,000 books, and 500 manuscripts. Further west is the *Musée Chanoine Puissant* with antiquities and ecclesiastical art.

Going south-west down the hill from Castle Square via the Rue des Clercs, you arrive at the large late Gothic **Collegiate Church of St Waudru** (15th–17th c.). The *interior, 108 m (354 feet) long, 36 m (119 feet) wide and 25 m (82 feet) high has sixty columns and is extremely well proportioned. The old stained-glass windows in the choir are of the 16th c. Parts of a rood screen (reliefs and statues) by Jacques Dubroecq, dating from

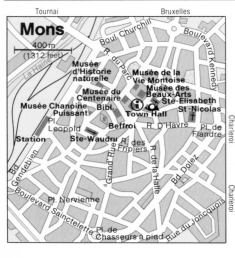

Map labels: Tournai, Bruxelles, Mons, 400 m (1312 feet), La Haine, Boul. Churchill, R. du Parc, Boulevard Kennedy, Musée d'Historie naturelle, Musée de la Vie Montoise, Musée du Centenaire, Musée des Beaux-Arts, Ste-Elisabeth, Musée Chanoine Puissant, Bibl., Town Hall, St-Nicolas, Pl. Leopold, Beffroi, R. D'Havre, Pl. de Flandre, Station, Ste-Waudru, R. des Fripiers, R. de la Hatte, Grand'Place, Bd. Dolez, Bd. Gendebien, Boulevard Sainctelette, Pl. Nervienne, Pl. de Chasseurs à pied, Rue du Joncquois, Charleroi, Charleroi

right is the **Museum of Fine Arts** (Musée des Beaux-Arts), devoted primarily to local art, and the *Folklore Museum* (Musée de la vie montoise). At the north-west end of the Rue Neuve, you come to the Rue du 11 Novembre, on the right-hand side of which is the *Park*. On the east side of the Park are the *State Archives* in the buildings of a former 17th c. monastery, with a former church dating from 1715.

On the right of the Rue de Nimy, running north-east from the Grand'Place, stands the 16th c. *Church of St Elizabeth* with a bell tower of the 18th c. and a notable organ loft. To the south-east in the Rue d'Havre is the *Church of St Nicolas-en-Havre* which dates from the 17th–18th c. In the choir are some outstanding wood carvings. The Rue d'Havre runs east to the Place de Flandre, in which stands an *equestrian statue of Baldwin I*, the Count of Hainaut and Flanders who in the 4th Crusade of 1204 became Emperor of Constantinople. Nearby to the east is the *Park Wauxhall*.

1535–48, are displayed in various places in the church; this screen was one of the most important Renaissance masterpieces in Belgium and was strongly influenced by Italian art. It was broken up by the French in 1792. In the treasury are valuable reliquaries, among them one of St Vincent from the School of Hugo d'Oignies (13th c.). In the north aisle is the Car d'Or, a gilded carriage from the 18th c. used in the annual procession on Trinity Sunday to carry the reliquary of St Vincent through the town.

In the north corner of the Grand'Place is the beginning of the Rue Neuve. On the

On the left of the Boulevard Dolez, running south-west from the Place de Flandre, are the premises of the *Mining Academy*. The main building of this Academy, further west in the middle of the town in the Rue de Houdain, houses a

Binche – "Gilles" in the Carnival Procession

Museum of Natural History (*Musée d'Histoire naturelle et de Géologie*). Especially worth seeing is the large palaeontological collection.

SURROUNDINGS of Mons. – 10 km (6 miles) north-east is the village of **Casteau** (Hôtel Eurocrest, III, 71 r.), with a 13th c. church, the ruins of a castle and some old farms. 3 km (2 miles) south-west of Casteau is the headquarters of the NATO forces in Europe (SHAPE).

22 km (14 miles) north-west of Mons is the village of **Beloeil** with a * château of the same name owned by the Princes de Ligne. It has been the property of the same family for over 600 years. The palace was burned down in 1900 and was rebuilt in its present form in 1902. Only the two side wings and the pavilions at the entrance were preserved in their original state. They date from 1682. The Château Beloeil contains several valuable collections, among them objets d'art, coins, a library and archives, but it is famous mainly for its unique gardens of 120 hectares (296 acres). Because of these the château is often called the Versailles of Belgium. The French gardens were laid out in the 17th c. and the English Park dates from the 18th c.

Binche is a little town with a population of 11,000, 16 km (10 miles) east of Mons. It is famous for its * carnival, in which hundreds of "Gilles" (clowns) in colourful costumes dance in a procession through the town. The carnival probably commemorates the feast given in 1549 by Mary of Hungary to celebrate the victory of Pizarro over the Incas of Peru. There is also the church of St Ursmer (12th–15th c.), the Town Hall with an old belfry, the remains of the 12th c. town wall and the Carnival Museum.

Mullerthal

(Valley of the Black Ernz)
(Vallée de l'Ernz Noire)

Country: Luxembourg. – Canton: Echternach.

(i) **Syndicat d'Initiative,**
L-Beaufort;
tel. (0 03 52) 8 60 61.

HOTELS. – IN MÜLLERTHAL: *La Réserve du Müllerthal*, Rue des Rochers 1, I, 50 r. *Central*, Rue de l'Ernz Noir 1, II, 17 r. – IN BEAUFORT: *Meyer*, Grand'rue 130, I, 44 r.; *Du Commerce*, Grand'rue 71, III, 23 r.; *Binsfeld*, Montée du Château 1, III, 17 r.; *St Jean* (no rest.), Grand'rue 95, III, 15 r.; *Cigrand*, Grand'rue 57, III, 8 r. – YOUTH HOSTEL. – IN BERDORF: *Bisdorff*, Rue de Heisbich 2, I, 45 r.; *L'Ermitage*, Route de Grundhof 44, II, 16 r.; *Parc*, II, 35 r.; *Kinnen*, III, 37 r.; *Du Pérécop*, Rue d'Echternach 80, III, 34 r.; *Herber*, Rue Principale 91, III, 34 r.; *Scharff*, III, 36 r.; *Dostert* (no rest.), IV, 21 r. – Several CAMP SITES.

The Black Ernz (in French Ernz Noire), is a little river in the Grand Duchy of Luxembourg, which rises some 10 km (6 miles) north-east of the capital and joins the Sûre between Diekirch and Echternach not far from Grundhof. The lower part of the river valley, the so-called * Mullerthal, is one of the most attractive excursion areas in Luxembourg. It lies in the southernmost tip of the German/Luxembourg Nature Reserve. Because of the deep river valley and steep sandstone rocks, it is also called the Switzerland of Luxembourg (La Suisse Luxembourgeoise).

The Mullerthal is accessible by a good road but the beautiful countryside can be better enjoyed if you leave the car, preferably in *Grundhof*, and take the footpath (to Mullerthal 3½–4 hours). The path rises steeply to the left and then runs along the eastern edge of the Ernz Valley which is lined with the sandstone rocks of the * **Schnellert**. The most remarkable rock formations are the *Kasselt* (355 m (1165 feet), view), the *Siebenschlüff*, seven narrow clefts with sheer walls, the *Zickzackschlüff* and the *Adlerhorst* (a ladder down into a robbers' cave). Further on is the *Hölle*, a cleft in the rock approximately 60 m (197 feet) long, the *Binzeltschlüff* on the other side of the road to Berdorf, the *Predigtstuhl* split by deep ravines, the *Wehrschrumschlüff*, the *Eisgrotte*, and, shortly before Mullerthal, the *Keltenhöhle*, where prehistoric remains have been found.

The hamlet of **Mullerthal** is located at a junction of several roads where the Ernz Valley becomes wider. 9 km (6 miles) to the west in the Valley of the White Ernz is the village of *Larochette*; 10 km (6 miles) south on the main road from Luxembourg to Ernz is *Graulinster*, and 3 km (2 miles) further south-east *Consdorf*. In the lovely surroundings of Mullerthal there are several interesting ravines where good walks can be taken.

You can get from Grundhof to Beaufort by road (6 km – 4 miles). The road first goes in the direction of the Mullerthal up to the bridge on the Ernz, then winds uphill through the woods, and some ½ km (about a ¼ mile) south of the bridge reaches a park in which stands the *Château of Grundhof*. Another way is to take the footpath which also starts at the Ernz bridge. It turns right out of the Mullerthal and is much more attractive than the road (from Grundhof to Beaufort, 1½ hours). The path first leads through

Mullerthal (The Valley of the Black Ernz) – Waterfall "Les Cascades"

the *Hallerbachtal* past numerous rock formations, waterfalls, and lush vegetation, then turns right and up into the picturesque ravine of *Haupeschbach*. On reaching the top one has an unexpected view of the ruined castle *Beaufort* or *Befort* (12th–16th c.) and the *New castle* (17th c.). A little further up you reach the village of **Beaufort**, a very popular summer resort.

The road from Grundhof to Berdorf (6 km (4 miles), more interesting to walk via *Schnellert, 3¾ hours) branches off the Mullerthal road to the left after the Ernz bridge. It then runs rather steeply uphill through the woods and crosses the plateau above. You then arrive at the beautifully situated summer resort of **Berdorf**, with an old Parish Church, visible from afar. In this church below the high altar is a Roman altar with four reliefs of deities. The village is a starting point for the charming Valley of the *Eschbach. In its upper part, ¾ hour to the south, is *Hollay*, an enormous hollowed rock known locally as "The Roman Grotto", with old millstone quarries probably used in the Roman era. From Berdorf you can take the road through the pretty lower part of the Ehsbach Valley with several picturesque ravines on both sides; then downhill and 4 km (3 miles) further you join the Sûre Valley road.

The ruined castle of Beaufort (Luxembourg)

Naarden

Country: The Netherlands. – Province: North Holland.
Altitude: 0–10 m (0–33 feet). – Population: 17,000.
Postal code: NL-1410 AA to 1412.
Telephone code: 0 21 58.
ⓘ **VVV Naarden,**
    Markstraat 11,
    NL-1411 CX Naarden;
    tel. 4 28 36.

HOTELS. – *Euromotel Naarden*, Amersfoortsestraatweg 92, I, 105 b.; *De Doelen*, III, 11 b.; *De Beurs*, III, 15 b.

RESTAURANT. – *Auberge le Bastion*, St Annastraat 3.

EVENTS. – *Festival Week* (last week in August); *a performance of St Matthew's Passion* (Good Friday in the Grote Kerk).

Naarden is an attractive little town, formerly the chief town of Gooiland. It lies on the IJsselmeer in the Dutch province of North Holland and has star-shaped fortifications designed by the French military architect Vauban (1633–1707).

The old fortress town was mentioned as early as the 10th c. Its port was constructed in 1411 and it soon became important in the fishing trade. It lost this function when the harbour had to be closed because of reconstruction of the fort. A later period of prosperity was brought by the cloth trade. Today it is mainly a residential town in the commuter belt of the capital Amsterdam, 20 km (12 miles) away. Tourism is also an important economic factor.

SIGHTS. – The town is dominated by the 14th–15th c. **Grote Kerk** (*St Vituskerk*) in the Marktstraat. Inside is an interesting choir screen (1518). In the same street is the beautiful *Renaissance Town Hall* (1602) with rich interior decoration. Near the Turfpoortstraat is the so-called *Comenius Chapel* housing the tomb of the preacher, pedagogue, and leader of the Bohemian Brethren, John Amos Comenius (Komensky; 1592–1670), who spent the last years of his life in exile in Holland. The *Comenius Museum* is in the "Spaanse Huis" at No. 27 Turfpoortstraat.

Naarden – the fortress city in North Holland

The *Fortification Museum* in the citadel (Westwalstraat), has an interesting collection of weapons and uniforms.

Within the area of the town on the south bank of the IJsselmeer is the well-known nature and bird sanctuary Naardermeer. It is a reed-covered swampy area which is a paradise for ornithologists.

Namur (Namen)

Country: Belgium. – Province: Namur.
Altitude: 83 m (272 feet). – Population: 35,000 (Greater Namur 100,000).
Postal code: B-5000.
Telephone code: 0 81.

ⓘ Syndicat d'Initiative,
Square Léopold;
tel. 22 28 59.

HOTELS. – *Grand Hôtel de Flandre*, Place de la Gare 14, III, 36 r.; *Queen Victoria*, Avenue de la Gare 11–12, III, 20 r.; *Le Fourquet*, Avenue Albert 1er, IV, 6 r.; *La Poule d'Or*, Place du Théâtre, IV, 10 r.; *Balmoral*, Avenue Félicien Rops 40, IV, 7 r.; *Au Coq d'Or*, Rue de Fer 139, V, 15 r.; *De Charleroi*, Place de la Gare 21, V, 13 r.

RESTAURANTS. – *Côté Jardin*, Rue de la Halle 2; *Rive Gauche*, Boulevard Baron Huart 28; *Marignan*, Carrefour Porte-de-Fer 1. – IN BENZET: *Le Chef*, Chaussée de Namur 4. – IN MALONNE: *Relais du Roi Louis*, Chaussée de Charleroi 18.

Namur, in Flemish Namen, is the capital of the Belgian province of the same name. It lies at the confluence of the Sambre and the Meuse and is the starting point for visitors to the picturesque Upper Meuse Valley.

Namur already had military significance in the Roman era, and it was fortified very early. From the 10th c. it was the main town of a county which was acquired by Burgundy in 1420. It became the seat of a Bishop in 1559. The town suffered many sieges so that almost no old buildings have survived. With its outer forts, built in 1889–1902, Namur became one of the key strategic points in the Belgian defence line on the Meuse, but was conquered by the Germans both in 1914 and in 1940. It manufactures glass, porcelain, enamel, paper and steel products, most of which are based in the suburb of Jambes.

SIGHTS. – The old town lies on the left bank of the Sambre and the Meuse. Here in the Place St Aubain stands the **Cathedral** (*St Aubain*), a large domed structure in Classical style (1751–67), with a bell tower (1273). In its beautiful, light interior are statues by L. Delvaux d. 1778), a wrought-iron 18th c. choir

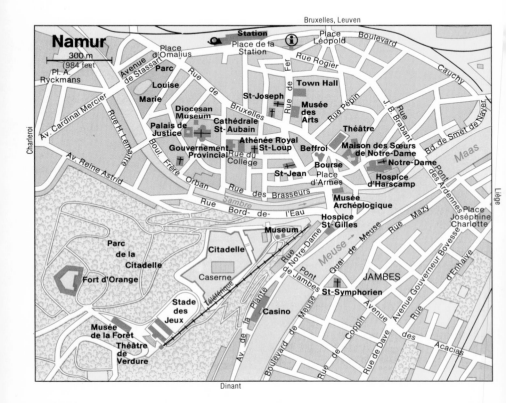

screen, and behind the high altar a memorial plaque to Don Juan de Austria who died near Namur in 1578 and whose body was transferred in 1579 to the Escorial near Madrid. Next to the choir of the Cathedral, on the right, is the *Musée Diocésain* with the valuable treasury of St Aubain (the exhibits include the "hat of St Peter", believed to date from the 11th c.).

To the north behind the Cathedral in the Place du Palais de Justice are the *Law Courts* (17th c.) with the Government Archives. Opposite the Cathedral on the corner of the Place St Aubain and the Rue du Collège, is the *Provincial Palace* (Gouvernement Provincial) built in 1726–40 as the residence of the Bishop. At the end of the Rue du Collège on the left stands the former Jesuit **Church of St Loup**, built in 1621–53. It is the most important ecclesiastical building in the town and has a rich Baroque decoration. Next to it on the left is the old Jesuit College, now the *Athénée Royal*, with a beautiful courtyard (1611).

The Rue de la Croix, which is the eastern continuation of the Rue du Collège, joins the busy line of streets consisting of the Rue de Fer and the Rue de l'Ange, running south from Leopold Square (at the station) across the old town to the Place d'Armes. On the right, set slightly back, is the **Church of St Jean**, the only surviving Gothic building in Namur (15th c.), with a Baroque interior. On the north side of the Place d'Armes, the busiest square in town, stands the *Stock Exchange*. Behind it is the *belfry*, built over the remains of the old Jacob tower. It was part of the 14th c. second town wall. The *Convent of the Sœurs de Notre-Dame*, further east in the Rue J. Billart, possesses a magnificent treasury with several 13th c. masterpieces by Friar Hugo d'Oignies.

East of the Place d'Armes is the *Hospice d'Harscamp*, a former Franciscan Nunnery, and the Baroque Church of *Notre-Dame*, rebuilt in 1750–6, with the tombs in the crypt of the Counts William I and William II of Namur (d. 1391 and 1418 respectively). South of the Place d'Armes, to the left of the Sambre bridge, is the brick building of the former *Butcher's Hall* (Ancienne Boucherie; 1560), now the **Archaeological Museum**. It contains a good collection of local antiquities. Next to it, on the east, is the *Palais de la Culture* (1964).

Beyond the Sambre bridge you come via the "Pointe de Grognon", the oldest part of the town, to the Avenue Baron Louis Huart, which skirts the Meuse. At the confluence of the Sambre and the Meuse stands the *equestrian statue of King Albert* (1955); on the right is the *Hospice St Gilles* (16th–17th c.). In its chapel is the interesting tombstone of the sculptor Colard Jacoris (1395). Further upstream is the **old bridge** (*Pont de Jambes*, damaged in the War, rebuilt), which connects Namur with its suburb Jambes. Still further south, in Avenue Baron de Moreau, is the **casino** (1911) and a park called *La Plante*.

A historic mortar in the Citadel of Namur

The town is dominated by the **Citadel** which stands on a rocky spur between the Sambre and the Meuse, and which has been fortified since the Roman era. It can best be reached by a cable way 2·2 km (1 mile) long, or by tram (streetcar) from the station via the suburb of "Salzinnes". It can also be reached by car either from the War Memorial on the right bank of the Sambre up the Route des Panoramas (*views), or from the casino by the equally scenic Route Merveilleuse. At the top of the hill, occupying an area of 65 hectares (161 acres) is a beautiful park, a large *sports stadium* (Stade des Jeux), an *Open-air Theatre*, a *Forestry Museum* (Palais Forestier) and an *amusement park*. Here too is the *Château de Namur*, visible from afar, and an observation tower. A little below are the 17th c. buildings of the Citadel, now partly barracks. At the northern bastion which the road skirts on the inner side, are two medieval towers housing the *Museum of Arms, Armour and Military History*.

SURROUNDINGS of Namur. – Leaving the town from the station in a westerly direction by road No. 22, you reach first the suburb of *Salzinnes*. 6·5 km (4 miles) from the middle of the town a road branches off to the left to the old **Abbey Malonne**, which lies to the south in a wooded ravine and has a church in the so-called Jesuit style of 1651. Another 4 km (3 miles) away from Namur is the village of **Floreffe**, where the former Premonstratensian Abbey is one of the best preserved old abbeys in Belgium. It was founded in 1121 and is now a seminary. The present buildings date from the 18th c. The church was originally Romanesque and was rebuilt in the 17th–18th c.

An interesting excursion can be made into the *Upper Meuse Valley (see page 214) and to **Dinant** (see page 136). In July and August it can also be made by boat (3½ hours).

Nieuwpoort (Nieuport)

Country: Belgium. – Province: West Flanders.
Altitude: 0–9 m (0–30 feet). – Population: 8000.
Postal code: B-8450.
Telephone code: 0 58.
ⓘ **Dienst voor Toerisme en Cultuur,**
   Marktplein 7;
   tel. 23 55 94.

HOTELS. – In NIEUWPOORT-BAD: *Parkhotel*, Albert I Laan 177, IV, 21 r.; *Léopold*, Albert I Laan 268, IV, 12 r.; *Cosmopolite*, Albert I Laan 144, IV, 30 r.; *Le Phare*, Albert I Laan Ö92, IV, 15 r.; *Centrale* (no rest.), Kaai 11, V, 8 r. – In NIEUWPOORT-STAD: *De l'Yser*, Sluizen 10, V, 10 r. – Numerous BOARDING HOUSES in Nieuwpoort-Bad. – CAMP SITE.

RESTAURANTS. – In NIEUWPOORT-BAD: *Jan Turpin*, Albert I Laan 68a; *Ter Polder*, Victorlaan 17; *Windhoek*, Albert I Laan 153. – In NIEUWPOORT-STAD: *De Kwinte*, Kaai 50; *Visserke*, IJzer 5.

EVENTS. – Numerous *Art Exhibitions* in the Fishmarket; also permanent Art Exhibitions at: *Henri Vancraeynest*, Oostendestraat 8; *Galerij Caroline*, Zeedijk 14; *Arc en Ciel*, Albert I Laan 207. – *Carillon Concerts*; mid-July–mid-September, Wednesday and Saturday, 8.30–9.30 p.m.; Friday, 11.15–11.45 a.m.; mid-September–mid-June, Sunday and Friday, 11.15–11.45 a.m. – In summer, *various entertainments* (programme can be obtained from the Dienst voor Toerisme). – Folklore: *Witches' Pageant* (third Sunday in May); *Homage of the Fishermen* (Whit Monday); National *Day of Homage to King Albert and the Heroes of the IJzer* (Yser) (first Sunday in August); *The Procession of St Bernard* (last Sunday in August). – Also, *International Deep Sea Fishing Competition, Tennis Tournaments, Sailing Regattas*.

SPORTS and LEISURE. – Basket and volleyball, bowling, table tennis, riding, speed skating (artificial ice track), sailing, tennis, angling, shooting, water sports.

The Belgian town of Nieuwpoort, in French Nieuport, lies in the province of West Flanders on the River Yser,

3 km (2 miles) from its estuary in the North Sea.

Nieuwpoort is an important fishing port (also oyster farming and deep sea fishing), and the headquarters of fish processing. In the economic life of the town, metal processing and chemical industries also play a significant part. The same applies to tourism which is concentrated at Nieuwpoort-Bad, a part of the town lying some 3 km (2 miles) north among the North Sea dunes. The importance of tourism is reflected in the size of the yacht harbour which ranks among the largest on the North Sea coast. At present it has a capacity of 900 moorings which will soon be extended to 2600.

Nieuwpoort Yacht Harbour

HISTORY. – Nieuwpoort was founded in the 12th c. by Count Philip of Flanders to replace Lombardsijde as a fortified new port for Ypres after the Yser had changed its course. In the course of centuries it endured ten sieges. In the First World War it held a key position in the Yser line – since it had six locks by which the entire Yser area could be flooded. After the War the town had to be completely rebuilt.

SIGHTS. – The vast Grote Markt with a *belfry* and the *Cloth Hall* (1280), partly preserved and partly rebuilt, provides an attractive picture. In the lower hall there is now an interesting *ornithological museum* containing a remarkable collection of sea birds and crustaceans. In the upper hall is a *War Museum* (1914–18) and the *Pieter-Braecke Museum* (sculptures). The *Town Hall* was rebuilt in 1922. Behind it stands the *Church of Our Lady*, which was destroyed in both World Wars, but each time rebuilt in its original Gothic style of the 15th c. In the detached tower is a carillon of sixty-seven bells. Nearby, north-west of the Grote Markt in No. 18 Kokstraat, is the *Municipal Museum of Ethnography*.

Nijmegen

Country: The Netherlands. – Province: Gelderland.
Altitude: 10–25 m (33–82 feet). – Population: 214,000.
Postal code: NL-6500 AA to 6599.
Telephone code: 0 80.

ⓘ **VVV Rijk van Nijmegen,**
Keizer Karelplein 34,
NL-6511 NH Nijmegen;
tel. 22 54 40.

HOTELS. – *Schaeferhotel* (no rest.), Grote Markt 39, I, 33 b.; *Sionshof*, Nijmeegsebaan 53, III, 50 b.; *Rozenhof*, Nijmeegsebaan 114, IV, 34 b.; *Rondeel*, Bloemerstraat 1, V, 26 b. – CAMP SITE: *De Kwakkenberg.*

RESTAURANTS. – *In d'Oude Laeckenthal*, Grote Markt 23; *St Stephens*, Oranjesingel 1; *Belvédère*, Kelfkensbos 41.

FLEA MARKET. – St Stevenskerkhof, Mondays 9 a.m.–1 p.m.

The town of Nijmegen lies in the south of the Dutch province of Gelderland, approximately 7 km (4 miles) from the German border. It has a Catholic University and, together with nearby Arnhem, it is one of the two gateways to the Netherlands on the Lower Rhine. The town lies on the left bank of the Waal, which is the southern branch of the Rhine delta. It is dominated by seven hills, the terraced slopes of which look from afar like the tiers of a giant amphitheatre.

Nijmegen is, after Arnhem, the most important town of the Gelderland province. There are numerous administrative offices, educational and research institutes linked to the University. Several business enterprises, together with vegetable and flower markets, also play an important role.

Nevertheless, the decisive factor in the economy of Nijmegen is its industry. Its demand for labour is sufficient to make the town the hub of a large commuter area. The principal areas of employment are in metal-working, electrical engineering, textiles, food and chemicals.

The Port of Nijmegen on the Waal is accessible to ships of up to 6000 tons. This makes it one of the most important points on the inland waterway between Rotterdam and the Ruhr Basin. As a transshipment port it is of regional importance for the Gelderland province.

HISTORY. – Nijmegen was a Roman settlement known as *Batavodurum*, and later as *Noviomagus*. In the Carolingian era it was the Imperial residence and later an Imperial and Hanseatic city. In 1579 it joined the Union of Utrecht. In 1585 it surrendered to the Spanish, but in 1591 was retaken by Maurice of Nassau. In 1678 the Peace Treaty between France and the Netherlands was signed here. The period of economic prosperity of Nijmegen began only with the age of industrialisation, after its fortifications had been destroyed in 1877–84. In the Second World War the central part of the town in particular suffered heavy damage. Its reconstruction, mostly in modern style, has been completed. In the Arnhem Operation of 7–25 September 1944, the Bridge over the Waal at Nijmegen was one of the targets. Its capture was duly effected, but the plan for airborne troops to link up with the British troops at Arnhem failed.

SIGHTS. – In the middle of the old town is the Grote Markt. In it stands the *Waag*, built in 1612, originally the Municipal Weigh-house and Meat market, now used as an exhibition hall. From here to the west via the attractive *Kerkboog* (church archway; 16th–17th c.), you arrive at the **Grote** or **St Stevenskerk** (13th–15th c., Reformed). It was heavily damaged in the Second World War. The tower and the façade were rebuilt and the interior was restored in 1969. In the choir is the tomb of Catherine of Bourbon (d. 1469), the wife of the Duke Adolphe of Geldern. In the churchyard stands the old *Latin School* (1544).

North of the Grote Markt is the **Commanderie van St Jan** (originally 1196), which since 1974 has housed the *Municipal Museum* (Gemeente-Museum). East of the Grote Markt on the right-hand side of the busy Burchtstraat stands the **Town Hall** (1554–1882; restored and enlarged in 1953), with an interesting

The Market Square at Nijmegen

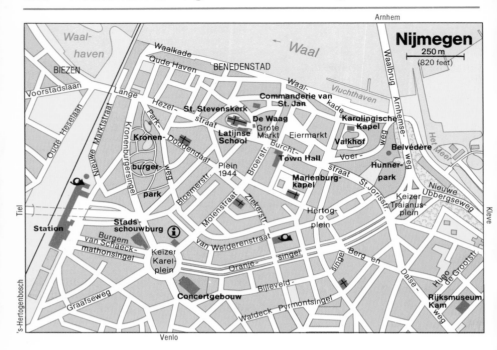

interior. The Burchtstraat leads east from the Town Hall to the *Valkhof, an attractive park on a rise by the Waal. It is laid out on the site of the former Imperial stronghold, founded in 768 by Charlemagne. Under the Saxon, Frankish and Staufen dynasties, it was often the seat of the Imperial Court. Here the Empress Theophano, wife of Emperor Otto II, died in 991, and here in 1165 Henry VI, the son of Frederick Barbarossa and Beatrix of Burgundy, was born. Of the palace only the *Carolingian chapel*, consecrated in 799 by Pope Leo III, now remains. Southeast of here are the ruins of a Romanesque choir apse believed to date from the time of Barbarossa (1155). There is a beautiful view over the Waal plain from the chapel. Not far east of the Valkhof at the north end of the Hunnerpark, stands the *Belvedere*, which is visible from afar. It is a former 16th c. rampart tower from which there is an extensive view (restaurant). From the Hunnerpark the impressive 700 m long (2296 feet) **Waal bridge** leads to the suburb of LENT on the other side. The best view of Nijmegen is to be had from this bridge. From Lent you can take the highway to Arnhem.

South of the Hunnerpark lies the busy Keizer Traianusplein from which, to the south-east, you can reach the Mariaplein and the Berg en Dalseweg via the Meester Franckenstraat. Left, at No. 45 Museum

Kamstraat, is the **Rijksmuseum Kam**, housing an important collection of Roman and prehistoric antiquities, mostly from the Nijmegen area.

SURROUNDINGS of Nijmegen. – To the Heilig-Land-Stichting and to Bergen Dal (8 km – 5 miles). To the east of Nijmegen extends pleasant rolling wooded country, criss-crossed by several roads and many footpaths. You leave the town from the Keizer Karelplein by the Groesbeekseweg in a south-easterly direction, and continue along the edge of the woods. In 4 km (3 miles) you arrive at a crossroads, turn left, and in 300 m (330 yards) left again to the *Heilig-Land-Stichting (Holy Land foundation; 50 hectares (124 acres)). This is a graphic replica of the holy places to be found in the New Testament (guided tours, restaurant). From the Hill of Calvary there is a beautiful view. – The road to Berg en Dal then crosses the *Meerwijk* where there is a small lake. 4 km (3 miles) further comes **Berg en Dal** (Parkhotel Val Monte, I, 172 b.; Erica, II, 47 b.; Hamer, II, 24 b.), a pretty summer resort lying on the crest of a hill with an extensive view. There is an interesting African Museum. East of Berg en Dal near the German border, there are far-ranging views from the *Duivelsberg* (76 m (250 feet), café) overlooking the *Wijlermeer*.

Nivelles (Nijvel)

Country: Belgium. – Province: Brabant.
Altitude: 99 m (325 feet). – Population 16,000.
Postal code: B-1400.
Telephone code: 0 67.

ⓘ **Syndicat d'Initiative et de Tourisme**,
Hôtel de Ville,
Place Albert 1er;
tel. 22 54 13.

HOTELS. – *Nivelles-Sud (Motel)*, Chaussée de Mons 22, III, 60 r.; *L'Aigle d'Or*, Place L. Schiffelers 5, IV, 10 r.

RESTAURANTS. – *Restaurant de la Collégiale*, Avenue Léon Jeuniaux 2; *L'Ortolan*, Chaussée de Mons 2; *Restaurant de la Gueulardière*, Faubourg de Mons 96; *Restaurant de l'Union*, Grand'Place; *Restaurant des Arts*, Grand'Place 51; *Restaurant Le Pascal*, Grand'Place 3.

Nivelles lies in the south of the Belgian province of Brabant, amid rolling fertile agricultural country. Although severe bombing in 1940 reduced some 20% of all buildings to rubble, among them historic monuments of inestimable value, the town recovered very quickly after the Second World War. It developed from an agricultural base into a modern industrial town. The most important branches of industry are metal-working, the manufacture of railway equipment, machinery and paper-making.

The Sloping Lock at Ronquières near Nivelles

HISTORY. – The history of the town goes back to the earliest centuries of the Christian era. It experienced its first period of prosperity when Pippin the Elder, the high steward of King Dagobert I, made it his residence. His widow founded a convent here about 645 and her daughter Gertrude became its first Abbess. At the beginning of the 16th c. Nivelles was a flourishing city with a population of about 20,000 and eight guilds. The destiny of the town has always been linked with the history of the convent, and when this was closed down in 1798 the decline of the town began. In 1815 Nivelles was besieged by the troops of the Dutch General de Perponcher. In the First World War, Nivelles was spared, but in 1940 about 20% of the town (50% of the old town), was destroyed.

SIGHTS. – The former *Convent Church of St Gertrude* in the Market Square, was consecrated in 1046. It is one of the best examples of Romanesque architecture in Belgium. The unique feature of its ground plan are the two choirs and twin transepts. The massive 12th c. western tower was probably built over an earlier Ottonian structure. In the Sacristy are fragments of the famous **Shrine of St Gertrude*, which, before its destruction in 1940, was one of the most precious works of the Gothic goldsmiths. Only one-third of the figurines and adornments could be salvaged. Of the sculptures on the *portals* there remain only the lintels, with scenes from the Legend of Samson on the north door and the Archangel Michael on the south door. The *crypt* (*c*. 1100) is underneath the east choir. It is the largest in Belgium (22 m × 10·5 m – 72 feet × 34 feet). The beautiful *cloisters* next to the church are a transitional work dating from the beginning of the 13th c. From that period, however, only the north gallery remains in its original state.

SURROUNDINGS of Nivelles. – To the west, on the *canal from Charleroi to Brussels* is the village of **Ronquières**, with an interesting *sloping elevator, or lock, for ships, consisting of two large water tanks 1430 m (4690 feet) long, each capable of carrying boats up and down a difference in height of 68 m (223 feet).

North Brabant/ Noord-Brabant

Country: The Netherlands – Province: North Brabant

ⓘ **VVV Noord-Brabant en Streek,**
VVV West-Brabant,
Willemstraat 17,
NL-4811 AJ Breda;
tel. (0 76) 22 57 33.
VVV 's-Hertogenbosch en de Meijerij,
Markt 77,
NL-5211 JX 's-hertogenbosch;
tel. (0 73) 12 30 71.
VVV Hart van Brabant,
Spoorlaan 440,
NL-5038 CH Tilburg;
tel. (0 13) 43 61 31.
VVV Kempenland,
Stationsplein 24,
NL-5611 AC Eindhoven;
tel. (0 40) 44 92 31.

The Dutch province of North Brabant comprises the entire southern

part of the so-called "Geest Holland", with the exception of a narrow strip in the east which forms part of Limburg. The region is bordered in the north and east by the Maas; in the west it merges into the Schelde marshes in Zealand. In the south North Brabant ends at the Belgian frontier (Brabant and Kempen; see pages 104, 183.).

The southern part of Geest Holland is a monotonous plain between 5 and 35 m (16–115 feet) above sea level, running into the region of Kempen on the Belgian side. Its geological subsoil consists of substantial layers of gravel deposited by the rivers Rhine and Maas in the course of many hundreds of thousands of years. In the last Ice Age the entire area was covered by a layer of sand. In the east, near the German border, the **Peel** was then formed, one of the many high moors characteristic of the lowlands of north-west Germany. The Peel is now almost entirely cultivated and developed.

What was once the heathland of North Brabant is now mostly agricultural land. Approximately 12% of its entire area has been planted with pine woods; approximately 80% is used as farmland. The soil, though inferior, permits the growth of such undemanding crops as rye, oats, potatoes and ordinary feed plants for dairy farming. Also important is pig and poultry farming. Hamlets and small villages with well-kept farms are characteristic of rural settlements.

North Brabant has a fairly high population density with about 300 people per sq. km (777 per sq. mile). This figure shows that industry plays a predominant role in its economy. The traditional cloth-making around **Tilburg** (see page 252), and **Eindhoven** (see page 141), has been supplemented since the beginning of the century by manufacturing industries of all kinds. The best known example is the Philips complex in Eindhoven. The Geest towns of Brabant, among them the capital of the province **'s-Hertogenbosch** (see page 177), as well as *Roosendaal* and **Bergen op Zoom** (see page 101), have three distinct advantages over the fen areas of the country and these have helped to promote its industrial development: a large available labour force, low

cost land, and the ability to employ more economic building methods than in the swampy marshlands.

The North-East Polder/ Noordoostpolder

Country: The Netherlands. – Province: Overijssel.

ⓘ **Prov. VVV Overijssel en VVV Twente,** De Werf 1, NL-7607 HH Almelo; tel. (0 54 90) 1 87 65. **VVV West-Overijssel,** Grote Kerkplein 14, NL-8011 PK Zwolle; tel. (0 52 00) 1 89 77.

The Dutch region known as the North-East Polder in the furthest north-west of the province of Over-ijssel, is a marshy area of 47,600 hectares (117,620 acres). The land was reclaimed in the years 1937–42 from the IJsselmeer into which it projects from the east as a peninsula. In the south the Polder is separated by the narrow inlets of the Ketelmeer and the Zwartemeer from the neighbouring Flevoland and from the mainland. In the north it reaches the altitude of De Lemmer. Its eastern border forms a narrow tongue-shaped strip of Geest running from south-east to north-west.

The level of the fertile marshland lies between 4·5 and 5·70 m (15–19 feet) below sea level; the area has been drained by means of a complicated system of canals, locks and pumping stations. Three draining canals run from Emmeloord in the middle of the Polder to De Lemmer in the north, to the former IJsselmeer island of Urk in the south-west, and to Voort, neart Vollenhove, in the south-east. The pumping stations and the locks are located here.

The fertile new land was divided by the Government into 1600 lots farmed by as many leaseholders, each having between 12 and 48 hectares (30–119 acres). The principal crops are sugar-beet, grain, rape seed, flax and legumes. In the south-east, flowers, fruit and vegetables are also grown.

THE RECLAIMING OF LAND ON THE IJSSEL-MEER. – The vast project of draining the former **Zuiderzee**, which originally had an area of 5250 sq. km (2026 sq. miles), was designed by Lely, and the Dutch Government began to put it into effect in 1920. In 1924, the *Amsteldiep*, present-day *Amstelmeer*, was the first stretch of water to be enclosed by a dam, so that the former Island of *Wieringen* was connected to the mainland. Then to the south the *North-West* or *Wieringermeer-Polder* (20,000 hectares – 49,420 acres) was laid out and completed in 1930. It was originally intended as an experimental area. In 1932 the **Enclosing Dike** (*Afsluitdijk* see page 65); 30 km (19 miles) long, was completed and this separated the IJsselmeer from the North Sea and made it again into a tideless inland freshwater lake. In 1942 the *North-East Polder* between the islands of Urk and Schokland and the mainland, was completed; in the autumn of 1956 the 90 km (56 miles) long dike of the polder of East Flevoland, was finished (area of 54,000 hectares – 133,434 acres). North of Gooiland emerged the polder of *South Flevoland* which, together with East Flevoland, forms the *South-East Polder*. Another polder, *Markerwaard* or the *South-West Polder*, between the islands of Marken and Enkhuizen is planned. The *IJsselmeer* (110,000 hectares – 271,810 acres), which remains in the middle, is the estuary area of the IJssel. It is connected to the North Sea by two locks in the Enclosing Dike and serves as a huge reservoir for periods of drought. It will be connected with the *IJmeer* (6800 hectares – 16,803 acres) by a narrow channel between the South-West and the South-East Polder. The IJ will be dammed before Amsterdam in order to maintain coastal shipping, and also to be able to flood the country should this be necessary for its defence.

From Kampen to De Lemmer (35 km – 22 miles). The road towards Sneek leaves Kampen by a bridge over the *IJssel*, on to the right bank (good view back to the town) and then follows a wide canal. 8 km (5 miles) beyond Kampen you cross the *Ramsdiep* by a long bridge with twin bascules. The Ramsdiep is a bay of the **IJsselmeer** created by the estuary of the *Zwarte Water*. Then you continue straight on across the North-East Polder. In 3 km (2 miles) you reach *Ens* a neat polder village lying to the east of the road. Turn left past some attractive farms to the new settlement of **Schokland**, 3 km (2 miles) west, which lies on the site of the former island in the Zuiderzee. Some 200 m (220 yards) left of the road to Urk there is a museum standing in a group of trees. It is in a former church and contains a collection of prehistoric finds made during the draining of the Zuiderzee. 13 km (8 miles) further west, on the bank of the IJsselmeer, is the small fishing harbour of **Urk** (Hotel 't Wapen van Urk, 30 b.). It

was originally an island and still keeps its traditional Dutch character (picturesque traditional costumes). On the main road to Sneek, 9 km (6 miles) past Ens, is a bascule bridge across the *Urkervaart*. At the next road junction the road from *Steenwijk* (26 km – 16 miles) enters from the right, and on the left is the road to Urk on which, 1 km (about a $\frac{1}{2}$ mile) west, is **Emmeloord** (Hotel 't Voorhuys, I, 52 b.), the new main town of the North-East Polder with a population of 8000. From the above-mentioned junction the road to Sneek then follows the Canal *Lemster-vaart* and winds its way to a bay of the IJsselmeer. A further 15 km (9 miles) brings you to **De Lemmer** (population 7000; Hotel De Wildeman, III, 38 b.; Centrum, V, 20 b.), an important port on the IJsselmeer for inland shipping.

Ostend/Ostende/Oostende

Country: Belgium. – Province: West Flanders.
Altitude: sea level. – Population: 72,000.
Postal code: B-8400.
Telephone code: 0 59.

ⓘ **Officieel Bureau**
   voor Toerisme en Feesten,
   Wapenplein 3;
   tel. 70 11 99 and 70 60 17.

HOTELS (some of them closed in winter). – AM DEICH: *Andromeda*, Albert I Promenade 60, I, 60 r.; *Thermae Palace*, Koningin Astridlaan 7, I, 110 r.; *Bellevue-Britannia*, Albert I Promenade 55–56, II, 58 r.; *Royal Albert*, Zeedijk 167, IV, 20 r.; *Die Prince* (no rest.), Albert I Promenade 41–42, IV, 46 r.; *Royal Midland*, Zeedijk 354, IV, 24 r.; *Marsouin*, Albert I Promenade 87, IV, 20 r.
IN TOWN: *Ter Streep* (no rest.), Leopold II Laan 14, II, 38 r.; *Ambassadeur*, Wapenplein, 8A, III, 24 r.; *Strand Hotel* (no rest.), Visserskaai 1, III, 20 r.; *Westminster*, Van Iseghemlaan 22, III, 60 r.; *Ter Kade* (no rest.), Visserskaai 49 III, 30 r.; *Riff* (no rest.), Leopold II Laan 20, III, 28 r.; *Danielle*, IJzerstraat 7, III, 25 r.; *Prado* (no rest.), Leopold II Laan 22, III, 32 r.; *Ensor* (no rest.), Kapucijnenstraat 27, III, 24 r.; *Impérial*, Van Iseghemlaan 76, III, 62 r.; *Viking*, Boekareststraat 2, IV, 25 r.; *Europe*, Kapucijnenstraat 52, IV, 60 r.; *Pacific*, Hofstraat 11, IV, 50 r.; *Ostende Palace Hotel*, Londenstraat 6, IV, 180 r.; *Pick's*, Wapenplein 13, IV, 16 r.; *Du Parc* (no rest.), Marie-Joséplein 3, IV, 54 r.; *Queen Mary*, Van Iseghemlaan 40, IV, 12 r.; *Terminus Maritime*, Natienkaai 2, IV, 25 r.; *Des Alliés*, Visserskaai 36, IV, 18 r.; *Nouveau Coq d'Or*, Hofstraat 1a, IV, 46 r.; *Métropole*, Kerkstraat 32, IV, 63 r.; *Stella Maris*, Vindictivelaan 17, IV, 85 r.; *Royal Astor*, Hertstraat 15, IV, 94 r.; *Glenmore*, Hofstraat 25, IV, 50 r.; *Derby*, Van Iseghemlaan 1, IV, 16 r.; *Georg V* (no rest.), Vlaanderenstraat 42, V, 50 r.; *Motor-Inn* (no rest.), Visserskaai 7, V, 23 r.; *Carlton*, Koningsstraat 75–77, V, 57 r.; *Melbourne*, Koningsstraat 70–72, V, 38 r. – Several BOARDING HOUSES.

YOUTH HOSTEL: Raversijdestraat 20, 218 b. – Two CAMP SITES.

RESTAURANTS. – *Périgord*, im Casino; *Grill Freddy*, Albert I Promenade 9; *Prince Charles*, Visserskaai 19.

EVENTS. – Ostend offers a great deal of entertainment throughout the year. In winter (November–April) there are many lectures, film and slide shows, concerts, theatrical and other performances; Gastronomic weekends; Exhibitions and Sporting Competitions.

Seaside Show (January); *Trade Fair for Beach, Garden, Camping and Leather Goods* (January); *Trotting Races* (April); *International Motor Rally for Tourists* (April); *International Relay Race* (April); *Festival of Women* (Easter); *Carillon and Kiosk Concerts* (Easter); *Homage of the Fishermen* (Easter Monday); *Trotting Races* (May); *Spring Night Horse Show and Trotting Races* (May); *International Motor Rally "Night of Ostend"; The Ostend Fair* (May); *Benelux Amateur Film Festival* (May); *International Rowing Competition* (May); *International Festival of Percussion Bands* (Whitsun – seventh Sunday after Easter); *International Angling Competition* (May); *International Basketball Tournament; Carillon Concerts* (June–August); *International Sailing Regattas, Gymnastics, etc.* (July and August); *"The Six Days of the St Paul's Square"* (August); *International Riding and Show Jumping Tournament* (August); *"Rally der Vlaanderen"* (Veteran Cars, September).

SPORTS and LEISURE. – Angling, billiards, bowling, golf, sailing, keep-fit, riding, cycling, roller skating, rowing, shooting, swimming, gliding, tennis, waterskiing, etc.

Ostend (in Flemish Oostende; in French, Ostende), on the Belgian North Sea coast in the province of West Flanders, is the most important seaport in Belgium. It was originally a village at the east end of the coastal stretch called Ter Streep, on the western tip of which is the village of Westende. In the 15th c.

Ostend Harbour

Ostend was fortified. At the end of the 16th c. it was the last stronghold of the Dutch in the Southern Netherlands, but it surrendered in 1604 after three years of valiant defence in which 72,000 men lost their lives. The town acquired a new status from the middle of the 19th c. because of its seaside resort, now the largest in Belgium and one of the most popular in Europe. It is also the principal port for passenger and car ferry services to England (Dover and Folkestone).

In the First World War, Ostend and Zeebrugge were German submarine bases and suffered much damage. In the Second World War, the town was bombed several times and almost all its important buildings were damaged. The great tidal wave of 1953 broke through the dike between Ostend and Knokke-Heist and caused considerable flooding. It was, however, possible to repair all the damage in a very short time.

The Ostend deep sea fishery is the most important in Belgium (there are three specialised schools of fishery). Oyster farming has been practised in Ostend since 1763. Associated industry includes shipyards and fish processing plants and is, next to tourism, the most important factor in the city's economy.

SIGHTS. – The main line of streets in the old town runs from the commercial docks in the south, north-west to the dike and is called first the Kapellestraat and beyond the Wapenplein, the Vlaanderenstraat. Not far east of the Kapellestraat stands the **Church of St Peter and Paul**, originally built in the 14th c. and in 1896–1905 restored, after a fire, in the neo-Gothic style. The burial chapel of the first Belgian Queen Louise-Marie, who died in Ostend in 1850, was built on to the choir. Next to the church is a brick tower which is the only remaining part of the old church. In front of the church is a War Memorial. In the Wapenplein is the **Festival Hall** (*Feestpaleis*), which stands on the site of the Old Town Hall (1711) which was destroyed in the Second World War. The belfry is 63 m (207 feet) high (carillon; open in July and August). Inside the Festival Hall are a library and a Museum of Fine Arts which includes paintings by James Ensor. In the western part of the

Oostende

300 m
(984 feet)

Noordzee

Staketsel
Havengeul
Staketsel

Vuurtorensteenweg

Visserij-dok

Tijdok

Zeewezendok

Montgomerydok

Albert I. Promenade
Lange Straat
Wapen-plein
Groente-markt
Kursaal
Monaco-plein
str. Adolf Buylstr.
Feestpaleis
Ooststraat
Kapellestraat
Visserskaai
Ferry Terminal

Railway Station

Albert I. Promenade
Koning
Leopold-Laan
Leopold-Plein
Leopold-park
St. Petrus en Paulus
Leopold III. Laan
Voorhaven

Zeedijk
Koning Steenweg
Leopold I Plein
Euphrosine Beernaertstr.
Vindictivelaan
Mercator
Slachthuiskaa

Konink. Residentie
Thermae
Astrid-laan
Wellingtonstr.
Pieterslaan
Vuurkruisen-plein
Town Hall
Graaf de Smet de Naeyerlaan
Conterdamkaai
Knokke-Heist

Mariakerke, Flughafen
Koningin
Sportstraat
Alfons
Petit-Paris-plein
St.-Jozef
Rome straat
Kairostraat
Verenigde Natieslaan
3 en 23 Linieregiments-plein

Hippodroom
steenweg
Steenweg
Prinses Stefaniepl.
Koninginnelaan

Wellington
Heilig Hart
Prof. Mac Leobplein
Frère Orbanstraat
Maria-
Hendrika-

Nieuwpoort-
Suiverstraat
Steenbakkersstr
Torhoutse
Leffinge-
straat
Park

Lille   Brugge, Gent

town is the **Leopold Park** with a fine flower clock and mini-golf. North-west of the park is the small Leopoldplein with an equestrian statue of King Leopold I.

The *dike (Zeedijk) 7·5–10 m (25–33 feet) high and 30 m (99 feet) wide, built of large blocks of stone on the dunes, lines the seashore for 15 km (9 miles) as far as Westende. The oldest part, between the Sailors' Memorial and the Kursaal, forms a bulge protected against the impact of the waves and erosion of the soil. In the bend of the dike above the main bridge stands the **Kursaal**, built in 1876–8, enlarged several times, and completely reconstructed in 1950. Inside are a large concert hall with 1700 seats, exhibition and reading rooms, a casino, a restaurant, etc. Further west on the dike is the *Chalet Royal* (Koninklijke Residentie), built on an eminence by King Leopold II, and completely restored in 1956–7. The seaside resort owes much of its reputation to the encouragement of the King, whose equestrian statue stands in front of the Chalet. Next to it is a 500 m (1640 feet) long *colonnade*, with a glass hall. In the middle of the colonnade stands the **Palais des Thermes**, built in 1930–3 with sections for hydro, helio- and electro-therapy, and with an alkaline well 352 m (1155 feet) deep. There is also an indoor swimming pool. Opposite, to the west, is the *Wellington Hippodrome*, restored between 1947 and 1953, and beyond this, still really part of Ostend, is the village of *Mariakerke*, with an old Gothic brick church and an airport.

Joined to the dike, north-east beyond the Seamen's Memorial, are the **Staketsel**, two piers jutting into the sea which were built to protect the entrance to the harbour. The western pier, 625 m (2050 feet) long with a café, is a popular promenade. The **harbour** contains several large and small docks, and extends some 2 km (about a mile) inland as far as the opening of the Ostend–Bruges Canal.

The **railway station** (*Station Oostende-Kaai*, with boat connections to Dover) is located at the 800 m (2624 feet) *outer harbour*, east of the old *commercial port* (Handelsdok I and II) and south of the old town. Nearby in the new yacht harbour is the former Belgian training ship, the three-masted "Mercator".

Further east, beyond the *naval docks* (Zeewezendok) and the *Tijdok* is the **fishing harbour** *(Vissershaven* or *Vlotdok)*. On its west side is the fishmarket (*Vismijn*), where every morning a fish auction, supervised by a municipal officer, takes place when the boats return. South of the outer harbour are the *industrial docks*.

In the southern part of the old town extends the **Maria-Hendrikapark** covering an area of 50 hectares (124 acres) and encircled by the highway access route. In it is a tall *water tower*, several lakes with boating facilities, and a café/restaurant. Nearby, to the north-west, stands the new *Town Hall* (Stadhuis). Along the north-east side of the park runs the Graaf de Smet de Naeyerlaan which, further east, crosses the harbour area by a series of massive flyovers (overpasses) (view). Nearby is the memorial to the English cruiser "Vindictive" (bow and two masts of the ship), which was sunk in 1918 between the piers to block the entrance into the harbour.

East of the harbour entrance and of the fishing harbour rises the **New Lighthouse** 56 m (184 feet) high (*Vuurtoren*). Beyond it extend the dunes with remains of fortifications from the two World Wars. The *Fort Napoleon* dates from the Napoleonic era. Behind it is the *Instituut voor Zeekuur*.

Oudenaarde (Audenarde)

Country: Belgium. – Province: East Flanders.
Altitude: 14 m (46 feet). – Population: 28,000.
Postal code: B-9700.
Telephone code: 0 55.
ⓘ **Dienst voor Toerisme,**
   Stadhuis;
   tel. 31 14 91.

The Town Hall in Oudenaarde.

HOTELS. – *Elnik*, Deinzestraat 55, IV, 14 r.; *De la Pomme d'Or*, Markt 62, IV, 7 r.; *De Zalm*, Hoogstraat 4, V, 8 r.; *Tijl*, Stationsstraat 60–62, V, 8 r.

EVENTS. – The *Adriaan-Brouwer Feast*, a large traditional festival (last Sunday in June).

Oudenaarde (in French Audenarde) has several beautiful buildings dating from the late Middle Ages. On 11 July 1708 Marlborough and Prince Eugene defeated the French army under Vendôme near Oudenaarde. The town was famous earlier for its carpet weaving, and its tapestries are still an attraction.

SIGHTS. – The magnificent *Town Hall* in the Market Place was built in 1526–37 by H. van Peede in Flamboyant Gothic. Its tower is 40 m (131 feet) high. Especially interesting is the Council Hall, adorned with unique tapestries with motifs of trees, peacocks, pheasants and castles, mostly on a green background. North of the Town Hall is the old *Cloth Hall* (13th c.), now a Museum of Local Tapestries (guided tours). In the south-west corner of the market stands the *Church of St Walburga* (12th–14th c.), with a Gothic nave and a tower 88 m (289 feet) high (carillon). On the right bank of the Schelde stands the Church of *Onze Lieve Vrouw Pamele*, built in the Schelde Gothic style (begun 1235). Also worth mentioning is the *Hospital*, with a chapel (1409), and the old *Bishop's House*, with the 11th c. Tower of Baldwin (Boudewijnstoren). The Bishop's House was the birthplace of the Governor General, Margaret of Parma (1522–86), the daughter of Emperor Charles V by a servant girl.

Valley of the Ourthe/Vallée de l'Ourthe

Country: Belgium. – Provinces: Luxembourg, Namur, Liège.

ⓘ Fédération Touristique
du Luxembourg Belge,
Quai de l'Ourthe 9,
B-6980 La Roche-en-Ardenne;
tel. (00 32 84) 41 13 75.
Syndicat d'Initiative,
Rue Halle aux Blés,
B-5480 Durbuy-sur-Ourthe;
tel. (00 32 86) 21 24 28.
Syndicat d'Initiative,
B-6660 Houffalize-sur-Ourthe;
tel. (00 32 62) 28 81 16.
Syndicat d'Initiative
et de Tourisme,
Hôtel de Ville,
B-6980 La Roche-en-Ardenne;
tel. (00 32 84) 41 13 42.
Ourthe et Aisne,
Rue du Baty 8,
B-5450 Hotton;
tel. (0 84) 46 62 04.
Ourthe-Néblon,
Avenue Blonden 33,
B-4000 Liège;
tel. (0 41) 52 20 60.

HOTELS. – In LA ROCHE-EN-ARDENNE: *De l'Air Pur*, Route de Houffalize 11, II, 14 r.; *Le Vieux Château*, Pesserue 6, III, 13 r.; *Des Ardennes*, Rue de Beausaint 1, III, 12 r.; *Belle Vue*, Avenue de la Gare 10, IV, 22 r.; *Des Genets*, Corniche du Deister, IV, 11 r.; *Moderne*, Rue Chamont 26, IV, 11 r.

YOUTH HOSTEL in Hotton. – CAMP SITES in Barvaux, Durbuy, Grand-Han, Hotton, Houffalize, Marcourt, Ortho and Rendeux.

The Ourthe is a river in East Belgium, 130 km (81 miles) long. It has two sources in the Ardennes, the Ourthe Orientale and the Ourthe Occidentale which unite near the village of Engreux. The Ourthe then flows north-west through a steep deeply cut valley and later north across the high plateau of the Ardennes and the regions sometimes described as the Fore-Ardennes, Famenne and Condroz. It joins the Meuse near Liège.

The Valley of the Ourthe ranks among the most picturesque regions of Belgium. The banks of the river are lined with numerous tourist resorts, the largest and most important of which is the little town of **La Roche-en-Ardenne** (altitude 223 m (731 feet), population 4000). It is situated where several side valleys meet the Ourthe Valley, and is dominated by a

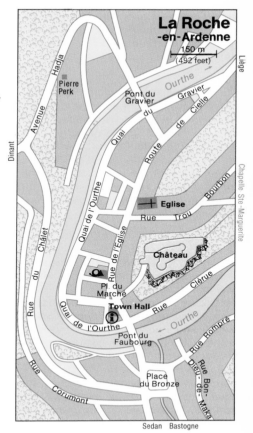

Sedan   Bastogne

ruined castle. It is the starting point for various excursions. The best *view of the town and valley, as well as of the landscape of the Ardennes, is from the rugged hill to the west, the *Montagne de Corumont*, which is surrounded by the Ourthe. An interesting excursion of 12 km (7 miles) to the east of La Roche on the N560 runs first upstream along the Ourthe for 6 km (4 miles), as far as *Maboge*, then 4 km (3 miles) away from the river up to the plateau towards *Nadrin*, and from here a further 2 km (about a mile) downhill again into the Ourthe Valley to the wooded slate rock *Le Hérou (*Rocher du Hérou*), which is 1400 m (4592 feet) long, and on two sides drops straight down into the Ourthe. From here there is a footpath (approximately $1\frac{1}{2}$ hours) upstream on the right bank of the river to the confluence of the two branches of the Ourthe, amid charming, wooded countryside.

12 km (7 miles) east of Nadrin is the small town of **Houffalize**, a pleasant summer resort in the Valley of the Ourthe Orientale. In Houffalize there is an interesting

early Gothic Parish Church and the remains of a medieval castle. Enjoyable walks in the beautiful surrounding countryside can be made from the town.

7·5 km (5 miles) from La Roche-en-Ardenne, downstream along the Ourthe in the direction of Liège, on a rounded hill on the left is the small Chapel of *St Thibaut*, a place of pilgrimage. On the other side of the river is the vacation resort of *Marcourt* (population 650) which was formerly the principal town of the old county of Montaigu (1050). There are several interesting houses dating from the Spanish era, and a 14th c. church.

On the border between the regions of the Ardennes and the Famenne lies the village of *Hotton* (population 2000). This village has apparently existed for thousands of years. Remains from the Neolithic Age and from the Roman era were found in the vicinity. There is a magnificent view over the Ardennes and the Famenne from a steep rock overlooking the village. On one side is wooded hilly country and, on the other, vast stretches of meadows and pastures. Also interesting is a *stalactite cave* discovered in 1958.

10 km (6 miles) downstream is **Durbuy**, known as the smallest town in Belgium, with a population of only 320. It nestles pleasantly on both banks of the Ourthe and most of it is closed to vehicles. Its narrow lanes and old houses together with the remains of the town wall give the impression that time has stopped here. The castle of the Counts of Ursel, the old Cloth Hall, the Law Courts and the 16th–18th c. Parish Church are all of interest.

The N34 leaves the Valley of the Ourthe beyond Durbuy. A pleasant excursion can be made 3 km (2 miles) to the east in the valley to the village of **Bomal** (population 1000). Here the Ourthe is joined by the River Aisne which flows through a romantic rocky valley. Bomal is the starting point for numerous walks, and there is also a well-signposted circular drive.

De Panne (La Panne)

Country: Belgium. – Province: West Flanders.
Altitude: 0–5 m (0–16 feet). – Population: 7000.
Postal code: B-8470.
Telephone code: 0 58.

(i) **Dienst voor Toerisme,**
Gemeentehuis,
Zeelaan 19–21;
tel. 41 13 02 and 41 13 04.

HOTELS. – *Strandmotel*, Nieuwpoortlaan 153, III, 51 r.; *Du Parc*, A. Dumontlaan 30, III, 48 r.; *Seahorse* (no rest.), Toeristenlaan 7, III, 20 r.; *Val Joli*, Barkenlaan 55, III, 23 r.; *Ambassadeurs*, Duinkerkelaan 43, III, 36 r.; *Astoria*, Zeedijk 49, III, 23 r.; *Terlinck*, Zeelaan 173, III, 55 r.; *Royal*, Zeelaan 178–180, IV, 35 r.; *Sablon*, Duinkerkelaan 19, IV, 26 r.; *Des Princes*, Nieuwpoortlaan 46, IV, 36 r.; *Europe*, Meeuwenlaan 60, IV, 30 r.; *Cecil*, Marktplaats 14, IV, 15 r.; *Artevelde*, Sloepenlaan 24, IV, 28 r. – Several BOARDING HOUSES. – Several CAMP SITES.

RESTAURANTS. – *A la Bonne Auberge*, Zeedijk 3; *Le Catinou*, Bortierplaats 1; *Dunepanne*, Dynastielaan 60; *L'Ecailleur*, Sloepenlaan 27; *Poulet de Malines*, Zeelaan 57; *Prado*, Nieuwpoortlaan 44; *Le Président*, Nieuwpoortlaan 32; *Westdiep*, Dynastielaan 34.

EVENTS. – Entertainment every week during the summer months.

SPORTS and LEISURE. – Water sports, sand-yachting, riding, tennis, etc.

ENTERTAINMENT. – *Amusement Park Meli* on the road to Adinkerke.

The Belgian seaside resort of De Panne (in French La Panne), nestles pleasantly in a dune valley. It was once a fishing village patronised by artists, but it quickly developed into a modern vacation resort with many amenities.

The town became famous in the First World War because it was the only unoccupied part of Belgian territory. King Albert of Belgium resided here while his Government moved to Le Havre.

SIGHTS. – De Panne has the widest **beach** (400 m (438 yards) at low tide) of the entire Belgian coast. The beach extends as far as Nieuwpoort 12 km (7 miles) away, and to Dunkerque (17 km – 11 miles) in France. The brothers Dumont constructed their first sand yacht here more than eighty years ago, and by doing so they founded a new kind of sport (sand yacht racing) for which the beach of De Panne is uniquely suited.

De Panne – The beach on the Belgian North Sea Coast

Behind the 1 km (about a $\frac{1}{2}$ mile) long paved dike extend the **Oosthoek Dunes** which are partly wooded and ideal for enjoyable walks. The dunes are sometimes called by the locals "The Sahara" because of their vast expanse. They cover an area of 640 hectares (1581 acres).

SURROUNDINGS of De Panne. **To Dunkerque** (20 km – 12 miles). You first take road No. 72 from De Panne in a south-easterly direction inland. After 1·5 km (1 mile) you reach *Duinhoek* with a Belgian and British Military Cemetery. From here you can either use a secondary road via the French villages of *Bray-Dunes* and *Zuydcoote*, which have been the scenes of hard fighting in the past, to Dunkerque, or you can continue on road No. 72 which is faster and better. 1·5 km (1 mile) further on you reach *Adinkerke*. At the end of the village is the Belgian frontier and customs control. Proceed west along the canal; after 3 km (2 miles) you cross the *Belgian–French frontier* and then follow Route Nationale No. 40 to the French frontier and customs control, 6 km (4 miles) beyond Adinkerke. From here it is 11 km (7 miles) to **Dunkerque**, the well-known French port (population 45,000) and the scene of heavy fighting in both World Wars. (In 1940 345,000 allied soldiers were evacuated from the beaches here.)

Roermond

Country: The Netherlands. – Province: Limburg.
Altitude: 20 m (66 feet). – Population: 37,000.
Postal code: NL-6040 AA to 6099.
Telephone code: 0 47 50.
ⓘ **VVV Roermond,**
Kloosterwandplein 12,
NL-6041 JA Roermond;
tel. 1 32 05.

HOTELS. – *De la Station*, Stationsplein 9, III, 24 b.; *Cox*, Maalbroek 102, III, 22 b.

RESTAURANTS. – *Kraanpoort*, Kraanpoort 1; *Tin-San*, Varkensmarkt 1. – In BOUKOUL (6 km (4 miles) from the town): *Graeterhof*, Graeterweg 23.

The town of Roermond in the province of Limburg lies at the confluence of the Roer and the Maas. It is an important Dutch cultural and economic base in the northern part of the Dutch frontier district, sandwiched between Belgium and the Federal Republic of Germany.

Among the most important cultural institutions in Roermond are the Bishopric, founded as early as 1569, and the Episcopal Seminary connected to it, as well as agricultural schools, several museums and libraries. The town also has an important Chamber of Industry and Commerce, and a large market for agricultural products. The widely diversified industries in Roermond include metal works, electrical engineering, chemicals, textiles, paper manufacture and food processing (there is an important mushroom canning plant).

HISTORY. – Roermond is mentioned for the first time in the middle of the 12th c. under the name of Ruregemunde. It developed rapidly and obtained town status in 1230. Shortly afterwards it became the main town of the Upper quarter of the Geldern, and joined the North German Hanseatic League in 1441. It belonged to the Habsburgs from 1543 to 1794 and in 1839 became part of the Netherlands.

Munsterkerk in Roermond

SIGHTS. – Roermond still has the charac-ter of a typical Limburg town. In its midst stands the magnificent *Munsterkerk. This former Convent Church of Cistercian Nuns is built in the transitional style from Romanesque to Gothic, and was con-secrated in 1224. The building was restored in 1864–91 by the well-known architect P. J. H. Cuypers. Under the crossing is the tomb of Gerard III of Nassau, Count of Geldern (d. 1229), and his wife Margaret of Brabant (13th c.). In the Market Place stands the 15th c. Cathedral of *St Christoffel*. The cathedral was destroyed in the Second World War and subsequently rebuilt. Also interesting is the *Municipal Museum* at No. 8 Andersonweg. It has valuable collections of old weapons as well as paintings. The Kapellerlaan runs south along the Roer to the *Redemptorist Chapel* (Kapel in 't Zand, 1·5 km (1 mile) away). In it is the miraculous image "Onze Lieve Vrouw in 't Zand". 4·5 km (3 miles) further south in the Roer Valley is the village of *St Odilienberg* with an interesting Roman-esque church; inside is a beautiful statue of the Virgin (1300).

Rotterdam

Country: The Netherlands. – Province: South Holland.
Altitude: Sea level. – Population: 1,031,000.
Postal code: NL-3000 AA to 3099.
Telephone code: 0 10.
ⓘ VVV Rotterdam,
Stadhuisplein 19,
NL-3012 AR Rotterdam;
tel. 13 60 00.
Further Information:
Centraal Station (Central Station),
Station Hall;
tel. 13 60 06.
Informatiek,
Shopping Complex Zuidplein.

HOTELS. – *Rotterdam Hilton*, Weena 10, L, 487 b.; *Parkhotel*, Westersingel 70, I, 146 b.; *Rijnhotel Rotterdam DMP*, Schouwburgplein 1, I, 240 b.; *Central*, Kruiskade 12, I, 115 b.; *Savoy Golden Tulip Hotel*, Hoogstraat 81, I, 200 b.; *Atlanta Golden Tulip Hotel*, Aert van Nesstraat 4, I, 250 b.; *Euromotel Rotterdam*, Vliegveldweg 61, I, 250 b.; *Van Walsum*, Marthenesserlaan 199, II, 44 b.; *Het Witte Paard*, Groenezoom 245, III, 14 b.; *Pax* (no rest.), Schiekade 110, III, 90 b.; *Baan* (no rest.), Rochussenstraat 345, III, 26 b.; *'s-Gravenburg*, 's-Gravendijkwal 100–102, III, 56 b.; *Heemraad* (no rest.), Heemraadssingel 90, III, 24 b.; *Gare du Nord*, Villapark 7, III, 22 b.; *Emma* (no rest.), Nieuwe Binnenweg 6, IV, 50 b.; *Scandia*, Willemsplein 1, IV, 93 b.; *Zuiderparkhotel*, Dordtse-straatweg 483, IV, 162 b.; *Wilgenhof*, Heem-raadsingel 92–94, IV, 77 b.; *Holland* (no rest.), Provenierssingel 7, IV, 50 b.; *De Gunst*, Brieselaan 190–192, IV, 23 b.; *Commerce*, Henegouwerplein 56–62, IV, 80 b.; *Astoria*, Pleinweg 205, IV, 20 b.; *Bavri* (no rest.), 's-Gravendijkwal 70–72, III, 34 b.; *Europa* (no rest.), Snellinckstraat 1, IV, 40 b.; *Simone* (no rest.), Nieuwe Binnenweg 162a, IV, 17 b.; *Breitner* (no rest.), Breitnerstraat 23, V, 22 b.; *Bienvenu* (no rest.), Spoorsingel 24, V, 18 b.; *Floris*, Graaf Floristraat 68–70, V, 60 b.; *Het Wapen van Charlois*, Doklaan 59, V, 19 b.; *H. van de Woude* (no rest.), Graaf-Floristraat 99 a, V, 32 b.; *Geervliet* (no rest.), 's-Gravendijkwal 14, V, 32 b.; *Metropole* (no rest.), Nieuwe Binnenweg 13a, V, 22 b.; *Vernon* (no rest.), Heemraadssingel 324, V, 26 b.

YOUTH HOSTEL. – Rochussenstraat 107–109, 160 b.; CAMP SITE: Kanalweg.

RESTAURANTS. – *Coq d'Or*, Van Vollenhovenstraat 25; *Old Dutch* (traditional Dutch furnishings), Rochussenstraat 20; *Euromast*, Parkhaven 20.

FLEA MARKET. – Binnenrotte (Tuesday and Satur-day, 10 a.m.–5 p.m.).

"SPIDO" HARBOUR CRUISE (from Willemsplein). – *Harbour Cruise:* Merwehaven, Eemhave, Maashaven (daily, approximately 1¼ hours); *Long Cruise:* Rot-terdam, Schiedam, Vlaardingen, Pernis, Botlek (daily from April to September, approximately 2¼ hours); *Evening Cruise:* by boat around the docks of Rotterdam (in July and August, every Friday, from 8 p.m., approximately 2¼ hours); *Rotterdam–Europoort:* Boat trip around the new dock area as far as the sea (in July and August, every Friday, from 10 a.m. 5½ hours); *Rotterdam–Deltaworks:* interesting tour of the water-ways with view of modern industrial plants, bridges, locks, etc. (July and August, Monday–Thursday, from 10 a.m., approximately 9 hours).

The port of Rotterdam in the Dutch province of South Holland is the second largest city in the country. It lies on both banks of the Nieuwe Maas (the southern branch of the Rhine). Here the river receives a small tributary, the Rotte; the North Sea tidal area extends a good dis-tance upstream. The difference in water level between high and low tides is between 1·20 and 2·50 m (3·9 and 8·2 feet).

Since the inauguration of the "Europoort" harbour area in 1966, Rotterdam is the world's largest *port in volume of goods handled. The city has developed into a gigantic transit complex for commerce and industry, and its potential for growth is still strong. The major imports are crude oil, ores, grain, timber and fats. Exports are primarily coal and food. In addition, Rotterdam is an important trans-shipment place for raw tobacco. The main industries include shipbuilding, with the largest shipyard in Europe, machinery, rolling stock, bicycles, electrical engineering, petro-chemicals (the largest plant on the Continent), food processing, clothing and paper-making, etc. The rapid development of Rotterdam is due to its extraordinarily favourable position on a waterway having access to the North Sea. This waterway is open all year round and needs no locks. Ships up to 90,000 tons, and with a draught of up to 12 m (39 feet) can enter the port.

The Inner City of Rotterdam was almost completely destroyed by German air-raids in 1940. Energetic reconstruction, with modern shopping streets, residential areas and high-rise buildings, has made Rotterdam one of the most modern cities in Europe. – The central area of the city is surrounded by the districts of Kralingen in the east, Delfshaven in the west, and Feijenoord in the south, which, in turn, are enclosed by outer suburbs (such as Overschie, Hillegersberg, IJsselmonde and Pernis). The Hook of Holland is still part of the city area, but Schiedam, Vlaardingen and Maassluis are independent. Together with its surrounding satellite towns, Rotterdam is a highly

The Port of Rotterdam in Figures	
Ships from more than 90 countries; more than 12,000 regular departures annually.	

Annual Turnover of Goods (Million metric tons)	
Sea-going Shipping	280
Mineral oils, oil products	175
Ores	32
General cargo	28
Grain	23
Containers	12
Inland Shipping	110
Transit	
By sea	56
By inland waterways	58
By road	5
By rail	3
By pipeline	41

600 km (375 miles) Docks
400 km (250 miles) Harbour railroad tracks
32 million cu. m (1130 million cu. feet) tank storage capacity

395 Dock cranes
35 Container cranes
15 Roll-on, Roll-off ramps
87 Oil ramps

518 Tugs
35 Floating and dry docks

Number of Employees in the Port Area:	
Port	13,000
Transport	25,000
Petro-chemical industries	23,000
Metal industry	50,000
Construction industry	35,000

Approximately a third of the total of 4,500 Dutch customs officers work in Rotterdam.

The Port of Rotterdam

industrialised urban area with a population far exceeding 1 million.

HISTORY. – Rotterdam developed from an early medieval settlement. It began to expand in the 13th c., when the little River Rotte was separated from the New Maas by a dam. Thus the name Rotterdam. The town received its charter in 1340. Soon after it was linked by a canal to the then important commercial town of Delft, and began to benefit from the prosperity of that town. In this first period of prosperity, the most famous citizen of the town was born, the humanist Erasmus of Rotterdam (born c. 1465 – died 1536 in Basle). Most of Rotterdam was destroyed by fire in 1563. The second development phase only began when many thousands of refugees from the Spanish Netherlands settled in the town in 1585. Cloth-making and carpet weaving contributed greatly to its economic progress. The port was less important then, handling only about a fifth of the goods which were loaded for Amsterdam in the 17th c. Expansion of the harbour began after the separation of Belgium when

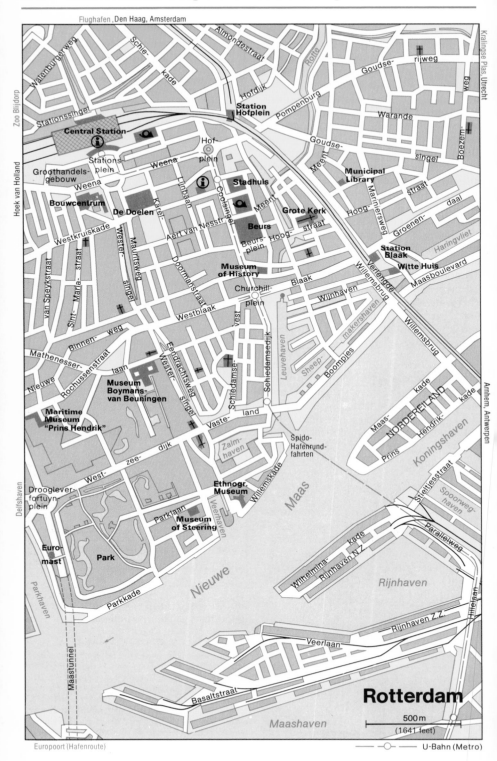

Flughafen ,Den Haag, Amsterdam

Rotterdam

500 m
(1641 feet)

Europoort (Hafenroute)

—— —○—— U-Bahn (Metro)

the Dutch closed the estuary of the Schelde (1830–9). The obstacle for large ships presented by the silting of the Maas estuary was removed a little later (1866), when the Nieuwe Waterweg was constructed and steadily deepened. At the mouth of the Maas, on the North Sea coast, grew the new suburb of the Hook of Holland.

SIGHTS. – The main street of the city, on the right bank of the Maas, is the wide **Coolsingel** leading south from the busy Hofplein. At the beginning of the Coolsingel there stands on the left the **Town Hall** (*Stadhuis*), built in 1914–20 in

Dutch Renaissance style. It has a massive tower (fine carillon) and a lavishly decorated interior. On the other side of the Meent, on the left, is the **Exchange** (*Beurs*) built in 1941; the south façade opens into the Beursplein. To the west, opposite the Exchange, is the department store of *De Bijenkorf* (Marcel Breuer, 1958). In front of it stands the modern 26 m (85 feet) high sculpture "Construction", by the French artist of Russian origin, Naum Gabo (1957). Further south, a little way back on the left, at the end of the Coolsingel, stands the 17th c. *Schielandshuis* with the interesting *Museum of History* (entrance No. 31 Korte Hoogstraat).

East of Coolsingel is one of the oldest parts of the city. It was heavily damaged in 1940. Here in the Grote Kerkplein stands the **Grote Kerk**, or the *Church of St Laurence* (Dutch Reformed), originally built in the 15th c., and burned down in 1940. It has a tower 64 m (210 feet) high (carillon) and an organ 23 m (75 feet) high (1973). Further east on the other side of the railway line, lies the Nieuwe Markt. Here is the *Municipal Library* housing a valuable collection of the works of Erasmus of Rotterdam. Nearby to the south is the Hoogstraat, one of the main traffic arteries and shopping streets in the city. Further south, parallel to the Hoogstraat, runs the wide **Blaak**. Here, near the *Leuvehafen*, stands the impressive sculpture "Monument for a Devastated City" by Ossip Zadkine (1953). Not far east, in the Geldersekade between the Oudehaven and the Wijnhaven or Makershaven, stands the **Witte Huis** (*White House*), a 10-storey office building 46 m (151 feet) high. It was built in 1900 and was the first high-rise building in Europe. South-east of here is the **Maasboulevard**, 3 km (2 miles) long, completed in 1964. From its eastern end there is an *excellent view of Rotterdam. On the left are two large bridges across the Maas to the harbour area in the southern part of the city.

The wide Weena leads west from the Hofplein to the vast Stationsplein. On the north side of the Stationsplein is the **Central Station** (*Centraalstation*). On the west side of the square stands the massive Wholesale Trade Building (*Groothandelsgebouw*), with 6000 employees, completed in 1952–3. Opposite, to the south, is the *Bouwcentrum*, an in-

ternational information and advice office for the construction industries; it was built in 1947 and has several showrooms.

South of the Stationsplein lies a modern commercial district between the Coolsingel in the east and the Westersingel. Its main street is the **Lijnbaan**, laid out in 1953, a modern pedestrian-only shopping street with covered walks and exhibitions of modern art. To the west in the Schouwburgplein is the new concert and conference building, **De Doelen**, which was destroyed in 1940 and rebuilt in 1966 (2000 seats, excellent acoustics; exhibition hall).

About 1 km (about a $\frac{1}{2}$ mile) to the south at No. 18 Mathenesserlaan, in a building completed in 1935, is the world-famous **Museum Boymans-Van Beuningen**. It has an excellent picture gallery, sculpture, objects of applied art (including Persian, Spanish, Italian and Dutch majolica, porcelain, glass, silver, pewter, lace and furniture), drawings and a collection of prints.

The gallery is based on a collection of F. J. O. Boymans (d. 1847) and has been extended several times. Its light, modern premises rank it among the most important museums in the Netherlands. Particularly well represented are the painters of the 14th–16th c.: *Hubert* and *Jan van Eyck, Geertgen tot St Jans*, the *Master of Aix*, the *Master of the Virgo inter Virgines, Hieronymus Bosch, Hans Memling, Quentin Massys, Lucas van Leyden, Jan van Scorel, Pieter Breughel the Elder* and others. From the 17th c. there are three paintings by *Pieter Saenredam*, two by *Frans Hals*, three by *Rembrandt* (including one of his son Titus), a self-portrait by *Carel Fabritius*, landscapes by *Hercules Seghers, P. Koninck, Jacob van Ruisdael* and *Hobbema* as well as paintings by *Jan Steen* and *Rubens* (26 works). Among the Italians from the 15th–18th c. *Vincenzo Foppa, Giambattista Moroni, Titian* ("Boy with Dogs"), *Tintoretto, Veronese, Guardi* and *Tiepolo* ("Golgotha") should be mentioned. Among the 18th c. French painters represented are: *Watteau, Chardin, Boucher, Nicolas Lancret, J. Pater* and *Hubert Robert*. From the 19th c.: *Daumier, Boudin, Claude Monet, Pissarro, Signac* and *Gauguin*. The gallery also possesses several paintings by *Vincent van Gogh*. Among the modern painters, the following should be noted: *Picasso, Matisse, Chagall, Kandinsky, Franz Marc, Ensor, Tytgat, Permeke, Rik Wouters* and *Kees van Dongen*. In 1958 the museum acquired the important **collection of D. G. van Beuningen** with 104 paintings and 27 sculptures, among them one by H. and J. van Eyck (the "Three Marys at the Sepulchre"), and the "Tower of Babel" by Pieter Breughel the Elder.

South-west of the Museum Boymans-Van Beuningen at No. 8 Burgmeester 's Jacobsplein is the interesting **Prins Hendrik Maritime Museum**, a collection depicting the history of navigation since the 17th c. (models of ships, charts,

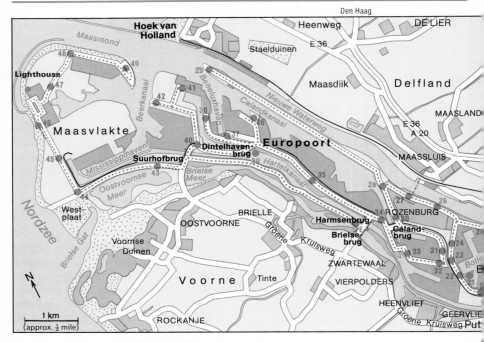

----●----- Harbour route with points of interest

Rotterdamse Haven route ANWB

The *Harbour Route of Rotterdam (*Rotterdamse Havenroute*), marked by the sign reproduced here, is a recommended drive of 90–150 km (56–93 miles) through the extensive harbour area of Rotterdam.

● A **Departure point** (from Spaanse Polder)

● 1 **Europoint** (office block)

● 2 **Oud Delfshaven** (originally the port for the town of Delft, incorporated into Rotterdam in 1886)

● 3 **Coolhaven** (an inland port constructed between the two World Wars)
    Maas Tunnel (built 1937–42)

● 4 **Sluisjesdijk** (on a peninsula between Nieuwe Maas and Waalhaven; 1888 the first oil tanks)

● 5 **Waalhaven** – *East Side* (originally constructed in 1907–30 for bulk cargo: timber, heavy cargo, container)

● 6 **Waalhaven** – *South Side* (harbour and transport school, container terminal)

● 7 **Prins Johan Frisohaven** (vehicles, including Japanese cars)

● 8 **Heijplaat** (garden city for shipyard employees)

● 9 **Prinses Beatrixhaven** (opened in 1965 as general cargo port; roll-on, roll-off, large banana unloaders)

● 10 **Prinses Margriethaven** (container terminal; large quay cranes)

● 11 **Pernis** (a fishing village on land reclaimed in the 14th c.)

● 12 **1008 km mark on the Rhine** (1008 river kilometres (625 miles) from the first Rhine bridge at Konstanz on Lake Constance; harbour radar station)

● 13 **Benelux Tunnel** (opened 1967)

● 14 **2nd Petroleumhaven** (Petro-chemical works of Shell and Chevron)

● 15 **Rotterdamse Ster** ("The Star of Rotterdam", access to highway ring road)

● 16 **Petrochemiekomplex** (Shell, Chevron; start of an oil pipeline to Germany; environmental control complex)

● 17 **Botlekbrug** (bascule bridge with 45 m (148 feet) clearance)
    Botlektunnel

● 18 **Geulhaven** (tug and harbour service boats)

● 19 **3rd Petroleumhaven** (Esso Refinery)

● 20 **Chemiehaven** (chemical plants; dischargers for copra and tapioca)

● 21 **Botlek-Hafen** (grain and ore loading; shipyards)

● 22 **Grain Warehouses** (on the Enclosing Dike of the former Brielse Maas now Brielse Meer, built in 1950; elevators, conveyor belts)

● 23 **St Laurenshaven** (mineral raw materials)

● 24 **Petrochemiekomplex** (storage tanks, chemical plants)

● 25 **Shipyards** (Prins-Willem-Alexander Dry Dock; waste disposal area)

● 26 **Rozenburg** (village called "The Green Heart of Europoort", surrounded by reclaimed industrial areas and dikes)

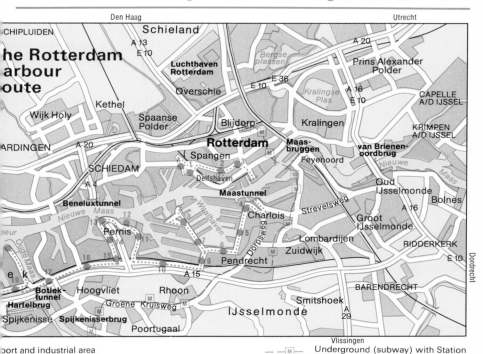

Den Haag   Utrecht

CHIPLUIDEN   Schieland
                            A 13
he Rotterdam   E 10   Luchthaven   Prins Alexander
arbour   Rotterdam   Polder
oute   Overschie   E 10 E 36
                 Kethel   Kralingse A 16   CAPELLE
   Wijk Holy   Spaanse   Plas   E 10   A/D IJSSEL
                         Polder   Blijdorp   Kralingen   KRIMPEN
ARDINGEN   A 20   Rotterdam   Maas-   van Brienen- A/D IJSSEL
                                        Spangen   bruggen   oordbrug
              SCHIEDAM   Feyenoord   Nieuwe
                 A 4   Delfshaven   Oud   Maas
       Beneluxtunnel   Maastunnel   IJsselmonde Bolnes
              Nieuwe Maas 12   Strevelsweg   A 16
   eur   Pernis   13   Charlois   Groot
                                              Lombardijen   IJsselmonde
                                        Zuidwijk   RIDDERKERK
                           15   Pendrecht   E 10
   e k   16   A 15
                  19   BARENDRECHT
       Botlek-   Hoogvliet   Rhoon   Smitshoek
       tunnel
   Hartelbrug   Groene Kruisweg   A 29
   Spijkenisse Spijkenisserbrug
                         Poortugaal   IJsselmonde

                                                        Vlissingen
port and industrial area   ——M—— Underground (subway) with Station

● 27 **Ferry Rozenburg-Maassluis**

● 28 **Calandkanaal** (canal for seagoing vessels between the Europoort docks and the North Sea)

● 29 **Separation Dam** (between Calandkanaal and Nieuwe Waterweg; mooring places for Europoort docks in Scheurhaven)

● 30 **Calandbrug** (bascule bridge with 50 m (164 feet) clearance)
Calandbrug (vehicle terminal under construction)

● 31 **Europoort Oost** – *Merseyweg* (plastics factory)

● 32 **Europoort Oost** – *Theemsweg* (chemical plants and cement factory)

● 33 **Rozenburgsesliis** (Rozenburg lock between Hartelkanaal and Calandkanaal; lock size 299 m × 233 m – 981 feet × 764 feet)

● 34 **7th Petroleumhaven** (crude oil transit)

● 35 **"De Beer"** (International Seamen's Institute)

● 36 **4th Petroleumhaven** (Shell, Esso, Chevron, Gulf; mooring station)
5th Petroleumhaven (Gulf Refinery)

● 37 **Beneluxhaven** (ferry services to Britain)

● 38 **Beneluxhaven** (discharge towers, conveyors and silos for grain shipments)

● 39 **Hartelkanaal** (Rhine waterway between the harbour industries of the Maasvlakte and Europoort, and the hinterland)

● 40 **6th Petroleumhaven** (BP Refinery)

● 41 **Europoort** (ore shipment; large discharge towers on the Calandkanaal)

● 42 **Beerkanaal** (pilot station)

● 43 **Oostvoornse Meer** (lake created in the first stage of the Delta plan)

● 44 **Mississippihaven** (natural gas tanks; ore shipments; coal terminal under construction)

● 45 **Maasvlakte Power Station**

● 46 **Beach** (along the west coast of the Maasvlakte)
Stone dam (a stone block jetty 4·5 km (3 miles) long)

● 47 **Port and industrial area** (a new lighthouse is planned)

● 48 **Manmade Dunes** (imitation oil tank; view of the estuary of the Rhine known as 'Maasmond')

● 49 **8th Petroleumhaven** (Maasvlakte oil terminal for giant tankers)

● E **Terminal point** between Brielsebrug and Harmsenbrug

Oil refineries in Botlek Harbour

Euromast and the Erasmus University in Rotterdam

maps, atlases, etc.). Adjacent to it is the Institute of Navigation and Shipbuilding (*Institut voor Scheepvaart en Scheepsbouw*) with collections from various fields of modern shipbuilding and navigation. Further west, in the G. J. de Jonghweg, stands the *Academy of Fine Arts*. Nearby to the south is the entrance to the *Maas Tunnel, a vehicle underpass (over 1·5 km (1 mile) long, opened in 1942). It runs under the Maas, here almost 800 m (2624 feet) wide, and connects the city to its southern suburbs. Next to it is a separate tunnel for pedestrians and cyclists. At the northern entrance of the Maas Tunnel rises the *Euromast, 185 m (607 feet) high, constructed on the occasion of the Floriade (International Gardening Exhibition) in 1960. Inside are a ship's bridge, two panoramic restaurants at a height of 92 m (302 feet) and a "Space Tower" (added in 1970).

South of the Museum Boymans-Van Beuningen, the **Westzeedijk** runs from the Leuvehaven to the Schiehaven. It separates an urban district along the Maas from the city proper. In the east, by the Maas, is the Willemsplein, the departure point for harbour cruises. Nearby stands *De Boeg*, an impressive memorial to the seamen who died in the War. South-west of the Willemsplein runs the Maas embankment Willemskade, at the west end of which, in No. 25A, is the **Museum of Geography and Ethnography** (*Museum voor Land en Volkenkunde*). From here you arrive at the *Veerhaven*, the

departure point for ferries across the Maas, and crossing the Westplein you reach the Parklaan, where in No. 14 is the *Steuer Museum*.

The Parklaan continues to the *Park (beautiful trees, meadows and lakes). Overlooking the Parkkade is a café on a terrace, with a colourful view over the busy river. The International Gardening Exhibition took place in this park in 1960.

West of the Park are several smaller docks, such as *Parkhaven, St Jacobshaven, Schiehaven, Coolhaven* and others. Bordering them on the west is the old district of *DELFSHAVEN, birthplace of Admiral Piet Hein. In the *Oude Kerk*, at the outer harbour, a memorial stone and a bronze tablet commemorate the last service of the English Puritans who, after being exiled from York, embarked in 1620 at Delfshaven for their journey to North America (the Pilgrim Fathers). Also the Museum of Local History (*"De Dubbelde Palmboom"*, No. 12 Voorhaven), and the House of the Grain Sack Carriers (*Zakkendragershuisje*, Nos. 13–15 Voorstraat); there is an old pewter worker's shop in operation, and an exhibit showing the development of Delfshaven.

The **southern districts** of the city on the left bank of the Maas can be reached either by the busy *Willemsbrug*, next to which is another bridge for the railway, or by the Maas Tunnel. The Willemsbrug crosses the elongated island of **Noordereiland**. Behind the island lies the 1 km (about a $\frac{1}{2}$ mile) long *Koningshaven*, the oldest dock on the left bank of the river; it dates from 1873 and is crossed by impressive rail and road bridges.

Next to the Koningshaven lies the dock area of FEIJENOORD, with the *Binnehaven* and the *Spoorweghaven* docks. Further west is the *Rijnhaven* and the large *Maashaven* (58 hectares – 143 acres) occupying the site of the former village of Katendrecht. The small docks of *Charlois* follow. West of these extends the huge **Waalhaven**. With an area of 310 hectares (766 acres), it is one of the largest manmade docks in the world (ferry from Delfshaven). Beyond the suburb of PERNIS, to the west of the Waalhaven at the confluence of the Oude Maas and the Nieuwe Maas, where the Nieuwe Waterweg ("Het Scheur") begins, extend the new massive port installations of the *Europoort ("Gate of Europe"). They lie between the Nieuwe Waterweg, the Brielse Maas (Brielse Meer) and the North Sea near the Hook of Holland.

North-west of the Inner City, between the Central Station and the suburb of OVER-SCHIE is the new district of BLIJDORP. Here is the popular *Zoo Blijdorp (Diergaarde, restaurant). It is one of the most progressive zoos in Europe, beautifully laid out, with animals in open enclosures. There is a good view of it from the platform of the glassed-in observation tower 48 m (157 feet) high.

North-east of Rotterdam beyond the district of KRALINGEN is the large lagoon of Kralingse Plas (Water sports). The lagoon is surrounded by the Kralinse Bos, a forest occupying 220 hectares (544 acres), popular with the people of Rotterdam (several restaurants). On the south bank of the Kralinse Plas stands the 1740 windmill "De Ster" (a restored mill for grinding snuff tobacco and spices, closed Sunday). Two other windmills, "Prinsenmolen" (1648) and "De Vier Winden" (1776) are located further north at the Bergse Voorplas and on the bank of the Rotte respectively.

SURROUNDINGS of Rotterdam. – A very interesting excursion (22 km – 14 miles) can be made to the east via Rijsoord and Alblasserdam to Kinderdijk. There are still 19 **windmills in the vicinity of Kinderdijk. They operate on Saturday afternoons in summer, and can be visited on weekdays.

Salland

Country: The Netherlands. – Province: Overijssel.

(i) Prov. VVV Overijssel
en VVV Twente,
De Werf 1,
NL-7607 HH Almelo;
tel. (0 54 90) 1 87 65.
VVV West-Overijssel,
Grote Kerkplein 14,
NL-8011 PK Zwolle;
tel. (0 52 00) 1 89 77.

The region of Salland in the Dutch province of Overijssel extends east of the IJssel and is surrounded by the Geest areas of Drente, Twente and Veluwe.

The extensive sand plains characteristic of Salland were formed in the next to last Ice Age. Isolated moraine hills up to 80 m

(262 feet) high, such as the Lemelerberg and the Koningsbelt, rise above the monotonous plain. North of the Vechte are several peat marshes.

Settlements scattered among traditional villages are the dominant feature of this almost exclusively agricultural countryside. Stock raising and a modest amount of arable farming are the principal agricultural occupations. The only large towns are Zwolle (see page 273) and Deventer (see page 134) in the IJssel Plain.

Scheveningen

Country: The Netherlands. – Province: South Holland. Altitude: Sea level. – Part of the City of The Hague. Postal code: NL-2500 AA to 2599. Telephone code: 0 70.

(i) VVV Den Haag/Scheveningen,
Nassauplein 31,
N-2585 EC Den Haag:
tel. 65 89 10.
Information bureau,
Gevers Deynootplein.

HOTELS. – *Steigenberge: Kurhaus Hotel, Kurhausplein. L, 465 b.; Clingendael Europa Hotel, Zwolsestraat 2, I, 358 b.; Eurotel Scheveningen, Gevers Deynootweg 63, I, 143 b.; Badhotel, Gevers Deynootweg 15, I, 179 b.; Gouden Wieken, Scheveningseweg 237, III, 85 b.; Alpa (no rest.), Gevers Deynootplein, III, 46 b.; Bali, Badhuisweg 1, III, 60 b.; Atlanta Zee (no rest.), Seinpostduin 1, III, 18 b.; Burgia (no rest.), Harstenhoekweg 4, III, 16 b.; Van der Spek, Antwerpsestraat 18, III, 28 b.; Strandhotel, Zeekant 111, IV, 45 b.; City, Renbaanstraat 17–23, IV, 60 b.; Maaswijk (no rest.), Stevinstraat 1, IV, 34 b.; Esquire, Van Aerssenstraat 59–61, V, 16 b.; 't Witte Huys, Bosschestraat 2, V, 13 b.; Zeezicht (no rest.), Seinpostduin 28, V, 30 b.; Hage, Seinpostduin 22, V, 30 b.; Duinhorst-Duinroos, Alkmaarsestraat 12, V, 27 b.; Elisa, Gevers Deynootweg 120, V, 50 b.

RESTAURANTS. – Maribaya, Dr Lelykade 17; Ducdalf, Dr Lelykade 5; Paddock, Terrace Zeekant 87; Havenrestaurant (Fish specialities), Treilerdwarsweg 2a.

Casino. – In the Kurhaus (Roulette, Black Jack, Pontoon (Ving-et-un) 2 p.m.–2 a.m. daily).

EVENTS. – Scheveningen Fête (1 July).

The fashionable North Sea resort of *Scheveningen, which was originally a simple fishing village, is now part of the city of The Hague. It became famous when Admiral de Ruyter defeated the joint fleets of France and England off its coast in 1673.

Scheveningen, with its white sandy beach and promenade, is the ideal seaside

The Kurhaus in Scheveningen (The Hague)

vacation resort for all those who seek the sea and sunshine. Here one can swim, walk on the dunes, ride, play tennis or take part in a fishing trip from the Scheveningen fishing harbour. Other attractions are the new swimming pool with artificial waves, and the casino.

SIGHTS. – The 3 km long (2 mile) boulevard (Strandweg) follows the edge of the dunes from the fishing harbour in the south-west to the Strand Hotel in the north-east. Flanking it are several hotels with terraces overlooking the sea. The hub of activity is the huge *Kurhaus, an Art

Nouveau style building, with a hotel, restaurant, casino, gallery, promenades and the Kursaal (public building for visitors). In the neighbourhood, there are residential and pedestrian districts with parks, shops, cafés, a gymnasium, a swimming pool with artificial waves, sauna, solarium, etc. The 381 m (1250 feet) **pier** has four island-like extensions with sun terraces, shops, a restaurant, an "Underwater Wonderland" and an observation tower 45 m (148 feet) high. Nearby is the Circus Theatre with 1750 seats where concerts and other performances take place. Both the pier and the theatre were renovated to attract visitors to the resort. Also worth seeing is the nearby *Sea Aquarium*.

About 1 km (about $\frac{1}{2}$ mile) south-west of the Kurhaus, beyond the village where traditional costumes are still worn, stands the *Monument*, an obelisk erected in 1865 on the site where King William I landed in 1813. Beyond it is the *Vuurtoren* (lighthouse) and behind the lighthouse the *fishing harbour* (a large fishmarket, auctions). The harbour is the departure point for popular fishing trips in the North

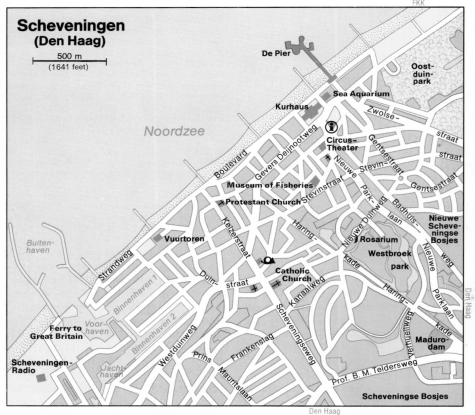

FKK

Scheveningen
(Den Haag)

500 m
(1641 feet)

De Pier

Oost-duin-park

Noordzee

Sea Aquarium

Kurhaus

Zwolse-

Circus-Theater

Gevers Deijnootweg

Gentsestraat

straat

straat

Nieuwe Stevin-

Museum of Fisheries

Protestant Church

Stevinstraat

Park-

Gentsestraat

Badhuis-

Buiten-haven

Vuurtoren

Keizerstraat

Strandweg

Haring-

Nieuwe Duinweg

laan

Rosarium

Nieuwe Scheveningse Bosjes

Westbroek park

Nieuwe weg

Duin-

straat

Catholic Church

Kanaalweg

Haring-

Park-laan

Ferry to Great Britain

Voor-haven

Binnenhaven 1

Binnenhaven 2

Westduinweg

Prins

Frankenslag

Mauritslaan

Scheveningseweg

Vernuellweg

kade

Maduro-dam

Scheveningen-Radio

Jacht-haven

Prof. B. M. Teldersweg

Den Haag

Scheveningse Bosjes

Den Haag

The beach and pier in Scheveningen

Sea, and also of a ferry to Great Britain. In no. 92 Neptunusstraat is the *Museum of Fisheries.*

SURROUNDINGS of Scheveningen. – Several streets, among them the *Scheveningseweg, laid out as early as 1666 and designed by the poet C. Huyghens, lead south-east to The Hague (4 km (3 miles) to the midpoint of the city). Across the pleasant **Scheveningse Bosjes**, next to the *Hotel Wittebrug*, is the fascinating miniature city of *Madurodam.

Madurodam, opened in 1952, was financed by Mr and Mrs L. M. L. Maduro of Curaçao. It was originally conceived as a memorial to their son who died in Dachau in 1945. On an area the size of a football field there is an exact replica in miniature of a typical Dutch landscape, complete with city scenes, buildings, factories, a working railway, canals, harbours, etc. The round trip of about 3 km (2 miles) is well marked with all points of interest numbered (café/restaurant).

Valley of the Semois/ Vallée de la Semois

Country: Belgium. – Provinces: Luxembourg, Namur.
ⓘ **Secrétariat du Groupement Régional
Semois et Vierre,**
  Point de Vue 67,
  B-6824 Chassespierre;
  tel. (0 61) 31 20 80,
  Semois et Vierre,
  Bureau du Château Fort,
  B-6830 Bouillon; tel. (0 61) 46 62 57.
  Semois Namuroise,
  Mont des Champs,
  B-6868 Bohan-sur-Semois;
  tel. (0 61) 50 02 21.

HOTELS. – In ALLE-SUR-SEMOIS: *La Charmille*, Rue Libiochant 12, III, 11 r.; *Auberge d'Alle-S-Semois*, Rue Libiochant 98, IV, 10 r.; *Du Fief de Libiochant*, Rue Libiochant 99, IV, 30 r. – In BOHAN: *Auberge du Printemps*, Route de France 185, IV, 6 r. – In

FLORENVILLE: *Hostellerie du Vieux Moulin*, III, 19 r. – In FRANAN: *Roches Fleuries*, IX, 18 r.; *Beau Séjour*, IV, 16 r. – In HERBEUMONT: *Hostellerie du Prieuré de Conques*, Route de Florenville 176, II, 13 r.; *Châtelaine*, Rue Bravy 127, III, 26 r.; *Le Bravy*, Rue Bravy 128, III, 26 r. – In ROCHEHAUT: *Balcon-en-Forêt*, Route de Alle 120, III, 11 r.; *L'An 1600*, Rue Palis 40, IV, 17 r. – In VRESSE-SUR-SEMOIS: *Au Relais*, Rue Grande 45, IV, 7 r.; *Eau Vive*, Rue Petit-Fays 52, V, 30 r.

The River Semois begins near Arlon in southern Belgium and wends its way to the north-west, joining the Meuse in France. There is beautiful scenery and interesting old buildings in the Belgian part of the Semois Valley.

The little river first crosses the Plain of Gaume in the Belgian part of Lorraine and enters the Ardennes at Tintigny. Here the valley is deeply cut into the rock and forms so many bends that, while the entire length of the river is some 200 km (124 miles), as the crow flies it is only about 80 km (50 miles) from its source to its confluence with the Meuse.

Since it is so deep that it is protected against the constantly blowing westerly winds, the climate of the valley is relatively mild. The main agricultural crop is tobacco, which otherwise would only grow in more southerly regions.

The steep sides of the valley sometimes press so close to the river that the roads frequently have to cross the crests of the hills. A drive through the Semois Valley should be combined, therefore, with walks and boat trips so that the most beautiful parts are not missed. For the same reason, many of the larger villages lie high above the river bends on

In the Valley of the Semois

The Abbey of Orval in the Valley of the Semois

the plateau of the Ardennes. A typical example is Florenville from which there is a beautiful view over the Semois.

A good starting point for an excursion into the Upper and Lower Semois Valley is the little town of **Bouillon** (see page 103). 11 km (7 miles) upstream from Bouillon, in the Upper Semois Valley, is the village of **Dohan**. It is built on terraces on the right bank of the river; there is a fine 17th c. château which is now a country estate. After the villages of *Auby* and *Herbeumont*, well known as summer resorts, is the little tourist town of **Florenville**. It is close to the French border and lies in an open plain above the Semois. It was once fortified. From the tower of the church there is a magnificent view over the countryside. It is worth while making a detour to the former *Abbey of Orval, 8·5 km (5 miles) from here. The monastery, founded in the 12th c., was one of the three largest in Belgium but was destroyed by the French in 1793. In 1926, new buildings for the Abbey were built on one part of the estate. The church stands on the foundations of an 18th c. building.

Jamoigne, at the end of the picturesque *Valley of Vierre*, is a pleasant village with an old château rebuilt in the 19th c. There is an interesting church with a fine 12th c. font. From here it is an easy drive to the village of *Tintigny*. A few miles upstream is the geographical boundary between the Ardennes and the layered Uplands of Lorraine.

The scenery in the lower part of the Semois Valley is no less impressive than that of the upper one. 5 km (3 miles) below Bouillon is the pleasant village of *Corbion*, a good base for magnificent

walks. Further downstream is the picturesque village of **Rochehaut** and a few miles past the *Viewpoint of Frahan*, is *Alle*, the focal point of the tobacco plantations in the Semois Valley. Further downstream is *Vresse*, with charming surroundings inviting long walks. From here it is only a short distance to *Bohan*, the last village in Belgian territory.

Sint-Niklaas (Saint-Nicolas)

Country: Belgium. – Province: East Flanders.
Altitude: 5–30 m (16–98 feet). – Population: 49,000.
Postal code: B-2700.
Telephone code: 0 31.
ⓘ **Commissie voor Bevordering van Vreemdelingenverkeer en Toerisme,**
Stadhuis,
Grote Markt;
tel. 76 34 71.

HOTELS. – *Vlaanderens Gasthof*, Stationsplein 5, III, 20 r.; *Serwir*, Koningin Astridlaan 49, III, 45 r.

RESTAURANTS. – *'t Mezennestje*, De Meulenaerstraat 2; *Billiet*, Prinses Jos. Charlottelaan 61; *'t Begijnhofken*, Kokkelbeekstraat 39; *Carlton*, Stationsstraat 73; *De Kardinaal*, Kardinal Mercierplein 10.

EVENTS. – *International Competition in Balloon Landing* (first Sunday in September); *The entry of St Nicholas* into his home town (second half of October); In the district of Nieuwkerke, *International Clog Tour* (around Easter); In the district of Sinaai, famous *missionary procession* (beginning of September).

Sint-Niklaas (in French Saint-Nicolas) lies in the middle of the Waasland between the rivers Schelde and Durme in the province of East Flanders. It is a prosperous industry and trade town and is also important administratively. The largest industry is textiles (weaving, knitwear and carpet-making), but metal, timber and tobacco processing plants are also significant.

HISTORY. – Sint-Niklaas lies at the crossroads of two old trade routes; one led from Brabant to Zealand, the other linked Antwerp with Ghent and Bruges. It was at first a trading place and in 1217 became an independent parish with Sint Niklaas as its Patron Saint. In 1248 Margaret of Constantinople, the Countess of Flanders, ceded the land of the present-day Market Place to the new parish on the condition that the huge plot would never be built upon. In the 17th c., Sint-Niklaas developed into an important textile area and consolidated its position in the following century. It received town status under Napoleon in 1804. Because of its favourable location for European trade, Sint-Niklaas became one of the most important industrial towns in Belgium in the 20th c.

SIGHTS. – The Market Place lies 1·5 km (1 mile) west of the main traffic artery. It is one of the largest squares in Belgium, occupying an area of over 3 hectares (7 acres). On its north-western side is the neo-Gothic **Town Hall** built in 1876 (carillon of thirty-five bells). Opposite, to the south-east, stands the *Church of St Niklaas*. It was consecrated in 1238, enlarged several times in the 16th c. and again in the years 1895–1900. On the right of the church is the *Parochiehuis*, the parish building (1663), which later became the Town Hall and is now the Commercial Court. Beyond the Parochiehuis is the *Ciperage*, originally a prison (1662) and now a library. Here, too, is the *Landhuis*, the former Law Courts (1637). Behind the Town Hall is the *Church of Our Lady* (1844) with some frescoes and a tower which is visible from a considerable distance. North-east of the Market Place at No. 49 Zamanstraat, is the **Museum** with antiquities from the Waasland and some paintings, among them **"Nero and the Burning of Rome"* by Rubens, as well as an interesting **col- lection of works by the famous geographer Mercator. In the pleasant town park is the *Château Walburg* (16th–19th c.; astro- nomical clock "Heirmanklok").

Sint-Truiden (Saint-Trond)

Country: Belgium. – Province: Limburg.
Altitude: 34–106 m (112–348 feet).
Population: 36,000.
Postal code: B-3800.
Telephone code: 011.
ⓘ **Dienst voor Toerisme,**
   Stadhuis,
   Grote Markt;
   tel. 67 55 91.

HOTELS. – *In de Klok*, Grote Markt 11, IV, 7 r.; *Majestic*, Grote Markt 10, IV, 6 r.; *Tio*, Stationsstraat 59, IV, 10 r.; *Riddershof*, Maasrodeweg 7, Halmaal, IV, 6 r. – CAMP SITE.

RESTAURANTS. – *Amico*, Naamsestraat 3; *Astoria*, Grote Markt 18; *Breugelhof*, Beekstraat 10; *Hof van Maasrode*, Maasrodeweg 11; *Thier Brauhof*, Spaan- sebrugstraat.

EVENTS. – *Carnival* (Monday before Lent); *Concerts in the Basilica* (every Wednesday in June); *Christmas Exhibition*.

The Belgian town of Sint-Truiden (in French, Saint-Trond), lies in the region of Hesbaye in the province of Limburg, 35 km (22 miles) north-

west of Liège. It is the market town of a wide fruit-producing area. It is also an important industrial town, with a sugar refinery, distilleries and breweries, chemical, metal and tex- tile plants and ceramics factories.

HISTORY. – Sint-Truiden rose up around an ancient Abbey, founded by St Trudo in 657. It received town status in the 11th c. and was fortified in 1086. The Benedictine Abbey was first subordinated to the Abbot and Bishop of Metz, whose place was taken after the 13th c. by the Bishop of Liège. At that time, Sint-Truiden developed into an important cloth- making capital. The monastery was closed when the town became French in 1795. In 1814, Sint-Truiden belonged to the Netherlands and in 1830 it became part of Belgium. The checkered history of the town is documented by several historical monuments.

SIGHTS. – In the middle of the town is the Grote Markt. Here stands the *Town Hall* (17th–18th c.), built next to a *belfry* (1606) which now towers above one of the side gables of the building. In the tower is a fine carillon of forty-one bells. The gables of the Town Hall were added between 1754 and 1758. Behind the Hall stands the Gothic **Church of Our Lady**. Its choir dates from the 14th c.; the naves were completed in the 15th c.; The tower is more recent. The reliquary of St Trudo and fine choir-stalls are notable features of the interior.

North of the Grote Markt is the *Seminary* in which some remains of the old Abbey are concealed. Not far west of the Market Place stands the *Church of St Martin*, the tower of which is a gem of Gothic architecture. The church itself is a neo- Romanesque 19th c. structure.

In the south of the old town stands the *Church of St Peter*, well known for its Romanesque ribless vaulting (12th c.). East of the Grote Markt is the *Franciscan Church*, built in 1731. The interior of this Baroque building is impressive because of its size (100 m (328 feet) long, 16 m (52 feet) wide and 26 m (85 feet) high). – The 15th c. *Brustempoort* at the end of the Luikerstraat is an underground forti- fication; it can be visited every Sunday and holiday from Easter until September.

In the former *Begijnhof* about $\frac{1}{2}$ km (about a $\frac{1}{4}$ mile) north-east of the middle of town is an earlier church with some beautiful medieval frescoes. In the adjacent build- ing is an *astronomical clock* 6 m (20 feet) high (K. Festraets, 1942). It has more than 20,000 parts.

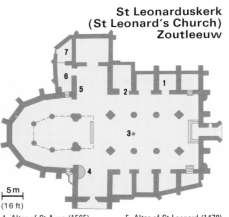

**St Leonarduskerk
(St Leonard's Church)
Zoutleeuw**

5 m
(16 ft)

1 Altar of St Anne (1565)
2 Romanesque Christ (11th c.)
3 Statue of the Virgin (1530)
4 Tabernacle (1550–2)
5 Altar of St Leonard (1478)
6 Treasury in the
Former Chapter Hall
7 Sacristy

Town Hall in Bolsward

SURROUNDINGS of Sint-Truiden. – 6 km (4 miles) north-west is the little old town of **Zoutleeuw** (in French *Léau*, population 3000). The Gothic *Church of St Leonard is one of the few churches in Belgium not pillaged during the religious wars. It also survived the storms of the French Revolution undamaged. The wealth of the interior decoration and the high quality of the works of art are exceptional. Among the most remarkable items are several carved altars, a stone *tabernacle by Cornelis Floris and a 6 m (20 feet) high candelabra (1483), a rare masterpiece of Mosan brasswork. On the south side of the pleasant Market Place stands a small Renaissance Town Hall (1538–9).

Sneek

Country: The Netherlands. – Province: Friesland.
Altitude: Below sea level. – Population: 28,000.
Postal code: NL-8600 AA to 8699.
Telephone code: 0 51 50.
ⓘ **VVV Sneek Amicitia,**
Leeuwenburg 12,
NL-8601 BC Sneek;
tel. 1 40 90.

HOTELS. – *Bonnema*, Stationsstraat 62–66, III, 55 b.; *Hanenburg*, Wijde Noorderhorne 2, IV, 26 b. – YOUTH HOSTEL: *Wigledam*, Oppenhuizerweg 76. – CAMP SITE: *De Domp*, Leeuwardeweg; *De Potten*, Offingawier.

RESTAURANTS. – *Montmartre*, Kleine Kerkstraat 9; *Onder de Linden*, Marktstraat 28.

EVENTS. – *Sneek-Week Sailing Regatta* (beginning of August).

SPORTS and LEISURE. – Sailing Schools and Sailboat Rental.

The Dutch town of Sneek lies in the province of Friesland, in the middle of the Frisian lakeland. It has agricultural colleges, an Agricultural Advice Bureau and a Teachers' Training College, as well as one of the largest yacht harbours in the country.

In summer the town is a popular place for water sports on the Frisian lakes, particularly on the Sneeker. Meer, 4 km (3 miles) away. Apart from tourism, food, textile, paper, chemical and metal industries also contribute to the town's economy. Sneek is also an important market town for dairy products.

SIGHTS. – In the Marktstraat stands the imposing 15th c. **Town Hall** (*Stadhuis*) with a magnificent Rococo façade (1760). A few yards south, in the Kerkstraat, is the Gothic *Martinikerk*, also dating from the 15th c. It has a beautiful 16th c. sacristy. The continuation of the

Sailing Regatta near Sneek

Kerkstraat, the Oude Koemarkt, leads southward to a canal called Geeuw. On the right is the *Waterpoort* (Watergate) (1613), part of earlier fortifications. Beyond the canal, turn left and proceed along the water via Hoogend, then along the street called Singel. At its end, on the right, is the *Museum of Navigation and Antiquities*, with a collection of ship models, navigational instruments and paintings of marine subjects.

SURROUNDINGS of Sneek. – An interesting excursion can be made to the little town of **Bolsward** (Hotel de Wijnberg, III, 68 b.), 11 km (7 miles) west of Sneek. Here there is a State Dairy School. The town was once a harbour and a Hanseatic town on the Middelsee. Its *Town Hall, built in 1614–16, is the most remarkable Renaissance building in Friesland. Also interesting is the 15th c. Martinikerk, with choirstalls and a carved pulpit (1450 and 1662 respectively), as well as fine tombstones from the small Broerekerk (1281).

Spa

Country: Belgium. – Province: Liège.
Altitude: 260 m (853 feet). – Population: 9500.
Postal code: B-4880.
Telephone code: 0 87.
(i) **Office du Tourisme, du Thermalisme et des Fêtes de la Ville de Spa,**
Rue Royale 2;
tel. 77 29 13.

HOTELS. – *Park-Hotel*, Avenue Reine Astrid 33, III, 39 r.; *Grand Cerf*, Rue de la Sauvenière 111, III, 7 r.; *Hostellerie Ardennaise*, Rue de la Poste 15, III, 15 r.; *Le Cardinal*, Place Royale 17–21, III, 32 r.; *Gai Séjour*, Boulevard Rener 6, III, 9 r.; *Du Lac*, Warfaaz 75, III, 12 r.; *La Vieille France*, Route du Lac 7, IV, 6 R.; *Olympic*, Avenue Amédée Hesse 13, IV, 33 r.; *Le Bergerac*, Place du Monument 22, IV, 6 r.; *L'Auberge*, Place du Monument 4, IV, 27 r.; *Cortina II*, Rue du Marché 64, IV, 4 r.; *Du Louvre*, Place P. Le Grand 6–7, IV, 8 r.; *Canterbury*, Rue Général Bertrand 2–3, IV, 11 r.; *Bij de Vlaming Roger*, Avenue Reine Astrid 68, V, 10 r.; *Du*

Chemin du Fer, Place de la Gare 25, V, 8 r.; *De l'Avenue*, Avenue Reine Astrid 48, V, 12 r. – In BALMORAL: *Eurotel*, Route de Balmoral 33, I, 97 r.

YOUTH HOSTEL. – Avenue Prof. Henrijeau 24.

CAMP SITES. – *Du Parc des Sources*, Route de la Sauvenière 141; *Havette*, Rue Chelui 21; *Du Chalet Suisse*, Route de Balmoral 20; *Polleur*, Rue du Congrès 90; *Francopole*, Ster-Francorchamps.

RESTAURANTS. – *Pitchoun*, Place du Monument 15; *Crémaillère*, Route de Nivezé 69. – In MALCHAMPS. *Ferme de Malchamps*, Rue Sauvenière 201. – In LA REID: *A la Retraite de l'Empereur*, Basse Desnié 842; *Auberge Menobu*, Rue Menobu 546.

EVENTS. – Casino: *French Chansons* in July; performances by the National Theatre in August.

Casino. – Rue Royale.

SPORTS and LEISURE. – Athletics, tennis, volleyball, basketball, handball. A gymnasium is available. Swimming, skiing, gliding and riding.

The Belgian health resort of Spa lies 35 km (22 miles) south of Liège among the low, wooded hills of the Northern Ardennes, in the pleasant valley of the little River Wayai, here joined by the Pickerotte. Spa has been popular since the 16th c. because of its alkaline springs which are also rich in iron salts and which are particularly good for anaemia, gout and rheumatism. The name "Spa" entered the English language as a general description for a "place with mineral springs, curative waters, baths".

The 18th c. was a period of splendour for Spa: Tsar Peter the Great and Emperor Joseph II, among others, stayed here. In the First World War, the town was occupied by German troops and used for

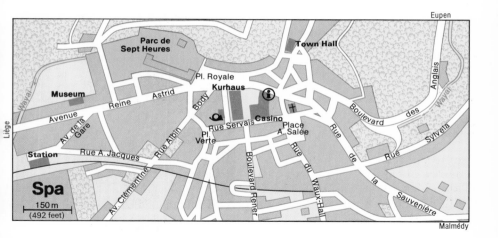

Casino in the Belgian Health Resort of Spa

Valley of the Sûre/ Vallée de la Sûre

Countries: Luxembourg and Belgium.

ⓘ Syndicat d'Initiative,
Porte St-Willibrord,
L-Echternach;
tel. 7 22 30.
Syndicat d'Initiative,
Place Guillaume,
L-Diekirch;
tel. 8 30 23.
Syndicat d'Initiative,
Grand. Rue 13,
L-Ettelbruck;
tel. 8 20 68.
Syndicat d'Initiative,
L-Esch-sur-Sûre;
tel. 8 91 12.

the convalescence of thousands of wounded and sick soldiers. Between March and November of 1918, the German army headquarters were located here. In July of 1920, the Conference on Disarmament and Reparations between the Allies and Germany was held in the town.

SIGHTS. – The activities of the spa are concentrated mainly in the Place Royale and in the buildings and parks around it. On the south side stands the **Casino**, built in 1903–8 and restored after a fire in 1919–21. It contains a café/restaurant, a banqueting hall, gaming rooms, a ballroom and a theatre hall. Opposite is the **Kurhaus** (*Etablissement des Bains*), built by Leon Suys in 1862–8; water from the Spring of Marie-Henriette was piped into this building.

To the west of the Place Royale extends the pleasant **Parc de Sept Heures** with a monument to the composer G. Meyerbeer, and an Armistice Memorial (1926). Further west, in the Avenue Reine Astrid, is the *Museum* of Spa with a collection of gilded wooden boxes, the oldest dating from the 16th c. Opposite the Casino, to the north-east, in the Place Pierre-le-Grand, stands a round building with a Pump Room and a Winter Garden, where the **Pouhon**, the most effective of the mineral springs, originates. South of the Pouhon is the neo-Romanesque *Parish Church* (1882).

HOTELS. – In ESCH-SUR-SÛRE: *Du Moulin*, Rue du Moulin 6, III, 28 r.; *Des Ardennes*, Rue du Moulin 1, III, 44 r. – In GOEBELSMÜHLE: *Schroeder*, Rue de la Gare 9, III, 12 r. – In BOURSCHEID: *Du Moulin*, II, 18 r.; *St Fiacre*, Rue Principale 4, III, 10 r.; *St Laurent*, Rue Principale 27, IV, 11 r.; *De Bourscheid*, Rue Principale 5, V, 5 r. – In REISDORF: *Auberge The Cosy Corner*, IV, 10 r. – In WALLENDORF-PONT: *Dimmer* (no rest.), Route d'Echternach 12, III, 18 r.; *Wenzel* (no rest.), III, 10 r. – In ROSPORT: *De la Poste*, Route d'Echternach 7, III, 8 r. – In BORN: *Chez Jean*, Route d'Echternach 28, III, 14 r.; *Scherff*, Route d'Echternach, III, 25 r.; *Beau Rivage*, Rive Principale 55, III, 10 r. – In WASSERBILLIG: *Hengen*, Grand'rue 2, IV, 29 r. – In MARTELANGE: *Martinot*, Route de Bastogne 2, III, 16 r.; *Au Repos des Voyageurs*, Route d'Arlon 58, IV, 7. – Several CAMP SITES.

The River Sûre is 173 km (107 miles) long. Its source is on the north-east slope of the Ardennes between the Belgian towns of Bastogne and Neufchâteau. At first it flows east to the Belgian/Luxembourg frontier at Martelange. The frontier then follows the winding river bed for several miles north. A little later, the river turns east and, after being

Esch-sur-Sûre in the Sûre Valley

joined by the Clerve, it alters course again to the south. At Ettelbruck it leaves the wooded massif of the Ardennes (called Ösling in Luxembourg), and enters the open country of Gutland, the northern projection of the Uplands of Lorraine. East of Ettelbruck, the Sûre follows the Luxembourg/German frontier and joins the Moselle at Wasserbillig as its left bank tributary.

Both the deep and narrow valleys of the Upper Sûre, winding through the Ardennes, and its lower part which is somewhat wider and gentler, are among the most beautiful parts of Luxembourg, making this pleasant region a very popular vacation area in summer. Most of the tourist resorts of the country can be found along the banks of the River Sûre.

One of the best known is the summer resort of Esch-sur-Sûre, romantically set in the Upper Sûre Valley. Because of its hidden location it is also often called Esch-in-the-Hole. A ruined castle, perched picturesquely on a slate crag split in two by a deep cleft, towers above the valley. About 1 km (about a $\frac{1}{2}$ mile) west of the Esch is the *Lac de la Haute Sûre, a hydroelectric reservoir created in 1960–1 (capacity: 60 million cu. m (2000 million cubic feet)). A scenic road skirts the south side of the lake to Ingenborn. 12·5 km (8 miles) downstream, where the Clerve joins the Sûre, lies the little village of Goebelsmühle.

Here the road leaves the winding valley and ascends its right-hand slope to Bourscheid, 6 km (4 miles) away, on the plateau above the river. It is a quiet little village with a beautiful view over the deeply incised Valley of the Sûre. The impressive ruins of the medieval *Castle Bourscheid, high on a rounded hill above a loop of the river, are about 1·5 km (1 mile) below the village and can be reached by a good road from the church. 2 km (1 mile) beyond Bourscheid, there is a *superb rear view of the ruin lying half-way below. The road then continues along the edge of the plain and begins to wind its way downward, with good views, to Ettelbruck (see page 145), 7 km (4 miles) away.

From here you first follow the main road to Liège in a northerly direction; at the outskirts of the town you cross the Sûre. 1 km (about a $\frac{1}{2}$ mile) further, turn right at the crossroads into the river valley, which now becomes much wider. 4 km (2 miles) further on comes Diekirch (see page 135). 3 km (2 miles) beyond Diekirch turn right at the crossroads and shortly afterwards you arrive at Bettendorf (2 km – 1 mile) with a château (1728) and an old church tower built on Roman foundations. Further downstream the valley narrows again as the river enters layers of harder rock. At Reisdorf (5 km – 3 miles) it receives the White Ernz (Ernz Blanche).

From Wallendorf-Pont (2 km – 1 mile), the Sûre forms the Luxembourg/German border. The valley narrows and the slopes become more densely wooded. In this stretch there are several beautiful camp sites. 6·5 km (4 miles) below Wallendorf is the village of Grundhof at the confluence of the Black Ernz (Ernz Noire; Mullerthal, see page 219) and the Sûre. Continuing in the direction of Echternach you can see on the German bank opposite the former summer residence of the Abbots of Echternach (17th–18th c.).

Echternach in the Sûre Valley

5·5 km (3 miles) beyond Grundhof, on the German side, is a little château, formerly belonging to the Abbots of Echternach. 4·5 km (3 miles) past it is Echternach (see page 140). Road No. 10 to Wasserbillig then continues along the Sûre Valley, which below Echternach (beautiful rear view) is gentler and less spectacular. Vineyards and orchards surround the villages. Beyond Rosport (8 km – 5 miles) and Hinkel (3 km – 2 miles), the valley narrows again and is in parts densely wooded. Here is the tourist resort of Born, with river bathing and camp sites. 8 km (5 miles) beyond is Wasserbillig, situated at the confluence of the Sûre and the Moselle. This former Roman settlement, "Biliacus", is now a thriving frontier town with an attractive Baroque church (carillon) and Roman ruins.

Tienen (Tirlemont)

Country: Belgium. – Province: Brabant.
Altitude: 35–89 m (115–219 feet).
Population: 32,800.
Postal code: B-3300.
Telephone code: 0 16.

(i) **Vereniging vor Vreemdelingenverkeer en Toerisme,**
Stadthuis,
Grote Markt;
tel. 81 10 07.

HOTELS. – *Alpha*, Leuvensestraat 95, IV, 17 r.; *Cambrinus*, Grote Markt 22, IV, 7 r.

RESTAURANT. – *Normandy*, Grote Markt 40.

EVENT. – A famous *Equestrian Procession* on Easter Monday in the district of Hakendover.

The town of Tienen (in French, Tirlemont), lies half-way between Liège and Brussels, on the border between the Belgian provinces of Brabant and Hesbaye.

It lies in the middle of a fertile loess-covered agricultural countryside. The main crop of the area is sugar-beet which is processed annually in the refineries of Tienen into approximately 200,000 tons of sugar.

HISTORY. – Tienen was a settlement on a Roman road which in places is still well preserved. It was first mentioned in writing in a charter of Charles the Bald in 872. It received town status from the Counts of Louvain as early as 1015, and somewhat later was fortified for the first time. In the Middle Ages the craft of cloth-making acquired major significance and helped to create the town's prosperity and steadily growing reputation. Since the 19th c. Tienen has developed into an important location for Belgium's sugar industry. Several buildings of historical and artistic merit still remain from its medieval era of prosperity.

SIGHTS. – In the Grote Markt, which is the traffic hub of the town, stand the *Town Hall* (1836) and the Gothic **Church of our Lady**. Of the church there remains only the choir (1345) and a transept with three portals (14th–15th c.). The construction of the nave was never started. Inside is a valuable Late-Gothic stone statue of the Virgin (Wouter Paus, 1362–3). Also interesting are the Baroque choir-stalls and the fine panelling.

South-east of the Market Place in the Wolmarkt, which is surrounded by 17th–18th c. *Town houses*, stands the **Church of St Germanus**. Its imposing western front dates from the first half of the 13th c.

and is the latest Romanesque structure in the Meuse area. The Gothic choir and the nave were not built until the 14th–15th c.

SURROUNDINGS of Tienen. – 3 km (2 miles) east of the town beyond the Greater Gete is the suburb of **Hakendover**, a famous place of pilgrimage. The Church of St Saviour, with a Romanesque west tower, houses a beautiful carved altar (1430), and Baroque choir-stalls from the Abbey of Oplinter. Driving in the direction of Louvain, you come to the village of **Kumtich** at the opposite end of Tienen. The village, which is now a part of Tienen, is a former Roman settlement. In it stands the 13th c. Romanesque Church of St Gillis, surrounded by a circular wall (1636).

Tilburg

Country: The Netherlands. – Province: North Brabant.
Altitude: 15 m (49 feet). – Population: 213,000.
Postal code: NL-5000 AA to 5239.
Telephone code: 0 13.

(i) **Streek VVV Hart van Brabant,**
Spoorlaan 440,
NL-5036 CH Tilburg;
tel. 43 61 31.

HOTELS. – *Ibis*, Dr H. v. Doorneweg 105, II, 154 b.; *De Postelse Hoeve*, Dr Deelenlaan 10, II, 34 b.

RESTAURANTS. – *Shakespeare*, Stadhuisplein 42; *Modern*, Heuvel 39; *Korenbeurs*, Heuvel 24; *Aub. 't Koetshuys*, Heuvelstraat 40; *Kota Radja*, Heuvelring 110; *La Petite Suisse*, Heuvel 41.

EVENTS. – *Epiphany Songs* (6 January); *Pottery Market* (January–March, first Saturday of every Month; April–December, every Saturday); *Jazz festival* (first weekend in September).

The industrial town of Tilburg lies on the Wilhelmina Canal in the province of North Brabant and after Eindhoven is the largest business and cultural city in the Southern Netherlands. It obtained town status in 1809. Being the capital of Dutch Catholicism, it has a Catholic Business College; there are also several specialised colleges in the fields of economics, teaching, architecture and music. The traditional wool industry still plays a dominant role in the economic life of the town, producing about 60% of all woollen goods in Holland. Recently some metal manufacture and other areas of employment were introduced into the town in order to reduce the risks of a single-industry economy.

SIGHTS. – The present *Town Hall* was once the palace of King William II, who died here in 1849. Also interesting is the

Amusement Park De Efteling

E Entrance and Exit	3 Playground	5 Swimming
1 Fairytale Forest	4 Rowing and	Pool
2 Haunted Castle	Boating Lake	6 Deer Park

Tongeren (Tongres)

Country: Belgium. – Province: Limburg.
Altitude: 75–108 m (246–354 feet).
Population: 29,500.
Postal code: B-3700.
Telephone code: 0 12.
(i) **Vereniging voor Vreemdelingenverkeer,**
Stadhuis;
tel. 23 29 61.

HOTELS. – *Beukenhof*, Sint-Truidersteenweg 501,
IV, 10 r.; *Lido*, Grote Markt 19, IV, 9 r.; *Chemin de Fer*,
Stationslaan 44, IV, 14 r.

RESTAURANTS. – *Ascot-Picolo*, Sint-Truiderstraat
8; *De Toerist*, Grote Markt 4.

MARKETS. – *Cattle Market* (summer months); *Cloth
Market* (winter months, Sunday, 7 a.m.–1 p.m.).

Grote Kerk, a beautiful neo-Gothic structure. The *Museum of Natural History*
contains some interesting geological,
botanical and zoological collections.
Exhibits in the *Textile Museum* include
not only precious textiles from all over the
world, but also spinning wheels, looms
and other equipment. The *Museum of
Ethnography* specialises in Indonesia,
New Guinea, Africa, Central and South
America.

SURROUNDINGS of Tilburg. To the north, near the
village of *Kaatsheuvel* (Hotel De Horst, V, 12 b.), is the
Recreation and Amusement Park *De Efteling
(Easter–October), covering an area of 65 hectares
(161 acres). It has three large lakes (swimming and
rowing facilities), the largest haunted castle in
Europe, a fairytale city, a restaurant with terraces, a
tea-room, etc.

On the "Langstraat", the road from 's-Hertogenbosch
to Geertruidenberg, the village of *Drunen* has an
*Automobile Museum "Lips Autodron", and 5 km (3
miles) further north-east the village of *Waalwijk*
boasts a Leather Museum. East of Tilburg, to the right
of the road to 's-Hertogenbosch, in dune-like country
is the village of **Oisterwijk** with a church by P. J. H.
Cuypers. South of the village is the nature reserve
Oisterwijkse Vennen with an area of 600 hectares
(1483 acres), an outdoor theatre, a swimming pool,
etc.

The rural market town of Tongeren
(in French, Tongres), is the headquarters of an administrative district in the Belgian province of
Limburg. Known as the oldest town
in Belgium, it lies on the banks of the
little River Jeker and is surrounded
by the fertile fields of the Hesbaye.

Tongeren, with its many small-sized
industrial plants, provides widely diversified employment for the population of
the surrounding area. The cultural and historic attractions of the town, reflecting its
long history, have created a tourist industry which has increased considerably
in the last few years and now represents a
substantial part of the town's economy.

HISTORY. – Tongeren, the Roman *Aduatuca Tungrorum*, was founded by Caesar in 57 B.C. as the
central town of the "civitas Tungrorum". The Roman
settlement developed very quickly owing to its location on important crossroads, and soon became one
of the most prosperous towns in Lower Germania. It
was fortified in the 2nd c. by a wall, 4·5 km (2¾ miles)
long, parts of which still remain. Between the 4th and
6th c., Tongeren was one of the earliest bishoprics. Destruction by the Germans and the Vikings, as well as
the transfer of the bishopric to Maastricht brought
about the decline of the town under the Merovingians. A new era of prosperity came in the 9th c.,
however, and from the Middle Ages until the French
Revolution Tongeren was one of the most important
towns in the Principality of Liège. In the 13th c. it was
fortified for the third time. In 1677 the town was
almost completely destroyed by Louis XIV's army.
Reconstruction began almost immediately. Industrialisation from 1830 onwards helped the town to
acquire, in addition to its market and administrative
role, its present industrial significance.

SIGHTS. – In the Market Place stands the
*Memorial to Ambiorix, the Chief of the
Eburones*, who decisively defeated the

Dwarfs' Cottage in the Park De Efteling

A torso in the Gallo-Roman Museum in Tongeren

Tournai (Doornik)

Country: Belgium. – Province: Hainaut.
Altitude: 29–147 m (95–482 feet).
Population: 70,000.
Postal code: B-7500.
Telephone code: 0 69.
ⓘ **Centre de Tourisme,**
Vieux Marché aux Poteries 14;
tel. 22 20 45.

HOTELS. – *Aux Armes de Tournay*, Place de Lille 23, IV, 23 r.; *Du Parc*, Place Crombez 9, V, 31 r.; *De la Tour St-Georges*, Place de Nedonchel, V, 10 r. – CAMP SITES.

RESTAURANTS. – *Trois Pommes d'Orange*, Rue de Wallonie 28; *Prandini*, Rue Corriers 8; *Dudans*, Place Crombez 9; *Charles-Quint*, Grand'Place 3.

EVENTS. – *Flower Market* (Good Friday); *Masked Procession, Traditional and Floral Processions* (second Sunday in June); *Great Historic Procession* (Sunday after 8 September); *Carillon* (June–August, Sundays and holidays, noon and 7 p.m.).

The Belgian town of Tournai (in Flemish, Doornik), lies on both banks of the Schelde, near the Belgian/French frontier. Administratively and culturally its influence extends beyond its own area and there are important industries.

Tournai is the administrative hub of an "Arrondissement" and the seat of a Bishop. It also has a Chamber of Industry and Commerce and Law Courts. Its cultural institutions include several large museums (Ethnography, Archaeology, History and Art), libraries and an Episcopal Seminary. Cement works, machinery plants, food processing and the traditional textile industries, especially carpet-weaving, form the economic nucleus of Tournai. Tourism also plays an important role.

Roman legions of Sabinus and Cotta in 54 B.C. It is by the famous sculptor Jules Bertin and was erected in 1866. The **Basilica of Our Lady**, on the site of an earlier Romanesque church, was begun in 1240 and completed 300 years later. The choir, the transept and the eastern part of the nave date from the 13th c. The apse was added in the 14th c., the aisles in the 15th c., and the tower in the 16th c.

The Basilica houses valuable treasures, particularly a Gothic carved altar (16th c.), superb Renaissance stained-glass windows and excellent brasswork by J. José. The *treasury at the entrance to the south aisle is one of the richest in Belgium. It contains liturgical utensils, early medieval ivories and a quantity of gold and silverware, as well as the famous "Head of Christ" (11th c.).

Next to the church are Romanesque cloisters (beautiful sculptures). Around the town there are remains of several medieval fortifications, among them the *Moerenpoort* (Military Museum). The **Roman Rampart-tower** was part of the second Roman town wall. Especially interesting are parts of the first *town walls* (2nd c.), approximately one-third of which have survived. A visit to the **Gallo-Roman Museum** is also recommended. It contains a number of interesting Roman finds.

HISTORY. – Tournai is one of the oldest towns in the country. It was known in the Roman era as *Turris Nerviorum* and as early as the 4th c. was an important fortress. In the middle of the 5th c. it was the headquarters of the Salian Franks. It lost its position when King Clovis I transferred his seat to Soissons in 486. At the beginning of the 6th c., Tournai became the see of a Bishop. It then belonged to the County of Flanders and after 1188 to France. In the 15th c., it was quite prosperous, owing to its famous carpet-making. At that time, its School of Painting (Robert Campin and Rogier van der Weyden) became world-famous. In 1521, Tournai came into the possession of Charles V. He ceded it to the Netherlands and since then the town shared the checkered destiny of that country. It was conquered in 1667 by Louis XIV, and then fortified by Vauban. In 1714 it became part of the Austrian Netherlands. In 1794, it again belonged to France, and in 1814 became part of the United Netherlands, until it was incorporated into Belgium in 1830. The splendour of the old princely residence and

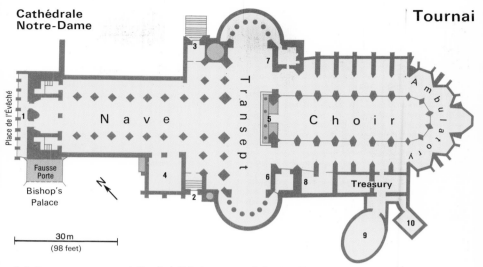

**Cathédrale
Notre-Dame**

Tournai

Place de l'Evêché

N a v e

T r a n s e p t

C h o i r

A m b u l a t o r y

3

7

1

5

Fausse
Porte

4

6

8

Treasury

Bishop's
Palace

2

10

9

30 m
(98 feet)

1 Portico
2 Porte du Capitole
3 Porte Mantile
  (Romanesque sculptures)

4 Chapelle de St-Louis
  ('Crucifixion' by Jordaens)
5 Renaissance Rood Screen
6 Frescoes

7 Remains of Frescoes
8 Chapelle du St-Sacrement
  ('Purgatory' by
  Rubens)

9 Chapelle du St-Esprit
  (tapestry 'Saints Piat
  and Eleutherius')
10 Chapter House

episcopal city is well illustrated by a number of important buildings which, despite large-scale destruction in the Second World War (1940), have remained largely undamaged. Most works by the famous medieval School of Painting were destroyed in 1566 by the Iconoclasts.

SIGHTS. – The Inner City, on the left bank of the Schelde, is bypassed by through traffic which is diverted along the ring road following the line of the former town wall. The focal point of the city is the large triangular **Market Place** (*Grand'Place*). Here there is a *bronze statue of Christine de Lalaing* (A. Dutrieux, 1863), who led the defence of the town in the siege of 1581. On the north-west side of the square stands the Church of *St Quentin*, a 12th c. Romanesque structure. It was rebuilt several times before it was burned down in the Second World War and again re-

Cathedral of Tournai

constructed. On the south side of the Grand'Place stands the former *Cloth Hall* (Halle aux Draps), a Renaissance building begun in 1610 and rebuilt after partially collapsing in 1881.

Nearby, to the south, stands the **belfry** (*Beffroi*), 72 m (236 feet) high. It was built in the 12th–14th c. and restored in 1844–74. It has 260 steps, a carillon, and offers a beautiful view. Nearby is the interesting *Museum of Folklore* (La Maison Tournaisienne).

East of the Market Place is the ****Cathedral** (*Cathédrale de Notre-Dame*), the most notable ecclesiastical structure in Belgium. A basilica in the shape of a cross (ambulatory, chapels), and a group of imposing towers, the central one of which is 83 m (272 feet) high, it was built in the 11th–12th c. and restored in the 19th c. The north and south doors, (the "Porte Mantile" and "Porte du Capitole") are adorned with valuable 12th c. *sculptures. In the western portico are some good relief sculptures, including (in the lower row), the Prophets, Early Fathers and Adam and Eve; these date from the 14th c. and those above them from the 16th–17th c.

The three-aisled INTERIOR of the Cathedral is 134 m (440 feet) long, 66 m (216 feet) wide and 24–33 m (79–108) high. In the transept are 16th c. stained-glass windows illustrating the history of the Bishopric of Tournai. There are also remains of 12th c. frescoes. The superb Renaissance rood screen, separating the choir from the nave, is by Cornelis de Vriendt (1570–3). In the chapels of the ambulatory are

The interior of the Cathedral of Tournai

stained-glass windows (16th–19th c.) and a number of tombstones by the Old School of Tournai. These were damaged by the Iconoclasts. Behind the high altar (1727) is a large marble memorial with the names of all the Bishops and Canons of Tournai. Next to the ambulatory is the *treasury*, containing some first-rate items, including superb tapestries illustrating the legend of Saints Piat and Eleutherius. In the treasury chamber are two late Romanesque reliquaries, the shrine of the Virgin with scenes from the life of Christ (Nicholas of Verdun, 1205), and the shrine of St Eleutherius (1247), with statues of Christ and the Saints.

North of the Cathedral, at the beginning of the Rue de l'Hôpital Notre-Dame which

leads to the station, stands a *bronze sculpture* by Charlier representing four blind people led by a boy (1908). On the south side of the Cathedral is the *memorial* to the painter Rogier van der Weyden (1399–1464), who was born in Tournai. From here, going past the belfry and south-west by the Rue St-Martin, you arrive at the park (Parc Communal). In it stands the **Town Hall** (*Hôtel de Ville*). The building, formerly the Monastery of St Martin was erected in the 18th c., destroyed in the Second World War and then rebuilt. In front of it, on the east side, is the *Museum of Natural History* with a good collection of birds. Nearby on the south-west, is the *Musée des Beaux Arts** which is predominantly a collection of modern paintings but also houses several works by van der Weyden, Rubens and Manet, including "Chez le Père Lathuille" (1879), and "Les Canotiers d'Argenteuil" by the last named. About 500 m (1640 feet) north-east of the Town Hall is the large *Church of St Piat* (12th–17th c.).

West of the Grand'Place is the Place de Lille with the *Church of St Margaret*, originally Romanesque, rebuilt in 1733. In front of it stands the *Memorial* to the

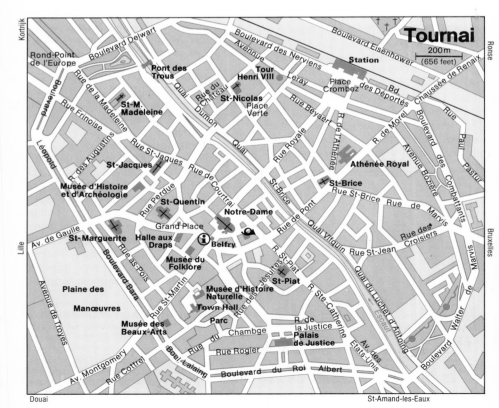

soldiers who lost their lives in Antwerp in 1832 (1897). Not far from here, via the Rue des Carmes, you reach the *Musée d'Histoire et d'Archéologie* housed in a former pawn shop (Mont de Piété; 1622). It has collections of pottery, tombstones and remnants of masonry and paintings salvaged from the ruined churches and buildings after the destruction in 1940.

Further north stands the **Church of St Jacques**, a picturesque building with a Romanesque tower, early Gothic nave and transept, and a choir added in 1368. Down the Rue St Jacques and the Rue de la Madeleine, and right, past the early Gothic Church of *Ste-Marie-Madeleine*, is the **Pont des Trous**, a fortification with two towers (1290). It was part of the old city wall built to control the entry into the town from the River Schelde.

On the right bank of the Schelde is the QUARTIER DU CHÂTEAU (castle district), which attests to the earlier existence of a medieval castle. From the citadel erected here by Henry VIII (1513–18), only the *Tour Henri VIII* now remains. It has a massive cylindrical keep with two vaulted chambers, one above the other. Inside is a Museum of Arms. Nearby is the early Gothic *Church of St Nicholas* with 14th–15th c. tombstones. Further south stands the *Church of St Brice*, burned down in 1940 and restored to its former Romanesque-Gothic style. Nearby, in the Rue Barre St Brice, there are some well-preserved late 12th c. Romanesque town houses. Remains of the 13th c. medieval *town wall* can be seen at the south-east end of the part of the town on the right bank of the river.

SURROUNDINGS of Tournai. – 6 km (4 miles) north rises the **Mont St-Aubert**, still within the boundaries of the town. It is 147 m (482 feet) high and is the only hill in the vicinity. It is named after the little 18th c. Church of the Holy Trinity which crowns it. Nearby are several large limestone quarries.

Twente/Twenthe

Country: The Netherlands. – Province: Overijssel.
ⓘ **Prov. VVV Overijssel en VVV Twente,**
De Werf 1,
NL-7607 HH Almelo;
tel. (0 54 90) 1 87 65.
Prov. VVV Gelderland en VVV Arnhem en de Zuid-Veluwe,
Stationsplein 45,
NL-6811 KL Arnhem;
tel. (0 85) 45 29 21.

The region of Twente (in Dutch Twenthe) lies in the provinces of Overijssel and Gelderland, in the eastern part of the Netherlands. It extends between Salland in the north and Achterhoek in the south. In the west it reaches as far as the IJssel and its eastern border is formed by the Dutch/German frontier.

The region's characteristic features are vast stretches of monotonous sandy plains which rise in the east into a moraine elevation up to 85 m (279 feet) high. The hills consist of the eroded remains of gravel and rock deposited here by the glaciers in the next-to-last Ice Age.

Since about 1830 domestic crafts, traditional in this area, have developed into an important textile industry and an important factor in the region's economy. Cotton processing, spinning and weaving mills and dyeing plants are located mainly in the towns **Enschede** (see page 144), **Hengelo, Almelo** and **Oldenzaal**. Except for these industrial areas, the rest of Twente is still largely agricultural. Villages and scattered farms are the dominant feature of the landscape. In the north pastures and meadows are only occasionally broken by cultivated fields. South of Enschede the ratio of cultivation increases because of the improved quality of the soil.

Utrecht

Country: The Netherlands. – Province: Utrecht.
Altitude: 5 m (16 feet). – Population: 248,000.
Postal code: NL-3500 AA to 3599.
Telephone code: 0 30.
ⓘ **VVV Utrecht,**
Vredenburg 90,
NL-3511 BD Utrecht;
tel. 31 41 32.
VVV-Kiosk in Hoog Catharijne,
Stationsstraverse 5,
NL-3554 EZ Utrecht.

HOTELS. – *Holiday Inn*, Jaarbeursplein 24, L, 430 b.; *Smits*, Vredenburg 14, I, 89 b.; *Noord-Brabant*, Vredenburg 3, II, 18 b.; *Des Pays Bas*, Janskerkhof 10, II, 75 b.; *Hes*, Maliestraat 2–4, III, 40 b.; *De Baronie*, Biltstraat 29–31, IV, 24 b. – YOUTH HOSTEL: in Bunnik, Rijnauwenselaan 14, 130 b. – CAMP SITE: *De Berekuil*, Ariënslaan 5–7.

RESTAURANTS. – *'t Begijntje*, Van Asch van Wijckskade 26; *In der Sackendraegher*, Zakkendragersteeg 22; *Wilhelminapark*, Wilhelminapark 65; *Brabant*, Radboudkwartier 23; *Jean d'Hubert*,

Vleutenseweg 228; *Den Hommel*, Pijperlaan 1; *Juliana*, Amsterdamsestraatweg 464.

EVENTS. – *Spring and Autumn Fair "Jaarbeurs"*; *Carillon Concerts*: on the Domplain (June–August, every Thursday (8–9 p.m.), on holidays (noon–1 p.m.), and from the tower of the Gerardus-Majella Church, Vleutenseweg/Thomas a Kempisweg (every first Saturday in the month 3–4 p.m.)).

FLEA MARKETS. – Near the Château De Haar.

SPORTS and LEISURE. – Fishing, bowling, skittles, golf, riding, swimming, sailing, wind-surfing, water-skiing.

Utrecht, the north-east cornerstone of "Randstad Holland", is the capital of the province of the same name and the fourth largest city in the Netherlands. It lies on the Kromme Rijn (which divides here into the Old Rhine and the Vecht), and on the Amsterdam-Rhine Canal, exactly on the geographical divide between the marshes and the sandy areas of the Geest. This position on the natural dividing line has had a favourable effect on the development of habitation over the years. The North Sea tidal waves could not reach the surface of the slightly elevated Geest, and before dike construction was invented it was an ideal place for a settlement.

Utrecht has always been one of the most important political, cultural and economic cities in the country. The Provincial Administration and its famous University (founded in 1636) are overshadowed in their importance by the religious functions of the city. Utrecht is the seat of a Catholic and a Dutch Old Catholic Archbishop, as well as the headquarters of the Ecumenical Council of the Netherlands. As such it is the focal point of Catholicism in the country. Through the University, several educational and research institutions have been established in Utrecht, including sections of the Royal Dutch Academy of Sciences, the Central Institute for Food Research, Space Research Laboratories and the Institute for International Law, to name the most important.

Utrecht is not only an educational, administrative and religious capital, however; it is also important in the service industries, commerce and transport. Industry is concentrated primarily in the west of the city where railway lines, roads and canals converge. There are steel and rolling mills, machinery and rolling stock construction, electrical and food industries, petro-chemicals, textiles, railway repair yards, furniture-making and a number of other concerns.

No less important economically is tourism. Visitors are attracted by the picturesque old town, surrounded by moats and intersected by canals, and by its architectural monuments. Equally attractive are the pleasant surroundings of the city.

HISTORY. – Utrecht was known to the Romans as *Trajectum ad Rhenum*. Later it was called *Wiltaburg* by the Frisians and the Franks. It is one of the oldest cities in Holland. The Frankish King Dagobert I (628–638) founded the first church in the land of the Franks here; the first Bishop of the church became St Willibrord in 696. The bishops (archbishops since 1559) were powerful and influential prelates in the Middle Ages, and the town soon became famous for its magnificent churches. It belonged first to Lotharingia, then to the Holy Roman Empire, and was frequently the imperial residence. In 1528, Bishop Henry of Bavaria ceded secular authority to Charles V, who built the fort of Vredenburg in Utrecht. Charles V's tutor, Adriaan Floriszoon Boeyens, the future Pope Adrian VI (Hadrian), who was one of the most erudite men of his time, was born in Utrecht in 1459. The *Union of Utrecht*, a special pact between the seven northern Protestant provinces seeking separation from the Southern Netherlands, was concluded here in 1579 under the chairmanship of Jan van Nassau the Elder, brother of William the Silent. In 1672, Louis XIV wrought heavy damage upon the city. The *Peace Treaty of Utrecht* ended the War of the Spanish Succession in 1713.

SIGHTS. – The old town is surrounded by the ancient moat called the *Singel*, along which extend attractive promenades. The middle of the old town is intersected by the *Oude* and the *Nieuwe Gracht*. The water level of the Nieuwe Gracht is so low that the vaults in the embankment walls are used as warehouses. In summer pleasant boat excursions can be taken. Approximately in the middle of the old town is the Domplein with the ***Cathedral of St Michael** (Dutch Reformed), one of the most magnificent churches in the country. It was built in 1254 on the site of the 10th c. Romanesque Church of St Martin. It was completed in 1517, but of the original building, only the choir (completed 1317), the transept (1455–79) and two crossbeams of the outer southern aisle have survived. The original five-aisled church was destroyed by a storm in 1674.

The relatively plain INTERIOR of the Cathedral contains several tombstones which were partially damaged in the 16th c. by the Iconoclasts. There are

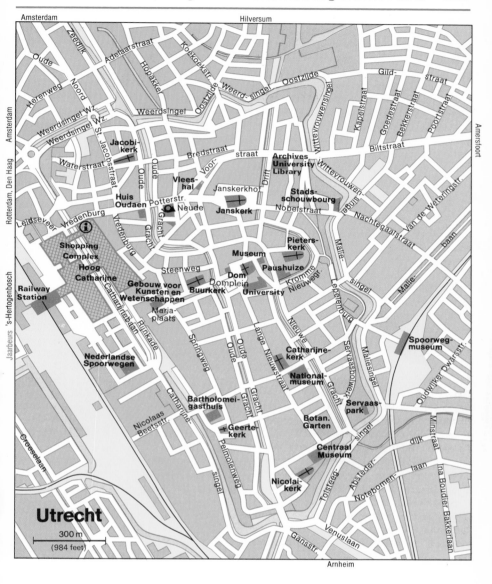

Utrecht

300 m
(984 feet)

also the viscera of the German Emperors Conrad II and Henry V, who died in Utrecht. Their bones are buried in the Cathedral of Speyer.

replica of a *runic stone* of 980, the original of which is in Jutland in Denmark.

The *Cathedral tower* (14th c.), is 112 m (367 feet) high and has stood alone since 1674. Its carillon of forty-seven bells is by the brothers Hemony. The tower was once symbolic of the power of the bishops; it is the highest in the country and its construction has been much imitated. At a height of 100 m (328 feet) is a platform which can be reached by 465 steps (difficult ascent) and which offers a superb view. The picturesque *cloisters* (14th–15th c.) on the south side of the choir connect the Cathedral to the University. West of the cloisters is a *statue of Count Jan van Nassau* (1833), and also a

The Canal House in Utrecht

The **University**, founded in 1636, has about 20,000 students; it is housed in the buildings of the Old Chapter House and in 19th c. extensions. The Union of Utrecht was signed in its former Chapter Hall. (The Hall is now used as the University Assembly Hall.) Adjoining the choir of the Cathedral is the *Dutch Museum of Gold, Silver and Clocks*, and the *Organ Museum* called "From Musical Box to Barrel Organ" (organ recitals Thursdays, 8 p.m.). Next to it is the *Museum of Contemporary Art* (art since 1965). Nearby, to the south-east, on the Pausdam on the corner of Kromme Nieuwegracht are the offices of the **provincial administration**. They are housed in the so-called *Paushuize* ("Papal House") built in 1517 for the then Prior of St Saviour, the future Pope Adrian VI. To the north, in the Pieterskerkhof, stands the **St Pieterskerk**, consecrated in 1054 (Romanesque crypt, Gothic transept and choir). It now belongs to the Walloon community.

On the right of the **Nieuwegracht**, which leads from Pausdam to the south, stands the former *House of the Teutonic Order* (No. 3, entrance from Hofpoort). On the right, the narrow Catharijnesteeg leads to the Catholic *Church of St Catherine*, built between 1524 and 1537, which is the Catholic Cathedral. It has a neo-Gothic tower (1900). Adjacent, to the south, is the *National Museum "Het Catharijneconvent"* (No. 63 Nieuwe Gracht) which was opened in 1979 and illustrates the history of Christianity in Holland. At the south end of the Nieuwegracht, on the right, lie the *Botanical Gardens* of the University. Opposite is the *Servaas Park* (observatory).

From here the Agnietenstraat and its continuation, the Nicolaasstraat, lead south to Oudegracht. On the left at No. 1 Agnietenstraat, is the *Central Museum occupying the chapel (1512–16), the refectory of the former Convent of St Agnes and an adjacent building. Its collections which comprise those of the *Archiepiscopal Museum*, the *Municipal Museum* and the *Archaeological Collection*, are important to the study of the history of ecclesiastical art in the Netherlands. Further to the south-west, at the end of the Agnietenstraat, stands the *Church of St Nicolai* (Reformed) with two Romanesque towers (12th c.). In one of them is a carillon by the brothers Hemony.

In the southern part of the **Oudegracht (Tolsteegzijde)**, on the corner of the Eligenstraat, is a Frisian *sacrificial stone* ("de gesloten steen") fastened by a chain which figures in an old Devil's Legend. Not far west from the Oudegracht stands the old *Geerte-Kerk* (restored in 1957, Dutch Reformed), and the *Hospice of St Bartholomew* (Bartholomei-Gasthuis; 1407). Inside, in the Regent's Room are superb tapestries by the carpet-weaver Maximilian van der Gucht of Delft.

To the west of the Cathedral, beyond the Maartensbrug (to the right beautiful view of the Vismarkt), stands the ancient *Buurkerk* (13th–15th c.) with a massive brick tower. West of this is the **Mariaplaats**, with the *Gebouw voor Kunsten en Wetenschappen*, built in 1840, used for theatrical performances and lectures. At the south-west corner of the building stands the Romanesque *Kloostergang van St Marie* (cloisters), a remnant of the Church of St Mary (founded in the 11th c. by King Henry IV and pulled down in the 19th c.). To the north-west there extends as far as Square Vredenburg the large new *shopping complex, **Hoog Catherijne**. The complex is connected with the **Central Station** (*Centraal Station*) to the west. South-west of the station is the new building of the *Jaarbeurs* (exhibition grounds). South-west of the Mariaplaats, beyond the Catharijnebaan, stands the large *administrative building of the Dutch railways* (Nederlandse Spoorwegen, 1920, 60 m (197 feet) tower).

North of the Cathedral, the Domstraat leads to the *Janskerkhof* (Saturday morning a flower market). In the middle stands **St Janskerk** (Dutch Reformed), a Romanesque building (*c.* 1050; choir, 1539; façade, 1682). Nearby to the north-east, are the *National and Municipal Archives* (entrance Drift), and not far way, in the Wittevrouwenstraat, the *University Library* with approximately 850,000 books and 2500 valuable manuscripts (among them the 11th c. "Utrecht Psalter"). East of the Janskerkhof, the Nobelstraat leads to the Lucasbolwerk (pleasant park) and to the *Stadsschouwburg* (theatre built in 1940 by Dudok).

West of the Janskerkhof, via the Lange Jansstraat, is **Neude**, a square with the large Post Office building (1918–24). Opposite the *Post Office*, to the south, is the *Neudeflat*, a fifteen-storey tower

In the Railway Museum of Utrecht

(1963) with a panoramic restaurant. North-east of the square, on the right of the Voorstraat, is the *Butcher's House* (1637). West of the Neude is the pictures-que **Oudegracht (Weerdzijde)**. Here, opposite the Post Office, stands the *Huys Oudaen*, a 14th c. castle-like mansion with a beautiful doorway (1680). The Peace Treaty of Utrecht was signed in this house. Near the north end of the Oude-gracht stands **St Jacobikerk** (Re-formed), founded in 1173 and rebuilt in the 14th–15th c. in the form of a Gothic hall-church.

West of the Neude on the site of the former imperial castle (destroyed in 1577), is the vast **Vredenburg (Vree-burg)**, one of the busiest squares in the city.

The newer town development lies beyond the Singel. On the east side of the old town runs the well-known **Maliebaan**, an avenue 700 m (766 yards) long and lined with lime trees, spared by the French troops in 1672–3 by order of Louis XIV. At No. 42 is the *Department of Modern Art of the Central Museum*. The former Maliebaan-Station houses the *Railway Museum*. At the north-east end of the Maliebaan, on the right, lies the small *Hoogelandse Park*. South of here, along the Koningslaan, is the *Wilhelmina Park*.

SURROUNDINGS OF Utrecht. – The pleasant coun-tryside around Utrecht is fertile and criss-crossed by canals and branches of the Rhine. Almost everywhere it has the ambience of a garden, with numerous country estates and parks. Good roads connect the city with villages and towns lying on the wooded fringes of the Veluwe (see page 261), part of which is now a nature reserve. 5 km (3 miles) north-west in *Haarzuilens*, is the Château De Haar, built by P. J. H. Cuypers in 1890–2. 8 km (5 miles) north-east is *Bilthoven*, and 16 km (10 miles) north-east the Royal

residence *Soestdijk*. South-west of here stands Castle *Drakestein*, the present residence of Queen Beatrix. 2 km (1 mile) east is **Amersfoort** (see page 67). Other places of interest are *Zeist, Dreibergen* and *Doorn*, and in the region of Gooiland **Hilversum** (16 km (10 miles) north, see page 179), *Baarn* (18 km (11 miles) north-east), and *Bussum* (22 km – 14 miles north). A worthwhile excursion can be made to the west via *Alphen a.d. Rijn* (*bird sanctuary "Avi-fauna"*) to **Leyden** (see page 189) or **Gouda** (see page 158).

Veluwe

Country: The Netherlands. – Province: Gelderland.
(i) **VVV Noord-eu Midden Veluwe,**
Stationsplein 6,
NL-7311 NZ Apeldoorn;
tel. (0 55) 21 04 21.

Most of the Dutch region of Veluwe lies in the province of Gelderland. It extends south of the Veluwemeer, a narrow inlet of the IJsselmeer sepa-rating Flevoland from the main-land. In the east it is bordered by the River IJssel. In the west it merges into the hill range of Utrecht, while in the south it reaches as far as the Lek, the Delta branch of the Rhine.

The Veluwe is an extensive sandy area which acquired its present form in the Ice Ages. The monotonous stretches of dunes with heath and woods are broken in the south and east by moraines up to 80–100 m (262–328 feet) high from the next-to-last Ice Age. There is a thriving tourist industry. A special attraction is the *National Park De Hoge Veluwe north of Arnhem. This nature reserve, covering 5400 hectares (13,343 acres), includes a *game reserve* in the south. Adjacent to it, in the north, is the *Museum Park* with the very interesting *National Museum Kröller-Müller, which can be reached by car from Otterloo. It primarily houses collections of modern art, among them many outstanding paintings by Vincent van Gogh. Worth seeing also are the sculptures in the park, as well as the *hunting lodge St Hubertus* (open to visitors).

Almost all of the old traditional villages have been converted into holiday resorts. Tourism is an important source of income for the local population. There is only a small amount of farming, which is based on undemanding crops and the pro-duction of butter and eggs.

The sandy region of Veluwe is sparsely populated, and has no towns within it. These are all situated on the perimeter, where communications are good; the rest of the area is unsuitable for settlements. Among the towns are the IJsselmeer ports *Harderwijk* and *Elburg*, **Arnhem** (see page 94), **Apeldoorn** (see page 91), and *Ede*.

Venlo

Country: The Netherlands. – Province: Limburg.
Altitude: 20 m (66 feet). – Population: 62,000.
Postal code: NL-5900 AA to 5999.
Telephone code: 0 77.
ⓘ **VVV Venlo,**
Keulsepoort 3,
NL-5911 BX Venlo;
tel. 1 12 41.

HOTELS. – *De Bovenste Molen DMP*, Bovenste Molenweg 12, II, 130 b.; *Valuas*, Urbanusweg 9–11, II, 22 b.; *Wilhelmina*, Kaldenkerkerweg 1, III, 68 b.; *Stationshotel*, Keulsepoort 16, III, 58 b.; *Deckers*, Mgr Nolensplein 44, III, 19 b.; *Old Dutch*, Markt 21, III, 14 b.; *In de Grolschquelle*, Eindhovenseweg 3–8, IV, 32 b.; *Irene*, Mgr Nolensplein 55, V, 13 b. – CAMP SITE.

RESTAURANTS. – *Escargot*, Parade 42. – In BLERICK: *Tramhalte*, Antoniusplein 4.

The Dutch town of Venlo, on the River Maas, is the northern cultural, administrative and economic hub of the province of Limburg.

Venlo is an important traffic junction between Rotterdam and the Ruhr Basin and has provided, especially since the end of the Second World War, excellent conditions for the establishment of industries and international business companies which export the market-garden produce from the surrounding area. The most important industrial enterprises are machinery, the manufacture of optical apparatus, wire drawing, electrical equipment, in addition to textiles, building materials and timber.

HISTORY. – Venlo was an unimportant trade settlement until it received its charter in 1343. In 1481, it joined the Hanseatic League. As a frontier settlement it was built up into a fortress, but had to surrender on several occasions – in 1543 to the troops of Charles V, in 1586 to Farnese, in 1632 to Frederick Henry and in 1794 to Marlborough. In 1713, it became part of the United Netherlands. In-dustrialisation and the rapid rise in population which accompanied it, began after 1868 when the for-tifications were destroyed. The town was heavily damaged in the Second World War, but within a few years the present modern town rose out of the rubble.

SIGHTS. – In the Grote Kerkstraat stands the **St Maartenskerk** (*Hoofdkerk*) (1411). It was heavily damaged in 1944 but expertly restored. Inside is a bronze font (1629) and a carved wooden altar screen showing Christ and the Two Thieves. In the vicinity of the church there are several interesting *gabled houses* (16th and 18th c.).

North of the Church of St Martin, via the Gasthuisstraat, is the fine 14th c. **Town Hall** (*Stadhuis*). In the Council Chamber, which has leather-covered walls, are several good paintings. The *Goltzins Museum*, on the same street, south-east of the Town Hall, contains interesting collections of local and regional history and some valuable porcelain.

SURROUNDINGS of Venlo. 6 km (4 miles) south-east, beyond the Dutch/German border, is the town of **Nettetal**, incorporating the district of *Kaldenkirchen*. Nettetal can be reached via the border crossing *Keulse Barrière*.

Verviers

Country: Belgium. – Province: Liège.
Altitude: 200–240 m (656–787 feet).
Population: 57,000.
Postal code: B-4800.
Telephone code: 0 87.
ⓘ **Syndicat d'Initiative**
(Bureau du Tourisme),
Hôtel de Ville;
tel. 3 61 61.
Syndicat d'Initiative
(Pavillon),
Place des Victoires;
tel. 3 02 13.
(May to September only.)

HOTELS. – *Amigo*, Rue Herla 1, II, 59 r.; *Le Grand Hôtel*, Rue du Palais 145, III, 25 r.; *Le Square*, Rue du Manège 22, IV, 6 r.; *Le Grand Hôtel Europe*, Place Verte 38–40, IV, 22 r.; *Le Charlemagne*, Place du Martyr 48, IV, 15 r.; *Park* (no rest.), Rue Xhavée 90, IV, 14 r.; *Des Ardennes*, Place de la Victoire 15, V, 5 r.

RESTAURANT. – *Maison Monlan*, Crapaurue 37.

EVENTS. – Operas, operettas, concerts and drama in the Town Theatre (Théâtre Communal).

SPORTS and LEISURE. – Soccer, handball, basket-ball, tennis, swimming (outdoor and indoor pools), skiing.

The Belgian industrial town of Ver-viers in the province of Liège is set like an amphitheatre on both banks of the Vesdre, approximately half-way between Aachen (Aix) and

Liège. Verviers is the district administrative capital of an urban area with a population of some 80,000.

Vervier developed systematically after the 18th c. into the main town of a textile region reaching as far as Eupen. Its basis was the traditional wool industry which, from the 15th c., made use of the town's advantages. Its location on the Vesdre kept it supplied with water, and the sheep-rearing areas in the Ardennes and the Eifel provided the raw materials. In addition to textiles, leatherware, machinery, paper-making and building materials are also important, as is tourism, since the town is the gateway to the picturesque Herve region and to the Ardennes (see pages 92–93).

HISTORY. – The history of Verviers goes back to the Roman settlement of *Virovirius*. In the 10th c. a parish was founded on the same site by Benedictine monks from Stavelot. Up to the 18th c. Verviers belonged to the principality of Liège. On 4 December 1651 the Prince of Liège gave it town status. In 1795 it was acquired by France. After the defeat of Napoleon, it belonged briefly to Holland, and after 1830 it became part of the Kingdom of Belgium. From then on, the industrialisation of the town began, and its population increased from 20,000 in 1830 to 53,000 in 1900.

SIGHTS. – The main part of the town lies on the left bank of the Vesdre. Its central point is the Place Verte, from which the Rue Crapaurue, the main shopping street, leads to the **Town Hall** (*Hôtel de Ville*). This detached neo-Classical building dates from the 18th c., and ranks among the most elegant structures of its kind. In front of it is a *Perron* (1732; steps and a platform).

Further north, on the Rue des Raines, are several beautiful town houses (16th–18th c.), evidence of the prosperous history of the town. Nearby to the east, in the Place Saint-Remacle, stands the *Church of St Remacle* (1838), the principal church in the town. It has an interesting façade of limestone quarried in the vicinity.

West of here, in a former 17th c. Hospice for elderly men, in the Rue Renier, is the **Municipal Museum** (*Musée des Beaux Arts et de la Céramique*), with local antiquities, paintings, and an excellent collection of pottery and china. Further west, by the river, stands the small *Church of Notre Dame* (18th c.). In the tower is a fine forty-bell carillon.

From the UPPER TOWN there is a very good view of Verviers. In the Place Vieuxtemps stands a memorial to the violinist of the same name who was born in the town.

Veurne (Furnes)

Country: Belgium. – Province: West Flanders.
Altitude: 0–30 m (0–99 feet). – Population: 10,000.
Postal code: B-8480.
Telephone code: 0 58.
(i) **Dienst voor Toerisme,**
Grote Markt;
tel. 31 21 54.

HOTEL. – *'t Belfort*, Grote Markt 26, V, 9 r.

EVENTS. – **Procession of Penitents** (every year on the last Sunday in July); *Harvest Procession* (15 August).

The little town of Veurne (in French, Furnes), not far from the Belgian North Sea coast at the junction of four canals, was once the main settlement in the Castellany of the Counts of Flanders (Veurne-Ambacht). Today it is the capital of an administrative and judicial district and merits a visit for its beautiful Market Place. Its architectural monuments from the Spanish era, destroyed by bombardment in the First World War, have been skilfully restored.

The famous Penitents' Procession (Boeteprocessie), in which scenes from the Passion of Christ are performed, began in the 12th c. Since the plague in 1637, it has taken place on the last

Penitents' Procession in Veurne

Sunday in July. It has now become, to some extent, a secular celebration.

SIGHTS. – In the middle of the town is the ancient *Grote Markt. On its east side, on the left of the Ooststraat, stands the Gothic building of the *Spaans Paviljoen* (15th c.). It was a town hall until 1586 and then the headquarters of the Spanish garrison; it is now the district court. To the right of it is the old *Butcher's House*, a Renaissance building (1615), now a museum and library. On the north side are several beautiful Renaissance houses. In the north-west corner stands the **Town Hall** (*Stadhuis*, guided tours in summer), a twin-gabled Renaissance building with a fine loggia (1596–1612). Among other items of interest are Spanish leather wall hangings, and several souvenirs relating to 15th and 16th c. law. On the north, at right angles to the Town Hall, stand the *Law Courts* (Gerechtschof), the old "Landhuis" or "Châtellenie", built in 1613–16, with an interesting interior.

Behind the Law Courts, on the north, stands the massive Gothic *belfry* (1616–28). It burned down in 1940, but has been restored. The **Church of St Walburga** was planned on a vast scale in 1230–80, but only the lofty *choir was completed by the Middle Ages. The transept is modern. Inside are beautiful choir-stalls (1629) and a 15th c. shrine. Behind the church is a pleasant park. Nearby, to the east of the Market Place, is the Gothic *Church of St Nicholas* (massive unfinished tower, carillon). In the Noordstraat, also near the Market Place, is an old inn, *Noble Rose*, built in 1572, and now occupied by a bank.

Church of St Nicholas in Veurne

Vianden

Country: Luxembourg. – Canton: Vianden.
Altitude: 202–505 m (663–1656 feet).
Population: 1600.

ⓘ Syndicat d'Initiative,
Victor Hugo-Museum;
tel. (0 03 52) 8 42 57.

HOTELS. – *Collette*, Grand'rue 68–70, I, 17 r.; *Heintz*, Grand'rue 55, II, 30 r.; *Oranienburg*, Grand'rue 126, II, 45 r.; *Victor Hugo*, Rue Victor Hugo 1, III, 36 r.; *Hof van Holland*, Rue de la Gare 6, III, 47 r. – YOUTH HOSTEL. – Several CAMP SITES.

RESTAURANT. – *Veiner Stuff*, Rue Gare 26.

EVENTS. – "Chasing of Judas" (Good Friday).

The picturesque little Luxembourg town of Vianden lies in the Valley of the Our near the German border. It is a popular summer resort and a favourite destination of sightseers.

SIGHTS. – Vianden has a fine 13th c. Gothic **Parish Church** with a Renaissance altar by the famous artist Ruprecht Hoffmann of Trier. The cloisters of this former Trinitarian monastery are some of the oldest to be found between

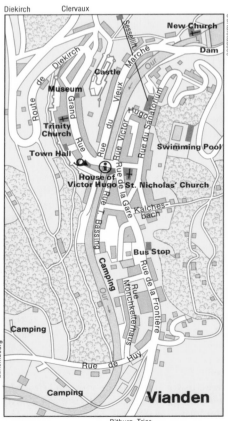

Vianden

View of Vianden

SURROUNDINGS of Vianden. – 5 km (3 miles) north of the town lies the upper reservoir of the *Centrale Hydro-Electrique de Pompage. The Our Valley Dam has two reservoirs and an underground power station. Above it rises *St Nicholas' Hill* (460 m – 1509 feet) with a *beautiful view. The storage system consists of the twin upper reservoirs, and the *lake, which is 8 km (5 miles) long and has a capacity of more than 6 million cu. m (200 million cubic feet). It extends from the dam near Vianden as far as Stolzembourg.

the Meuse, the Rhine and the Moselle. In the *House of Victor Hugo* a small museum contains hand-written letters, furniture, documents and drawings which belonged to the author. He lived here in 1871.

The town is dominated by a ruined *castle (12th–17th c.), the former family seat of the Counts of Vianden and later of the House of Nassau-Orange. It is now the family property of the Grand Duke. The best views are from the *Belvedere and from the chairlift which goes up to 420 m (1378 feet).

The Our Valley Dam near Vianden

Waterloo

Country: Belgium. – Province: Brabant.
Altitude: 90–130 m (295–426 feet).
Population: 18,000.
Postal code: B-1410.
Telephone code: 02

(i) Syndicat d'Initiative
   et de Tourisme de Waterloo,
   Rue Colline 12;
   tel. 5 12 68 67 and 5 13 89 40.

HOTELS. – *La Grimaudière*, Chaussée de Bruxelles 254, IV, 19 r.; *Veorkarre*, Route du Lion 369, IV, 6 r.; *Du Lion* (no rest.), Route du Lion 254, IV, 7 r.

RESTAURANTS. – *La Charmille*, Chaussée de Bruxelles 154; *Sphinx*, Chaussée de Tervuren 178; *Clos Joli*, Chaussée de Tervuren 155; *Maison du Seigneur*, Chaussée de Tervuren 389.

The Belgian Commune of Waterloo, in the province of Brabant, 18 km (11 miles) south of Brussels, has become famous because of the great battle of 1815.

The former battlefield of Waterloo, sometimes also called Belle-Alliance, has been visited by so many sightseers that the commune has become an important tourist resort. The main source of income of the local population is still agriculture, however, with industry (metal and timber processing plants, textiles, leather and food) playing only a relatively small economic role.

HISTORY. – The village of Waterloo was remote and unknown until 18 June 1815. On that day, 3 km (2 miles) south of Waterloo, Napoleon's army attacked British, Prussian and Dutch troops under Wellington's

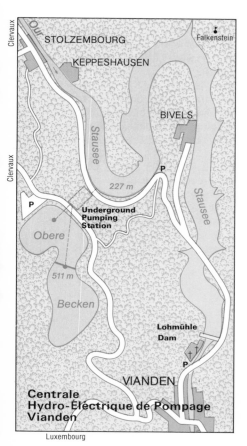

Clervaux
STOLZEMBOURG   Falkenstein
KEPPESHAUSEN
BIVELS
Stausee
P
227 m
Stausee
P
Underground
Pumping
Station
Obere
511 m
Becken
Lohmühle
Dam
P
VIANDEN
Centrale
Hydro-Électrique de Pompage
Vianden
Luxembourg

Waterloo – the Lion's Mound on the battlefield.

command. The Prussians had been defeated at Ligny two days earlier, but Wellington mounted a successful defence; the Prussian army under Blucher and Gneisenau arrived and decided the issue. The devastating defeat of the French led to the downfall of Napoleon and the demise of his empire.

SIGHTS. – Wellington had his command post from 17–19 June 1815 in the village of Waterloo. A **museum** has been installed on the site. Road N5 to Charleroi runs south of Waterloo, along the so-

The Battlefield of Waterloo (1815)

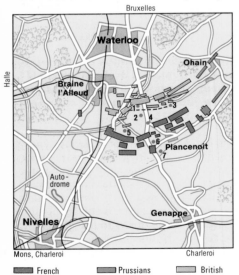

French   Prussians   British

---- Chemin Creux

1 Butte du Lion
  (Wellington's Command Post)
2 Ferme de la Haie Sainte
3 Ferme de la Papelotte
4 Cabaret de la Belle Alliance
5 Ferme de Hougoumont
6 Napoleon's Command Post
7 Ferme du Caillou

called *Crossroads*, with three memorials (Belgian, Hanoverian, and one to Sir Alexander Gordon, Wellington's aide-de-camp). On the right of the road, the former "defile of Ohain" leads towards the famous *Lion's Mound (Butte du Lion)*, visible from some distance. It is a man-made hillock 40 m (131 feet) high, built by the Dutch in 1824–6 with the soil obtained when the surrounding terrain was levelled. The cast-iron lion on top was supplied by France. There are 260 steps leading to the top of the hillock (panoramic view over the battlefield). At the foot of the Lion's Mound, in a circular building, is an interesting *Panorama of the battle*. Opposite is a *museum* (souvenirs).

On the other side of the Crossroads lies the **Ferme de la Belle-Alliance**, once the command post of Napoleon. 3 km (2 miles) beyond, to the left of the road, is the farm of *Le Caillou* (museum) in which Napoleon spent the night of 17 June 1815.

West Frisian Islands/ Nederlandse Waddeneilanden

Country: The Netherlands. Provinces: North Holland, Friesland and Groningen.

ⓘ **VVV Amsterdam e. o.,**
Rokin 5,
NL-1012 KK Amsterdam;
tel. (0 20) 26 64 44.
VVV Friesland-Leeuwarden,
Stationsplein 1,
NL-8911 AC Leeuwarden;
tel. (0 51 00) 3 22 24.
VVV Texel (Waddeneilanden),
Groenplants 9,
NL-1791 CC Den Burg;
tel. (0 22 20) 28 44.

Arranged like a string of pearls, the West Frisian islands extend along the Dutch coast at a distance of 2–25 km (1–16 miles) from the shore: Texel, Vlieland, Terschelling, Ameland, Schiermonnikoog and Rottum. Beyond the Dutch/German border they continue as the East Frisian Islands. Separated from the coastline by the Waddenzee, the arch-shaped line of islands shelters it from the waves of the open North Sea.

Nieuweschild on the West Frisian Island of Texel

About 2500 years ago the Waddenzee was a vast moorland, protected from the destructive forces of the sea by a natural dike of sand and flotsam washed up by the surf. A steady rise in the sea level, caused by the melting of glaciers after the last Ice Age and by the subsidence of the land, led, somewhat later, to the flooding of large stretches of the former peat moor. The most devastating tidal waves occurred in the Middle Ages; they created both the Waddenzee and the Zuiderzee (enclosed by a dike in 1932 and now the IJsselmeer).

The present chain of islands is the remnant of the former natural dike, pierced in several places by the advancing sea. On the seaward side, the West Frisian Islands are lined with younger dunes which moved steadily eastward, pushed by currents and westerly winds. By planting dune grass and constructing breakwaters the shifting of sand masses has been arrested.

In addition to sheep rearing, fishing and sporadic farming, summer tourism is economically important. The white beaches, miles long, are among the most beautiful in the world. The islands have many nature parks where thousands of sea birds nest in winter, e.g. on the north coast of Texel (Eijerland) and on the islands of Vlieland and Terschelling (Boschplaat).

Wiltz

Country: Luxembourg. – Canton: Wiltz.
Altitude: 340–500 m (1115–1640 feet).
Population: 4000.

ⓘ **Syndicat d'Initiative,**
Bureau au Château;
tel. 9 61 45 and 9 61 99.

HOTELS. – *Du Commerce*, Rue des Tondeurs 9, II, 13 r.; *Du Vieux Château*, Grand'rue 1, II, 13 r.; *Belle Vue*, Rue de la Fontaine 5–7, III, 10 r.; *Beau-Séjour*, Rue du X Septembre 21, III, 47 r.; *Du Pont*, Rue de Pont 11, IV, 12 r. – CAMP SITES.

EVENTS. – *International Festivals* in the Outdoor Theatre.

SPORTS and LEISURE. – Tennis, amateur flying.

The little Luxembourg town of Wiltz is a popular tourist resort in the Ösling, and the European capital of the scout movement. It consists of two parts – Oberwiltz, on a high hill above the little Ardennes river of the same name, and Niederwiltz, which lies on both of its banks. Wiltz is the seat of the Canton administration and provides shopping facilities for the surrounding area.

SIGHTS. – In Oberwiltz there is a *château*, restored in the 16th–17th c. It now houses a *Museum of the Battle of the Bulge*. Inside is an interesting Baroque wooden staircase. Next to it is the *outdoor theatre* (annual international festivals). In the lower part of the Grand'rue stands the *Cross of Justice* (1502), a symbol of the

Wiltz in the Grand Duchy of Luxembourg

town's freedom and judicial authority. In the *Parish Church* of the upper town there is a fine altar (1743) by a local sculptor.

The late Gothic *Deanery Church* in the lower town of Niederwiltz contains several interesting 18th c. altars.

SURROUNDINGS of Wiltz. – The picturesque surroundings of the town can be explored by any of the many footpaths. An excursion to *Esch*, in the neighbouring **Valley of the Sûre** (see page 250), and to the *Lac de la Haute Sûre*, is well worth while.

Ypres/Ieper

Country: Belgium. – Province: West Flanders.
Altitude: 17–45 m (56–147 feet).
Population: 22,000.
Postal code: B-8900.
Telephone code: 0 57.
ⓘ **Dienst voor Toerisme,**
Stadhuis,
Grote Markt;
tel. 20 26 26.

HOTELS. – *De Sultan*, Grote Markt 33, III, 12 r.; *Continental*, R. Colaertplein 29, III, 17 r.; *De Maan*, Grote Markt 5, IV, 8 r.; *Regina*, Grote Markt 45, IV, 17 r.; *Hostellerie St-Nicolas*, G. de Stuersstraat 6, IV, 6 r.; *'t Zweerd*, Grote Markt 2, V, 10 r. – In KEMMEL (Heuvelland): *Hostellerie du Mont Kemmelberg*, Berg 4, III, 20 r. – In WESTOUTER (Heuvelland): *Alhambra*, Rodebergstraat 32, IV, 21 r. – In POPERINGE: *Palace*, Ieperstraat 34, IV, 14 r. – In LANGEMARK-POELKAPELLE: *Munchenhof*, Korte Ieperstraat 6, V, 24 r.

RESTAURANTS. – *Britannique*, Grote Markt 17; *Les Halles*, Grote Markt 35; *Regina*, Grote Markt 45; *Sultan*, Grote Markt 33. – In IEPER-DIKKEBUS: *Dikkebusvijver*, Dikkebusvijverdreef 31. – In WESTOUTER: *Berkenhof*, Bellestraat 53. – In DRANOUTER (Heuvelland): *De Hollemeersch*, Lettinckstraat 58.

EVENTS. – *Tattoo*, daily at 8 p.m., at the Menenpoort; "*Kattestoet*" *Procession and Throwing of Cats* (second Sunday in May).

The Belgian town of Ypres (in Flemish Ieper), lies in the plain of West Flanders, on the River Ieper

(Yperlee), a tributary of the Yser. Ypres is the chief town of a district and has important trade and service functions. Its most important industries are textiles and textile machinery, as well as food processing. Tourism also plays a significant economic role.

HISTORY. – In the Middle Ages, Ypres was, together with Ghent and Bruges, one of the most important towns in Flanders, because of its prosperous clothmaking. Its Cloth Hall, the symbol of power and wealth in the 13th–14th c., was the largest and most beautiful building of its kind in Belgium. In the 14th c. the town took the side of the Kings of France against Ghent, which was allied to England, and was besieged in 1383. It withstood the siege but its surroundings were destroyed and the cloth weavers left. In the 16th c. it was devastated by the Iconoclasts and the troops of the Duke of Alba, sacked by the Geuze and Alexander Farnese and, in the 17th c., was besieged several times by the French. Despite all this, most of its ancient buildings, evidence of its former splendour, were preserved until the First World War when the town, the junction of several important roads, found itself in the middle of the so-called Salient of Ypres held by the English. For four years it was continuously in the line of fire; by 1918 it was a heap of rubble. It was rebuilt according to the original plans, and the damage caused by air-raids in 1940 has also been repaired.

SIGHTS. – In the Grote Markt stands the *Cloth Hall (Lakenhall, 132 m (433 feet) long, restored in its 13th c. style). Inside is a museum with paintings and antiquities from buildings destroyed in the years 1914–18. The *belfry* is 70 m (230 feet) high. Opposite, to the south, is the former *Butcher's House*. To the north, behind the Cloth Hall, stands the **Cathedral of St Martin**, restored in 1922. The original building dates from the 13th c., its south

The "Cats" Feast in Ypres

portal and tower from the 15th c. Inside are several brass fonts (*c.* 1600).

The Menenstraat leads from the Grote Markt east to the **Menin Gate (Menenpoort)**, a memorial arch 40 m (131 feet) long and 32 m (105 feet) wide, built into the old city wall. It was designed by Sir Reginald Blomfield in 1923–7. Inscribed on the inside walls are the names of 58,600 British soldiers who lost their lives in the years 1914–17. In their honour, the Last Post is sounded beneath the gate every day at 8 p.m. – Along the city side of the Majoorgracht, which marks the eastern and southern boundaries of the inner part of the town, runs a tree-lined embankment on the site of the former ramparts (some remains can still be seen).

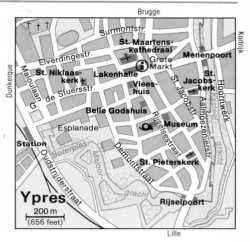

Tattoo in front of the Cloth Hall in Ypres

The Rijselstraat (Lille Street) leads south of the Grote Markt to the rampart (Lille Gate). On the right-hand side, at No. 38, is the former *Belle Godshuis*, a hospital founded about 1279 and rebuilt in 1616. It has an interesting interior. Further south, on the left, is the *Church of St Peter*, originally 12th c. Romanesque and later enlarged in Gothic style. The Rijselstraat ends at the *Lille Gate* (Rijselpoort). From the bridge across the Majoorgracht the remains of the ramparts and, on their west side, the English cemetery can be seen.

SURROUNDING of Ypres. **The Battlefields of the First World War.** The area around the town is visited for its many memories of the First World War. West Flanders was, in the years 1914–18, the scene of heavy fighting, and there are hundreds of war cemeteries here. Massive casualties were suffered in the First Battle of Ypres between 19 October and 22

November 1914, when the Salient was established. The long trench warfare between 1915 and 1917 also claimed thousands of victims on both sides. The British war cemeteries are scattered around Ypres, whereas the graves of the German soldiers are concentrated in a few huge cemeteries.

An interesting round trip of the battlefields (63 km – 39 miles) can be made by car from the Menin Gate. 9 km (6 miles) north-east, across one of the most hotly contested areas, past several British cemeteries, is **Zonnebeke**, a village once completely destroyed. It now has an attractive church with a detached belfry (1921). In *Broodseinde*, 2 km (1 mile) further on, turning left towards *Passendale* (Passchendaele), are German and British cemeteries. 1 km (about a ½ mile) beyond, at the hamlet of Nieuwe-Molden, turning left again, you soon reach the largest British war cemetery, *Tyne Cot*. It was laid out by Sir Reginald Blomfield, has 26,000 war graves and a memorial to 35,000 missing soldiers. From here there is one of the best views over the battlefields of the First World War. 7 km (4 miles) beyond is **Poelkapelle**. 2·5 km (2 miles) south-west, on Road No. 70 leading from here back to Ypres (9 km – 6 miles), are, beyond *Sint-Juliaan*, several British cemeteries. Where the road crosses the road from Zonnebeke to Langemark stands a memorial to 2000 Canadians who lost their lives in 1915 in the first German gas attack. 3 km (2 miles) further on is **Langemark**, a large village with a population of 5500 which was much contested in the war. It has a large German cemetery with some 4500 graves. 1·5 km (1 mile) further south-west, in the direction of Poperinge, is the British cemetery of *Cementhouse* (on the left). A beautiful silhouette of Ypres can be seen on the left. 5 km (3 miles) beyond Langemark, left across the canalised *River Ieper* and 1 km (about a ½ mile) further on in *Boezinge* Road No. 69 enters and runs from Ypres to Ostend. Follow it to the left along the canal past five British cemeteries and in 7 km (4 miles) you arrive back in **Ypres**.

The round trip can be continued further to the south-west by Road No. 70 along the Lake of *Dikkebus*. In *De Klijte* (10 km – 6 miles) turn left and follow a country road slightly uphill. 3 km (2 miles) further you come to **Kemmel**, a village which was completely destroyed during the fighting. 2·5 km (2 miles) south-west rises the strategically important *Kemmelberg* (156 m (512 feet), restaurant), the easternmost spur of the hill range of West Flanders (Monts de Flandre) offering a panoramic view over Ypres and the Flemish plain. On its western slope is a large French communal cemetery with 10,000 graves. 5 km (3 miles) away in the village of *Mesen* (*Messines*) there are several war cemeteries. The elevated ground north of here, between Mesen and *Wijtschate*, was taken by the British in 1917 with the aid of a massive artillery barrage and mine blasting. One of the largest mine craters of that battle, the *"Lone Tree Crater"*, is now a small lake preserved as a memorial. The road continues northwards along Road No. 69 back towards Ypres. 5·5 km (3 miles) beyond Wijtschate a little lane on the right leads to the village of Zillebeke (2·5 km (2 miles) east) and to *Hill 60*, 4·5 km (3 miles) south-east, which was an important artillery observation post and the centre of heavy fighting. There are two English memorials here. The main road then continues straight on to **Ypres** (1·5 km (1 mile), via the Rijselstraat).

East of Ypres, in the direction of Geluwe (Road No. 9), is the **amusement park of Bellewaerde** (small zoo). There is a café/restaurant in a former manor house.

Zealand/Zeeland

Country: The Netherlands. – Province: Zealand.
ⓘ **Provinciate Zeeuwse VVV,**
Postfach 123,
NL-4330 AC Middelburg;
tel. (0 11 80) 2 80 51.

The Dutch region of Zealand in the estuary area of the Rhine, the Maas and the Schelde, includes the islands and peninsulas in the south-west Netherlands (Walcheren, South and North Beveland, Schouwen-Duiveland, Tholen, St Filipsland and Goeree-Overflakkee), as well as the narrow mainland strip of Zealand Flanders between the Wester-schelde and the Belgian frontier. Except for the island of Goeree-Overflakkee, in South Holland, the region of Zealand is identical to the Dutch province of the same name.

Present-day Zealand has been reclaimed from the sea by man-made dikes only within the last 1800 years. The major part of the area lies below sea level. Before the dikes were built, the older peat marshes were flooded by the North Sea and covered with layers of mud. In the course of centuries the waters gradually subsided and depressions ("Kommen") formed on the land. The oldest parts of the islands, enclosed by dikes before the 13th c., were especially affected. These areas were repeatedly exposed to devastating floods, the latest on 1 February 1953. Neither the protective lines of dunes in the north-west of Walcheren, Schouwen and Goeree nor the dikes could resist the impact of the waves. To prevent similar floods in the

Zealand – the bridge between the Dutch islands of North Beveland and Schouwen-Duiveland

A Zealand costume

Zierikzee

Country: The Netherlands. – Province: Zealand.
Altitude: below sea level. – Population: 9000.
Postal code: NL-4300 AA to 4329.
Telephone code: 0 11 10.
ⓘ **VVV Zierikzee,**
Havenpark 29,
NL-4301 JG Zierikzee;
tel. 24 50.

HOTELS. – *Mondragon*, Havenpark 21, III, 18 b.;
Monique (no rest.), Driekoningenlaan 5–7, V, 26 b. –
CAMP SITE.

RESTAURANTS. – *Mondragon*, Oude Haven 13;
Poorthuys, Havenplein 7; *Ecu de France*, Korte
Groensal 2.

MARKETS. – *Horse Market* (first Wednesday in
June); *Market for Tourists* (every Tuesday, from the
beginning of July to the beginning of August).

**Zierikzee is the main town of the
Island Schouwen-Duiveland lying in
the delta of the Rhine and the Maas
in the Dutch province of Zealand,
and consisting of six communes
with a total population of 26,000.**

The main sources of income are tourism
and agriculture. The fertile moor soil of the
island suits the growing of grain, root
crops, flax and vegetables. These products are partly processed in the industrial
plants of Zierikzee. Tourism is concentrated around the yacht harbour and
visitors are attracted by both the picturesque panorama of Zierikzee and the
beautiful sandy beaches lined with
wooded dunes up to 38 m (125 feet)
high in the western part of the island.

The economic prosperity of Zierikzee
really began when communications with
the island improved under the Delta plan.
When the Zealand Bridge (over 5 km (3
miles) long) was opened in 1966 the
island became more closely linked with
Noord-Beveland and the mainland. It was
also linked to the neighbouring islands by
causeways.

SIGHTS. – The spire of the **Sint Lievens-
monstertoren** (60 m (197 feet) high)
can be seen from a great distance. The
structure, begun in 1454 by the famous
architect Anthonis Keldermans, should
have reached a height of 206 m (676
feet), but remained unfinished. Also
worth seeing is the *Town Hall* (1554) by
Bloemmaert, with a wooden bell tower
(carillon). Inside is a *Museum of Ethnography and History*. On the other side of

future, all large river estuaries in Zealand
have been separated from the North Sea
by Enclosing Dikes as part of the so-called
Delta Plan. The only exceptions are the
Nieuwe Waterweg, connecting the Port
of Rotterdam with the open sea, and the
Westerschelde, the shipping lane to
Antwerp.

Zealand is an intensively farmed agricultural country. The villages, as well as the
arable land belonging to them, lie on
elevated ground. These areas, less exposed to the danger of flooding, are
farmed, while the low lying areas are used
as pastures and meadowland. The sizes of
the farms vary between 20 and 50
hectares (49 and 124 acres) in the more
recent, less densely populated polders,
while in the older parts of the islands they
are considerably smaller. The main crops
are grain, sugar-beet and potatoes.

Industrial areas of some importance
include the canal zone crossing Zealand
Flanders from *Terneuzen* to *Ghent* (coking plants, metal and chemical industries,
glass, sugar and textile plants), the
eastern part of Zealand Flanders (textile
industries), the town of **Flushing/
Vlissingen** (see page 149) on the island
of Walcheren, with several shipyards, and
a little further north, **Middelburg** (see
page 215) which, as the capital of
Zealand, is the hub of a thriving tourist
trade.

Zuidhavenpoort in Zierikzee

the street is the 15th c. *Tempeliershuis*. Nearby, at the Havenplein, is the old fishmarket (1616).

Among the historical architectural gems in Zierikzee are the three ancient city gates, remains of the former fortifications. Particularly attractive is the façade of the *Noordhavenpoort* by Bloemmaert (1559), located at the entrance to the harbour. The *Zuidhavenpoort* has a square tower with 14th c. bay-type corner turrets and was designed to control entry into the harbour. In the north of the town is the *Nobelpoort*, the oldest of the town gates (twin towers).

SURROUNDINGS of Zierikzee. – An interesting **round trip** of about 55 km (34 miles) can be made around the part of the island known as "**Schouwen**". Drive first 13·5 km (8 miles) north to the old village of *Brouwershaven* which has a beautiful hall-church (13th–15th c.). There is also a Renaissance Town Hall (1599) and a statue of the popular poet, Jacob Cats (1577–1660). 13 km (8 miles) further west is *Renesse*, with the Château of Moermont. From here drive south-west across pleasant countryside with wooded dunes, via *Burgh/Haamsted* to *Westenschouwen* by the sea 10 km (6 miles) away. There is a good view across the sea to the Island of Schouwen and towards the Island of Noord-Beveland. In 4 km (3 miles) you arrive at *Burghsluis*. From here the road partly follows the southern shore of the island back to Zierikzee. You can cross from the Island of Schouwen-Duiveland to the Island Noord-Beveland in the south by the *Zealand Bridge which was completed in 1966; it is 5022 m (16,171 feet) long and has forty-eight arches carried on double piers (toll).

Zutphen

Country: The Netherlands. – Province: Gelderland.
Altitude: 7 m (23 feet). – Population: 30,000.
Postal code: NL-7200 AA to 7299.
Telephone code: 0 57 50.
ⓘ **VVV Zutphen,**
Wijnhuis, Markt;
tel. 1 93 55.

HOTELS. – *Ibis*, In de Stoven 14, II, 60 b.; *'s-Gravenhof*, Kuiperstraat 11, III, 23 b.

The name of Zutphen is derived from "Zuid Veen" (South Fen). The town lies in the Dutch province of Gelderland, at the confluence of the Berkel and the IJssel, at the beginning of the Twente Canal. It was once the chief town of the county of the same name, which has been part of Geldern since 1127. Zutphen received its town charter in 1190 and joined the Hanseatic League at the end of the 14th c. It was conquered by the Spanish in 1572 but retaken nineteen years later by Maurice of Nassau.

The town is now the capital of the regions of Veluwe and Achterhoek, and possesses cultural and administrative institutions. Important industries are engineering brickworks, chemicals and timbers. Paper and textile mills are also important.

SIGHTS. – In the Groenmarkt, the elongated main square of the town, stand several old *gabled houses*. At the east end of the square is the *Wijnhuistoren*, destroyed by fire in 1920 and restored in its original 17th c. style. It has a carillon (1925). North of the Groenmarkt, in the Rozengracht, is the Municipal Museum, housed in a *former 14th c. monastery*. South of the Groenmarkt is a square called the 's-Gravenhof with the church of **St Walburg** or the **Grote Kerk** dating from the 12th–15th c. (Dutch Reformed). Inside are 15th and 16th c. wall and ceiling paintings, a bronze *font (1527), and, in the choir, a wrought-iron 15th c. chandelier. The chapter house of the church, which dates from the years 1561–3, has some curiously carved capitals and contains an unusual *library* with some 400 valuable manuscripts and incunabula fastened to the reading desks with chains.

Opposite the church, to the north, is the 18th c. *Town Hall*, restored in 1956. Behind it stands the 15th c. Gothic *Burgerzaal*, originally the meat market and later the butter market. East of the church is *Drogenapstoren*, a fine city gate (1444–6). Immediately next to it is the Zaadmarkt (salt market), with good 16th–17th c. brick houses. From the former fortifications the ruins of *Berkelpoort* (1312) and *Nieuwstadspoort* can still be seen.

Zwolle

Country: The Netherlands. – Province: Overijssel.
Altitude: sea level. – Population: 79,000.
Postal code: NL-8000 AA to 8069.
Telephone code: 0 52 00.

(i) **VVV Zwolle,**
Bethlehemskerkplein 35,
NL-8011 PH Zwolle;
tel. 1 39 00.

HOTELS. – *Golden Tulip Hotel Wientjes*, Stationsweg 7, II, 100 b.; *Postiljon Motel Zwolle*, Hertsenbergweg 1, IV, 144 b.; *Weenink*, Rode Torenplein 10–11, IV, 27 b. – CAMP SITE.

RESTAURANT. – *Koningshof*, Koningsplein 8.

Zwolle is the capital of the Dutch province of Overijssel. It lies on the little River Zwarte Water (black water) which, like the River IJssel nearby to the west, opens into the IJsselmeer some 20 km (12 miles) north-west of the town.

Zwolle is the central town of a larger region which includes parts of Drente, Veluwe and the neighbouring North-East Polder. The town is the headquarters of many administrative and educational institutions, and important business enterprises. Of greater importance is its cattle market, one of the largest in the country. Zwolle is also a favoured location for industry (vehicles, machinery, food, textiles, building materials, timber, leather, and chemicals).

HISTORY. – Zwolle is first mentioned in 1040. It then consisted of three adjoining communes, two of which acquired town status in 1230. In 1346, Zwolle

1 Grote Markt 2 Ossenmarkt 3 Melkmarkt 4 Bethlehemskerk

became a member of the Hanseatic League; in 1572 it was acquired by William of Orange, and in 1579 it joined the Union of Utrecht.

SIGHTS. – In the Grote Markt stands the **Grote Kerk** or **St Michaelskerk** (Dutch Reformed Church), built in the 15th c. In the interior is a richly carved pulpit by Adam Straes from Weilburg in Hessen (1622). The artist felt it necessary to insert an inscription explaining that he created the brutal and sinful faces in this work without any evil intention. Beneath the organ lies the fine "Consistoriekamer" (Church Council Chamber); in the choir is the tomb of the painter Gerard ter Borch (Terborch), who was born in Zwolle about 1617 and who died in 1681. The curious *Guard-house* was built in 1614 adjacent to the north side of the church.

Behind the church on the corner of the Sassenstraat, stands the 15th c. **Town Hall** with a magnificent "Schepenzaal" (Aldermen's Hall, now the Marriage Room). Further east is the small 14th c. *Bethlehemsekerk*, a remnant of the monastery of the same name. At the end of the Sassenstraat stands the imposing Saxon gate (**Sassenpoort**) with five pinnacles, built in 1408. It now houses the *archives of the Province of Overijssel*. A good view of the gate is possible from the Burg van Roijensingel.

East of the Grote Markt, on the right of the Diezerstraat, the main shopping street in the town, stands the neo-Gothic *Staten-zaal* (1898). West of the Grote Markt lies the Ossenmarkt, with the 15th c. Catholic *Church of Our Lady*. Its tower, 91 m (298 feet) high, is called "Peperbus" (Pepperpot) and from it there is a beautiful view. Not far north of the Ossenmarkt, in No. 41 Melkmarkt, is the **Overijsseler Museum** (*Museum of History*) housed in a 16th c. building.

On the north-east edge of the town (No. 32 Middelweg), stands the Catholic *Parish Church of St Michael*, built in 1964. In its portico is a memorial to Thomas à Kempis (1380–1471), the author of the four-volume "Imitation of Christ", who from 1407 until his death, lived in the monastery at Agnietenberg, 3 km (2 miles) north-east of Zwolle (memorial).

Practical Information

The Procession of Giants
in the Belgian Town of Ath (Hainaut)

your rear lights and brake lights are working from the reflection on the front of the other vehicle, and you can check up on your headlights and front indicators in your own garage or in a shop window.

When driving at night on wet roads you should stop in a parking place every 50 or 100 km (30 or 60 miles) and clear your headlights and rear lights.
Even the thinnest coat of dirt on the glass reduces the strength of your headlights by half, and a heavy coating may reduce their output by as much as 90%.

Safety on the Road. Some Reminders for the Vacation Traveller

Always wear your seat-belt, and make sure that your passengers wear theirs.
This is compulsory in the Benelux countries.
Note: Compensation for injury may be reduced by up to 50% if seat-belts are not worn.

Change the brake fluid in your car at least every two years.
This vitally important fluid tends to lose its effectiveness in the course of time as a result of condensation of water, dust and chemical decomposition.

Change your tires when the depth of tread is reduced to 2 mm (0·08 inch).
Tires must have enough depth of tread to get a good grip on the road and hold the car steady even on a wet surface. In the case of wide sports tires, with their long water channels, a 3-mm (0·12 inch) tread is advisable.

You will see better, and be more easily seen, if your car lights are functioning properly.
It is important, therefore, to check your sidelights and headlights regularly. This can be done even without getting out of the car. When you stop at traffic lights in front of a bus or truck you can see whether

The best place for fog lights is on the front bumper.
This gives them the maximum range without dazzling oncoming traffic. If they are mounted below the bumper they will have a range of only 5 or 10 m (16 or 32 feet). Fog lights are most effective when used in conjunction with parking lights only: for safe driving, therefore, they must have an adequate range.

It is always advisable to carry a first-aid kit. It is compulsory for all drivers, including visitors, to carry a warning triangle. Remember, however, that if these items are kept on the rear shelf they can become dangerous projectiles in the event of an accident.

The first-aid kit should be kept inside the car, either secured in a holder or under a seat; the warning triangle should be kept ready to hand in the boot (trunk). If there is no more room in the boot any items of equipment or pieces of luggage inside the car should be stowed carefully and securely.

If there is so much luggage in the back of the car that the view through the rear window is obstructed it is a wise precaution, as well as a statutory requirement, to have an outside mirror on the passenger's side. This is useful in any event when driving in heavy traffic on multi-lane highways. It should be convex type.

Drivers who keep their left foot on the clutch pedal after changing gear may be letting themselves in for a heavy repair bill.
This very rapidly wears down the clutch release bearing, giving rise to whining and grating noises.

As a light bulb grows older its efficiency falls off very markedly. A dark-coloured deposit inside a bulb — wolfram from the filament — is an indication of age.
All bulbs should therefore be checked at least once a year. It is advisable to change those which have darkened glass as well as those which are clearly defective.

You can save fuel when driving on highways by keeping the accelerator pedal at least 2 cm (about ¾ inch) short of the "foot down" position.
The nearer to its maximum speed a car is travelling the more steeply does fuel consumption increase. A slightly lighter touch on the accelerator will make little difference to your speed but quite a difference to the amount of fuel you use.

If you wear glasses you will increase the safety of night driving by getting special coated lenses; and all drivers should avoid wearing tinted glasses after dusk and at night.
All glass reflects part of the light passing through it, and even through a clear windshield only about 90% of the light outside reaches the driver's eyes inside the car. If the driver is wearing glasses there is a further light loss of 10%. With a tinted windshield and tinted glasses only about half the light outside reaches the driver's eyes, and in these conditions driving at night is not possible.

If you have an accident

However carefully you drive, you may nevertheless find yourself involved in an accident. If this does happen do not lose your temper, however great the provocation: remain polite, keep cool and take the following action:

1. Warn other road users: switch on your hazard warning lights and set out your warning triangle at a sufficient distance from the scene of the accident.

2. Attend to the injured. Expert assistance should be summoned immediately. Unless you have a knowledge of first aid you should be extremely cautious about attending anyone injured in an accident. Call an ambulance if required.

3. If anyone has been injured, if there has been major damage to the cars involved or if there is disagreement between you and the other party, inform the police.

4. Get the names and addresses of other parties involved; note the registration number and make of the other vehicles and the time and place of the accident. Ask the other parties for the name of their insurers and their insurance number.

5. Note down the names and addresses of witnesses; take photographs and/or make sketches of the scene of the accident.
After a minor accident the police are usually more concerned with getting the road clear for traffic than making a full record of the incident. What you should try to record in your photographs is not damage to the cars involved – that can be established later – but the general situation at the scene of the accident. It is particularly important to photograph each of the cars in the direction of travel from a sufficient distance.

6. If possible fill in the "European Accident Statement" (which you will have received along with your green card if you own the car) and have it signed by the other party. Do not sign any admission of liability. If the other party ask you to sign an accident form not written in English and you are in doubt of its meaning, add the words "without prejudice to liability" above your signature.

7. Inform your own insurance company by letter if possible, within 24 hours of the accident. If your car is rented, inform the rental agency by phone immediately.

8. If the accident involves injury to persons (other than yourself and your passengers) or damage to property, inform the bureau named on the back page of your green card.

9. If you own the car follow the instructions of your insurance company – which you will normally have received along with your green card – concerning repair of damage to your car.

Vaccinations, etc.?
Check first-aid kit.
Confirm hotel, etc., reservations.
Check-up on car, caravan (trailer), etc.
List of service garages for car.
Maps.
Inform friends and neighbours.

Before a vacation by car:
Look over car and caravan (trailer).
Wash car.
Fill up windshield washer reservoir.
Check tire pressures.
Check first-aid kit.
Check adjustment of seat-belts and head-rests.
Check visibility.
International Distinguishing Sign.
Warning triangle.
Flashing light.
Flashlight.
Fire extinguisher.
Wheel brace (wrench).
Tow-rope.
Spare light bulbs and fuses.
Check tool-kit and jack.
Second outside mirror (if towing a caravan) (trailer).

Checklists

Do you have everything ready for your journey? Is everything under control at home? These checklists may help you to make sure that you haven't forgotten anything.

Six weeks or so before the date of departure:
Passport still valid?
Visas, if required?
International driving permit, if required.
Registration document (if taking own car).
Green card (international insurance certificate) (if taking own car).
Bail bond for car, if required (if taking own car).
Travel insurance.
Tickets (air, boat, train).
Visit doctor and dentist if required.

A week or so before leaving:
Arrange for payment of bills (telephone, electricity, gas, water, insurance premiums, rent, shops, etc.).
Stop papers, milk, etc.
Make arrangements for dealing with mail.
Valuables into bank safe deposit.
Arrange for house plants and animals to be looked after.
Get foreign currency and/or travellers' checks.
Leave details of vacation and addresses and spare keys with friends or neighbours.
Make photocopies of important papers.
Begin packing.
Use up perishable foodstuffs.
Empty, de-frost and switch off refrigerator.

Immediately before departure:
Put on comfortable clothing.
Don't eat too heavy a meal.
Turn off water.
Turn off gas.
Pull out electric plugs (except freezer).
Pull out radio and television aerial plug.
In summer switch off heating system, in winter turn down (checking oil level where appropriate) and take precautions against freezing of heating and water system.
Take sunglasses – children's toys – personal medicines.
Empty dust-bins (garbage cans).
Check documents (papers, money, checks, tickets, etc.), make sure that you have everything necessary and distribute them among the members of the party.
Give second set of car keys to passenger.
Pack food – tissues – toilet paper – bag for rubbish (garbage).
Lock garage.
Children into back seat of car.
Check doors and windows.
Close curtains – blinds – shutters.
Switch on burglar alarm, if any.
Fill up with fuel and check oil.

Season

The best time to go to Belgium and Luxembourg is in spring and summer, i.e. from May to September. Autumn in these countries is very often windy and rainy, although that season also has its charm, especially because of the wine festivals in Belgium and in Luxembourg. For a visit to one of the seaside resorts on the Belgian North Sea coast, July and August are the best months. Since it is likely that hotels will be full, it is advisable to book in advance.

For a visit to the Netherlands, spring is the best time, when the flower fields between Haarlem and Leyden are in bloom. Autumn, too, from the end of August can be very beautiful owing to the extraordinary brightness and light of the countryside, so favoured by the Classical Dutch painters. The main season in the resorts on the Dutch coast and on the islands lasts from July to the end of August.

Climate

The climate in Belgium and the Netherlands is oceanic, with relatively cool summers and mild winters. Westerly winds are predominant. Most rain falls in the coastal areas in autumn, and inland in summer. Detailed information about the climatic conditions of the Benelux countries is given on page 12.

Summer Time

The Benelux countries are on Central European Time (1 hour ahead of Greenwich Mean Time). From the end of March until the end of September summer time (2 hours ahead of GMT) is in force.

Travel Documents

A **passport** or **identity card** is required for entry into Belgium, the Netherlands and Luxembourg. A *visa* in the passport is necessary for a stay of more than three months. Benelux visas are valid in all three countries. They are issued by the consulates of Belgium, Luxembourg and the Netherlands. Children under sixteen years of age require a special children's passport if they are not included in the passport of their parents. In the Netherlands, when the stay exceeds eight days, one must *register* with the local police.

Driving licence and **car registration papers** of EEC countries are accepted. Visitors from other countries are advised to have an *international certificate for motor vehicles*. All foreign cars must display the appropriate *international distinguishing sign* of the approved type and design. Third party insurance is compulsory in all Benelux countries. Boats over 5·5 m (18 feet) long travelling under their own power in Belgium and Luxembourg must have a *triptych* (customs' certificate) or a *Carnet de Passage* (customs' certificate for several countries).

Currency

Belgium

Currency Unit: **Belgian Franc** (Bfr) = 100 *centimes*.
Bank notes: 20, 50, 100, 500, 1000 and 5000 Bfr.
Coins: 25 and 50 centimes; 1, 5, 10 and 20 Bfr.

Netherlands

Currency Unit: **Dutch Guilder** (Hfl)= 100 *cents*.
Bank notes: 5, 10, 25, 100 and 100,000 Hfl.
Coins: 1, 5, 10, 25 cents; 1 and $2\frac{1}{2}$ Hfl.

Luxembourg

Currency Unit: **Luxembourg Franc** (Lfr)=100 *centimes*.
Bank notes: 20, 50, 100 Lfr.
Coins: 25 centimes; 1, 5, 10 Lfr.

The Belgian Franc is also valid in Luxembourg and is currently in circulation.

Currency Regulations

Import and export of local or foreign currency is not subject to limitations in any of the Benelux countries. Euro-cheques, Travellers' Checks or credit cards are convenient and widely accepted.

Exchange Rates (Variable)

Visitors to Belgium, The Netherlands and Luxembourg should check the prevailing exchange rates prior to the start of their journey, as these rates are liable to fluctuation day by day. Details are generally to be found in local and national newspapers.

Postal Rates

Country	Letters up to 20g (0·7 oz) Domestic/Foreign	Postcards Domestic/Foreign
Belgium	9–18 Bfr	6·50–10 Bfr
Netherlands	0·55–0·75 Hfl	0·40–0·50 Hfl
Luxembourg	6–12 Lfr	5–8 Lfr

The domestic postal rates are also valid for mail to other EEC countries except Britain, Denmark and Ireland. Unlike Belgian currency, Belgian postage stamps are not valid in Luxembourg.

Transport

Road Traffic

The network of roads in the three Benelux countries is fairly comprehensive and all destinations can be easily reached. In **Belgium** the backbone of the road network is now the extensive system of toll-free highways (motorways). The main roads are also generally good. Road numbers of the all-purpose main roads are prefixed by "N". Highways (Autoroute/Autosnelweg) are prefixed by "A", or by "E" if the section is part of the European road network.

In the **Netherlands** most important road links are wholly or partly by toll-free highways (Autosnelweg), mostly with two lanes and continuous lane markings. Motorway numbers are prefixed by "A", and all-purpose roads are prefixed by "N". "E" numbers of the European road network are also shown.

In **Luxembourg** there is a comprehensive system of good main and secondary roads. Short sections of toll-free highway, radiating from Luxembourg, are also available.

Traffic Rules. – In Benelux countries as in the rest of mainland Europe, *Traffic travels on the right* with passing on the left. Seat belts are compulsory and a warning triangle must be carried. Where two roads of equivalent size intersect, traffic from the right has priority. Buses always have priority over motor vehicles. Sounding the horn should be kept to a minimum. Roads, even outside the built-up areas and especially in Holland, are

═══ **Motorways**
─── **Main Roads**

used by many cyclists who expect drivers to be considerate. You should drive carefully and respect them. Also the numerous drawbridges require attention. Frequently canals and dikes are crossed by hump-backed bridges which may not always allow sufficient clearance for heavily laden vehicles and caravans (trailers). **Drinking and driving:** Severe penalties (including imprisonment) are imposed upon persons convicted of driving under the influence of alcohol.

Maximum Speed Limits in km per hour

Country	Highway (Motorway)	Roads	Built-Up Areas	Cars with Trailers
Belgium	120 (74 mph)	90 (56 mph)	60 (37 mph)	–
Netherlands	100 (62 mph)	80 (49 mph)	50 (31 mph)	80 (49 mph)
Luxembourg	120 (74 mph)	90 (56 mph)	60 (37 mph)	–

Studded tires: Although residents are not permitted to use studded tires in the Netherlands, visitors may do so provided that they do not exceed 80 km per hour (49 mph), and if studs are allowed in their home country.

In Belgium they can be used from 1 November to 31 March (maximum speed 60 km per hour (37 mph), on motorways 90 km per hour (56 mph).

Studded tires may be used between January and March in Luxembourg, however they must be fitted to all four wheels and speed must not exceed 60 km per hour (37 mph). A disc must be attached to the rear of the vehicle indicating "60".

Bus Service

A network of bus routes, operated by national and private companies, comple-ments the railway network of the Benelux countries.

Ferry Service

There are passenger and car ferry con-nections by Sealink from Dover and Folkestone to Ostend; by Townsend Thoresen Ferries from Dover and Felix-stowe to Zeebrugge. Seaspeed and Hoverlloyd run hovercraft services from Dover and Ramsgate to Calais with con-

Air Routes
—— SABENA
—— KLM
—— LUXAIR

necting coaches to Brussels. There is also a Sealink ferry from Harwich to Hoek van Holland, and North Sea Ferries run services from Hull to Rotterdam and Zeebrugge. A car ferry service Sheerness–Flushing, opened in March 1981 (Olau Line).

Air Service

The Benelux countries are connected to the international air network via the airports of Brussels National and Amsterdam Schiphol. National and international flights are operated by the Belgian Airline, **SABENA** (Société Anonyme Belge d'Exploitation de la Navigation Aérienne), and the Dutch Airline **KLM** (Koninklijke Luchtvaart Maatschappij). The Luxembourg Airline **LUXAIR** operates flights between Luxembourg and London.

There are direct air connections between Brussels and Amsterdam and all the

Railways
— **Main Lines**
— **Secondary Lines**

important airports in the United Kingdom. Rotterdam and Antwerp have direct flights to London. There are also flights from London to Ostend, Charleroi and Liège, and from Amsterdam via Norwich to Aberdeen.

There are also direct flights from Brussels and Amsterdam to the USA, Canada, South Africa and the Republic of Ireland. Internal flights in the Benelux countries exist between Brussels and Amsterdam, Antwerp and Eindhoven, from Amsterdam to Eindhoven, Enschede, Groningen, Maastricht and Luxembourg, from Charleroi to Ostend, from Eindhoven and Maastricht to Rotterdam, and also between Enschede and Groningen.

Rail Services

The network of railways in the Benelux countries is extensive. It is operated by the state-owned **SNCB** (Société Nationale des Chemins de Fer Belges), **NS** (Nederlandse Spoorwegen) and **CFL** (Société Nationale des Chemins de Fer Luxembourgeois). The companies organise rail and coach excursions to many tourist attractions.

Price Reductions Tourist "Rover Ticket", reduced daily and weekend return fares, and reduced fares for students and senior citizens, are available. Especially attractive for tourists is a *Benelux season ticket* which can be used on all railways in the Benelux countries for a period of 8 or 15 days. The tickets can be purchased at the major stations, at British Rail offices, or at the Benelux railway offices abroad.

Bicycles at Stations

At several railway stations in Belgium, the Netherlands and Luxembourg, you can rent a bicycle. A reduced price will be charged for holders of valid tickets.

Overnight transport for cars, with sleeping accommodation for passengers (**Auto-Couchettes**) is available between Brussels and destinations in Switzerland, Italy and the South of France.

Language

The Benelux countries belong to the Dutch, French and German linguistic areas. Dutch (Flemish) is the official language in the Netherlands and in the northern part of Belgium, French in the southern part of Belgium. In Luxembourg, French is also the official language, but the majority of the population speak a dialect related to German. In the former German border areas of Eupen-Malmédy, and in the region of Arlon, German is spoken to some extent. Generally in Holland and in Flanders, you will get along with English, while in the Walloon part of Belgium, some knowledge of French will be useful.

Dutch, the language of the NETHERLANDS and of the northern part of Belgium, stands linguistically between the Frankish and the Low Saxon dialects of Low German. As early as the 12th c. there was a written language in the Netherlands, and this in the 17th c. developed into modern Dutch, as opposed to Flemish. Most of its vocabulary is Germanic. In the Dutch province of Friesland the local language is *West Frisian*, which has recently been accepted for official use. *Flemish*, as it is spoken in the Southern Netherlands and Northern Belgium, is divided into a number of spoken dialects.

BELGIUM is a multi-lingual country, inhabited by the *Flemish* in the river basin of the Schelde, and the *Walloons* in the basin of the Meuse. In the areas of Eupen, St-Vith and Arlon, some German is still spoken. The linguistic frontier between the Flemish and the Walloons has hardly changed since the Middle Ages. It runs approximately from Visé on the Meuse west, across Waremme, Halle and Ronse to Menen on the French border. North of this line a dialect akin to Dutch is spoken; south of it, French. Brussels and its suburbs are officially bilingual, but the Inner City is a predominantly French-speaking island within the Flemish area, near its southern border.

Flemish, like Dutch, is a branch of the Low German language group. It ceased to be used as a written language after the Dutch Wars of Independence. All Flemish literature was burned at that time by order of the Duke of Alba. It was only under the Dutch administration between 1814 and 1830 that Flemish ceased to be discriminated against. Nevertheless, shortly afterwards, the north of Belgium spoke Dutch rather than Flemish. After bitter linguistic wrangling in the 19th c., Dutch prevailed over French which had been the official language in the Flemish area. In the forefront of the Flemish linguistic revival were several well-known writers of the 19th–20th c., among them Felix Timmermans (1886–1947).

Walloon is an old French dialect with some elements of Celtic and German. It is still spoken in some districts in Eastern Belgium; but is virtually extinct elsewhere. As a written language it has never acquired any significance, French having fulfilled this function since the 12th c.

French developed from Vulgar Latin after the German Occupation of Celtic Gaul. Although it acquired a number of words of Celtic and later also some of Germanic origin, it has kept its Romance character. For centuries it was the most important Romance language spoken by the educated élite and in diplomatic circles.

Numbers

French	Dutch		French	Dutch
0 zéro	null	18	dix-huit	achttien
1 un, une	een	19	dix-neuf	negentien
2 deux	twee	20	vingt	twintig
3 trois	drie	21	vingt et un	een en twintig
4 quatre	vier	22	vingt-deux	twee en twintig
5 cinq	vijf	30	trente	dertig
6 six	zes	31	trente et un	een en dertig
7 sept	zeven	40	quarante	veertig
8 huit	acht	50	cinquante	vijftig
9 neuf	negen	60	soixante	zestig
10 dix	tien	70	septante[1]	zeventig
11 onze	elf	80	quatre-vingt	tachtig
12 douze	twaalf	90	nonante[1]	negentig
13 treize	dertien	91	nonante et un[1]	een en negentig
14 quatorze	veertien	100	cent	honderd
15 quinze	vijftien	101	cent un	honderd een
16 seize	zestien	200	deux cents	twee honderd
17 dix-sept	zeventien	1000	mille	duizend

Ordinals

	French	Dutch
1st	Premier (-ière)	eerste
2nd	deuxième	tweede
3rd	troisième	derde

Fractions

	French	Dutch
$\frac{1}{2}$	un demi	een half
$\frac{1}{3}$	un tiers	een derde
$\frac{1}{4}$	un quart	een kwart

[1] Numbers used only in Belgium (in France 70 = soixante-dix, 90 = quatre-vingt-dix, 91 = quatre-vingt-onze).

Vocabulary

English	French	Dutch
American	Américain	Amerikaan
America	L'Amérique	Amerika
English	Anglais	Engels
British	Britannique	Brits
England	L'Angleterre	Engeland
Britain	La Grande Bretagne	Groot Brittannië
Belgium	La Belgique	België
Luxembourg	Le Luxembourg	Luxemburg
The Netherlands	Les Pays-Bas	Nederland
Holland	La Hollande	Holland
Dutch	Néerlandais	Nederlands
French	Français	Frans
Do you speak . . .	Parlez-vous . . .	Spreekt u . . .
I do not understand	Je ne comprends pas	Ik versta niet

English	French	Dutch
Yes	Oui	Ja
No	Non	Neen
Please	S'il vous plaît!	Als 't u blieft!
Thank you	Merci!	Dank u!
Many thanks	Merci beaucoup!	Mag ik u wel bedanken
Excuse me	Pardon!	Pardon!
I beg your pardon	Excusez!	
Good morning	Bonjour!	Goeden morgen
Good afternoon	Bonjour!	Goeden dag!
Good evening	Bonsoir!	Goeden avond!
Good night	Bonne nuit!	Goede nacht!
Goodbye	Au revoir!	Tot ziens!
Mr	Monsieur	Mijnheer
Mrs	Madame	Mevrouw
Miss	Mademoiselle	Juffrouw
Where is?	Où est . . . ?	Waar is . . . ?
The street	La rue . . .	De . . . straat
The square	La Place . . .	De . . . plaats
A travel agency	Un bureau de voyage	Een reisbureau
The church	L'église	De kerk
The museum	Le musée	Het Museum
When	Quand?	Wanneeer?
When is . . . open?	A quelle heure . . . est ouvert(e)?	Wanner is geopend . . . ?
The Town Hall	L'hôtel de ville	Het stadhuis
The post office	Le bureau de poste	Het postkantoor
A bank	Une banque	Een bank
The Station	La gare	Het station
A hotel	Un hôtel	Een hotel
I need a room	Je voudrais une chambre	Ik zou graag en kamer
Single room	A un lit	Met een bed
Double room	A deux lits	Met twee bedden
With bath	Avec bain	Met een badkammer
The key	La clef	De sleutel
The toilet	La toilette, le cabinet	De toilet
A doctor	Un médecin	De arts
Right	A droite	Rechts
Left	A gauche	Links
Straight on	Tout droit	Rechtuit
Above	En haut	Boven
Below	En bas	Beneden
Old, ancient	Ancien, ancienne	Oud
	Vieux, vieille	
New	Nouveau, nouvelle	Nieuw
How much is?	Combien coûte?	Hoeveel kost . . . wat kost . . .
Expensive	Cher, chère	Duur
Restaurant	Restaurant	Restaurant
Breakfast	Petit déjeuner	Ontbjit
Lunch	Déjeuner, diner	Middagmaal
Dinner	Souper	Avondeten
To eat	Manger	Eten
To drink	Boire	Drinken
Much, many	Beaucoup	Veel
Little, few	Peu	Weinig
The Bill	Addition	Rekening
To pay	Payer	Betalen
At once	Tout de suite	Dadelijk

Traffic Signs and Warnings

English	French	Dutch
Stop	Halte! Stop!	Halt! Stop!
Customs	Douane	Tol
Beware of, drive carefully	Attention! Prudence!	Pasop!
Slow	Au pas! Ralentir!	Langzaam rijden!
Danger	Danger de mort!	Levensgevaar!
One-way street	Sens unique	Straat met eenrichtingsverkeer
No through road	Route barrée!	Afgesloten rijweg!
	Passage interdit!	
Road works	Travaux!	Bestratingswerkzaamheden!
Dangerous bends ahead	Virage dangereux!	Gevaarlijke bocht!

Car Terms

English	French	Dutch
To tow away	Remorquer	Wegslepen
Axle	Essieu	As
Starter	Démarreur	Starter
Car	Voiture, auto	Auto
Battery	Accumulateur, batterie	Accumulator
Fuel (Petrol)	Essence	Benzine
Fuel tank	Réservoir à essence	Benzinetank
Brake	Frein	Rem
Exhaust	Joint, garniture	Pakking
Spare part	Pièce de rechange	Onderdeel
Direction indicator	Indicateur de direction	Richtingsaanwijzer
Spring	Ressort	Veer
Driving licence	Permis de conduire	Rijbewijs
Gear	Vitesse	Versnelling
Garage	Garage	Garage
Accelerator	Accélérateur	Gaspedaal
Horn	Avertisseur, klaxon	Hoorn, toeter
Piston	Piston	Zuiger
Radiator	Radiateur	Radiator
Clutch	Embrayage	Koppeling
Litre (measure of fuel)	Litre	Liter
Air	Air	Lucht
Motor-cycle	Moto(-cyclette)	Motorijwiel
Oil	Huile	Olie
Change of oil	Vidange d'huile	Olie verversen
Breakdown	Panne	Defect (motor)
Parking place	Parking, place de stationnement	Parkeerplaats
Wheel	Roue	Rad, wiel
Tire	Pneu	Band
Garage	Atelier de réparation, Service de dépannage	Reparatieinrichting
Headlight	Phare	Schijnwerper
Grease	Huile de graissage	Smeerolie
Screw, bolt	Vis	Schroef
Nut	Ecrou	Moer
Spanner	Clef à écrou	Moersleutel
Fuse	Fusible	Zekering
Speedometer	Compteur de vitesse	Snelheidsmeter
Gas (Petrol) station	Poste d'essence	Benzinepomp
Valve	Soupape	Ventiel
Pressure Release	Valve	Ventiel
Carburettor	Carburateur	Vergasser
Jack	Cric	Krick
To wash	Laver	Wassen
Windshield	Pare-brise	Windscherm
Sparking plug	Bougie	Bougie
Ignition	Allumage	Ontsteking
Cylinder	Cylindre	Cilinder

Months of the Year

English	French	Dutch
January	Janvier	Januari
February	Février	Februari
March	Mars	Maart
April	Avril	April
May	Mai	Mei
June	Juin	Juni
July	Juillet	Juli
August	Août	Augustus
September	Septembre	September
October	Octobre	October
November	Novembre	November
December	Décembre	December

Days of the Week

English	French	Dutch
Monday	Lundi	Maandag
Tuesday	Mardi	Dinsdag
Wednesday	Mercredi	Woensdag
Thursday	Jeudi	Donderdag
Friday	Vendredi	Vrijdag
Saturday	Samedi	Zaterdag
Sunday	Dimanche	Zondag
Holiday	Jour de Fête	Feestdag, rustdag
Day	Jour, journée	Dag

Holidays

English	French	Dutch
New Year	Nouvel An	Nieuwjaar
Easter	Pâques	Pasen
Ascension	Ascension	Hemelvaart
Whitsuntide	Pentecôte	Pinksteren
Corpus Christi	Fête-Dieu	Sacramentsdag
Assumption	Assomption	Hemelvaart
All Saints	Toussaint	Allerheiligen
Christmas	Noël	Kerstmis
New Year's Eve	La Saint-Sylvestre	Oudejaarsavond

At the Post Office

English	French	Dutch
Post Office	Bureau de poste	Postkantoor
Central Post Office	Bureau de poste central	Hoofdpostkantoor
Postage stamp	Timbre-poste	Postzegel
Letter	Lettre	Brief
Postcard	Carte postale	Briefkart
Postman	Facteur	Postbode
Registered mail	Recommandé	Aangetekend
Printed matter	Imprimé	Drukwerk
Express	Par exprès	Expres
Air mail	Par avion	Luchtpost
Telegram	Télégramme	Telegram
Telephone	Téléphone	Telefoon

Culinary terminology, see page 295

Accommodation

Hotels and Inns

Hotels in the larger towns and resorts in the Benelux countries provide the usual international comfort. Advanced booking is recommended, especially in high season. The *inns* (in French "auberge") in medium-sized and small places also provide pleasant accommodation. The traditional Dutch inns, especially in places off the beaten track, are recommended. They may be quaint and old-fashioned (steep staircases), but they are cosy, clean and a good value. Accurate information can be obtained from an annual accommodation list published in all three countries. In the Netherlands, reliable booking is provided by the *National Reserveringscentrum* (PO Box 3387, NL-1001 AD Amsterdam: Telephone 0 20/21 12 11).

Hotel Prices

Belgium

	Category		Price for 1 Night in Bfr	
	in this book	1 Person		2 Persons
No	L (de luxe)	over 2000		over 2500
official	I	1500–2000		2000–2500
categories	II	1000–1500		1500–2000
	III	500–1200		1000–1500
	IV	300–800		500–1000
	V	200–400		300–500

The Netherlands

	Category		Price for 1 Night in Hfl	
Official	in this book	1 Person		2 Persons
C/1	{ L (de luxe)	over 110		over 150
	{ I	35–150		60–200
C/2	II	30–110		55–150
C/3	III	25–75		50–120
C/4	IV	20–60		45–110
C/5	V	15–45		40–100

Luxembourg

	Category		Price for 1 Night in Lfr/Bfr	
	in this book	1 Person		2 Persons
No	L (de luxe)	over 1100		over 1500
official	I	600–1200		1000–1500
categories	II	500–950		700–1350
	III	350–600		500–900
	IV	300–400		400–650
	V	200–300		300–550

These are final prices including service charges and taxes. The price in Dutch Guilders is mostly for bed and breakfast. Also in Belgium, especially in seaside resorts, breakfast is often included in the price.

Country-House Hotels

In Belgium, the Netherlands and Luxembourg there are a number of country-house hotels well known for their high standards and for their attractive locations. Frequently they provide opportunities for fishing, hunting or riding. Generally they only have a limited number of rooms, and advance booking is therefore recommended.

Belgium

Villers le Temple
Hôtel La Commanderie
12 r.; Riding facilities
Rue Joseph Pierco 28
B-4155 Villers le Temple
tel. (0 85) 51 10 01

Heyd-Durbuy
Hôtel Le Lignely
11 r.; Fishing, hunting and riding
B-5494 Heyd-Durbuy
tel. (0 86) 49 90 26

Malmédy
Hostellerie Trôs Marets
7 r.; Riding nearby
Route de Mont 1
B-4891 Malmédy
tel. (0 80) 77 79 17

La Roche-en-Ardenne
Hôtel L'Air Pur
14 r.; Fishing, hunting and riding
B-6980 La Roche-en-Ardenne
tel. (0 84) 41 12 23

Herbeumont
Hostellerie du Prieuré de Conques
11 r.; Boat rentals, fishing
B-6803 Herbeumont
tel. (0 61) 41 14 17

Noirefontaine
Auberge du Moulin Hideux
13 r.; Fishing
B-6831 Noirefontaine
tel. (0 61) 46 70 15

Soire – St-Géry
Hostellerie Le Prieuré Saint-Géry
6 r.; Fishing and hunting
B-6574 Soire – St-Géry
tel. (0 71) 58 85 71

Stambruges
Hostellerie Le Vert Gazon
7 r.; Riding nearby
B-7980 Stambruges
tel. (69) 57 59 84

Nukerke
Hostellerie Shamrock
6 r.
Ommegangstraat 148
B-9680 Nukerke
tel. (0 55) 21 55 29

Keerbergen
Hostellerie Berkenhof
7 r.; Golf, fishing and riding
Valkeniersdreet 5
B-2850 Keerbergen
tel. (0 15) 51 18 03

Oostkamp
Château de Brides (no rest.)
10 r.
B-8020 Oostkamp
tel. (0 50) 82 20 01

Masnuy – St-Jean
Hôtel Amigo
35 r.
Chaussée Brunenault 4
B-7433 Masnuy – St-Jean
tel. (0 65) 72 87 21

The Netherlands

Wassenaer
Auberge de Kieviet
6 r.; Golf course and riding facilities nearby
Stoeplaan 27
NL-2243 Wassenaar
tel. (0 17 51) 7 92 03

Beetsterzwag
Hôtel-Restaurant Lauswolt
22 r.; Golf course
Harinxmaweg 10
NL-9244 Beetsterzwag
tel. (0 51 26) 12 45

Valkenburg
Hotel Prinses Juliana
34 r.
Broekhem 11
NL-6301 HD Valkenburg
tel. (0 44 06) 1 22 44

Luxembourg

Gaichel-Eischen
Hôtel La Gaichel
14 r.
L-Gaichel-Eischen
tel. 3 91 29

Echternach
Hôtel Bel Air
44 r.
Route de Berdorf 1
L-Echternach
tel. 72 93 83

Youth Hostels

Youth hostels in the Benelux countries provide low-priced accommodation for young people. In Belgium and in the Netherlands there is no age limit and the stay is not restricted to three days. In the Luxembourg youth hostels only persons up to 35 years of age are accepted and the length of stay is limited to three nights (in busy periods, one night). A youth hostel card from the country of origin is required.

Information: **Vlaamse Jeugdherbergcentrale**
Van Stralenstraat 40
B-2000 **Antwerpen**
tel. (0 31) 32 72 18

**Centrale Wallonne des
Auberges de la Jeunesse**
Rue Van Oost 52
B-1030 **Bruxelles**
tel. (02) 2 15 31 00

**Stichting Nederlandse
Jeugdherberg Centrale**
Prof. Tulpstraat 2–6
NL-1018 GX **Amsterdam**
tel (0 20) 22 60 45

**Centrale des Auberges
de Jeunesse Luxembourgeoises**
Place d'Armes 18 a
L-**Luxembourg**
tel. 2 55 88

Holiday Flats and Villas (Vacation Rentals)

Numerous vacation apartments and villas are available on the coast as well as inland. Here also, advanced booking is recommended in high season. Information can be obtained from the Tourist Bureaux.

Farm Vacations

Opportunities for farm vacations ("Agrivacances") exist, especially in Belgium. Camping at farms is also possible.

Camping and Caravaning

The Benelux countries are especially suited for camping and caravaning (trailering). In most tourist resorts, as well as off the beaten track in quiet river valleys or in the dune areas on the coast, there are well-appointed and equipped camp sites.

Holders of an international camping card qualify for a range of price reductions. In high season many sites are filled to capacity. Camping in the open is limited to a few areas because of the population density, and requires permission from the owner of the land.

Food and Drink

Belgium

Belgium has always been the country of the gourmet. People enjoying a festive meal or having a picnic in the open often figure in paintings of old Flemish masters. Even today the Belgians make any excuse to enjoy a good meal. In Flanders in particular food and drink are highly valued.

There are an extraordinary number of **restaurants** in Belgium. Belgian restaurants, especially in Brussels, have an excellent reputation. Some of the best places hide their proficiency behind an unpretentious appearance. In addition to expensive luxury restaurants there are several places of good value serving excellent meals. Those who wish to eat "à la carte" can choose from a wide selection of interesting dishes. Many restaurants serve "specialities of the house". On the average, prices are higher than in the UK or the US. Apart from restaurants serving standard international cuisine, and others with typical Belgian fare, there are numerous Italian, Greek, Yugoslav, Chinese and Indonesian restaurants.

For those who want to eat quickly and cheaply, there are snack bars and "fritures".

Meal Times At noon the Belgians eat only a light meal, taking their main meal in the evening. With it they drink mostly beer or wine.

Belgian Specialities

MEAT DISHES. – Flemish "Karbonaden", beef stew cooked in beer; Smoked Ardennes Ham; Veal Kidney à la Liégeoise; Potato purée with Black Pudding and Stewed Apples.

GAME. – Flemish Hare with Onions and Prunes; Rabbit with Plums; Pheasant à la Brabançonne; Fieldfare à la Liégeoise.

Belgian Smoked Ham from the Ardennes

POULTRY. – Brussels Chicken: especially tender chickens bred around Brussels; Waterzooi: pieces of chicken served in vegetable broth thickened with cream; Roast Goose à la Visé: goose boiled and then roasted.

FISH. – Green Eels: boiled eel with many herbs and spinach; Herring in Cream; Trout; Seafood: mussels, lobsters, crabs, prawns served with a variety of sauces.

FRUIT. – Grapes and strawberries from hothouses available all year round.

VEGETABLES. – Red Cabbage à la Flamande; Asparagus à la Malinoise; Brussels Endives; Brussels Sprouts; Brussels Chicory.

PASTRIES. – Cheesecake; Rice Pudding; Sugar Cake; Rice Cake; Gingerbread; Brussels Waffles with Sugar, Butter, Fresh Cream and/or Fruit; Liège Waffles with Caramel.

SWEETS (CANDIES). – Babeluttes (Toffee); Chocolates.

DRINKS. – Kinds of Beer: Geuze, Kriek, Trappist, Diester, Louvain and Malmédy.

Gastronomic Weekends

From the beginning of November to the end of April "Gastronomic Weekends" are arranged on the Belgian coast. In autumn and winter game dishes are served during weekends in the Ardennes. These "Gastronomic Weekends" have become increasingly popular.

The Netherlands

The **Restaurants** (*Restauratie*) in the Netherlands are known for their good cuisine. Many of them also serve French dishes. The prices in the Netherlands lie somewhere between those in Belgium and those in the UK or the US. Most Dutch hotels also have restaurants and those in the main tourist resorts have a predominantly international character. Family boarding houses often provide food of good value.

In many places in the Netherlands, there are restaurants serving Chinese, Greek, Indonesian and other food. Nowhere outside Indonesia can you find such a good "Reistafel" as in Holland. With Indonesian dishes beer is usually drunk.

In the larger towns there are *Melksalons* (milk bars), where coffee, tea, chocolate, sandwiches and eggs are served.

Cafés are often combined with restaurants (*café/restaurant*). In the evening the front part functions as a café, separated by a curtain and often unlit so that the customers can watch activity in the street.

Meal Times. – The Dutch begin their day with a good breakfast. Between 9 a.m. and noon they have another "Kopje Koffie" with milk and sugar. The midday meal consists of the so-called "Koffietafel" (coffee dish), which is mainly sandwiches, sometimes accompanied by a cold or hot dish. Between 3 and 5 p.m. they drink tea and sometimes eat a pastry. In the evening between 6 and 8 p.m. comes the main meal of meat, vegetables and potatoes, often accompanied by soup and a desert.

More than 700 restaurants serve a *tourist menu*. The meal, which costs about 15 Hfl, consists of an appetiser, a main dish and a dessert. The price for this meal is roughly the same everywhere, but the combinations vary. (Brochures giving addresses of the restaurants providing tourist menus can be obtained from the Tourist Bureaux.) Prices in restaurants, inns and snack bars include service charges and VAT (Value Added Tax).

Dutch Specialties

FISH. – Salt Herring: available in the first weeks after the start of the season in May, under the name "Green" or "New" herring; Sole and Eel prepared in various ways. Seafood: lobsters, crabs, oysters, mussels (from May to September oysters and mussels from the Province of Zealand are available).

MEAT. – A great variety of meat and meat dishes. Preparation: beef is usually grilled only lightly on both sides (*biefstuk*). Those who prefer their meat well-done should ask for *doorbakken*. "Duitse Biefstuk" means hamburger. Specialties: *Rolpens* (brawn in vinegar marinade, sliced and grilled, served with apple sauce and roast potatoes); *Huzarensla* (meat salad).

VEGETABLES. – Fresh vegetables from hothouses available all year. In May and June especially good asparagus.

FRUIT. – Strawberries, Grapes, Apples and Pears of very good quality.

CASSEROLE DISHES (*stamppot*). – Sauerkraut with Bacon; Cabbage with Smoked Sausage; *Hutspot* (a dish of carrots, onions, potatoes and sirloin); *Snert* (pea soup).

PANCAKES (*pannekoeken*). – Pancakes with Bacon; Apple Pancakes; *Flensjes* (a kind of thin pancake); *Poffertjes* (doughnuts).

SANDWICHES. – *Uitsmijter* ("throw aways"; sandwiches with cold meat and poached egg); a great variety of sandwiches available in *broodjeswinkels*.

SWEETS. – *Hagelslag* (chocolate crumble), popular with children; *Haagse Hopjes* (chocolates).

DRINKS. – Beer; Genever (Juniper Schnapps of various kinds); Liqueurs; the most famous is the "Advocaat" (Egg Liqueur).

CHEESES. – Gouda; Edam; Cheeses with caraway seeds, cloves, etc.

Luxembourg

Luxembourg also offers very good eating. Hotels, restaurants and boarding houses in the Grand Duchy provide modern comforts. The Luxembourg cuisine is closely linked to French cuisine, and enjoys a good reputation.

Luxembourg Specialties

HOT DISHES. – Blood sausage with potato purée and horseradish; Smoked pork with beans; Ardennes ham, boiled or raw; Tripe à la Luxembourgeoise; Pieces of piglet in jelly; Liver dumpling with Sauerkraut and potatoes; Hare à la Luxembourgeoise (in hunting season); Trout and crayfish à la Luxembourgeoise (from 1 April to 30 September).

PASTRIES. – "Twisted Thoughts" (pastry eaten on Shrove Tuesday): Plum cake (September).

DRINKS. – Luxembourg beer; Wines from the Luxembourg Moselle; "Eibling", an ordinary wine; a great selection of quality wines; Sparkling wines from the Luxembourg Moselle; Brandies: "Quetsch", "Mirabelle", "Kirsch", "Prunelle", as well as the red-currant liqueur from Castle Beaufort.

The Menu

English	French	Dutch
MENU	Carte	Spijskaart, menu
Wine list	Carte des vins	Wijnkaart
SOUP	Potage, soupe	Soep
Broth	Bouillon	Bouillon
APPETISERS	Hors-d'œuvres	Voorspijzen, voorgerechten
MEAT COURSES:	Viandes	Vleesspijzen
Roast	Rôti	Vlees
Lamb	Rôti de mouton	Lamsvlees
Veal	Rôti de veau	Kalfsvlees
Pork	Rôti de porc	Varkensvlees
Stew	Bœuf en daube	gestoofs, gesmoord
Cutlet	Escalope	Kalfsoester
Liver	Foie	Lever
Kidneys	Rognons	Nieren
POULTRY	Volaille	Gevogelte
Goose	Oie	Gans
Chicken	Poule, poulet	Kip
GAME	Gibier	Wild
Hare	Lièvre	Haas
Venison	Chevreuil	Ree
SAUSAGE	Saucisson, saucisse	Worst
Ham	Jambon	Ham
FISH:	Poisson	Vis
Fried	Frit	Gebakken
Boiled	Cuit	Gekookt
Eel	Anguille	Aal
Perch	Perche	Baars
Flounder	Flet	Bot
Trout	Truite	Forel
Pike	Brochet	Snoek
Herring	Harang	Haring
Cod	Cabillaud	Kabeljauw
Carp	Carpe	Karper
Salmon	Saumon	Zalm
Sole	Sole	Tong
VEGETABLES:	Légumes	Groente
Cauliflower	Chou-fleur	Bloemkool
Beans	Haricots	Bonen
Peas	Pois	Erwten
Cucumber	Concombre	Komkommer
Potatoes	Pommes de terre	Aardappelen
Cabbage	Chou	Kool
Kohlrabi	Chou-rave	Koolraap
Brussels Sprouts	Chou de Bruxelles	Spruitjes
Red cabbage	Chou rouge	Rodekool
Salad – lettuce	Salade	Sla, salade
Sauerkraut	Choucroute	Zuurkool
Spinach	Epinard	Spinazie
Tomatoes	Tomates	Tomaten
Noodles	Nouilles	Macaroni
Rice	Riz	Rijs
DESSERT:	Dessert	Dessert
Ice cream	Glace	Ijs
Cheese	Fromage	Kaas
Fruit salad	Compote	Compote
Custard pie	Flan	Pudding
Whipped cream	Crème Chantilly	Slagroom
FRUIT	Fruits	Fruit
Pineapple	Ananas	Ananas
Apple	Pomme	Appel
Orange	Orange	Sinaasappel
Banana	Banane	Banaan
Pear	Poire	Peer
Strawberry	Fraise	Aardbei
Cherry	Cerise	Kers
Peach	Pêche	Perzik
Plum	Prune	Pruim

English	French	Dutch
FRUIT	Fruits	Fruit
Grape	Raisins	Druifen
Lemon	Citron	Citroen
DRINKS:	Boissons	Dranken
Beer	Bière	Bier
Coffee	Café	Koffie
Milk	Lait	Melk
Mineral water	Eau minérale	Mineraalwater
Cream	Crème	Room
Tea	Thé	Thee
Water	Eau	Water
Wine	Vin	Wijn
White wine	Vin blanc	Wittewijn
Red wine	Vin rouge	Rodewijn
BREAD:	Pain	Brood
White bread	Pain blanc	Wittebrood
Rolls	Pistolet, petit pain	Broodje
Cake	Gâteau	Koek
Tart	Tarte	Taart
Butter	Beurre	Boter
Marmalade	Confiture, marmelade	Jam
Honey	Miel	Honing, honig
Salt	Sel	Zout
Sugar	Sucre	Suiker
Vinegar	Vinaigre	Azijn
Oil	Huile alimentaire	Olie
EGG:	Oeuf	Ei
Hard boiled	Dur	Hard
Boiled	À la coque	Week
Omelette	Omelette	Omelet
Scrambled	Oeufs brouillés	Roerei
Poached	Oeufs sur le plat	Spiegelei

Seaside and Health Resorts, Beaches

In the **Netherlands**, there are over fifty seaside resorts dotted along some 220 km (136 miles) of coastline. The wide, sandy beaches stretch from the West Frisian Islands in the north to the estuary of the Schelde in the south. The most fashionable resort is *Scheveningen. Zandvoort, Noordwijk aan Zee, Katwijk aan Zee* and *Egmond aan Zee* are also very popular. There are also seaside resorts on the Waddenzee islands.

The **Belgian North Sea coast**, which stretches from the Dutch to the French border has some twenty resorts. The largest and best known among them is *Ostend*, followed closely by the elegant *Knokke-Heist* and the family resort of *Blankenberge*. The two extreme points of the coastline, Knokke-Heist and De Panne, are connected by a fast light railway service. Along this coastal area there are sandy beaches which at low tide are up to 250 m (820 feet) wide. The

"Koningsweg" runs along the beach, protected by the dunes.

Dangers on the Coast. – There is surf along the Dutch coast, and those who wish to swim must be strong enough to resist the hidden currents. You should ask about local conditions at the beginning of your vacation. In the season there are usually lifeguards on duty along the dangerous stretches of beach.

● **Spas**

BELGIUM

83 Ostend
Sea level.
Rheumatism, Paralysis, Neuralgia, Liver and Circulatory Ailments, Asthma, Hay Fever.

84 Chaudfontaine
Altitude: 80 m (262 feet).
The only hot spring in Belgium (36·6°C – 98°F).
Rheumatism, Gout at early stage.

85 Spa
Altitude: 260 m (853 feet).
Heart and Circulatory ailments, Gout, Rheumatism, Anaemia, Metabolic disorders.

LUXEMBOURG

86 Mondorf-les-Bains
Altitude: 194 m (636 feet).
Liver and Metabolic disorders.

○ Seaside Resorts ● Spas

○ Seaside Resorts

THE NETHERLANDS

1 Schiermonnikoog Island
2 Ameland Island
3 Terschelling Island
4 Vlieland Island
5 Texel Island

6 Den Helder
7 Den Helder-Huisduinen
8 Julianadorp aan Zee
9 Callantsoog
10 St. Maartenszee
11 Petten
12 Camperduin
13 Groet
14 Schoorl
15 Bergen Binnen
16 Bergen aan Zee
17 Egmond aan Zee
18 Egmond Binnen
19 Egmond aan den Hoef
20 Castricum aan Zee
21 Bakkum Noord
22 Wijk aan Zee
23 Beverwijk
24 IJmuiden
25 Velsen
26 Bloemendaal
27 Zandvoort
28 Noordwijkerhout
29 Noordwijk aan Zee
30 Katwijk aan Zee
31 Wassenaar
32 Den Haag/
   Scheveningen

33 Kijkduin
34 Ter Heijde
35 Monster
36 's-Gravenzande
37 Hook of Holland
38 Oostvorne
39 Rockanje
40 Hellevoetsluis
41 Ouddorp
42 Scharendijke
43 Renesse
44 Burgh
45 Haamstede
46 Kamperland
47 Vrouwenpolder
48 Oostkapelle
49 Domburg
50 Westkapelle
51 Zoutelande
52 Koudekerke
53 Vlissingen
54 Breskens
55 Groede
56 Nieuwvliet
57 Cadzand
58 Retranchement

BELGIEN

59 Het Zoute
60 Knokke
61 Duinbergen
62 Heist
63 Zeebrugge
64 Blankenberge
65 Wenduine
66 De Haan
67 Bredene

68 Oostende
69 Mariakerke
70 Middelkerke
71 Westende
72 Westende-Bad
73 Lombardsijde
74 Nieuwpoort
75 Nieuwpoort-Bad
76 Oostduinkerke
77 Oostduinkerke-Bad
78 Koksijde
79 Koksijde-Bad
80 Sint-Idesbald
81 De Panne
82 De Panne-Bad

Dutch windmills near Kinderdijk

Windmills in the Netherlands

Windmills are perhaps the best known symbol of the Netherlands. There were at one time about 10,000 windmills in the country, used primarily for draining the polders lying below sea level, and for grinding grain, pressing oil and cutting timber. When the polders were enclosed by dikes after the 11th c. it became necessary to reduce the underground water level to make the land habitable and suitable for cultivation. Man or horse-powered bucket elevators were used at first to convey the water into the draining dikes. In the 17th c. there were already north of Amsterdam a great number of wind-pumps.

The several types of windmills are distinguishable by their construction. The oldest among them is the support mill ("standermolen"), built on a square plan. In front are the mill sails and in the back the *Steert*, a weathervane by which the entire millhouse can be rotated around a vertical axis in order to find the wind direction. These mills were used predominantly for grinding grain and can still be found in the Central Netherlands. The mills in the south of Holland were built on the same technical principles, but on an octagonal plan.

Later the support mills were replaced by another type, where the mill-house was fixed and only the upper part, with sails attached to a shaft, rotated with the wind. Inland they were often built on higher places or on the town ramparts to make better use of the wind. When these mills were out of action they could be used to communicate news by the positioning of their sails. This system is said to have been used by the Dutch as late as the Second World War to contact pilots of allied aircraft.

Today there remains about 1,000 windmills in the Netherlands, with approximately 300 still in occasional use. Almost all date from the 18th–19th c. and have been carefully restored and preserved. Every year on the second Saturday in May National Windmill Day is celebrated and the mills are set in motion.

The best known windmill group is near **Kinderdijk**, north of Alblasserdam. There nineteen windmills operate every Saturday in summer. Some mills of varying construction can be seen in the outdoor museum in Arnhem, and also near Zaandam. Rampart mills are to be found in Schiedam.

Windmills in the Netherlands

Kinderdijk	Place with 1 or more windmills
GELDERLAND	Province with windmills in various places

Castles, Monasteries and Beguinages

● Castles and Mansions

There are several hundred castles and mansions in Belgium; over thirty are regularly open to visitors, at least during the summer months.

1 Loppem (neo-Gothic)
East of Damme

2 Oidonk (13th c.)
South-west of Ghent

3 's Gravensteen (11th c. unfinished)
Moated castle in Ghent

4 Laarne (12th–17th c.)
Laarne, east of Ghent

5 Leeuwergem (18th c.
Leeuwergem, south of Ghent

6 Royal Palace
(rebuilt 1905)
Brussels

7 Gaasbeek (13th and 16th c.)
South-west of Brussels

8 Beersel (14th c. unfurnished)
Beersel, south of Brussels

9 Grand-Bigard (14th–18th c.)
North-west of Brussels

10 Rixensart (17th c.)
South-east of Brussels

11 Horst (13th c. unfurnished)
Horst near Aarschot (Hageland)

12 Schoonbeek (17th–18th c.)
Beverst, south of Ghent

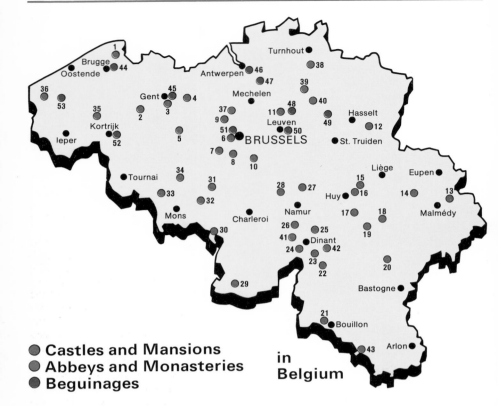

Castles and Mansions
Abbeys and Monasteries
Beguinages

in Belgium

13 Reinhardstein (very ancient, reconstructed in 17th c.)
Robertville, north-east of Malmédy

14 Franchimont (12th c. ruin)
Theux, north of Spa

15 Aigremont (18th c.)
On the Meuse, south of Liège

16 Jehay (16th c.)
Jehay-Bodegnée, north-east of Huy

17 Modave (17th c.)
Modave, south of Huy

18 Logne (ruin)
On the Ourthe, south of Liège

19 Durbuy (16th c.)
Durbuy, on the Ourthe

20 La Roche-en-Ardenne (11th c. ruin)
La Roche-en-Ardenne, on the Ourthe

21 Bouillon (groundwork 11th c. unfurnished)
Bouillon

22 Lavaux-Sainte-Anne (14th–15th c. reconstructed 17th–18th c.)
Lavaux-Sainte-Anne, west of Han-sur-Lesse

23 Veves (16th c.)
Veves, south of Dinant

24 Freyr (16th–18th c.)
Freyr, south of Dinant on the left bank of the Meuse

25 Spontin (11th–12th c.)
Spontin, north-east of Dinant

26 Annevoie (16th c.)
Near Annevoie-Rouillon on the Meuse south of Namur

27 Franc-Waret (18th c.)
Franc-Weret, north-east of Namur

28 Corroy-le-Château (13th c.)
Gembloux, north-west of Namur

29 Chimay (medieval)
Chimay (Fagne)

30 Soire-sur-Sambre (13th–14th c.)
Soire-sur-Sambre, Hainaut

31 Le Roeulx (15th–18th c.)
Le Roeulx, south-east of Soignies

32 Château de Lalaing (11th–15th c.)
Ecaussinnes-Lalaing, north-east of Mons

33 Belœil (rebuilt 1900 after a fire)
Belœil, north-west of Mons

34 Attre (18th c.)
Attre, Hainaut (south of Ath)

35 Rumbeke (16th c.)
Rumbeke, south-east of Roeselare

36 Beauvoorde (16th–17th c.)
Beauvoorde, south of Veurne

Abbeys and Monasteries

Several monasteries and abbeys are still occupied; their churches and parts of the monastery premises can be visited.

37 Grimbergen (12th c.)
Grimbergen, north of Brussels

38 Postel (12th c.)
Postel, south of Turnhout

39 Tongerlo (19th c.)
Tongerlo, west of Lier

40 **Averbode** (14th c.)
North-east of Aarschot
41 **Maredsous** (19th c.)
Maredsous, north-west of Dinant
42 **Chevetogne** (19th c, former château)
South of Dinant
43 **Orval** (11th c.)
Villers devant-Orval,
south-east of Florenville

● **Beguinages**

"Beguines" are women living as "secular nuns". They live in Beguinages (Begijnhof), groups of buildings surrounded by walls. These precincts with their narrow lanes and whitewashed cottages are often very picturesque. Some of them are well preserved and worth visiting.

44 **Brügge** (13th c.)
45 **Gent** (13th c.)
46 **Antwerpen**
47 **Lier** (13th c., 17th c.)
48 **Aarschot** (13th c.)
49 **Diest** (13th c., 17th c.)
50 **Löwen** (13th c., 14th–18th c.)
51 **Brüssel**
52 **Kortrijk** (13th c., 17th c.)
53 **Diksmulde**

For the Nature Lover

Walking

The territory of the Benelux countries is crossed by European Long-Distance Walking Tracks Nos. 2 and 3. The Dutch part of the *European Long-Distance Walking Track No. 2* begins at Bergen op Zoom and crosses the Dutch/German border near Essen. The Belgian part of European Track No. 2 is divided into a Flemish and Walloon part, and has its own markings (white/red). The main track runs via Diest, Liège, Malmédy to the south. 20 km (12 miles) east of Antwerp it meets a side track near Grobbendonk coming in from Ostend across Flanders. This is useful to tourists who cross from Britain to Ostend and want to use the track from Bergen op Zoom to Nice. The Flemish part of the track runs across a fairly flat landscape, whereas the Walloon one crosses wooded and undulating countryside.

European Long-Distance Track No. 2 reaches the Belgian/Luxembourg border near Ousen. In Luxembourg the white/red marking is replaced by yellow circles. The Luxembourg section then traverses the Valley of the Ourthe between Ösling and Eifel, along the Lower Sûre, then follows a stretch of the Moselle and leaves the country near Rumelange.

European Long-Distance Track No. 3 crosses the south of Belgium and Luxembourg. It begins in Belgium, approximately 1 km (about a ½ mile) south of Sorendal near the Baraque Laurent, and leaves the country near Martelange. It corresponds in principle to the Eifel–Ardennes track which connects Federal Germany with Luxembourg, Belgium and France. These tracks are also marked white/red. In Eastern Belgium, the track partly follows the Valley of the Semois. An excursion can be made to the Abbaye d'Orval near the Belgian/French border. From Habaye-la-Neuve it crosses the Forêt d'Anlier north to the Belgian/Luxembourg border. From here the track is marked with a green triangle on a white background as far as Echternach, and then by a yellow triangle from Echternach to Remerschen. The International Long-Distance Tracks E3 (Atlantic Coast–Bohemian Forest) and E2 (Holland–Mediterranean) meet at the viewpoint of Geislay and separate again near Remerschen on the Moselle. The E3 leaves the Grand Duchy of Luxembourg near Schengen.

Popular walks, group walks and excursions are organised in all three countries (in Luxembourg almost every weekend).

Cycling

The bicycle (French "bicyclette", Dutch "fiets") is a very popular means of transport, especially in the less hilly parts of the Benelux countries, and it is often used for outings. In many places, it is possible to rent a bicycle.

Climbing

In Belgium rock climbing is possible on the cliffs on the banks of the Meuse, the Ourthe, Molignée and Samson. The Alpine Club runs a mountaineering school in Freyr.

Information: **Club Alpin Belge**
Square Ambiorix 37,
B-1040 **Brussels**
tel. (02) 7 34 70 04

Hunting

In each of the three Benelux countries, a hunting permit is required. This can only be obtained when a local owner or occupant acts as an intermediary. In the Netherlands, insurance is also required.

The Ardennes are very good shooting grounds for boars and red deer. The Dutch hunting season lasts from August–September to January–February. No hunting is allowed on Sundays and holidays.

Fishing

Facilities for fresh- and salt-water fishing are many. For *fresh-water fishing*, a permit is required in all three Benelux countries, and if private property is involved, the permission of the owner or occupant as well. As the dates of closed seasons and of minimum sizes vary from country to country, it is advisable to ask on the spot. *Salt-water fishing* off the Belgian and Dutch North Sea coasts is free. In the open sea inlets in the Southern Netherlands, the same closed seasons apply as for fresh-water fishing.

Water Sports

The numerous lakes, canals and rivers in the Netherlands provide facilities for various water sports, especially boating. The rivers of the Ardennes are excellent for canoes and kayaks. A special sport on the Belgian coast is sand yachting (racing light, wheeled land yachts).

In the Netherlands there is a central charter agency for boats, of which seven large boat rental companies are members: Holland International Jachtcharter, Treubstraat 16, Postbus 157, NL-2280 AD Rijswijk.

Riding

Riding is available in all three Benelux countries. Lessons are also provided. Pony-treks of several days' duration are very popular.

Information: **Fédération Belge**
des Sports Equestres
Avenue Hamoir 38
B-1180 **Bruxelles**
tel. (02) 3 74 47 34

Nederlandsche Hippische Sportbond
P.O. Box 117
NL-2240 AC **Wassenaar**
tel. (0 70) 24 54 34

Fédération Luxembourgeoise
des Sports Equestres
Route de Thionville 90
L-Luxembourg

Winter Sports

In Belgium in the Province of Liège, winter sports are available. Under normal conditions there is enough snow in the Ardennes from December to March to make skiing possible. The best known skiing slopes are at Jalhay, Francorchamps, Robertville-Ovifat, Malmédy, Manderfeld, Eupen, Trois-Ponts, and Spa. In some places it is possible to rent skiing equipment at favourable rates.

Information: **Fédération du Tourisme**
de la Province de Liège,
Avenue Blonden 33,
B-400 **Liège**
tel. (0 41) 52 20 60

Golf Courses and Casinos

● **Golf Courses**

THE NETHERLANDS

1 **Groningen**
Noordlaaren (15 km (9 miles) south of Groningen)
9 holes

2 **Hengelo**
Golf course (3 km (2 miles) north-east of Hengelo)
9 holes

3 **Deventer**
Diepenveen (6 km (4 miles) north of Deventer)
9 holes

4 **Zwolle**
Hattem (8 km (5 miles) south of Zwolle)
9 holes

5 **Apeldoorn**
Hoog Soeren (5 km (3 miles) west of Apeldoorn)
18 holes

● Golf Courses
● Casinos

Leeuwarden ● ● Groningen
● 1
Sneek ● ● Assen
THE
NETHERLANDS
Den Helder ●
Meppel ●
Alkmaar ●
Zwolle ●
Haarlem ● ● 9 4
33 ● 10 ● ● 3 2 ●
11 ● AMSTERDAM Deventer ● Enschede ●
12 ● Leiden 8 5 ●
34 ● ● 7
THE HAGUE Utrecht 6 ●
13 ● Rotterdam ● Arnhem
Nijmegen ●
's-Hertogenbosch ●
Breda ● ● 15
14 ● Middelburg
36 ● ● 19 Eindhoven ●
21 ● 20 ● 16
37
39 ● 38 ● Oostende
22 ● Antwerpen ●
● Gent 18
Mechelen ●
Ieper ● Kortrijk ● BRUSSELS 28 ●
23 25 ● ● Leuven ● 35
Maastricht ●
26 ● 27 17 ●
● Tournai Liège ● ● 42
24 ● 30 31 43 ●
● Mons Charleroi ● ● ● 40
Namur Malmédy ●
41 ● **BELGIUM**
Dinant ● ●
29 Clervaux ●
Bastogne ●
LUXEM-BOURG
LUXEMBOURG
● 32

Golf Course in Belgian Kempen

6 Arnhem
Golf course (5 km (3 miles) north of Arnhem)
18 holes

7 Utrecht
Huis ter Heide (10 km (6 miles) east of Utrecht)
18 holes

8 Hilversum
Golf course (3 km (2 miles) north-west of
Hilversum)
18 holes

9 Amsterdam
Duivendrecht (8 km (5 miles) south of
Amsterdam)
18 holes

10 Haarlem
Zandvoort (6 km (4 miles) west of Haarlem)
9 holes

11 Noordwijk aan Zee
18 holes

12 The Hague
Wassenaar (8 km (5 miles) north of The Hague)
18 holes

13 Rotterdam
Golf course (10 km (6 miles) outside
Rotterdam)
9 holes

14 Middelburg
Domburg (15 km (9 miles) north of Middelburg)
9 holes

15 Breda
Molenschot (8 km (5 miles) east of Breda)
18 holes

16 Eindhoven
Valkenswaard (9 km (6 miles) south of
Eindhoven)
18 holes

17 Maastricht
Wittem (10 km (6 miles) east of Maastricht)
9 holes

BELGIUM

18 Hasselt
Houthalen (20 km (12 miles) north of Hasselt
18 holes

19 Antwerp
Kapellen (14 km (9 miles) north of Antwerp)
18 holes

20 Knokke-Heist
Het Zoute (1 km (about a ½ mile) east of
Knokke-Heist)
18 holes

21 Ostend
De Hann (11 km (7 miles) north of Ostend)
18 holes

22 Ghent
St Martens Latem (10 km (6 miles) west of
Ghent)
18 holes

23 Oudenaarde
Wortegem (3 km (2 miles) west of Oudenaarde)
18 holes

24 Mons
Erbisoel (6 km (4 miles) north of Mons)
18 holes

25 Brussels
Terturen (13 km (9 miles) east of Brussels)
18 holes

26 Brussels
Ohain (22 km (14 miles) south of Brussels)
18 holes

27 Brussels
Grez-Doiceau (25 km (16 miles) south-east of
Brussels)
18 holes

28 Mechelen
Keerbergen (10 km (6 miles) south-east of
Mechelen)
18 holes

29 Dinant
Houyet (9 km (6 miles) south-east of Dinant)
18 holes

30 Liège
Golf course (10 km (6 miles) outside Liège)
18 holes

31 Spa
Balmoral (5 km (3 miles) north-east of Spa)
18 holes

LUXEMBOURG

32 Luxembourg
Golf course (7 km (4 miles) outside the capital)
18 holes

Information: **Fédération Royale Belgique
de Golf**
Château de Ravenstein
B-1980 **Tervuren**

Nederlandse Golf Federatie
Soestdijkerstraatweg 172
NL-1213 XE **Hilversum**
tel. (0 35) 83 05 65.

**Golf-Club Grand-Ducal
de Luxembourg
L-Senningerberg**
tel. 3 40 90.

● Casinos

THE NETHERLANDS

33 Zandvoort
34 Scheveningen
35 Valkenburg

BELGIUM

36 Knokke-Heist
37 Blankenberge
38 Ostend
39 Middelkerke
40 Namur
41 Dinant
42 Chaudfontaine
43 Spa

National Parks
Nature Reserves
Caves

Leeuwarden ● ● Groningen

● Sneek

Den Helder

THE NETHERLANDS

● Assen

Alkmaar ●

● Meppel

● Zwolle

Haarlem ●

AMSTERDAM

● Deventer   Enschede ●

● Leiden

● Utrecht

THE HAGUE

● Arnhem

● Rotterdam

Nijmegen ●

s-Hertogenbosch ●

● Breda

● Middelburg

● Eindhoven

Oostende ● 3

4 ● Antwerpen

● Gent

● Mechelen

5
6   8
7

2

Maastricht

Ieper ●

● Kortrijk

BRUSSELS

● Leuven

9

● Tournai

BELGIUM   Liège ●
15   17
16

13

Mons ●

Namur ●

Charleroi ●

19

20
10

● Dinant   ● 18

21
22

12

Malmédy

11   Bastogne ●

Clervaux ●

14

LUXEM-
BOURG

National Parks,
Nature Reserves,
Caves Open to the
Public

National Parks and
Nature Reserves

In Belgium, the Netherlands and Luxembourg, there are a number of nature reserves described variously as "Nature Park", "National Park", "Nature Reserve"; in Belgium sometimes also as "Domaine". Most of them are open to visitors.

The nature parks in the Netherlands and North Belgium are mostly heath; those in the Ardennes mostly deciduous and mixed forests. In the heath areas many species of birds can be spotted; in the

woods game can be seen, and occasionally there are prehistoric caves.

THE NETHERLANDS

1 De Hoge Veluwe (National Park)
   Area 5400 hectares (13,343 acres)
   Location: North of Arnhem

2 German-Dutch Nature Park
   Area 70,000 hectares (172,970 acres)
   Location: near Roermond

BELGIUM

3 Zwin (Bird Sanctuary)
Area: 125 hectares (309 acres)
Location: near Knokke-Heist

4 Kalmthouter Heide
Area 1700 hectares (4200 acres)
Location: north of Antwerp

5 Molenheide (with Zoo)
Area 100 hectares (247 acres)
Location: near Helchteren, north of Hasselt

6 Bokrijk
(with an Open-air Museum and an Arboretum)
Area 514 hectares (1270 acres)
Location: north-east of Hasselt

7 Maten (Nature and Bird Sanctuary)
Area 300 hectares (741 acres)
Location: near Genk

8 Mechelse Heide
Area 400 hectares (988 acres)
Location: near Maasmechelen

9 Bois de Soignes (*Zonienwoud*)
Area 4000 hectares (9880 acres)
Location: south-east of Brussels

10 Furfooz (Nature Park)
Area 819 hectares (2024 acres)
Location: south-east of Dinant

11 Lesse and Lomme (National Park)
Area 250 hectares (618 acres)
Location: near Han-sur-Lesse

12 Hautes Fagnes-Eifel (Nature Park)
Area 70,000 hectares (172,970 acres)
Location: east of Malmédy

13 Hautes Fagnes (Nature Reserve)
Area 4200 hectares (10,378 acres)
Location: east of Malmédy
(part of the Nature Park Hautes Fagnes)

LUXEMBOURG

14 The German-Luxembourg Nature Park
Area 72,500 hectares (179,148 acres)
Location: north of Luxembourg

● Caves

In South Belgium slate and limestone form the upper strata in the Ardennes, especially in the Condroz. Water from the Meuse, Ourthe, Lesse and other rivers easily penetrated the porous limestone layers and created clefts in several places. Gradually water penetrated deeper into the ground and stalactite caves formed. Some rivers flow partly below ground, such as the Lesse, which near Han-sur-Lesse flows through the famous Grottoes of Han. Some of these underground grottoes are open to tourists.

BELGIUM

15 Grotte de Ramioul
in Ramet, 14 km (9 miles) south-west of Liège.
Prehistoric finds,
Cave museum.

16 Grotte de Comblain-au-Pont
near Comblain-au-Pont,
18 km (11 miles) south of Liège.
Mineral formations, bone finds.

17 Grotte de Remouchamps
in Remouchamps,
13 km (9 miles) west of Spa,
Mineral formations, underground river.

18 Grotte des Mille et Une Nuits
in Hotton, 40 km (25 miles) south of Liège.
Mineral formations, stalactites,
underground river.

19 Grotte La Merveilleuse
near Dinant, 20 km (12 miles) south of Namur.
Mineral formations, underground lake.

20 Grotte du Pont d'Arcole
in Hastière-Lavaux,
28 km (17 miles) south of Namur.
Mineral formations, stalactites,
underground river.

21 Grottes de Rochefort
in Rochefort,
40 km (25 miles) south-east of Namur.
Crystal formations, underground river.

22 Grottes de Han
near Han-sur-Lesse,
45 km (28 miles) south-east of Namur.
Mineral formations, underground river.

Miniature Models, Fairytale Parks and Zoos in the Netherlands

● Miniature Models

1 Miniatuur Walcheren
Molenwater
Middelburg
Model of the Island of Walcheren (scale 1:20)
with an electric railway, dredging equipment, etc.

2 Madurodam
Haringkade 175
The Hague/Scheveningen
Town model (scale 1:25) with old and modern parts, communication system, harbour, canals with ships and boats.

● Fairytale Parks

3 Recreation Park Duinrell
(with Fairytale Park)
Wassenaar.

4 De Sprookjeshof (Recreation Park)
Groningerstraat 10,
Zuidlaaren.

5 Fairytale Park Hellendoorn
Luttenbergerweg 18,
Hellendoorn.

Miniature Models
Fairytale Parks
Zoos,
   Bird Sanctuaries,
   Aquariums,
   Dolphinariums
in the Netherlands

6 Dream Castle Fantastico
Ganzeweide 113–115,
Heerlerheide.

7 Fairytale Forest
Sibbergrubbe,
Valkenburg.

8 De Efteling (Recreation Park)
Europaweg,
Kaatsheuvel.

Miniature Town of Madurodam in The Hague

Zoos, Bird Sanctuaries, Aquariums, Dolphinariums

9 Delphirama Bouwes (with Aquarium)
Burgemeester van Fenemaplein,
Zandvoort.

10 Sea Aquarium
Van der Wijckplein 16,
Bergen aan Zee.

11 Recreation Area De Koog
(with Sea Aquarium)
Ruyslaan 92,
De Koog (Texel).

12 Animal Park Artis (with Aquarium)
Plantage Kerklaan 40,
Amsterdam.

13 Animal Park Amersfoort
Barchman/Wuytierslaan 224,
Amersfoort.

14 **Dolphinarium**
Strandboulevard 1,
Harderwijk.

15 **Sybrandy Bird Sanctuary and Pheasant Farm**
J. Schotanusweg 71,
Rijs.

16 **Animal Park De Vluchtheuvel**
Donderseweg 12,
Norg.

17 **Zeepark** (with Aquarium)
Kustweg 7,
Delfzijl.

18 **Noorder Animal Park** (with Aquarium)
Hoofdstraat 18,-
Emmen.

19 **Aquarium of the Natural History Museum**
De Ruyterlaan 2,
Enschede.

20 **Recreation Area 't Smallert**
Smallertsweg,
Vaassen.

21 **Park Berg en Bos** (with a Monkey House)
J. C. Wilslaan,
Apeldoorn.

22 **Playground De Burg** (with Aquarium)
Eerbeek.

23 **Bird Sanctuary Tropical East** (with Zoo)
Kapelweg 1,
Silvolde.

24 **Burgers Zoo** (with Safari Park)
Schelmseweg 85,
Arnhem.

25 **Ouwehands Zoo** (with Aquarium and Dolphinarium)
Grebbeweg 109,
Rhenen.

26 **Recreation Area Gulpen** (with an Aviary and Monkey-House)
Euverem 1-5,
Gulpen.

27 **Cave Aquarium Valkenburg**
Cauberg,
Valkenburg.

28 **European Bird Sanctuary**
Born.

29 **Bird and Monkey-House Animali**
Roostenlaan 303,
Eindhoven.

30 **Recreation Area Beekse Bergen** (with Safari Park)
Beekse Bergen 1,
Hilvarenbeek.

31 **Bird Sanctuary Oisterwijk**
Gemullehoekenweg 147,
Oisterwijk.

32 **Dolfirodam**
Scharendijke.

33 **Stork Village "Het Liesveld"**
Groot-Ammers.

34 **Animal Park Blijdorp** (with Aquarium)
Van Aerssenlaan 49,
Rotterdam.

35 **Bird Sanctuary and Recreation Park Avifauna**
Hoorn 65,
Alphen aan den Rijn.

36 **Animal Park Wassenaar**
Rijksstraat 667,
Wassenaar.

Folklore

Among the three Benelux countries, **BELGIUM** has without doubt the liveliest heritage of folklore. This can be seen principally in innumerable popular festivals, processions and fairs (known as "Kermises"), sometimes on a large scale and almost always in a festive and relaxed atmosphere. Reasons for a festival can be insignificant, such as a "Criterium" (a bicycle race), or the raising of a maypole. Most of the large-scale events take place throughout the year on one or other of the Saints' Days or on the anniversary of a historic event. At other times there are countless events on a small scale, as, for example, the "Kermesses aux boudins", when once a year the innkeepers of the innumerable inns in the country invite their regular customers for a meal. Usually it turns out to be no more than an enormous sausage meal with a lot of beer and good humour.

The first large festival of the year is the Carnival (*Carnaval*), which is especially celebrated, and colourfully, in the Walloon part of the country, in its highly traditional form. The carnival capital is Binche (between Charleroi and Mons), with its characteristic "Gilles" (clowns). The colourful linen costumes of the Gilles are adorned with twelve lions in the form of a coat of arms, colourful ribbons, lace and a belt with bells. For the closing dance in the Market Place, the Gilles carry on their heads eight enormous white ostrich feathers. The Gilles dance on Shrove Tuesday (Mardi Gras) over a period of twenty-four hours to the accompaniment of drums and brass bands. From small baskets which they carry with them, they throw oranges to the spectators.

The "Chinels" at the Carnival in Fosses-la-Ville

They also appear on the Sunday and Monday before. For four weeks before the carnival, processions and balls follow each other in Binche. They are called "Répétitions de batteries" (roughly translated: "group rehearsals").

Equally famous is the Carnival of Malmédy with its six "Crazy Days". In Eupen an enormous procession takes place on the Monday before Lent, bearing the unmistakable influence of the Rhineland tradition.

In the Flemish part of the country, the Carnival of Aalst attracts tens of thousands of spectators every year. Carnival Sunday is the "Day of the Giants"; Monday is the "Day of Onion Throwing". On Tuesday the procession of the "Vuil Jeannetten" (roughly "Dirty Aunties") in their funny old costumes parades through the town.

Ash Wednesday is by no means the end of merrymaking. On the following Saturday there is in Ostend the fashionable "Dead Rat Ball". In the middle of Lent (Sunday Laetare), great carnival processions take place in Hasselt, Tilff, Stavelot and Fosse. The typical character in Stavelot is the "Blanc moussis", who wears a long-nosed mask and a white hood and plays all sorts of pranks. In former times, supposedly, the monks, who were not allowed to take part in the festivities, but who could not resist the temptation to frolic, hid behind the masks, in order not to be recognised. From Fosses come the "Chinels" (an abbreviation of Polichinelle, Pulcinella), who dance like living

dolls. The first carnival procession of the year in Belgium takes place on 6 January. Thousands of costume-clad people celebrate Fools Monday in Ronse, south of Ghent.

Since Belgium is predominantly Catholic, religious **processions** (especially in Passion Week) play an important role, although they are perhaps not now taken as seriously as they once were. The best known Passion processions are those of Rupelmonde near Antwerp on the Thursday before Easter, in Hakendover on Easter Monday, and in Veurne on the night between Maundy Thursday and Good Friday. Veurne has two other impressive processions to offer on the Sunday before 3 May, and the famous Penitents' Procession on the last Sunday in July. Here praying penitents wearing dark hoods proceed across the town, dragging heavy crosses on their backs. This custom is based on Spanish tradition and goes back to the times when Belgium was still Spanish territory. The Penitents' Procession at Lessines on Good Friday is also interesting. The penitents are masked and hooded and carry torches, resulting in a somewhat ghostly show.

World-famous is the Procession of the Holy Blood, which takes place in Bruges on the Monday after 2 May. Many carts and pedestrian groups proceed across the festively decorated town, portraying the entire story from the Fall of Man to the Redemption. Representatives of the clergy carry a shrine, believed to hold several drops of Christ's Blood, which Dietrich of Alsace, Count of Flanders, is said to have received from the Patriarch of Jerusalem in 1150.

Most seaside resorts have processions for the blessing of the sea, and well-known pilgrimages take place in Halle, Hakendover, Scherpenheuvel and St Hubert.

In Wallonia there are processions which are somewhat more secular in character. In Mons on Trinity Sunday, the shrine containing the relics of St Waltrudis, the Patron Saint of the town, is carried in a solemn procession across the city in a gilded carriage. The procession ends with a "Lumeçon Fight" between St George and a green dragon, who naturally is defeated (symbolic victory of good over evil). Typical of the region between the

Sambre and the Meuse are the "military processions". Their tradition goes back to the times when precious shrines, which were carried in the procession, had to be protected from highwaymen. The marchers wear uniforms, some of them from Napoleonic times, and walk through the town firing into the air. The military processions in Gerpinnes, near Charleroi, and in Jumet (around 20 July) are well known.

Many **secular festivals** complete the list. The most famous of these is undoubtedly the "Ommegang" in Brussels. Its origins are medieval processions which prayed for protection against this or that plague. The present "Ommegang" is a revival of a procession which took place in 1549 in the presence of Charles V. Over 2000 men in costumes, with some 300 flags representing the city guilds, drummers and many decorated carts, proceed into the historic Market Place in July, and file past "the imperial family". In Ath at the end of August, the "Giants' Fair" takes place, which ends with the marriage of the giant Goliath. The Flemish remember their famous compatriots of past centuries in many different ways. In June, for example, the painter Adriaen Brouwer (1605–38) is the patron of a beer festival in Oudenaarde. In Wingene the painter Breughel is remembered every two years, and the citizens of the town perform live scenes from Breughel's paintings. The tradition of the Corporations of Archers is kept alive in Flanders with the St Hubert Fair. In Bruges the procession with the "Golden Tree" commemorates the town's period of prosperity in the Burgundian period. The "Kattefeest" (Cats' Festival) in Ypres is quite extraordinary. The cat was very often equated with the Devil. Count Boudewijn III wanted to end this veneration of idols, and he ordered that living cats be thrown from the tower of the Town Hall, to demonstrate that the superstition was unwarranted. This gruesome act was maintained until the beginning of the 19th c. Now only cloth replicas are thrown, and a huge procession, demonstrating the role of the cat in civilisation and folklore takes place.

Autumn in Belgium is the time for various beer, hops, and harvest Festivals. In the little town of Wieze near Aalst, its October Festival, the "Wieze Oktoberfeesten" has become well known far and wide. There is a huge tent which can hold 10,000 people, and the special beer from the brewery of Wieze flows in the evening. Three bands, usually from Bavaria, and a Flemish compère keep the participants in a relaxed mood until the small hours.

Children take great joy in the November St Martin's Festival. They receive presents on that day, mostly toys and candies. The tradition of St Martin's Fires is still kept up in many places, for example in Eupen, Genk, Retie and Visé.

Christmas is celebrated in Belgium as in France, with a good deal of merrymaking, a festive meal, dancing and music. Children receive presents from St Nicholas, just as they do in Holland. The St Nicholas shopping rush (in Flemish Sint Niklaas) starts as early as October, and several weeks before the actual festival the streets and shops are festively decorated.

Popular music in Belgium has no special style of its own. Popular songs are usually those of France or Holland. Apart from them there is, in particular, especially in Wallonia, a whole range of dances showing a strong French influence, both in movement and in the accompanying music. They feature drums, wind instruments and brass, distinguished by penetrating, highly vibrating, very full, high-pitched tones. In Flanders, popular dances are often accompanied by the Flemish spinet, violin, flute and a diatonic accordion. Those who like **popular art** should not miss a visit to the Folklore Museums in Liège, Brussels, Ghent and Tournai, and the Open-air Museums in Bokrijk and St Hubert.

Compared with Belgium folklore in the **NETHERLANDS** seems rather modest. Because of the higher proportion of Protestants among the population, and the reformist and matter-of-fact attitude of the Catholic Church, the great ecclesiastical festivals play a far less important role than in Belgium. Dutch traditional celebrations are much less spectacular than Belgian ones, with fewer processions and large popular festivals, but richer in local character.

> One particular feature of the Dutch way of life, is the habit of not having curtains in the windows of their homes, giving the passer-by an unobstructed view of the interior.

The Dutch are very tradition-conscious. In contrast to Belgium, there are regions in Holland where the wearing of **costumes**, especially in the country, is still quite natural and common today. It must, of course, be emphasised that the Dutch

A girl in Dutch costume

everyday costume is rather simple and practical, and cannot be compared with the festive costumes of Yugoslavia, Italy or France. Typical of many Dutch costumes are knickerbockers for men and bonnets for women, as well as the well-known clogs. Country people wearing traditional costumes can be seen mostly in Zealand, North Holland and Friesland, and in the area of the IJsselmeer (Volendam and Marken).

The carnival is of importance only in a few places, mostly in the border areas with Federal Germany where there is still some Rhineland influence (Venlo, Maastricht).

Flower festivals and flower processions are very popular in the Netherlands. In the warm season popular customs and costumes can be seen on the occasion of the cheese market in Alkmaar and in several fishing villages. One of the particularly festive occasions for the Dutch is the Opening of Parliament in The Hague, the "Prinsjesdag", when the Queen, with a large escort, is driven to the Parliament Building in a splendid carriage.

In tiny **LUXEMBOURG** the main event is the spring procession of Echternach which takes place at Whitsuntide (the seventh week after Easter) and has kept its ancient character. The country has taken over many customs from its neighbours.

Calendar of Events

(A selection of interesting events)

January

Belgium

Zottegem	The Feast of the Magi (6 January)
Ronse	Bommelsfeesten (Carnival)
Genk	Election of the Prince of the town. Presentation of the Order against Bestial Seriousness (27 January)

February

Belgium

Malmédy	Cwarmê de Malmédy (Carnival)
Eupen	Procession on Monday before Lent
Aarschot	Fools Tuesday
Binche	Procession of the "Gilles" (Shrove Tuesday)

February–March

Belgium

Fosses-la-Ville	Carnival procession of the "Chinels" (4th Wednesday before Easter)
Stavelot	Carnival procession of the "Blancs-Moussis" (4th Wednesday before Easter)
Tilff-sur-Ourthe	Carnival procession of the "Porais"

Luxembourg

Pétange	Carnival procession (4th Wednesday until 3rd Sunday before Easter)

February–April

Belgium

Many places	Carnival

March

Belgium

Beldenne	Great Bear Carnival
Fosses-la-Ville	Carnival of the "Chinels"
Ostend	Popular carnival in the fishing district
Visé	International Goose Carnival

March–April

Belgium

Lessines	Procession of the Entombment (Good Friday)
Lembeek	March of St Veronus (Easter Monday)
Hakendover	Horseback Procession (Easter Monday)
Ghent	Fair

Luxembourg

Grevenmaches — Field and Vineyard Exhibition (Easter Saturday until the following Thursday)

Luxembourg, Nospelt — The "'E' maischen" (sale of pottery)

A Dutch Floral Procession

April

Belgium

Antwerp — Flemish Song Festival

Charleroi — Fair

Liège — Trade Fair with Exhibition of Antiques

Genk, Hasselt — Trade Fair with Exhibition of Antiques Maypole Festival (30 April)

April—May

The Netherlands

Keukenhof — Flowering Tulip Fields

April—August

The Netherlands

Bergen op Zoom — Curio Market ("'t Ouwe Thalia")

May

Belgium

Antwerp — Special Market (1 May)

Genk — Festival of 1 May, Fair

Rutten — Play of St Evermarus (1 May)

St Amandsberg — "Negenmeinmaarkt" (Horse Market)

Ypres — Cats' Festival (2nd Sunday in May)

Brussels — Weekend of the "Francs-Bourgeois" (3rd Sunday in May)

Lembeke — Windmill Festival (3rd weekend in May)

Nieuwpoort — Procession of Witches (3rd Sunday in May)

Bruges — Procession of the Holy Blood (Ascension)

Doel — Eel Festival

Louvain — Beer Festival

Melsele — Strawberry Festival

Tournai — Fair

The Netherlands

Keukenhof — Open-air Flower Show

Hank — International Competition of Wind Surfing (middle of the month)

Many places — National Windmill Day

Luxembourg

Remerschen — Tasting Day of the Association of Wine Merchants (1 May)

Kopstal — Moto-Cross (1 May)

Luxembourg — International Trade Fair

May—June

Mons — Procession of the Golden Carriage; Fight of St George and the Dragon "Doudou" (Sunday before Whitsuntide)

Ronse — "Fiertel" Procession of St Hermes (Sunday before Whitsuntide)

Walcourt — March of Our Lady (Sunday before Whitsuntide)

Ecaussinnes-Lalaing — Wedding Vespers (Whit Monday)

Gerpinnes — March of St Rotande (military march, Whit Sunday)

Soignies — March of St Vincent (Whit Monday)

Luxembourg

Luxembourg, Diekirch — Closing Procession of the Octave (5th Sunday after Easter)

Bad Mondorf — International Chess Festival (Ascension)

Wiltz — Broom Feast with Traditional Procession (Whit Monday)

Echternach — Jumping Procession (Whit Tuesday)

Wormeldange — Wine Market (1st Thursday after Whitsun)

Everywhere — National Day (23 June)

June

Belgium

Ligny — Procession of "the 100 Days" (1st Sunday in June)

Tournai — Days of the Four Processions (1st weekend in June)

Mons — Procession of the "Car d'Or" (2nd Sunday in June)

Turnhout — Farm Festivals (2nd weekend in June)

Oostduinkerke — Shrimp Festival (3rd Sunday in June)

Verviers — International Costume Procession (3rd Sunday in June)

Ham — Procession of St Christopher (4th Sunday in June)

Ostend — Blessing of the Sea, Shrimp Festival and Procession (4th or last Sunday in June)

Wepion	Strawberry Festival (4th Sunday in June)	Baardegem	Harvest Festival (last weekend in July)
Oudenaarde	The Adriaan-Brouwer Festival (Beer Festival; 30 June)	Beselare	Procession of Witches (last Sunday in July)
		Veurne	Penitents' Procession (last Sunday in July)
The Netherlands			
Haarlem	"Luilakmarkt" (Flower Market along the canals, 1–2 July)	**The Netherlands** Voerendaal	Old Limburg Archery Festival
Den Helder	"Haaks-Waddenweek" (Sailing Competition)	**Luxembourg** Luxembourg	Theatre in the Casemates
Scheveningen	International Kite Festival		
Alkmaar	"Graskaasdag" (Cheese Market)	**July/August**	
Many places	Holland Festival (Concerts, etc.)	**Belgium** Bruges	Festival of Flanders (International Music Days)
Gouda	Pottery Festival		
Warffum	"Op Roakeldais" (International Festival)	Brussels	Brussels Fair
Bolsward	Harvest Festival (end of the month)	Ostend	International Tennis Tournament; Horse Racing
The Hague	Horse Days (end of the month)	**The Netherlands**	
Zwolle	"Blue Finger Dance" (demonstration of old crafts, every Wednesday)	Alkmaar	Art Market (Fridays)
		Doorn	Castle Round Trip and "Cours d'Elégance"
		Den Helder	Fishing Week and Flag Day
Medemblik	Romantic Market	Kinderdijk	Windmill Day (Saturdays)
Noorbeek	Castle Festival, Folklore Festival	Markelo	Historic Farm Wedding
		Many places	Market with traditional performances
June–July			
Belgium		Many places in Friesland	Pole jump "Fierljeppen"
Antwerp	Fair		
		Luxembourg	
June–August		Many places	Concerts and traditional performances
The Netherlands			
Amsterdam	Vondelpark (theatrical and other performances)	Nospelt	Exhibitions of Pottery and Ceramics
Bolsward	Performance of the Traditional Dance Group "Skotsploegh"	Wiltz	International Open-air performances
Gouda	Art Market	**August**	
Den Helder	Knick-knack Market (Flea Market)	**Belgium**	
		Many places	Water Sports Festivals
June–September		Bruges	Canal Festival (every 2–3 years)
The Netherlands			
Amsterdam	Cruising in traditional sail boats	Hamois	Procession with Fanfares (1st Sunday in August)
The Hague	International Rose Exhibition	Brussels	Raising of the "Meyboom" (9 August)
July		Marche-en-Famenne	Bird Market (15 August)
Belgium			
Poperinge	St Mary's Procession (1 July)	Veurne	Harvest Procession (15 August)
Bruges	Organ Recitals in the Cathedral	Heusden	Giants' Procession (3rd Sunday in August)
Brussels	"Ommegang" (beginning of the month)	Nassogne	Heather Festival (3rd Sunday in August)
Schoten	International Festival of Traditional Dances (2nd Sunday in July)	Sint-Andries	Hunters' Festival (3rd weekend in August)
		Ath	The "Goyasse" Wedding (Giants, 4th or last Sunday in August)
Tielt	European Festival (2nd Sunday in July)		
Barvaux-sur-Ourthe	Meeting of Twins	Blankenberge	Flower Procession (last Sunday in August)
Jumet	March of Madelaine (military march, Sunday nearest to 21 July)	Beaumont	Wine Festival (last Sunday in August)

Overijse

Theux

The Netherlands
Many places
Bergen op Zoom

Giethoorn

Zandvoort

Luxembourg
Nospelt

Ettelbruck

Stadtbredimus

Girsterklaus/Rosport

Luxembourg

August/October

Belgium
Ghent

August/December

The Netherlands
Many places

September

Belgium
Lessines

Ghent

Antwerp

Tournai

Grape and Wine
Festival (last Sunday in
August)
Medieval Market in
Castle Franchimont
(last weekend in
August)
"Ommegang" of the
Giants (30 August)

Floral Procession
"Maria-Ommegang"
(Procession)
Illuminated Gondola
Cruise on the Canals
Grand Prix of Holland
(Formula 1)

Antique Market (1st
Sunday in August)
International
Moto-Cross (2nd
Sunday in August)
Wine and Vintner
Festival (2nd weekend
in August)
St Mary's Procession
(Sunday after 15
August)
"Barn Fair" (Kermis)

Festival of Flanders
(International Music
Festival)

Horse Racing and
Riding Tournaments

"Festin" (historic
procession)
Floral Procession (1st
Sunday in September)
Liberation Festival and
Guild Festival (3–4
September)
Great Historic
Procession (2nd
Sunday in September)

The Netherlands
Valkenburg

Wassenaar

Luxembourg
Schwebsingen

Grevenmacher

September/October

Belgium
Wieze

October

Belgium
Diksmuide

The Netherlands
Lisse
St Oedenrode
Zuilaren

Luxembourg
Luxembourg
Vianden

November

Belgium
Han-sur-Lesse

Scherpenheuvel

Eupen

The Netherlands
Zeist

December

Belgium
Malmédy

Eupen
Sint-Niklaas
Verviers

Vielsalm

Bruges

The Netherlands
Everywhere

Many places

"The Night of
Valkenburg" (bicycle
races, etc.)
Horse Races (Grand
Prix of the Netherlands)

Wine Festival (1st
Sunday in September)
Wine and Grape
Festival with Traditional
Procession (2nd
weekend in September)

October Feast (Beer
Festival)

October Festival (Beer
Festival)

Flower Bulb Market
Clog Fair of Brabant
Horse Market

International Trade Fair
Nut Market (2nd
Sunday in October)

The Feast of St Hubert
(1st Sunday in
November)
Candle Procession (1st
Sunday in November)
St Martin's Day (11
November)

St Hubert's Hunt

St Nicholas Procession
(1 December)
Christmas Market
Fair
"Bethlehem in
Verviers"
Christmas in Salmland
(Folk Festival)
Star Procession (end of
the month)

Feast of St Nicholas (5
December)
"Midwinter Blowing"
(a traditional custom to
announce the birth of
Christ)

The Breughel Festival in Belgian Huizingen

Wingene

Many places in Wallonia

Breughel Festival
(every second year, 2nd
Sunday in September)
Wallonian Festivals

Official Holidays

Belgium	The Netherlands	Luxembourg
1 January	1 January	1 January
Easter Monday	Easter Monday	Easter Monday
1 May	30 April	1 May
Ascension Day	Ascension Day	Ascension Day
Whit Monday	Whit Monday	Whit Monday
21 July	25–26 December	23 June (if this is a Sunday, the following
15 August		working day is taken)
1 and 11 November		15 August
25 December		1 November
		25–26 December

Shopping, Souvenirs

In the Benelux countries the traveller can purchase valuable souvenirs and in-expensive presents. Luxury shops can be found in the big cities.

In **Belgium**, luxury gift items are: diamonds (Antwerp) and jewelry (Brussels and Kortrijk); ceramics; embossed copperware from Dinant (Dinanderies); crystal from Val Saint-Lambert; Lace from Bruges, Brussels and Mechelen; also cambric and linen from Kortrijk. Wood carving is carried on in Spa, sporting guns are produced in Liège, and pewter items in Huy.

Dutch "Klompen" (Clogs)

In various places in the **Netherlands**, art and antique markets take place during the season; those of Breda and The Hague are particularly well known. China from the Delft factory, Delft blue, is more expensive than other makes. Amsterdam is a leading place for diamond cutting and polishing, and there are many art and antiques shops in the city. With a little luck you can strike a bargain at an auction or in a flea market.

Apart from this, there are many places with special local products. In the Dutch province of Friesland, local pottery is made in Makkum and Workum, furniture in Hindeloopen, and clocks in Joure. Broek in Waterland on the IJsselmeer is the capital of clog-making. Beautiful goldware can be found in the province of Zealand, silverware in the town of Schoonhoven, candles and pipes in Gouda; crystal can be obtained in Leerdam and Maastricht, which is also a good place to buy ceramics. In Lisse and Sassenheim the gardening enthusiast can purchase tulip and other bulbs. And no tourist should miss trying the many different Dutch cheeses.

In **Luxembourg** there are typical local souvenirs, among them the wrought-iron miniature chimneyplates called "Tâk" from the Fonderie de Mersch embellished with coats of arms and other motifs. Porcelain and stoneware decorative plates with landscapes of the Grand Duchy especially, are also good gift items.

In all three countries it is possible to purchase paintings or prints from one of the many art galleries. If a private person purchases a work of art at one of the exhibitions of young Dutch artists, the state pays one-fifth of the price, up to a maximum of 1200 Hfl. Everyday items, such as shoes or leather, clothing, tobacco and chocolates, can also be bought inexpensively in many places.

Information

Belgium

General Commissariat for Tourism
(*Commissariat Général au Tourism*; CGT)

HEAD OFFICE:
Rue Marché aux Herbes 61,
B-1000 **Bruxelles**
tel. (02) 513 90 90

Within Belgium information can be obtained from Belgian Tourist Offices, under different names according to whether the area is Dutch or French speaking: Either **Dienst voor Toerism**, or **Syndicat d'Initiative**.

Automobile and Touring Club

Touring Club Royal de Belgique (*TCB*)
Rue de la Loi 44,
B-1000 **Bruxelles**.
tel. (02) 513 82 40 and 512 78 90

Royal Automobile Club de Belgique (*RACB*)
Rue d'Arlon 53,
B-1000 **Bruxelles**.
tel. (02) 513 38 55

Diplomatic Representation (Brussels):

United Kingdom: Britannia House, 28 Rue Joseph II; Australia: 52 Avenue des Arts; Canada: 6B Rue de Loxum; New Zealand: 47–48 Blvd du Régent; USA: 27 Blvd du Régent; Republic of Ireland: 19 Rue du Luxembourg.

The Netherlands

Dutch Tourist Office
(*National Bureau voor Toerism*; NBT)

HEAD OFFICE:
Bezuidenhoutseweg 2,
NL-2594 AV **The Hague**
tel. (0 70) 70 81 41 91

In the major towns there are Dutch Tourist Offices: **Vereniging voor Vreemdelingenverkeer** (*VVV*)

Automobile and Touring Clubs

Koninklijke Nederlandse Toeristenbond (*ANWB*)
Wassenaarseweg 220,
NL-2596 EC **The Hague**
tel. (0 70) 26 44 26

Koninklijke Nederlandse Automobilclub (*KNAC*)
Sophialaan 4
NL-2514 JP **The Hague**
tel. (0 70) 46 92 80

Diplomatic Representation (The Hague)

American Embassy: Lange Voorhout 102; Australia: Koninginnegr 23; Canada: Sophialn 7; Great Britain: Lange Voorhout 10; Ireland: Dr Kuyperstr. 9; New Zealand: Lange Voorhout 18.

Luxembourg

The National Tourist Office of the Grand Duchy of Luxembourg
(*Office National du Tourisme*; ONT)

HEAD OFFICE:
Avenue de la Gare 51
L-**Luxembourg**
tel. 48 79 99

Information Office at the Air terminal on the Station square.

Automobile Club

Automobile Club du Grand-Duché de Luxembourg (*ACL*)
Route de Longwy 13
L-**Luxembourg-Helfenterbruck**
tel. 31 10 31

Diplomatic Representation (Luxembourg)

British: Blvd Franklin Roosevelt; USA: Blvd E. Servaes.

Information about **War Cemeteries** in Belgium, the Netherlands and Luxembourg of the First and Second World Wars can be obtained from the *Commonwealth War Graves Commission*, Head Office: 2 Marlow Road, Maidenhead, Berks, SL6 7DX, England – tel. (0628) 34221.

Emergency Calls by Radio

In urgent cases the radio stations in the Benelux countries will broadcast emergency calls. Information can be obtained from the Automobile Clubs and the police.

STD Telephone Codes

From the UK
To **Belgium**   01032
to the **Netherlands**   01031
to **Luxembourg**   010352

From **Belgium**
to the **UK**   00 44

From the **Netherlands**
to the **UK**   09 44

From **Luxembourg**
to the **UK**   00 44

Emergency Calls

Belgium

On Belgian highways there are *emergency telephones*. Several Automobile Organisations run a Road Rescue Service.

Emergency Telephone Numbers:
Police   901
   in large cities   906
Accident assistance   900

The Netherlands

There are *emergency telephones* on Dutch highways.

There is no emergency telephone number (police, accident) for the whole country.

Luxembourg

Emergency telephone
(police, accident)
for the whole country: 012

Tourist Information Offices

Belgian tourist offices

BELGIUM

Commissariat-Général au Tourisme
Rue Marché aux Herbes 61
1000 **Bruxelles**
tel. (02) 513 90 90
Bureau d'Information
tel. (02) 512 30 30, telex B. BRU B-63245

Commissariaat-Generaal voor Toerisme
Grasmarkt 61
1000 **Brussel**
tel. (02) 513 90 90
Informatiebureau
tel. (02) 512 30 30, telex B. BRU B-63245

Generalkommissariat für Fremdenverkehr
Rue Marché aux Herbes 61 Grasmarkt
1000 **Brussel**
tel. (02) 513 90 90
Auskunftsbüro
tel. (02) 512 30 30, telex B. BRU B-63245

Belgian National Tourist Office
Rue Marché aux Herbes 61 Grasmarkt
1000 **Brussels**
tel. (02) 513 90 90
Information Office
tel. (02) 512 30 30, telex B. BRU B-63245

Toeristische Federatie van de Provincie Antwerpen
Karel Oomsstraat 11
2000 **Antwerpen**
tel. (031) 16 28 10

Toeristische Federatie van Brabant — Fédération du Tourisme du Brabant
Grasmarkt 61 Rue Marché aux Herbes
1000 **Brussel/Bruxelles**
tel. (02) 513 07 50
Info
tel. (02) 512 30 30, telex B. BRU B-63245

Fédération du Tourisme de la Province du Hainaut
Rue des Clercs 31
7000 **Mons**
tel. (065) 31 61 01

Provinciaal Verbond voor Toerisme in Limburg
Domein Bokrijk
3600 **Genk**
tel. (011) 22 29 58

Fédération du Tourisme de la Province de Liège
Bd de la Sauvenière 77
4000 **Liege**
tel. (041) 32 52 10 – 15

Fédération Touristique du Luxembourg belge
Quai de l'Ourthe 9
6980 **La Roche-En-Ardenne**
tel. (084) 41 10 12 – 41 10 11

Fédération du Tourisme de la Province de
Namur
Rue Notre-Dame 3
5000 Namur
tel. (081) 22 29 98

Federatie voor Toerisme in Oost-Vlaanderen
Koningin Maria-Hendrikaplein 27
9000 Gent
tel. (091) 22 16 37

Westtoerisme
Vlamingstraat 55
8000 Brugge
tel. (050) 33 73 44

Dienst voor Toerisme
Suikkerrui 19
2000 Antwerpen
tel. (031) 32 01 03

Dienst voor Toerisme
Markt 7
8000 Brugge
tel. (050) 33 07 13

Tourist Information Brussels (T.I.B.)
Grasmarkt 61 Rue Marché aux Herbes
1000 Brussel/Bruxelles
tel. (02) 513 89 40
Info
tel. (02) 512 30 30, telex B. BRU B-63245

Syndicat d'Initiative de Dinant
Rue Grande 37
5500 Dinant
tel. (082) 22 28 70

Stedelijke Dienst voor Toerisme
Borluutstraat 9
9000 Gent
tel. (091) 25 36 41

Office du Tourisme de la Ville de Liège
en Feronstrée, 92
4000 Liège
tel. (041) 32 24 56

Syndicat d'initiative de Namur
Square Léopold
5000 Namur
tel. (081) 22 28 59

Stedelijke Dienst voor Toerisme
Wapenplein
8400 Oostende
tel. (059) 70 11 99

Office de Tourisme de Tournai
Vieux Marché aux Poteries
14-7500 Tournai
tel. (069) 22 20 45

INFORMATION OFFICES AT THE FRONTIER

E10 (Breda–Antwerpen–Brussel-Bruxelles)
E5 (Aachen–Liège–Brussel-Bruxelles)
E10 (Paris–Valenciennes–Mons–Brussel-Bruxelles)
Nationale Luchthaven–Zaventem (Aankomsthall)
Aéroport nationale–Zaventem (Hall d'arrivée)
Nationale Flughafen–Zaventem (Ankunftshalle)
Airport Zaventem (Arrival Hall)

CANADA
Office National Belge de Tourisme
Belgian National Tourist Office
Montreal H4A 1G4
5801 Avenue Monkland
tel. 487-3387

DENMARK
Det Officielle Belgiske Turistbureau
1606 København V
Vester Farimagsgade 7–9
tel. 12 30 27

DEUTSCHLAND (Bundesrepublik)
Belgisches Verkehrsamt
D-4000 Düsselford 1
Berliner Allee 47
tel. 0211–32 60 08

ESPAÑA
Comisaria General de Turismo Belga
Madrid 13
Calle Navas de Tolosa n° 3 – Piso 2°
tel. 22 12 68 1

FRANCE
Office National Belge de Tourisme
75002 Paris
21 Boulevard des Capucines
tel. 742 41 18 – 742 41 82
59000 Lille
12 Rue Saint-Sauveur
tel. 52 67 48 – 53 53 41
67000 Strasbourg
2 Rue du Noyer
tel. 32 52 64

GRAND-DUCHÉ du LUXEMBOURG
Office National Belge de Tourisme
Luxembourg
17 Avenue de la Liberté
tel. 24955

ITALIA
Ufficio Nazionale Belga per il Turismo
I-00187 Roma
Via Barberini 3
tel. 47 54 37 5

JAPAN
Belgian National Tourist Office
Tameike Tokyu Bldg 9F
1–14, Akasaka 1
Chome, Minato-ku, Tokyo
tel. (03) 586–70 41/2, telex J23811 – CGTTYO

NEDERLAND
Nationaal Belgisch Verkeersbureau
Amsterdam
Leidseplein 5
tel. 25 12 51

NORGE
Det Belgiske Turiskontor
Oslo 2
Drammensveien 30
tel. 56 29 82 – 56 29 83

ÖSTERREICH
Sabena
A-1010 Wien
Opernring 9
tel. 57 35 06 – 57 35 07 – 57 35 08 – 57 35 09

PORTUGAL
Comissariado Geral Belge de Turismo
1200 Lisboa
Rua do Salitre 84 – 3°-Dto
tel. 53 56 30

SCHWEIZ – SUISSE
Offizielles Belgisches Verkehrsbüro
Office National Belge de Tourisme
Ch-4051 Basel–Bale
Aeschenvorstadt 48–50
tel. 23 77 95

SVERIGE
Belgiska Statens Turistbyrà
S-104.32 – Stockholm 19
Box 19.520 (Markvadsgaten 16)
tel. 34.15.75

UNITED KINGDOM
Belgian National Tourist Office
London W1X 3RB
38 Dover Street
tel. 499–5379

U.S.A.
Belgian National Tourist Office
New York, N.Y. 10022
745 Fifth Avenue
tel. 758 81 30

ZUID AFRIKA – SOUTH AFRICA
Sabena
Johannesburg
Carlton Centre – Commissionerstreet – 25th Floor
tel. 218166 – 219166

Dutch tourist offices

HEAD OFFICE
Bezuidenhoutseweg 2, 2594 AV Den Haag
Postbus 90415, 2509 LK Den Haag
tel. 070–814191, telex 32488

BRANCH OFFICES
AUSTRALIA
Suite 302, 5 Elizabeth Street
Sydney N.S.W. 2000, tel. 02–276921

BELGIË/BELGIQUE – LUXEMBURG/
LUXEMBOURG
Ravensteinstraat 68, 1000-Brussel
tel. 02–5124409

BUNDESREPUBLIK DEUTSCHLAND UND
WEST-BERLIN
Laurenzplatz 1–3, 5000-Köln-1
tel. 0221–236262, telex 8882511

CANADA
One Dundas Street West, P.O. Box 19
Suite 2108, Toronto, Ontario M5G 1Z3
tel. 0(416) 598–2830/2831

850 Hastings Street, Suite 214
Vancouver, B.C. V6C 1E1
tel. 0(604) 684–5720, telex 04–55133

ESPAÑA
Apartado Postal 8101, Madrid 8
tel. 01–247.9699

FRANCE
31/33 Avenue des Champs Elysées
75008 Paris
tel. 01–2254125, 2259625, telex 641828

GREAT BRITAIN AND IRELAND
Savory and Moore House, 2nd Floor
143 New Bond Street, London W1Y 0QS
tel. 01–499 9367/8/9/0, telex 269005

JAPAN
No. 10, Mori Building
1–18–1 Toranomon, Minato-KU, Tokyo
tel. 03–508.8015/8016, telex 7224563

MEXICO
Apartado Postal 24533, Mexico 7 D.F.
tel. 05–5288308, telex 2201771227

ÖSTERREICH
c/o Niederl. Handelskammer für Österreich
Schwarzenbergplatz 10, A-1040 Wien
tel. 0222–655708, telex 133867

SCHWEIZ/SUISSE
c/o Handelskammer Holland/Schweiz
Uraniastrasse 20, 8001 Zürich
Postfach, 8023 Zürich
tel. 01–2110990/91, telex 813703

SOUTH AFRICA
Union Square (2nd Floor), cnr.
Plein and Klein Street, P.O. Box 8624
Johannesburg
tel. 011–236991

SVERIGE, DANMARK, NORGE, SUOMI
Kungsgatan 29 VI, III 56 Stockholm
tel. 08–230420, telex 17740

U.S.A.
576 Fifth Avenue, New York N.Y. 10036
tel. 0(212) 245–5320, telex 620081

681 Market Street, Room 941
San Francisco, Cal. 94105
tel. 0(415) 781–3387

INFORMATION OFFICES IN PROVINCES

Provinciale Groninger VVV.
Grote Markt 23, Groningen
tel. 050–139700

VVV Friesland-Leeuwarden
Stationsplein 1, Leeuwarden
tel. 05100–32224

Provinciale VVV Drenthe
Brink 42, Assen
tel. 05920–14324

Provinciale VVV Overijssel en VVV Twente
De Werf 1, Almelo
tel. 05490–10266

VVV Overijsselse Heuvelrug en Salland
Marktstraat 19, Raalte
tel. 05720–18765

VVV West-Overijssel
Bethlehemskerkplein 35, Zwolle
tel. 05200–18977

Provinciale VVV Gelderland en VVV Arnhem en de
Zuid-Veluwe
Stationsplein 45, Arnhem
tel. 085–452921

VVV Achterhoek, Wijnhuis/Markt, Zutphen
tel. 05750–19355

VVV Noord- en Midden-Veluwe
Stationsplein 6, Apeldoorn
tel. 055–212249

VVV Rijk van Nijmegen
Keizer Karelplein 33, Nijmegen
tel. 080–225440

VVV Gelders Rivierengebied
Stationsstraat 37, Tiel
tel. 033–6441

VVV Eemland
Stationsplein 8, Amersfoort
tel. 03490–12747

VVV De Utrechtse Heuvelrug
Kromme Rijn en Lek, Slotlaan 321, Zeist
tel. 03404–12174

Streek VVV Utrechts weidegebied. Vecht en Plassen
en stad Utrecht, Smakkelaarsveld 3, Utrecht
tel. 030–314132

VVV Amsterdam e.o.
Rokin 5, Amsterdam
tel. 020–266444

VVV Het Gooi
Stationsplein 1–3, Hilversum
tel. 035–11651

Federatie van VVV's in Noord-Holland boven het
Noordzeekanaal
Bierkade 7, Alkmaar
tel. 072–19841

VVV Texel
Groenplaats 9, Den Burg
tel. 02220–2844

VVV Kennemer-Amstelland
Stationsplein 1, Haarlem
tel. 023–319059

VVV Den Haag e.o.
Postbus 1973, Den Haag, Station H.S. en Gev.
Deynootplein, Scheveningen
tel. 070–546200

VVV Rotterdam e.o.
Stadhuisplein 19, Rotterdam
tel. 010–136000

Provinciale VVV Zuid-Holland en VVV Deft e.o.
Markt 85, Delft
tel. :15–126100

VVV Dordrecht e.o.
Stationsweg 1, Dordrecht
tel. 078–32800

VVV Leiden e.o.
Stationsplein 210, Leiden
tel. 071–146846

Provinciale VVV Zeeland
Postbus 123, Middelburg
tel. 01180–28051

Provinciale VVV Noord-Brabant en Streek VVV
West-Brabant
Willemstraat 17, Breda
tel. 076–132150

VVV 's-Hertogenbosch en de Meierij
Markt 77, Den Bosch
tel. 073–123071

VVV Hart van Brabant
Spoorlaan 440, Tilburg
tel. 013–436131

VVV Kempenland
Stationsplein 24, Eindhoven
tel. 040–24300

VVV Noord-Limburg
Keulsepoort, Venlo
tel. 077–11241

Provinciale VVV in Limburg
Kasteel ,,Den Halder'', Valkenburg
tel. 04406–13993

Sealink car ferries

Belgium
British Rail,
Place Rogier 23, 1000 **Brussels.**
tel. 217–97–02, 217–09–88

Holland
British Rail,
Leidseplein 5, **Amsterdam.**
tel. 23 41 33
Harwich Ferry Agentur B.V.
Postbus 4 **Hoek van Holland**
tel. 01747–4140

North Sea Ferries

Belgium
Prins Filipsdok
Lanceloot Blondeellaan,
8380 **Zeebrugge** (Bruges).
tel. (050) 545601, telex 81469 et 81897

Holland
Beneluxhaven, Rotterdam/Europoort.
(Boîte postale 1123, 3180 AC
Rozenburg Z.H.)
tel. (01819) 62077, telex 26571

Britain
King George Dock
Hedon Road, **Hull** HU9 5QA.
tel. 0482 795141, telex 52349

Hoverlloyd

London
Royal National Hotel
Bedford Way, London WC1

Paris
24 Rue de Saint Quentin
75010 Paris
tel. 208 1196

Brussels
Hoverlloyd Terminal,
Rue de Brabant 13
1030 Bruxelles
tel. 219 02 25/219 55 88, telex 61710

Courtrai
Supermarché GB, 2, Walle
8500 Courtrai

Mons
Buffet de la Gare de Mons
Place Leopold
7000 Mons

Calais
Hoverport International
62226 Calais Cedex
tel. 96 67 10 à Calais, telex 130250 F

Ramsgate
International Hoverport
Ramsgate, Kent
tel. 0843 54881, telex 96412

Sabena belgian world airlines

BRUSSELS B-1000 Belgium

Air Terminal: National (12 km – 7 miles).
Check in: 30 minutes
Check in: 60 minutes to Tel Aviv

Aircraft reservations: Air Terminus –
tel. 02–511.42.20 and 02–513.65.71

Aircraft reservations: Hilton Hotel-Bd. de
Waterloolaan, 38 – tel. 02–512.35.00
CARGO: Airport, tel. 02–751.80.80

Townsend Thoresen European Ferries

Belgium and Luxembourg

Townsend Thoresen Car Ferries
18-24 (B1) Rue des Colonies
1000 **Brussels**
tel. (02) 513 29 80, telex 25800

Townsend Thoresen Car Ferries
Car Ferry Terminal
Doverlaan 7, 8380 **Zeebrugge**
tel. (050) 54 48 73, telex 81306

Holland

Townsend Thoresen Car Ferries
Leidsestraat 32, 1017 PB **Amsterdam**
tel. (020) 22 38 32, telex 14601

England

Townsend Thoresen Car Ferries,
127 Regent Street, **London** W1R 8LB.
tel. 01–734 4431, 01–437 7800, telex 23802

Townsend Thoresen Car Ferries
1 Camden Crescent, **Dover**, Kent CT16 1LD
tel. 0304 203388, telex 96200

Townsend Thoresen Car Ferries
Car Ferry House, Canute Road
Southampton SO9 5GP
tel. 0703 34488, telex 47637

Townsend Thoresen Car Ferries
The Continental Ferry Port, Mile End, **Portsmouth**
tel. 0705 815231, telex 86807

Townsend Thoresen Car Ferries
Car Ferry Terminal, The Docks, **Felixstowe** Suffolk
IP11 8TB
tel. 039 42 78711, telex 98232

Republic of Ireland

B+I Line, 16 Westmoreland Street, **Dublin** 2
tel. Dublin 778271

KLM

Amsterdam

KLM, Leidseplein 1–3, tel. 493633. Reservations
and travel information tel. 434242
Coach from: Museumplein 15a
Coach from: Central Station (Northern Exit). A
limited train service to the South of Amsterdam will
be available.
Check in: Domestic flights European flights: 30
mins./Intercontinental flights: 1 hour. Tel Aviv
flights: 2 hrs.

Luxair

Aéroport de Luxembourg
tel. 4798–510, telex 2247

Booking Office/Representative
Luxembourg
tel. 436161
Luxair telex 2372

City Terminal
Place de la Gare
tel. 481820